Mastering
Linux® System Administration

Mastering
Linux® System
Administration

Christine Bresnahan

Richard Blum

SYBEX®
A Wiley Brand

Library of Congress Control Number: 2021938273

To the Lord God Almighty, "in whom are hidden all the treasures of wisdom and knowledge."
—Colossians 2:3

Acknowledgments

First, all glory and praise go to God, who through His Son, Jesus Christ, makes all things possible and gives us the gift of eternal life.

Many thanks go to the fantastic team of people at John Wiley & Sons for their outstanding work on this project. Thanks to Kenyon Brown, the acquisitions editor, for offering us the opportunity to work on this book. Also, thanks to Kathryn Duggan, the project editor, for keeping things on track and making this book more presentable. Thanks, Kathi, for all your hard work and diligence. The technical editor, Jason Eckert, did a wonderful job of double-checking all the work in the book, plus making suggestions to improve the content. Thanks to Barath Kumar Rajasekaran and his team for their endless patience and diligence to make our work readable. We would also like to thank Carole Jelen at Waterside Productions, Inc., for arranging this opportunity for us, and for helping us out in our writing careers.

Christine would like to thank her husband, Timothy, for his encouragement, patience, and willingness to listen, even when he has no idea what she is talking about. Rich would like to thank his wife, Barbara, for the life-sustaining baked goods she readily prepared to help him keep up his energy while writing!

About the Authors

Christine Bresnahan started working with computers more than 30 years ago in the IT industry as a system administrator. Christine is an adjunct professor at Ivy Tech Community College where she teaches Linux certification and Python programming classes. She also writes books and produces instructional resources. During her downtime, Christine enjoys spending time with her husband and family, hiking, and gardening.

Richard Blum has worked in the IT industry for more than 30 years as both a systems and network administrator, working with lots of different operating systems (including Linux, of course). Over the years, he's also volunteered for several nonprofit organizations to help support small networks that had little financial support. Rich is the author of many Linux-based books for total Linux geeks and teaches online courses in Linux and web programming. When he's not busy being a computer nerd, Rich enjoys playing piano and bass guitar and spending time with his wife, Barbara, and their two daughters, Katie Jane and Jessica.

About the Technical Editor

Jason W. Eckert is an experienced technical trainer, systems architect, software engineer, and best-selling author in the technology industry. With 45 industry certifications, more than 30 years of technology and programming experience, 4 published apps, and 25 published textbooks covering UNIX, Linux, Security, Windows Server, Microsoft Exchange Server, PowerShell, BlackBerry Enterprise Server, and video game development, Mr. Eckert brings his expertise to every class that he teaches at triOS College. He was also named 2019 Outstanding Train-the-Trainer from the Computing Technology Industry Association (CompTIA). For more information about Mr. Eckert, visit `jasoneckert.net`.

Contents at a Glance

Contents

Introduction

Over the last few decades, the Linux operating system has evolved from being a hobbyist curiosity to becoming the operating system of choice for most servers on the Internet. The explosion in popularity of cloud computing is due to the robustness of Linux servers, and knowing how to install, configure, and manage Linux servers has become a necessary skill for most data center system administrators.

This book covers what you'll need to know to work in a Linux server environment. One of the difficulties of working on Linux servers is that more often than not, you don't have access to a graphical desktop, so knowing how to interact with the server using text commands is a crucial skill to have for Linux system administrators. This book covers all aspects of Linux server management from the command line, from installing the system to configuring and monitoring common software packages found on Linux servers.

One of the confusing aspects of Linux is that there are many different "flavors," or distributions, of Linux available. However, there are two main Linux server distributions that have risen to the top in popularity in professional data centers. This book covers how to interact with both Ubuntu and Red Hat servers, providing separate instructions for each server environment when necessary.

Who Should Read This Book

This book is intended for the classroom environment, so the primary audience for the book is educators working at the high school, college, or university level. The book provides sufficient exercises, quizzes, and instructor material to create a one-semester course in Linux system administration.

That said, this book can also be used as a standard reference for any individual wanting to learn more about Linux system administration. There are several ways you can use this book. The most straightforward is to start at the beginning and follow all the steps to install, configure, and use a Linux server as described over the course of the book. Alternately, you can skip around from chapter to chapter and follow only the steps of the individual chapters. The book will also make for a handy reference guide as you work in a Linux server environment, performing your day-to-day duties in supporting your system users.

NOTE This book provides Instructor Materials that include PowerPoints for each chapter, a course syllabus, and bonus questions. Please visit the book page at www.wiley.com.

What You Will Learn

This book covers the basics of installing a Linux server, working in a command-line environment, and managing users, hardware, and software. The book starts by covering the basic Linux skills you'll need to install and work in a Linux server and then goes on to cover more intermediate skills such as configuring and troubleshooting user accounts, storage devices, and networks. Finally, the book finishes by providing advanced system administration skills in writing shell script programs, setting up a web or database server, and even using virtualization in the Linux environment.

What You Need

To follow along in the chapters and complete the exercises in this book, you'll need some type of Linux server environment. The book specifically covers both the Ubuntu and Red Hat servers. If you intend to use the Red Hat server environment, you don't necessarily need to purchase a commercial copy of Red Hat Enterprise Linux. Instead, you can use the open source CentOS Linux server, which is an authorized copy of Red Hat intended for the open source world. At the time of this writing, the current versions of each are Ubuntu 20.04LTS and CentOS 8.1. These are the versions used in the exercises; if you opt to use newer versions of either server, you may experience different results in some exercises.

The best way to learn Linux is to install it on a separate physical system. If you don't plan on having your server host thousands of clients, you can use any old Windows workstation to install Linux (the book covers how to do that). Just remember that if you replace an existing Windows workstation with Linux, you will lose all data currently on the workstation, so make sure you back up any important data first.

Alternatively, you can load a virtualization software package, such as VirtualBox, in an existing Windows workstation. The virtualization software allows you to install and run the Linux server software in a virtual environment on top of Windows, sharing the hardware and disk space with your Windows workstation. In this setup, you don't need to worry about your Windows workstation data—it will remain safely separate from the Linux server.

The Mastering Series

The Mastering series from Wiley provides outstanding instruction for readers with intermediate and advanced skills, in the form of top-notch training and development for those already working in their field and clear, serious education for those aspiring to become pros. Every Mastering book features the following:

- The Wiley "by professionals for professionals" commitment. Mastering authors are themselves practitioners, with plenty of credentials in their areas of specialty.

- A practical perspective for a reader who already knows the basics—someone who needs solutions, not a primer.

- Real-World Scenarios, ranging from case studies to interviews, that show how the tool, technique, or knowledge presented is applied in actual practice.

- Skill-based instruction, with chapters organized around real tasks rather than abstract concepts or subjects.

- Self-review test "Master It" problems and questions, so you can be certain you're equipped to do the job right.

How to Contact Wiley or the Authors

Sybex strives to keep you supplied with the latest tools and information you need for your work. If you believe you have found an error in this book and it is not listed on the book's web page, you can report the issue to the Wiley customer support team at `wileysupport.com`.

You can email the authors with your comments or questions at `rich@richblum.com`.

Part 1

Basic Admin Functions

Chapter 1

Understanding the Basics

The Linux operating system has taken the world by storm. Whether it's embedded Linux software operating in phones and refrigerators or full-blown Linux servers running famous Internet sites, you can find Linux systems just about everywhere. If you've chosen (or have been chosen) to be a Linux system administrator, the task before you can seem daunting at first. But don't panic—while complex, the Linux system is organized and structured. Just knowing the basics of how Linux works will go a long way in helping you with your goals of becoming a Linux system administrator. This chapter walks you through the basics of what Linux is and explains the different versions of Linux that are available.

IN THIS CHAPTER, YOU WILL LEARN TO

- ◆ List the components of a standard Linux system
- ◆ Explain how GNU utilities are used in Linux
- ◆ Describe the various Linux user interface environments
- ◆ Explain why there are different Linux distributions

What Is Linux?

If you've never worked with Linux, you may be confused as to why there are so many different versions of it available. You've probably heard various terms such as *distribution, LiveDVD,* and *GNU* when looking at Linux packages, and may have been confused. Wading through the world of Linux for the first time can be a tricky experience. This chapter takes some of the mystery out of the Linux system before you start working on commands and scripts.

For starters, these four main parts make up a Linux system:

- ◆ The Linux kernel
- ◆ The GNU utilities
- ◆ A user interface
- ◆ Application software

Each of these four parts has a specific job in the Linux system. Figure 1.1 shows a basic diagram of how the parts fit together on top of the computer hardware to create the overall Linux system.

FIGURE 1.1

The Linux system

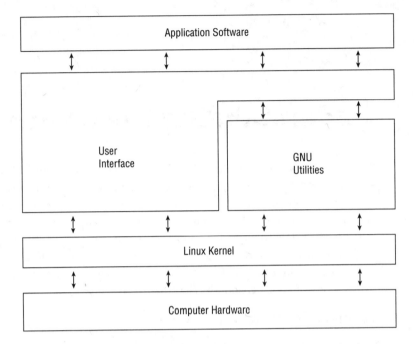

This section describes these four main parts in detail and gives you an overview of how they work together to create a complete Linux system.

Looking into the Linux Kernel

The core of the Linux system is the *kernel*. The kernel controls all of the hardware and software on the computer system, allocating hardware when necessary and executing software when required.

If you've been following the Linux world at all, no doubt you've heard the name Linus Torvalds. Linus is the person responsible for creating the first Linux kernel software while he was a student at the University of Helsinki. He intended it to be a copy of the Unix system, at the time a popular operating system used at many universities.

After developing the Linux kernel, Linus released it to the Internet community and solicited suggestions for improving it. This simple process started a revolution in the world of computer operating systems. Soon Linus was receiving suggestions from students as well as professional programmers from around the world.

Allowing anyone to change programming code in the kernel would result in complete chaos. To simplify things, Linus acted as a central point for all improvement suggestions. It was ultimately Linus's decision whether to incorporate suggested code in the kernel. This same concept is still in place with the Linux kernel code, except that instead of just Linus controlling the kernel code, a team of developers has taken on the task.

The kernel is primarily responsible for these four main functions:

♦   System memory management

♦   Software program management

- ♦ Hardware management
- ♦ Filesystem management

The following sections explore each of these functions in more detail.

SYSTEM MEMORY MANAGEMENT

One of the primary functions of the operating system kernel is memory management. Not only does the kernel manage the physical memory available on the server, but it can also create and manage virtual memory, or memory that does not actually exist.

It does this by using space on the hard disk, called the *swap space*. The kernel swaps the contents of virtual memory locations back and forth from the swap space to the actual physical memory. This allows the system to think there is more memory available than what physically exists (shown in Figure 1.2).

FIGURE 1.2

The Linux system memory map

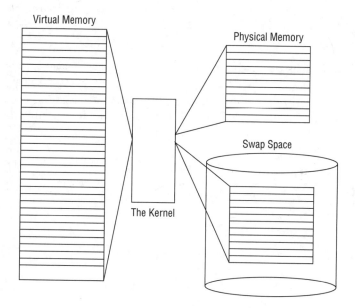

The memory locations are grouped into blocks called *pages*. The kernel locates each page of memory either in the physical memory or in the swap space. The kernel then maintains a table of the memory pages that indicates which pages are in physical memory and which pages are swapped out to disk.

The kernel keeps track of which memory pages are in use and automatically copies memory pages that have not been accessed for a period of time to the swap space area (called *swapping out*), even if there's other memory available. When a program wants to access a memory page that has been swapped out, the kernel must make room for it in physical memory by swapping out a different memory page and swapping in the required page from the swap space. Obviously, this process takes time and can slow down a running process. The process of swapping out memory pages for running applications continues for as long as the Linux system is running.

Real World Scenario

LOOKING AT MEMORY

There are a couple of simple commands you can use to get an idea of just how your Linux system is managing memory. While we'll be exploring these commands in more detail later in the book, here's a quick exercise for you to get started exploring your Linux system:

1. Log into your Linux system. (If you don't have a Linux system available yet, you can come back to here after going through either Chapter 2, "Installing an Ubuntu Server," or Chapter 4, "Installing a Red Hat Server.")

2. From the command prompt, enter the command **free**. You should see something similar to this output:

```
$ free
              total        used        free      shared  buff/cache   available
Mem:        2035504      135668     1449568        1048      450268     1742704
Swap:       2097148           0     2097148
```

The output from the free command shows the total amount of physical memory installed on the system, as well as the amount of swap space currently configured.

3. The free command just provides an overview of the memory for your Linux system. For a more detailed look, enter the command **cat /proc/meminfo**. You should see a long listing, similar to this:

```
$ cat /proc/meminfo
MemTotal:       2035504 kB
MemFree:        1449632 kB
MemAvailable:   1742352 kB
Buffers:          25452 kB
Cached:          386028 kB
SwapCached:           0 kB
Active:          166036 kB
Inactive:        290704 kB
Active(anon):     51796 kB
Inactive(anon):     128 kB
Active(file):    114240 kB
Inactive(file):  290576 kB
Unevictable:      18640 kB
Mlocked:          18640 kB
SwapTotal:      2097148 kB
SwapFree:       2097148 kB
Dirty:              156 kB
Writeback:            0 kB
AnonPages:        63940 kB
Mapped:           63344 kB
Shmem:             1048 kB
```

```
    KReclaimable:      38664 kB
    Slab:              74316 kB
    SReclaimable:      38664 kB
    SUnreclaim:        35652 kB
    KernelStack:        2044 kB
    PageTables:         1268 kB
    NFS_Unstable:          0 kB
    Bounce:                0 kB
    WritebackTmp:          0 kB
    CommitLimit:     3114900 kB
    Committed_AS:     376812 kB
    VmallocTotal:  34359738367 kB
    VmallocUsed:       27676 kB
    VmallocChunk:          0 kB
    Percpu:              516 kB
    HardwareCorrupted:     0 kB
    AnonHugePages:         0 kB
    ShmemHugePages:        0 kB
    ShmemPmdMapped:        0 kB
    FileHugePages:         0 kB
    FilePmdMapped:         0 kB
    CmaTotal:              0 kB
    CmaFree:               0 kB
    HugePages_Total:       0
    HugePages_Free:        0
    HugePages_Rsvd:        0
    HugePages_Surp:        0
    Hugepagesize:       2048 kB
    Hugetlb:               0 kB
    DirectMap4k:       90048 kB
    DirectMap2M:     2007040 kB
    $
```

The kernel continually updates the `meminfo` file to show exactly what's going on in memory at that moment in time, so the file constantly changes.

SOFTWARE PROGRAM MANAGEMENT

The Linux operating system calls a running program a *process*. A process can run in the foreground, displaying output on a display, or it can run in background, behind the scenes. The kernel controls how the Linux system manages all the processes running on the system.

The kernel creates the first process, called the *init process*, to start all other processes on the system. When the kernel starts, it loads the init process into virtual memory. As the kernel starts each additional process, it gives it a unique area in virtual memory to store the data and code that the process uses.

There are a few different types of init process implementations available in Linux, but these days, the two most popular are as follows:

SysVinit—The *SysVinit* (SysV) initialization method was the original method used by Linux and was based on the Unix System V initialization method. Though it is not used by many Linux distributions these days, you still may find it around in older Linux distributions.

Systemd—The *systemd* initialization method was created in 2010 and has become the most popular initialization and process management system used by Linux distributions.

The SysVinit initialization method used a concept called *runlevels* to determine what processes to start. The runlevel defines the state of the running Linux system and what processes should run in each state. Table 1.1 shows the different runlevels associated with the SysVinit initialization method.

TABLE 1.1: The SysVinit Runlevels

RUNLEVEL	DESCRIPTION
0	Shuts down the system
1	Single-user mode used for system maintenance
2	Multiuser mode without networking services enabled
3	Multiuser mode with networking services enabled
4	Custom
5	Multiuser mode with GUI available
6	Reboots the system

The /etc/inittab file defines the default runlevel for a system. The processes that start for specific runlevels are defined in subdirectories of the /etc/rc.d directory. You can view the current runlevel at any time using the runlevel command, as shown here:

```
$ runlevel
N 5
$
```

The systemd initialization method became popular because it has the ability to start processes based on different events such as these:

◆ When the system boots

◆ When a particular hardware device is connected

◆ When a service is started

◆ When a network connection is established

◆ When a timer has expired

The systemd method determines what processes to run by linking events to *unit files*. Each unit file defines the programs to start when the specified event occurs. The systemctl program allows you to start, stop, and list the unit files currently running on the system.

The systemd method groups unit files together into *targets*. A target defines a specific running state of the Linux system, similar to the SysVinit runlevel concept. At system startup, the *default. target* unit defines all the unit files to start. You can view the current default target using the systemctl command.

```
$ systemctl get-default
graphical.target
$
```

The graphical.target target defines the processes to start when a multiuser graphical environment is running, similar to the old SysVinit runlevel 5.

 Real World Scenario

EXAMINING PROCESSES

In Chapter 14, "Working with Processes and Jobs," you'll see how to use the ps command to view the processes currently running on the Linux system. You can use it now to take a quick peek at what programs are currently running on your Linux system.

1. Log into your Linux system. (If you don't have a Linux system available yet, you can come back to here after going through either Chapter 2 or Chapter 4.)

2. At the command prompt, enter the command **ps ax**. You should see something similar to this output:

```
$ ps ax
    PID TTY       STAT    TIME COMMAND
      1 ?         Ss      0:00 /sbin/init maybe-ubiquity
      2 ?         S       0:00 [kthreadd]
      3 ?         I<      0:00 [rcu_gp]
      4 ?         I<      0:00 [rcu_par_gp]
      5 ?         I       0:00 [kworker/0:0-memcg_kmem_cache]
      6 ?         I<      0:00 [kworker/0:0H-kblockd]
      7 ?         I       0:00 [kworker/0:1-events]
      8 ?         I       0:00 [kworker/u2:0-events_power_efficient]
. . .
   1033 tty1      S       0:00 -bash
   1054 tty1      R+      0:00 ps ax
$
```

We've just shown the start of the listing, along with the last two lines, but you should see a long list of different programs running on your Linux system (including the ps command that you started). The kernel is keeping track of all those programs!

Hardware Management

Still another responsibility for the kernel is hardware management. Any device that the Linux system must communicate with needs driver code inserted inside the kernel code. The driver code allows the kernel to pass data back and forth to the device, acting as a middleman between applications and the hardware. There are two methods used for inserting device driver code in the Linux kernel.

- Drivers compiled in the kernel
- Driver modules added to the kernel

Previously, the only way to insert device driver code was to recompile the kernel. Each time you added a new device to the system, you had to recompile the kernel code. This process became even more inefficient as Linux kernels supported more hardware. Fortunately, Linux developers devised a better method to insert driver code into the running kernel.

Programmers developed the concept of kernel modules to allow you to insert driver code into a running kernel without having to recompile the kernel. Also, a kernel module could be removed from the kernel when the device was finished being used. This greatly simplified and expanded using hardware with Linux.

The Linux system identifies hardware devices as special files, called *device files*. There are three different classifications of device files.

- Character
- Block
- Network

Character device files are for devices that can only handle data one character at a time. Most types of modems and terminals are created as character files. Block files are for devices that can handle data in large blocks at a time, such as disk drives.

The network file types are used for devices that use packets to send and receive data. This includes network cards and a special loopback device that allows the Linux system to communicate with itself using common network programming protocols.

Linux creates special files, called *nodes*, for each device on the system. All communication with the device is performed through the device node. Each node has a unique number pair that identifies it to the Linux kernel. The number pair includes a major and a minor device number. Similar devices are grouped into the same major device number. The minor device number is used to identify a specific device within the major device group.

Filesystem Management

Unlike some other operating systems, the Linux kernel can support different types of filesystems to read and write data to and from hard drives. Besides having more than a dozen filesystems of its own, Linux can read and write to and from filesystems used by other operating systems, such as Microsoft Windows. The kernel must be compiled with support for all types of filesystems that the system will use. Table 1.2 lists the standard filesystems that a Linux system can use to read and write data.

TABLE 1.2:   Linux Filesystems

FILESYSTEM	DESCRIPTION
ext	Linux extended filesystem—the original Linux filesystem
ext2	Second extended filesystem; provides advanced features over ext
ext3	Third extended filesystem; supports journaling
ext4	Fourth extended filesystem; supports advanced journaling
btrfs	A newer, high-performance filesystem that supports journaling and large files
exfat	The extended Windows filesystem, used mainly for SD cards and USB sticks
hpfs	OS/2 high-performance filesystem
jfs	IBM's journaling file system
iso9660	ISO 9660 filesystem (CD-ROMs)
minix	MINIX filesystem
msdos	Microsoft FAT16
ncp	NetWare filesystem
nfs	Network File System
ntfs	Support for Microsoft NT filesystem
proc	Access to system information
smb	Samba SMB filesystem for network access
sysv	Older Unix filesystem
ufs	BSD filesystem
umsdos	Unix-like filesystem that resides on top of msdos
vfat	Windows 95 filesystem (FAT32)
XFS	High-performance 64-bit journaling filesystem

Any hard drive that a Linux server accesses must be formatted using one of the filesystem types listed in Table 1.2.

The Linux kernel interfaces with each filesystem using the Virtual File System (VFS). This provides a standard interface for the kernel to communicate with any type of filesystem. VFS caches information in memory as each filesystem is mounted and used.

The GNU Utilities

Besides having a kernel to control hardware devices and launch programs, a computer operating system needs utilities to perform standard functions, such as controlling files and programs. While Linus created the Linux system kernel, he had no system utilities to run on it. Fortunately for him, at the same time he was working, a group of people were working together on the Internet trying to develop a standard set of computer system utilities that mimicked the popular Unix operating system.

The GNU organization (GNU stands for GNU's Not Unix) developed a complete set of Unix utilities but had no kernel system to run them on. These utilities were developed under a software philosophy called open source software (OSS).

The concept of OSS allows programmers to develop software and then release it to the world with no licensing fees attached. Anyone can use the software, modify it, or incorporate it into their own system without having to pay a license fee. Uniting Linus's Linux kernel with the GNU operating system utilities created a complete, functional, free operating system.

While the bundling of the Linux kernel and GNU utilities is often just called Linux, you will see some Linux purists on the Internet refer to it as the GNU/Linux system to give credit to the GNU organization for its contributions to the cause.

The GNU project was mainly designed for Unix system administrators to have a Unix-like environment available. This focus resulted in the project porting many common Unix system command-line utilities. The core bundle of utilities supplied for Linux systems is called the *coreutils* package.

The GNU coreutils package consists of these three parts:

◆ Utilities for handling files

◆ Utilities for manipulating text

◆ Utilities for managing processes

Each of these three main groups of utilities contains several utility programs that are invaluable to the Linux system administrator and programmer.

Linux User Interfaces

Having a world-class operating system that can manage your computer hardware and software is great, but you also need some way to communicate with it. Back in the old days of computers, you communicated with the mainframe computer by punching holes into cards, feeding them into a card reader, and then waiting for the output to appear on a printer. Fortunately, those days are long gone.

Thanks to the Apple macOS and Microsoft Windows operating systems, these days most desktop computer users expect some type of graphical display to interact with their system. Linux doesn't disappoint, offering a plethora of graphical desktops you can choose from. The following sections describe a few of the more popular ones.

THE X WINDOW SOFTWARE

Two basic elements control your video environment—the video card in your PC and your monitor. To display fancy graphics on your computer, the Linux software needs to know how to talk to both of them. The X Window software is the core element in presenting graphics.

The X Window software is a low-level program that works directly with the video card and monitor in the PC and controls how Linux applications can present fancy windows and graphics on your computer.

Linux isn't the only operating system that uses X Window; there are versions written for many different operating systems. In the Linux world, there are a few different software packages that can implement it. There are two X Window packages that are most commonly used in Linux:

- X.org

- Wayland

The X.org package is the older of the two, based on the original Unix X Window System version 11 (often called X11). More Linux distributions are migrating to the newer Wayland software, which is more secure and easier to maintain.

When you first install a Linux distribution, it attempts to detect your video card and monitor and then creates an X Window configuration file that contains the required information. During installation, you may notice a time when the installation program scans your monitor for supported video modes. Sometimes this causes your monitor to go blank for a few seconds. Because there are lots of different types of video cards and monitors out there, this process can take a little while to complete.

The core X Window software produces a graphical display environment, but nothing else. While this is fine for running individual applications, it is not too useful for day-to-day computer use. There is no desktop environment allowing users to manipulate files or launch programs. To do that, you need a desktop environment on top of the X Window system software.

THE KDE PLASMA DESKTOP

The K Desktop Environment (KDE) was first released in 1996 as an open source project to produce a graphical desktop similar to the Microsoft Windows environment. The KDE desktop incorporates all of the features you are probably familiar with if you are a Windows user. Figure 1.3 shows the current version, called KDE Plasma, running in the openSUSE Linux distribution.

FIGURE 1.3
The KDE Plasma desktop on an openSUSE Linux system

The KDE Plasma desktop allows you to place both application and file icons in a special area on the desktop. If you single-click an application icon, the Linux system starts the application. If you single-click a file icon, the KDE desktop attempts to determine what application to start to handle the file.

The bar at the bottom of the desktop is called the Panel. The Panel consists of these four parts:

The KDE Start menu—Much like the Windows Start menu, the KDE Start menu contains links to start installed applications.

Program shortcuts—These are quick links to start applications directly from the Panel.

The taskbar—The taskbar shows icons for applications currently running on the desktop.

Applets—These are small applications that have an icon in the Panel that often can change depending on information from the application.

All of the Panel features are similar to what you would find in Windows. In addition to the desktop features, the KDE project has produced a wide assortment of applications that run in the KDE environment.

THE GNOME DESKTOP

The GNU Network Object Model Environment (GNOME) is another popular Linux desktop environment. First released in 1999, GNOME has become the default desktop environment for many Linux distributions (the most popular being Red Hat Linux).

GNOME CONTROVERSY

The GNOME desktop underwent a radical change with version 3, released in 2011. It departed from the standard look and feel of most desktops using standard menu bars and taskbars to make the interface more user-friendly across multiple platforms, such as tablets and mobile phones. This change led to controversy (see the "Other Desktops" section), but slowly many Linux enthusiasts accepted the new look and feel of the GNOME 3 desktop.

Figure 1.4 shows the standard GNOME desktop used in the Ubuntu Linux distribution.

The GNOME 3 desktop cleans up the desktop interface by reducing the available menus to just these three:

Activities—Displays favorites, as well as any running application icons

Calendar—Shows the current date/time, along with any system notification messages

System—Shows network connections, system settings, and options to restart the system

The GNOME 3 desktop was designed to work on multiple types of devices, so you'll find there aren't a lot of menus. To launch applications, you must search for them using the Activities Overview, which is a search feature from the Activities menu.

Figure 1.4
A GNOME 3 desktop on
an Ubuntu Linux system

Not to be outdone by KDE, the GNOME developers have also produced a host of graphical applications that integrate with the GNOME desktop.

OTHER DESKTOPS

One of the main features of Linux is choice, and nowhere is that more evident than in the graphical desktop world. There are a plethora of different types of graphical desktops available in the Linux world. If you're not happy with the default desktop in your Linux distribution, it usually doesn't take much effort to change it to something else.

When the GNOME desktop project radically changed its interface in version 3, many Linux developers who preferred the look and feel of GNOME version 2 created spin-off versions based on GNOME 2. Of these, two became somewhat popular.

Cinnamon—The Cinnamon desktop was developed in 2011 by the Linux Mint distribution in an attempt to continue development of the original GNOME 2 desktop. It's now available as an option in several Linux distributions, including Ubuntu, Fedora, and openSUSE.

MATE—The MATE desktop was also developed in 2011 by an Arch Linux user who disliked the switch to GNOME 3. However, it incorporates a few features of GNOME 3 (such as replacing the taskbar) but maintains the overall look and feel of GNOME 2.

Figure 1.5 shows the Cinnamon desktop as it appears in the Linux Mint distribution.

The downside to these fancy graphical desktop environments is that they require a fair amount of system resources to operate properly. In the early days of Linux, a hallmark and selling feature of Linux was its ability to operate on older, less powerful PCs that the newer Microsoft desktop products couldn't run on. However, with the popularity of KDE Plasma and GNOME 3 desktops, this has changed, as it takes just as much memory to run a KDE Plasma or GNOME 3 desktop as the latest Microsoft desktop environment.

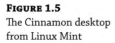

FIGURE 1.5
The Cinnamon desktop
from Linux Mint

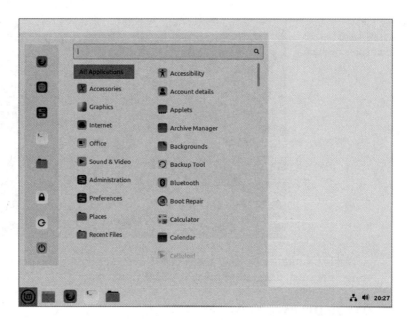

If you have an older PC, don't be discouraged. The Linux developers have banded together to take Linux back to its roots. They've created several low-memory–oriented graphical desktop applications that provide basic features that run perfectly fine on older PCs.

While these graphical desktops don't have a plethora of applications designed around them, they still run many basic graphical applications that support features such as word processing, spreadsheets, databases, drawing, and, of course, multimedia support.

Table 1.3 shows some of the smaller Linux graphical desktop environments that can be used on lower-powered PCs and laptops.

TABLE 1.3:   Other Linux Graphical Desktops

DESKTOP	DESCRIPTION
Fluxbox	A bare-bones desktop that doesn't include a Panel, only a pop-up menu to launch applications
Xfce	A desktop that's similar to the GNOME 2 desktop, but with fewer graphics for low-memory environments
JWM	Joe's Window Manager, a lightweight desktop ideal for low-memory and low-disk space environments
fvwm	Supports some advanced desktop features such as virtual desktops and Panels, but runs in low-memory environments
fvwm95	Derived from fvwm, but made to look like a Windows 95 desktop

These graphical desktop environments are not as fancy as the KDE Plasma and GNOME 3 desktops, but they provide basic graphical functionality just fine. Figure 1.6 shows what the Xfce desktop used in the MX Linux distribution looks like.

FIGURE 1.6
The Xfce desktop as seen in the MX Linux distribution

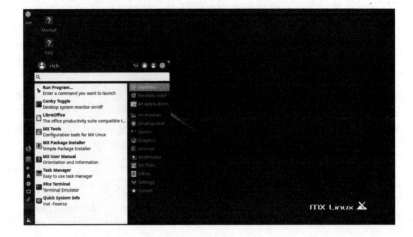

If you are using an older PC, try a Linux distribution that uses one of these desktops and see what happens. You may be pleasantly surprised.

THE COMMAND-LINE INTERFACE

While having a fancy graphical desktop interface is nice, there are drawbacks. The extra processing power required to interact with the graphics card takes away crucial CPU time that can be used for other programs. Nowhere is this more important than in a server environment.

Because of that, many Linux servers don't load a graphical desktop and instead rely on a text-based interface, called the *command-line interface* (CLI). The CLI provides a way for users to start programs, manage files on the filesystem, and manage processes running on the Linux system using simple text commands. The CLI is produced by a program called a *shell*. The shell allows you to enter text commands, and then it interprets the commands and then executes them in the kernel.

The shell contains a set of internal commands that you use to control things such as copying files, moving files, renaming files, displaying the programs currently running on the system, and stopping programs running on the system. Besides the internal commands, the shell also allows you to enter the name of a program at the command prompt. The shell passes the program name off to the kernel to start it.

You can also group shell commands into files to execute as a program. Those files are called *shell scripts*. Any command that you can execute from the command line can be placed in a shell script and run as a group of commands. This provides great flexibility in creating utilities for commonly run commands, or processes that require several commands grouped together.

There are quite a few Linux shells available to use on a Linux system. Different shells have different characteristics, some being more useful for creating scripts and some being more useful for managing processes. The default shell used in all Linux distributions is the Bash Shell. The Bash Shell was developed by the GNU project as a replacement for the standard Unix shell, called the Bourne shell (after its creator). The Bash Shell name is a play on this wording, referred to as the "Bourne again shell."

In addition to the Bash Shell, there are several other popular shells you could run into in a Linux environment. Table 1.4 lists the more popular ones.

TABLE 1.4: Linux Shells

SHELL	DESCRIPTION
ash	A simple, lightweight shell that runs in low-memory environments but has full compatibility with the Bash Shell
korn	A programming shell compatible with the Bourne shell but supporting advanced programming features like associative arrays and floating-point arithmetic
tcsh	A shell that incorporates elements from the C programming language into shell scripts
zsh	An advanced shell that incorporates features from bash, tcsh, and korn, providing advanced programming features, shared history files, and themed prompts

Most Linux distributions include more than one shell, although usually they pick one of them to be the default. If your Linux distribution includes multiple shells, feel free to experiment with different shells and see which one fits your needs.

Linux Distributions

Now that you have seen the four main components required for a complete Linux system, you may be wondering how you are going to get them all put together to make a Linux system. Fortunately, there are people who have already done that for you.

A complete Linux system package is called a *distribution*. There are lots of different Linux distributions available to meet just about any computing requirement you could have. Most distributions are customized for a specific user group, such as business users, multimedia enthusiasts, software developers, or average home users. Each customized distribution includes the software packages required to support specialized functions, such as audio- and video-editing software for multimedia enthusiasts, or compilers and integrated development environments (IDEs) for software developers.

The different Linux distributions are often divided into two categories.

◆ Core Linux distributions

◆ Specialized distributions

The following sections describe these different types of Linux distributions and show some examples of Linux distributions in each category.

Core Linux Distributions

A core Linux distribution contains a kernel, one or more graphical desktop environments, and just about every Linux application that is available, precompiled for the kernel. It provides one-stop shopping for a complete Linux installation. Table 1.5 shows some of the more popular core Linux distributions.

TABLE 1.5:   Core Linux Distributions

DISTRIBUTION	DESCRIPTION
Slackware	One of the original Linux distribution sets, popular with Linux geeks
Red Hat Enterprise	A commercial business distribution used mainly for Internet servers
Gentoo	A distribution designed for advanced Linux users, containing only Linux source code
openSUSE	Different distributions for business and home use
Debian	Popular with Linux experts and commercial Linux products

In the early days of Linux, a distribution was released as a set of floppy disks. You had to download groups of files and then copy them onto disks. It would usually take 20 or more disks to make an entire distribution! Needless to say, this was a painful experience.

Nowadays, Linux distributions are released as an *ISO image file*. The ISO image file is a complete disk image of a DVD as a single file. You use a software application to either burn the ISO image file onto a DVD or create a bootable USB stick. You then just boot your workstation from the DVD or USB stick to install Linux. This makes installing Linux much easier.

However, beginners still often run into problems when they install one of the core Linux distributions. To cover just about any situation in which someone might want to use Linux, a single distribution has to include lots of application software. They include everything from high-end Internet database servers to common games.

While having lots of options available in a distribution is great for Linux geeks, it can become a nightmare for beginning Linux users. Most core distributions ask a series of questions during the installation process to determine which applications to load by default, what hardware is connected to the PC, and how to configure the hardware. Beginners often find these questions confusing. As a result, they often either load way too many programs on their computer or don't load enough and later discover that their computer won't do what they want it to do.

Fortunately for beginners, there's a much simpler way to install Linux.

Specialized Linux Distributions

A new subgroup of Linux distributions has started to appear. These are typically based on one of the main distributions but contain only a subset of applications that would make sense for a specific area of use.

In addition to providing specialized software (such as only office products for business users), customized Linux distributions also attempt to help beginning Linux users by autodetecting and autoconfiguring common hardware devices. This makes installing Linux a much more enjoyable process.

Table 1.6 shows some of the specialized Linux distributions available and what they specialize in.

TABLE 1.6: Specialized Linux Distributions

DISTRIBUTION	DESCRIPTION
Fedora	A free distribution, originally used as a testing ground for Red Hat Enterprise Linux, now a popular distribution in its own right
Ubuntu	A free distribution originally intended for school and home desktop use, now also used as a server
MX Linux	A free distribution for home use
Linux Mint	A free distribution for home entertainment use
Puppy Linux	A free small distribution that runs well on older PCs

That's just a small sampling of specialized Linux distributions. There are hundreds of specialized Linux distributions, and more are popping up all the time on the Internet. No matter what your specialty, you'll probably find a Linux distribution made for you.

Many of the specialized Linux distributions are based on the Debian Linux distribution. They use the same installation files as Debian but package only a small fraction of a full-blown Debian system.

THE LINUX LiveDVD

Most Linux distributions also have a LiveDVD version available. The LiveDVD version is a self-contained ISO image file that you can burn onto a DVD (or USB stick) to boot up a running Linux system directly, without having to install it on your hard drive. Depending on the distribution, the LiveDVD either contains a small subset of applications or, in the case of specialized distributions, the entire system. The benefit of the LiveDVD is that you can test it with your system hardware before going to the trouble of installing the system.

The Bottom Line

List the components of a standard Linux system. The main components of a Linux system include the Linux kernel, the GNU utilities, a user interface, and application programs. The kernel controls how memory, programs, and hardware all interact with one another. The GNU utilities provide useful functions such as text and file manipulation. The Linux user interfaces range from fancy graphical desktops, such as GNOME or KDE Plasma, to simple command-line interfaces, such as the Bash Shell.

Master It   The Linux kernel is constantly updated and managed by a group of developers. They publish their work at the `kernel.org` website. Go to that website and determine the version number of the latest stable release. What version is currently under development?

Explain how GNU utilities are used within Linux.   The GNU utilities provide command-line functions for creating, modifying, moving, and deleting files, as well as working with data inside text files. The main GNU utilities are in the coreutils package.

Master It   The GNU community is constantly making improvements to the core GNU utilities used in Linux. You can find the latest released utilities at `www.gnu.org/software/coreutils/`. Go to that website and determine the current version of the GNU coreutils package.

Describe the various Linux user interface environments.   There are many graphical desktop environments available in Linux. The two most popular ones are GNOME and KDE Plasma. Both provide common desktop features most desktop users are comfortable with. However, for server environments, it's most common to use a command-line interface (CLI) provided by a Linux shell program. The most common Linux shell is bash.

Master It   The GNU Bash Shell is continually being updated, with updates available at `www.gnu.org/software/bash/`. According to that website, what is the most recent version of bash available for download?

Explain why there are different Linux distributions.   A Linux distribution bundles the various parts of a Linux system into a simple package that you can easily install on your PC. The Linux distribution world consists of full-blown Linux distributions that include just about every application imaginable, as well as specialized Linux distributions that only include applications focused on a special function.

Master It   There are many websites that track Linux distributions. The `www.distrowatch.com` website is a popular place to get information on new releases for lots of different distributions. Go to that site and list the current top five Linux distribution downloads.

Chapter 2

Installing an Ubuntu Server

Ubuntu Server is a popular Linux distribution, and most likely you will install it many times in your Linux career. Gaining experience with this distro's installation process will help you become a Linux expert.

The first few times you install a particular operating system, it feels like a daunting task. And rightly so! Without proper guidance, the process can often result in frustration and lost time. Our goal in this chapter is to assist you through your first installation of the Ubuntu Server distribution. We provide step-by-step guidance, help you avoid pitfalls, and ultimately build your sysadmin skillset.

IN THIS CHAPTER, YOU WILL LEARN TO

- ◆ Review needed Ubuntu Server hardware resources

- ◆ Determine the requirements for a virtual Ubuntu system

- ◆ Obtain Ubuntu Server software

- ◆ Conduct an installation of an Ubuntu Server

- ◆ Audit the Ubuntu Server's installation

Pre-Installation Requirements

A graphical user interface (GUI) uses a lot of resources on a computer system, and if the server is not needed for providing a desktop to users, those applications and utilities are typically not installed. This is the case with the Ubuntu Server distribution. If you want a GUI on it, you'll have to add that software to it after the installation.

The Ubuntu Server distribution is designed for a system that not only doesn't need a GUI, but is headless. Though that sounds like something in a horror movie, you often find these types of servers in modern server rooms. A headless system is simply a computer without a directly attached monitor. A sysadmin connects to the computer through the network to reach its text-based command-line interface.

Before jumping into a Linux installation, it's wise to review what is needed to make the project successful. We're assuming that you already have your customer's requirements in hand and now need to determine what is required for an Ubuntu installation on a physical or virtualized server.

UNDERSTANDING BASIC VIRTUALIZATION TERMS

If you're unfamiliar with virtualization computer terms, it's a good idea to read through the first several pages of Chapter 22, "Exploring the Virtualization Environment." But here are a few basic definitions to get you started:

Virtual machine (VM)—A computer system that appears and acts as a physical computer server to its users and operating system but is actually a grouping of files and programs managed by a hypervisor

Hypervisor—Software application used to create and manage virtual machines

Host machine—The physical server on which the hypervisor and its virtual machines run

---

In the next few sections, we'll look at the hardware requirements needed for installing the Ubuntu server distribution directly on a physical server and for installing it within a virtualized environment.

Hardware Requirements

If you plan on installing the Ubuntu Server 20.04LTS distribution directly on a headless server, your computer must support a 64-bit processor architecture. Any of the following will work fine:

◆ AMD amd64

◆ ARM arm64

◆ IBM Z s390x

◆ Intel amd64

◆ LinuxONE s390x

◆ POWER8 or 9 ppc64el

Besides having the proper processor on your system, you need to have enough resources available to avoid a sluggish system. Table 2.1 shows the recommended resources to support a well-running Ubuntu Server distro.

TABLE 2.1:   Recommended Server Resources for Ubuntu Server Distribution

RESOURCE	MINIMUM	RECOMMENDED
CPU	1 GHz	1 or more GHz
Memory	1 GB	2 or more GB
Disk space	2.5 GB	10 or more GB

Keep in mind that these recommendations are only for the operating system. Increase these resources to meet the needs of the application(s) you will run on the server.

Not everyone has access to a physical server. But you can set up a virtual environment on a laptop or some old desktop you have stuffed away in your closet. Using a virtualized system on your daily laptop provides a great deal of flexibility. You can learn about Linux while sitting in the park!

Virtual Server Requirements

If you plan on running the Ubuntu Server distribution as a virtual machine, you need to ensure that the host machine's operating system is supported by the hypervisor.

For this book, we're focusing on the Oracle VirtualBox hypervisor software. Here are a few of the operating systems on which it can run:

◆ Windows 8.1

◆ Windows 10

◆ macOS High Sierra

◆ Ubuntu 18.04LTS

This list is always evolving. It's a good idea to visit the Oracle VirtualBox manual website, `virtualbox.org/manual`, and view the currently supported host operating systems.

Running a virtualized environment will increased the needed resources on your system. You need to make sure that the host machine can handle not only the hypervisor but the Ubuntu Server VM as well. Table 2.2 lists the recommended host machine resources for a virtualized Ubuntu Server system.

TABLE 2.2:   Recommended Host Machine Resources for an Ubuntu Server VM

RESOURCE	MINIMUM	RECOMMENDED
CPU	2 GHz dual core	2 GHz dual core
Memory	4 GB	16 or more GB
Free disk space	25 GB	30 or more GB

These recommendations assume you are running only one VM at a time. You need more resources on your system if you plan on running multiple VMs at the same time or run a VM along with several other apps. Keep in mind that these resource recommendations are guidelines. They are not rules, so you may need a little more or a little less.

After you have your host system properly outfitted with resources, it's time to start downloading software. We'll cover those steps in the next section.

Finding the Software

After you determine that you have the appropriate resources but before you start the installation process, you need to have the proper software. You need to make sure that you get the correct version and type. For the larger software files, it's also critical to verify that no corruption has occurred when the software was downloaded. If you have a corrupt software file, you'll end up needlessly wasting your time.

Oracle VirtualBox

We recommend that you use Oracle VirtualBox as the hypervisor on your system. You can download the latest version of this software from `virtualbox.org`.

It is important that you get the correct platform package of VirtualBox. You'll see a list of potential host systems on the VirtualBox website, such as the following:

◆   Windows

◆   macOS

◆   Linux

Make sure to select the VirtualBox package for the system on which the Ubuntu Server virtual machine will be running. Often people make an incorrect choice, because they confuse the host system with the virtual machine. Here's an example that may help: if you have a laptop running Windows where you plan on installing Ubuntu Server as a VM, then Windows is the host, and you want to download the VirtualBox package for Windows. Our examples in this chapter are based on a Windows 10 host system.

Ubuntu Server

To install Ubuntu Server as a VM, besides the hypervisor software (and the correct amount of resources on the host machine), you need an Ubuntu Server ISO image file. An ISO image file (also called an *ISO image*) is a specially formatted package file that contains all the files needed to boot a system. The Ubuntu Server ISO image file is used to boot and then install the distribution. In our case, we're installing it as a VM.

To get your hands on the Ubuntu Server ISO image file, go to `ubuntu.com/download/server`. If you are provided options for the download, choose the manual install option as shown in Figure 2.1.

You can start the process of downloading the ISO image file by clicking the Download button. Depending on the web browser you are using, you may have to deal with some pop-up windows that want to confirm it is OK to download this file.

Since the ISO file is large, it's important to verify that no corruption has occurred while the software was downloading. If you have a corrupt ISO image file, you'll need to download the file again.

FIGURE 2.1
Option to choose an
Ubuntu Server ISO
image file download

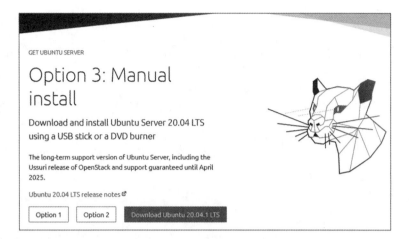

Real World Scenario

CHECKING THE UBUNTU SERVER ISO IMAGE FILE

Once the Ubuntu Server ISO image file is completely downloaded, you need to verify it. To do this, we'll employ hashing. Hashing uses a one-way mathematical algorithm to create a fixed-length hash, which is basically a series of letters and numbers. A hash is also called a *message digest*, a *hash value*, a *fingerprint*, a *signature*, or *cipher text*. One cool thing about hash values is that hashing produces the same hash value for files that are the same. You can take a file with a picture in it and copy it to another location. If we use hashing to produce a hash value for the original picture file and for the copied picture file and those two hash values match, we know that the picture was not corrupted when it was copied to the new location.

Follow these steps to produce a hash value to check your image file:

1. On your Windows 10 system, open the Windows 10 PowerShell app by typing **Windows PowerShell** in the search bar and clicking the resulting Windows PowerShell app icon.

2. After the Windows PowerShell app window is open and you have a prompt, assuming you down-loaded your Ubuntu Server image file to the Downloads folder, type **cd Downloads** and press Enter. The prompt should now show that you are in the Downloads folder.

3. Run the PowerShell hashing utility on the Ubuntu Server image file by typing **Get-FileHash ubuntu**, and press the Tab key so that PowerShell autocompletes the Ubuntu Server's image filename for you. Go on to the next step before you press Enter.

4. Complete the rest of the PowerShell command by pressing the spacebar, typing **-Algorithm SHA256**, and pressing Enter. Be patient! It may take a while for the command to output the SHA256 hash value. You should see something similar to the following:

Don't exit the PowerShell window yet. You need to compare your resulting hash value with the current SHA256 hash value on the Ubuntu website.

5. Open your favorite web browser and go to `releases.ubuntu.com/focal/SHA256SUMS`. (If this web page has been moved, you may need to search the `releases.ubuntu.com` site to find the Ubuntu Server ISO image file's SHA256 hash value.)

6. Compare the hash value on the website with your hash value in PowerShell for the Ubuntu Server ISO image file. If they match, no file corruption occurred when you downloaded the file, and congratulations—you're ready to move forward in the installation process! However, if the hash values don't match, you need to download the file again and repeat this checking process.

7. Type **exit** at the PowerShell prompt to leave the app.

Verifying that the Ubuntu Server ISO image file is a good copy will save you time. If you tried to use a corrupt image file in an installation, it may work partway through the process and then quit before completion. That's frustrating. It's always best to check that your file is good before proceeding within an install.

PREPARING FOR A HARDWARE INSTALLATION

If you are planning on installing the Ubuntu Server distribution directly on a computer's hardware, instead of creating a VM, you need to do one additional step after checking the ISO image file: create a bootable media device. While bootable DVDs were popular many years ago, most hardware instal-lations can be handled through a bootable USB drive. The process of creating this bootable USB (or DVD) is called *burning* an ISO file to a USB drive.

You cannot just copy the file to the USB. Instead, you need a special software app that will burn the ISO properly. To find the right software, open your web browser and go to your favorite search engine. Type **burn a bootable USB** and press Enter. The resulting list will have several sites with instructions that point to free software. Once you have your Ubuntu Server ISO image file properly burned to a USB (or DVD) drive, you're able to boot your system and perform the installation process similar to what is covered in the next section.

Now that you've verified your copy of the Ubuntu Server ISO image file and downloaded the Oracle VirtualBox hypervisor software, you're ready to start the installation. We'll cover that process next.

Running the Installation

To create an Ubuntu Server VM, you need to first install the hypervisor, Oracle VirtualBox. Once that software is up and running, you can set up and install Ubuntu as a VM using its ISO image file and the hypervisor.

Oracle VirtualBox

The Oracle VirtualBox hypervisor software will allow you to do much more than set up Ubuntu Server as a Linux VM. You can also install another version of Windows within a VM and use it to try out features or configurations you normally wouldn't do on your main system.

 **Real World Scenario**

INSTALLING ORACLE VirtualBox ON WINDOWS 10

If you have ever installed an app on Windows, the process of installing the Oracle VirtualBox hypervisor will feel familiar. It follows the typical Windows installation process.

1. Assuming you downloaded your VirtualBox software file to the Downloads folder, navigate to that folder and double-click the software file. The file will have a name similar to the following, but with version numbers instead of #: `VirtualBox-#.#.#-######.exe`.

2. Click the Next button in the VirtualBox Welcome window, which looks similar to the following:

3. If desired, in the Custom Setup window, make any modification you'd like. If you want to install VirtualBox using the defaults, just click the Next button.

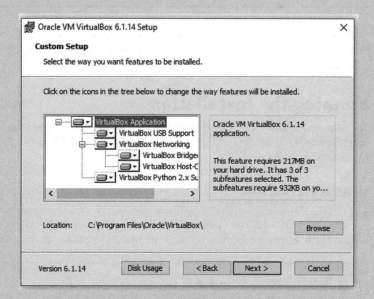

4. In the second Custom Setup window, remove check marks from the boxes if you want to have fewer methods for accessing VirtualBox or no registered file associations. Click the Next button when you are done. If you want to keep the defaults, just click the Next button.

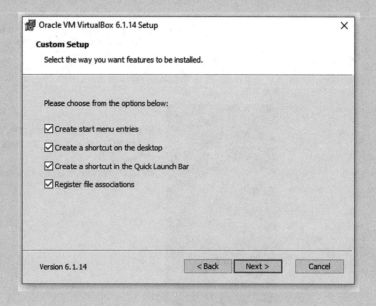

5. After reading the Warning window and you are ready to proceed with the installation, click the Next button.

6. You get one more chance to bail out of this installation. If you want to continue, click the Install button.

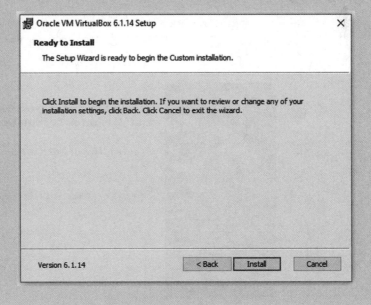

7. If you are not performing this VirtualBox software installation in an account that has adminis-trator privileges, you will receive a pop-up window asking for the administrator password. Enter the password and click the Yes button.

8. At this point, you will receive an installation status box that shows the progress of the VirtualBox software install, similar to the following:

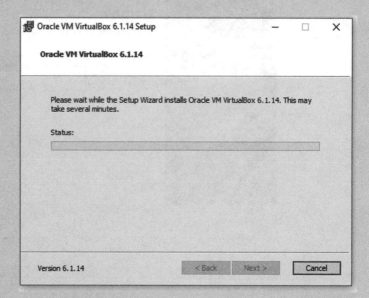

9. After the software installation is completed, you'll receive a window letting you know that it is done. Click the Finish button to open the VirtualBox hypervisor app.

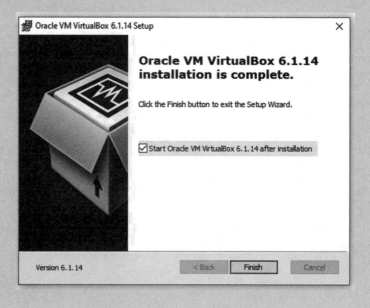

10. You should see a window showing the Oracle VirtualBox hypervisor interface, called the VirtualBox Manager, which looks similar to this:

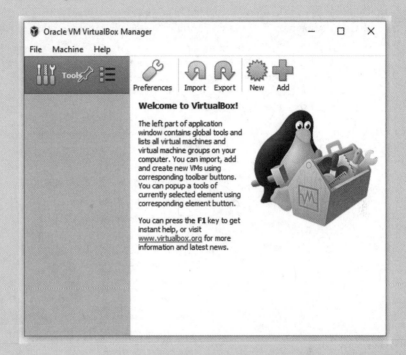

Congratulations! You have successfully installed the hypervisor software! You are ready to start the process of creating your Ubuntu Server VM.

If you need to take a break, close out the VirtualBox interface window by clicking the X in the upper-right corner. However, if you want to plow on ahead, keep it open. We'll launch into installing Ubuntu Server in the next section.

Ubuntu Server

Installing the Ubuntu Server as a VM may feel overwhelming the first time you do it, but as you complete the process a few more times, you'll feel more at ease. We'll help you through this initial instance to build confidence.

 **Real World Scenario**

SETTING UP AN UBUNTU SERVER CONFIGURATION WITHIN ORACLE VirtualBox

Prior to installing Ubuntu Server as a VM within the VirtualBox hypervisors, you need to perform a few basic tasks to create and configure a place for the new VM within the VirtualBox app. After you have completed these tasks, you will have a folder on your host machine for the new VM as well as two files within the folder: one file for the VM configuration information and one file acting as a hard disk for the VM.

Follow these steps to configure the VM. Though only a few steps are needed to complete this part of the installation project, they are important! So don't skim through this exercise.

1. Open the Oracle VirtualBox app on your host system. How this is accomplished depends on the configuration you chose when installing the VirtualBox software. You may have to find it via the menu search feature on Windows 10, or you can simply click the VirtualBox icon on the desktop or taskbar. Once you have the app open, you should see a window showing the Oracle VirtualBox Manager that looks similar to this:

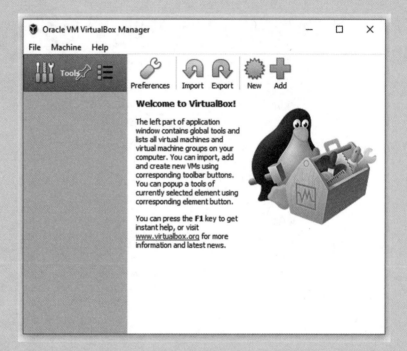

2. In the VirtualBox Manager window, using the top menu within the window, select Machine ➤ New. This will start the process of configuring the Ubuntu Server VM and produce the Create Virtual Machine window.

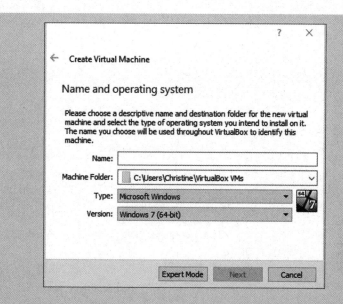

3. Enter the name **Ubuntu Server** in the Create Virtual Machine window's Name box.

4. Click the Next button to reach the Memory Size window, which looks similar to the following:

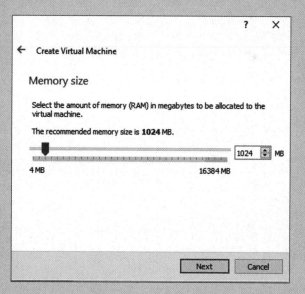

5. By either typing in the memory setting box or using the up-arrow button, change the Ubuntu Server memory to **2048**MB.

6. Click the Next button in the Memory Size window to reach the Hard Disk window.

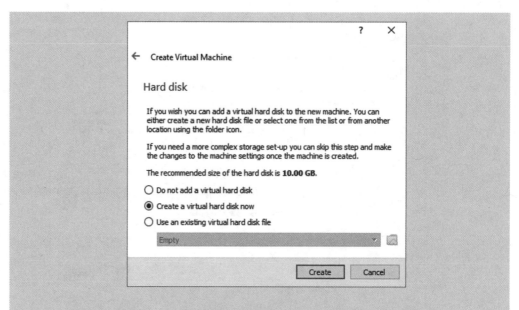

7. Double-check that the Create A Virtual Hard Disk Now option is selected. (You can tell that a particular option is selected by the circle next to it being filled with a dark color as shown in the previous figure.) If you need to select the Create A Virtual Hard Disk Now option, click the empty circle next to it.

8. Click the Create button in the Hard Disk window, which will open another configuration window called Hard Disk File Type.

9. Within the Hard Disk File Type window, ensure that the VirtualBox disk image (VDI) is selected.

10. Click the Next button, and the Storage On Physical Hard Disk window will appear. This configuration window looks similar to the following:

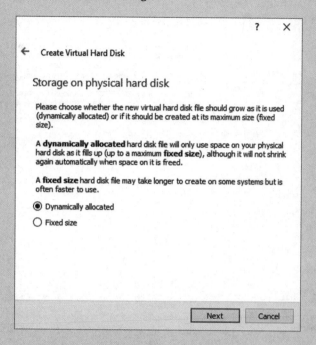

11. Double-check that the Dynamically Allocated setting is selected.

12. Click the Next button to open the File Location And Size window.

13. Click the Next button, and the Storage On Physical Hard Disk window will appear. In this window, you will see where the VM's virtual disk file will be created as well as its size. This configuration window looks similar to the following:

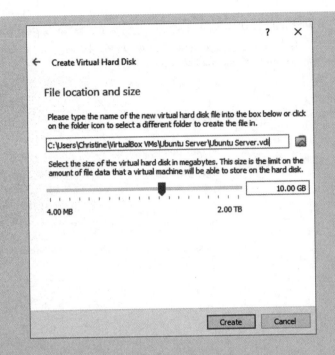

14. Change the file size to 16 GB by typing **16** within the size box.

15. You are now ready to create the basic configuration and virtual disk file of the VM. Do so by clicking the Create button.

   You should now be back at the VirtualBox Manager window with the Ubuntu Server VM in the left pane, as shown here:

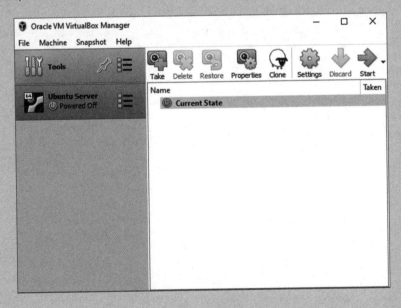

We have a few more configuration items to accomplish before the VM is completely configured.

16. Click the Settings button in the VirtualBox Manager's top-right pane, which opens the Settings window for the Ubuntu Server VM.

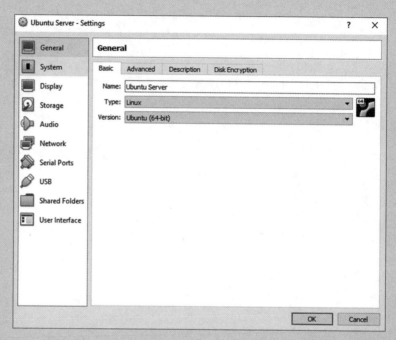

17. In the Settings window, click Network in the left pane to open the Network settings window for the Ubuntu Server.

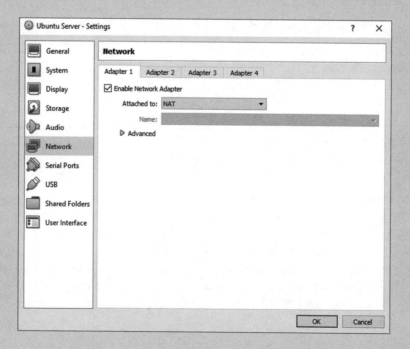

The next few steps help you to set up a second network interface card (NIC) on the Ubuntu Server. This allows your VM to act as an independent node on your network.

18. In the Network settings window's right pane, click the Adapter 2 tab.

19. In the Adapter 2 tab window, click the empty box next to Enable Network Adapter.

20. Still in the Network settings' Adapter 2 tab window, use the arrow to open the drop-down menu in the Attached To box, and select Bridged Adapter. Except for the Name box, your selections should look similar to the following:

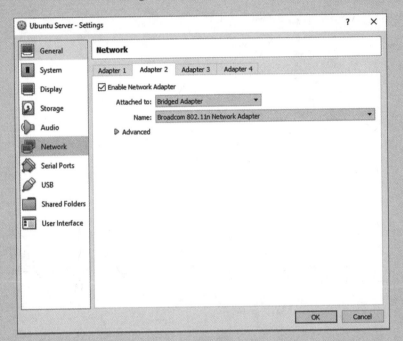

21. Click the OK button to save the network settings.

You should now be back to the VirtualBox Manager window. Pat yourself on the back! You have successfully configured the Ubuntu Server VM.

All this hard work will soon pay off. You are now ready to install the Ubuntu Server distribution on the virtual machine you just configured within VirtualBox.

 **Real World Scenario**

INSTALLING UBUNTU SERVER AS A VM

After configuring the Ubuntu Server VM within the VirtualBox hypervisor, you can perform the actual installation of the Linux OS. Conducting the installation process on a VM is similar to conducting it on a physical server. Just a few differences exist, such as loading the ISO image file into the virtualized DVD drive.

Follow these steps to install your Ubuntu Server from the ISO image file:

1. Open the Oracle VirtualBox hypervisor app on your host system if it's not already open.

2. If you have multiple VMs configured in your hypervisor, click one time on the Ubuntu Server VM to select it.

3. Click the Settings button in the VirtualBox Manager's top-right pane, which opens the Settings window for the Ubuntu Server VM.

4. In the Settings window, click Storage in the left pane to open the Storage settings window for the Ubuntu Server. It will look similar to the following:

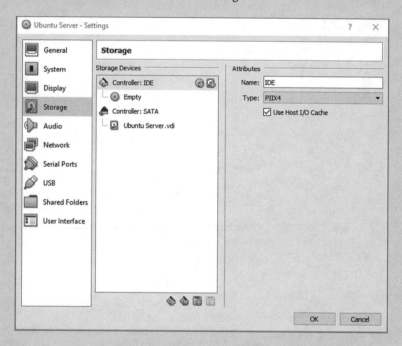

5. In the Storage settings window's middle pane under Controller: IDE, click the word *Empty* to open the Attributes pane for the IDE optical drive.

6. In the Storage settings window's Attributes pane, click the DVD image to produce a drop-down menu, and select Choose/Create A Virtual Optical Disk. An Optical Disk Selector window will appear that looks similar to the following:

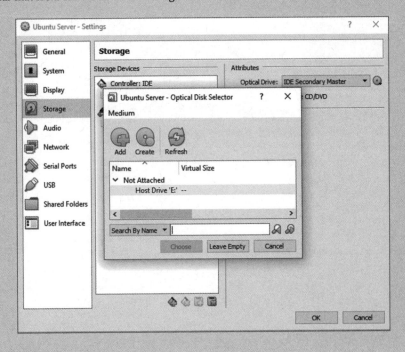

7. In the Optical Disk Selector window, click the Add icon, which will open the Windows Explorer utility, and you will see "Please choose an optical disk file" in the window's title bar.

8. Navigate to the location of your Ubuntu Server ISO image file, select the file by clicking it, and then click Open. The Optical Disk Selector window now looks similar to the following:

9. In the Optical Disk Selector window, click Choose, and you are returned to the Storage settings window's Attributes pane with the Ubuntu Server ISO image filename displayed under Controller: IDE.

10. Click OK to keep the virtually loaded ISO image file and return to the main VirtualBox Manager window.

11. Boot your Ubuntu Server VM by clicking the Start button in the VirtualBox Manager's top-right pane.

You may see lots of messages go by on your screen. Let the process continue until you reach this window:

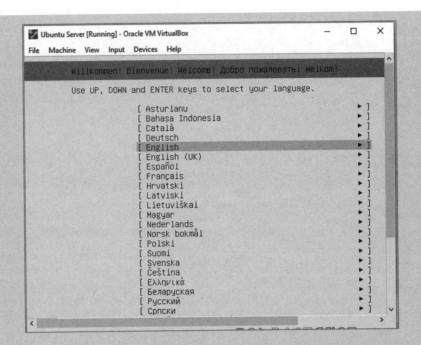

12. Using your arrow keys, select the language you prefer and press Enter.

13. In the Keyboard configuration window, select your desired keyboard layout (the defaults are typically OK), and press Enter.

14. In the Network Connections window, review the displayed information, and press Enter.

15. In the Configure Proxy window, review the displayed information, and if you need to enter a proxy address, do so. Otherwise, press Enter.

16. In the Configure Ubuntu Archive Mirror window, press Enter.

17. If you receive the Install Update Available window, select Update To The New Installer, and press Enter. You have to wait until the installer is updated. This may take a few minutes depending on the speed of your Internet connection. When it is complete, you should see the next installation window, which looks similar to the following:

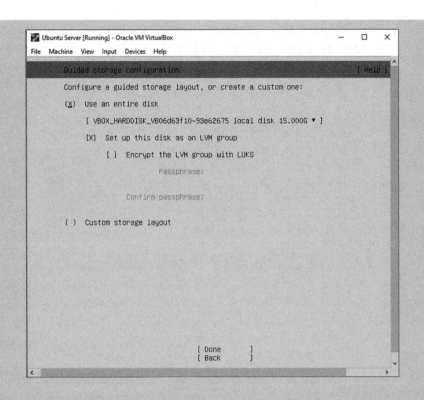

18. In the Guided Storage Configuration screen, keep the defaults, tab to Done, and press Enter.

19. Read through the information provided in the storage configuration window, and press Enter. You'll receive a warning message similar to the following:

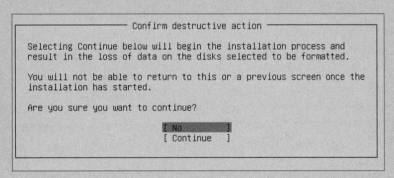

Don't let this warning message scare you. Remember that your virtual hard drive for this Ubuntu Server is merely a file on your host machine.

20. Tab to Continue, and press Enter.

21. Within the Profile Setup screen, type your first and last names in the Your Name field.

22. Tab to the Your Server's Name field, and type **ubuntu-server**.

23. Tab to the Pick A Username field, and type **sysadmin**.

24. Now tab to the Choose A Password field, and type in a password. Be sure to choose one that you will remember!

25. Tab to the Confirm Your Password field, and type in the same password as you did in the previous step. Your screen should now look similar to the following:

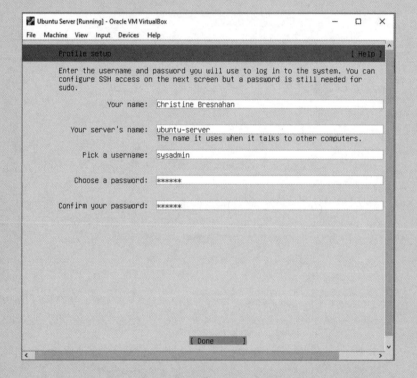

26. Once all the fields in the Profile Setup window are filled, tab to Done and press Enter.

27. In the SSH Setup window, tab to Done and press Enter.

You'll receive a message in the next screen when the initial installation is complete that looks similar to the following:

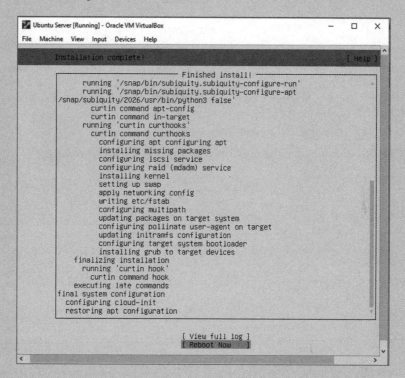

28. Press Enter to select Reboot Now.

29. Because the Ubuntu Server ISO image file has not yet been removed from the virtual DVD drive, you'll most likely get a "Failed" message along with a request to remove the installation medium. Click the X in the VM's upper-right corner. You'll receive the Close Virtual Machine screen, which looks similar to the following:

30. Click the circle next to Power Off The Machine.

31. Click OK to power off the Ubuntu Server virtual machine. At this point, the VirtualBox hypervisor typically automatically removes the ISO image file from the virtual DVD drive for you. But you should check to make sure it is gone.

32. Click the Settings button in the VirtualBox Manager's top-right pane, which opens the Settings window for the Ubuntu Server VM.

33. In the Settings window, click Storage in the left pane to open the Storage settings window for the Ubuntu Server. Here you should see the word *Empty* in the window's middle pane under the Controller: IDE.

34. Click OK to return to the VirtualBox Manager window.

35. Boot up your Ubuntu Server VM by clicking the Start button in the VirtualBox Manager's top-right pane.

You may see lots of messages go by on your screen. Let the process continue until you reach this window:

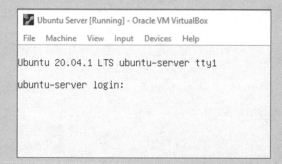

Because this first terminal, called tty1, gets messages displayed on it, it's best to jump to a different terminal where you can work in peace.

36. Press Ctrl+Alt+F2 to reach the tty2 terminal.

37. In the Username field, type **sysadmin** and press Enter.

38. In the Password field, be aware that nothing will show as you type in your password. There are no symbols such as asterisks or dots shown. Type in the password you created for this system earlier, and press Enter.

39. After you log into the system successfully, you receive a prompt similar to the following:
sysadmin@ubuntu-server:~$

This prompt is where you enter your commands, and it's called the command-line interface.

The next several commands assume that your host machine is connected to a network.

40. As part of the installation process, update the software information by typing **sudo apt update**, and press Enter. When it asks for a password, type in the same password you used to log into the system.

41. When you receive a prompt, update the software by typing **sudo apt dist-upgrade**, and press Enter. It may ask you for a sudo password, and if it does, type in the same password you used to log into the system.

42. When the software update process asks "Do you want to continue? [Y/n]," type **Y** and press Enter.

This software update may take a while, so go get a cup of coffee and check the latest statuses on social media.

43. When you receive a command-line prompt, the installation process is complete. Type **sudo poweroff** at the prompt and press Enter. It may ask you for a sudo password, and if it does, type in the same password you used to log into the system.

Congratulations! You've installed Ubuntu Server as a VM within the VirtualBox hypervisor. Now that the installation process is complete, it's a good idea to check and make sure everything is OK. We'll cover that next.

Checking the Installation

Though the system may appear fine after an initial installation, it's wise to check. It may be tricky to understand everything you are looking at in this section, but reviewing this information will help as we cover these utilities and concepts in detail later in the book. Also, you can return to this section the next time you perform an Ubuntu distribution installation for guidance.

First, boot your Ubuntu Server VM. After the system has booted, log into the tty2 terminal, and do the following:

Check for boot errors. There are three commands that can help you check for boot errors, and none of them requires the sudo command to run. The first is dmesg. This will display the kernel ring buffer, but that data is useful only if you check it soon after the system has booted.

To see boot messages long after a system boot, type **less /var/log/bootstrap.log** at the prompt and press Enter. You can move forward through this log by pressing the spacebar. When you are done looking at the information, press the Q key to return to the command-line prompt.

Finally, you can look for boot errors and all kinds of messages via the journalctl command. To peruse this information, you will need to press the spacebar to move forward and then the Q key to quit your viewing.

Determine the default boot level. The default boot level on a Linux system determines what applications are started when the system boots. The command to see this information is systemctl get-default. It does not require the sudo command to use.

Most likely, you will see graphical.target when you issue this command, meaning that if graphical user interface (GUI) software is available, the GUI will start on bootup. However, on Ubuntu Server, since GUI software is *not* installed by default, this response from the systemctl get-default command does not indicate a GUI is provided.

Check version information.   Determining the version numbers of the system's main components is helpful when tracking down problems. First, make sure you have the right Ubuntu Server distribution version installed by typing **cat /etc/issue** at the prompt. The version is in the first few words of the displayed line.

Check the Linux kernel version too. This is important to know because different features (and bugs!) exist in the various kernel versions. To see this information, you need to type **uname -r** at the command-line prompt. You can also view this information via the cat /proc/ version command.

Finally, look at the version of the Bash shell running on the system. This is easy to accomplish with the bash --version command.

Once you've completed your checks, celebrate! You worked hard to get this Ubuntu Server distribution installed correctly.

The Bottom Line

Review needed Ubuntu server hardware resources.   Determining the hardware resources required for an Ubuntu installation on a physical or virtualized server helps to ensure a successful completion of the install. It also avoids wasting time.

> **Master It**   Imagine that you need to install the Ubuntu Server on a physical server that has a dual-core 1 GHz CPU, a 200 GB hard drive, and 10 GB of RAM. Are the server's resources sufficient? Why or why not?

Determine the requirements for a virtual Ubuntu system.   Installing the Ubuntu Server distribution on as a VM on a host system has different requirements than a direct installation on a physical server. It is critical to evaluate the host system so that the installation is successful.

> **Master It**   Your project team is planning on installing two Ubuntu Server VMs on a host system that has a dual-core 1 GHz CPU, a 200 GB hard drive, and 10 GB of RAM. Are the host system's resources sufficient? Why or why not?

Obtain Ubuntu Server software.   To install the Ubuntu Server Linux distribution, you must have the proper ISO image file. This is true whether you are installing it directly on hardware or as a VM. Besides getting the ISO file, you need to ensure that it is not corrupted so that the installation proceeds well.

> **Master It**   You've downloaded the Ubuntu Server ISO image file but are concerned that during the download process, file corruption occurred. What should you do to see whether the ISO image file is corrupt?

Conduct an installation of an Ubuntu Server.   There are several steps to successfully install an Ubuntu Server, and it is critical that you complete all of them. Skipping a step can cause problems immediately, and problems later, if you can even get the system to boot.

> **Master It**   Your sysadmin team has correctly installed the Ubuntu Server software from the ISO image file, and the system booted without any problems. What's the next step?

Audit the Ubuntu Server's installation.   If you had some problems while booting the system, there are a few commands you can use to look at helpful boot messages. But even a successful installation still requires a few additional checks.

Master It   At your company, you have completed the entire Ubuntu Server installation process on a new system without any problems for the development team. The team wants to know what version of the Linux kernel is used on this new system. How do you get that information?

Chapter 3

Installing and Maintaining Software in Ubuntu

In the old days of Linux, installing software could be a painful experience. Fortunately, the Linux developers have made life a little easier for us by bundling software into prebuilt packages that are much easier to install. However, there's still a little work on your part to get the software packages installed, especially if you want to do so from the command line on a server.

IN THIS CHAPTER, YOU WILL LEARN TO

- ◆ Explore different Linux software package management systems

- ◆ Use Debian software packages to install software

- ◆ Install applications using Debian snap containers

- ◆ Install software from source code

Exploring Package Management

Before diving into the world of Linux software package management, this chapter goes through a few of the basics of how Linux manages application software. Each of the major Linux distributions utilizes some form of a package management system to control installing software applications and libraries. A *package management system* uses a database that keeps track of the following:

- ◆ What software packages are installed on the Linux system

- ◆ What files have been installed for each package

- ◆ Versions of each of the software packages installed

Software packages are stored on servers, called *repositories*, and are accessed across the Internet via package management system utilities running on your local Linux system. You can use these utilities to search for new software packages or even updates to software packages already installed on the system.

A software package will often have *dependencies*, or other packages that must be installed first for the software to run properly. The package management system utilities will detect these dependencies and offer to install any additionally needed software packages before installing the desired package.

The downside to a package management system is that there isn't a single standard utility. Not all software package management systems work in all Linux distributions.

The package management system utilities and their associated commands are vastly different between the various Linux distributions. The two primary package management system base utilities commonly used in the Linux world are *dpkg* and *rpm*.

Debian-based distributions such as Ubuntu use, at the base of their package management system utilities, the dpkg command. This command interacts directly with the package management system on the Linux system and is used for installing, managing, and removing software packages.

The Red Hat–based distributions, such as CentOS, use the rpm command at the base of their package management system. Similar to the dpkg command, the rpm command can list installed packages, install new packages, and remove existing software.

Note that these two commands are the core of their respective package management system, not the entire package management system itself. Many Linux distributions that use the dpkg or rpm methods have built additional specialty package management system utilities upon these base commands to make your life much easier. The following sections walk through the package management systems you'll find in Debian-based systems, such as Ubuntu. Chapter 5, "Installing and Maintaining Software in Red Hat," covers using the rpm package management system.

Inspecting the Debian-Based Systems

The dpkg command is at the core of the Debian-based family of package management system tools. It provides options to install, update, and remove Debian package files on your Linux system.

The dpkg command assumes you have the package file either downloaded onto your local Linux system or available as a URL. More often than not, that isn't the case. Usually you'll want to install an application package from the repository for your Linux distribution. To do that, you'll use the Advanced Package Tool (APT) suite of tools.

◆   apt-cache

◆   apt-get

◆   apt

The apt command is essentially a front end for both the apt-cache and apt-get commands. The nice thing about APT is that you don't need to remember which tool to use when—it covers everything you need to do with package management. The basic format for the apt command is

```
apt [options] command
```

The *command* defines the action for apt to take. If needed, you can specify one or more *options* to fine-tune what happens. This section looks at how to use the APT command-line tool to work with the software packages on your Linux system.

Managing Packages with *apt*

A common task that Linux system administrators face is to determine what packages are already installed on the system. The apt list command displays all the packages available in the repository, but by adding the --installed option, you can limit the output to only those packages already installed on your system.

```
$ apt --installed list
Listing...
accountsservice/focal-updates,focal-security,now 0.6.55-0ubuntu12~20.04.4 amd64
 [installed,automatic]
adduser/focal,now 3.118ubuntu2 all [installed,automatic]
alsa-topology-conf/focal,now 1.2.2-1 all [installed,automatic]
alsa-ucm-conf/focal-updates,now 1.2.2-1ubuntu0.4 all [installed,automatic]
amd64-microcode/focal,now 3.20191218.1ubuntu1 amd64 [installed,automatic]
apparmor/focal-updates,now 2.13.3-7ubuntu5.1 amd64 [installed,automatic]
apport-symptoms/focal,now 0.23 all [installed,automatic]
apport/focal-updates,focal-security,now 2.20.11-0ubuntu27.12 all
[installed,automatic]
...
$
```

As you can guess, the list of installed packages will be long, so we've abbreviated the output to show just a sample of what the output looks like. Next to the package name is additional information about the package, such as the version name, and whether the package is installed and flagged for automatic upgrades.

If you already know the package name and want to quickly display detailed information about it, use the show command.

```
apt show package_name
```

Here's an example of displaying the details of the package zsh:

```
$ apt show zsh
Package: zsh
Version: 5.8-3ubuntu1
Priority: optional
Section: shells
Origin: Ubuntu
Maintainer: Ubuntu Developers <ubuntu-devel-discuss@lists.ubuntu.com>
Original-Maintainer: Debian Zsh Maintainers <pkg-zsh-devel@lists.alioth.
debian.org>
Bugs: https://bugs.launchpad.net/ubuntu/+filebug
Installed-Size: 2,390 kB
Depends: zsh-common (= 5.8-3ubuntu1), libc6 (>= 2.29), libcap2 (>=
1:2.10), libtinfo6
 (>= 6)
Recommends: libgdbm6 (>= 1.16), libncursesw6 (>= 6), libpcre3
Suggests: zsh-doc
Homepage: https://www.zsh.org/
Download-Size: 707 kB
APT-Sources: http://us.archive.ubuntu.com/ubuntu focal/main amd64 Packages
Description: shell with lots of features
 Zsh is a UNIX command interpreter (shell) usable as an
```

```
interactive login shell and as a shell script command
processor. Of the standard shells, zsh most closely resembles
ksh but includes many enhancements. Zsh has command-line editing,
built-in spelling correction, programmable command completion,
shell functions (with autoloading), a history mechanism, and a
host of other features.

$
```

The apt show command does not indicate that the package is installed on the system. It shows only detailed package information from the software repository. One detail you cannot get with apt is a listing of all the files associated with a particular software package. To get this list, you will need to go to the dpkg command itself.

```
dpkg -L package_name
```

Here's an example of using dpkg to list all the files installed as part of the apt-utils package:

```
$ dpkg -L apt-utils
/.
/usr
/usr/bin
/usr/bin/apt-extracttemplates
/usr/bin/apt-ftparchive
/usr/bin/apt-sortpkgs
/usr/lib
/usr/lib/apt
/usr/lib/apt/planners
/usr/lib/apt/planners/apt
/usr/lib/apt/solvers
/usr/lib/apt/solvers/apt
...
$
```

You can also do the reverse—find what package a particular file belongs to, as shown here:

```
dpkg --search absolute_file_name
```

Note that you need to use an absolute file reference for this to work.

```
$ dpkg --search /usr/bin/apt-ftparchive
apt-utils: /usr/bin/apt-ftparchive
$
```

The output shows the apt-ftparchive file was installed as part of the apt-utils package.

Installing Software Packages with *apt*

Now that you know more about listing software package information on your system, this section walks you through a software package installation. First, you'll want to determine the package name to install. How do you find a particular software package? Use apt with the search command.

```
apt search package_name
```

The beauty of the search command is that you do not need to insert wildcards around package_name. Wildcards are implied. By default, the search command displays packages that contain the search term in either the package name or the package description, which can be misleading at times. If you want to limit the output to only package names, include the --names-only option.

```
$ apt --names-only search zsh
Sorting... Done
Full Text Search... Done
fizsh/focal,focal 1.0.9-1 all
  Friendly Interactive ZSHell

zsh/focal 5.8-3ubuntu1 amd64
  shell with lots of features

zsh-antigen/focal,focal 2.2.3-2 all
  manage your zsh plugins

zsh-autosuggestions/focal,focal 0.6.4-1 all
  Fish-like fast/unobtrusive autosuggestions for zsh

zsh-common/focal,focal 5.8-3ubuntu1 all
  architecture independent files for Zsh

zsh-dev/focal 5.8-3ubuntu1 amd64
  shell with lots of features (development files)

zsh-doc/focal,focal 5.8-3ubuntu1 all
  zsh documentation - info/HTML format

zsh-static/focal 5.8-3ubuntu1 amd64
  shell with lots of features (static link)

zsh-syntax-highlighting/focal,focal 0.6.0-3 all
  Fish shell like syntax highlighting for zsh

zsh-theme-powerlevel9k/focal,focal 0.6.7-2 all
  powerlevel9k is a theme for zsh which uses powerline fonts

zshdb/focal,focal 1.1.2-1 all
  debugger for Z-Shell scripts

$
```

Once you find the package you'd like to install, installing it using apt is as easy as this:

```
sudo apt install package_name
```

Since installing new software requires root privileges, you must use the sudo command in Ubuntu. The output will show basic information about the package and ask if you want to proceed with the installation.

 Real World Scenario

INSTALLING SOFTWARE USING APT

Using the apt command makes installing software in Ubuntu easy. In this exercise, you'll install the Z shell on your Ubuntu server.

1. Log into your Linux system as the sysadmin account created in Chapter 2, "Installing an Ubuntu Server."

2. From the command prompt, enter the command **sudo apt install zsh**. The sudo command is required to allow your user to run the apt command with root user privileges. Enter your user password when prompted. You should see something similar to this output:

```
[sudo] password for sysadmin:
Reading package lists... Done
Building dependency tree
Reading state information... Done
The following additional packages will be installed:
  zsh-common
Suggested packages:
  zsh-doc
The following NEW packages will be installed:
  zsh zsh-common
0 upgraded, 2 newly installed, 0 to remove and 56 not upgraded.
Need to get 4,450 kB of archives.
After this operation, 18.0 MB of additional disk space
will be used.
Do you want to continue? [Y/n] y
Get:1 http://us.archive.ubuntu.com/ubuntu focal/main amd64 zsh-
common all 5.8-3ubuntu1 [3,744
  kB]
Get:2 http://us.archive.ubuntu.com/ubuntu focal/main amd64
zsh amd64 5.8-3ubuntu1 [707 kB]
Fetched 4,450 kB in 4s (1,039 kB/s)
Selecting previously unselected package zsh-common.
(Reading database ... 179515 files and directories currently
installed.)
Preparing to unpack .../zsh-common_5.8-3ubuntu1_all.deb ...
Unpacking zsh-common (5.8-3ubuntu1) ...
```

```
                Selecting previously unselected package zsh.
                Preparing to unpack .../zsh_5.8-3ubuntu1_amd64.deb ...
                Unpacking zsh (5.8-3ubuntu1) ...
                Setting up zsh-common (5.8-3ubuntu1) ...
                Setting up zsh (5.8-3ubuntu1) ...
                Processing triggers for man-db (2.9.1-1) ...
                $
```

3. Test the install by entering the command **zsh**. You will see a menu prompting if you want to customize your Z shell environment. Enter **0** to use the default configuration. You should then get the Z shell prompt.

```
                ubuntu-server%
```

4. Return to your normal Bash Shell by typing the command **exit**.

5. Check whether the installation processed properly, type the command **apt --installed list**. You should see the package appear, indicating that it is installed.

When installing a package, apt will ask to install other packages as well. This is because apt automatically resolves any necessary package dependencies for us and installs the needed additional library and software packages. This is a wonderful feature included in many package management systems.

Upgrading Software with *apt*

While apt helps protect you from problems installing software, trying to coordinate a multiple-package update with dependencies can get tricky. To safely upgrade all the software packages on a system with any new versions in the repository, use the upgrade command (again, using sudo to obtain root privileges).

```
    sudo apt upgrade
```

Notice that this command doesn't take any software package names as an argument. That's because the upgrade option will upgrade all the installed packages to the most recent version available in the repository, which is safer for system stabilization.

Figure 3.1 shows a sample output from running the apt upgrade command.

In the Figure 3.1 output, notice that apt lists the packages that will be upgraded, but also any new packages that are required to be installed because of upgrades.

The upgrade command won't remove any packages as part of the upgrade process. If a package needs to be removed as part of an upgrade, use the following command:

```
    sudo apt full-upgrade
```

Although this may seem like an odd thing, sometimes it's required to remove packages to keep things synchronized between distribution upgrades.

FIGURE 3.1

Upgrading
Ubuntu using apt

```
  linux-modules-5.4.0-54-generic linux-modules-extra-5.4.0-54-generic
The following packages will be upgraded:
  alsa-ucm-conf grub-common grub-pc grub-pc-bin grub2-common krb5-locales libasound2
  libasound2-data libgssapi-krb5-2 libk5crypto3 libkrb5-3 libkrb5support0 libldap-2.4-2
  libldap-common linux-generic linux-headers-generic linux-image-generic linux-libc-dev
  python3-software-properties software-properties-common
20 upgraded, 5 newly installed, 0 to remove and 0 not upgraded.
Need to get 79.1 MB/79.9 MB of archives.
After this operation, 360 MB of additional disk space will be used.
Do you want to continue? [Y/n] y
Get:1 http://us.archive.ubuntu.com/ubuntu focal-updates/main amd64 libasound2 amd64 1.2.2-2.1ubuntu2
.2 [335 kB]
Get:2 http://us.archive.ubuntu.com/ubuntu focal-updates/main amd64 libasound2-data all 1.2.2-2.1ubun
tu2.2 [20.2 kB]
Get:3 http://us.archive.ubuntu.com/ubuntu focal-updates/main amd64 alsa-ucm-conf all 1.2.2-1ubuntu0.
5 [25.7 kB]
Get:4 http://us.archive.ubuntu.com/ubuntu focal-updates/main amd64 grub2-common amd64 2.04-1ubuntu26
.7 [590 kB]
Get:5 http://us.archive.ubuntu.com/ubuntu focal-updates/main amd64 grub-pc amd64 2.04-1ubuntu26.7 [1
25 kB]
Get:6 http://us.archive.ubuntu.com/ubuntu focal-updates/main amd64 grub-pc-bin amd64 2.04-1ubuntu26.
7 [971 kB]
Get:7 http://us.archive.ubuntu.com/ubuntu focal-updates/main amd64 grub-common amd64 2.04-1ubuntu26.
7 [1,876 kB]
Get:8 http://us.archive.ubuntu.com/ubuntu focal-updates/main amd64 linux-modules-5.4.0-54-generic am
d64 5.4.0-54.60 [14.4 MB]
Get:9 http://us.archive.ubuntu.com/ubuntu focal-updates/main amd64 linux-image-5.4.0-54-generic amd6
4 5.4.0-54.60 [8,883 kB]
Get:10 http://us.archive.ubuntu.com/ubuntu focal-updates/main amd64 linux-modules-extra-5.4.0-54-gen
eric amd64 5.4.0-54.60 [38.5 MB]
Get:11 http://us.archive.ubuntu.com/ubuntu focal-updates/main amd64 linux-generic amd64 5.4.0.54.57
[1,900 B]
Get:12 http://us.archive.ubuntu.com/ubuntu focal-updates/main amd64 linux-image-generic amd64 5.4.0.
54.57 [2,628 B]
Get:13 http://us.archive.ubuntu.com/ubuntu focal-updates/main amd64 linux-headers-5.4.0-54 all 5.4.0
-54.60 [10.9 MB]
89% [13 linux-headers-5.4.0-54 6,897 kB/10.9 MB 63%]                         1,146 kB/s 5s_
```

UPDATING A NEW INSTALLATION

Obviously, running apt's upgrade option is something you should do on a regular basis to keep
your system up-to-date. However, it is especially important to run it after a fresh distribution installation. Usually there are lots of security patches and updates that are released since the last full
release of a distribution.

Uninstalling Software with *apt*

Getting rid of software packages with apt is as easy as installing and upgrading them. The only
real choice you have to make is whether to keep the software's data and configuration files
around afterward.

To remove a software package but not the data and configuration files, use apt's remove
command. To remove a software package and the related data and configuration files, use the
purge option.

```
$ sudo apt purge zsh
Reading package lists... Done
Building dependency tree
Reading state information... Done
The following package was automatically installed and is no longer required:
  zsh-common
Use 'sudo apt autoremove' to remove it.
The following packages will be REMOVED:
  zsh*
```

```
0 upgraded, 0 newly installed, 1 to remove and 56 not upgraded.
After this operation, 2,390 kB disk space will be freed.
Do you want to continue? [Y/n] y
(Reading database ... 180985 files and directories currently installed.)
Removing zsh (5.8-3ubuntu1) ...
Processing triggers for man-db (2.9.1-1) ...
(Reading database ... 180928 files and directories currently installed.)
Purging configuration files for zsh (5.8-3ubuntu1) ...
$
```

Notice, though, as part of the purge output, apt warns us that the zsh-common package that was installed as a dependency wasn't removed automatically, just in case it might be required for some other package. If you're sure the dependency package isn't required by anything else, you can remove it using the autoremove command.

```
$ sudo apt autoremove
Reading package lists... Done
Building dependency tree
Reading state information... Done
The following packages will be REMOVED:
  zsh-common
0 upgraded, 0 newly installed, 1 to remove and 56 not upgraded.
After this operation, 15.6 MB disk space will be freed.
Do you want to continue? [Y/n] y
(Reading database ... 180928 files and directories currently installed.)
Removing zsh-common (5.8-3ubuntu1) ...
Processing triggers for man-db (2.9.1-1) ...
$
```

The autoremove command will check for all packages that are marked as dependencies and no longer required.

The *apt* Repositories

The default software repository locations for apt are set up for you when you install your Linux distribution. The repository locations are stored in the file /etc/apt/sources.list.

In most cases, you will never need to add or remove a software repository, so you won't need to touch this file. However, apt will only pull software from these repositories. Also, when searching for software to install or update, apt will only check these repositories. If you need to include some additional software repositories for your package management system, this is the place to do it.

SOFTWARE VERSIONS

The Linux distribution developers work hard to make sure package versions added to the repositories don't conflict with one another. Usually it's safest to upgrade or install a software package from the repository. Even if a newer version is available elsewhere, you may want to hold off installing it until that version is available in your Linux distribution's repository.

When you look at the file, you'll notice that it's full of helpful comments and warnings. The repository sources specified use the following structure:

```
deb (or deb-src) address  distribution_name  package_type_list
```

The deb or deb-src value indicates the software package type. The deb value indicates it is a source of compiled programs, whereas the deb-src value indicates it is a source of source code.

The *address* entry is the software repository's web address. The *distribution_name* entry is the name of this particular software repository's distribution's version. In the example, the distribution name is focal. This does not necessarily mean that the distribution you are running is Ubuntu's Focal Fossa; it just means the Linux distribution is using the Ubuntu Focal Fossa software repositories. For example, in Linux Mint's sources.list file, you will see a mix of Linux Mint and Ubuntu software repositories.

Finally, the *package_type_list* entry may be more than one word and indicates what type of packages the repository has in it. For example, you may see values such as main, restricted, universe, or partner.

When you need to add a software repository to your sources file, you can try to wing it yourself, but that more than likely will cause problems. Often, software repository sites or various package developer sites will have an exact line of text that you can copy from their website and paste into your sources.list file. It's best to choose the safer route and just copy and paste.

The front-end interface, apt, provides intelligent command-line options for working with the Debian-based dpkg utility.

Using Snap Containers

Canonical, the creators of the Ubuntu Linux distribution, has developed an application container format called *snap*. The snap packaging system bundles all the files required for an application into a single snap distribution file. The difference between a snap package and a dpkg package is that snap packages don't have any dependencies—all of the files needed to run an application are in the package installation. This can create duplication of files that could be shared with other applications, but it also resolves any issues that could occur from conflicting library files installed by multiple packages.

The snapd application manages the snap packages installed on the system and runs in the background. You use the snap command-line tool to query the snap database to display installed snap packages, as well as to install, upgrade, and remove snap packages.

To check whether snap is running on your system, use the snap version command.

```
$ snap version
snap    2.47.1+20.04
snapd   2.47.1+20.04
series  16
ubuntu  20.04
kernel  5.4.0-53-generic
$
```

If snap is running, you can see a list of the currently installed snap applications by using the snap list command.

```
$ snap list
Name      Version   Rev     Tracking        Publisher    Notes
core18    20200929  1932    latest/stable   canonical*   base
lxd       4.0.4     18150   4.0/stable/...  canonical*   -
snapd     2.47.1    9721    latest/stable   canonical*   snapd
$
```

To search the snap repository for new applications, use the snap find command.

```
$ snap find stress-ng
Name        Version   Publisher           Notes   Summary
stress-ng   V0.11.24  cking-kernel-tools  -       A tool to load, stress test and
  benchmark a computer system
$
```

To view more information about a snap application (snap for short), use the snap info command.

```
$ snap info stress-ng
name:      stress-ng
summary:   A tool to load, stress test and benchmark a computer system
publisher: Colin King (cking-kernel-tools)
store-url: https://snapcraft.io/stress-ng
contact:   colin.king@canonical.com
license:   GPL-2.0
description: |
  stress-ng can stress various subsystems of a computer.  It can stress load
  CPU, cache, disk, memory, socket and pipe I/O, scheduling and much more.
  stress-ng is a re-write of the original stress tool by Amos Waterland but
  has many additional features such as specifying the number of bogo
  operations to run, execution metrics, a stress verification on memory and
  compute operations and considerably more stress mechanisms.
snap-id: YMJsyW4vySPdys8BCA7jx8UiOVSVhUT6
channels:
  latest/stable:    V0.11.24                        2020-11-13 (5273) 3MB -
  latest/candidate: V0.11.24                        2020-11-13 (5273) 3MB -
  latest/beta:      V0.11.24                        2020-11-13 (5273) 3MB -
  latest/edge:      V0.11.24-44-20201121-7613-g2627a 2020-11-21 (5298) 3MB -
$
```

To install a new snap, use the snap install command as the root user (or with root privileges).

 **Real World Scenario**

INSTALLING SOFTWARE SNAPS

The stress-ng application allows you to stress test the CPU, memory, disk, and other features on your Linux system. Use the snap install command to install the stress-ng snap application package on your Linux system following these steps:

1. Log into your Ubuntu server using the sysadmin account you created in Chapter 2.

2. At the command line, enter the command **sudo snap install stress-ng**. Enter your user password when prompted. You should see the following output:

```
[sudo] password for sysadmin:
stress-ng V0.11.24 from Colin King (cking-kernel-tools) installed
$
```

3. At the command line, enter the command **snap list** to see if the stress-ng snap package has been installed. You should see the following output:

```
Name       Version    Rev    Tracking       Publisher          Notes
core18     20200929   1932   latest/stable  canonical*         base
lxd        4.0.4      18150  4.0/stable/... canonical*         -
snapd      2.47.1     9721   latest/stable  canonical*         snapd
stress-ng  V0.11.24   5273   latest/stable  cking-kernel-tools -
$
```

When you install a snap package, the snapd program mounts it as a drive. You can see the new snap mount by using the mount command.

```
$ mount
...
/var/lib/snapd/snaps/stress-ng_5273.snap on /snap/stress-ng/5273 type squashfs
  (ro,nodev,relatime,x-gdu.hide)
$
```

If you need to remove a snap, just use the snap remove command.

```
$ sudo snap remove stress-ng
stress-ng removed
$
```

As the snap is removed, you'll see some messages about the progress of the removal. Instead of removing a snap, if you prefer, you can just disable it without removing it. Just use the snap disable command. To reenable the snap, use the snap enable command.

Installing from Source Code

Before package management systems and application containers, open source application developers had to distribute their software as source code and allow users to compile the applications on their own systems. Source code packages were commonly released as a *tarball*. Tarball packages bundle files into an archive file using the tar command-line command. Once the files are bundled into a tarball, it's common to use a compression utility to compress the file to easily distribute it.

Once you've obtained a software source-code package tarball, there are a few steps you'll need to go through to install the software:

1. Unpack the files in the tarball using the `tar` command. The `-xvf` options expand the tarball specified on the command line. Optionally, if the tarball has been compressed, you'll need to include an option to uncompress the file. Use `-J` for `.xz` compressed files, or use `-z` for `.gz` compressed files.

2. Create the script for compiling the software on your system using the `configure` script included with the package. This detects what tools are installed on the system and what CPU features and capabilities are available. This creates a `Makefile` script to build the software.

3. Run the `Makefile` script to compile the source code using the `make` command.

4. Install the software using the `make install` command.

The software package developer determines the installation location and whether you need to have root privileges to run the application.

 Real World Scenario

INSTALLING SOFTWARE FROM SOURCE CODE

If you develop or work with open source software source code much, there's a good chance you will still find software packed up as a tarball. This section walks you through the process of unpacking and installing a tarball software package.

For this example, the GNU software package `hello` will be used. The `hello` package is a simple program that produces a "Hello World!" output but demonstrates how GNU packages source code files for distribution.

1. Download the `hello` tarball package to your Ubuntu server. Go to the GNU software download website `ftp.gnu.org/gnu/hello/`. Click the link to download the current version of the package. The current filename is `hello-2.10.tar.gz`.

2. Unpack the software tarball using the command **`tar -zxvf hello-2.10-tar.gz`**. This command will create a directory named `hello-2.10` and unpack all of the files into that directory.

3. Change to that directory by typing **`cd hello-2.10`**. In this directory, you should see a README and an INSTALL file. It's important to read these files. In these files will be instructions you will need to finish the software's installation.

4. Run the configuration script by typing the command **`./configure`**. You will see output messages as the script scans your system to check for the appropriate tools for building the software. If anything goes wrong, the configure step will display an error message explaining what's missing from your system.

> **5.** Compile the application by typing **make**. You should see a lot of messages scroll by as the script compiles the individual pieces of the application, but you shouldn't see any error messages. When the make command is finished, you'll have the actual hello software program available in the directory! However, it's somewhat inconvenient to have to run it from that directory. Instead, you'll want to install it in a common location on your Linux system.
>
> **6.** Install the application by typing **sudo make install**. Now the hello application is installed on your Linux system.

Unfortunately, uninstalling an application installed by source code may or may not be easy. It's up to the developers whether to include an uninstall make script. Try running the sudo make uninstall command from the software directory to see whether that works.

> ### THE CORE LINUX PROGRAMMING LANGUAGES
>
> Most Linux utility programs are written using the C or C++ programming language. To compile them on your system, you will need the gcc package installed, as well as the make package. Most Linux desktop distributions don't install these by default. If the configure program shows an error that these parts are missing, consult your specific Linux distribution docs on what packages you need to install.

The Bottom Line

Explore different Linux software package management systems.   Developers bundle the files required for an application into a package to make it easier to install. A package management system allows you to easily track, install, and remove application packages on your Linux system. There are two popular Linux package management systems: dpkg for Debian-based systems, and rpm for Red Hat–based systems.

> **Master It**   The Debian Linux distribution maintains an official website that tracks all software packages as they're developed for the Debian environment. Go to the packages .debian.org website and determine what version of the systat application is available as a stable Debian package.

Use Debian software packages to install software.   The Debian-based Linux distributions use the dpkg utility to interface with the package management system from the command line, and they use the apt-cache and apt-get utilities to interface with a common repository to easily download and install new software. A front end to these utilities is apt. It provides simple command-line options for working with software packages in the dpkg format.

> **Master It**   The C shell provides an alternative to the Bash Shell, handy for writing advanced shell scripts. For Ubuntu, the C shell is bundled as part of the csh package. What commands should you use to install the csh package from the standard Ubuntu software repository?

Install applications using Debian snap containers. Application containers are a relatively new player in software package management. An application container bundles all the files necessary for an application to run in one installable package. This means the application doesn't rely on any external dependencies such as library files, and the container bundle can be installed in any Linux distribution and run. Currently, the two most popular container packages are snap, common in the Ubuntu Linux distribution, and flatpak, used in Red Hat Linux environments.

Master It The PowerShell package provides a powerful scripting language similar to that found on Microsoft Windows servers. Ubuntu distributes the PowerShell package as a snap container. What command should you use to install PowerShell on your Ubuntu server?

Install software from source code. The chapter closed with a discussion on how to install software packages that are only distributed in source code tarballs. The tar command allows you to unpack the source code files from the tarball, and then the configure and make commands allow you to build the final executable program from the source code.

Master It There are lots of handy utilities created and shared by Linux developers. One such utility is the sysstat tool. The sysstat tool provides statistics for various features of your Linux system. You can find the sysstat tool on the developer's website, sebastien.godard.pagesperso-orange.fr. After downloading the package tarball, what commands would you need to use to compile the software and install it on your Linux server?

Chapter 4

Installing a Red Hat Server

Red Hat Enterprise Linux (RHEL) is the most popular Linux distribution, and chances are that you'll install it many times during your Linux career. Gaining experience with this distro's installation process will help you become a Linux expert. If you read through Chapter 2, "Installing an Ubuntu Server," some items within the installation steps will feel familiar. However, there are enough differences between installing the two Linux distributions that you can get tripped up.

Therefore, our goal in this chapter is to assist you through your first installation of a RHEL distribution. We'll provide step-by-step guidance, help you avoid pitfalls, and ultimately build your sysadmin skillset.

IN THIS CHAPTER, YOU WILL LEARN TO

- ◆ Review needed Red Hat Server hardware resources

- ◆ Determine the requirements for a virtual Red Hat system

- ◆ Obtain Red Hat Server software

- ◆ Conduct an installation of a Red Hat Server

- ◆ Audit the Red Hat Server's installation

Pre-Installation Requirements

Before taking a look at the needed resources, we need to have a chat about fees associated with RHEL. This particular distribution requires you to pay money to use it. For example, every year it would cost you about $350 to potentially more than $1,300 per system to run RHEL on a server. This is expensive if you just want a Linux distribution to work with for learning purposes! But don't give up hope, because we've got a free solution for you. The CentOS Linux distribution is free of charge and is a community-supported version of RHEL. For learning purposes, it will work perfectly for you!

UNDERSTANDING RED HAT CHARGES FOR RHEL

While it may seem odd to you that a company charges for its Linux distribution, Red Hat has solid reasoning and experience behind what it calls its subscription model. When you pay a subscription, besides getting the RHEL distro to run on a server and access to any of its software updates, you have access to experts.

As an example, suppose you have a mission-critical system running RHEL. The system starts to exhibit some performance issues. Your subscription with Red Hat includes a system performance expert, who will analyze and evaluate your server configuration and then make recommendations for improvement. In addition, you can talk to RHEL security experts and get technical support at any time.

Red Hat has been using this subscription model for more than 20 years, and the popularity of this Linux distribution shows that the model works. You can find more information about the Red Hat subscription model at redhat.com.

For our purposes in this book, the CentOS distribution without a GUI will provide what is needed since our target is a headless server (see Chapter 2 for a more detailed explanation as to why a GUI is typically not used in modern server rooms). Specifically, we're using a CentOS 8 Linux distribution.

Before starting your CentOS installation, it's a good idea to review what resources are needed. This step is important in order to achieve a successful Linux distribution installation.

UNDERSTANDING BASIC VIRTUALIZATION TERMS

If you're unfamiliar with virtualization computer terms, it's a good idea to read through the first several pages of Chapter 22, "Exploring the Virtualization Environment." If you'd like a quick jump start instead, a few basic definitions were covered in Chapter 2.

You may perform the CentOS installation on a physical system, or you may install it as a virtual machine on a host system. Thus, in the next few sections, we'll look at the hardware requirements needed for installing the CentOS distribution directly on a physical server and for installing it within a virtualized environment.

Hardware Requirements

If you plan on installing the CentOS 8 distribution directly on a headless server, your computer must support a 64-bit processor architecture. Here is a list of a few that will work well:

- AMD amd64
- ARM64 (not supported by RHEL)
- Intel amd64
- POWER9 (not supported by RHEL)

Besides having the proper processor on your system, you need to have enough resources available to avoid a sluggish system. Table 4.1 shows the recommended resources to support a well-running CentOS distro.

TABLE 4.1:   Recommended Server Resources for CentOS Distribution

RESOURCE	MINIMUM	RECOMMENDED
CPU	1.8 GHz	2 or more GHz
Memory	2 GB	2 GB per logical CPU
Disk space	10 GB	20 or more GB

Notice the "per logical CPU" tag in the recommended memory. This is because CentOS can support some rather powerful CPUs, and it treats every core (or thread) in a multicore (or thread) processor as a logical CPU. So if you have a dual-core processor, it is recommended that you have 4 GB of RAM on your system, while a quad-core processor needs 8 GB of memory.

Also, keep in mind that these recommendations are only for the operating system. Increase these resources to meet the needs of the application(s) you will run on the server.

If you don't have access to a physical server, you can set up a virtual environment on a laptop or an old desktop. Using a virtualized system on your laptop provides a great deal of flexibility. Wherever you go with your laptop, you can learn about Linux.

Virtual Server Requirements

If you plan on running the CentOS distribution as a virtual machine (VM), you need to ensure that the host machine's operating system is supported by the hypervisor.

For this book, we're focusing on the Oracle VirtualBox hypervisor software. Here are a few of the operating systems on which it can run:

◆   Windows 8.1

◆   Windows 10

◆   macOS High Sierra

◆   Ubuntu 18.04LTS

This list is always evolving. Thus, it's a good idea to visit the Oracle VirtualBox manual website, virtualbox.org/manual, and view the currently supported host operating systems.

Running a virtualized environment will increase the needed resources on your system. You'll need to make sure that the host machine can handle not only the hypervisor, but the CentOS VM as well. Table 4.2 lists the recommended host machine resources for a virtualized CentOS server.

TABLE 4.2: Recommended Host Machine Resources for a CentOS VM

RESOURCE	MINIMUM	RECOMMENDED
CPU	2 GHz dual core	2 or more GHz dual core
Memory	4 GB	16 or more GB
Free disk space	25 GB	30 or more GB

These resource recommendations are guidelines, not rules. Thus, you may need slightly more resources or get by with a fewer. Also, these recommendations assume you are running only one VM at a time. You'll need more resources on your system if you plan on running multiple VMs at the same time or running a VM along with several other apps.

After you have the right level of resources on your host system, you're ready to start downloading the needed software. We'll cover this in the next section.

Finding the Software

After you determine that you have the appropriate resources, but before you start the installation process, you need to have the proper software. You'll want to make sure that you get the correct version and type. For the larger software files, it's also critical to verify that no corruption has occurred when the software was downloaded. If you have a corrupt software file, you'll end up needlessly wasting your time or, worse, delaying the completion of an important installation project.

Oracle VirtualBox

We recommend that you use Oracle VirtualBox as the hypervisor on your system. If you did not download this software when you read Chapter 2, you can now download the latest version of this software from `virtualbox.org`.

It is important that you get the correct platform package of VirtualBox. You'll see a list of potential host systems on the VirtualBox website, such as the following:

- Windows
- macOS
- Linux

Make sure to select the VirtualBox package for the system on which the CentOS virtual machine will be running. Often, people make an incorrect choice because they confuse the host system with the virtual machine. Here's an example that may help: if you have a laptop running Windows where you plan on installing CentOS as a VM, then Windows is the host, and you'll want to download the VirtualBox package for Windows. Our examples in this chapter are based on a Windows 10 host system.

CentOS

To install CentOS as a VM, besides the hypervisor software (and the correct amount of resources on the host machine), you need a CentOS ISO image file.

> ### Understanding an ISO Image File
>
> An *ISO image file* (also called an ISO image) is a specially formatted package file that contains all of the files needed to boot a system. The ISO image file is used to boot and then install the distribution.

To find the needed CentOS ISO image file, first go to the website: `centos.org/download/`. The type of processor you have will determine your next step. Click the appropriate CPU type for your processor under the CentOS Linux section, shown in Figure 4.1.

FIGURE 4.1

Option to choose to access the appropriate CentOS ISO image file download site

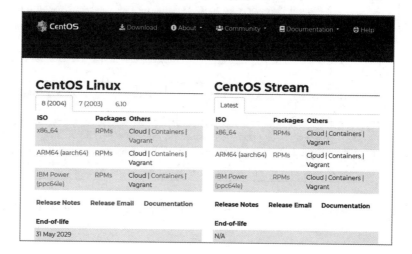

A new browser window will appear, allowing you to select from several sites to start the download process. You can click any of the sites. Once you do, you should get a window similar to what is shown in Figure 4.2.

Click the `CentOS-8*boot.iso` link to start the download of the CentOS ISO image file. Depending on the web browser you are using, you may have to deal with some pop-up windows that want to confirm it is OK to download this file. You'll most likely want to keep this website open or bookmark it in your browser, because we use the checksum information provided here soon.

FIGURE 4.2
Option to choose for
CentOS ISO image
file download

Index of /centos/8.2.2004/isos/x86_64

Name	Last modified	Size	Description
Parent Directory		-	
CHECKSUM	12-Jun-2020 18:42	485	
CHECKSUM.asc	19-Jun-2020 13:10	811	
CentOS-8.2.2004-x86_64-boot.iso	08-Jun-2020 17:26	624M	
CentOS-8.2.2004-x86_64-boot.iso.manifest	08-Jun-2020 17:39	626	
CentOS-8.2.2004-x86_64-boot.torrent	15-Jun-2020 10:35	25K	
CentOS-8.2.2004-x86_64-dvd1.iso	08-Jun-2020 18:11	7.7G	
CentOS-8.2.2004-x86_64-dvd1.iso.manifest	08-Jun-2020 18:11	425K	
CentOS-8.2.2004-x86_64-dvd1.torrent	15-Jun-2020 10:35	307K	
CentOS-8.2.2004-x86_64-minimal.iso	08-Jun-2020 18:09	1.6G	
CentOS-8.2.2004-x86_64-minimal.iso.manifest	08-Jun-2020 18:09	91K	
CentOS-8.2.2004-x86_64-minimal.torrent	15-Jun-2020 10:35	65K	

ENDURING A POTENTIALLY PAINFUL DOWNLOAD OF AN ISO FILE

ISO image files are sometimes large and can hover around 2 GB to 7 GB in size. Fortunately for us, the CentOS boot ISO image file isn't that big. However, if you have a slow Internet connection and desire to get a large ISO image file, it could take hours to download! In these cases, it's worth your time to go visit that friend who has fiber-based Internet and is willing to share their bandwidth.

It's important to verify that no corruption occurred while the ISO file was downloading. To do this, we'll use hashing.

UNDERSTANDING HASHING

Hashing uses a one-way mathematical algorithm to create a fixed-length hash, which is basically a series of letters and numbers. A hash is also called a *message digest*, a *hash value*, a *fingerprint*, a *signature*, or *cipher text*. One cool thing about hash values is that certain hashing algorithms produce the same hash value for files that are the same. Thus, you can take a file with a picture in it and copy it to another location across the network. If we use hashing to produce a hash value for the original picture file and for the copied picture file and those two hash values match, we know that the picture was not corrupted when it was copied to the new location.

While you work your way through the following exercise, you may find you have a corrupted CentOS ISO image file. If this is the case, you'll need to re-download the file and check it via hashing again.

Real World Scenario

CHECKING THE CentOS ISO IMAGE FILE

Once the CentOS ISO image file is completely downloaded, you need to verify it. Follow these steps to verify the ISO image file:

1. On your Windows 10 system, open the Windows 10 PowerShell app by typing **Windows PowerShell** in the search bar and clicking the resulting Windows PowerShell app icon.

2. After the Windows PowerShell app window is open and you have a prompt, assuming you downloaded your CentOS image file to the Downloads folder, type **cd Downloads** and press Enter. The prompt should now show that you are in the Downloads folder.

3. Run the PowerShell hashing utility on the CentOS image file by typing **Get-FileHash CentOS** and press the Tab key so that PowerShell autocompletes the CentOS's image filename for you. Go to the next step before you press Enter.

4. You can complete the rest of the PowerShell command by pressing the spacebar, typing **-Algorithm SHA256** (this option is not required), and pressing Enter. Be patient! It may take a while for the command to output the SHA256 hash value. You should see something similar to the following:

Don't exit the PowerShell window yet. You need to compare your resulting hash value with the current SHA256 hash value on the website from which you downloaded the CentOS ISO image file.

5. Go back to your web browser and look at the website page from which you downloaded the CentOS ISO image file, and click the CHECKSUM (or something similar) link to open the page containing the `CentOS-8*boot.iso` image file's SHA256 hash value.

6. Compare the hash value on the website with your hash value in PowerShell for the `CentOS-8*boot.iso` image file. (Be aware that case does not matter. A lowercase *b* is considered a match for an uppercase *B*.) If the values match, no file corruption occurred when you downloaded the file. However, if the hash values don't match, you'll need to download the file again and repeat this checking process.

7. Type **exit** at the PowerShell prompt to leave the app.

Verifying that the CentOS ISO image file is a good copy will save you time. If you tried to use a corrupt image file in an installation, it may work partway through the process and then quit before completion. That's frustrating. It's always best to check that your ISO image file is good before proceeding within an install.

PREPARING FOR A HARDWARE INSTALLATION

If you are planning on installing the CentOS distribution directly on a computer's hardware instead of creating a VM, you need to do one additional step after checking the ISO image file: create a bootable media device. While bootable DVDs were popular many years ago, most hardware installations are handled through a bootable USB drive. The process of creating this bootable USB (or DVD) is called *burning* an ISO file to a USB drive. You cannot just copy the file to the USB. Instead, you'll need a special software app that will burn the ISO properly. To find the right software, open your web browser and go to your favorite search engine. Type **burn a bootable USB** and press Enter. The resulting list will have several sites that point to free software with instructions. Once you have your CentOS ISO image file properly burned to a USB (or DVD) drive, you'll be able to boot your system and perform the installation process similar to what is covered in the next section.

Now that you've verified your copy of the CentOS ISO image file and have downloaded the Oracle VirtualBox hypervisor software, you're ready to start the installation. We'll cover that process next.

Running the Installation

To create a CentOS VM, you'll need to first install the hypervisor, Oracle VirtualBox. Once that software is up and running, you can set up and install CentOS as a VM using its ISO image file and the hypervisor.

Oracle VirtualBox

The Oracle VirtualBox hypervisor software will allow you to do much more than set up CentOS as a Linux VM. You can also install another version of Windows within a VM and use it to try features or configurations you normally wouldn't do on your main system.

CONSIDERING THE INSTALLATION OF ORACLE VirtualBox

If you read through Chapter 2 and completed the exercises, you already have Oracle VirtualBox installed on your host system, so you can skip ahead to the next section in this chapter. However, if you did not read through Chapter 2 or did not complete its exercises, go back to the "Installing Oracle VirtualBox on Windows 10" exercise in Chapter 2 and complete it. This exercise will take you step-by-step through the Oracle VirtualBox installation process. When you have finished that exercise, come back to this chapter for the next section.

If you need to take a break, close out the VirtualBox interface window by clicking the X in the upper-right corner. However, if you want to plow ahead, keep it open. We'll launch into installing CentOS in the next section.

CentOS

Installing the CentOS as a VM may feel overwhelming the first time you do it, and there are a few tricky items to negotiate along the way. We'll help you through this initial instance to build your confidence and help you avoid potential pitfalls.

 Real World Scenario

SETTING UP A CentOS CONFIGURATION WITHIN ORACLE VirtualBox

Prior to installing CentOS as a VM within the VirtualBox hypervisors, you need to perform a few basic tasks to create and configure a place for the new VM within the VirtualBox app. After you have completed these tasks, on your host machine you will have a folder for the new VM as well as two files within the folder—one file for the VM configuration information and one file acting as a hard disk for the VM.

Follow these steps to configure the CentOS VM. There are only a few steps needed to complete this part of the installation project, but they are important! So, don't skim through this exercise.

1. Open the Oracle VirtualBox app on your host system. How this is accomplished depends on the configuration you chose when installing the VirtualBox software. You may have to find it via the menu search feature on Windows 10 or simply click the VirtualBox icon on the desktop or taskbar. Once you have the app open, you should see a window showing the Oracle VirtualBox Manager that looks similar to this (note that you may or may not have an Ubuntu Server VM showing in your Manager window):

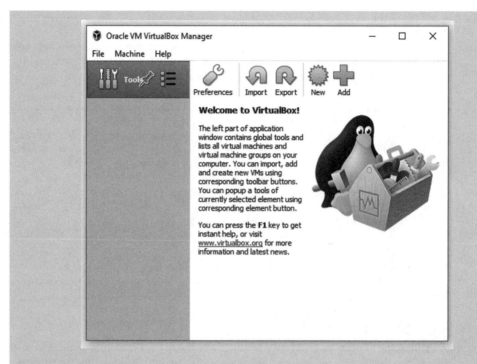

2. In the VirtualBox Manager window, using the top menu within the window, select Machine ➤ New. This will start the process of configuring the CentOS VM and produce the following Create Virtual Machine window:

3. Enter the name **CentOS Server** in the Create Virtual Machine window's Name box.

4. Click the Next button to reach the Memory Size window, which looks similar to the following:

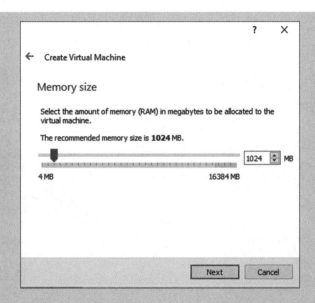

5. By either typing in the memory setting box or using the up-arrow button, change the CentOS Server memory to 2048 MB.

6. Click the Next button in the Memory Size window to reach the Hard Disk window.

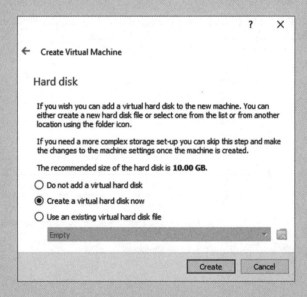

7. Double-check that the Create A Virtual Hard Disk Now option is selected. (You can tell that a particular option is selected by the circle next to it being filled with a dark color, as shown in the previous figure.) If you need to select Create A Virtual Hard Disk Now, click the empty circle next to the option.

8. Click the Create button in the Hard Disk window, which will open another configuration window called Hard Disk File Type.

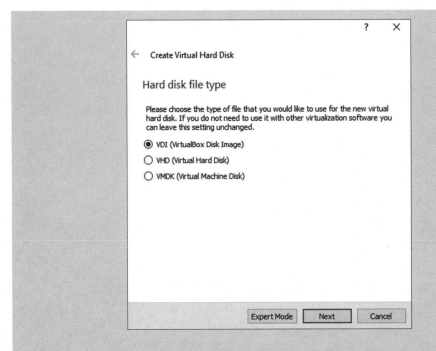

9. Within the Hard Disk File Type window, ensure that the VirtualBox Disk Image (VDI) is selected.

10. Click the Next button, and the Storage On Physical Hard Disk window will appear. This configuration window looks similar to the following:

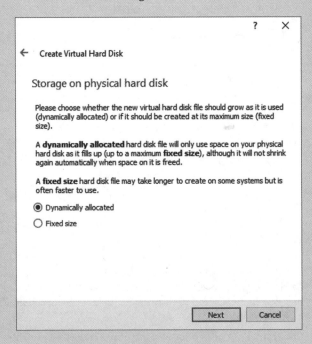

11. Double-check that the Dynamically Allocated setting is chosen.

12. Click the Next button to open the File Location And Size window. In this window, you will see where the VM's virtual disk file is created as well as its size. This configuration window looks similar to the following:

13. Change the file size to 20 GB by typing 20 within the size box.

14. You are now ready to create the basic configuration and virtual disk file of the VM. Do so by clicking the Create button.

You should now be back at the VirtualBox Manager window with the CentOS Server VM in the left pane, as shown here:

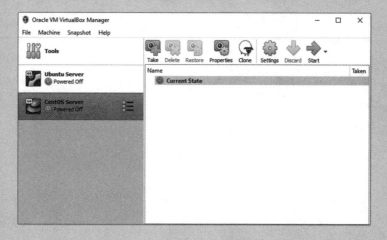

We have a few more configuration steps to take before the VM is completely configured.

15. Click the Settings button in the VirtualBox Manager's top-right pane, which opens the Settings window for the CentOS Server VM.

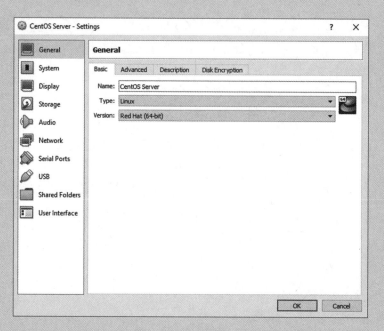

16. In the Settings window, click Network in the left pane to open the Network Settings window for the CentOS Server.

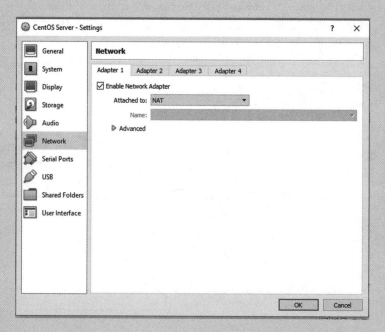

The next few steps help you to set up a second network interface card (NIC) on the CentOS Server. This allows your VM to act as an independent node on your network.

17. In the Network Settings window's right pane, click the Adapter 2 tab.

18. In the Adapter 2 tab window, click the empty box next to Enable Network Adapter.

19. Still in the Network Settings' Adapter 2 tab window, use the arrow to open the drop-down menu in the Attached To box, and select Bridged Adapter. Except for the Name box, your selections should look similar to the following:

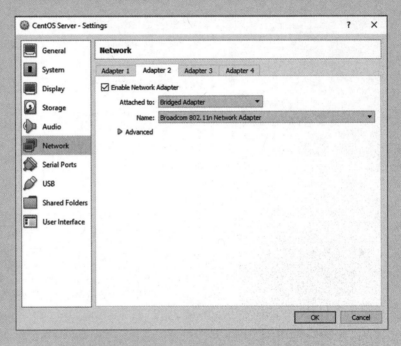

20. Click System in the left pane to open the System Settings window for the CentOS Server.

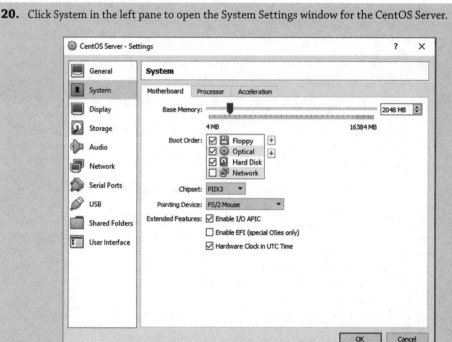

21. In the Pointing Device selection, click the down arrow and select USB Tablet from the drop-down menu. This is a critical step that will avoid problems with your mouse working inside and outside of the virtual machine.

22. Click the OK button to save the changes you made to the CentOS VM settings.

You should now be back to the VirtualBox Manager window. Pat yourself on the back! You have successfully configured the CentOS Server VM.

Your hard work is about to pay off. You are now ready to install the CentOS distribution on the virtual machine you just configured within VirtualBox.

Real World Scenario

INSTALLING CentOS AS A VM

After configuring the CentOS VM within the VirtualBox hypervisor, you can perform the actual installation of the Linux OS. Conducting the installation process on a VM is similar to conducting it on a physical server. There are just a few differences, such as loading the ISO image file into the virtualized DVD drive.

Follow these steps to install CentOS as a VM:

1. If not already opened, open the Oracle VirtualBox hypervisor app on your host system.

2. If you have multiple VMs configured in your hypervisor, click one time on the CentOS Server VM to select it.

3. Click the Settings button in the VirtualBox Manager's top-right pane, which opens the Settings window for the CentOS Server VM.

4. In the Settings window, click Storage in the left pane to open the Storage Settings window for the CentOS Server. It will look similar to the following:

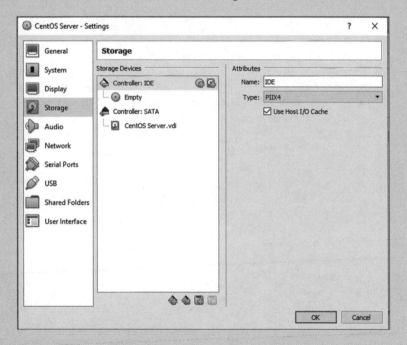

5. In the Storage Settings window's middle pane under Controller: IDE, click the word *Empty* to open the Attributes pane for the IDE optical drive.

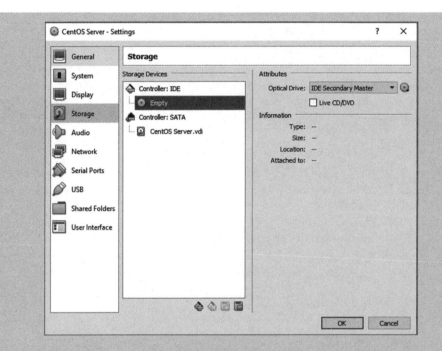

6. In the Storage Settings window's Attributes pane, click the DVD image to produce a drop-down menu, and select Choose/Create A Virtual Optical Disk. An Optical Disk Selector window will appear that looks similar to the following:

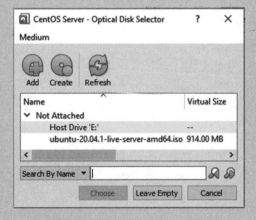

7. In the Optical Disk Selector window, click the Add icon, which will open the Windows Explorer utility, and you will see "Please choose an optical disk file" in the window's title bar.

8. Navigate to the location of your CentOS ISO image file, select the file by clicking it, and then click Open. The Optical Disk Selector window now looks similar to the following:

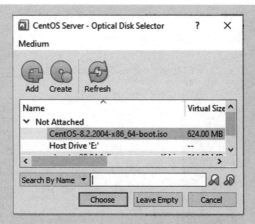

9. In the Optical Disk Selector window, click Choose, and you're returned to the Storage Settings window's Attributes pane with the CentOS ISO image filename displayed under Controller: IDE.

10. Click OK to keep the virtually loaded ISO image file and return to the main VirtualBox Manager window.

11. Boot your CentOS Server VM by clicking the Start button in the VirtualBox Manager's top-right pane.

    You may see lots of messages go by on your screen. Let the process continue until you reach this window:

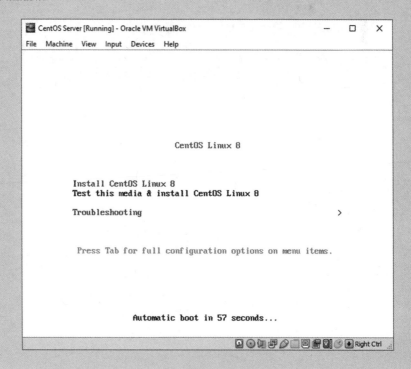

12. Press Enter to start the installation process.

You may see several more messages go by on your screen. Let the process continue until you reach this window:

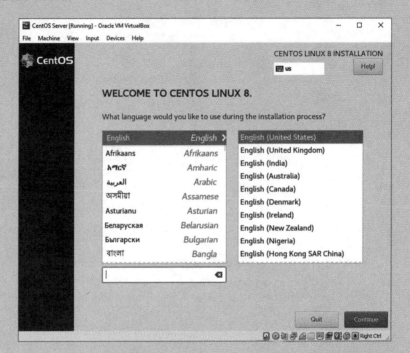

13. Using your arrow keys, select the language you prefer and press Enter. The next window, Installation Summary, will look similar to the following:

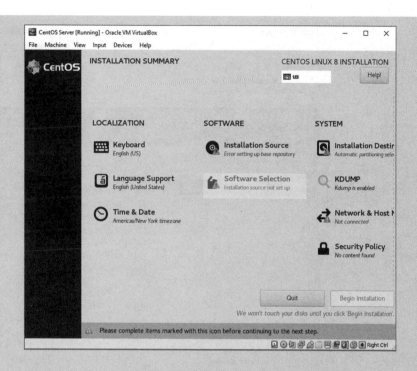

14. Click Network & Host Name to reach a screen that looks similar to this:

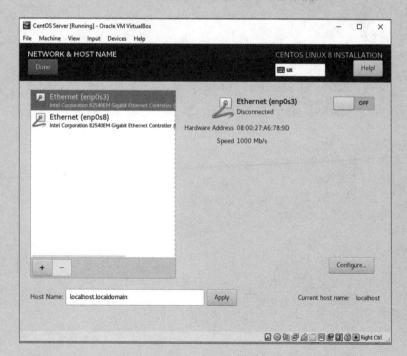

15. Within the Network & Host Name window, click the second Ethernet listed to select it. Now click Off in the screen's upper-right corner to turn this network on. It should now look similar to this:

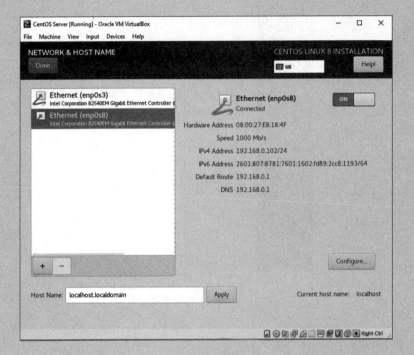

16. Still within the Network & Host Name window, click Done to save your settings and return to the Installation Summary screen.

17. Within the Installation Summary screen, click Installation Destination to reach a window that looks similar to this one:

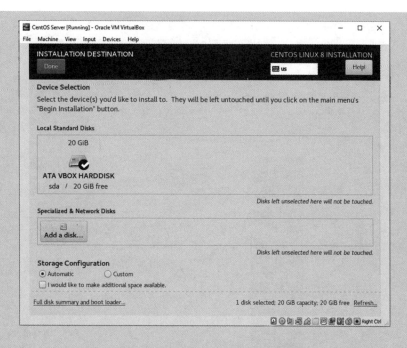

18. Click Done in the Installation Destination window's upper-left corner to accept the defaults and return to the Installation Summary screen.

19. Within the Installation Summary screen, click Software Selection to reach a window that looks similar to this one:

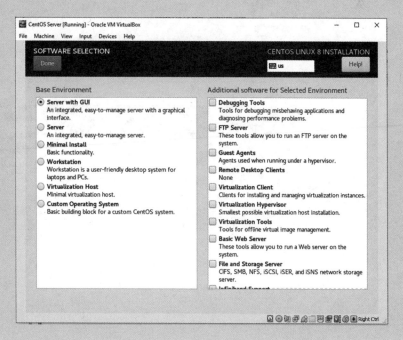

20. In the Base Environment pane, click the circle next to Server to select it. This selection chooses a CentOS server without any GUI elements, as is desired here.

21. Click Done in the Software Selection window to return to the Installation Summary screen.

22. At this point, the Begin Installation button in the Installation Summary window's lower-right corner should no longer be grayed out. Click Begin Installation. The installation will start, and a Configuration window will appear that is similar to the following:

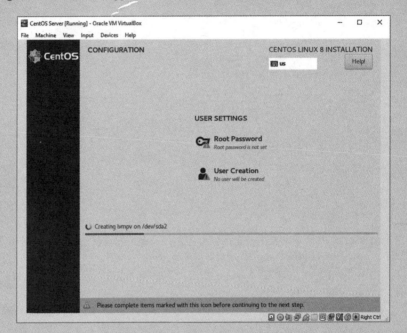

23. Click Root Password to reach a screen that looks similar to this:

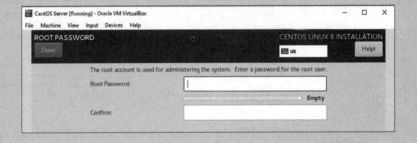

24. In the Root Password field, type in a password for the root account. Be sure to choose one that you will remember!

25. Tab to the Confirm field, and type in the same password you entered in the previous step. If the passwords don't match, you will not be able to proceed past the next step, so type carefully!

26. Click Done in the upper-left corner of the window to return to the Configuration window.

27. Click User Creation to reach a screen that looks similar to the following:

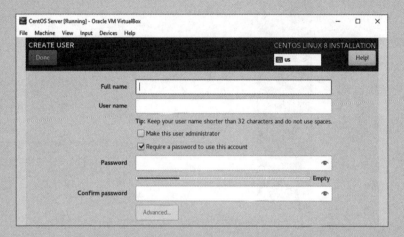

28. Within the Create User screen, type your first and last name in the Full Name field.

29. Tab to the User Name field, and type `sysadmin`.

30. Tab to the Password field, and type in a password. Be sure to choose one that you will remember!

31. Tab to the Confirm Password field, and type in the same password you entered in the previous step. If the passwords don't match, you will not be able to proceed past the next step, so type carefully!

32. Click Done in the upper-left corner of the window to return to the Configuration window.

33. In the Configuration window, you may have to wait a while for the software to finish downloading and installing. When this part of the process is completed, you'll see a screen containing a "Complete!" message like this:

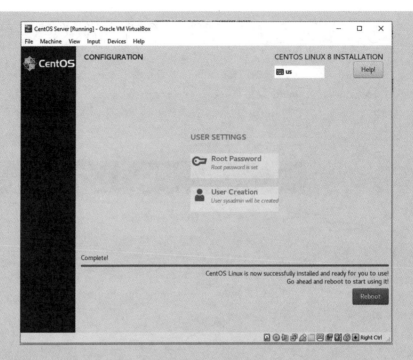

34. Because the CentOS ISO image file has not yet been removed from the virtual DVD drive, click the X in the VM's upper-right corner. You'll receive the Close Virtual Machine screen, which looks similar to the following:

35. Click the circle next to Power Off The Machine.

36. Click OK to power off the CentOS Server virtual machine.

37. Click the Settings button in the VirtualBox Manager's top-right pane, which opens the Settings window for the CentOS Server VM.

38. In the Settings window, click Storage in the left pane to open the Storage Settings window for the CentOS Server.

39. In the Storage Settings window's Attributes pane, click the DVD image to produce a drop-down menu, and select Remove Disk From Virtual Drive in the Storage Devices pane. The Controller: IDE item should show Empty, similar to the following:

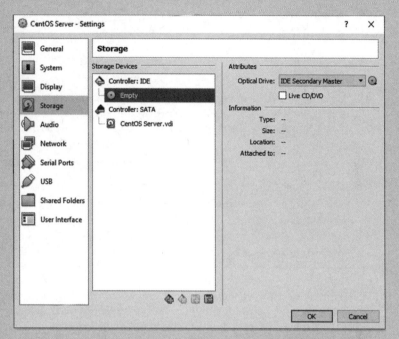

40. Click OK to return to the VirtualBox Manager window.

41. Boot your CentOS Server VM by clicking the Start button in the VirtualBox Manager's top-right pane.

You may see messages on your screen. Let the process continue until you reach this window:

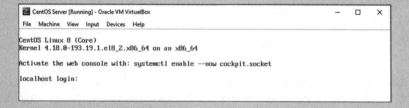

42. In the localhost login field (which is for the username), type **root** and press Enter. The password field will then display.

43. In the password field, be aware that nothing will show as you type in your password. There are no symbols such as asterisks or dots shown. Type in the password you created for the root account earlier, and press Enter.

44. After you log into the system successfully, you'll receive a prompt similar to this:

```
[root@localhost:~]#
```

This prompt is where you enter your commands, and it's called the *command-line interface*.

The next several commands assume that your host machine is connected to a network.

45. Updating software on a newly installed Linux system is an important step, and before you begin this process, you can see whether there are any updates to perform. To do this, type **dnf list upgrades** and then press Enter. (Note that if no updates are listed, you can skip the next two steps.)

46. Once you receive the prompt, update the software by typing **dnf upgrade** and pressing Enter.

47. Whenever the software update process asks "Is this ok [y/N]," type **y** and press Enter.

This software update may take a while, so go get a cup of coffee and check the latest statuses on social media.

48. When you receive the "Complete!" message and a command-line prompt, the installation process is complete. Type **poweroff** at the prompt and press Enter to shut down the system.

Congratulations! You've installed CentOS as a VM within the VirtualBox hypervisor, and you can use this Red Hat distribution twin to learn more about RHEL. Now that the installation process is complete, it's a good idea to check and make sure everything is OK. We'll cover that next.

Checking the Installation

Though the system may appear fine after an initial installation, it's wise to perform a few checks. While it's a little difficult to understand everything you are looking at in this section, reviewing this information will help you as we cover these utilities and concepts in detail later in the book. Also, you can return to this section for guidance the next time you perform a CentOS distribution installation.

First, boot your CentOS Server VM. After the system has booted, log into the terminal using the root account name and password, and do the following:

Check for boot errors. There are three commands that can help you check for boot errors. The first is dmesg, and to view this information, you don't need super user privileges. This will display the kernel ring buffer, but that data is useful only if you check it soon after the system has booted.

To see boot messages long after a system boot, type **less /var/log/boot.log** at the prompt and press Enter. You can move forward through this log by pressing the spacebar. When you are done looking at the information, press the Q key to exit to the command-line prompt.

You can look for boot errors and all kinds of messages via the `journalctl` command. To peruse this information, you will also need the spacebar to move forward and the Q key to quit your viewing.

Determine the default boot level.   The default boot level on a Linux system determines what applications are started when the system boots. The command to see this information is `systemctl get-default`. It does not require super user privileges to use.

Most likely, you will see `multi-user.target` when you issue this command, meaning that even if GUI software is available, the GUI will *not* start on boot. You'll learn more about targets later in this book.

Check version information.   Determining the version numbers of the system's main components is helpful when tracking down problems. First, make sure you have the right CentOS distribution version installed by typing **cat /etc/redhat-release** at the prompt. The distribution name and version is displayed.

Check the Linux kernel version too. This is important to know because different features (and bugs!) exist in the various kernel versions. To see this information, you'll need to type **uname -r** at the command-line prompt. You can also view this information via the `cat /proc/version` command.

Finally, look at the version of the Bash Shell running on the system. This is easy to accomplish by using the `bash --version` command.

Once you've completed your checks, celebrate! You worked hard to get this CentOS distribution installed correctly.

The Bottom Line

Review needed CentOS hardware resources.   Determining the hardware resources required for a CentOS installation on a physical or virtualized server helps to ensure a successful completion of the install. It also avoids important project delays due to under-resourced systems.

> **Master It**   Imagine that you need to install the CentOS distribution on a physical server that has a dual-core 2 GHz CPU, 200 GB hard drive, and 2 GB of RAM. Are the server's resources at the recommended level? Why or why not?

Determine the requirements for a virtual CentOS system.   Installing the CentOS distribution as a VM on a host system has different requirements than a direct installation on a physical server. It is critical to evaluate the host system so that the installation is successful.

> **Master It**   Your project team is planning on installing two CentOS VMs on a host system that has a quad-core 2.8 GHz CPU, 200 GB of free disk space, and 32 GB of RAM. Are the host system resources sufficient? Why or why not?

Obtain CentOS software.   To install the CentOS Linux distribution, you must have the proper ISO image file. This is true whether you are installing it directly on hardware or as a

VM. Besides getting the ISO file, you need to ensure that it is not corrupted so that the installation proceeds well.

Master It   You've downloaded the CentOS ISO image file, but you are concerned that during the download process, file corruption occurred. What should you do to see whether the ISO image file is corrupt?

Conduct an installation of a CentOS distribution.   There are several steps to successfully install a CentOS distribution, and it is critical to make sure you complete all of them. Skipping a step can cause problems immediately as well as problems later, if you can even get the system to boot.

Master It   Your sysadmin team has correctly installed the CentOS software from the ISO image file, and the system booted without any problems. What's the next step?

Audit the CentOS distribution's installation.   If you had some problems while booting the system, there are a few commands you can use to look at helpful boot messages. But even a successful installation still requires a few additional checks.

Master It   At your company, you have completed the entire CentOS distro installation process on a new system without any problems, but you then ran into issues the last time the server was rebooted. You need to review the boot messages to track down the problem(s). What log file can you use to view these messages?

Chapter 5

Installing and Maintaining Software in Red Hat

Installing and maintaining software on Red Hat–based servers is similar to the Ubuntu server process, just with different tools. Just like Ubuntu, Red Hat uses a package management system to make installing and updating software easy, especially if your server is connected to the Internet. However, if your Red Hat server is not connected to the Internet, there's still a way for you to install and upgrade software using packages.

IN THIS CHAPTER, YOU WILL LEARN TO

- ◆ Recognize Red Hat packages

- ◆ Use automated Red Hat package managers

- ◆ Manually install Red Hat packages

- ◆ Install flatpack application containers

Exploring Red Hat Packages

Red Hat Enterprise Linux, CentOS, and Fedora use the Red Hat Package Manager (RPM) utility to install and manage software. Application files are bundled into an rpm package for distribution. rpm package files have an .rpm file extension and use a specific naming format as follows:

name-version-release.architecture.rpm

Since software packages are compiled for specific architectures, there are usually multiple rpm packages for each software package. The *version* is the program's version number, so you can easily track what version of the software is currently installed and what version is available for download. The *release* is the distribution release identifier. Even though rpm packages can be installed on any Red Hat–based Linux system, sometimes packages are compiled for specific distribution environments. Packages created for CentOS normally have a release of el8. Here's an example of listing some .rpm files:

```
# ls -l *.rpm
total 11920
drwxr-xr-x. 2 sysadmin sysadmin      253 Dec  5 10:23 .
drwx------. 3 sysadmin sysadmin       74 Dec  5 10:21 ..
```

```
-rwxr-x---. 1 sysadmin sysadmin 1621792 Dec  5 10:21 bash-4.4.19-10.el8.x86_64.rpm
-rwxr-x---. 1 sysadmin sysadmin 5943540 Dec  5 10:21 binutils-2.30-73.el8.x86_64.rpm
-rwxr-x---. 1 sysadmin sysadmin  361000 Dec  5 10:21 curl-7.61.1-12.el8.x86_64.rpm
-rwxr-x---. 1 sysadmin sysadmin  507956 Dec  5 10:21 openssh-8.0p1-4.el8_1.x86_64.rpm
-rwxr-x---. 1 sysadmin sysadmin  713708 Dec  5 10:21 openssl-1.1.1c-15.el8.x86_64.rpm
-rwxr-x---. 1 sysadmin sysadmin 3039264 Dec  5 10:21 zsh-5.5.1-6.el8_1.2.x86_64.rpm
#
```

Notice that the architecture for each is x86_64, indicating that the software packages were compiled for a 64-bit CPU environment.

There are two ways to install rpm packages.

◆ Using an automated package management tool

◆ Manually using the rpm command-line tool

Using an automated package management tool is usually preferred. These tools have the ability to connect via the Internet to a software repository to find the requested package and install it, along with any dependent packages. However, there are times when a Red Hat server doesn't have Internet access, such as in secure environments. In those cases, you'll have to download the software rpm packages on a different platform, transfer them to the server, and then install them manually using the rpm command-line tool. The following sections cover both methods of installing RPM software packages.

Automated Package Management

Like the Debian-based distributions, the Red Hat–based systems have several different front-end tools available. The common ones are these:

◆ yum: Used in Red Hat, CentOS, and Fedora

◆ dnf: An updated version of yum with some additional features

◆ zypper: Used in openSUSE

These front ends are all based on the rpm command-line tool. The following section discusses how to manage software packages using these various rpm-based tools. The focus will be on dnf, but the other packages use similar commands and formats.

Listing Installed Packages

To find out what is currently installed on your system, at the shell prompt use the list option of the dnf command, as shown here:

```
$ dnf list installed
Installed Packages
NetworkManager.x86_64                   1:1.22.8-5.el8_2          @BaseOS
NetworkManager-config-server.noarch     1:1.22.8-5.el8_2          @BaseOS
NetworkManager-libnm.x86_64             1:1.22.8-5.el8_2          @BaseOS
NetworkManager-team.x86_64              1:1.22.8-5.el8_2          @BaseOS
NetworkManager-tui.x86_64               1:1.22.8-5.el8_2          @BaseOS
PackageKit.x86_64                       1.1.12-4.el8              @AppStream
PackageKit-glib.x86_64                  1.1.12-4.el8              @AppStream
```

```
abattis-cantarell-fonts.noarch       0.0.25-4.el8                        @AppStream
acl.x86_64                           2.2.53-1.el8                        @BaseOS
adcli.x86_64                         0.8.2-5.el8                         @BaseOS
at.x86_64                            3.1.20-11.el8                       @BaseOS
attr.x86_64                          2.4.48-3.el8                        @BaseOS
audit.x86_64                         3.0-0.17.20191104git1c2f876.el8     @BaseOS
audit-libs.x86_64                    3.0-0.17.20191104git1c2f876.el8     @BaseOS
...
$
```

There will be lots of packages installed on your server; it usually helps to redirect the output to the more or less command to look at the list in a controlled manner. You can also redirect the output to a text file for viewing in a text editor.

```
dnf list installed > installed.txt
```

The format of the listing is a little different from the format of the original package names, but you can probably pick out the different components. The package name and architecture are listed first, followed by the version and release. The third column shows what repository category the package came from.

You can also look for a single installed package.

```
$ dnf list installed bash
Installed Packages
bash.x86_64                          4.4.19-10el8                        @BaseOS
$
```

If the package isn't installed, dnf will tell you.

```
$ dnf list installed zsh
Error: No matching Packages to list
$
```

You can then check if the package is available in the software repository by using the list option with the software package name.

```
$ dnf list zsh
Last metadata expiration check: 0:00:18 ago on Sat 05 Dec 2020 10:33:03 AM EST.
Available Packages
zsh.x86_64                           5.5.1-6.el8_1.2                     BaseOS
$
```

Finally, if you need to find out what software package provides a particular file on your filesystem, use the provides option.

```
dnf provides file_name
```

Here's an example of trying to find what software provided the file /usr/bin/gzip:

```
$ dnf provides /usr/bin/gzip
Last metadata expiration check: 0:04:02 ago on Sat 05 Dec 2020 10:32:22 AM EST.
gzip-1.9-9.el8.x86_64 : The GNU data compression program
Repo        : @System
Matched from:
```

```
Filename    : /usr/bin/gzip

gzip-1.9-9.el8.x86_64 : The GNU data compression program
Repo        : BaseOS
Matched from:
Filename    : /usr/bin/gzip
$
```

dnf checked two separate repositories: the local system (denoted by @System) and the default fedora repository (denoted by BaseOS). That allows you to easily check whether there's an update available for the file.

Installing Software with *dnf*

Installation of a software package using dnf is simple. All you need is the install option, followed by the package name.

```
dnf install package_name
```

This installs not only the software package specified, but also any package dependencies. The output will show you the package information, along with any dependent packages required to install, and prompt you to continue the installation.

 Real World Scenario

INSTALLING SOFTWARE USING *DNF*

In this exercise, you'll install the Z shell software package using the dnf tool on your CentOS server.

1. Log into your CentOS server as the root user account, using the password you created in Chapter 4, "Installing a Red Hat Server."

2. From the command prompt, enter the command **dnf install zsh**. You should see output that's similar to this:

```
# dnf install zsh
CentOS-8 - AppStream                    2.4 kB/s | 4.3 kB    00:01
CentOS-8 - AppStream                    883 kB/s | 6.2 MB    00:07
CentOS-8 - Base                         154  B/s | 3.9 kB    00:25
CentOS-8 - Base                         865 kB/s | 2.3 MB    00:02
CentOS-8 - Extras                       2.3 kB/s | 1.5 kB    00:00
CentOS-8 - Extras                       8.3 kB/s | 8.1 kB    00:00
Dependencies resolved.
============================================================================
 Package    Architecture      Version          Repository        Size
============================================================================
Installing:
```

```
zsh          x86_64           5.5.1-6.el8_1.2        BaseOS        2.9 M

Transaction Summary
================================================================================
Install  1 Package

Total download size: 2.9 M
Installed size: 7.2 M
Is this ok [y/N]: y
Downloading Packages:
zsh-5.5.1-6.el8_1.2.x86_64.rpm                   392 kB/s | 2.9 MB    00:07
--------------------------------------------------------------------------------
Total                                            362 kB/s | 2.9 MB    00:08
Running transaction check
Transaction check succeeded.
Running transaction test
Transaction test succeeded.
Running transaction
  Preparing        :                                                    1/1
  Installing       : zsh-5.5.1-6.el8_1.2.x86_64                         1/1
  Running scriptlet: zsh-5.5.1-6.el8_1.2.x86_64                         1/1
  Verifying        : zsh-5.5.1-6.el8_1.2.x86_64                         1/1
Installed products updated.

Installed:
  zsh-5.5.1-6.el8_1.2.x86_64

Complete!
#
```

3. Test the installation by entering the command **zsh**. You will see a prompt from the new Z shell. If you receive an error message, something went wrong.

4. Return to the Bash Shell by entering the command **exit**.

5. Check whether the installation processed properly by entering the command **dnf list installed zsh**. You should see the package appear, as shown here:

```
# dnf list installed zsh
Installed Packages
zsh.x86_64              5.5.1-6.el8_1.2                      @BaseOS
#
```

ROOT PRIVILEGES

To install new software packages, you must have root privileges, either by logging in as the root user account or by using the sudo command before the dnf command to gain root privileges for your user account.

Upgrading Software with *dnf*

In most Linux distributions, when you're working away in the graphical user interface (GUI), you get those nice little notification icons telling you a software upgrade to a new version is needed. Here at the command line, it takes a little more work.

To see the list of all the available upgrades for your installed packages, type the following command:

```
dnf list upgrades
```

If you see that a particular software package needs upgrading, then type in the following command:

```
dnf upgrade package_name
```

If you'd like to upgrade all the packages listed in the upgrade list, just enter the following command:

```
dnf upgrade
```

One nice feature in dnf is the upgrade-minimal command. It upgrades a package to the latest bug fix or security patch version instead of the latest and greatest version.

Uninstalling Software with *dnf*

The dnf tool also provides an easy way to uninstall software you no longer need by using the remove option.

```
# dnf remove zsh
Dependencies resolved.
================================================================================
 Package          Architecture     Version              Repository        Size
================================================================================
Removing:
 zsh              x86_64           5.5.1-6.el8_1.2       @BaseOS          7.2 M

Transaction Summary
================================================================================
Remove   1 Package

Freed space: 7.2 M
Is this ok [y/N]: y
Running transaction check
Transaction check succeeded.
Running transaction test
Transaction test succeeded.
Running transaction
  Preparing        :                                                        1/1
  Running scriptlet: zsh-5.5.1-6.el8_1.2.x86_64                             1/1
  Erasing          : zsh-5.5.1-6.el8_1.2.x86_64                             1/1
  Running scriptlet: zsh-5.5.1-6.el8_1.2.x86_64                             1/1
```

```
  Verifying            : zsh-5.5.1-6.el8_1.2.x86_64                    1/1
Installed products updated.

Removed:
  zsh-5.5.1-6.el8_1.2.x86_64

Complete!
#
```

Unlike the Ubuntu apt tool, dnf doesn't provide an option to remove the application files but keeps any configuration or data files. When you remove a package, everything associated with that package is removed.

Handling Broken Dependencies

Sometimes as multiple software packages get loaded, a software dependency for one package can get overwritten by the installation of another package. This is called a *broken dependency*.

If this should happen on your system, first try the following command:

```
dnf clean all
```

Then try to use the upgrade option in the dnf command. Sometimes, just cleaning up any misplaced files can help.

If that doesn't solve the problem, try the following command:

```
dnf repoquery --deplist package_name
```

This command displays all the package's library dependencies and what software package provides them. Once you know the libraries required for a package, you can then install them. Here's an example of determining the dependencies for the zsh package:

```
# dnf repoquery --deplist zsh
CentOS Linux 8 - AppStream                   1.3 MB/s | 6.2 MB     00:04
CentOS Linux 8 - BaseOS                      867 kB/s | 2.3 MB     00:02
package: zsh-5.5.1-6.el8_1.2.x86_64
  dependency: /bin/sh
   provider: bash-4.4.19-12.el8.x86_64
  dependency: coreutils
   provider: coreutils-8.30-8.el8.x86_64
  dependency: grep
   provider: grep-3.1-6.el8.x86_64
  dependency: info
   provider: info-6.5-6.el8.x86_64
  dependency: libc.so.6(GLIBC_2.15)(64bit)
   provider: glibc-2.28-127.el8.x86_64
  dependency: libdl.so.2()(64bit)
   provider: glibc-2.28-127.el8.x86_64
  dependency: libdl.so.2(GLIBC_2.2.5)(64bit)
   provider: glibc-2.28-127.el8.x86_64
  dependency: libgdbm.so.6()(64bit)
   provider: gdbm-libs-1:1.18-1.el8.x86_64
```

```
dependency: libm.so.6()(64bit)
 provider: glibc-2.28-127.el8.x86_64
dependency: libm.so.6(GLIBC_2.2.5)(64bit)
 provider: glibc-2.28-127.el8.x86_64
dependency: libm.so.6(GLIBC_2.23)(64bit)
 provider: glibc-2.28-127.el8.x86_64
dependency: libncursesw.so.6()(64bit)
 provider: ncurses-libs-6.1-7.20180224.el8.x86_64
dependency: libpcre.so.1()(64bit)
 provider: pcre-8.42-4.el8.x86_64
dependency: librt.so.1()(64bit)
 provider: glibc-2.28-127.el8.x86_64
dependency: librt.so.1(GLIBC_2.2.5)(64bit)
 provider: glibc-2.28-127.el8.x86_64
dependency: libtinfo.so.6()(64bit)
 provider: ncurses-libs-6.1-7.20180224.el8.x86_64
dependency: rtld(GNU_HASH)
 provider: glibc-2.28-127.el8.i686
 provider: glibc-2.28-127.el8.x86_64
#
```

As you can see from the output, there are lots of different packages that must be installed for the Z shell to work properly. Good thing dnf ensured they were all installed for us!

Working with RPM Repositories

Just like the apt systems, dnf has its software repositories set up at installation. For most purposes, these preinstalled repositories will work just fine for your needs. But if and when the time comes that you need to install software from a different repository, here are some things you will need to know.

ROGUE REPOSITORIES

These days, it's always a good idea to stick with approved repositories. An approved repository is one that is sanctioned by the distribution's official site. If you start adding unapproved repositories, you lose the guarantee of stability. And you will be heading into broken dependencies territory.

To see what repositories you are currently pulling software from, use the repolist option.

```
# dnf repolist
repo id                 repo name
appstream               CentOS Linux 8 - AppStream
baseos                  CentOS Linux 8 - BaseOS
extras                  CentOS Linux 8 - Extras
#
```

If you don't find a repository you need software from, then you will need to do a little configuration file editing. There are two places where the dnf repository definitions can be located.

◆ In the /etc/dnf/dnf.conf configuration file

◆ As separate files in the /etc/yum.repos.d directory

Good repository sites such as rpmfusion.org will lay out all the steps necessary to use them. Sometimes these repository sites will offer an RPM file that you can download and install. The installation of the RPM file will do all the repository setup work for you!

Working Directly with Packages

There may be some environments where your Linux server won't have Internet access to contact the repository to automatically download packages. For example, often high-security environments block all network traffic except internal traffic. In these environments, you'll need a way to manually install or update software packages.

The main tool for working with .rpm files is the rpm program. The rpm utility is a command-line program to install, modify, and remove .rpm software packages. Its basic format is as follows:

```
rpm action [OPTION] package
```

Table 5.1 describes the actions for the rpm command.

TABLE 5.1:   The rpm Command Actions

SHORT	LONG	DESCRIPTION
-e	--erase	Removes the specified package
-F	--freshen	Upgrades a package only if an earlier version already exists
-i	--install	Installs the specified package
-q	--query	Queries if the specified package is installed
-U	--upgrade	Installs or upgrades the specified package
-V	--verify	Verifies if the package files are present and the package's integrity

The following sections show how to use the rpm command to manually manage software packages.

Finding Package Files

If you need to obtain copies of RPM files on a Red Hat–based distro, such as CentOS or Fedora, you have a few different options. If you have a separate Linux system connected to the Internet, use the yumdownloader utility. This downloads a specified rpm package file directly from the repository. The yumdownloader tool is part of the yum-utils package, which you'll most likely need to install first; then you can download any rpm package from the repository.

```
$ yumdownloader zsh
Last metadata expiration check: 0:21:30 ago on Sat 05 Dec 2020 08:49:35 AM EST.
zsh-5.5.1-6.el8_1.2.x86_64.rpm                1.1 MB/s | 2.9 MB      00:02

$ ls -l zsh*
-rw-r--r--. 1 root root 3039264 Dec  5 09:11 zsh-5.5.1-6.el8_1.2.x86_64.rpm
$
```

The other method for obtaining rpm package files is using the distribution website. Most Linux distributions provide direct access to RPM files used in the distribution via a download site. For CentOS, click the RPMs link on the Download page (mirror.centos.org/centos/8/ at the time of this writing), next to the distribution version you have installed on the server. This takes you to a repository of all the current rpm packages for that distribution.

Inspecting Package Files

Use the -q action to perform a simple query on the package management database for installed packages.

```
$ rpm -q bash
bash-4.4.19-12.el8.x86_64
$ rpm -q zsh
package zsh is not installed
$
```

There are several options you can add to the query action to obtain more detailed information. Table 5.2 shows a few of the more commonly used query options.

TABLE 5.2:   The rpm Command Query Action Options

SHORT OPTION	LONG OPTION	DESCRIPTION
-c	--configfiles	Lists the names and absolute directory references of package configuration files
-i	--info	Provides detailed information, including version, installation date, and signatures
N/A	--provides	Shows what facilities the package provides
-R	--requires	Displays various package requirements (dependencies)
-s	--state	Provides states of the different files in a package, such as normal (installed), not installed, or replaced
N/A	--what-provides	Shows to what package a file belongs

You can also add the -i action, which provides a detailed list of information on the package.

```
$ rpm -qi bash
Name        : bash
Version     : 4.4.19
Release     : 12.el8
Architecture: x86_64
Install Date: Sat 05 Dec 2020 08:43:49 AM EST
Group       : Unspecified
Size        : 6861588
License     : GPLv3+
Signature   : RSA/SHA256, Tue 21 Jul 2020 12:08:45 PM EDT, Key ID
05b555b38483c65d
Source RPM  : bash-4.4.19-12.el8.src.rpm
Build Date  : Tue 21 Jul 2020 12:03:55 PM EDT
Build Host  : x86-02.mbox.centos.org
Relocations : (not relocatable)
Packager    : CentOS Buildsys <bugs@centos.org>
Vendor      : CentOS
URL         : https://www.gnu.org/software/bash
Summary     : The GNU Bourne Again shell
Description :
The GNU Bourne Again shell (Bash) is a shell or command language
interpreter that is compatible with the Bourne shell (sh). Bash
incorporates useful features from the Korn shell (ksh) and the C shell
(csh). Most sh scripts can be run by bash without modification.
$
```

From the output of the detailed query, you can see specific information, such as the date the package was installed and a brief description of the package.

LISTING INSTALLED PACKAGES

You can use the rpm command to list all the packages installed on your Linux system by using the -a option with the rpm -q command, although the packages are returned in the order in which they were installed, which can make it hard to find a specific package. We like to use the command rpm -qa | sort to sort the output by package name.

Installing Package Files

There are a couple of ways to install an rpm package that you have downloaded. For a new package, use the -i action to install the package. However, if an older version of the package already exists on your system, you'll receive an error message.

It's more common to use the -U action, which installs the new package, or upgrades the package if it's already installed on the system. It has also become somewhat common to add the

-vh options as well. The -h option shows the progress of the update, and the -v option shows what it's doing.

```
rpm -Uvh package
```

It's also important to remember that you must have root privileges to manually install packages, either as the root user or as a user account with root privileges.

 Real World Scenario

MANUALLY INSTALLING RPM PACKAGES

The zsh package is an alternative shell that you can find in the standard CentOS repository. Follow these steps to manually install it:

1. Log into your CentOS server, either as the root user account or as a user account with root privileges.

2. Download the zsh package from the CentOS repository. You can do this either by using the command **yumdownloader zsh** or by manually downloading the package from mirror.centos .org/centos/8/BaseOS/x86_64/os/Packages/ and copying the file to your CentOS server. At the time of this writing, the current zsh package is zsh-5.5.1-6.el8_1.2.x86_64.rpm.

3. Install the zsh package by entering the command **rpm -Uvh zsh-5.5.1-6.el8_1.2.x86_64 .rpm**. You should see output similar to this:

```
# rpm -Uvh zsh-5.5.1-6.el8_1.2.x86_64.rpm
Verifying...                        ################################ [100%]
Preparing...                        ################################ [100%]
Updating / installing...
1:zsh-5.5.1-6.el8_1.2                ################################ [100%]
#
```

4. Verify the installation by entering the command **zsh**. You should then get the Z shell prompt and not an error message.

5. Return to your normal Bash Shell by typing the command **exit**.

6. Check whether the installation processed properly by typing the command **dnf list installed zsh**. You should see the package appear, indicating that it is installed.

Even though you installed the zsh package using the rpm command-line tool, it appears when you use the dnf command to list the installed packages. This shows that both commands install packages to the same package management database.

Removing Package Files

To remove an installed package, just use the -e action for the rpm command.

```
# rpm -e zsh
# rpm -q zsh
package zsh is not installed
```

```
# dnf list installed zsh
Error: No matching Packages to list
#
```

The -e action doesn't show if it was successful, but it will display an error message if something goes wrong with the removal. You can check to make sure the removal was successful by using the -q action to query the package database or by using the
dnf list installed command.

Using Flatpak Containers

As discussed in Chapter 3, "Installing and Maintaining Software in Ubuntu," containers are software packaging systems that bundle all the files required to run an application into a single package. While this creates duplication of files, it helps eliminate the issue of conflicting library files and makes it easier to move application containers around between servers.

The *flatpak* application container format was created as an independent open source project with no direct ties to any specific Linux distribution. That said, battle lines have already been drawn, with Red Hat, CentOS, and Fedora oriented toward using flatpak instead of Canonical's snap container format.

While CentOS desktop distributions install flatpak by default, the CentOS server environment doesn't. However, you can easily install flatpak as a package using the standard dnf or rpm methods.

 Real World Scenario

INSTALLING FLATPAK

The flatpak container format provides quick installation of many popular application programs. To use flatpak on your CentOS server, you'll need to first install the software package and then install the repository configuration by following these steps:

1. Log onto your CentOS server as the root user account.

2. From the command-line prompt, enter the command **dnf install flatpak**. There are lots of dependencies required, so you'll see quite a few packages install.

3. Once flatpak is installed, you will need to point it to a flatpak container repository. The most popular one is Flathub. Configure that by entering the command **flatpak remote-add --if-not-exists flathub https://flathub.org/repo/ flathub.flatpakrepo**. You should see output that's similar to this:

```
# flatpak remote-add --if-not-exists flathub https://flathub.org/repo/
flathub.flatpakrepo

Note that the directories

'/var/lib/flatpak/exports/share'
```

```
            '/root/.local/share/flatpak/exports/share'

        are not in the search path set by the XDG_DATA_DIRS environment
        variable, so
        applications installed by Flatpak may not appear on your
        desktop until the
        session is restarted.


        #
```

4. Test the flatpak command by entering the command **flatpak list**.

```
# flatpak list
#
```

Not too exciting. When you first install flatpak, there won't be any containers installed, but now you know that flatpak is installed.

To find an application in the flatpak repository, you use the flatpak search command.

```
# flatpak search mosh
Name    Description        Application ID     Version   Branch    Remotes
Mosh    The Mobile Shell   org.mosh.mosh      1.3.2     stable    flathub
#
```

When working with a container, you must use its Application ID value and not its name. To install the application, use the flatpak install command.

```
# flatpak install org.mosh.mosh
Looking for matches...
Found similar ref(s) for 'mosh' in remote 'flathub' (system).
Use this remote? [Y/n]: y
Found ref 'app/org.mosh.mosh/x86_64/stable' in remote 'flathub' (system).
Use this ref? [Y/n]: y
Required runtime for org.mosh.mosh/x86_64/stable (runtime/org.freedesktop.
Platform/x86_64/20.08) found in remote flathub
Do you want to install it? [Y/n]: y
...
Installation complete.
#
```

To check whether the installation went well, you can use the flatpak list command again.

```
# flatpak list
Name                Application ID                     Version   Branch  Installation
Freedesktop Plat... org.freedesktop.Platform           20.08.2   20.08   system
default             ...freedesktop.Platform.GL.default            20.08   system
openh264            ...g.freedesktop.Platform.openh264 2.1.0     2.0     system
Mosh                org.mosh.mosh                      1.3.2     stable  system
#
```

Finally, to remove an application container, use the `flatpak uninstall` command.

```
# flatpak uninstall org.mosh.mosh

        ID                  Branch      Op
   1. [-] org.mosh.mosh     stable      r

Uninstall complete.
#
```

Using application containers is similar to using package management systems, but what goes on behind the scenes is fundamentally different. However, the end result is that you have an application installed on your Linux system that can be easily maintained and upgraded.

The Bottom Line

Recognize Red Hat packages.   Developers bundle the files required for an application into a package to make it easier to install. A package management system allows you to easily track what software packages are installed on your Linux system, as well as install, update, and remove them. Red Hat–based Linux distributions use the Red Hat Package Management (RPM) system for managing application software. The rpm command-line tool provides access to the package management database, allowing you to quickly determine the status of installed packages.

> **Master It**   The curl software package allows you to easily transfer data using a multitude of protocols (such as FTP, HTTP, and SCP) from the command line. What command would you use to determine whether curl is installed on your Linux system? If the package is installed, what command would you use to view the version and a description of the package?

Use automated Red Hat package managers.   Most Red Hat–based Linux distributions are based on the rpm utility but use different front-end tools at the command line. Red Hat, CentOS, and Fedora use dnf for installing and managing software packages. The dnf tool automatically installs any software packages required by the package you install.

> **Master It**   The perf utility allows you to monitor the performance of a Linux system. What command would you use to check whether the perf software is available as an rpm package for your Linux system, and what command would you use to install it? What command would you use to remove it?

Manually install Red Hat packages.   Not all Linux systems are connected to the Internet, allowing the automated package management tools to connect to a repository. In those situations, you'll need to manually find and download RPM software packages and then use the rpm command to manually install the package. The most common options used to install software are the -Uvh options, which will update the package if it's already installed and provide verbose information on the installation progress.

> **Master It**   What steps would you need to take to install the perf utility if your Linux system is not connected to the Internet?

Install flatpak application containers. Application containers are relatively new in software package management. Containers bundle all of the software required for an application to run, including all files the application is dependent on. This makes containers portable and easily moved between systems. Red Hat Linux–based distributions use the flatpak container format.

Master It Cointop is a terminal-based application for tracking cryptocurrencies. What command would you use to check if there's a flatpak container for it, and what command would you use to install it?

Chapter 6

Working with the Shell

Now that you have a grasp of installing a Linux distribution and managing its software, it's time to start digging into the basics of command-line work. As a system admin, you need to be proficient at using the Bash shell. Often this includes being fast at the CLI and knowing how to get help without engaging the Internet. In addition, understanding how variables operate in this environment and how to use special shell features, such file descriptors, will work to your advantage. These abilities not only will improve your career at the command line but will allow you to spend less time there.

Our goal in this chapter is to assist you in learning or reinforcing some basic and important skills at the command line. Knowing these basics will serve you well through the rest of this book (and your sysadmin career).

IN THIS CHAPTER, YOU WILL LEARN TO

- ◆ Decode the shell prompt and the manual pages

- ◆ Enter, recall, and redirect shell commands

- ◆ Set and use environment variables

Exploring the Shell

Before the days of graphical desktops, the only way to interact with a Unix system (Linux's predecessor) was through a text *command-line interface* (CLI) provided by the shell. The CLI allowed text input only and could display only text and rudimentary graphics output.

Things are significantly different in today's Linux environment. Just about every Linux desktop distribution uses some type of graphical desktop environment. However, to enter shell commands on a server Linux system that doesn't run a graphical environment, you still need a way to reach the shell's CLI.

Fortunately, you can access the Linux system via text mode. This provides nothing more than a simple shell CLI on the monitor, just like the days before graphical desktops. This mode is called the *Linux console* because it emulates the old days of a hardwired console terminal and is a direct interface to the Linux system.

When the Linux system starts, it automatically creates several *virtual consoles*. A virtual console is a terminal session that runs in Linux system memory. Instead of having several physical terminals connected to the computer, most Linux distributions start five or six (or sometimes even more) virtual consoles that you can access from a single computer keyboard and monitor.

REACHING A VIRTUAL CONSOLE

On most Linux servers, if you are not taken automatically to a virtual terminal login session, you can access one using a simple keystroke combination. Usually, you must hold down the Ctrl+Alt key combination and then press a function key (F1 through F7) for the virtual console you want to use. Function key F2 produces virtual console 2, key F3 produces virtual console 3, key F4 produces virtual console 4, and so on. Which function keys work depends on how the Linux system is configured

Text mode virtual consoles use the whole screen and start with the text login screen displayed. Figure 6.1 shows an example of a text login screen from a CentOS virtual console.

FIGURE 6.1
Text mode virtual
console login screen

```
CentOS Server [Running] - Oracle VM VirtualBox          —   □   ×
File   Machine   View   Input   Devices   Help

CentOS Linux 8 (Core)
Kernel 4.18.0-193.19.1.el8_2.x86_64 on an x86_64

Activate the web console with: systemctl enable --now cockpit.socket

localhost login:
```

You log into a console terminal by entering your username after the login prompt and typing your password after the Password prompt. If you have never logged in this way before, be aware that typing your password is a different experience than in a graphical environment! In a graphical environment, you may see dots or asterisks indicating the password characters as you type. However, at the virtual console, nothing is displayed when you type your password.

SWITCHING TO A DIFFERENT VIRTUAL CONSOLE

It's tedious to wait for long programs to finish running so that you can get on with your work. Well, on Linux, you can just jump to a different terminal without leaving your seat. For example, if you are logged on virtual console 2, you can switch to virtual console 3 using the Ctrl+Alt+F3 key sequence, log in there, and get back to work. If you want to check your program's progress on virtual console 2, simply press the Ctrl+Alt+F2 key sequence and take a peek, and then jump back to virtual console 3. This is handy when you've got a lot to get done!

You'll know that you have successfully logged into the Linux system and reached the CLI when you get a shell prompt. We'll cover that next.

The Shell Prompt

Once you log in to a Linux virtual console, you get access to the shell CLI *prompt*. The prompt is your gateway to the shell. This is the place where you enter shell commands.

The default prompt symbol for the Bash shell is the dollar sign ($). This symbol indicates that the shell is waiting for you to enter text. Different Linux distributions use different formats for the prompt. On the Ubuntu Linux server you installed in Chapter 2, "Installing an Ubuntu Server," the shell prompt probably looked similar to this:

```
sysadmin@ubuntu-server:~$
```

whereas on the CentOS Linux server you installed in Chapter 4, "Installing a Red Hat Server," it looked similar to this:

```
[sysadmin@localhost ~]$
```

Besides acting as your access point to the shell, the prompt can provide additional helpful information. In the two preceding examples, the current user ID name, sysadmin, is shown in the prompt. Also, the name of the system is shown, ubuntu-server on the Ubuntu system and localhost on the CentOS machine. (You may also see a ~, which is a special character that represents your home directory.) You'll learn later in this chapter about how to modify this shell prompt.

Think of the shell CLI prompt as a helpmate, assisting you with your Linux system, giving you helpful insights, and letting you know when the shell is ready for new commands. Another helpful item in the shell is the manual.

The Shell Manual

Most Linux distributions include an online manual for looking up information on shell commands, as well as lots of other GNU utilities included in the distribution. You should become familiar with the manual, because it's invaluable for working with commands, especially when you're trying to figure out various command-line parameters.

The man command provides access to the manual pages stored on the Linux system. Entering the man command followed by a specific command name provides that utility's manual entry. Figure 6.2 shows an example of looking up the apt command's manual pages. This page was reached by typing the command **man apt** on an Ubuntu system.

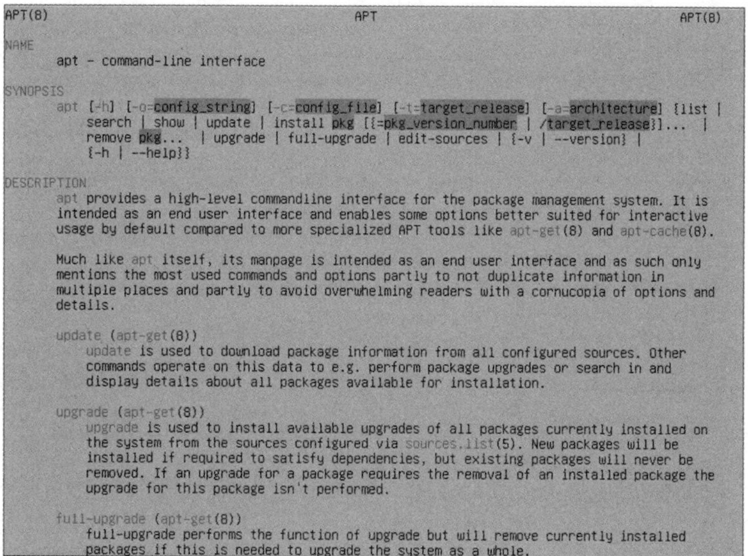

FIGURE 6.2

Manual pages for the apt command

Notice the apt command's DESCRIPTION paragraph in Figure 6.2. It is rather sparse and full of technical jargon. The Bash manual is not a step-by-step guide, but instead a quick reference.

When you use the man command to view a command's manual, the information is displayed with something called a *pager*. A pager is a utility that allows you to view text a page (or a line) at a time. Thus, you can page through the man pages by pressing the spacebar, or you can go line by line using the Enter key. In addition, you can use the arrow keys to scroll forward and backward through the information. Specifically, the man pages use the less pager utility. If you'd like to find out more about less, type **man less** at the command line, and press Enter.

When you are finished with the man pages, press the Q key to quit. When you leave the man pages, you receive a shell CLI prompt, indicating the shell is waiting for your next command.

> **GETTING HELP WITH THE *MAN* PAGES**
>
> For those who are new or fairly new to Linux, the Bash manual is often difficult to use. However, a nice feature is that the manual has reference information on itself! Type **man man** (yes, that is man typed two times) and press Enter to see information concerning the man pages.

The manual page divides information about a command into separate sections. Each section has a conventional naming standard, as shown in Table 6.1.

TABLE 6.1: The Linux Man Page Conventional Section Names

SECTION	DESCRIPTION
Name	Displays the command name and a short description
Synopsis	Shows command syntax
Configuration	Provides configuration information
Description	Describes the command generally
Options	Describes the command option(s)
Exit Status	Defines the command exit status indicator(s)
Return Value	Describes the command return value(s)
Errors	Provides command error messages
Environment	Describes environment variable(s) used
Files	Defines files used by the command
Versions	Describes command version information

Section	Description
Conforming To	Provides the standards that are followed
Notes	Describes additional helpful command material
Bugs	Provides the location to report found bugs
Example	Shows command use examples
Authors	Provides information on command developers
Copyright	Defines command code copyright status
See Also	Refers to similar available commands

Not every command's man page has all the section names described in Table 6.1. Also, some commands have section names that are not listed in the conventional standard.

In addition to the conventionally named sections for a man page, there are man page section areas. Each section area has an assigned number, starting at 1 and going to 9; they are listed in Table 6.2.

TABLE 6.2:   The Linux Man Page Section Areas

Section Number	Area Contents
1	Executable programs or shell commands
2	System calls
3	Library calls
4	Special files
5	File formats and conventions
6	Games
7	Overviews, conventions, and miscellaneous
8	Super user and system administration commands
9	Kernel routines

Typically, the man utility provides the lowest numbered content area for the command. For example, looking back to Figure 6.2 where the command man apt was entered, notice that in the upper-left and upper-right display corners, the word APT is followed by a number in parentheses, (8). This means the man pages displayed are coming from content area 8 (super user and system administration commands).

Your Linux system may include a few nonstandard section numbers in its man pages. For example, 1p is the section covering Portable Operating System Interface (POSIX) commands, and 3n is for network functions.

GETTING ADDITIONAL HELP

The man pages are not the only reference. There are also the information pages called *info pages*. You can learn about the info pages by typing **info info**.

Built-in commands, which are commands that are built into the Bash shell, have their own special resource called the help pages. For more information on using help pages, type **help help** (just don't say it out loud as you type it!).

In addition, most commands accept the -h or --help option. For example, you can type **man --help** to see a brief help screen.

Occasionally, a command has the same name as a special file or overview section in the man pages, and thus the name is listed in multiple section content areas. For example, the man pages for passwd contain information on the command as well as a file. Typically by default, the man information for the lowest section number is displayed, so if you type in **man passwd**, you'll see information on the passwd command from section 1. To get around the default section search order, type **man *section# topicname***. Thus, to see the passwd file man pages in section 5, type **man 5 passwd**.

You can also step through an introduction to the various section content areas by typing **man 1 intro** to read about section 1, **man 2 intro** to read about section 2, **man 3 intro** to read about section 3, and so on.

 Real World Scenario

FINDING HELP INFORMATION

What if you want help on a command but cannot remember its name? Or maybe you'd like to peruse a general topic in the man pages. How do you find out what's available? There a few different commands that will let you search the man pages: whatis, apropos, and man -k.

Imagine you are trying to get help on a command that will let you copy files, but you cannot remember the command's name. The following steps will take you through finding the command's name and getting help on it:

1. Log into a Linux system using the sysadmin account and the password you created for it.

2. Once you reach the command prompt, type **man -k copy** and press Enter.

You should see several lines of text listed. The information displayed in the previous step is the result of a keyword search, where copy was the keyword. The man -k command searches through each man page's Name and Description sections, looking for the specified keyword. And if found, it displays the man page's Name information.

3. Now try a different man page search utility for the same keyword. Type **apropos copy** and press Enter. Is the information different from the previous step or the same? (You may need to use the Shift+Page Up key combination to see the text that has scrolled out of view on the screen. You can press either Enter or Shift+Page Down to get back to the prompt.) You should find the same information, because apropos is essentially an equivalent command to man -k.

4. Look back through the last step's output (use Shift+Page Up, if needed) and find the line starting with cp (1). Record the information following cp (1).

5. Try another man page search utility. This one requires you to know the name of the command. Type **whatis cp** and press Enter. You should see at least a single line of text. (It is OK if you get two or more lines of text.)

6. Compare the line starting with cp (1) to the information you recorded in step 4. Does it match? It should, because the whatis command pulls out the Name information from the man pages for the designated command.

These different search methods allow you to quickly find commands via keyword searches and pull out brief information regarding the command. If you want more in-depth information, go directly into the man pages once you learn the command's name. Using our example command from earlier, you would type **man cp** and press Enter. The cp command is covered in depth in Chapter 7, "Exploring Linux File Management."

Now that you know how to get help, you can begin more in-depth experimentation with various shell commands. We'll cover that topic next.

Working with Commands

Although you've already entered several Bash shell commands in the CLI so far in this book, it's a good idea to stop and examine the process. There are also several tricks and tips to explore that will help you get your shell work done faster. We'll look at those items in this section along with some rather useful, but tricky, methods to save and/or manipulate your command-line work.

Entering Commands

Commands you enter at the command-line prompt are actually programs. When you enter the program name at the shell prompt and press Enter, this instructs the Bash shell to run the named program. Either these programs are built into the shell or they are external and reside in the Linux virtual directory structure (the Linux directory structure is covered in more detail within Chapter 7).

DETERMINING WHETHER A COMMAND IS A PROGRAM BUILT INTO THE SHELL

The quickest way to find out whether a command is a Bash shell built-in program or an external program is to use the type command. For example, if you type **type help** and press Enter, you'll receive the message help is a shell built-in or something similar. This indicates that the help utility is a program built into the Bash shell.

Another example is to use the `type` command on the man utility. At the CLI, enter **type man** and press Enter. You'll either receive the message /usr/bin/man or, if the man command was recently used, receive man is hashed (/usr/bin/man). Either way, when `type` provides the directory name of a command, this indicates the program is external to the Bash shell.

These programs have a basic syntax for their use, as follows:

```
CommandName  Option(s)  Argument(s)
```

An example is the man -k cp command used earlier in this chapter. The breakdown of this command syntax is as follows: man is the *CommandName*, -k is the *Option*, and cp is the *Argument*. The *Option(s)* and *Argument(s)* are not required. When added, they are used to modify the behavior of the command and/or redirect on what the program is operating.

It's important to understand that commands are programs, because many of these programs have different authors. Therefore, a command may or may not use the basic syntax. For example, the type command *requires* that you provide it with an argument, or nothing is displayed—not even an error message!

If you are unfamiliar with a particular command, it's a good idea to view its man page. The Synopsis section will provide you with the syntax for the command, as shown in Figure 6.3 for the uname command.

FIGURE 6.3

Manual pages for the uname command

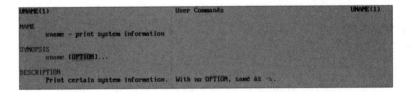

In a command's man page Synopsis section, brackets indicate that a particular item is not required. Thus, from the information in Figure 6.3, you can successfully use the uname command without providing any options. Knowing the right syntax for a command will speed up your command-line work.

 Real World Scenario

USING COMMAND COMPLETION FOR SPEED

If you lack keyboarding skills, working at the CLI is frustrating. Fortunately, the Bash shell provides a nice feature called *command completion*. Command completion allows you to type out part of a command or filename and then press the Tab key. If there is only one command (or file) that meets the partially typed-out data, the Bash shell completes it for you!

Follow these steps to try Bash shell command completion:

1. If you are not already, log into a Linux system using the sysadmin account and the password you created for it.

2. Type **cat /p** and stop.

3. Press the Tab key. The Bash shell will partially complete the command, which should now look like cat /proc/.

4. At the partially completed command's end, type **ve** and stop.

5. Press the Tab key. The Bash shell will complete the command, which should now look like cat /proc/version.

6. Press the Enter key and view the current Linux kernel's version.

Learning to work quickly in the Bash shell has many advantages. For instance, if there is a problem, knowing the various methods for issuing commands quickly will help in eliminating the difficulty faster. And who wouldn't like to finish work for the day a little sooner? That's another nice benefit of Bash shell command-line speed.

Retrieving Past Commands

One method for getting things done faster is using command-line history. All the commands you type at the prompt are stored in a history list. You can retrieve commands from this list and reissue them with minimal typing. In addition, you can modify the commands to make them operate slightly different.

To see your history list, type in the history command with no options.

```
$ history
[...]
    11  exit
    12  man -k copy
    13  apropos copy
[...]
    19  type help
[...]
    28  cat /proc/version
[...]
    34  history
$
```

In this example, the listing is snipped and only some of the commands are shown. Typically, the last 1,000 commands are kept in the history list.

You can recall and reuse the last command in your history list. This can save time and typing. To recall and reuse your last command, type !! and press the Enter key.

```
$ type man
man is /usr/bin/man
$ !!
type man
man is /usr/bin/man
$
```

When !! was entered, the Bash shell first displayed the command it was recalling from the shell's history list. And after the command was displayed, it was executed. You can also just press the up-arrow key and press the Enter key to recall and reuse your last command from command history.

To recall a command that is higher up the list, type ! # and press Enter. The # is the number corresponding to the command you want to reuse.

```
$ history
[...]
    12  man -k copy
    13  apropos copy
[..]
    16  whatis cp
[...]
    28  cat /proc/version
[...]
$
$ !16
whatis cp
cp (1)                    - copy files and directories
[...]
$
```

Command 16 was pulled from the history list. Notice that similar to executing the last command in history, the Bash shell first displays the command it is recalling from the shell's history. After the command is displayed, it is executed.

You can also edit commands, before running them, which is useful for adding different options and/or arguments. However, you're forced to use the up-arrow key to recall the command prior to modifying it.

The history list is kept in memory. But when you log out, the list is saved in a special file, the .bash_history file, which is located in each user's home directory. When you log in again, the file's contents are loaded into the history list in memory.

Table 6.3 contains a few of the more commonly used history command options. These options are useful for managing the history list as well as the history file.

TABLE 6.3:   A Few history Command Options

OPTION	DESCRIPTION
-a	Appends the current history list to the history file
-c	Clears the history list of contents
-n	Appends history file commands to the current history list, but only if they have not already been put into the list
-w	Writes the current history list to the history file

If you have multiple terminal sessions open, automatically update the history lists in your other open terminal sessions by issuing the history -a command in the terminal session whose history you want to save. Then in the other terminal sessions, use the history -n command to update their history lists.

Redirecting Commands

One of the neat things you can do at the Linux CLI is redirect commands. By default, command output goes to your terminal screen, and input into the CLI comes from your keyboard or mouse. However, you can modify this behavior.

The Linux system handles every object as a file, including the input and output process. Linux identifies each file object using a *file descriptor*, which is an integer that uniquely identifies open files in a session. The Bash shell reserves the first three file descriptors (0, 1, and 2) for the purposes shown in Table 6.4. These three special file descriptors handle the input and output from the CLI.

TABLE 6.4:   Linux Standard File Descriptors

FILE DESCRIPTOR	ABBREVIATION	DESCRIPTION
0	STDIN	Standard input
1	STDOUT	Standard output
2	STDERR	Standard error

REDIRECTING *STDOUT*

We'll start with redirecting STDOUT, because it typically is the easiest one to understand (and demonstrate). Most Bash commands direct their output to the STDOUT file descriptor by default, but you can redirect that output.

Imagine you just got done issuing several new-to-you Bash commands, and you would like to keep a copy of all the commands you used for future study. Recall that the history command, used earlier in this chapter, displays the history list, which would contain all these commands. You can issue the history command and redirect its output this way:

```
[sysadmin@localhost ~]$ history > keepHistory.txt
[sysadmin@localhost ~]$
[sysadmin@localhost ~]$ cat keepHistory.txt
    1  man man
    2  man -k copy
    3  apropos copy
    4  whatis cp
    5  type man
    6  uname
    7  cat /proc/version
[...]
   12  history > keepHistory.txt
[sysadmin@localhost ~]$
```

By using the greater-than symbol (>), the Bash shell's STDOUT is redirected to the file named keepHistory.txt instead of showing on the screen. To display the file's newly created contents, we used the cat command. (The cat command allows us to display a text file's contents, as was done earlier in this chapter to display the information residing in the /proc/version file.) So all the commands that were in the history list are now saved in a text file. That's useful!

The > STDOUT redirection symbol has a bit of a problem, though. If you use it to redirect output to a pre-existing file, it will *wipe* the file's contents and replace it with STDOUT! Thus, to append STDOUT data to a file, use the >> redirection symbol combination as follows:

```
[sysadmin@localhost ~]$ cat /proc/version >> keepHistory.txt
[sysadmin@localhost ~]$
[sysadmin@localhost ~]$ cat keepHistory.txt
    1  man man
    2  man -k copy
    3  apropos copy
    4  whatis cp
    5  type man
    6  uname
    7  cat /proc/version
[...]
   12  history > keepHistory.txt
Linux version 4.18.0-193.28.1.el8_2.x86_64 (mockbuild@kbuilder.bsys
.centos.org) (gcc version 8.3.1 20191121 (Red Hat 8.3.1-5) (GCC))
#1 SMP Thu Oct 22 00:20:22 UTC 2020
[sysadmin@localhost ~]$
```

So with redirecting CLI output, you can create new files of information or add to them. This is handy, but redirection gets even better.

REDIRECTING *STDERR*

The shell handles error messages using the special STDERR file descriptor. This is the location where the shell sends error messages generated by the shell or programs and scripts running in the shell. By default, the STDERR file descriptor points to the same place as the STDOUT file descriptor (even though they are assigned different file descriptor values). This means that, by default, all error messages go to the terminal screen.

There may be times you want to save error messages or just not have them display. This is especially true when you run a command that you know will encounter files you don't have privileges to look at, and those error messages are annoying.

To redirect STDERR, you use the same symbol as you did with redirecting STDOUT, but add the standard error file descriptor to it, like this:

```
[sysadmin@localhost ~]$ hist
-bash: hist: command not found
[sysadmin@localhost ~]$
[sysadmin@localhost ~]$ hist 2> myerr.txt
[sysadmin@localhost ~]$
[sysadmin@localhost ~]$ cat myerr.txt
-bash: hist: command not found
[sysadmin@localhost ~]$
```

In the preceding example, the `history` command was purposely misspelled, and it generated an error message. That STDERR was directed to the screen. Using the `hist 2> myerr.txt` command caused the error message to redirect to the `myerr.txt` file.

Appending an error message file operates in a similar fashion to appending the redirection of STDOUT. You just need to include the STDERR file descriptor again.

```
[sysadmin@localhost ~]$ hist 2>> myerr.txt
[sysadmin@localhost ~]$ cat myerr.txt
-bash: hist: command not found
-bash: hist: command not found
[sysadmin@localhost ~]$
```

If you don't want to save error messages and just desire not to see them, put them into what is called the *black hole*, which is the /dev/null file. Using the previous example, our command would now look like `hist 2>> /dev/null`.

If needed, you can redirect both STDERR and STDOUT to the same file. The Bash shell nicely provides a symbol for this purpose—the ampersand symbol (&). To get both STDOUT and an error message, we'll display a file that exists, /proc/version, and one that does not, NSF.txt, using the cat command.

```
[sysadmin@localhost ~]$ cat /proc/version NSF.txt &> newerr.txt
[sysadmin@localhost ~]$ cat newerr.txt
Linux version 4.18.0-193.28.1.el8_2.x86_64 (mockbuild@kbuilder.bsys
.centos.org) (gcc version 8.3.1 20191121 (Red Hat 8.3.1-5) (GCC))
#1 SMP Thu Oct 22 00:20:22 UTC 2020
cat: NSF.txt: No such file or directory
[sysadmin@localhost ~]$
```

So now you can redirect STDOUT and STDERR. Also, if you want, you can redirect them both to the same file. But wait! Redirection gets even better.

REDIRECTING THROUGH PIPES

Some of the most powerful things you can do with redirection involve using pipes. This is not referring that hardware that brings fresh water into your home and wastewater out. Instead, with the CLI, pipes, all you do is chain together the STDOUT of one command to the STDIN of another command. This creates a command pipeline.

The STDIN file descriptor references the standard input to the shell. For a terminal interface, the standard input is the keyboard. The shell receives input from the keyboard on the STDIN file descriptor and processes each character as you type it. The symbol to redirect STDIN for a command is the less-than symbol (<).

However, to chain together STDOUT as STDIN, the Bash shell provides another symbol: the pipe (|). This symbol is typically located on your keyboard's backslash (\) key and looks like a long, lowercase L.

To demonstrate this, we'll use the `history` command again. We'll redirect its STDOUT as STDIN into the `less` pager utility using a pipe so you can view the history list a page at a time.

```
[sysadmin@localhost ~]$ history | less
   1  man man
   2  man -k copy
```

Continues

(continued)
```
    3  apropos copy
    4  whatis cp
    5  type man
    6  uname
    7  cat /proc/version
    8  history
    9  type man
[...]
   23  cat myerr.txt NoSuchFile.txt &> newerr.txt
:
```

If you do use this command on your system, be aware that you can move forward or backward through the `less` pager utility by pressing the up-arrow and down-arrow keys and the Page Up and Page Down keys. However, you'll need to press the Q key to get back to the CLI prompt.

One of the neat things about redirection using pipes is that you can chain together multiple commands! You are not limited to only two commands in a pipeline.

SPLITTING THE REDIRECTION

If you want to not only view the information produced in a command pipeline but also keep a copy, you can do that too. This requires the use of a special command called `tee`. Like a plumber's tee that directs liquid into two different flows, the `tee` command will save STDOUT to a file and flow it as STDIN to the next command in the pipeline.

In this example, we are keeping a copy of the history list in the `keepHistory.txt` file and viewing it through the `less` pager:

```
[sysadmin@localhost ~]$ history | tee keepHistory.txt | less
    1  man man
    2  man -k copy
[...]
   23  cat myerr.txt NoSuchFile.txt &> newerr.txt
:
[sysadmin@localhost ~]$
[sysadmin@localhost ~]$ cat keepHistory.txt
    1  man man
    2  man -k copy
[...]
   23  cat myerr.txt NoSuchFile.txt &> newerr.txt
   24  cat newerr.txt
[...]
   30  history | less
   31  history | tee keepHistory.txt | less
[sysadmin@localhost ~]$
```

As you learn additional Bash shell commands, consider how you might redirect their STDOUT and STDERR. In addition, try them in a command pipeline. We'll continue our exploration of the Bash shell by exploring various variables.

Environment Variables

The Bash shell uses a feature called *environment variables* to store information about the shell session and the working environment. This feature also allows you to store data in memory that can be easily accessed by any program.

There are two environment variable types in the Bash shell: global variables and local variables. This section describes each type of environment variable and shows how to view and use them.

Global Environment Variables

The shell session that starts when a user logs into a virtual console terminal is a *parent shell*. When the bash command is entered at the CLI prompt, such as when running a shell script (shell scripts are covered in detail in Chapter 19, "Writing Scripts"), a new shell process is created. This is a *child shell*. Global environment variables are visible not only from the shell session in which they were defined, but from any spawned child subshells.

Local variables are different in that they are available only in the shell that creates them. This fact makes global environment variables useful in applications that create child subshells, which require parent shell information.

The Linux system sets several global environment variables when you start your Bash session. (More details about what variables are started at that time are covered in Chapter 13, "Managing Users and Groups.") These system environment variables almost always use all capital letters to differentiate them from user-defined variables.

To view all the currently set global environment variables, use the printenv or the env command, as shown in the following code snippet:

```
[sysadmin@localhost ~]$ env
[...]
HOSTNAME=localhost.localdomain
[...]
USER=sysadmin
[...]
PWD=/home/sysadmin
HOME=/home/sysadmin
[...]
SHELL=/bin/bash
[...]
HISTSIZE=1000
[...]
[sysadmin@localhost ~]$
```

You can use the printenv or the echo command to display an individual global environment's contents as follows:

```
[sysadmin@localhost ~]$ printenv USER
sysadmin
[sysadmin@localhost ~]$ echo $HOME
/home/sysadmin
[sysadmin@localhost ~]$
```

Notice that if you use the echo command, you have to add a dollar sign ($) to the front of the global environment variable's name. The dollar sign is not required with the printenv command.

There are several default global environment variables that are potentially defined on your system(s). Table 6.5 lists a few of the more common environment variables you'll find. Because Linux distributions often add their own environment variables, you'll need to check your Linux distribution's documentation for the entire list.

TABLE 6.5:   A Few Common Default Linux Global Environment Variables

NAME	DESCRIPTION
BASH	The full pathname to execute the current instance of the Bash shell
BASH_VERSION	The version number of the current instance of the Bash shell
GROUPS	A variable array containing the list of groups of which the current user is a member
HISTFILE	The name of the file in which to save the shell history list (.bash_history by default)
HISTSIZE	The maximum number of commands stored in the history list
HOME	The current user's home directory
HOSTNAME	The name of the current host
PATH	A colon-separated list of directories where the shell looks for commands
PS1	The primary shell command-line interface's prompt string
PS2	The secondary shell command-line interface's prompt string
PWD	The current working directory
SHELL	The full pathname to the Bash shell
USER	Username of current login session

A couple of interesting variables in Table 6.5 involve the history command we covered earlier in this chapter. Notice the HISTFILE and HISTSIZE variables. Their current settings on this CentOS distribution are as follows:

```
[sysadmin@localhost ~]$ echo $HISTFILE
/home/sysadmin/.bash_history
[sysadmin@localhost ~]$
[sysadmin@localhost ~]$ echo $HISTSIZE
1000
[sysadmin@localhost ~]$
```

You can see that this distribution stores its history list in the .bash_history file (HISTFILE), when the user either logs out of the system or directs the history command to do so. The number of commands that are allowed for the history list to contain is set to 1000 (HISTSIZE), which is more than enough for most cases.

User-Defined Environment Variables

Local environment variables, as their name implies, are seen only in the local process in which they are defined and are not available to child subshells. The Linux system defines a few standard local environment variables for you, but when you define your own, these are called *user-defined local environment variables*.

After you log in to the Linux system or spawn a child shell, you're allowed to create user-defined local variables that are visible within your shell process. You can assign either a numeric value or a string value to a variable by using the equal sign (=). To keep from tromping on global system-defined environment variables, it's best to name your user-defined variables with all lowercase letters.

```
[sysadmin@localhost ~]$ myvar="Hello World"
[sysadmin@localhost ~]$
[sysadmin@localhost ~]$ echo $myvar
Hello World
[sysadmin@localhost ~]$
```

After you define a user variable, any time you need to reference it, just enter its name preceded by a dollar sign, such as $myvar. When you set a user variable using this method, you are creating a user-defined local environment variable.

If you'd like to remove the variable's value, use the unset command. Here's an example:

```
[sysadmin@localhost ~]$ echo $myvar
Hello World
[sysadmin@localhost ~]$ unset myvar
[sysadmin@localhost ~]$
[sysadmin@localhost ~]$ echo $myvar

[sysadmin@localhost ~]$
```

THE GLOBALIZATION OF VARIABLES

There may be times when you'd like or need a user-defined local variable available to subshells. Making this adjustment is fairly easy. If you need to make an already defined variable global, use the export command, such as export *VariableName*.

To make a variable global when you define it, you have a couple of choices. You can put the two commands together on the same command line, separated by a semicolon, as in this example: newvar="42"; export newvar.

The other choice for globalization involves a lot less typing. Just use the export command at the beginning, as in this example: export newvar="42". Simple!

The set command displays both global and local environment variables, user-defined variables, and local functions. It also sorts the display alphabetically. You should know that the env and printenv are different from set in that they do not sort the variables, nor do they include local environment variables, local user-defined variables, or local shell functions.

 Real World Scenario

REDEFINING DEFAULT ENVIRONMENT VARIABLES

There may be times that you'll need or want to modify a default environment variable. You may want to keep that modification local or make it global depending on your needs. However, because changing a global default environment variable can have serious repercussions on the system you are administrating, it's a good idea to practice these modifications with a less important global environment variable.

Follow these steps to redefine a global default environment variable:

1. If you are not already, log into a Linux system using the sysadmin account and the password you created for it.

2. View your current Bash shell prompt, and record what it looks like. You'll use this information later for comparison.

3. Change your Bash shell prompt's appearance by typing **PS1="$ "** and pressing Enter.

4. Compare your current prompt with how it appeared in step 2. Ideally, the appearance changed. (If not, redo step 3 with a different character and space between the quotation marks.)

5. See whether this prompt setting will survive going into a subshell by typing **bash** and pressing Enter. You should see that the prompt returned to the appearance you recorded in step 3. That's because you did not globalize the environment variable setting.

6. Leave the child shell, by typing **exit** and pressing Enter. You should see that the prompt returns to the appearance you set for it back in step 4.

7. Recall your command by pressing the up-arrow key until you see PS1="$ ".

8. Edit the command so it looks like export PS1="Hello: ", and press Enter.

9. See whether this new Bash shell prompt setting will survive going into a subshell by typing **bash** and pressing Enter. You should see that the prompt still looks like it did when you set it in step 8. This is due to you using the export command, which made the prompt variable setting global.

10. Leave the child shell by typing **exit** and pressing Enter. It won't look like anything happened, because you get no messages and the prompt does not change.

11. Remove your prompt setting by typing **unset PS1** and pressing Enter. Wow! Now you have no prompt. That's because you removed the value of PS1.

12. Type **exit** to log out of your session. The next time you log in, your prompt will be "back to normal."

Now you have some great tools to help in your exploration of the Linux CLI. In fact, you can change your prompt to your liking for all your future work through this book.

The Bottom Line

Decode the shell prompt and the manual pages. The prompt is where you enter shell commands. It provides access to the utilities needed to manage a system. In addition, the shell prompt often gives additional information that can help you at the CLI.

Master It Imagine that you recently successfully logged in to a Linux system. This particular system uses the CentOS Linux distribution. What sort of items might you see in the shell prompt?

Decode the shell prompt and the manual pages. The man pages are an online manual that provide information on various shell utilities, special files, system administrator commands, and so on. They are a source of quick help and can be searched to determine the information you need.

Master It You are attempting to become proficient at using the man pages. However, the pager utility it employs is causing you some frustration, so you attempt to learn more about it without leaving the CLI. How can you accomplish learning more about the pager utility used for the man pages?

Enter, recall, and redirect shell commands. To function efficiently and effectively at the CLI, recalling shell commands is a critical task. A system admin must be proficient at quickly retrieving, potentially modifying, and using previously issued commands.

Master It Your main production app on the server is experiencing some performance problems, and you are working as fast as possible to determine and correct the issue(s). You need to recall and reenact a command you used previously. You can see from this history list that it is command 42. What's the fastest way to recall and reuse this command?

Enter, recall, and redirect shell commands. Being efficient and effective at the command line is more than just being fast. It also requires smart habits. One of these is using command redirection to manage STDIN, STDOUT, and STDERR.

Master It You created a nice pipeline of commands to filter and format some needed text file information. You want to view the information but keep a copy of it at the same time. How can you accomplish this?

Set and use environment variables. Variables help to define your CLI environment. In addition, they allow you to store data in memory that can be easily accessed by any program. Defining a variable, removing a definition, and globalizing a variable are all important management activities.

Master It You are creating a user-defined environment variable for an application. Because of the nature of the application, this variable must be available in subshells. What needs to be done to ensure this happens?

Chapter 7

Exploring Linux File Management

One of the most important functions of working in the Linux command-line interface is handling files and directories. Just about every administrative task you perform on your Linux system requires working with some type of file. This chapter dives into the topic of handling files and directories from the Linux command line.

IN THIS CHAPTER, YOU WILL LEARN TO

◆ Describe how Linux handles files and directories

◆ Explain the different options available to list files and directories

◆ Submit commands to manage files and directories

◆ Use Linux commands to find files and directories

◆ Use Linux commands to compress and archive files and directories

Filesystem Navigation

For most Linux distributions, when you start a shell session, you are placed in your user Home directory. Most often, you will need to break out of your Home directory to get to other areas in the Linux system. This section describes how to do that using command-line commands. Before that, though, is a short tour of just what the Linux filesystem looks like.

The Linux Filesystem

If you're new to the Linux system, you may be confused by how it references files and directories, especially if you're used to the way that the Microsoft Windows operating system does that. Before exploring the Linux system, it helps to have an understanding of how it's laid out.

The first difference you'll notice is that Linux does not use drive letters in pathnames. In the Windows world, the physical drives installed on the PC determine the pathname of the file. Windows assigns a letter to each physical disk drive, and each drive contains its own directory structure for accessing files stored on it.

For example, in Windows you may be used to seeing file paths such as this:

```
C:\Users\Rich\My Documents\test.doc
```

This indicates that the file `test.doc` is located in the directory `My Documents`, which itself is located in the directory `Rich`. The `Rich` directory is contained under the directory `Users`, which is located on the hard disk partition assigned the letter `C` (usually the first hard drive on the PC).

The Windows file path tells you exactly which physical disk partition contains the file named `test.doc`. If you wanted to save a file on a USB memory stick, you would click the icon for the drive assigned to the memory stick, such as `E:`, which automatically uses the file path `E:\test.doc`. This path indicates that the file is located at the root of the drive assigned the letter `E`, which is often assigned to the first USB storage device plugged into the PC.

This is not the method used by Linux. Linux stores files within a single directory structure, called a *virtual directory*. The virtual directory contains file paths from all the storage devices installed on the PC, merged into a single directory structure.

The Linux virtual directory structure contains a single base directory, called the *root*. Directories and files beneath the root directory are listed based on the directory path used to get to them, similar to the way Windows does it.

SLASHES IN LINUX

You'll notice that Linux uses a forward slash (/) instead of a backward slash (\) to denote directories in filepaths. The backslash character in Linux denotes an escape character and causes all sorts of problems when you use it in a filepath. This may take some getting used to if you're coming from a Windows environment.

For example, the Linux file path `/home/rich/Documents/test.doc` only indicates that the file `test.doc` is in the directory `Documents`, under the directory `rich`, which is contained in the directory `home`. It doesn't provide any information as to which physical disk on the PC the file is stored on.

The tricky part about the Linux virtual directory is how it incorporates each storage device. The first hard drive installed in a Linux PC is called the *root drive*. The root drive contains the core of the virtual directory. Everything else builds from there.

On the root drive, Linux creates special directories called *mount points*. Mount points are directories in the virtual directory where you assign additional storage devices.

The virtual directory causes files and directories to appear within these mount point directories, even though they are physically stored on a different drive.

Often the system files are physically stored on the root drive, while user files are stored on a different drive, as shown in Figure 7.1.

In Figure 7.1, there are two hard drives on the PC. One hard drive is associated with the root of the virtual directory (indicated by a single forward slash). Other hard drives can be mounted anywhere in the virtual directory structure. In this example, the second hard drive is mounted at the location `/home`, which is where the user directories are located.

The Linux filesystem structure has evolved from the Unix file structure. Unfortunately, the Unix file structure has been somewhat convoluted over the years by different flavors of Unix. While Linux started out that way too, a push has been made to standardize the Linux directory structure, called the Linux Filesystem Hierarchy Standard (FHS). Table 7.1 lists some of the more common Linux virtual directory names defined in the FHS.

FIGURE 7.1

The Linux file structure

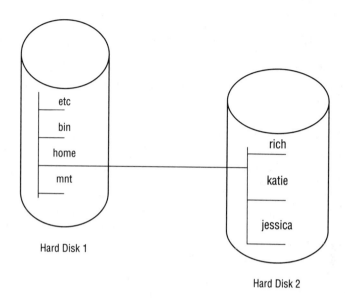

Hard Disk 1

Hard Disk 2

TABLE 7.1: Common Linux Directory Names

DIRECTORY	USAGE
/	The root of the virtual directory. Normally, no files are placed here
/bin	The binary directory, where many GNU user-level utilities are stored
/boot	The boot directory, where boot files are stored
/dev	The device directory, where Linux creates device nodes
/etc	The system configuration files directory
/home	The Home directory, where Linux creates user directories
/lib	The library directory, where system and application library files are stored
/media	The media directory, a common place for mount points used for removable media
/mnt	The mount directory, another common place for mount points used for removable media
/opt	The optional directory, often used to store optional software packages
/root	The root user account's Home directory
/sbin	The system binary directory, where many GNU admin-level utilities are stored
/tmp	The temporary directory, where temporary work files can be created and destroyed
/usr	The user-installed software directory
/var	The variable directory, for files that change frequently, such as log files

When you start a new shell prompt, your session starts in your *Home directory*, which is a unique directory assigned to your user account. When you create a user account, the system normally assigns a unique directory for the account.

In the Windows world, you're probably used to moving around the directory structure using a graphical interface. To move around the virtual directory from a command-line interface (CLI) prompt, you'll need to learn to use the cd command.

Traversing Directories

The change directory command (cd) is what you'll use to move your shell session to another directory in the Linux filesystem. The format of the cd command is pretty simplistic.

```
cd destination
```

The cd command may take a single parameter, *destination*, which specifies the directory name you want to go to. If you don't specify a destination on the cd command, it will take you to your Home directory.

The destination parameter, though, can be expressed using two different methods.

◆ An absolute filepath

◆ A relative filepath

The following sections describe the differences between these two methods.

ABSOLUTE FILEPATHS

You can reference a directory name within the virtual directory using an *absolute filepath*. The absolute filepath defines exactly where the directory is in the virtual directory structure, starting at the root of the virtual directory. It's sort of like a full name for a directory.

Thus, to reference the ssl directory that's contained within the lib directory, which in turn is contained within the usr directory, you would use the absolute filepath.

```
/usr/lib/ssl
```

With the absolute filepath, there's no doubt as to exactly where you want to go. To move to a specific location in the filesystem using the absolute filepath, you just specify the full pathname in the cd command.

```
sysadmin@ubuntu-server:~$ cd /usr/lib/ssl
sysadmin@ubuntu-server:/usr/lib/ssl$
```

On most Linux distributions, the prompt shows the current directory for the shell (the tilde represents your user Home directory). You can move to any level within the entire Linux virtual directory structure using the absolute filepath.

However, if you're just working within your own Home directory structure, often using absolute filepaths can get tedious. For example, if you're already in the directory /home/rich, it seems somewhat cumbersome to have to type the following command just to get to your Documents directory. Fortunately, there's a simpler solution.

```
cd /home/rich/Documents
```

RELATIVE FILEPATHS

Relative filepaths allow you to specify a destination directory relative to your current location, without having to start at the root. A relative filepath doesn't start with a forward slash indicating the root directory.

Instead, a relative filepath starts with either a directory name (if you're traversing to a directory under your current directory) or a special character indicating a relative location to your current directory location. The two special characters used for this are as follows:

♦ The dot (.) to represent the current directory

♦ The double dot (..) to represent the parent directory

The double dot character is extremely handy when you're trying to traverse a directory hierarchy. For example, if you are in the systemd directory under the etc directory and need to go to the ssl directory, also under the etc directory, you can do this:

```
sysadmin@ubuntu-server:/etc/systemd$ cd ../ssl
sysadmin@ubuntu-server:/etc/ssl$
```

The double dot character takes you back up one level to the etc directory, and then the /ssl portion takes you back down into the ssl directory. You can use as many double dot characters as necessary to move around. For example, if you are in your Home directory (/home/sysadmin) and want to go to the /etc directory, you could type the following:

```
sysadmin@ubuntu-server:~$ cd ../../etc
sysadmin@ubuntu-server:/etc$
```

Of course, in a case like this, you actually have to do more typing to use the relative filepath rather than just typing the absolute filepath, /etc, which would get you to the same place!

Linux Files

One of the things that made the Unix operating system unique when it was first created in the 1970s was that it treats everything on the computer system as a file—hardware devices, data, network connections, everything. That simplified the way programs interact with hardware, and with each other, because no matter where your data comes from, the Unix operating system handles it the same way. While at first that may seem odd, it's what revolutionized the computer world and made the Unix operating system so popular.

However, because everything is a file, there are some issues that you'll run into. One of those issues is trying to identify file types. This section walks you through how Linux handles filenames and provides some hints on how you can determine file types on a Linux system.

Determining File Types

Linux files cover a pretty wide range of file types—everything from text data to executable programs. Because Linux files aren't required to use a file extension, it can sometimes be difficult to tell what files are programs, what files are text data, and what files are binary data. Fortunately, there's a command-line utility that can help.

The `file` command returns the type of the file specified. If the file is a data file, it also attempts to detect just what the file contains.

```
$ file myprog.c
myprog.c: C source, ASCII text
$ file myprog
myprog: ELF 64-bit LSB shared object, x86-64, version 1 (SYSV), dynamically linked,
 interpreter /lib64/ld-linux-x86-64.so.2,
 BuildID[sha1]=a0758159df7a479a54ef386b970a26f076561dfe, for GNU/Linux 3.2.0, not
 stripped
$
```

In this example, the `myprog.c` file is a C program text file, and the `myprog` file is a binary executable program.

Filenames

The first thing you'll notice as you peruse the directories on your Linux system is that Linux has a different filenaming standard than Windows. In the Windows world, you're probably used to seeing a three- or four-character file extension added onto each file (such as `.docx` for Word documents). Linux doesn't require file extensions to identify file types on the system (although they're allowed if you like to use them).

Linux filenames can be any length of characters, although 255 is a practical limit for filenames (when filenames get longer than that, some programs have trouble handling them). Linux filenames can contain uppercase and lowercase letters, numbers, and most special characters (the only characters not allowed are the forward slash and the NULL character). Linux filenames can contain spaces as well as foreign language characters. However, the filename should always start with a letter or number.

Here's an example of some valid Linux filenames:

```
testing
A test file.txt
4_data_points
my.long.program.name
```

Hidden Files

Another feature of Linux filenames that is different from Windows is *hidden files*. Hidden files don't appear in normal file listings. In the Windows world, you use file properties to make a file hidden from normal viewing. When a normal user displays the directory listing, the hidden files don't appear, but when an administrator displays the directory listing, the hidden files magically appear in the output. This feature helps protect important system files from being accidentally deleted or overwritten.

Linux doesn't use file properties to make a file hidden. Instead, it uses the filename. Filenames that start with a period are considered hidden files in that they don't appear in a normal listing when you use the ls command and aren't displayed when you're using a graphical file manager tool. You can, however, use options to display hidden files with the ls command, discussed later in the "File and Directory Listing" section.

To display hidden files with the ls command, you need to include the –a command-line parameter.

```
$ ls
mydata.txt  mydirectory  myprog  myprog.c
$ ls -a
.                    .bash_logout  mydata.txt   myprog.c                  .viminfo
..                   .bashrc       mydirectory  .profile                  .zcompdump
.bash_history        .cache        myprog       .sudo_as_admin_successful  .zshrc
$
```

In this example, the ls command by itself shows only a few files in the directory. Adding the –a parameter shows all of the hidden files in the directory. Many Linux programs store any settings that you make as a hidden file in each users' Home directory.

File Inodes

Linux has to keep track of a lot of information for each file on the system. The way it does that is by using index nodes, also called *inodes*. The Linux operating system creates an inode for each file on the system to store the file properties. The inodes are hidden from view, and only the operating system can access them. Each inode is also assigned a number, called the *inode number*. This is what Linux uses to reference the file, not the filename. The inode numbers are unique on each physical disk partition.

Linux also creates a table on each disk partition, called the *inode table*. The inode table contains a listing that matches each inode number assigned to each file on the disk partition. As you create and delete files, Linux automatically updates the inode table behind the scenes. However, if the system should abruptly shut down (such as due to a power failure), the inode table can become corrupt. Fortunately for us, there are utilities that can help reorganize the inode table and help prevent data loss. Unfortunately, though, if the inode table does become unrepairable, you won't be able to access the files on the disk partition, even if the actual files are still there!

To view the inode number for files, use the –i option in the ls command. You can combine it with the –l option to produce a long listing to show more details about the file:

```
$ ls -il
total 36
263784 -rw-rw-r-- 2 sysadmin sysadmin    71 Dec 19 13:17 copy.c
262804 -rw-rw-r-- 1 sysadmin sysadmin    15 Dec 19 13:26 mydata.txt
395365 drwxrwxr-x 2 sysadmin sysadmin  4096 Dec 19 13:26 mydirectory
264036 -rwxrwxr-x 1 sysadmin sysadmin 16696 Dec 19 13:18 myprog
263784 -rw-rw-r-- 2 sysadmin sysadmin    71 Dec 19 13:17 myprog.c
$
```

The first number displayed in the long listing is the inode number for each file. Notice that the inode number for the myprog.c file is the same as the copy.c file. That means there is a hard link between those two files. The hard link points to the same physical disk location as the original file, so the inode numbers are the same. We'll look at hard links more closely in the "Linking Files" section.

File and Directory Listing

The most basic feature of the shell is the ability to see what files are available on the system. The list command (ls) is the tool that helps do that. This section describes the ls command and all of the options available to format the information it can provide.

Basic Listing

The ls command at its most basic form displays the files and directories located in your current directory in the command line (also called the *working directory*).

```
sysadmin@ubuntu-server:~$ ls
copy.c  mydata.txt  mydirectory  myprog  myprog.c
sysadmin@ubuntu-server:~$
```

Notice that the ls command produces the listing in alphabetical order (in columns rather than rows). If you're using a terminal emulator that supports color, the ls command may also show different types of entries in different colors. The LS_COLORS environment variable controls this feature. Different Linux distributions set this environment variable depending on the capabilities of the terminal emulator.

If you don't have a color terminal emulator, you can use the -F parameter with the ls command to easily distinguish files from directories. Using the -F parameter produces the following output:

```
sysadmin@ubuntu-server:~$ ls -F
copy.c  mydata.txt  mydirectory/  myprog*  myprog.c
sysadmin@ubuntu-server:~$
```

The -F parameter now flags the directories with a forward slash to help identify them in the listing. Similarly, it flags executable files (like the myprog file in the previous code snippet) with an asterisk to help you find the files that can be run on the system easier.

The basic ls command can be somewhat misleading. It shows the files and subdirectories contained in the current directory, but not the hidden files.

The -R parameter is another command ls parameter to use. It performs a recursive listing, showing files that are contained within subdirectories in the current directory. If you have lots of subdirectories, this can be quite a long listing. Here's a simple example of what the -R parameter produces:

```
sysadmin@ubuntu-server:~$ ls -F -R
.:
copy.c  mydata.txt  mydirectory/  myprog*  myprog.c

./mydirectory:
file1  file2  file3
sysadmin@ubuntu-server:~$
```

Notice that, first, the -R parameter shows the contents of the current directory, which includes a subdirectory (mydirectory). Following that, it traverses all of the subdirectories, showing if any files are contained within each subdirectory. The mydirectory subdirectory shows three files (file1, file2, and file3). If there had been further subdirectories within the mydirectory subdirectory, the -R parameter would have continued to traverse those as well. As you can see, for large directory structures, this can become quite a large output listing.

Modifying Listing Information

As you can see in the basic listings, the ls command doesn't produce a whole lot of information about each file by default. For listing additional information, another popular parameter is -l. The -l parameter produces a long listing format, providing more information about each file in the directory.

```
sysadmin@ubuntu-server:~$ ls -l
total 36
-rw-rw-r-- 2 sysadmin sysadmin    71 Dec 19 13:17 copy.c
-rw-rw-r-- 1 sysadmin sysadmin    15 Dec 19 13:26 mydata.txt
drwxrwxr-x 2 sysadmin sysadmin  4096 Dec 19 13:51 mydirectory
-rwxrwxr-x 1 sysadmin sysadmin 16696 Dec 19 13:18 myprog
-rw-rw-r-- 2 sysadmin sysadmin    71 Dec 19 13:17 myprog.c
sysadmin@ubuntu-server:~$
```

The long listing format lists each file and directory contained in the directory on a single line. Besides the filename, it shows additional useful information. The first line in the output shows the total number of blocks contained within the directory. Following that, each line contains the following information about each file (or directory):

♦ The file type, such as directory (d), file (-), character device (c), or block device (b)

♦ The permissions string for the file, indicting permissions for the user, group, and other users

 ♦ The number of hard links to the file

 ♦ The username of the owner of the file

 ♦ The group name of the group the file belongs to

 ♦ The size of the file in bytes

 ♦ The time the file was modified last

 ♦ The file or directory name

The -l parameter is a powerful tool to have. Armed with this information, you can see just about any information you need for any file or directory on the system.

The Complete Parameter List

There are lots of parameters for the ls command that can come in handy as you do file management. If you use the man command for ls, you'll see several pages of available parameters for you to use to modify the output of the ls command.

The `ls` command uses two types of command-line parameters:

◆ Single-letter parameters

◆ Full-word (long) parameters

The single-letter parameters are always preceded by a single dash. Full-word parameters are more descriptive and are preceded by a double dash. Many parameters have both a single-letter and full-word version, while some have only one type. Table 7.2 lists some of the more popular parameters that'll help you out with using the `ls` command.

TABLE 7.2: Some Popular `ls` Command Parameters

SINGLE LETTER	FULL WORD	DESCRIPTION
-a	--all	Don't ignore entries starting with a period.
-A	--almost-all	Don't list the . and .. files.
	--author	Print the author of each file.
-b	--escape	Print octal values for nonprintable characters.
	--block-size=*size*	Calculate the block sizes using size-byte blocks.
-B	--ignore-backups	Don't list entries with the tilde (~) symbol (used to denote backup copies).
-c		Sort by time of last modification.
-C		List entries by columns.
	--color=*when*	When to use colors (always, never, or auto).
-d	--directory	List directory entries instead of contents, and don't dereference symbolic links.
-F	--classify	Append file-type indicator to entries.
	--file-type	Only append file-type indicators to some filetypes (not executable files).
	--format=*word*	Format output as across, commas, horizontal, long, single-column, verbose, or vertical.
-g		List full file information except for the file's owner.
	--group-directories-first	List all directories before files.
-G	--no-group	In a long listing, don't display group names.

Single Letter	Full Word	Description
-h	--human-readable	Print sizes using K for kilobytes, M for megabytes, and G for gigabytes.
	--si	Same as -h, but use powers of 1000 instead of 1024.
-i	--inode	Display the index number (inode) of each file.
-l		Display the long listing format.
-L	--dereference	Show information for the original file for a linked file.
-n	--numeric-uid-gid	Show numeric userid and groupid instead of names.
-o		In a long listing, don't display owner names.
-r	--reverse	Reverse the sorting order when displaying files and directories.
-R	--recursive	List subdirectory contents recursively.
-s	--size	Print the block size of each file.
-S	--sort=size	Sort the output by file size.
-t	--sort=time	Sort the output by file modification time.
-u		Display the last access time instead of last modification time for all files.
-U	--sort=none	Don't sort the output listing.
-v	--sort=version	Sort the output by file version.
-x		List entries by line instead of columns.
-X	--sort=extension	Sort the output by file extension.

You can use more than one parameter at a time if you want. The double-dash parameters must be listed separately, but the single-dash parameters can be combined into a string behind the dash. A common combination to use is the -a parameter to list all files, the -i parameter to list the inode for each file, the -l parameter to produce a long listing, and the -s parameter to list the block size of the files. Combining all of these parameters creates the easy-to-remember -sail parameter.

```
sysadmin@ubuntu-server:~$ ls -sail
total 132
265238  4 drwxr-xr-x 4 sysadmin sysadmin  4096 Dec 19 13:45 .
262145  4 drwxr-xr-x 3 root     root      4096 Nov  4 18:56 ..
```

```
262184  8 -rw------- 1 sysadmin sysadmin  4957 Dec 19 13:27 .bash_history
265244  4 -rw-r--r-- 1 sysadmin sysadmin   220 Feb 25  2020 .bash_logout
265240  4 -rw-r--r-- 1 sysadmin sysadmin  3771 Feb 25  2020 .bashrc
265296  4 drwx------ 2 sysadmin sysadmin  4096 Nov  4 18:57 .cache
263784  4 -rw-rw-r-- 2 sysadmin sysadmin    71 Dec 19 13:17 copy.c
262804  4 -rw-rw-r-- 1 sysadmin sysadmin    15 Dec 19 13:26 mydata.txt
395365  4 drwxrwxr-x 2 sysadmin sysadmin  4096 Dec 19 13:51 mydirectory
264036 20 -rwxrwxr-x 1 sysadmin sysadmin 16696 Dec 19 13:18 myprog
263784  4 -rw-rw-r-- 2 sysadmin sysadmin    71 Dec 19 13:17 myprog.c
265242  4 -rw-r--r-- 1 sysadmin sysadmin   807 Feb 25  2020 .profile
265302  0 -rw-r--r-- 1 sysadmin sysadmin     0 Nov  4 18:58 .sudo_as_admin_successful
263813 12 -rw------- 1 sysadmin sysadmin 10056 Dec 19 13:17 .viminfo
262207 48 -rw-rw-r-- 1 sysadmin sysadmin 49006 Nov 23 13:36 .zcompdump
265288  4 -rw-rw-r-- 1 sysadmin sysadmin    29 Nov 23 13:36 .zshrc
sysadmin@ubuntu-server:~$
```

Besides the normal -l parameter output information, you'll see two additional numbers added to each line. The first number in the listing is the file or directory inode number. The second number is the block size of the file.

Directory Handling

In Linux, there are a few commands that work for both files and directories, and some that work only for directories. This section discusses the commands that can work only with directories.

Creating Directories

There's not much to creating a new directory in Linux; just use the mkdir command.

```
sysadmin@ubuntu-server:~$ mkdir dir3
sysadmin@ubuntu-server:~$ ls -il
total 40
263784 -rw-rw-r-- 2 sysadmin sysadmin    71 Dec 19 13:17 copy.c
395394 drwxrwxr-x 2 sysadmin sysadmin  4096 Dec 19 14:09 dir3
262804 -rw-rw-r-- 1 sysadmin sysadmin    15 Dec 19 13:26 mydata.txt
395365 drwxrwxr-x 2 sysadmin sysadmin  4096 Dec 19 13:51 mydirectory
264036 -rwxrwxr-x 1 sysadmin sysadmin 16696 Dec 19 13:18 myprog
263784 -rw-rw-r-- 2 sysadmin sysadmin    71 Dec 19 13:17 myprog.c
sysadmin@ubuntu-server:~$
```

The system creates the new directory and assigns it a new inode number.

Deleting Directories

Removing directories can be tricky, but there's a reason for that. There are lots of opportunities for bad things to happen when you start deleting directories. Bash tries to protect us from accidental catastrophes as much as possible. The basic command for removing a directory is rmdir.

```
sysadmin@ubuntu-server:~$ rmdir dir3
sysadmin@ubuntu-server:~$ rmdir mydirectory
rmdir: failed to remove 'mydirectory': Directory not empty
sysadmin@ubuntu-server:~$
```

By default, the rmdir command works only for removing empty directories. Since there is a file in the mydirectory directory, the rmdir command refuses to remove it. You can remove nonempty directories using the --ignore-fail-on-non-empty parameter.

You can also use the rm command when handling directories.

If you try using it without parameters, as with files, you'll be somewhat disappointed.

```
sysadmin@ubuntu-server:~$ rm mydirectory
rm: cannot remove 'mydirectory': Is a directory
sysadmin@ubuntu-server:~$
```

However, if you really want to remove a directory, you can use the -r parameter to recursively remove the files in the directory and then the directory itself.

```
sysadmin@ubuntu-server:~$ rm -r mydirectory
sysadmin@ubuntu-server:~$
```

DELETION QUERIES

If the directory is write-protected, you will be prompted to confirm the deletion request. You can override that prompt by adding the -f parameter, but be careful!

File Handling

Bash provides lots of commands for manipulating files on the Linux filesystem. This section walks through the basic commands you will need to work with files from the CLI for all your file-handling needs.

Creating Files

Every once in a while, you will run into a situation where you need to create an empty file. Sometimes applications expect a log file to be present before they can write to it. In these situations, you can use the touch command to easily create an empty file.

```
sysadmin@ubuntu-server:~$ touch test1
sysadmin@ubuntu-server:~$ ls -il test1
263320 -rw-rw-r-- 1 sysadmin sysadmin 0 Dec 19 14:22 test1
sysadmin@ubuntu-server:~$
```

The touch command creates the new file you specify and assigns your username as the file owner.

Notice that the file size is zero, since the touch command just created an empty file. The touch command can also be used to change the access and modification times on an existing file without changing the file contents.

```
sysadmin@ubuntu-server:~$ touch test1
sysadmin@ubuntu-server:~$ ls -il test1
263320 -rw-rw-r-- 1 sysadmin sysadmin 0 Dec 19 14:30 test1
sysadmin@ubuntu-server:~$
```

The modification time of test1 is now updated from the original time. If you want to change only the access time, use the -a parameter. To change only the modification time, use the -m parameter.

By default, touch uses the current time. You can specify the time by using the -t parameter with a specific timestamp value.

```
sysadmin@ubuntu-server:~$ touch -t 202112251200 test1
sysadmin@ubuntu-server:~$ ls -l test1
-rw-rw-r-- 1 sysadmin sysadmin 0 Dec 25  2021 test1
sysadmin@ubuntu-server:~$
```

Now the modification time for the file is set to a date significantly in the future from the current time.

Copying Files

Copying files and directories from one location in the filesystem to another is a common practice for system administrators. The cp command provides this feature.

In its most basic form, the cp command uses two parameters—the source object and the destination object.

```
cp source destination
```

When both the *source* and *destination* parameters are filenames, the cp command copies the source file to a new file with the filename specified as the destination. The new file acts like a new file, with an updated file creation and last modified times.

```
sysadmin@ubuntu-server:~$ cp test1 test2
sysadmin@ubuntu-server:~$ ls -il test*
263320 -rw-rw-r-- 1 sysadmin sysadmin 0 Dec 25  2021 test1
263324 -rw-rw-r-- 1 sysadmin sysadmin 0 Dec 19 14:27 test2
sysadmin@ubuntu-server:~$
```

The new file test2 shows a different inode number, indicating that it's a completely new file. You'll also notice that the modification time for the test2 file shows the time that it was created.

If the destination file already exists, the cp command will overwrite the existing file by default. That can be somewhat dangerous. By adding the -i parameter, the cp command will prompt you to answer whether you want to overwrite the destination file.

```
sysadmin@ubuntu-server:~$ cp -i test1 test2
cp: overwrite 'test2'? y
sysadmin@ubuntu-server:~$
```

If you don't answer **y**, the file copy will not proceed.

You can also copy a file to an existing directory by specifying the directory as the destination.

```
sysadmin@ubuntu-server:~$ mkdir dir1
sysadmin@ubuntu-server:~$ cp test1 dir1
sysadmin@ubuntu-server:~$ ls -il dir1
total 0
395391 -rw-rw-r-- 1 sysadmin sysadmin 0 Dec 19 14:31 test1
sysadmin@ubuntu-server:~$
```

The new file is now under the dir1 directory, using the same filename as the original.

These examples all used relative pathnames, but you can just as easily use the absolute pathname for both the source and destination objects. To copy a file to the current directory you're in, you can use the dot symbol.

```
sysadmin@ubuntu-server:~$ cp /home/sysadmin/dir1/test1 .
sysadmin@ubuntu-server:~$ ls -il test1
263320 -rw-rw-r-- 1 sysadmin sysadmin 0 Dec 19 14:33 test1
sysadmin@ubuntu-server:~$
```

As with most commands, the cp command has a few command-line parameters to help you. These are shown in Table 7.3.

TABLE 7.3: The cp Command Parameters

PARAMETER	DESCRIPTION
-a	Archive files by preserving their attributes.
-b	Create a backup of each existing destination file instead of overwriting it.
-d	Preserve.
-f	Force the overwriting of existing destination files without prompting.
-i	Prompt before overwriting destination files.
-l	Create a file link instead of copying the files.
-p	Preserve file attributes if possible.
-r	Copy files recursively.
-R	Copy directories recursively.
-s	Create a symbolic link instead of copying the file.
-S	Override the backup feature.
-u	Copy the source file only if it has a newer date and time than the destination (update).
-v	Verbose mode, explaining what's happening.
-x	Restrict the copy to the current filesystem.

Use the -p parameter to preserve the file access or modification times of the original file for the copied file.

```
sysadmin@ubuntu-server:~$ cp -p test1 test3
sysadmin@ubuntu-server:~$ ls -il test*
263320 -rw-rw-r-- 1 sysadmin sysadmin 0 Dec 19 14:33 test1
263324 -rw-rw-r-- 1 sysadmin sysadmin 0 Dec 19 14:30 test2
263725 -rw-rw-r-- 1 sysadmin sysadmin 0 Dec 19 14:33 test3
sysadmin@ubuntu-server:~$
```

Now, even though the test3 file is a completely new file, it has the same timestamps as the original test1 file.

The -R parameter is extremely powerful. It allows you to recursively copy the contents of an entire directory in one command.

```
sysadmin@ubuntu-server:~$ cp -R dir1 dir2
sysadmin@ubuntu-server:~$ ls -l dir*
dir1:
total 0
-rw-rw-r-- 1 sysadmin sysadmin 0 Dec 19 14:31 test1

dir2:
total 0
-rw-rw-r-- 1 sysadmin sysadmin 0 Dec 19 14:38 test1
sysadmin@ubuntu-server:~$
```

Now dir2 is a complete copy of dir1.

You can also use wildcard characters in your cp commands.

```
sysadmin@ubuntu-server:~$ cp test* dir2
sysadmin@ubuntu-server:~$ ls -al dir2
total 8
drwxrwxr-x 2 sysadmin sysadmin 4096 Dec 19 14:42 .
drwxr-xr-x 5 sysadmin sysadmin 4096 Dec 19 14:38 ..
-rw-rw-r-- 1 sysadmin sysadmin    0 Dec 19 14:42 test1
-rw-rw-r-- 1 sysadmin sysadmin    0 Dec 19 14:42 test2
-rw-rw-r-- 1 sysadmin sysadmin    0 Dec 19 14:42 test3
sysadmin@ubuntu-server:~$
```

This command copied all of the files that started with test to dir2.

Linking Files

You may have noticed that a couple of the parameters for the cp command referred to linking files. This is a pretty cool option available in the Linux filesystems. If you need to maintain two (or more) copies of the same file on the system, instead of having separate physical copies, you can use one physical copy and multiple virtual copies, called *links*. A link is a placeholder in a directory that points to the real location of the file. There are two different types of file links in Linux.

♦ A symbolic, or soft, link

♦ A hard link

The *hard link* creates a separate file that contains information about the original file and where to locate it. When you reference the hard link file, it's just as if you're referencing the original file.

```
sysadmin@ubuntu-server:~$ cp -l test1 test4
sysadmin@ubuntu-server:~$ ls -il test*
263320 -rw-rw-r-- 2 sysadmin sysadmin 54 Dec 19 14:33 test1
263324 -rw-rw-r-- 1 sysadmin sysadmin  0 Dec 19 14:30 test2
263725 -rw-rw-r-- 1 sysadmin sysadmin  0 Dec 19 14:33 test3
263320 -rw-rw-r-- 2 sysadmin sysadmin 54 Dec 19 14:33 test4
sysadmin@ubuntu-server:~$
```

The -l parameter created a hard link for the test1 file called test4. The file listing shows that the inode numbers of both the files are the same, indicating that, in reality, they are both the same file. Also notice that the link count (the third item in the listing) now shows that both files have two links.

HARD LINKS AND PARTITIONS

You can only create a hard link between files in the same disk partition. You can't create a hard link between files under separate mount points. In that case, you'll have to use a soft link.

Conversely, the -s parameter creates a symbolic, or soft, link.

```
sysadmin@ubuntu-server:~$ cp -s test1 test5
sysadmin@ubuntu-server:~$ ls -il test*
263320 -rw-rw-r-- 2 sysadmin sysadmin 54 Dec 19 14:33 test1
263324 -rw-rw-r-- 1 sysadmin sysadmin  0 Dec 19 14:30 test2
263725 -rw-rw-r-- 1 sysadmin sysadmin  0 Dec 19 14:33 test3
263320 -rw-rw-r-- 2 sysadmin sysadmin 54 Dec 19 14:33 test4
263840 lrwxrwxrwx 1 sysadmin sysadmin  5 Dec 19 14:46 test5 -> test1
sysadmin@ubuntu-server:~$
```

There are a couple of things to notice in the file listing, First, you'll notice that the new test5 file has a different inode number than the test1 file, indicating that the Linux system treats it as a separate file. Second, the file size is different. A linked file needs to store only information about the source file, not the actual data in the file. The filename area of the listing shows the relationship between the two files.

Instead of using the cp command to link files, you can use the ln command. By default, the ln command creates hard links. If you want to create a soft link, you'll still need to use the -s parameter.

HANDLING LINKED FILES

Be careful when copying linked files. If you use the cp command to copy a file that's linked to another source file, all you're doing is making another copy of the source file. This can quickly get confusing.

Instead of copying the linked file, you can create another link to the original file. You can have many links to the same file with no problems. However, you also don't want to create soft links to other soft-linked files. This creates a chain of links that not only can be confusing but also can be easily broken, causing all sorts of problems.

Renaming Files

In the Linux world, renaming files is called *moving*. The mv command is available to move both files and directories to another location.

```
sysadmin@ubuntu-server:~$ mv test2 test6
sysadmin@ubuntu-server:~$ ls -il test*
263320 -rw-rw-r-- 2 sysadmin sysadmin 54 Dec 19 14:48 test1
263725 -rw-rw-r-- 1 sysadmin sysadmin  0 Dec 19 14:33 test3
263320 -rw-rw-r-- 2 sysadmin sysadmin 54 Dec 19 14:48 test4
263840 lrwxrwxrwx 1 sysadmin sysadmin  5 Dec 19 14:48 test5 -> test1
263324 -rw-rw-r-- 1 sysadmin sysadmin  0 Dec 19 14:30 test6
sysadmin@ubuntu-server:~$
```

Notice that moving the file changed the filename but kept the same inode number and the timestamp value. Moving a file with soft links is a problem.

```
sysadmin@ubuntu-server:~$ mv test1 test8
sysadmin@ubuntu-server:~$ ls -il test*
263725 -rw-rw-r-- 1 sysadmin sysadmin  0 Dec 19 14:33 test3
263320 -rw-rw-r-- 2 sysadmin sysadmin 54 Dec 19 14:48 test4
263840 lrwxrwxrwx 1 sysadmin sysadmin  5 Dec 19 14:48 test5 -> test1
263324 -rw-rw-r-- 1 sysadmin sysadmin  0 Dec 19 14:30 test6
263320 -rw-rw-r-- 2 sysadmin sysadmin 54 Dec 19 14:48 test8
sysadmin@ubuntu-server:~$
```

The test4 file that uses a hard link still uses the same inode number, which is perfectly fine. However, the test5 file now points to an invalid file, and it is no longer a valid link. If your terminal supports colors, it is most likely displayed in a red font.

You can also use the mv command to move directories.

```
sysadmin@ubuntu-server:~$ mv dir2 dir4
sysadmin@ubuntu-server:~$
```

The entire contents of the directory are unchanged. The only thing that changes is the name of the directory.

Deleting Files

Most likely at some point in your Linux career, you'll want to be able to delete existing files. Whether it's to clean up a filesystem or to remove a software package, there's always opportunities to delete files.

In the Linux world, deleting is called *removing*. The command to remove files in Bash is rm. The basic format of the rm command is pretty simple.

```
sysadmin@ubuntu-server:~$ rm -i test3
rm: remove regular empty file 'test3'? y
```

```
sysadmin@ubuntu-server:~$ ls -il test*
263320 -rw-rw-r-- 2 sysadmin sysadmin 54 Dec 19 14:48 test4
263840 lrwxrwxrwx 1 sysadmin sysadmin  5 Dec 19 14:48 test5 -> test1
263324 -rw-rw-r-- 1 sysadmin sysadmin  0 Dec 19 14:30 test6
263320 -rw-rw-r-- 2 sysadmin sysadmin 54 Dec 19 14:48 test8
sysadmin@ubuntu-server:~$
```

Just as with the `rmdir` command, you can use the `-i` parameter to prompt you for safety. There's no trashcan in the CLI like there often is in the graphical desktop environment. Once you remove a file, it's gone forever.

 Real World Scenario

WORKING WITH FILES

It's important to feel comfortable with creating, modifying, and deleting files in Linux. This exercise walks you through doing just that with some sample files so you don't have to worry about breaking anything as you experiment. Just follow these steps:

1. Log into your Linux server using the user account you created earlier during the installation.

2. From your Home directory CLI prompt, create a directory by entering the command **mkdir test**. Change to that directory by entering the command **cd test**, and then enter the command **ls -l** to look at the directory contents.

   ```
   sysadmin@ubuntu-server:~$ mkdir test
   sysadmin@ubuntu-server:~$ cd test
   sysadmin@ubuntu-server:~/test$ ls -l
   total 0
   sysadmin@ubuntu-server:~/test$
   ```

3. From the CLI prompt, enter the command **touch test1**. This creates a test file to work with.

   ```
   sysadmin@ubuntu-server:~/test$ touch test1
   sysadmin@ubuntu-server:~/test$ ls -l
   total 0
   -rw-rw-r-- 1 sysadmin sysadmin 0 Dec 19 17:45 test1
   sysadmin@ubuntu-server:~/test$
   ```

4. From the CLI prompt, create another file that's a hard link to the first file by entering the command **ln test1 test2**. List the inodes of the files using the command by typing **ls -il** to ensure they are hard linked.

   ```
   sysadmin@ubuntu-server:~/test$ ln test1 test2
   sysadmin@ubuntu-server:~/test$ ls -il
   total 0
   395415 -rw-rw-r-- 2 sysadmin sysadmin 0 Dec 19 17:45 test1
   395415 -rw-rw-r-- 2 sysadmin sysadmin 0 Dec 19 17:45 test2
   sysadmin@ubuntu-server:~/test$
   ```

5. Save some data in the test1 file by entering the command **echo "Testing" >> test1**. Enter the command **ls -l** to see the file size of both the test1 and test2 files. They should have both changed.

```
sysadmin@ubuntu-server:~/test$ echo "Testing" >> test1
sysadmin@ubuntu-server:~/test$ ls -l
total 8
-rw-rw-r-- 2 sysadmin sysadmin 8 Dec 19 17:46 test1
-rw-rw-r-- 2 sysadmin sysadmin 8 Dec 19 17:46 test2
sysadmin@ubuntu-server:~/test$
```

6. Remove the test1 file by entering the command **rm test1**. Enter the command **ls** to list the remaining file.

```
sysadmin@ubuntu-server:~/test$ rm test1
sysadmin@ubuntu-server:~/test$ ls -il
total 4
395415 -rw-rw-r-- 1 sysadmin sysadmin 8 Dec 19 17:46 test2
sysadmin@ubuntu-server:~/test$
```

Notice that the test2 file still remains, with the data intact.

File Features

There are a few features unique to Linux that you'll need to be aware of when working with files. This section walks you through these features.

Using Wildcards

The ls, cp, mv, and rm commands are handy, but specifying a single file or directory name in the commands makes them somewhat clunky to work with on the Linux command line. If you want to work with more than one file or directory, you need to use a technique the Linux world calls *globbing*.

Globbing is basically the use of wildcard characters to represent one or more characters in a file or directory name. That feature allows us to specify a pattern for Linux to match multiple files or directories against. There are two basic globbing characters that you can use.

◆ The question mark—represents a single character

◆ The asterisk—represents zero or more characters

The question mark is a stand-in character to represent any single character to match in the filename. For example, you can specify the filename file?.txt in a rm command to remove any file that starts with file, followed by one character, and ending with .txt. Here's an example:

```
sysadmin@ubuntu-server:~$ ls -il file*
265217 -rw-rw-r-- 1 sysadmin sysadmin 0 Dec 19 15:05 file.txt
265214 -rw-rw-r-- 1 sysadmin sysadmin 0 Dec 19 15:05 file11.txt
```

```
  263855 -rw-rw-r-- 1 sysadmin sysadmin 0 Dec 19 15:04 file1.txt
  265146 -rw-rw-r-- 1 sysadmin sysadmin 0 Dec 19 15:04 file2.txt
sysadmin@ubuntu-server:~$ rm file?.txt
sysadmin@ubuntu-server:~$ ls -il file*
  265217 -rw-rw-r-- 1 sysadmin sysadmin 0 Dec 19 15:05 file.txt
  265214 -rw-rw-r-- 1 sysadmin sysadmin 0 Dec 19 15:05 file11.txt
sysadmin@ubuntu-server:~$
```

The rm command uses the glob file?.txt as the parameter. Linux looks for any file in the directory that matches the pattern to remove. Two files, file1.txt and file2.txt, match the pattern. However, the file11.txt file doesn't match the pattern, as there are two characters between the file and .txt parts of the filename, and the file.txt file doesn't match the pattern, as there aren't any characters between the file and .txt parts of the filename.

You use the asterisk glob character to match zero or more characters in the filename.

```
sysadmin@ubuntu-server:~$ rm file*
sysadmin@ubuntu-server:~$ ls -il file*
ls: cannot access 'file*': No such file or directory
sysadmin@ubuntu-server:~$
```

By using the asterisk, Linux matched all of the files, even the file.txt file! You can use the asterisk in any list, copy, move, or delete operation in the command line.

Quoting

Another issue you may run into with Linux is files or directories that contain spaces in their names. This is perfectly legal in Linux, but it can cause headaches when you're working from the command line.

If you try to reference a file or directory that contains a space in the filename, you'll get several error messages:

```
sysadmin@ubuntu-server:~$ ls -l long*
-rw-rw-r-- 1 sysadmin sysadmin 0 Dec 19 15:09 'long file name.txt'
sysadmin@ubuntu-server:~$ rm long file name.txt
rm: cannot remove 'long': No such file or directory
rm: cannot remove 'file': No such file or directory
rm: cannot remove 'name.txt': No such file or directory
sysadmin@ubuntu-server:~$
```

The problem is that, by default, the rm command uses a space to indicate the end of a filename, so it thinks you're trying to remove three separate files—long, file, and name.txt!

To get around that, you need to use quoting, which places quotes around any filenames that contain spaces:

```
sysadmin@ubuntu-server:~$ rm 'long file name.txt'
sysadmin@ubuntu-server:~$ ls -il long*
ls: cannot access 'long*': No such file or directory
sysadmin@ubuntu-server:~$
```

You can use either single or double quotes around the filename, as long as you use the same type on both ends of the filename.

Case Sensitivity

One last thing to watch out for when using the Linux file handling command-line commands is the case of any file or directory names that you're working with. Linux is a case-sensitive operating system, so files and directories can have both uppercase and lowercase letters in the names. Likewise, as you're working with the files, make sure you reference the correct format of the files or directory names.

```
sysadmin@ubuntu-server:~$ ls -il *.txt
263725 -rw-rw-r-- 1 sysadmin sysadmin  0 Dec 19 15:13 file1.txt
263855 -rw-rw-r-- 1 sysadmin sysadmin  0 Dec 19 15:12 File1.txt
sysadmin@ubuntu-server:~$ rm file1.txt
sysadmin@ubuntu-server:~$ ls -il *.txt
263855 -rw-rw-r-- 1 sysadmin sysadmin  0 Dec 19 15:12 File1.txt
sysadmin@ubuntu-server:~$
```

This is a good example of when using filename globbing can come in handy. If you're not sure of the case of a character, you can use the question mark to represent any character of any case.

```
$ rm ?ile1.txt
$
```

This command will remove both the `file1.txt` and `File1.txt` files.

Finding Files

With so many files stored on the Linux system, it can often become difficult to find the files you're looking for. Fortunately, Linux provides a few different file-searching features to help. This section looks at the ones you'll most likely use as a Linux systems administrator.

The *which* Command

You can use the `which` command to find where programs and utilities are stored. This can come in handy if you have two versions of a program installed on your system or if you're not sure if a command is built into the Linux shell or supplied as a separate utility. The format for using the `which` command is pretty simple.

```
$ which touch
/usr/bin/touch
$
```

The output of the `which` command shows the full path to where the command is stored on the system. If you have two versions of a program on the system, the `which` command shows which one will run when you type it at the command line. If you need to use a different version, you have to use the full path to the program file.

The *locate* Command

Many Linux distributions contain the `locate` command by default. If your distribution doesn't, it's usually found in the `mlocate` software package.

The locate command uses a database that keeps track of the location of files on the system. When you use the locate command, it searches the database to find the requested file. This process is often quicker than trying to search through all of the files on the filesystem.

The key to the locate command is the information in the database. It can only find files that have been indexed into the database. The information in the database is updated by the appropriately named updatedb program. The Linux system runs the updatedb program in background mode on a regular basis to update the file database with any new files stored on the system.

Be careful when using the locate command, though; you may get more than you bargained for! Here's an example:

```
sysadmin@ubuntu-server:~$ locate touch
/snap/core18/1932/bin/touch
/snap/core18/1932/lib/udev/hwdb.d/70-touchpad.hwdb
/snap/core18/1932/lib/udev/rules.d/70-touchpad.rules
/snap/core18/1932/usr/bin/touch
/snap/core18/1944/bin/touch
/snap/core18/1944/lib/udev/hwdb.d/70-touchpad.hwdb
/snap/core18/1944/lib/udev/rules.d/70-touchpad.rules
/snap/core18/1944/usr/bin/touch
/usr/bin/touch
...
sysadmin@ubuntu-server:~$
```

The locate command returns any file that contains the word *touch* in the filename! You'll need to filter through the results to find the file that you're looking for.

Another downside to the locate command is that it can't find any newly added files until the next running of the updatedb program. Some Linux systems run the updatedb program on a regular basis, every few minutes, while others schedule it to run only once or twice a day. How often you need to run it depends on how often you get new files on your Linux system and how quickly you'd need to find them.

The *whereis* Command

The whereis command is similar to the which command in that it looks for a specific occurrence of the file you're searching for. However, it looks only in binary file directories, library directories, and documentation directories, so that helps speed up the search process some. This is great for finding not only commands but the documentation files that go along with them.

```
sysadmin@ubuntu-server:~$ whereis touch
touch: /usr/bin/touch /usr/share/man/man1/touch.1.gz
sysadmin@ubuntu-server:~$
```

In this example, the whereis command returned the location of the touch program file and the location of the manual page associated with the touch program.

The *find* Command

The last resort to finding files on your Linux system is the find command. It does a physical search through the virtual directory tree looking for the specified file. As you can imagine, the wider the search area, the longer it will take for the find command to return an answer. You specify the search area as the first parameter on the find command line.

```
sysadmin@ubuntu-server:~$ find /home/sysadmin -name myprog -print
/home/sysadmin/myprog
sysadmin@ubuntu-server:~$
```

This example restricts the find command to looking in the /home/sysadmin directory structure for the file named myprog. The -name option specifies the filename to look for, and the -print command tells the find command to display the results.

What makes the find command so versatile is that it can find files based on lots of different criteria besides just the filename, such as the creation time, the file owner, the file size, or even file permissions. For example, you can use the find command to look for all files over 1 MB on your filesystem. Table 7.4 shows some of the options you can use in the find command.

TABLE 7.4:   Useful find Command Options

OPTION	DESCRIPTION
-amin *n*	File was last accessed *n* minutes ago.
-atime *n*	File was last accessed *n* days ago.
-ctime *n*	File was last changed *n* minutes ago.
-inum *n*	Match the file inode number to the number specified.
-name *pattern*	Match the file name to the *pattern* specified.
-perm *pattern*	Match the file permissions to the *pattern* specified.
-size *n*	Match the file size to the amount specified.
-user *name*	Match the file owner to the *name* specified.

You can also use special modifiers on the find options, such as a plus sign for "greater than" or a minus sign for "less than." For example, to list all of the files larger than 5,000 characters, you'd use the following:

```
sysadmin@ubuntu-server:~$ find . -size +5000c -print
./.zcompdump
./myprog
./.viminfo
sysadmin@ubuntu-server:~$
```

The +5000c parameter tells the find command to look for files in the current directory that are more than 5,000 characters in size.

Archiving Files

Storing data can get ugly. The more data you need to store, the more disk space it requires. While disk sizes are getting larger these days, there is still a limit to how much space you have. To help with that, you can use some Linux file archiving tools to compress data files for storage and sharing. This section takes a look at how Linux handles compressing and archiving both files and directories.

Compressing Files

If you've done any work in the Microsoft Windows world, no doubt you've used zip files. The PKZip compression utility became the de facto way to compress data and executable files in Windows, so much so that Microsoft eventually incorporated it into the Windows operating system, starting with XP, as the compressed directories feature. Compressed directories allow you to easily compress large files or a large group of files into a smaller file that takes up less space and is easier to copy to another location.

Linux provides a few different tools you can use to compress files to save space. While this may sound great, it can sometimes lead to confusion and chaos when trying to download and extract Linux files from the Internet. Table 7.5 lists the different file compression utilities available in Linux.

TABLE 7.5:   Linux File Compression Utilities

UTILITY	FILE EXTENSION	DESCRIPTION
bzip2	.bz2	Uses the Burrows-Wheeler block sorting text compression algorithm and human coding
compress	.Z	Original Unix file compression utility, but starting to fade away into obscurity
gzip	.gz	The GNU Project's compression utility; uses the open-source Lempel-Ziv_Welch coding
xz	.xz	A general-purpose compression utility gaining in popularity
zip	.zip	The Unix version of the PKZip program for Windows

The compress utility can work with files compressed on standard Unix systems, but it's not often installed by default on Linux systems. If you download a file with a .Z extension, you can usually install the compress package from the distribution software repository. The zip utility creates compressed directories that can be extracted on Windows systems, but it's not the best compression algorithm to use if you're keeping the files on a Linux system.

The `gzip` utility is the most popular compression tool used in Linux. It is a creation of the GNU Project, in its attempt to create a free version of the original Unix compress utility. This package includes three main files.

◆ `gzip` for compressing files

◆ `gzcat` for displaying the contents of compressed text files

◆ `gunzip` for uncompressing files

The `gzip` command compresses the file you specify on the command line. You can also specify more than one filename or even use wildcard characters to compress multiple files at once.

```
$ gzip my*
$
```

This `gzip` command compresses every file in the directory that starts with `my`.

Creating Archive Files

Although the `gzip` command not only can compress data but also archive the data into a single file, it's not the standard utility used for archiving large amounts of data in the Unix and Linux worlds. By far the most popular archiving tool used in Unix and Linux is the `tar` command.

The `tar` command was originally used to back up files to a tape device for archiving. However, it can also write the output to a file, which has become a popular way to bundle data for distribution in Linux. It's common to see source code files bundled into a `tar` archive file (affectionately called a *tarball*) for distribution.

The following is the format of the `tar` command:

```
tar function [options] object1 object2
```

The *function* parameter defines what the `tar` command should do, as shown in Table 7.6.

TABLE 7.6:   The `tar` Command Functions

FUNCTION	DESCRIPTION
-a	Appends an existing tar archive file to another tar archive file
-c	Creates a new tar archive file
-d	Checks the differences between a tar archive file and the filesystem files
-r	Appends files to an existing tar archive file
-t	Lists the contents of an existing tar archive file
-u	Appends files to an existing tar archive file that are newer than a file with the same in the archive
-x	Extracts files from an existing tar archive file

Each function uses one or more options to define a specific behavior for the tar archive file. Table 7.7 shows the options that you can use with the `tar` command.

TABLE 7.7: The `tar` Command Options

OPTION	DESCRIPTION
-C *dir*	Changes to the specified directory
-f *file*	Outputs results to the file (or device) specified
-j	Redirects output to the `bzip2` command for compression
-P	Preserves all file permissions
-v	Lists files as they are processed
-z	Redirects the output to the `gzip` command for compressions

While the combination of several functions along with several options seems like an impossible task to remember, in reality you'll find yourself just using a handful of combinations to do common tasks. The following section takes a look at the more common archiving scenarios that you'll run into.

Archiving Scenarios

Normally, there are just three basic things you'll need to do with the `tar` command.

◆   Archive files to create a tarball.

◆   List the files contained in a tarball.

◆   Extract the files from a tarball.

This helps narrow down the function and option features that you need to remember for the tar command.

To start, you can create a new archive file using this command:

```
tar -cvf test.tar test/ test2/
```

This command creates an archive file called `test.tar` containing the contents of both the test directory and the `test2` directory. The `-v` option is a nice feature in that it displays the files as they are added to the archive file.

Next, to display the contents of a tarball file, you just use this command:

```
tar -tf test.tar
```

The `-t` function lists the contents of the tarball to the standard output by default, which is your monitor. The files aren't extracted, just listed.

Finally, to extract the files contained in a tarball, you'll use this command:

```
tar -xvf test.tar
```

It extracts the contents of the tar file `test.tar` into the current directory. If the tar file was created from a directory structure, the entire directory structure is re-created starting at the current directory.

As you can see, using the `tar` command is a simple way to create archive files of entire directory structures. That's why this has become a common method for distributing source code files for open source applications in the Linux world!

 Real World Scenario

WORKING WITH FILE ARCHIVES

In this exercise, you will create a tar archive file containing several files in one directory and then extract the tar archive file contents into another directory to simulate moving the files to another server. Just follow these steps:

1. Log into your Linux server using the user account you created during installation.

2. From the CLI prompt, create a new directory by entering the command **mkdir mytest1**, and then create another new directory by entering the command **mkdir mytest2**.

3. Create a few new files in the `mytest1` directory by entering these commands:

    ```
    touch mytest1/test1
    touch mytest1/test2
    touch mytest1/test3
    touch mytest1/test4
    ```

4. Change to the `mytest1` directory by entering the command **cd mytest1**, and then enter the command **ls -l** to ensure the files exist:

    ```
    sysadmin@ubuntu-server:~$ cd mytest1
    sysadmin@ubuntu-server:~/mytest1$ ls -l
    total 0
    -rw-rw-r-- 1 sysadmin sysadmin 0 Dec 19 18:14 test1
    -rw-rw-r-- 1 sysadmin sysadmin 0 Dec 19 18:14 test2
    -rw-rw-r-- 1 sysadmin sysadmin 0 Dec 19 18:14 test3
    -rw-rw-r-- 1 sysadmin sysadmin 0 Dec 19 18:14 test4
    sysadmin@ubuntu-server:~/mytest1$
    ```

5. Archive the files by entering the command **tar -cvf test.tar test***. You should see the following output:

    ```
    sysadmin@ubuntu-server:~/mytest1$ tar -cvf test.tar test*
    test1
    test2
    test3
    test4
    sysadmin@ubuntu-server:~/mytest1$
    ```

6. Copy the `test.tar` archive file to the **mytest2** directory using the command **cp test .tar ../mytest2**.

7. Change to the `mytest2` directory by entering the command **cd ../mytest2**, and then list the directory contents by entering the command **ls -l**.

8. Extract the archive file using the command **tar -xvf test.tar**. Enter the command **ls -l** to ensure the files have been extracted.

```
sysadmin@ubuntu-server:~/mytest2$ ls -l
total 12
-rw-rw-r-- 1 sysadmin sysadmin     0 Dec 19 18:14 test1
-rw-rw-r-- 1 sysadmin sysadmin     0 Dec 19 18:14 test2
-rw-rw-r-- 1 sysadmin sysadmin     0 Dec 19 18:14 test3
-rw-rw-r-- 1 sysadmin sysadmin     0 Dec 19 18:14 test4
-rw-rw-r-- 1 sysadmin sysadmin 10240 Dec 19 18:15 test.tar
sysadmin@ubuntu-server:~/mytest2$
```

You can use this same process to move files from one server to another server as a single archive file.

The Bottom Line

Describe how Linux handles files and directories.   File management is an important part of the Linux system, and it helps to know the basics of how to manage files from the CLI. This chapter first showed you how to use both absolute and relative filepaths in commands to reference files and directories. Next, it showed the standard Linux file naming conventions used by Linux distributions, along with how Linux uses inodes to handle files.

Master It   Your boss has given you a list of files he saw being used on the server and wants you to find out what type of files they are. The files are as follows:

`/usr/bin/grep`

`/usr/bin/zcat`

`/etc/hosts`

`~/.bashrc`

What command should you use to determine those file types?

Explain the different options available to list files and directories.   The `ls` command is how to list the contents of directories from the command prompt. While there are lots of parameters associated with the `ls` command, you'll soon find yourself using just a handful of them to view the information that you need.

Master It   A user on your Linux server has an important project and needs access to the file `/share/HR/employees.txt`. However, the user doesn't know who owns the file to ask for permission to access the file. What command and parameters should you use to determine the owner of the file?

Submit commands to manage files and directories.   The chapter showed you how to use the Linux CLI to create, move, and remove both directories and files. The chapter also went through how to use globbing to specify file and directory ranges instead of single files in the commands, as well as how to use quoting to work with file and directory names that incorporate spaces.

Master It   You have been assigned the task of creating a new directory for the Engineering team on the Linux server. Under that directory they'd also like to have separate directories for the automotive project group and the truck project group. What commands should you enter to create these directories?

Use Linux commands to find files and directories.   There are a few common Linux commands used to help find files on the Linux system. The which, locate, and whereis commands can be useful for general searches, but the find command allows you to customize your search by specifying specific file or directory properties to look for.

Master It   You have been tasked to find all files on your filesystem that are larger than 10 MB in size. What command would you use to easily find those files?

Use Linux commands to compress and archive files and directories.   There are many different utilities available for compressing and archiving files in Linux. For archiving files, the gzip family of commands is a popular option. For archiving multiple files into a single file, the tar command is common. You can also compress a tar archive file to facilitate moving it to off-site storage.

Master It   What commands should you use to create a backup archive file of the new /Engineering directory and compress it?.

Chapter 8

Working with Text Files

A proficient Linux systems administrator is capable of using at least one text editor in Linux. This skill is needed to manage daily work such as modifying configuration files and creating shell scripts. You have the choice of several editors. Many individuals find a particular editor whose functionality they love and use that one exclusively. This chapter provides a brief sampling of two text editors that are popular with admins.

When managing any computer server, you'll often have files that contain large amounts of text data. It's typically difficult to handle the information and make it useful. It's easy to get data overload when working with system commands. Fortunately, Linux provides several command-line utilities that help you manage large amounts of data.

IN THIS CHAPTER, YOU WILL LEARN TO

- Use the vim editor's basic features

- Employ the nano editor for everyday text file editing

- Find data in a text file and reduce its size

- Back up and organize text file data

The *vim* Editor

When managing a Linux system, it's wise to gain proficiency using at least one text editor. Using features such as searching, cutting, and pasting allows you to modify configuration files more quickly. In Chapter 19, "Writing Scripts," you'll need the text editor skills that you learn in this chapter to quickly create Bash shell scripts. This section walks you through the basics of using the vim editor, which is typically available for most Linux distros.

LOOKING AT A LITTLE *VIM* EDITOR HISTORY

The vi editor was one of the early editors on Unix systems. It uses the console graphics mode to emulate a text-editing window, allowing you to see the lines of your file; move around within the file; and insert, edit, and replace text.

Although it is quite possibly the most complicated editor in the world (at least in the opinion of those who hate it), vi provides many features that have made it a staple for programmers and system administrators for decades.

When the GNU Project ported the vi editor to the open source world, it chose to make some improvements to it. Because it extended the original vi editor found in the Unix world, the developers also renamed it to vim (which stands for "vi improved").

Checking Your *vim* Editor Program

Before you begin your exploration of the vim editor, it's a good idea to understand what "flavor" of vim your Linux system has installed. On some distributions, you will have a full functioning vim editor installed, but not on others, which can cause you some difficulties.

Three commands can help you determine whether your Linux distro has a fully functioning vim editor.

The alias Command To display whether a command calls a different command and/or uses additional command options, you type **alias *command-name*** at the command-line interface (CLI). For our purposes here, we need to see if the typical command to run the vim editor, vi, is aliased to the vim command or not. Thus, alias vi will let us know this information. If vi is not aliased, it's our first clue that a fully functioning vim editor is probably not installed.

The which Command This particular command is useful in many circumstances. When you type **which *command-name***, it shows you exactly where the program associated with the command name resides in the Linux virtual directory system. For our investigation, we'll need to use the *which vim* command to get the location, so we can properly use the next command, readlink.

The readlink Command When researching whether you have a fully functioning vim editor, you need to determine if a symbolic link is involved with the vim program name. Sometimes when a vim editor is installed, the vim program file, which by all initial appearances is fully functioning, is symbolically linked to a lesser vim flavor. We could adopt the ls -l technique used in Chapter 7, "Exploring Linux File Management," to investigate the soft links, but vim file soft links are often chained so that one soft link points to another soft link, which points to an additional soft link, and so on. In this case, it's best to use the readlink -f command, which will quickly find the final file in a chain of links.

Using these three commands to check the vim editor on a CentOS distribution reveals the following:

```
$ alias vi
alias vi='vim'
$
$ which vim
/usr/bin/vim
$
$ readlink -f /usr/bin/vim
/usr/bin/vim
$
```

The vi command is aliased, which is a good sign. And there are no soft links that indicate that the vim editor program is linked to a less than full-featured editor program. From the investigation here, you can rest assured that this CentOS distribution has a fully functioning vim editor.

Running these same commands on this Ubuntu distribution shows different results:

```
$ alias vi
-bash: alias: vi: not found
$
$ which vim
/usr/bin/vim
$
$ readlink -f /usr/bin/vim
/usr/bin/vim.basic
$
```

Notice that there is no alias for the vi command, but the /usr/bin/vim program file points to /usr/bin/vim.basic. If you have the vim.basic program as shown here on your Ubuntu system, you are OK. However, if in your investigation you find the vim.tiny program, you'll want to install the vim package to get vim.basic so that you can follow along with the vim editor examples in this chapter. Package installation for Ubuntu distributions was covered in Chapter 3, "Installing and Maintaining Software in Ubuntu."

Setting up an alias for the vim command on your Ubuntu system is fairly easy: just type **alias vi='vim'** on your system. However, this alias will not survive once you log out of the system. You'll need to add it to one of your login startup files, covered in Chapter 13, "Managing Users and Groups."

Using the *vim* Editor

To start using the vim text editor, type **vim** or **vi**, depending on your distribution, followed by the name of the file you want to edit or create. Figure 8.1 shows a vim text editor screen in action with a text file that was previously created.

FIGURE 8.1
Using the vim text editor

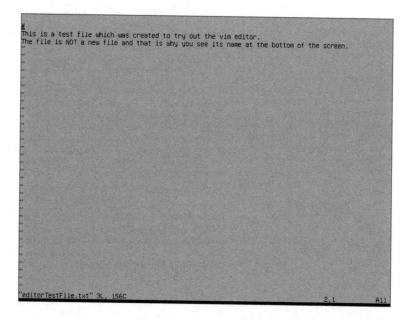

In Figure 8.1, the file being edited is the editorTestFile.txt file. The vim editor works the file data in a memory buffer, and this buffer is displayed on the screen. If you open vim without a filename, or the filename you entered doesn't yet exist, vim starts a new buffer area for editing.

The vim editor has a message area near the bottom line. If you have just opened an already created file, it will display the filename along with the number of lines and characters read into the buffer area. If you are creating a new file, you will see [New File] in the message area.

The vim editor has three standard modes.

Command Mode   This is the mode vim uses when you first enter the buffer area; this is sometimes called *normal mode*. Here you enter keystrokes to enact commands. For example, pressing the J key will move your cursor down one line. This is the best mode to use for quickly moving around the buffer area.

Insert Mode   Insert mode is also called *edit* or *entry mode*. This is the mode where you can perform simple editing. There are not many commands or special mode keystrokes. You enter this mode from Command mode by pressing the I key. At this point, the message --Insert-- will display in the message area. You leave this mode by pressing the Esc key.

Ex Mode   This mode is sometimes also called *colon commands* because every command entered here is preceded with a colon (:). For example, to leave the vim editor and not save any changes, you type **:q** and press the Enter key.

Since you start in Command mode when entering the vim editor's buffer area, it's good to understand a few of the commonly used commands to move around in this mode. Table 8.1 contains several commands for moving around in the editor.

TABLE 8.1:   Commonly Used vim Command Mode Moving Commands

KEYSTROKE	DESCRIPTION
h	Move cursor left one character.
l	Move cursor right one character.
j	Move cursor down one line (the next line in the text).
k	Move cursor up one line (the previous line in the text).
w	Move cursor forward one word to front of next word.
e	Move cursor to end of current word.
b	Move cursor backward one word.
^	Move cursor to beginning of line.
$	Move cursor to end of line.
gg	Move cursor to the file's first line.
G	Move cursor to the file's last line.
nG	Move cursor to file line number *n*.

KEYSTROKE	DESCRIPTION
Ctrl+B	Scroll up almost one full screen.
Ctrl+F	Scroll down almost one full screen.
Ctrl+U	Scroll up half of a screen.
Ctrl+D	Scroll down half of a screen.
Ctrl+Y	Scroll up one line.
Ctrl+E	Scroll down one line.

Quickly moving around in the vim editor buffer is useful. However, there are also several editing commands that help to speed up your modification process. For example, by moving your cursor to a word's first letter and pressing CW, the word is deleted, and you are thrown into Insert mode. You can then type in the new word and press Esc to leave Insert mode.

Once you have made any needed text changes in the vim buffer area, it's time to save your work. You can type **ZZ** in Command mode to write the buffer to disk and exit your process from the vim editor.

The third vim mode, Ex mode, has additional handy commands. You must be in Command mode to enter into Ex mode. You cannot jump from Insert mode to Ex mode. Therefore, if you're currently in Insert mode, press the Esc key to go back to Command mode first.

Table 8.2 shows several Ex commands that can help you manage your text file. Notice that all the keystrokes include the necessary colon (:) to use Ex commands.

TABLE 8.2: Commonly Used vim Ex Mode Commands

KEYSTROKES	DESCRIPTION
:x	Write buffer to file and quit editor.
:wq	Write buffer to file and quit editor.
:wq!	Write buffer to file and quit editor (overrides protection).
:w	Write buffer to file and stay in editor.
:w!	Write buffer to file and stay in editor (overrides protection).
:q	Quit editor without writing buffer to file.
:q!	Quit editor without writing buffer to file (overrides protection).
:! *command*	Execute shell *command* and display results, but don't quit editor.
:r! *command*	Execute shell *command* and include the results in editor buffer area.
:r *file*	Read *file* contents and include them in editor buffer area.

After reading through the various mode commands, you may see why some people despise the `vim` editor. There are a lot of obscure commands to know. However, some people love the `vim` editor because it is so powerful.

It's tempting to learn only one text editor and ignore the others. But knowing at least two text editors is useful in your day-to-day Linux work. For complex editing and writing programs, the `vim` editor is one of the most popular text editors. However, if you just need to make a small change to a file, the nano text editor shines. We cover this one next.

The *nano* Editor

In contrast to `vim`, which is a complicated editor with powerful features, nano is a simple editor. For individuals who need a simple console mode text editor that is easy to navigate, nano is the tool to use. It's also a great text editor for those who are just starting on their Linux command-line adventure.

The nano text editor is installed on most Linux distributions by default. Everything about the nano text editor is easy. To open a file at the command line with nano, enter **nano *filename***.

If you start nano without a filename or if the file doesn't exist, nano simply opens a new buffer area for editing. If you specify an existing file on the command line, nano reads the entire contents of the file into a buffer area, where it is ready for editing, as shown in Figure 8.2.

FIGURE 8.2
The nano editor window

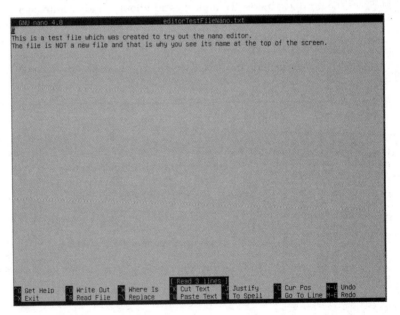

Notice at the bottom of the nano editor window, various commands with a brief description are shown. These commands are the nano control commands. The caret (^) symbol shown represents the Ctrl key. Therefore, ^X stands for the keyboard sequence Ctrl+X. Though the nano control commands list capital letters in the keyboard sequences, you can use either lowercase or uppercase characters for control commands.

Having most of the basic commands listed right in front of you is great—no need to memorize what control command does what. Table 8.3 presents the most common nano control commands.

The control commands listed in Table 8.3 are really all you need. However, if you desire more powerful control features than those listed, nano has them. To see more control commands, press Ctrl+G in the nano text editor to display its main help window containing additional control commands.

TABLE 8.3: nano Common Control Commands

COMMAND	DESCRIPTION
Ctrl+C	Displays the cursor's position within the text editing buffer
Ctrl+G	Displays nano's main help window
Ctrl+J	Justifies the current text paragraph
Ctrl+K	Cuts the text line and stores it in the cut buffer
Ctrl+O	Writes out the current text editing buffer to a file
Ctrl+R	Reads a file into the current text editing buffer
Ctrl+T	Starts the available spell checker
Ctrl+U	Pastes text stored in the cut buffer and places in current line
Ctrl+V	Scrolls text editing buffer to the next page
Ctrl+W	Searches for word or phrases within the text editing buffer
Ctrl+X	Closes the current text editing buffer, exits nano, and returns to the shell
Ctrl+Y	Scrolls the text editing buffer to previous page

A few of these additional control commands are called *Meta-key* sequences. In the nano documentation, they are denoted by the letter M. For example, you'll find the key sequence to undo the last task denoted as M-U in the nano help system. But don't press the M key to accomplish this. Instead, M represents the Esc, Alt, or Meta key, depending on your keyboard's configuration. Thus, you might press the Alt+U key combination to undo the last task within nano.

 Real World Scenario

CREATING AND MODIFYING A FILE WITH THE *NANO* TEXT EDITOR

When you're learning to use text editors, experience is the best tutor. Follow these steps to create, save, and then modify a text file with the nano utility:

1. Log into a Linux system using the sysadmin account and the password you created for it.

2. Create a new text file with nano by typing **nano QuestAns.txt** and pressing the Enter key.

3. From "The Bottom Line" section of this chapter, type in the text for the "Master It" paragraph concerning the vim editor and then the text in the "Master It" paragraph for the nano editor.

4. Save the file by pressing the Ctrl+O key combination, and then press Enter when the editor asks you the file's name.

5. Exit the editor by pressing the Ctrl+X key combination.

6. Determine the solutions for both the "Master It" questions before you return to modify the **QuestAns.txt** text file.

7. Return to edit the text file by typing **nano QuestAns.txt** and pressing the Enter key.

8. Add each solution under its appropriate "Master It" paragraph in the text file. Try to use as many key combinations in Table 8.3 for movement through the editor as possible.

9. When you are finished adding the solutions, save the file by pressing the Ctrl+O key combination, and then press Enter when the editor asks you the file's name.

10. Exit the editor by pressing the Ctrl+X key combination.

Using text editors at the CLI is one way to work with text files. The rest of this chapter explores additional methods you can use to manipulate text file data.

Working with Data Files

When you have a large amount of data, it's often difficult to handle the information and make it useful. The Linux system provides several CLI tools to help you manage large amounts of data. This section covers the basic commands that every system administrator—as well as any everyday Linux user—should know how to use to make their lives easier.

Sorting

Often, to understand the data within text files, you need to reformat file data in some way. The sort utility sorts a file's data. It makes no changes to the original file. It only reads the file, sorts its data, and displays the sorted data to STDOUT (covered in Chapter 6, "Working with the Shell").

If you want to order a file's content alphabetically, simply enter the sort command followed by the name of the file you want to sort.

```
$ nano alphabetKey.txt
$ cat alphabetKey.txt
Alpha
Tango
Sierra
Bravo
Foxtrot
Echo
$
```

```
$ sort alphabetKey.txt
Alpha
Bravo
Echo
Foxtrot
Sierra
Tango
$
```

It's pretty simple. However, things aren't always as easy as they appear. Take a look at this example:

```
$ nano numberKey.txt
$ cat numberKey.txt
1 One
2 Two
4 Four
3 Three
10 Ten
20 Twenty
100 One Hundred
$
$ sort numberKey.txt
1 One
10 Ten
100 One Hundred
2 Two
20 Twenty
3 Three
4 Four
$
```

If you were expecting the numbers to sort in numerical order, you were disappointed. By default, the sort command interprets numbers as characters, producing a sorted output that you may not want. Add the -n option to the command to sort the text based on their numerical values, if that's what you are seeking.

```
$ sort -n numberKey.txt
1 One
2 Two
3 Three
4 Four
10 Ten
20 Twenty
100 One Hundred
$
```

There are several useful sort parameters you can use depending on what kind of sort is needed. Table 8.4 shows commonly used options.

TABLE 8.4:   Commonly Used `sort` Command Options

SINGLE DASH	DOUBLE DASH	DESCRIPTION
-b	--ignore-leading-blanks	Ignore leading blanks when sorting.
-d	--dictionary-order	Consider only blanks and alphanumeric characters; don't consider special characters.
-f	--ignore-case	By default, sort orders capitalized letters first. This parameter ignores case.
-g	--general-numeric-sort	Use general numerical value to sort.
-i	--ignore-nonprinting	Ignore nonprintable characters in the sort.
-k	--key=POS1[,POS2]	Sort based on position POS1, and end at POS2 if specified.
-n	--numeric-sort	Sort by string numerical value.
-o	--output=file	Write results to file specified.
-r	--reverse	Reverse the sort order (descending instead of ascending).
-t	--field-separator=SEP	Specify the character used to distinguish key positions.
-z	--zero-terminated	End all lines with a NULL character instead of a new line.

Viewing sorted data is helpful, but what do you do if you want to keep that sorted data? STDOUT redirection (covered in Chapter 6) can help here:

```
$ nano numberKeySciFi.txt
$ cat numberKeySciFi.txt
1984 101
Wars 1138
Pi 3.14
Trek 1701
Back 88
$
$ sort -n -t ' ' -k 2 numberKeySciFi.txt > sortedSciFi.txt
$ cat sortedSciFi.txt
Pi 3.14
Back 88
1984 101
Wars 1138
Trek 1701
$
```

Keeping sorted data is especially handy when you've used a complex sort like the previous one. Another useful function when dealing with text data is searching for it. We'll cover that topic next.

Searching

You may need to locate a text file within the virtual directory structure, or just search through a file for text. Either way, Linux provides you lots of options to accomplish your task.

LOCATING FILES

A simple utility to use in finding files quickly is the locate program. What makes it fast is that this command searches a database that is pre-filled with filenames and their locations.

FINDING *LOCATE*

Be aware that locate may not be installed by default on your Linux distribution. If you'd like to have it, the package name is locate. And you can use the instructions for installing software packages in Chapter 3, "Installing and Maintaining Software in Ubuntu," if your distro is Ubuntu or Ubuntu-based, or Chapter 5, "Installing and Maintaining Software in Red Hat," if you are using a Red Hat or a Red Hat–based distribution, such as CentOS.

To find a file with the locate command, just enter **locate** followed by the file's name you want to find. If the file is on your system and you have permission to view it, the locate utility will display the file's directory path and name as demonstrated here on an Ubuntu distribution:

```
$ locate .bash_history
/home/sysadmin/.bash_history
$
```

Another nice feature of locate is that it uses a pattern to find files. This allows you to employ partial filenames and regular expressions (covered later in this chapter) and, with the command options, ignore case. Table 8.5 shows a few of the more commonly used locate command options.

TABLE 8.5: The locate Command's Commonly Used Options

SHORT	LONG	DESCRIPTION
-A	--all	Display only filenames that match all the patterns, instead of displaying files that match only one pattern in the pattern list.
-b	--basename	Display only filenames that match the pattern and do not include any directory names that match the pattern.
-c	--count	Display only the number of files whose name matches the pattern instead of displaying filenames.
-i	--ignore-case	Ignore case in the pattern for matching filenames.
-q	--quiet	Do not display any error messages, such as permission denied, when processing.
-r	--regexp *R*	Use the regular expression, *R*, instead of the pattern list to match filenames.
-w	--wholename	Display filenames that match the pattern and include any directory names that match the pattern. This is default behavior.

Where you can run into problems with locate is when a file is newly created. Here's an example of using the touch command to create a file and then it tries to find it with the locate utility:

```
$ touch newFile.txt
$ ls newFile.txt
newFile.txt
$
$ locate newFile.txt
$
```

When a file is newly created (or downloaded), often it is not yet listed in the locate database. Typically, this database is updated only periodically. Also, when you have a newly installed Linux system, the database may not even yet exist!

To fix both of these issues, you'll need to obtain super user privileges and run the updatedb command. This will update the database, named /var/lib/mlocate/mlocate.db (or some variation), or create and update it.

```
$ sudo updatedb
[sudo] password for sysadmin:
$
$ locate newFile.txt
/home/sysadmin/newFile.txt
$
```

That's much better! Now that the database is updated, the newly created file can be found by the locate utility.

The locate command is useful when you want to find files by their name, but it's not useful when you're trying to find a file based on its size or who owns it. This is where the find command can help.

FINDING FILES

The find command is flexible. It allows you to locate files based on data, such as who owns the file, when the file was last modified, permissions set on the file, and so on. Its command-line format is a little different.

```
find [path] [option] [expression]
```

The *path* argument is a starting point directory, because you designate a starting point in a directory tree, and find will search through that directory and all its subdirectories (recursively) for the file or files you seek. You can use a single period (.) to designate your present working directory as the starting point directory.

The *expression* command argument and its preceding *option* control what type of filters are applied to the search as well as any settings that may limit the search. Table 8.6 shows the more commonly used *option* and *expression* combinations.

TABLE 8.6:   The find Command's Commonly Used Options and Expressions

Option	Expression	Description
-cmin	n	Display names of files whose status changed n minutes ago.
-empty	N/A	Display names of files that are empty and are a regular text file or a directory.
-gid	n	Display names of files whose group ID is equal to n.
-group	name	Display names of files whose group is name.
-inum	n	Display names of files whose inode number is equal to n.
-maxdepth	n	When searching for files, traverse down into the starting point directory's tree only n levels.
-mmin	n	Display names of files whose data changed n minutes ago.
-name	pattern	Display names of files whose name matches pattern. Many regular expression arguments may be used in the pattern and need to be enclosed in quotation marks to avoid unpredictable results. Replace -name with -iname to ignore case.
-nogroup	N/A	Display names of files where no group name exists for the file's group ID.
-nouser	N/A	Display names of files where no username exists for the file's user ID.
-perm	mode	Display names of files whose permissions match mode. Either octal or symbolic modes may be used.
-size	n	Display names of files whose size matches n. Suffixes can be used to make the size more human readable, such as G for gigabytes.
-user	name	Display names of files whose owner is name.

One nice feature of find is that it will display all the files in your present working directory (and any subdirectories) that have no data in them:

```
$ find . -empty
[...]
./newFile.txt
./.local/share/nano
[...]
$
```

Unlike locate, you can quickly find files that were newly created without updating a database.

```
$ touch anotherNewFile.txt
$
```

```
$ find /home/sysadmin -name anotherNewFile.txt
/home/sysadmin/anotherNewFile.txt
$
```

You can search for files whose status was recently changed, such as when data has been added to the file.

```
$ nano anotherNewFile.txt
$
$ find /home/sysadmin -cmin 1
[...]
/home/sysadmin/anotherNewFile.txt
$
```

You can modify these find command searches at any location within the virtual directory system. However, you may want to use super user privileges to get accurate results and avoid an overload of permission denied messages.

```
$ sudo find / -name mlocate.db
[sudo] password for sysadmin:
/var/lib/mlocate/mlocate.db
$
```

Both locate and find are useful for discovering a file's location or performing a basic file analysis. However, neither of these commands can search through and display a file's contents. We'll cover a utility that does offer that feature next.

SEARCHING FOR AND THROUGH FILES

When you need a utility that lets you search for files that contain certain data, grep is the winner. The command-line format for the grep command is as follows:

```
grep [options] pattern [file]
```

In the following example, the text files we've used or created for this chapter are listed in a single-column format via the ls -1 *.txt command. Two of those files contain the word Pi, but which ones? The grep command can easily determine the correct answer.

```
$ ls -1 *.txt
alphabetKey.txt
anotherNewFile.txt
editorTestFile.txt
editorTestFileNano.txt
newFile.txt
numberKey.txt
numberKeySciFi.txt
sortedSciFi.txt
$
$ cat numberKeySciFi.txt
1984 101
Wars 1138
```

```
  Pi 3.14
  Trek 1701
  Back 88
$
$ cat sortedSciFi.txt
  Pi 3.14
  Back 88
  1984 101
  Wars 1138
  Trek 1701
$
$ grep Pi *.txt
  numberKeySciFi.txt:Pi 3.14
  sortedSciFi.txt:Pi 3.14
$
```

In the preceding example, the *pattern* used with grep was Pi, and in the current directory, all the text files, *.txt, were searched. The grep command lists the search results by displaying each file's name that contains the *pattern* and then shows the entire text line that has the *pattern*.

There are some nice options you can use in your grep searches. Table 8.7 shows some of the more commonly used grep utility options.

TABLE 8.7:   The grep Command's Commonly Used Options

SHORT	LONG	DESCRIPTION
-c	--count	Display a count of text file records that contain a PATTERN match.
-d action	--directories=*action*	When a file is a directory, if *action* is set to read, read the directory as if it were a regular text file; if action is set to skip, ignore the directory; and if action is set to recurse, act as if the -R, -r, or --recursive option was used.
-E	--extended-regexp	Designate the PATTERN as an extended regular expression.
-i	--ignore-case	Ignore the case in the PATTERN as well as in any text file records.
-R, -r	--recursive	Search a directory's contents, and for any subdirectory within the original directory tree, consecutively search its contents as well (recursively).
-v	--invert-match	Display only text file's records that do not contain a PATTERN match.

When searching through larger sections of the virtual directory structure for files containing certain data, it's a good idea to employ the -d skip option so that grep doesn't complain at you when it encounters a directory file.

```
$ grep -d skip sysadmin /etc/*
grep: /etc/at.deny: Permission denied
/etc/group:sysadmin:x:1000:
[...]
/etc/passwd:sysadmin:x:1000:1000:[...]:/home/sysadmin:/bin/bash
[...]
$
```

Notice that the grep utility found the word sysadmin in two files. This is a real time-saver when you're trying to locate data. However, also notice that a Permission denied message was produced. You'll need to use super user privileges to search through files that require higher permission levels to look through.

You can also use grep to conduct searches on one particular file. Often in a large file, you have to look for a specific line of data buried somewhere in the middle of the file. Instead of manually scrolling through the entire file, you can let the grep command search for you.

```
$ grep bash /etc/passwd
root:x:0:0:root:/root:/bin/bash
sysadmin:x:1000:1000:[...]:/home/sysadmin:/bin/bash
$
```

When looking for a particular piece of data whose case you cannot remember, use the -i option to make grep case-insensitive.

```
$ sudo grep -d skip Ubuntu-Server /etc/*
[sudo] password for sysadmin:
$
$ sudo grep -i -d skip Ubuntu-Server /etc/*
/etc/hostname:ubuntu-server
/etc/hosts:127.0.1.1 ubuntu-server
$
```

The -d skip and -i options, along with super user privileges, make your grep search results cleaner and provide you with faster results.

REGULAR EXPRESSIONS

Instead of looking for a word using grep, you can conduct a search using a regular expression. A regular expression is a pattern template you define for a utility, such as grep, which uses a pattern template to filter text. Basic regular expressions (BREs) include characters, such as a dot followed by an asterisk (.*), to represent multiple characters and a single dot (.) to represent one character. They also may use brackets to represent multiple characters, such as [a,e,i,o,u] or a range of characters, such as [A-z]. To find text file records that begin with particular characters, you can proceed them with a caret (^) symbol. For finding text file records where particular characters are at the record's end, succeed them with a dollar sign ($) symbol.

In addition to BREs, there are extended regular expressions (EREs), which have more complex pattern templates. When using grep with EREs, you must add the -E option to the command. An ERE pattern example is "word1|word2", which tells grep that if a text line contains either word1 *or* word2, display it. If you'd like a more in-depth look at regular expressions, our favorite resource is Chapter 20 in the book *Linux Command Line and Shell Scripting Bible* by Blum and Bresnahan (Wiley, 2021).

You can conduct rather complex searches with grep by using regular expressions. The grep can even handle extended regular expressions, if you use the -E option.

```
$ grep -E "(^root|^sysadmin)" /etc/passwd
root:x:0:0:root:/root:/bin/bash
sysadmin:x:1000:1000:[...]:/home/sysadmin:/bin/bash
$
```

The grep -E command is the more modern version of the egrep utility. The two are functionally the same, but egrep is now deprecated. When a command is *deprecated*, this means that it may not be available in the future, so you should stop using it as soon as possible and start using its modern equal.

Compressing

Linux contains several file compression utilities that allow you to easily compress large files into smaller files that take up less space. While this may sound great, it often leads to confusion and chaos when you're trying to determine which utility to use. The following popular utilities are available on Linux:

- ◆ gzip
- ◆ bzip2
- ◆ xz

The advantages and disadvantages of each of these data compression methods are explored in this section.

gzip   The gzip utility was developed in 1992 as a replacement for the old compress program. Achieving text-based file compression rates of 60–70 percent, gzip has long been a popular data compression utility. To compress a file, simply type in **gzip** followed by the file's name. The original file is replaced by a compressed version with a .gz filename extension. To reverse the operation, type in **gunzip** followed by the compressed file's name.

bzip2   Developed in 1996, the bzip2 utility offers higher compression rates than gzip but takes slightly longer to perform the data compression. There was a bzip program, but it had some patent issues, so bzip2 was created to replace it.

The bzip2 utility employs multiple layers of compression techniques and algorithms. Until 2013, this data compression utility was used to compress the Linux kernel for distribution. To compress a file, simply type in **bzip2** followed by the file's name. The original file is replaced by a compressed version with a .bz2 file extension. To reverse the operation, type in **bunzip2** followed by the compressed file's name, which decompresses (deflates) the data.

xz   Developed in 2009, the xz data compression utility quickly became popular among Linux administrators. It boasts a higher default compression rate than bzip2 and gzip. In 2013, the xz compression utility replaced bzip2 for compressing the Linux kernel for distribution. To compress a file, simply type in **xz** followed by the file's name. The original file is replaced by a compressed version with an .xz file extension. To reverse the operation, type in **unxz** followed by the compressed file's name.

It's helpful to see a side-by-side comparison of some of the compression utilities using their defaults. Here is a compression comparison example on an Ubuntu distribution:

```
$ ls -hs /var/log/syslog
344K /var/log/syslog
$
$ cp /var/log/syslog syslog1
$ cp /var/log/syslog syslog2
$ cp /var/log/syslog syslog3
$
$ gzip syslog1
$ bzip2 syslog2
$ xz syslog3
$

$ ls -hs syslog?.*
72K syslog1.gz  40K syslog2.bz2  32K syslog3.xz
$
```

In the preceding example, first the /var/log/syslog file size is shown, which is 344 K. (You can use /var/log/lastlog in place of /var/log/syslog for this comparison on a CentOS distribution.) Then the file is copied three times to the local directory using a new filename each time. Next, three compression utilities are used. After the files are compressed with the various utilities, another ls -hs command displays the compressed files' names and their sizes. You can see that the xz program produces the highest compression of this file, because its file, syslog3 .xz, is the smallest in size.

Compression goes hand in hand with backing up files, because the resulting file containing a backup is often rather large. We'll cover backing up files next.

Archiving

Backing up files is often called *archiving*, especially in the Linux world. There are several programs you can employ for managing backups. Some of the more popular products are Amanda, Bacula, Bareos, Duplicity, and BackupPC. Yet, often these GUI and/or web-based programs have command-line utilities at their core, which include the following:

◆   cpio

◆   dd

◆   rsync

◆   tar

The tar command was originally used to write files to a tape device for archiving. However, it can also write the output to a file, which has become a popular way to archive data in Linux, and that's the command we'll focus on in this chapter.

The tar command copies the selected files and stores them in a single file. This file is called a *tar archive* file. If this archive file is compressed using a data compression utility, the compressed archive file is called a *tarball*.

The tar program has several useful options. Table 8.8 describes the more commonly used ones for creating data backups.

TABLE 8.8: The tar Command's Commonly Used Archive Creation Options

SHORT	LONG	DESCRIPTION
-c	--create	Creates a tar archive file. The backup can be a full or incremental backup, depending upon the other selected options.
-u	--update	Appends files to an existing tar archive file, but only copies those files that were modified since the original archive file was created
-g	--listed-incremental	Creates an incremental or full archive based upon metadata stored in the provided file
-z	--gzip	Compresses a tar archive file into a tarball using gzip
-j	--bzip2	Compresses a tar archive file into a tarball using bzip2
-J	--xz	Compresses a tar archive file into a tarball using xz
-v	--verbose	Displays each file's name as each file is processed

Notice that there are some compression options in Table 8.8. When you use a compression utility along with an archive and restore program for data backups, it is vital that you use a lossless compression method. A lossless compression is just as it sounds: no data is lost. The gzip, bzip2, and xz utilities provide lossless compression. Obviously, it is important not to lose data when doing backups!

To create an archive using the tar utility, you have to add a few arguments for the options and the command.

```
$ ls n*.txt
newFile.txt   numberKey.txt   numberKeySciFi.txt
$
$ tar -cvf archive.tar n*.txt
newFile.txt
numberKey.txt
numberKeySciFi.txt
$
```

In the preceding example, three options are used.

◆ The -c option creates the tar archive.

◆ The -v option displays the filenames as they are placed into the archive file.

◆ The -f option designates the archive filename, which is archive.tar.

Though not required, it is considered good form to use the `.tar` extension on tar archive files. The example command's last argument designates the files to copy into this archive.

If you are backing up lots of files or large amounts of data, it is a good idea to employ a compression utility. This is easily accomplished by adding an additional switch to your `tar` command options. Here `gzip` compression is used to create a tarball:

```
$ ls -hs /var/log/syslog.*
132K /var/log/syslog.1  168K /var/log/syslog.2.gz
$
$ tar -zcvf syslog.tar.gz /var/log/syslog.*
tar: Removing leading `/' from member names
/var/log/syslog.1
tar: Removing leading `/' from hard link targets
/var/log/syslog.2.gz
$
$ ls -hs syslog.tar.gz
196K syslog.tar.gz
$
```

There are a couple of things to note in this example. First, look at the `tar: Removing leading` messages. The `tar` utility strips off the first forward slash (/) in filenames so that they can be restored anywhere in the future. If that forward slash was left in there, the files would only go back to their original location in the virtual directory structure, which is not very flexible.

The next thing to note in the preceding example is that the tarball filename has the `.tar.gz` file extension. It is considered good form to use the `.tar` extension and tack on an indicator showing the compression method that was used. However, you can shorten it to `.tgz` if desired.

Whenever you create data backups, it is a good practice to verify them. Table 8.9 provides some `tar` command options for viewing and verifying data backups.

TABLE 8.9:   The `tar` Command's Commonly Used Archive Verification Options

SHORT	LONG	DESCRIPTION
-d	--compare --diff	Compares a tar archive file's members with external files and lists the differences
-t	--list	Displays a tar archive file's contents
-W	--verify	Verifies each file as the file is processed. This option cannot be used with the compression options.

Backup verification can take several different forms. You might ensure that the desired files (sometimes called *members*) are included in your backup by using the `-v` option on the `tar` command in order to watch the files being listed as they are included in the archive file. You can also verify that desired files are included in your backup after the fact. Use the `-t` option to list a tarball or archive file's contents, as shown here:

```
$ tar -tf archive.tar
newFile.txt
```

```
numberKey.txt
numberKeySciFi.txt
$
$ tar -tf syslog.tar.gz
var/log/syslog.1
var/log/syslog.2.gz
$
```

Table 8.10 lists some of the options that you can use with the `tar` utility to restore data from a tar archive file or tarball. Several options used to create the backup, such as `-g`, are also available when restoring data.

TABLE 8.10: The `tar` Command's Commonly Used File Restore Options

SHORT	LONG	DESCRIPTION
-x	--extract --get	Extracts files from a tarball or archive file and places them in the current working directory
-z	--gunzip	Decompresses files in a tarball using `gunzip`
-j	--bunzip2	Decompresses files in a tarball using `bunzip2`
-J	--unxz	Decompresses files in a tarball using `unxz`

Extracting files from an archive or tarball is fairly simple using the `tar` utility. Here is an example of extracting files from our previously created tarball:

```
$ mkdir Extract
$ mv syslog.tar.gz Extract/
$ cd Extract
$
$ tar -zxvf syslog.tar.gz
var/log/syslog.1
var/log/syslog.2.gz
$
$ ls -F
syslog.tar.gz   var/
$
$ ls var/log/
syslog.1  syslog.2.gz
$
```

In the previous example, a new subdirectory, `Extract`, is created. The tarball is moved to the new subdirectory, and then the files are restored from the tarball. Notice that instead of putting the files in the top level of the new subdirectory, `Extract`, they were instead placed in the `var/log` subdirectory. That's because `tar` removed the leading forward slash of the original files but kept the rest of the directory reference. This is a rather useful feature of the `tar` utility.

Real World Scenario

TRYING THE *TAR* COMMAND

Archiving data is a large part of protecting information. The Linux tar utility is a popular way to archive directory structures into a single file that can easily be ported to another system. Practicing the use of this particular command will help you become more efficient in your day-to-day system administration tasks.

The following steps will take you through trying out the archiving and restoring files:

1. Log into a Linux system using the sysadmin account and the password you created for it.

2. Copy the /etc/passwd file to use for backup practice by typing **cp /etc/passwd $HOME/passwd1.txt** and pressing Enter.

3. Do this again to make a second file by typing **cp /etc/passwd $HOME/passwd2.txt** and pressing Enter.

4. You need one more file, so type **cp /etc/passwd $HOME/passwd3.txt** and press Enter.

5. Check to ensure you have three password files by typing **ls passwd?.txt** and pressing Enter.

6. Now that you have some files to archive, use the tar utility to make a tarball. Type **tar -zcvf PArchive.tgz passwd?.txt** and press Enter. You should see the three files' names displayed as they are processed by the tar command.

7. Review the PArchive.tgz tarball's contents by typing **tar -tf PArchive.tgz** and pressing Enter. You should see the three files' names that were displayed in the previous command.

8. Before you decompress and extract the tarball's files, you'll need a place to put the files. Create a new directory in your present working directory by typing **mkdir PArchiveDir** and pressing Enter.

9. Copy the tarball file to the new subdirectory by typing **cp PArchive.tgz PArchiveDir/** and pressing Enter.

10. Move your current working directory into the new subdirectory. Type **cd PArchiveDir** and press Enter.

11. Double-check that you are in the correct directory by typing **pwd** and pressing Enter. You should see something similar to /home/sysadmin/PArchiveDir displayed.

12. Now you can decompress and unpack the tarball in this subdirectory. Type **tar -zxvf PArchive.tgz** and press Enter. You should see three files' names displayed as they are processed by the tar command.

13. Double-check that the files were extracted by typing **ls** and pressing Enter. Do you see the three password files as well as the PArchive.tgz file? You should.

Using the tar command is a simple way to create a backup file of various files. You can also create archive files of entire directory structures. This is a common method for distributing source code files for open source applications in the Linux world.

The Bottom Line

Use the vim editor's basic features.   The vim editor is one of the most popular text editors in use. Though it can be tricky to use, modifying text files using vim is worth the time to learn. Grasping the basics of the vim editor is all that is needed for a system admin.

> **Master It**   Imagine that you just opened up a configuration file in the vim editor. You only want to quickly add a paragraph of comments to the top of the file. What editor commands can you employ to accomplish this task quickly?

Employ the nano editor for everyday text file editing.   The nano text editor is a simple and quick editor to use in your daily work. You can quickly get into a file, make any needed modifications, save your work, and go on with other tasks. It's a favorite editor of system administrators because of its simplicity.

> **Master It**   You need to quickly edit a text file by copying two lines of text from the top of the file to the bottom of the text file. Assuming you are already in the nano editor with this file in the buffer, what editor commands covered in this chapter can you use to accomplish this task quickly?

Find data in a text file, and reduce its size.   To quickly find files that contain certain data, the grep command is a utility to learn. With its ability to conduct simple or complex searches, locating the information or the files you need is a snap.

> **Master It**   You need to find all the files in the /etc directory (but not its subdirectories) that contain the word host. The search must be case-insensitive, and you don't want to see any error messages concerning directory files. Assuming you need to use the sudo command along with your grep command, what will your command look like to conduct this search?

Back up and organize text file data.   The tar utility has been around for a long time. It provides useful options to create archive files. While tar has the ability to compress files on the fly, you can also use the gzip, bzip2, and xz compression utilities to compress tar archive files as well as other files.

> **Master It**   You created a tar archive file, myArchive.tar, but did not compress it with a tar option, because you needed to verify each file as it was processed with the -W option. Now that the archive file was successfully created and verified, what command will you use to compress it to the highest level, and what will the resulting file's name be?

Part 2

Intermediate Admin Functions

Chapter 9

Managing Hardware

The typical Linux system has lots of different hardware devices connected to it. The list can include hard drives, external drives, monitors, keyboards, printers, audio cards, and network cards. Part of your job as a Linux administrator is to make sure all of those devices are working, and working properly.

IN THIS CHAPTER, YOU WILL LEARN TO

◆   Use Linux device driver modules

◆   Find device information for the system

◆   Work with PCI and USB devices

Device Driver Modules

One of the main jobs of the Linux operating system is to provide a standard interface for applications to work with hardware. There are lots of different types of hardware devices available, making it impossible for each application to include software to interact with all of them.

Instead, the Linux operating system provides a generic interface to all the different types of hardware that applications can face. Application programmers just need to know how to interface with the Linux system, and then Linux takes over from there. This makes tasks such as sending out data on a network or capturing keyboard input much easier for application developers.

Similar to the Microsoft Windows world, the Linux kernel interfaces with hardware devices using what's called a *device driver*. A device driver is a small piece of software written to interact with a specific hardware device. Each device that interacts with the Linux system must have a Linux device driver. Fortunately, with the growing popularity of Linux, most hardware manufacturers provide device drivers for their own devices so that Linux users can use the hardware on their Linux systems. There are also a few open source projects for creating device drivers for specific devices where the manufacturer has failed to produce a Linux device driver. This is especially true with printers.

Once you obtain the device driver necessary for the hardware you want to install on your Linux system, there are two ways to include the device driver into the Linux kernel.

◆   Compile it into the kernel software

◆   Plug a module into the kernel software

Compiled device drivers are device driver software that you must include directly into the Linux kernel software. This method requires the source code for the device driver, as well as the source code for the kernel. When the kernel program is recompiled, you must specify the additional device driver software to include in the kernel.

The downside to compiled device drivers is that every time you need to add a new hardware device to your Linux system, you must recompile the entire kernel software program. That can get old after a while, not to mention it's a great way to introduce bugs into the kernel code!

As a solution, Linux developers created device driver modules. A device driver module can be inserted into a running kernel at any time, without affecting the system operation. Similarly, you can also remove a module from the kernel at any time, without affecting other operations of the kernel. This provides the flexibility to only install the device drivers that you need for your system to interact with exactly the hardware you use, without the ugliness of having to recompile the kernel for each device.

Device driver modules have taken the Linux world by storm and are pretty much the default way of handling hardware devices. Linux systems now provide a few different utilities for working with device driver modules from the command line. The following sections walk you through the commands that you can use to manage hardware modules in your Linux system.

Listing Installed Modules

Before you get too far with your Linux system, you may need to determine just what devices it can support by default. Most Linux distributions include a set of pre-installed device driver modules for most common hardware.

You can take a peek at what device modules are already installed in your Linux system by using the lsmod command-line command. The "Viewing the Installed Modules" case study contains a quick exercise showing you how to do that.

 Real World Scenario

VIEWING THE INSTALLED MODULES

You can use the lsmod command to view the kernel modules currently installed on your Linux system. Just follow these steps:

1. If you've not done so already, log into your Linux system as a normal user account.

2. From the command prompt, type the command **lsmod**. You should see something similar to the following output:

```
$ lsmod
Module                 Size  Used by
vboxsf                81920  1
vboxvideo             36864  0
dm_multipath          32768  0
scsi_dh_rdac          16384  0
scsi_dh_emc           16384  0
scsi_dh_alua          20480  0
intel_rapl_msr        20480  0
snd_intel8x0          45056  0
intel_rapl_common     24576  1 intel_rapl_msr
```

```
snd_ac97_codec        131072  1 snd_intel8x0
intel_powerclamp       20480  0
rapl                   20480  0
ac97_bus               16384  1 snd_ac97_codec
snd_pcm               106496  2 snd_intel8x0,snd_ac97_codec
input_leds             16384  0
snd_timer              36864  1 snd_pcm
serio_raw              20480  0
joydev                 24576  0
snd                    90112  4 snd_intel8x0,snd_timer,snd_ac97_codec,snd_pcm
...
$
```

The output of the lsmod command has three columns. The Module column shows the name of the module. The Size column shows the amount of memory space the module takes when loaded. The Used By column shows the number of other modules or processes that use the module and what their names are. This helps you determine module dependencies in case you try to remove a module without knowing just what other modules or processes rely on it.

Knowing what device modules your Linux distribution preinstalls can help with trouble-shooting hardware issues, as well as giving you an idea of what drivers you'll need to track down for your specific hardware.

Installing New Modules

Once you obtain a device driver module file for your hardware, you can install it in your Linux system kernel using one of two common commands.

◆ insmod

◆ modprobe

While each of these commands can insert a module, they each work a little differently. The following sections describe what you'll need to know to use each command.

USING *INSMOD*

The insmod command inserts a single device module file into the kernel. You must have the device module file copied onto your Linux system to use this command. Most Linux distributions use the /lib/modules directory structure to store module files. If you look in that directory on your Linux system, you'll see a subdirectory tree structure that separates the device drivers for each kernel version, as well as the different types of hardware.

For example, on our Ubuntu Linux server system, we see the following subdirectory for Bluetooth hardware drivers:

/lib/modules/5.4.0-58-generic/kernel/drivers/bluetooth

This subdirectory is for the currently installed Linux kernel on our system: 5.4.0-58. Inside that subdirectory are lots of different device driver module files for various types of Bluetooth systems, as shown in Listing 9.1.

LISTING 9.1:   Kernel Module Files on an Ubuntu Server

```
$ ls -l

total 756
-rw-r--r--  1 root root  24993 Dec  9 07:10 ath3k.ko
-rw-r--r--  1 root root  13281 Dec  9 07:10 bcm203x.ko
-rw-r--r--  1 root root  25625 Dec  9 07:10 bfusb.ko
-rw-r--r--  1 root root  15505 Dec  9 07:10 bluecard_cs.ko
-rw-r--r--  1 root root  20281 Dec  9 07:10 bpa10x.ko
-rw-r--r--  1 root root  15185 Dec  9 07:10 bt3c_cs.ko
-rw-r--r--  1 root root  16449 Dec  9 07:10 btbcm.ko
-rw-r--r--  1 root root  23785 Dec  9 07:10 btintel.ko
-rw-r--r--  1 root root  36169 Dec  9 07:10 btmrvl.ko
-rw-r--r--  1 root root  42105 Dec  9 07:10 btmrvl_sdio.ko
-rw-r--r--  1 root root  24505 Dec  9 07:10 btmtksdio.ko
-rw-r--r--  1 root root   6625 Dec  9 07:10 btmtkuart.ko
-rw-r--r--  1 root root  22785 Dec  9 07:10 btqca.ko
-rw-r--r--  1 root root   8649 Dec  9 07:10 btrsi.ko
-rw-r--r--  1 root root  22049 Dec  9 07:10 btrtl.ko
-rw-r--r--  1 root root  16361 Dec  9 07:10 btsdio.ko
-rw-r--r--  1 root root  85985 Dec  9 07:10 btusb.ko
-rw-r--r--  1 root root  13225 Dec  9 07:10 btwilink.ko
-rw-r--r--  1 root root  14153 Dec  9 07:10 dtl1_cs.ko
-rw-r--r--  1 root root  25961 Dec  9 07:10 hci_nokia.ko
-rw-r--r--  1 root root 237233 Dec  9 07:10 hci_uart.ko
-rw-r--r--  1 root root  14225 Dec  9 07:10 hci_vhci.ko
$
```

Each .ko file is a separate device driver module file that you can install into the 5.4.0-58 ker-nel. To install the module, just specify the filename on the insmod command line. Some modules also require parameters, which you must specify on the command line as well.

```
$ sudo insmod /lib/modules/5.4.0-58-generic/kernel/drivers/bluetooth/
btusb.ko
password:
insmod: ERROR: could not insert module btusb.ko: Unknown symbol in module
$
```

This example demonstrates a limitation of the insmod command. If the module you want to install depends on other modules that aren't already installed, insmod just produces the cryptic error message seen here. It's up to you to figure out what dependencies are required to install the module. Don't fret, though—there's an easier way to install kernel modules.

USING *MODPROBE*

To make the process of installing kernel modules easier, the modprobe command helps resolve module dependencies for you. Another nice feature of the modprobe command is that it understands module names and will search the module library directories for the module file that provides the driver for the module name.

Because of this versatility, there are lots of options available for the modprobe command. Table 9.1 shows the command-line options that you can use.

TABLE 9.1: The modprobe Command Options

OPTION	DESCRIPTION
-a	Insert all modules listed on the command line.
-b	Apply the blacklist commands specified in the configuration file.
-C	Specify a different configuration file other than the default.
-c	Display the current configuration used.
-d	Specify the directory to use for installing modules.
-f	Force the module installation even if there are version issues.
-i	Ignore the install and remove commands specified in the configuration file for the module.
-n	Perform a dry run of the module install to see if it will work, without actually installing it.
-q	Quiet mode—doesn't display any error messages if the module installation or removal fails.
-r	Remove the module listed.
-s	Send any error messages to the syslog facility on the system.
-V	Display the program version and exit.
-v	Provide additional information (verbose) as the module is processed.

As you can see, the modprobe command is a full-featured tool all by itself. Perhaps the handiest feature is that it allows you to handle modules based on the module name and not have to list the full module filename.

```
$ sudo modprobe -iv btusb
insmod /lib/modules/5.4.0-58-generic/kernel/crypto/ecc.ko
insmod /lib/modules/5.4.0-58-generic/kernel/crypto/ecdh_generic.ko
insmod /lib/modules/5.4.0-58-generic/kernel/net/bluetooth/bluetooth.ko
```

```
insmod /lib/modules/5.4.0-58-generic/kernel/drivers/bluetooth/btintel.ko
insmod /lib/modules/5.4.0-58-generic/kernel/drivers/bluetooth/btbcm.ko
insmod /lib/modules/5.4.0-58-generic/kernel/drivers/bluetooth/btrtl.ko
insmod /lib/modules/5.4.0-58-generic/kernel/drivers/bluetooth/btusb.ko
$
```

Notice that by adding the -v option for verbose mode, the output shows the insmod commands automatically generated by the modprobe command as it finds all of the required module dependencies. Each insmod command shows the specific module file used to install the module.

Removing Modules

Normally, it does no harm to install a module in the system even if the hardware device is not present. The kernel ignores unused modules. However, some Linux administrators prefer to keep the kernel as lightweight as possible, so the Linux developers created a method for removing unnecessary modules: the rmmod command.

However, our friend the modprobe command can also remove modules for us, so you don't really need to memorize another command. Instead, just use the -r option with the modprobe command.

```
$ sudo modprobe -rv btusb
rmmod btusb
rmmod btintel
rmmod btbcm
rmmod btrtl
rmmod bluetooth
rmmod ecdh_generic
rmmod ecc
$
```

The modprobe -r command invokes the rmmod command automatically, removing the module by name, along with any dependent modules that were installed. You can verify that the modules have been removed by using the lsmod command.

Communicating with Devices

For any device to work on your Linux system, the Linux kernel must both recognize it and know how to talk to it. Once the kernel module is installed, the kernel must know how to communicate with the device. Linux supports several different types of hardware interfaces and methods for communicating with devices. This section describes the different ways Linux handles data and information from devices.

Device Interfaces

Each device you connect to your Linux system uses some type of standard protocol to communicate with the system hardware. The kernel module software must know how to send data to and receive data from the hardware device using those protocols. There are two popular standards used to connect devices.

PCI Boards

The *Peripheral Component Interconnect (PCI)* standard was developed in 1993 as a method for connecting hardware boards to PC motherboards. The standard has been updated a few times to accommodate faster interface speeds, as well as increasing data bus sizes on motherboards. The *PCI Express (PCIe)* standard is currently used on most server and desktop workstations to provide a common interface for hardware cards that plug directly into the motherboard.

Lots of different devices use PCI boards to connect to a server or desktop workstation.

Internal hard drives: Hard drives using the *Serial Advanced Technology Attachment (SATA)*, the *Small Computer System Interface (SCSI)*, or the *Non-volatile Memory (NVMe)* interface standards often use PCI boards to connect with workstations or servers. The Linux kernel automatically recognizes SATA, SCSI, and solid-state drive (SSD) hard drives connected to PCI boards.

External hard drives: Network hard drives using the Fibre Channel standard provide a high-speed shared drive environment for server environments. To communicate on a Fibre Channel network, the server usually uses PCI boards that support the *Host Bus Adapter (HBA)* standard.

Network interface cards: Hardwired network cards allow you to connect the workstation or server to a local area network (LAN) using the common RJ-45 cable standard. These types of connections are mostly found in high-speed network environments that require high through-put to the network.

Wireless cards: There are PCI boards available that support the IEEE 802.11standard for wireless connections to a LAN. While these are not commonly used in server environments, they are popular in workstation environments.

Bluetooth devices: The Bluetooth technology allows for short-distance wireless communication with other Bluetooth devices in a peer-to-peer network setup. These are most commonly found in workstation environments.

Video accelerators: Applications that require advanced graphics often use video accelerator cards, which offload the video processing requirements from the CPU to provide faster graphics. While these are popular in gaming environments, you'll also find video accelerator cards used in video processing applications for editing and processing movies.

Audio cards: Similarly, applications that require high-quality sound often use specialty audio cards to provide advanced audio processing and play, such as handling Dolby surround sound to enhance the audio quality of movies.

The USB Interface

The *Universal Serial Bus (USB)* interface has become a popular device interface due to its ease of use and its increasing support for high-speed data communication. Since the USB interface uses serial communications, it requires fewer connectors with the motherboard, allowing for smaller interface plugs.

The USB standard has evolved over the years. The original version 1.0 only supported data transfer speeds up to 12 Mbps. The 2.0 standard increased the data transfer speed to 480 Mbps.

The current USB standard, 4.0, allows for data transfer speeds up to 40 Gbps, making it useful for high-speed connections to external storage devices.

There are myriad different devices that can connect to systems using the USB interface. You can find hard drives, printers, digital cameras and camcorders, keyboards, mice, and network cards that have versions that connect using the USB interface.

USING USB DEVICES IN LINUX

There are two steps to get Linux to interact with USB devices. The first step is that the Linux kernel must have the proper module installed to recognize the USB controller that is installed on your server or workstation. The controller provides communication between the Linux kernel and the USB bus on the system. Once the Linux kernel can communicate with the USB bus, any device you plug into a USB port on the system will be recognized by the kernel, but not necessarily useful. The second step is that the Linux system must then also have a kernel module installed for the individual device type plugged into the USB bus.

The /dev Directory

Once the Linux kernel can communicate with a device on an interface, it must be able to transfer data to and from the device. This is done using *device files*. Device files are files that the Linux kernel creates in the special /dev directory to interface with hardware devices.

To retrieve data from a specific device, a program just needs to read the Linux device file associated with that device. The Linux operating system handles all the unsightliness of interfacing with the actual hardware. Likewise, to send data to the device, the program just needs to write to the Linux device file.

As you add hardware devices such as USB drives, network cards, or hard drives to your system, Linux creates a file in the /dev directory representing that hardware device. Application programs can then interact directly with that file to store and retrieve data on the device. This is a lot easier than requiring each application to know how to directly interact with a device.

There are two types of device files in Linux, based on how Linux transfers data to the device:

Character device files: Transfer data one character at a time. This method is often used for serial devices such as terminals and USB devices.

Block device files: Transfer data in large blocks. This method is often used for high-speed data transfer devices such as hard drives and network cards.

The type of device file is denoted by the first letter in the permissions list, as shown in Listing 9.2.

LISTING 9.2: Partial Output from the /dev Directory

```
$ ls -al sd* tty*
brw-rw---- 1 root     disk     8,  0 Jan  4 14:37 sda
brw-rw---- 1 root     disk     8,  1 Jan  4 14:37 sda1
brw-rw---- 1 root     disk     8,  2 Jan  4 14:37 sda2
```

```
brw-rw---- 1 root      disk    8,  3 Jan  4 14:37 sda3
crw-rw-rw- 1 root      tty     5,  0 Jan  4 14:52 tty
crw--w---- 1 root      tty     4,  0 Jan  4 14:37 tty0
crw------- 1 sysadmin  tty     4,  1 Jan  4 14:38 tty1
...
$
```

The hard drive devices, such as sda and sda1, show the letter b, indicating that they are block device files. The tty terminal files show the letter c, indicating that they are character device files.

Besides device files, Linux also provides a system called the *device mapper*. The device mapper function is performed by the Linux kernel. It maps physical block devices to virtual block devices. These virtual block devices allow the system to intercept the data written to or read from the physical device and perform some type of operation on them. Mapped devices are used by the Logical Volume Manager (LVM) for creating logical drives, and by the Linux Unified Key Setup (LUKS) for encrypting data on hard drives.

The */proc* Directory

The /proc directory is one of the most important tools you can use when troubleshooting hardware issues on a Linux system. It's not a physical directory on the filesystem, but instead, it's a virtual directory that the kernel dynamically populates to provide access to information about the system hardware settings and status.

The Linux kernel changes the files and data in the /proc directory dynamically as it monitors the status of hardware on the system. To view the status of the hardware devices and settings, you just need to read the contents of the virtual files using standard Linux text commands.

There are different /proc files available for different system features. You can find information on high-level hardware features, such as the CPU type and memory size, and low-level features, including the IRQs, I/O ports, and DMA channels in use on the system by hardware devices. This section discusses the files used to monitor these low-level features and how you can access them.

INTERRUPT REQUESTS

Interrupt requests (called IRQs) allow hardware devices to indicate when they have data to send to the CPU. The Plug-and-Play (PnP) system must assign a unique IRQ address to each hardware device installed on the system. You can view the current IRQs in use on your Linux system by looking at the /proc/interrupts file using the Linux cat command, as shown in Listing 9.3.

LISTING 9.3:   Listing System Interrupts from the /proc Directory

```
$ cat /proc/interrupts
           CPU0
    0:       30    IO-APIC    2-edge      timer
    1:       57    IO-APIC    1-edge      i8042
    8:        0    IO-APIC    8-edge      rtc0
```

```
       9:          0    IO-APIC   9-fasteoi    acpi
      12:        158    IO-APIC  12-edge       i8042
      14:          0    IO-APIC  14-edge       ata_piix
      15:       2798    IO-APIC  15-edge       ata_piix
      16:       9148    IO-APIC  16-fasteoi    enp0s8
      18:      13106    IO-APIC  18-fasteoi    vmwgfx
      19:       1857    IO-APIC  19-fasteoi    enp0s3
      20:       1122    IO-APIC  20-fasteoi    vboxguest
      21:      17402    IO-APIC  21-fasteoi    ahci[0000:00:0d.0], snd_intel8x0
      22:         25    IO-APIC  22-fasteoi    ohci_hcd:usb1
     NMI:          0    Non-maskable interrupts
     LOC:     129212    Local timer interrupts
     SPU:          0    Spurious interrupts
     PMI:          0    Performance monitoring interrupts
     IWI:          0    IRQ work interrupts
     RTR:          0    APIC ICR read retries
     RES:          0    Rescheduling interrupts
     CAL:          0    Function call interrupts
     TLB:          0    TLB shootdowns
     TRM:          0    Thermal event interrupts
     THR:          0    Threshold APIC interrupts
     DFR:          0    Deferred Error APIC interrupts
     MCE:          0    Machine check exceptions
     MCP:          9    Machine check polls
     ERR:          0
     MIS:          0
     PIN:          0    Posted-interrupt notification event
     NPI:          0    Nested posted-interrupt event
     PIW:          0    Posted-interrupt wakeup event
     $
```

Some IRQs are reserved by the system for specific hardware devices, such as 0 for the system timer, and 1 for the system keyboard. Other IRQs are assigned by the system as devices are detected at boot time.

I/O Ports

The system I/O ports are locations in memory where the CPU can send data to and receive data from the hardware device. As with IRQs, the system must assign each device a unique I/O port. This is yet another feature handled by the PnP system.

You can monitor the I/O ports assigned to the hardware devices on your system by looking at the /proc/ioports file, as shown in Listing 9.4.

LISTING 9.4: Displaying the I/O Ports on a System

```
$ cat /proc/ioports
0000-0000 : PCI Bus 0000:00
```

```
0000-0000 : dma1
0000-0000 : pic1
0000-0000 : timer0
0000-0000 : timer1
0000-0000 : keyboard
0000-0000 : keyboard
0000-0000 : rtc_cmos
  0000-0000 : rtc0
0000-0000 : dma page reg
0000-0000 : pic2
0000-0000 : dma2
0000-0000 : fpu
0000-0000 : 0000:00:01.1
  0000-0000 : ata_piix
0000-0000 : 0000:00:01.1
  0000-0000 : ata_piix
0000-0000 : 0000:00:01.1
  0000-0000 : ata_piix
0000-0000 : vga+
0000-0000 : 0000:00:01.1
  0000-0000 : ata_piix
0000-0000 : PCI conf1
0000-0000 : PCI Bus 0000:00
  0000-0000 : 0000:00:07.0
    0000-0000 : ACPI PM1a_EVT_BLK
    0000-0000 : ACPI PM1a_CNT_BLK
    0000-0000 : ACPI PM_TMR
    0000-0000 : ACPI GPE0_BLK
  0000-0000 : 0000:00:07.0
    0000-0000 : piix4_smbus
  0000-0000 : 0000:00:01.1
    0000-0000 : ata_piix
  0000-0000 : 0000:00:02.0
    0000-0000 : vmwgfx probe
  0000-0000 : 0000:00:03.0
    0000-0000 : e1000
  0000-0000 : 0000:00:04.0
  0000-0000 : 0000:00:05.0
    0000-0000 : Intel 82801AA-ICH
  0000-0000 : 0000:00:05.0
    0000-0000 : Intel 82801AA-ICH
  0000-0000 : 0000:00:08.0
    0000-0000 : e1000
  0000-0000 : 0000:00:0d.0
    0000-0000 : ahci
  0000-0000 : 0000:00:0d.0
    0000-0000 : ahci
  0000-0000 : 0000:00:0d.0
```

```
    0000-0000 : ahci
0000-0000 : 0000:00:0d.0
    0000-0000 : ahci
0000-0000 : 0000:00:0d.0
    0000-0000 : ahci
$
```

There are lots of different I/O ports in use on the Linux system at any time, so your output will most likely differ from this example. With PnP, I/O port conflicts aren't very common, but it is possible that two devices are assigned the same I/O port. In that case, you can manually override the settings automatically assigned by using the setpci command.

DIRECT MEMORY ACCESS

Using I/O ports to send data to the CPU can be somewhat slow. To speed things up, many devices use Direct Memory Access (DMA) channels. DMA channels do what the name implies—they send data from a hardware device directly to memory on the system, without having to wait for the CPU. The CPU can then read those memory locations to access the data when it's ready.

As with I/O ports, each hardware device that uses DMA must be assigned a unique channel number. To view the DMA channels currently in use on the system, just display the /proc/dma file.

```
$ cat /proc/dma
 4: cascade
$
```

This output indicates that only DMA channel 4 is in use on the Linux system.

The /sys Directory

Yet another tool available for working with devices is the /sys directory. The /sys directory is another virtual directory, similar to the /proc directory. It provides additional information about hardware devices that any user on the system can access.

There are lots of different information files available within the /sys directory. They are broken down into subdirectories based on the device and function in the system. You can take a look at the subdirectories and files available within the /sys directory on your system using the ls command-line command, as shown in Listing 9.5.

LISTING 9.5:   The Contents of the /sys Directory

```
$ ls -al /sys
total 4
dr-xr-xr-x  13 root root    0 Jan  4 14:37 .
drwxr-xr-x  21 root root 4096 Dec 21 19:49 ..
drwxr-xr-x   2 root root    0 Jan  4 14:37 block
drwxr-xr-x  42 root root    0 Jan  4 14:37 bus
```

```
drwxr-xr-x  65 root root    0 Jan  4 14:37 class
drwxr-xr-x   4 root root    0 Jan  4 14:37 dev
drwxr-xr-x  16 root root    0 Jan  4 14:37 devices
drwxr-xr-x   5 root root    0 Jan  4 14:37 firmware
drwxr-xr-x   9 root root    0 Jan  4 14:37 fs
drwxr-xr-x   2 root root    0 Jan  4 15:25 hypervisor
drwxr-xr-x  14 root root    0 Jan  4 14:37 kernel
drwxr-xr-x 168 root root    0 Jan  4 14:37 module
drwxr-xr-x   3 root root    0 Jan  4 15:25 power
$
```

Notice the different categories of information that are available. You can obtain information about the system bus, the devices, the kernel, and even the kernel modules installed.

Working with Devices

Linux provides a wealth of different command-line tools for using the devices connected to your system, as well as monitoring and troubleshooting the devices if there are problems. This section walks you through some of the more popular tools you'll want to know about when working with Linux devices.

Finding Devices

One of the first tasks for a new Linux administrator is to find the different devices installed on the Linux system. Fortunately, there are a few command-line tools to help with that.

THE *LSBLK* COMMAND

The lsblk command-line command displays information about the block devices installed on the Linux system. By default, the lsblk command displays all of the block devices, as shown in Listing 9.6.

LISTING 9.6:   The Output from the lsblk Command

```
$ lsblk
NAME              MAJ:MIN RM   SIZE RO TYPE MOUNTPOINT
loop0               7:0    0  55.4M  1 loop /snap/core18/1932
loop1               7:1    0  67.8M  1 loop /snap/lxd/18150
loop2               7:2    0  55.4M  1 loop /snap/core18/1944
loop3               7:3    0  71.3M  1 loop /snap/lxd/16099
loop4               7:4    0  31.1M  1 loop /snap/snapd/10238
loop5               7:5    0  31.1M  1 loop /snap/snapd/10492
sda                 8:0    0   16G   0 disk
├─sda1              8:1    0    1M   0 part
├─sda2              8:2    0    1G   0 part /boot
```

```
 └─sda3                        8:3   0   15G  0 part
   └─ubuntu--vg-ubuntu--lv 253:0   0   15G  0 lvm  /
 sr0                          11:0   1 57.8M  0 rom
 $
```

As you can see at the end of Listing 9.6, the lsblk command also indicates blocks that are related, as with the device-mapped LVM volumes and the associated physical hard drive. You can modify the lsblk output to see additional information about the blocks by adding command-line options. The −S option displays only information about SCSI and SATA block devices on the system.

```
$ lsblk -S
NAME HCTL       TYPE VENDOR   MODEL           REV TRAN
sda  2:0:0:0    disk ATA      VBOX_HARDDISK 1.0   sata
sr0  1:0:0:0    rom  VBOX     VBOX_CD-ROM   1.0   ata
$
```

This is a quick way to view the different SCSI and SATA drives installed on the system.

THE *DMESG* COMMAND

The *kernel ring buffer* records kernel-level event messages as they occur. Since it's a ring buffer, the event messages overwrite after the buffer area fills up. You can view the current messages in the kernel ring buffer by using the dmesg command. It helps to monitor it whenever you install a new device, as shown in Listing 9.7.

LISTING 9.7:   Partial Output from the dmesg Command

```
[ 4477.735599] usb 1-2: new full-speed USB device number 3 using ohci-pci
[ 4478.253882] usb 1-2: config 1 interface 0 altsetting 0 endpoint 0x81 has
 invalid maxpacket 512, setting to 64
[ 4478.253887] usb 1-2: config 1 interface 0 altsetting 0 endpoint 0x2 has
 invalid maxpacket 512, setting to 64
[ 4478.278753] usb 1-2: New USB device found, idVendor=0781,
 idProduct=5575, bcdDevice= 1.00
[ 4478.278758] usb 1-2: New USB device strings: Mfr=1, Product=2,
 SerialNumber=3
[ 4478.278761] usb 1-2: Product: Cruzer Glide
[ 4478.278764] usb 1-2: Manufacturer: SanDisk
[ 4478.278766] usb 1-2: SerialNumber: 2005103203115CC07E36
[ 4478.301341] usb-storage 1-2:1.0: USB Mass Storage device detected
[ 4478.302371] scsi host3: usb-storage 1-2:1.0
[ 4478.302431] usbcore: registered new interface driver usb-storage
[ 4478.304878] usbcore: registered new interface driver uas
[ 4479.347996] scsi 3:0:0:0: Direct-Access     SanDisk  Cruzer Glide
 1.00 PQ: 0 ANSI: 6
```

```
[ 4479.348398] sd 3:0:0:0: Attached scsi generic sg2 type 0
[ 4479.371561] sd 3:0:0:0: [sdb] 30595072 512-byte logical blocks: (15.7
 GB/14.6 GiB)
[ 4479.396443] sd 3:0:0:0: [sdb] Write Protect is off
[ 4479.396447] sd 3:0:0:0: [sdb] Mode Sense: 43 00 00 00
[ 4479.421924] sd 3:0:0:0: [sdb] Write cache: disabled, read cache:
 enabled, doesn't support DPO or FUA
[ 4479.545906]  sdb: sdb1
[ 4479.636754] sd 3:0:0:0: [sdb] Attached SCSI removable disk
```

The output from the `dmesg` command shows the steps the kernel took to recognize the new USB device that was plugged into the system.

The `dmesg` command is a great troubleshooting tool to use when a device isn't working correctly. It can help you determine if a hardware device module isn't loaded or didn't load correctly.

Working with PCI Cards

The `lspci` command allows you to view the currently installed and recognized PCI and PCIe cards on the Linux system. There are lots of command-line options you can include with the `lspci` command to display lots of different information about the PCI and PCIe cards installed on the system. Table 9.2 shows the more common ones that come in handy.

TABLE 9.2:   The `lspci` Command-Line Options

OPTION	DESCRIPTION
-A	Define the method to access the PCI information.
-b	Display connection information from the card point of view.
-k	Display the kernel driver modules for each installed PCI card.
-m	Display information in machine-readable format.
-n	Display vendor and device information as numbers instead of text.
-q	Query the centralized PCI database for information about the installed PCI cards.
-t	Display a tree diagram that shows the connections between cards and buses.
-v	Display additional information (verbose) about the cards.
-x	Display a hexadecimal output dump of the card information.

The output from the `lspci` command without any options shows all of the devices connected to the system, as shown in Listing 9.8.

LISTING 9.8:   Using the lspci Command

```
$ lspci
00:00.0 Host bridge: Intel Corporation 440FX - 82441FX PMC [Natoma] (rev 02)
00:01.0 ISA bridge: Intel Corporation 82371SB PIIX3 ISA [Natoma/Triton II]
00:01.1 IDE interface: Intel Corporation 82371AB/EB/MB PIIX4 IDE (rev 01)
00:02.0 VGA compatible controller: VMware SVGA II Adapter
00:03.0 Ethernet controller: Intel Corporation 82540EM Gigabit Ethernet
Controller (rev 02)
00:04.0 System peripheral: InnoTek Systemberatung GmbH VirtualBox Guest Service
00:05.0 Multimedia audio controller: Intel Corporation 82801AA AC'97 Audio
Controller (rev 01)
00:06.0 USB controller: Apple Inc. KeyLargo/Intrepid USB
00:07.0 Bridge: Intel Corporation 82371AB/EB/MB PIIX4 ACPI (rev 08)
00:08.0 Ethernet controller: Intel Corporation 82540EM Gigabit Ethernet
Controller (rev 02)
00:0d.0 SATA controller: Intel Corporation 82801HM/HEM (ICH8M/ICH8M-E) SATA
Controller [AHCI mode] (rev 02)
$
```

You can use the output from the lspci command to troubleshoot PCI card issues, such as if a card isn't recognized by the Linux system.

Working with USB Devices

You can view the basic information about USB devices connected to your Linux system by using the lsusb command. Table 9.3 shows the options that are available with that command.

TABLE 9.3:   The lsusb Command Options

OPTION	DESCRIPTION
-d	Display only devices from the specified vendor ID.
-D	Display information only from devices with the specified device file.
-s	Display information only from devices that use the specified bus.
-t	Display information in a tree format, showing related devices.
-v	Display additional information about the devices (verbose mode).
-V	Display the version of the lsusb program.

The basic lsusb program output looks like this:

```
$ lsusb
Bus 001 Device 003: ID 0781:5575 SanDisk Corp. Cruzer Glide
```

```
Bus 001 Device 002: ID 80ee:0021 VirtualBox USB Tablet
Bus 001 Device 001: ID 1d6b:0001 Linux Foundation 1.1 root hub
$
```

Most systems incorporate a standard USB hub for connecting multiple USB devices to the USB controller. Fortunately, there are only a handful of USB hubs on the market, so all Linux distributions include the device drivers necessary to communicate with each of these USB hubs. That guarantees that your Linux system will at least detect when a USB device is connected.

 Real World Scenario

ADDING A USB STORAGE DEVICE TO THE LINUX SYSTEM

This exercise walks you through how to view the kernel messages and device entries that occur when you connect a USB storage device to the Linux system.

1. Log into your Linux graphical desktop and open a command prompt window.

2. At the command prompt, enter the **lsusb** command to view any USB controllers and devices connected to your system.

3. Plug a USB storage device, such as a memory stick, into a USB port, and then wait a minute or so for the kernel to detect it.

4. Type the command **dmesg**, and observe the kernel ring buffer entries entered when the kernel detected the new USB device. Note the device name assigned to the new device (such as sdb1).

5. Type the **lsusb** command again and see if the new device appears in the output.

6. Type the command **ls /dev/sd*** to view the SCSI devices on the system. You should see the USB device name that appeared in the dmesg output appear as a device file in the /dev folder.

Using Hot Pluggable Devices

Computer hardware is generally categorized into two types.

♦ Cold pluggable devices

♦ Hot pluggable devices

Cold pluggable devices are hardware that can be connected to the system only when the system is completely powered down. These usually include things commonly found inside the computer case, such as memory, PCI cards, and hard drives. You can't remove any of these things while the system is running.

Conversely, you can usually add and remove *hot pluggable* devices at any time. These are often external components, such as network connections, monitors, and USB devices. The trick with hot pluggable devices is that somehow the Linux kernel needs to know when the device is connected and automatically load the correct device driver module to support the device.

Linux provides an entire subsystem that interacts with hot pluggable devices, making them accessible to users. This subsystem is described in the following sections.

Detecting Dynamic Devices

The *udev device manager* is a program that is automatically started at boot time and runs in the background at all times. It listens to kernel event messages regarding hardware devices. As you plug new hardware devices into the running system or remove existing hardware devices, the kernel sends out notification event messages.

The udev program listens to these notification messages and compares the messages against rules defined in a set of configuration files, normally stored under the /etc/udev/rules.d directory. If a device matches a defined rule, udev acts on the event notification as defined by the rule.

Each Linux distribution defines a standard set of rules for udev to follow. Rules define actions such as mounting USB memory sticks under the /media folder when they're installed or disabling network access when a USB network card is removed. You can modify the rules defined, but it's usually not necessary.

Working with Dynamic Devices

While the udev program runs in the background on your Linux system, you can still interact with it using the udevadm command-line tool. The udevadm command allows you to send commands to the udev program. The format of the udevadm command is as follows:

udevadm *command* [*options*]

Table 9.4 shows the commands available to send to the udevadm program.

TABLE 9.4: The udevadm Commands

COMMAND	DESCRIPTION
control	Modify the internal state of udev.
info	Query the udev database for device information.
monitor	Listen for kernel events and display them.
settle	Watch the udev event queue.
test	Simulate a udev event.
test-builtin	Run a built-in device command for debugging.
trigger	Request device events from the kernel.

The control command allows you to change the currently running udev program. For example, by adding the -R option, you can force udev to reload the rules defined in the /etc/dev/rules.d directory.

The Bottom Line

Use Linux device driver modules.   Similar to other operating systems, Linux uses device drivers to communicate with hardware devices connected to the system. The Linux kernel supports device modules, which allow you to dynamically insert or remove device driver software in the kernel as needed.

Master It   What command should you use to determine what hardware modules are currently installed on your Linux server?

Find device information for the system.   Besides the physical interfaces, Linux also uses files to communicate with devices. When you connect a device to the system, Linux automatically creates a file in the /dev directory that's used for applications to send data to and receive data from the devices. The kernel uses the /proc directory to create virtual files that contain information about the devices and system status. The /sys directory is also used by the kernel to create files useful for troubleshooting device issues.

Master It   Your boss just sent you an email asking what CPU and memory are installed in the Linux server. You know that you can find the information in the /proc/cpuinfo and /proc/meminfo files, but what command(s) should you use to obtain that information?

Work with PCI and USB devices.   Linux provides a handful of command-line tools that are useful when you're trying to troubleshoot device problems. The lsdev command allows you to view the status and settings for all devices on the system. The lsblk command provides information about block devices, such as hard drives and network cards, that are connected. The dmesg command lets you peek at the kernel ring buffer to view kernel event messages as it detects and works with devices. The lspci and lsusb commands allow you to view the PCI and USB devices that are connected to the Linux system.

Master It   You've just plugged in a USB storage device, but the server doesn't recognize it. What command should you use to determine if the correct device module loaded or if there's some other problem?

Chapter 10

Booting Linux

When you turn on the power to your Linux system, it triggers a series of events that eventually leads to a login prompt. Normally, you don't worry about what happens behind the scenes of those events; you just log in and start using your applications and services.

However, there may be times when your Linux system doesn't start quite correctly, or perhaps an application that you expected to be running isn't. In those cases, it helps to have a basic understanding of just how Linux loads the operating system and starts programs so you can troubleshoot the problem.

IN THIS CHAPTER, YOU WILL LEARN TO

- ◆ Diagnose the Linux boot process
- ◆ Configure a bootloader
- ◆ Interact with a bootloader
- ◆ Stop and start services after boot
- ◆ Analyze service startup times

Understanding the Boot Process

Starting a server and loading its operating system is called *booting*. The term has a history in the old saying, "pull yourself up by your bootstraps," which means to physically pull yourself up from lying on the floor to an upright position using small straps on your boots. Pulling yourself up off the floor using nothing but bootstraps is physically impossible, and it seems like that's what a system is doing when it boots up—an impossible task. However, once the process is demystified, the order and logic behind it make sense.

As a Linux administrator, it is important to understand the details of booting a Linux server. This section walks through the steps of the boot process and how you can watch the boot process to see what steps failed.

Overview of the Boot Process

The Linux boot process can be split into three main steps.

1. The server firmware starts, performing a quick check of the hardware (called a Power-On Self Test, or POST), and then looks for a bootloader program to run from a bootable device.

2. The bootloader runs and determines what Linux kernel program to load.

3. The kernel program loads into memory and starts the necessary background programs required for the system to operate (such as web and database servers on a server system).

While on the surface these three steps may seem simple, a ballet of operations happens to keep the boot process working. Each step performs several actions as they prepare your system to run Linux.

Watching the Boot Process

You can monitor the Linux boot process by watching the system console screen as the system boots. You'll see lots of informative messages scroll by as the system detects hardware and loads software.

Usually the boot messages scroll by somewhat quickly and it's hard to see what's happening. If you need to troubleshoot boot problems, you can review the boot-time messages using the dmesg command. Most Linux distributions copy the boot kernel messages into a special ring buffer in memory, called the *kernel ring buffer*. The buffer is circular and set to a predetermined size. As new messages are logged in the buffer, older messages are rotated out.

The dmesg command displays the most recent boot messages that are currently stored in the kernel ring buffer, as shown snipped here:

```
$ dmesg
[    0.000000] Linux version 4.18.0-193.28.1.el8_2.x86_64
 (mockbuild@kbuilder.bsys.centos.org) (gcc version 8.3.1 20191121
 (Red Hat 8.3.1-5) (GCC)) #1 SMP Thu Oct 22 00:20:22 UTC 2020
[    0.000000] Command line: BOOT_IMAGE=(hd0,msdos1)/vmlinuz-4.18.0-
193.28.1.el8_2.x86_64 root=/dev/mapper/cl-root ro crashkernel=auto
resume=/dev/mapper/cl-swap rd.lvm.lv=cl/root rd.lvm.lv=cl/
swap rhgb quiet
[...]
[   47.263987] IPv6: ADDRCONF(NETDEV_UP): enp0s8: link is not ready
[   47.454715] IPv6: ADDRCONF(NETDEV_UP): enp0s8: link is not ready
[   48.161674] IPv6: ADDRCONF(NETDEV_CHANGE): enp0s8: link
becomes ready
$
```

Most Linux distributions also store the boot messages in a log file, usually in the /var/log folder. For Debian-based systems, such as Ubuntu, the file is usually /var/log/boot or /var/log/bootstrap.log, and for Red Hat–based systems, such as CentOS, the file is /var/log/boot.log.

While it helps to be able to see the different messages generated during boot time, it is also helpful to know just what generates those messages. This chapter discusses each of these three boot steps and goes through some examples showing just how they work.

The Firmware Startup

All IBM-compatible servers utilize some type of built-in firmware to control how the installed operating system starts. On older servers, this firmware was called the Basic Input/Output

System (BIOS). On newer servers, the Unified Extensible Firmware Interface (UEFI) maintains the system hardware status and launches an installed operating system.

THE BIOS STARTUP

The BIOS firmware had a simplistic menu interface. It allowed you to change some settings to control how the system found hardware and define what device the BIOS should use to start the operating system.

One limitation of the original BIOS firmware was that it could read only one sector's worth of data from a hard drive into memory to run. That's not enough space to load an entire operating system. To get around that limitation, most operating systems split the boot process into two parts.

First, the BIOS ran a bootloader program, a small program that initialized the necessary hardware to find and run the full operating system program. It was often found at another location on the same hard drive, but sometimes on a separate internal or external storage device.

The bootloader program usually had a configuration file, so you could tell it just where to look to find the actual operating system file to run. Also, you could use the configuration to produce a small menu, allowing the user to boot between multiple operating systems.

To get things started, the BIOS had to know where to find the bootloader program on an installed storage device. Most BIOS setups allowed you to load the bootloader program from several locations.

- An internal hard drive

- An external hard drive

- A CD or DVD drive

- A USB memory stick

- An ISO file

- A network server using either NFS, HTTP, or FTP

When booting from a hard drive, you had to designate the hard drive, and partition on the hard drive, from which the BIOS should load the bootloader program. This was done by defining a master boot record (MBR).

The MBR was the first sector on the first hard drive partition on the system. There was only one MBR for the computer system. The BIOS looked for the MBR and read the program stored there into memory. Since the bootloader program had to fit in one sector, it had to be very small, so it couldn't do too much. The bootloader program mainly pointed to the location of the actual operating system kernel file, stored in a boot sector of a separate partition installed on the system. There were no size limitations on kernel boot files.

The bootloader program wasn't required to point directly to an operating system kernel file. It could point to any type of program, including another bootloader program. You could create a primary bootloader program that pointed to a secondary bootloader program, which provided options to load multiple operating systems. This process is called *chainloading*.

As operating systems became more complicated, it eventually became clear that a new boot method needed to be developed. However, be aware that there are still some systems that use the old BIOS startup process.

THE UEFI STARTUP

Intel created the Extensible Firmware Interface (EFI) in 1998 to address some of the limitations of BIOS. By 2005, the idea caught on with other vendors, and the Universal EFI (UEFI) specification was adopted as a standard. These days, just about all IBM-compatible server systems utilize the UEFI firmware standard.

Not all Linux distributions support the UEFI firmware. If you're going to use a UEFI system, ensure that the Linux distribution you select supports it.

Instead of relying on a single boot sector on a hard drive to hold the bootloader program, UEFI specifies a special disk partition, called the EFI System Partition (ESP) to store bootloader programs. This allows for any size of bootloader program, plus the ability to store multiple bootloader programs for multiple operating systems.

The ESP setup utilizes the old Microsoft File Allocation Table (FAT) filesystem to store the bootloader programs. On Linux systems, the ESP is typically mounted in the `/boot/efi` directory (mounting concepts are covered in Chapter 11, "Working with Storage Devices"), and the bootloader files are typically stored using the `.efi` filename extension, such as `linux.efi`.

The UEFI firmware utilizes a built-in mini bootloader (sometimes referred to as a *boot manager*) that allows you to configure just which bootloader program file to launch.

With UEFI, you need to register each individual bootloader file you want to appear at boot time in the boot manager interface menu. You can then select the bootloader to run each time you boot the system.

Once the firmware finds and runs the bootloader, its job is done. The bootloader step in the boot process is somewhat complicated. The next section dives into covering that.

The GRUB2 Bootloader

The bootloader program helps bridge the gap between the system firmware and the full Linux operating system kernel. In Linux, there are several choices of bootloaders to use. However, the most popular one is Grand Unified Bootloader 2, which is more commonly referred to as GRUB2.

There's a little bit of evolution behind GRUB2, which is helpful in understanding this bootloader program.

Linux Loader In the original versions of Linux, the Linux Loader (LILO) bootloader was the only bootloader program available. It was extremely limited in what it could do, but it accomplished its purpose—loading the Linux kernel from the BIOS startup. LILO became the default bootloader used by Linux distributions in the 1990s. The LILO configuration file was stored in a single file, `/etc/lilo.conf`, which defined the systems to boot. Unfortunately, LILO doesn't work with UEFI systems, so it had limited use on modern systems and quickly faded into history.

GRUB The first version of the GRUB bootloader (now called GRUB Legacy) was created in 1999 to provide a more robust and configurable bootloader to replace LILO. GRUB quickly became the default bootloader for all Linux distributions, whether they were run on BIOS or UEFI systems.

GRUB2 GRUB2 was created in 2005 as a complete rewrite of the GRUB Legacy system. It supports advanced features, such as the ability to load hardware driver modules and use logic statements to dynamically alter the boot menu options, depending on conditions detected on the system (such as if an external hard drive is connected).

The GRUB2 bootloader program has maintained its popularity through the years, and it still holds the position of the most used bootloader among Linux distributions. Since Linux kernel v3.3.0, the UEFI can load any size of a program, including the kernel itself, so a bootloader is no longer necessary. However, using this method isn't common, due to the fact that bootloader programs, such as GRUB2, provide more versatility in booting a Linux system.

Configuring the GRUB2 Bootloader

The GRUB2 bootloader was designed to simplify the process of the booting, and this includes the management of the process. It provides both an interactive boot menu and a shell. This section walks through understanding GRUB2 bootloader configuration basics, how to interact with its menu and shell at boot time, and some troubleshooting techniques.

Exploring the GRUB2 Configuration

You'll often find that there is no need to make changes in your GRUB2 configuration. For example, when your system's Linux kernel is upgraded, GRUB2 looks for any kernels (new and old) on the system and attempts to create boot menu entries for each one. That way, if a new kernel fails, you can pick an older kernel from the boot menu to get the system up and running. Figure 10.1 shows a GRUB2 boot menu on a CentOS distribution with older an Linux kernel available for selection.

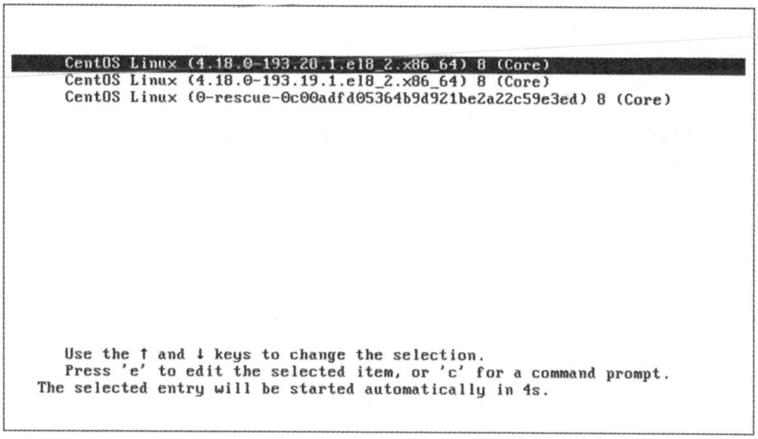

FIGURE 10.1
A CentOS
GRUB2 boot menu

```
    CentOS Linux (4.18.0-193.20.1.el8_2.x86_64) 8 (Core)
    CentOS Linux (4.18.0-193.19.1.el8_2.x86_64) 8 (Core)
    CentOS Linux (0-rescue-0c00adfd05364b9d921be2a22c59e3ed) 8 (Core)




       Use the ↑ and ↓ keys to change the selection.
       Press 'e' to edit the selected item, or 'c' for a command prompt.
     The selected entry will be started automatically in 4s.
```

GRUB2 uses the grub.cfg configuration file to design its boot menu and/or directly load the kernel. Depending on your distribution and configuration, this file resides in either the /boot/ grub/ or the /boot/grub2/ directory.

DETERMINING YOUR SYSTEM'S GRUB2 LOCATIONS AND COMMANDS

Linux distributions potentially vary widely when it comes to their implementation of GRUB2. You can quickly determine where the grub.cfg file resides by issuing the command **ls /boot/grub** and then **ls /boot/grub2**; when you see the grub.cfg file, you'll know in which directory it lives.

You may need to use super user privileges to view these directories; if so, either log into the root account or employ the sudo command along with ls.

Knowing which GRUB2 commands are available on your distro is helpful as well. Type **man -k grub** at the command line and press Enter to get a quick list of the available commands. (If this command does not display any commands for you, it's possible you need to use super user privileges and issue the **mandb** command to update the man page's index.)

You should never directly modify the grub.cfg file. This configuration file is generated by the grub-mkconfig command, the grub2-mkconfig command, and/or other GRUB2 utilities. So any changes you make directly in the file are lost the next time one of these programs is run.

The GRUB2 configuration file is built from a set of individual files in the /etc/grub.d/ directory. Also, a control file, /etc/default/grub, is used in building grub.cfg, which manages such items as the boot menu's appearance and what command-line arguments are passed to a Linux kernel at boot time.

The files in the /etc/grub.d directory are a series of high-level shell script files (basic shell scripting is covered in Chapter 19, "Writing Scripts"). These scripts are called *helper scripts*, because they help the GRUB2 utilities in generating the grub.cfg configuration file. The following example is a list of the helper scripts on an Ubuntu distribution. At the end of the example, the file command is used on one file to show that it is indeed a shell script.

```
$ ls -l /etc/grub.d
total 128
-rwxr-xr-x 1 root root 10627 Jul 31 00:34 00_header
-rwxr-xr-x 1 root root  6258 Jul 20 18:19 05_debian_theme
-rwxr-xr-x 1 root root 17622 Sep  8 10:24 10_linux
-rwxr-xr-x 1 root root 42359 Sep  8 10:24 10_linux_zfs
-rwxr-xr-x 1 root root 12894 Jul 31 00:34 20_linux_xen
-rwxr-xr-x 1 root root 12059 Jul 31 00:34 30_os-prober
-rwxr-xr-x 1 root root  1424 Jul 31 00:34 30_uefi-firmware
-rwxr-xr-x 1 root root   214 Jul 31 00:34 40_custom
-rwxr-xr-x 1 root root   216 Jul 31 00:34 41_custom
-rw-r--r-- 1 root root   483 Jul 31 00:34 README
$
$ file /etc/grub.d/10_linux
/etc/grub.d/10_linux: POSIX shell script, ASCII text executable
$
```

Notice that a number precedes each script file's name. These numbers guide the utilities that use the helper scripts so that the files are processed in a particular order. Be aware that on some Linux distributions, such as CentOS, you have to use super user privileges to see this information concerning the helper scripts.

Some administrators add customized boot menu entries by modifying the 40_custom script. You'll rarely, if ever, need to make changes to this helper script.

You'll often want to modify items in the GRUB2 control file, /etc/default/grub, which contains settings called *keys*. These keys manage the appearance and behavior of the boot menu. Table 10.1 describes the more commonly set keys.

TABLE 10.1:   Commonly Defined /etc/default/grub Keys

KEY	DESCRIPTION
GRUB_CMDLINE_LINUX	Sets the argument(s) to pass to the Linux kernel for all boot menu entries
GRUB_DEFAULT	Defines the default boot menu entry
GRUB_DISABLE_RECOVERY	When set to true, disables the generation of recovery mode boot menu entries
GRUB_DISABLE_SUBMENU	When set to true, disables the use of submenus in the boot menu, and lists all entries in the top menu
GRUB_DISTRIBUTOR	Sets the distribution's name and/or information in the boot menu
GRUB_GFXMODE	Defines the resolution on a graphical terminal, if used
GRUB_INIT_TUNE	Sets a sound to play when the menu starts
GRUB_TERMINAL	Defines the terminal input and output devices
GRUB_TIMEOUT	When no selection is made, sets the number of seconds until the default boot menu entry is selected (If set to 0, the boot menu is not displayed.)
GRUB_TIMEOUT_STYLE	Defines the method of handling the boot menu and the GRUB_TIMEOUT through one of three possible settings: ◆ menu—Displays the boot menu; honors the timeout setting ◆ countdown—Does not display the boot menu; shows the time remaining till the default boot selection is chosen ◆ hidden—Does not display the boot menu; honors the timeout setting

Once you've completed making changes to either the control file or the 40_custom helper script file, you need to update the grub.cfg configuration file. This is done by running the grub-mkconfig, grub2-mkconfig, update-grub, or update-grub2 command with super user privileges, depending on your distribution.

```
# grub-mkconfig > /boot/grub/grub.cfg
```

Notice that you must redirect the output of the program to the grub.cfg configuration file. By default, these update programs just output the new configuration file commands to standard output.

Interacting with GRUB2

When the GRUB2 boot menu displays during the boot process, you can wait for the timeout to expire (if set), and the default boot menu selection will process. Alternatively, you can use the arrow keys to select one of the other menu options and press Enter to boot it.

DISPLAYING THE BOOT MENU

Be aware that if your Linux system's boot menu doesn't display, as is typical for some distributions such as Ubuntu server, it's most likely due to GRUB2 control file (/etc/default/grub) settings. If the GRUB_TIMEOUT key is set to 0, the boot menu is not displayed, and you'll need to modify that definition and regenerate the grub.cfg file to change the behavior. If GRUB_TIMEOUT is *not* set to 0 and the GRUB_TIMEOUT_STYLE is set to hidden, to see the menu you'll need to press the Esc key at the right time. It is often tricky to know when to press the Esc key, so it may take some practice. Most admins just press Esc multiple times during the boot sequence in this situation.

You can also edit boot options from the GRUB menu on the fly. First, use the arrow key to the boot option you want to modify, and press the E key. Then use the arrow key to move the cursor to the line you need to modify, and edit it. Once you have completed your edits, press the B key to boot the system using the new values.

For on-the-fly changes during the boot process, besides modifying the boot menu, you can also access the GRUB2 interactive shell to submit commands. This shell is accessed by pressing the C key from the boot menu.

There are several commands available in the interactive shell, and you can see them all after you are in the shell by typing **help** and pressing Enter. You'll have to press the spacebar multiple times to return to the GRUB2 interactive shell prompt. To view the syntax needed for these commands as well a brief description, type **help** followed by the command name, such as help cat.

Once you have completed using the interactive shell, press Ctrl+X to use the settings made in the interactive shell to finish booting the system. If you'd like to discard any modifications made in the shell, press the Esc key to return to the boot menu.

 Real World Scenario

EXPLORING THE GRUB2 KEY SETTINGS AND MENU

Typically, you'll never have to do much with the GRUB2 bootloader. However, you don't want your first experience with it to be one in which an emergency is occurring. Therefore, it's a good idea to go exploring through the GRUB2 configuration and boot menu, take a look around, and try a few things.

The following steps will take you through exploring the GRUB2 key settings and interacting with its boot menu:

1. Log into a Linux system, using the sysadmin account and the password you created for it.

2. View the GRUB2 key settings by typing **less /etc/default/grub** and pressing Enter.

3. Looking at the /etc/default/grub key settings, determine the default boot menu entry by finding the GRUB_DEFAULT definition. Note that the first boot menu entry is selected by default, if GRUB_DEFAULT is set to 0. If it is set to 1, the second boot menu entry is selected, and so on. Record your findings.

4. Continuing to view the /etc/default/grub key settings, and determine if the GRUB_ TIMEOUT_STYLE is defined. Using the following process to record what you found in this step:

    a. If it is set to hidden, you will not see the boot menu when the system starts, and you will have to press the Esc key at the right time to view it (as long as GRUB_TIMEOUT is not set to 0).

    b. If GRUB_TIMEOUT_STYLE is set to countdown, you'll have to press the Esc key to view the boot menu when the system starts, and you'll see a countdown on the screen.

    c. If GRUB_TIMEOUT_STYLE is not defined or set to menu, you will be able to view the boot menu without any additional actions on your part.

5. Still looking at the /etc/default/grub key settings, determine the boot menu timeout and default boot menu autoselection by finding the GRUB_TIMEOUT and GRUB_DEFAULT definitions. Record what you find.

6. Press the Q key to quit the less pager and return to the command-line prompt.

7. If you found that your system's GRUB_TIMEOUT is set to 0, skip the rest of the steps in this exercise. (If desired, you can change that setting from 0 to 10 and rebuild the grub.cfg file using the appropriate commands, and then continue with this exercise.)

8. Type **poweroff** at the command prompt and press Enter to shut down the Linux system.

9. Once the system is stopped, read the next step, and then start your Linux system.

10. If your system's boot menu is not set to appear by default, take the appropriate action from what you determined in step 4.

11. Once you see the GRUB2 boot menu, press the E key to enter into edit mode.

12. Do not modify anything within this mode, but use your arrow keys to explore the information listed there. Try to find the line that starts with linux16 or linux (this line loads the Linux kernel) and view the entire line using your arrow keys.

13. Once you are done looking at the boot entry information, press the Esc key and then Enter to finish booting the system.

Once the kernel program is loaded into memory, the bootloader's job is done. Now the Linux kernel takes over and starts the initialization process. We'll cover that topic next.

The systemd Initialization Process

After your Linux system has traversed the boot process, it enters the final system initialization process, where it starts various services. A service, or *daemon,* is a program that performs a particular duty. The systemd initialization method is the most popular system service initialization and management mechanism.

Beyond initialization, systemd (also considered a *daemon*) is responsible for managing these services. We'll take a look at the various systemd components used for starting services at boot time, as well as the ones for managing them.

Exploring Unit Files

The easiest way to start exploring systemd is through the *systemd units*. A unit defines a service, a group of services, or an action. Each unit consists of a name, a type, and a configuration file. There are currently 12 different systemd unit types, as follows:

◆ automount

◆ device

◆ mount

◆ path

◆ scope

◆ service

◆ slice

◆ snapshot

◆ socket

◆ swap

◆ target

◆ timer

The systemctl command is the main utility to managing systemd and system services. Its basic syntax is as follows:

```
systemctl [OPTIONS...] COMMAND [NAME...]
```

You can use the systemctl utility to display a list of the various units currently loaded in your Linux system. A snipped example is shown here:

```
$ systemctl list-units
  UNIT                      LOAD   ACTIVE SUB     DESCRIPTION
[...]
  atd.service               loaded active running Job spoo[...]
  auditd.service            loaded active running Security[...]
[...]
  multi-user.target         loaded active active  Multi-Us[...]

121 loaded units listed. Pass --all to see loaded but inactive[...]
To show all installed unit files use 'systemctl list-unit-file[...]
$
```

In the example, you can see various units as well as additional information. Units are identified by their name and type using the format *name*.*type*. System services (daemons) have unit files with the .service extension. Thus, the job spooling daemon, atd, has a unit filename of atd.service.

Be aware that many displays from the systemctl utility use the less pager by default (The less pager was first covered in Chapter 6, "Working with the Shell"). Thus, to exit the displayed output, you must press the Q key. If you want to turn off the systemctl utility's use of the less pager, tack on the --no-pager option to the command.

Groups of services are started via target unit files. At system startup, the default.target unit is responsible for ensuring that all required and desired services are launched at system initialization. The default.target unit is actually a pointer to another target unit file, as shown here using the systemctl get-default command:

```
$ systemctl get-default
multi-user.target
$
```

Though multi-user.target is typically the default target unit file on Linux server systems, others are often employed as well. Table 10.2 shows the more commonly used system boot target unit files.

TABLE 10.2: Commonly Used System Boot Target Unit Files

NAME	DESCRIPTION
graphical.target	Provides multiple users access to the system via local terminals and/or through the network. Graphical user interface (GUI) access is offered, if available.
multi-user.target	Provides multiple users access to the system via local terminals and/or through the network. No GUI access is offered.
runleveln.target	Provides backward compatibility to SysV init (initialization) systems, where n is set to 1–5 for the desired SysV runlevel equivalence

If you need to change the group of services started at boot time, the command to use is systemctl set-default target-unit. You'll need to use super user privileges or be logged into the root account for this to work properly.

Focusing on Service Unit Files

Service unit files contain service information, such as when a service must be started, what targets want this service started, documentation resources, and so on. These configuration files are located in different directories.

A unit configuration file's directory location is critical, because if a file is found in two different directory locations, one will have precedence over the other. The following list shows the directory locations in ascending priority order:

1. /etc/systemd/system/

2. /run/systemd/system/

3. /usr/lib/systemd/system/

To see the various service unit files available, you can again employ the systemctl utility. However, a slightly different argument is needed than when viewing units, as shown here:

```
$ systemctl list-unit-files
UNIT FILE                                STATE
proc-sys-fs-binfmt_misc.automount        static
[...]
atd.service                              enabled
auditd.service                           enabled
[...]
$
```

Besides the unit file's base name in this command's output, you also see a unit file's state. This is called an *enablement state* and refers to when the service is started. There are at least 12 different enablement states, but you'll commonly see these:

◆ enabled: Service starts at system boot.

◆ disabled: Service does not start at system boot.

◆ static: Service starts if another unit depends on it. Can also be manually started.

To determine what directory or directories store a particular systemd unit file (or files), use the systemctl utility's cat command. An example on a CentOS distribution is shown here:

```
$ systemctl cat atd.service
# /usr/lib/systemd/system/atd.service
[Unit]
Description=Job spooling tools
After=syslog.target systemd-user-sessions.service

[Service]
EnvironmentFile=/etc/sysconfig/atd
ExecStart=/usr/sbin/atd -f $OPTS
IgnoreSIGPIPE=no

[Install]
WantedBy=multi-user.target
$
```

Notice that the first displayed line shows the atd.service unit file's directory location (/usr/lib/systemd/system/) and base name (atd.service). The next several lines are the unit configuration file's contents.

For service unit files, there are three primary configuration sections. They are as follows:

◆ [Unit]

◆ [Service]

◆ [Install]

Within the service unit configuration file's [Unit] section, there are basic *directives*. A directive is a setting that modifies a configuration, such as the After setting shown in the earlier example. Table 10.3 shows the more commonly used [Unit] section directives.

TABLE 10.3:   Commonly Used Service Unit File [Unit] Section Directives

DIRECTIVE	DESCRIPTION
After	Sets this unit to start after the designated units
Before	Sets this unit to start before the designated units
Description	Describes the unit
Documentation	Sets a list of uniform resource identifiers (URIs) that point to documentation sources. The URIs can be web locations, particular system files, info pages, and man pages
Conflicts	Sets this unit to *not* start with the designated units. If any of the designated units start, this unit is not started. (Opposite of Requires)
Requires	Sets this unit to start together with the designated units. If any of the designated units do not start, this unit is *not* started. (Opposite of Conflicts)
Wants	Sets this unit to start together with the designated units. If any of the designated units do not start, this unit is still started.

The [Service] directives within a unit file set configuration items, which are specific to that service. You will only find a unit file [Service] section in a service unit file. This middle section is different for each unit type. For example, in auto mount unit files, you would find an [Automount] section as the middle unit file section.

Table 10.4 describes the more commonly used [Service] section directives.

TABLE 10.4:   Commonly Used Service Unit File [Service] Section Directives

DIRECTIVE	DESCRIPTION
ExecReload	Indicates scripts or commands (and options) to run when unit is reloaded
ExecStart	Indicates scripts or commands (and options) to run when unit is started
ExecStop	Indicates scripts or commands (and options) to run when unit is stopped
Environment	Sets environment variable substitutes, separated by a space
Environment File	Indicates a file that contains environment variable substitutes

TABLE 10.4: Commonly Used Service Unit File [Service] Section Directives *(CONTINUED)*

DIRECTIVE	DESCRIPTION
RemainAfterExit	Set to either no (default) or yes. If set to yes, the service is left active even when the process started by ExecStart terminates. If set to no, then ExecStop is called when the process started by ExecStart terminates.
Restart	Service is restarted when the process started by ExecStart terminates. It is ignored if a systemctl restart or systemctl stop command is issued. Set to no (default), on-success, on-failure, on-abnormal, on-watchdog, on-abort, or always.
Type	Sets the startup type

The [Service] Type directive needs a little more explanation than what is given in Table 10.4. This directive can be set to at least six different specifications, of which the most typical are listed here:

◆ forking—ExecStart starts a parent process. The parent process creates the service's main process as a child process and exits.

◆ simple—(Default) ExecStart starts the service's main process.

◆ oneshot—ExecStart starts the service's main process, which is typically a configuration setting or a quick command, and the process exits.

◆ idle—ExecStart starts the service's main process, but it waits until all other start jobs are finished.

The [Install] directives within a unit file determine what happens to a particular service if it is enabled or disabled. An *enabled service* is one that starts at system boot. A *disabled service* is one that does *not* start at system boot. Table 10.5 describes the more commonly used [Install] section directives.

TABLE 10.5: Commonly Used Service Unit File [Install] Section Directives

DIRECTIVE	DESCRIPTION
Alias	Sets additional names that can be used to denote the service in systemctl commands
Also	Sets additional units that must be enabled or disabled for this service. Often the additional units are socket type units
RequiredBy	Designates other units that require this service
WantedBy	Designates which target unit manages this service

There is a great deal of useful information in the man pages for systemd and unit configuration files. Just type in **man -k systemd** to find several items you can explore. For example, explore the service type unit file directives and more via the man systemd.service command. You can find information on all the various directives by typing in **man systemd.directives** at the command line.

 Real World Scenario

LOOKING AT SERVICE UNIT FILES

The systemd daemon performs the heavy-duty method of creating and configuring the various service unit files. However, it is still a good idea to understand their directives so you can manage any needed tweaks or quickly deal with problems.

The following steps will take you through exploring a service unit file:

1. Log into a Linux system using the sysadmin account and the password you created for it.

2. List the various enabled systemd service unit files on your system by typing **systemctl list-unit-files *.service | grep enabled** and pressing Enter.

3. From the list in the previous step, pick a service unit file (for example, syslog.service).

4. View the service unit file by typing **systemctl cat *chosen-service-file*** and pressing Enter, where *chosen-service-file* is the service unit file you picked in the previous step (for example, systemctl cat syslog.service).

5. Looking at the displayed service unit file, answer the following questions:

   a. What directory does this file reside in? (Hint: Look at the first line in the file.)

   b. From the Description in the [Unit] section, for what is this service used?

   c. If a Documentation directive is in the [Unit] section, what documentation is available to learn more about this service?

   d. If a WantedBy directive is in the [Install] section, what target unit file wants this service started?

Understanding service unit files is helpful, especially if you have to troubleshoot a problem with a service not starting when the system boots. Another unit file type that needs special attention is the target unit file. We'll explore that topic next.

Focusing on Target Unit Files

As mentioned previously, the primary purpose of target unit files is to group together various services to start at system boot time. The default target unit file, default.target, is linked to the target unit file used at system boot. In this example, the default target unit file is located and displayed using the systemctl command on a CentOS distribution.

```
$ systemctl get-default
multi-user.target
$
```

```
$ systemctl cat multi-user.target
# /usr/lib/systemd/system/multi-user.target
[...]
[Unit]
Description=Multi-User System
Documentation=man:systemd.special(7)
Requires=basic.target
Conflicts=rescue.service rescue.target
After=basic.target rescue.service rescue.target
AllowIsolate=yes
$
```

Notice that the multi-user.target unit file has many of the same [Unit] directives as a service unit file has in its [Unit] section. These directives were described earlier in Table 10.3. Of course, these directives apply to a target type unit file instead of a service type unit file. For example, the After directive in the multi-user.target unit file sets this target unit to start after the designated units, such as basic.target. Target units, similar to service units, have various target dependency chains as well as conflicts.

In the previous example, there is one directive we have not covered yet—the AllowIsolate directive, if set to yes, permits the systemctl isolate command to use this target file. The isolate command is covered later in this chapter.

Changing a Unit Configuration File

Occasionally, you may need to change a particular unit configuration file for your Linux system's requirements or add components. However, be careful when doing this task. You should not modify any unit files in the /lib/systemd/system/ or /usr/lib/systemd/system/ directory.

To modify a unit configuration file, copy the file to the /etc/systemd/system/ directory and modify it there. This modified file will take precedence over the original unit file left in the original directory. Also, it will protect the modified unit file from software updates.

If you just have a few additional components, you can extend the configuration. Using super user privileges, create a new subdirectory in the /etc/systemd/system/ directory named *service.service-name*.d, where *service-name* is the service's name. For example, for the openSSH daemon, you would create the /etc/systemd/system/service.sshd.d directory. This newly created directory is called a drop-in file directory, because you can drop-in additional configuration files. Create any configuration files with names like *description*.conf, where *description* describes the configuration file's purpose, such as local or script. Add your modified directives to this configuration file.

After making these modifications, there are a few more needed steps. Find and compare any unit file that overrides another unit file by issuing the systemd-delta command. It will display any unit files that are duplicated, extended, redirected, and so on. Review this list. It will help you avoid any unintended consequences from modifying or extending a service unit file.

To have your changes take effect, issue the systemctl daemon-reload command for the service whose unit file you modified or extended. After you accomplish that task, you may need to issue the systemctl restart command to start or restart the service. This command is explained in the next section.

Changing the systemd Configuration File

The master systemd configuration file, system.conf, is located in the /etc/systemd/ directory. In this file, you will find all the default configuration settings commented out via a hash mark (#). Viewing this file is a quick way to see the current systemd configuration. Here is a snipped listing of this file:

```
$ cat /etc/systemd/system.conf
[...]
# See systemd-system.conf(5) for details.

[Manager]
#LogLevel=info
#LogTarget=journal-or-kmsg
#LogColor=yes
#LogLocation=no
#DumpCore=yes
#ShowStatus=yes
[...]
#IPAddressAllow=
#IPAddressDeny=
$
```

If you need to modify the configuration, just edit the file. However, it would be wise to peruse the file's man page first by typing **man systemd-system.conf** at the command line.

Looking at *systemctl*

There are several basic systemctl commands available for you to manage system services. We've already looked at a few of them, but several more deserve our attention. One that is often used after a system is booted is the status command. It provides a wealth of information. A couple of snipped examples are shown here:

```
$ systemctl status console-getty
• console-getty.service - Console Getty
   Loaded: loaded [...]disabled[...]
   Active: inactive (dead)
     Docs: man:agetty(8)
           man:systemd-getty-generator(8)
$
$ systemctl status atd
• atd.service - Job spooling tools
   Loaded: loaded [...]enabled[...]
   Active: active (running) since Wed [...]
 Main PID: 1123 (atd)
    Tasks: 1 (limit: 11479)
   Memory: 748.0K
   CGroup: /system.slice/atd.service
           └─1123 /usr/sbin/atd -f
$
```

The first `systemctl` command shows the status of the `console-getty` service. Notice the third line in the utility's output. It states that the service is `disabled`. The fourth line states that the service is `inactive`. In essence, this means that the `console-getty` service is not running (`inactive`) and is not configured to start at system boot time (`disabled`). The status of the `atd` service is also displayed, showing that `atd` is running (`active`) and configured to start at system boot time (`enabled`).

There are several simple commands you can use with the `systemctl` utility to manage systemd services and view information regarding them. Table 10.6 describes the more common commands. These `systemctl` commands generally use the following syntax:

```
systemctl COMMAND UNIT-NAME...
```

TABLE 10.6:   Commonly Used `systemctl` Service Management Commands

COMMAND	DESCRIPTION
daemon-reload	Load the unit configuration file of the running designated unit(s) to make unit file configuration changes without stopping the service. Note that this is different from the `reload` command.
disable	Mark the designated unit(s) to *not* be started automatically at system boot time.
enable	Mark the designated unit(s) to be started automatically at system boot time.
mask	Prevent the designated unit(s) from starting. The service cannot be started using the `start` command or at system boot. Use the `--now` option to immediately stop any running instances as well. Use the `--running` option to mask the service only until the next reboot or unmask is used.
restart	Stop and immediately restart the designated unit(s). If a designated unit is not already started, this will simply start it.
start	Start the designated unit(s).
status	Display the designated unit's current status.
stop	Stop the designated unit(s).
reload	Load the service configuration file of the running designated unit(s) to make service configuration changes without stopping the service. Note that this is different from the `daemon-reload` command.
unmask	Undo the effects of the `mask` command on the designated unit(s).

Notice the difference in Table 10.6 between the `daemon-reload` and `reload` commands. This is an important difference. Use the `daemon-reload` command if you need to load systemd unit file configuration changes for a running service. Use the `reload` command to load a service's modified configuration file. For example, if your system used the Network Time Protocol (NTP) and you modified its `ntpd` service configuration file, `/etc/ntp.conf`, for the new configuration to take immediate effect, you would issue the command **systemctl reload ntpd** at the command line.

Besides the commands in Table 10.6, there are some other handy systemctl commands you can use for managing system services. A few are shown in this example using super user privileges:

```
# systemctl stop atd
#
# systemctl is-active atd
inactive
#
# systemctl start atd
#
# systemctl is-active atd
active
#
```

The atd daemon is stopped using systemctl and its stop command. Instead of the status command, the is-active command is used to quickly display that the service is stopped (inactive). The atd service is then started back up, and again the is-active command is employed showing that the service is now running (active). Table 10.7 shows these useful service status checking commands.

TABLE 10.7: Convenient systemctl Service Status Commands

COMMAND	DESCRIPTION
is-active	Displays active for running services and failed for any service that has reached a failed state
is-enabled	Displays enabled for any service that is configured to start at system boot and disabled for any service that is *not* configured to start at system boot
is-failed	Displays failed for any service that has reached a failed state and active for running services

Services can fail for many reasons: for hardware issues, a missing dependency set in the unit configuration file, an incorrect permission setting, and so on. You can employ the systemctl utility's is-failed command to see if a particular service has failed.

One special command to explore is the systemctl is-system-running command. Here is an example of this command in action:

```
$ systemctl is-system-running
running
$
```

You may think the status returned here is obvious, but it means all is well with your Linux system currently. Table 10.8 shows other useful statuses.

TABLE 10.8: Operational Statuses Provided by `systemctl is-system-running`

STATUS	DESCRIPTION
running	System is fully in working order.
degraded	System has one or more failed units.
maintenance	System is in emergency or recovery mode.
initializing	System is starting to boot.
starting	System is still booting.
stopping	System is starting to shut down.

If you receive degraded status, you should review your units to see which ones have failed and take appropriate action. Use the `systemctl --failed` command to find the failed unit(s), as shown snipped here:

```
$ systemctl is-system-running
degraded
$
$ systemctl --failed
  UNIT                             LOAD   ACTIVE SUB [...]
• NetworkManager-wait-online.service loaded failed [...]
[...]
$
```

In this case, it looks like there are some potential network problems that need exploration. Chapter 12, "Configuring Network Settings," dives deeper into networking with Linux.

The `systemctl` utility has several commands that go beyond service management. You can jump between various system states and even analyze your system's boot-time performance. We'll look at these various commands next.

Jumping Targets

Occasionally, you may need to start or stop several services. If those services are grouped in a particular target unit, you can use `systemctl` to "jump" to that target, starting groups of services and stopping others on the fly.

The `isolate` command, used with super user privileges, is handy for jumping between system targets. When this command is used along with a target name for an argument, all services and processes not enabled in the listed target are stopped. Any services and processes enabled and not running in the listed target are started. A snipped example of jumping targets is shown snipped here on an Ubuntu distribution:

```
$ systemctl get-default
graphical.target
```

```
$
$ sudo systemctl isolate multi-user.target
[sudo] password for sysadmin:
$
$ systemctl status graphical.target
• graphical.target - Graphical Interface
    Loaded: loaded (/lib/systemd/system/[...]
    Active: inactive (dead) since Wed 20[...]
      Docs: man:systemd.special(7)
[...]
$
```

In the example, the systemctl isolate command caused the system to jump from the default system target to the multiuser target. Unfortunately, there is no simple command to show your system's current target in this case. However, the systemctl status command is useful. If you employ the command and give it the previous target's name (graphical.target in this case), you should see that it is no longer active (inactive) and thus not the current system target.

Be aware that the systemctl isolate command can be used only with certain targets. The target's unit file must have the AllowIsolate=yes directive set.

Two extra special targets to which you can jump are rescue and emergency. These targets, sometimes called *modes*, are described here:

Rescue Target   When you jump your system to the rescue target, the system mounts all the local filesystems, only the root user is allowed to log into the system, networking services are turned off, and only a few other services are started. The systemctl is-system-running command will return the maintenance status. Running disk utilities to fix corrupted disks is a useful task in this particular target.

Emergency Target   When your system goes into emergency mode, the system only mounts the root filesystem, and it mounts it as read-only. Similar to rescue mode, it only allows the root user to log into the system, networking services are turned off, and only a few other services are started. The systemctl is-system-running command will return the maintenance status. If your system goes into emergency mode by itself, there are serious problems. This target is used for situations where even rescue mode cannot be reached.

Be aware that if you jump into either rescue or emergency mode, you'll only be able to log into the root account. Also, your screen may go blank for a minute, so don't panic.

Other targets you can jump to include reboot, poweroff, and halt. For example, type in **systemctl isolate reboot** to reboot your system.

With GRUB2, you can reach a different target than the default target before the system boots via the bootloader menu. Just move your cursor to the menu option that typically boots your system and press the E key to edit it. Scroll down and find the line that starts with the linux16 or linux command. Press the End key or arrow keys to reach the line's end. Press the spacebar and type in **systemd.unit=*target-name*.target**, where *target-name* is the name of the target you want your system to activate, such as emergency.target. This is useful for crisis situations.

Analyzing with systemd

A handy systemd component is the `systemd-analyze` utility. With this utility, you can investigate your system's boot performance and check for potential system initialization problems. Table 10.9 contains the more common commands you can use with the `systemd-analyze` utility.

TABLE 10.9:   Common `systemd-analyze` Commands

COMMAND	DESCRIPTION
blame	Displays the amount of time each running unit took to initialize. Units and their times are listed starting from the slowest to the fastest.
time	Displays the amount of time system initialization spent for the kernel, and the initial RAM filesystem, as well as the time it took for normal system user space to initialize (Default)
critical-chain	Displays time-critical units in a tree format. Can pass it a unit file argument to focus the information on that particular unit.
dump	Displays information concerning all the units. The display format is subject to change without notice, so it should be used only for human viewing.
verify	Scans unit files and displays warning messages if any errors are found. Will accept a unit filename as an argument, but follows directory location precedence.

Be aware that some of the longer `systemd-analyze` displays are piped into the `less` pager utility. You can turn that feature off by using the `--no-pager` option. In the snipped example here, a few of these `systemd-analyze` commands are shown in action:

```
$ systemd-analyze time
Startup finished in 1.465s (kernel) + 13.911s (initrd)
+ 35.896s (userspace) = 5                    1.274s
multi-user.target reached after 30.317s in userspace
$
$ systemd-analyze --no-pager blame
          7.811s NetworkManager-wait-online.service
[...]
          5.022s firewalld.service
          4.753s polkit.service
[...]
           586ms auditd.service
[...]
           338ms rsyslog.service
[...]
            36ms sys-kernel-config.mount
$
```

The first command in the preceding example provides time information concerning your system's initialization. Note that you could leave off the `time` keyword, and the `systemd-analyze` utility would still display the system initialization time because that is the utility's default action.

The last command in the example employs the `blame` argument. This display begins with those units that took the longest to initialize. At the bottom of the list are the units that initialized the fastest. It is a handy guide for troubleshooting unit initialization problems.

 **Real World Scenario**

ANALYZING SYSTEM INITIALIZATION

Most production servers are expected to have minimal downtime. So when you need to take a server down, the faster it can boot back to full service, the better. Taking some time to analyze your system's initialization is worthwhile, especially if the analysis uncovers some services that are unneeded or whose configuration needs exploration to improve their startup times.

The following steps will take you through analyzing your system's initialization speeds:

1. Log into a Linux system, using the `sysadmin` account and the password you created for it.

2. View your system's total initialization time by typing **systemd-analyze time** and pressing Enter.

3. Try this command without the argument by typing **systemd-analyze** and pressing Enter. You should see the same output as displayed in the previous step.

4. View the output from the previous step to determine which target unit file is used on this system.

5. Looking at the output from step 3, how long did it take the services in the target unit file to start? (Hint: Find the line that says something similar to `multi-user.target reached after ____ in userspace`. You'll want to record the number of seconds listed on that line.)

6. Now analyze the speed of starting each service. Type **systemd-analyze blame** and press Enter. The results of this command will display using the `less` pager, so you will not receive your command-line prompt back.

7. From the preceding step's results, record what service is the slowest to start. (Hint: Find the first line of output from the command. That is the slowest service.)

8. From the results in step 6, record what service is the fastest to start. (Hint: This will be displayed on the last line of output from the command. You may need to press the spacebar a few times to go to the bottom of the `less` pager's output.)

9. Press the Q key to leave the `less` pager and return to the command line.

The systemd initialization approach is flexible and reliable for managing Linux systems and their services. Having a basic understanding of the methods and commands for managing systemd initialized systems will serve you well in your Linux career.

The Bottom Line

Diagnose the Linux boot process.   The process of booting a Linux server is typically free of problems. The firmware performs a POST, the bootloader finds and loads the Linux kernel, and systemd starts the desired services. Each part is critical in getting a system ready to offer services.

Master It   Imagine that you booted your Linux system, and as you were watching the boot messages, it seemed that several error messages were generated. However, the messages went by so fast, you did not have time to analyze them. The system is now up and running, but you'd like to review those messages to see if they were indeed errors. How can you do that?

Configure a bootloader.   The GRUB2 bootloader is the most typical and popular bootloader on Linux systems. It provides flexibility and supports advanced features. Often there is little need to make changes to its configuration.

Master It   After installing Linux on your new server, you notice that the GRUB2 boot-loader menu does not display when the system boots. You'd like to modify this behavior. What setting(s) should you look to potentially change and in what configuration file?

Interact with a bootloader.   At boot time, if configured to do so, the GRUB2 boot menu will display. This allows you to pick different Linux kernels to boot as well as modify parameters set in the menu entries, which is often helpful when troubleshooting problems that adversely affect the system's boot.

Master It   Your Linux system is currently not booted, and due to some troubleshooting, you need to select the `multi-user.target` for the next boot. How can you accomplish this?

Stop and start services after boot.   The systemd daemon and its `systemctl` utility help in managing system services. They allow you to control what services are started at boot time, start and stop services, and analyze service issues and troubleshoot problems.

Master It   By accident, the `ntpd` service was not enabled to start at boot time, and you need to immediately get this service up and running. Assuming you have super user privileges, how can you use systemd to start the service and check that it is indeed started?

Analyze service startup times.   The systemd daemon has some special utilities that can assist in tracking down the sources of various problems. One of those utilities is `systemd-analyze`, which has several commands you can use in troubleshooting situations.

Master It   Imagine that you've installed several new services on your Linux server, but they are not starting at boot time. The services are enabled, but something seems to be going wrong with their unit file configurations. What can you do to quickly narrow down the problem?

Chapter 11

Working with Storage Devices

The world runs on data. Whether it's an employee database or just your weekly bowling scores, the ability to save and retrieve data is a must for every application. Linux provides lots of different ways to store and manage files for applications. As a Linux system administrator, you will no doubt need to work with storage devices.

IN THIS CHAPTER, YOU WILL LEARN TO

- ◆ Create Linux partitions on storage devices
- ◆ Format partitions with a Linux filesystem and mount them in the virtual directory
- ◆ Examine storage devices using Linux tools

Storage Basics

The most common way to persistently store data on computer systems is using a *hard disk drive* (HDD). Hard disk drives are physical devices that store data using a set of disk platters that spin around, storing data magnetically on the platters with a moveable read/write head that writes and retrieves magnetic images on the platters.

These days, another popular type of persistent storage is called a *solid-state drive* (SSD). These drives use integrated circuits to store data electronically. There are no moving parts contained in SSDs, making them faster and more resilient than HDDs. While currently SSDs are more expensive than HDDs, technology is quickly changing that, and it may not be long before HDDs are a thing of the past.

Linux handles both HDD and SSD storage devices the same way. It mostly depends on the connection method used to connect the drives to the Linux system. This section describes the different methods that Linux uses in connecting and using both HDD and SSD devices.

Drive Connections

While HDDs and SSDs differ in how they store data, they both interface with the Linux system using the same methods. There are four main types of drive connections that you'll run into with Linux systems.

Parallel Advanced Technology Attachment (PATA)   Connects drives using a parallel interface, which requires a wide cable. PATA supports two devices per adapter.

Serial Advanced Technology Attachment (SATA) Connects drives using a serial interface, but at a much faster speed than PATA. SATA supports up to four devices per adapter.

Small Computer System Interface (SCSI) Connects drives using a parallel interface, but with the speed of SATA. SCSI supports up to eight devices per adapter.

Non-Volatile Memory Express (NVMe) Connects drives using a high-speed parallel interface, designed to support the higher speeds of SSD drives.

When you connect a drive to a Linux system, the Linux kernel assigns the drive device a file in the /dev folder. That file is called a *raw device*, as it provides a path directly to the drive from the Linux system. Any data written to the file is written to the drive, and reading the file reads data directly from the drive.

For PATA devices, this file is named /dev/hd*x*, where *x* is a letter representing the individual drive, starting with a. For SATA and SCSI devices, Linux uses /dev/sd*x*, where *x* is a letter representing the individual drive, again starting with a. Thus, to reference the first SATA device on the system, you'd use /dev/sda, then /dev/sdb for the second device, and so on. For NVMe devices, Linux assigns the /dev/nvme*x*n*y* name, where *x* is the drive number and *y* is the partition number.

Partitioning Drives

Most operating systems, including Linux, allow you to *partition* a drive into multiple sections. A partition is a self-contained section within the drive that the operating system treats as a separate storage space.

Partitioning drives can help you better organize your data, such as segmenting operating system data from user data. If a rogue user fills up the disk space with data, the operating system will still have room to operate on the separate partition.

Partitions must be tracked by some type of indexing system on the drive. Systems that use the old BIOS boot loader method (see Chapter 10, "Booting Linux"), use the *master boot record* (MBR) method for managing disk partitions. This method only supports up to four *primary partitions* on a drive. However, one primary partition can be labeled as an *extended partition*, which can be subdivided into multiple *logical partitions*.

Systems that use the UEFI boot loader method (see Chapter 10) use the more advanced *GUID Partition Table* (GPT) method for managing partitions, which supports up to 128 partitions on a drive. Linux assigns the partition numbers in the order that the partition appears on the drive, starting with number 1.

Linux creates /dev files for each separate disk partition. It attaches the partition number to the end of the device name and numbers the primary partitions starting at 1, so the first primary partition on the first SATA drive would be /dev/sda1. MBR logical partitions are numbered starting at 5, so the first logical partition is assigned the file /dev/sda5.

Automatic Drive Detection

Linux systems detect drives and partitions at boot time and assign each one a unique device filename. However, with the invention of removable USB drives (such as memory sticks), which can be added and removed at will while the system is running, that method needed to be modified.

Most Linux systems now use the udev application (see Chapter 9, "Managing Hardware"). The udev program runs in background at all times and automatically detects new hardware connected to the running Linux system. As you connect new drives, USB devices, or optical drives (such as CD and DVD devices), udev will detect them and assign each one a unique device filename in the /dev folder.

Another feature of the udev application is that it also creates *persistent device files* for storage devices. When you add or remove a removable storage device, the /dev name assigned to it may change, depending on what devices are connected at any given time. That can make it difficult for applications to find the same storage device each time.

To solve that problem, the udev application uses the /dev/disk folder to create links to the /dev storage device files based on unique attributes of the drive. There are four separate folders udev creates for storing links.

- ◆ /dev/disk/*by-id* links storage devices by their manufacturer make, model, and serial number.

- ◆ /dev/disk/*by-label* links storage devices by the label assigned to them.

- ◆ /dev/disk/*by-path* links storage devices by the physical hardware port they are connected to.

- ◆ /dev/disk/*by-uuid* links storage devices by the 128-bit universal unique identifier (UUID) assigned to the device.

With the udev device links, you can specifically reference a storage device by a permanent identifier rather than where or when it was plugged into the Linux system.

Partitioning Tools

After you connect a drive to your Linux system, you'll need to create partitions on it (even if there's only one partition). Linux provides several tools for working with raw storage devices to create partitions. This section covers the most popular partitioning tools you'll run across in Linux.

Working with *fdisk*

The most common command-line partitioning tool is the fdisk program. The fdisk program allows you to create, view, delete, and modify partitions on any drive that use either the MBR or GPT methods of indexing partitions.

To use fdisk, you must specify the drive device name (not the partition name) of the device you want to work with.

```
$ sudo fdisk /dev/sda
[sudo] password for sysadmin:
Welcome to fdisk (util-linux 2.23.1).
Changes will remain in memory only, until you decide to write them.
Be careful before using the write command.


Command (m for help):
```

The fdisk program uses its own command line that allows you to submit commands to work with the drive partitions. Table 11.1 shows the common commands you have available to work with.

TABLE 11.1: Common fdisk Commands

COMMAND	DESCRIPTION
a	Toggle a bootable flag.
b	Edit BSD disk label.
c	Toggle the DOS compatibility flag.
d	Delete a partition.
g	Create a new empty GPT partition table.
G	Create an IRIX (SGI) partition table.
l	List known partition types.
m	Print this menu.
n	Add a new partition.
o	Create a new empty DOS partition table.
p	Print the partition table.
q	Quit without saving changes.
s	Create a new empty Sun disk label.
t	Change a partition's system ID.
u	Change display/entry units.
v	Verify the partition table.
w	Write table to disk and exit.
x	Extra functionality (experts only)

The p command displays the current partition scheme on the drive.

```
Command (m for help): p

Disk /dev/sda: 20 GiB, 21474836480 bytes, 41943040 sectors
Units: sectors of 1 * 512 = 512 bytes
Sector size (logical/physical): 512 bytes / 512 bytes
I/O size (minimum/optimal): 512 bytes / 512 bytes
Disklabel type: dos
```

```
Disk identifier: 0xc243c8a9

Device     Boot   Start      End  Sectors Size Id Type
/dev/sda1  *       2048  2099199  2097152  1G 83 Linux
/dev/sda2       2099200 41943039 39843840 19G 8e Linux LVM

Command (m for help):
```

In this example, the /dev/sda drive is sectioned into two partitions, sda1 and sda2. The Id and Type columns refer to the type of filesystem the partition is formatted to handle. We cover that in the "Formatting Filesystems" section later in this chapter. Both partitions are formatted to support a Linux filesystem. The first partition is allocated about 1 GB of space, while the second is allocated 19 GB of space.

The fdisk command is somewhat rudimentary in that it doesn't allow you to alter the size of an existing partition. All you can do is delete the existing partition and rebuild it from scratch.

To be able to boot the system from a partition, the boot flag must be set for the partition. You do that with the a command. The bootable partitions are indicated in the output listing with an asterisk.

If you make any changes to the drive partitions, you must exit using the w command to write the changes to the drive.

Working with *gdisk*

If you're working with drives that use the GPT indexing method, you'll need to use the gdisk program.

```
$ sudo gdisk /dev/sda
[sudo] password for rich:
GPT fdisk (gdisk) version 1.0.3

Partition table scan:
  MBR: protective
  BSD: not present
  APM: not present
  GPT: present

Found valid GPT with protective MBR; using GPT.

Command (? for help):
```

The gdisk program identifies the type of formatting used on the drive. If the drive doesn't currently use the GPT method, gdisk offers you the option to convert it to a GPT drive.

CONVERTING DRIVES AND FIRMWARE

Be careful with converting the drive method specified for your drive. The method you select must be compatible with the system firmware (BIOS or UEFI). If it's not, your drive will not be able to boot.

The gdisk program also uses its own command prompt, allowing you to enter commands to manipulate the drive layout, as shown in Table 11.2.

TABLE 11.2:   Common gdisk Commands

COMMAND	DESCRIPTION
b	Back up GPT data to a file.
c	Change a partition's name.
d	Delete a partition.
i	Show detailed information on a partition.
l	List known partition types.
n	Add a new partition.
o	Create a new empty GUID partition table (GPT).
p	Print the partition table.
q	Quit without saving changes.
r	Recovery and transformation options (experts only)
s	Sort partitions.
t	Change a partition's type code.
v	Verify disk.
w	Write table to disk and exit.
x	Extra functionality (experts only)
?	Print a menu of commands.

You'll notice that many of the gdisk commands are similar to those in the fdisk program, making it easier to switch between the two programs. One of the added options that can come in handy is the i option, which displays more detailed information about a partition.

```
Command (? for help): i
Partition number (1-3): 2
Partition GUID code: 0FC63DAF-8483-4772-8E79-3D69D8477DE4 (Linux filesystem)
Partition unique GUID: 5E4213F9-9566-4898-8B4E-FB8888ADDE78
First sector: 1953792 (at 954.0 MiB)
Last sector: 26623999 (at 12.7 GiB)
Partition size: 24670208 sectors (11.8 GiB)
Attribute flags: 0000000000000000
Partition name: ''

Command (? for help):
```

The GNU *parted* Command

The GNU parted program provides yet another command-line interface for working with both MBR and GPT drive partitions.

```
$ sudo parted
GNU Parted 3.2
Using /dev/sda
Welcome to GNU Parted! Type 'help' to view a list of commands.
(parted) print
Model: ATA VBOX HARDDISK (scsi)
Disk /dev/sda: 15.6GB
Sector size (logical/physical): 512B/512B
Partition Table: gpt
Disk Flags:

Number  Start    End      Size     File system    Name  Flags
 1      1049kB   1000MB   999MB    fat32                 boot, esp
 2      1000MB   13.6GB   12.6GB   ext4
 3      13.6GB   15.6GB   2000MB   linux-swap(v1)

(parted)
```

As you probably guessed, the parted program has its own set of commands, shown in Table 11.3.

TABLE 11.3:   The parted Commands

COMMAND	DESCRIPTION
align-check *TYPE N*	Check partition *N* for *TYPE* alignment.
help [*COMMAND*]	Print general help, or help on *COMMAND*.
mklabel,mktable *LABEL-TYPE*	Create a new disk label (partition table).
mkpart *PART-TYPE* [*FS-TYPE*] *START END*	Make a partition.
name *NUMBER NAME*	Name the partition *NUMBER* as *NAME*.
print [devices|free|list, all|*NUMBER*]	Display the partition table, available devices, free space, all found partitions, or a particular partition.
quit	Exit the program.
rescue *START END*	Rescue a lost partition near *START* and *END*.
resizepart *NUMBER END*	Resize partition *NUMBER*.
rm *NUMBER*	Delete partition *NUMBER*.

TABLE 11.3: The parted Commands *(CONTINUED)*

COMMAND	DESCRIPTION
select *DEVICE*	Choose the device to edit.
disk_set *FLAG STATE*	Change the *FLAG* on the selected device.
disk_toggle [*FLAG*]	Toggle the state of *FLAG* on the selected device.
set *NUMBER FLAG STATE*	Change the *FLAG* on partition *NUMBER*.
toggle [*NUMBER* [*FLAG*]]	Toggle the state of *FLAG* on partition *NUMBER*.
unit *UNIT*	Set the default unit to *UNIT*.
version	Display the version number and copyright information of GNU Parted.

One of the selling features of the parted program is that it allows you to modify existing partition sizes using the resizepart command, so you can easily shrink or grow partitions on the drive.

With the availability of USB memory sticks, you can easily practice partitioning storage without damaging your existing Linux filesystem. Go through the following case study to get some practice.

 Real World Scenario

PARTITIONING A NEW STORAGE DEVICE

If you have a USB memory stick handy, you can practice creating and deleting partitions. Be careful, though, as this process will delete all files currently on the USB memory stick. Follow these steps to examine and create a new Linux partition on the drive:

1. Log into your Linux system.

2. Insert a USB memory stick into your system. If you're using a virtual machine (VM) environment, you may need to configure the VM to recognize the new USB device. For VirtualBox, click the Devices menu bar item, then select USB, and then the USB device name.

3. Type **dmesg | tail** to display the last few lines from the system console output. This should show the device name assigned to the USB device, such as /dev/sdb1.

4. If your system automatically mounted the drive, unmount the device using the command **sudo umount /dev/xxxx**, where *xxxx* is the device name shown from the dmesg output.

5. Type **sudo fdisk /dev/xxx** to partition the disk, where *xxx* is the device name, without the partition number (such as /dev/sdb). At the command prompt, type **p** to display the current partitions.

6. Remove the existing partition by typing **d**.

7. Create a new partition. Type **n** to create a new partition. Type **p** to create a primary partition. Type **1** to assign it as the first partition. Press the Enter key to accept the default starting location, and then press the Enter key again to accept the default ending location. Type **y** to remove the original VFAT signature if prompted.

8. Type **p** to display the new partition. The output should look something like this:

```
Disk /dev/sdb: 1000.3 MiB, 1048838144 bytes, 2048512 sectors
Units: sectors of 1 * 512 = 512 bytes
Sector size (logical/physical): 512 bytes / 512 bytes
I/O size (minimum/optimal): 512 bytes / 512 bytes
Disklabel type: dos
Disk identifier: 0xc3072e18


Device     Boot Start     End Sectors  Size Id Type
/dev/sdb1       2048 2048511 2046464 999.3M 83 Linux


Command (m for help):
```

9. Save the new partition layout. Type **w** to save the partition layout and exit the fdisk program. This creates a Linux partition on the USB memory stick, which won't be usable on a Windows system.

Formatting Filesystems

Before you can store data on a new drive partition, you must format it using a filesystem. There are myriad different filesystem types that Linux supports, with each having different features and capabilities. This section discusses the different filesystems that Linux supports and how to format a drive partition for the filesystems.

Common Filesystem Types

Each operating system utilizes its own filesystem type for storing data on drives. Not only does Linux support several of its own filesystem types, but it also supports filesystems of other operating systems. This section covers the most common Linux and non-Linux filesystems that you can use in your Linux partitions.

LINUX FILESYSTEMS

When you create a filesystem specifically for use on a Linux system, there are six main filesystems that you can choose from.

btrfs: A newer, high-performance filesystem that supports files up to 16 EiB in size and a total filesystem size of 16 EiB. It also can perform its own form of redundant array of independent disks (RAID) as well as logical volume management (LVM). It includes additional advanced features such as built-in snapshots for backup, improved fault tolerance, and data compression on the fly.

ecryptfs: The Enterprise Cryptographic Filesystem (eCryptfs) applies a POSIX-compliant encryption protocol to data before storing it on the device. This provides a layer of protection for data stored on the device. Only the operating system that created the filesystem can read data from it.

ext3: Also called ext3fs, this is a descendant of the original Linux ext filesystem. It supports files up to 2 TiB, with a total filesystem size of 16 TiB. It supports journaling, as well as faster startup and recovery.

ext4: Also called ext4fs, it's the current version of the original Linux filesystem. It supports files up to 16 TiB, with a total filesystem size of 1 EiB. It also supports journaling and utilizes improved performance features.

reiserFS: Created before the Linux ext3fs filesystem and commonly used on older Linux systems, it provides features now found in ext3fs and ext4fs. Linux has dropped support for the most recent version, reiser4fs.

swap: The swap filesystem allows you to create virtual memory for your system using space on a physical drive. The system can then swap data out of normal memory into the swap space, providing a method of adding memory to your system. This is not intended for storing persistent data.

The default filesystem used by most Linux distributions these days is ext4fs. The ext4fs filesystem provides *journaling*, which is a method of tracking data not yet written to the drive in a log file, called the *journal*. If the system fails before the data can be written to the drive, the journal data can be recovered and stored upon the next system boot.

Non-Linux Filesystems

One of the great features of Linux that makes it so versatile is its ability to read data stored on devices formatted for other operating systems, such as Apple and Microsoft. This feature makes it a breeze to share data between different systems running different operating systems.

Here's a list of the more common non-Linux filesystems that Linux can handle:

cifs: The Common Internet Filesystem (CIFS), also known as the Server Message Block (SMB), is a filesystem protocol created by Microsoft for reading and writing data across a network using a network storage device. It was released to the public for use on all operating systems.

hfs: The Hierarchical Filesystem (HFS) was developed by Apple for its macOS systems. Linux can also interact with the more advanced HFS+ and APFS+ filesystem.

iso-9660: The ISO-9660 standard is used for creating filesystems on CD-ROM devices.

nfs: The Network Filesystem (NFS) is an open source standard for reading and writing data across a network using a network storage device.

ntfs: The New Technology Filesystem (NTFS) is the filesystem used by the Microsoft NT operating system and subsequent versions of Windows. Linux can read and write data on an NTFS partition as of kernel 2.6.x.

udf: The Universal Disc Format (UDF) is commonly used on DVD-ROM devices for storing data. Linux can both read data from a DVD and write data to a DVD using this filesystem.

vfat: The Virtual File Allocation Table (VFAT) is an extension of the original Microsoft File Allocation Table (FAT) filesystem. It's not commonly used on drives, but is commonly used for removable storage devices such as USB memory sticks.

xfs: The X Filesystem (XFS) was created by Silicon Graphics for its (now defunct) advanced graphical workstations. The filesystem provided some advanced high-performance features that makes it still popular in Linux.

zfs: The Zettabyte Filesystem (ZFS) was created by Sun Microsystems (now part of Oracle) for its Unix workstations and servers. Another high-performance filesystem, it has features similar to the btrfs Linux filesystem.

It's generally not recommended to format a partition using a non-Linux filesystem if you plan on using the drive for only Linux systems. Linux supports these filesystems mainly as a method for sharing data with other operating systems.

Creating Filesystems

The Swiss Army knife for creating filesystems in Linux is the mkfs program. The mkfs program is a front end to several individual tools for creating specific filesystems, such as the mkfs.ext4 program for creating ext4 filesystems.

The beauty of the mkfs program is that you only need to remember one program name to create any type of filesystem on your Linux system. Just use the -t option to specify the filesystem type.

```
mkfs -t type device
```

After you specify the -t option, just specify the partition type and the device filename for the partition you want to format on the command line. The mkfs program does a lot of things behind the scenes when formatting the filesystem. Each filesystem has its own method for indexing files and folders and tracking file access. The mkfs program creates all of the index files and tables necessary for the specific filesystem.

NO GOING BACK!

Be careful when you're specifying the partition device filename. When you format a partition, any existing data on the partition is lost. If you specify the wrong partition name, you could lose important data or make your Linux system not able to boot.

Go through the following case study to experiment with formatting a new partition.

 Real World Scenario

FORMATTING A NEW STORAGE DEVICE

In the previous case study, you created a partition on a new USB memory stick storage device. Now you know that you need to use the mkfs command to format it so you can store data. Follow these steps to format the new partition you created:

1. If you're not already logged in to your Linux system, log in now.

2. Insert the USB memory stick that you formatted in the "Partitioning a New Storage Device" case study if it's not already loaded on your system. If you're using a virtual machine (VM) environment, you may need to configure the VM to recognize the new USB device. For VirtualBox, click the Devices menu bar item and then select USB and the USB device name.

3. Type **dmesg | tail** to display the last few lines of the system console output. This should show the device name assigned to the USB device, such as /dev/sdb1.

4. Create a new filesystem on the new partition. Type **sudo mkfs -t ext4 /dev/xxx1**, where *xxx* is the device name for the USB memory stick. You should see something similar to the following output:

```
mke2fs 1.45.6 (20-Mar-2020)
Creating filesystem with 255808 4k blocks and 64000 inodes
Filesystem UUID: 944a8b8d-0e8c-4828-b926-fa4656d39bac
Superblock backups stored on blocks:
        32768, 98304, 163840, 229376

Allocating group tables: done
Writing inode tables: done
Creating journal (4096 blocks): done
Writing superblocks and filesystem accounting information: done

$
```

Mounting Filesystems

Once you've formatted a drive partition with a filesystem, you can add it to the virtual directory on your Linux system. This process is called *mounting* the filesystem.

You can manually mount the partition within the virtual directory structure from the command line, or you can allow Linux to automatically mount the partition at boot time. This section walks through both of these methods.

Manually Mounting Devices

To temporarily mount a filesystem to the Linux virtual directory, use the mount command. The basic format for the mount command is as follows:

```
mount -t fstype device mountpoint
```

Use the -t command-line option to specify the filesystem type of the device:

```
$ sudo mount -t ext4 /dev/sdb1 /media/usb1
$
```

If you specify the mount command with no parameters, it displays all the devices currently mounted on the Linux system. Be prepared for a long output, though, as most Linux distributions mount lots of virtual devices in the virtual directory to provide information about system resources.

```
$ mount
...
/dev/sda2 on / type ext4 (rw,relatime,errors=remount-ro,data=ordered)
```

```
/dev/sda1 on /boot/efi type vfat
  (rw,relatime,fmask=0077,dmask=0077,codepage=437,iocharset=iso8859
-1,shortname=mixed,errors=remount-ro)
...
/dev/sdb1 on /media/usb1 type ext4 (rw,relatime,data=ordered)
$
```

To save space, we trimmed down the output from the mount command to show only the physical devices on the system. The main hard drive device (/dev/sda) contains two partitions, and our USB memory stick device (/dev/sdb) contains a single partition.

MOUNTING USING SPECIAL FEATURES

The mount command uses the -o option to specify additional features of the filesystem, such as mounting it in read-only mode, user permissions assigned to the mount point, and how data is stored on the device. These options are shown in the output of the mount command. Usually, you can omit the -o option to use the system defaults for the new mount point.

The downside to the mount command is that it only temporarily mounts the device in the virtual directory. When you reboot the system, you have to manually mount the devices again. This is usually fine for removable devices, such as USB memory sticks, but for more permanent devices, it would be nice if Linux could mount them for us automatically. Fortunately for us, Linux can do just that.

To remove a mounted drive from the virtual directory, use the umount command (note the missing n). You can remove the mounted drive by specifying either the device filename or the mount point directory.

Automatically Mounting Devices

For permanent storage devices, Linux maintains the /etc/fstab file to indicate which drive devices should be mounted to the virtual directory at boot time. The /etc/fstab file is a table that indicates the drive device file (either the raw file or one of its permanent udev filenames), the mount point location, the filesystem type, and any additional options required to mount the drive. Listing 11.1 shows the /etc/fstab file from a CentOS server.

LISTING 11.1: The /etc/fstab File

```
$ cat /etc/fstab
#
# /vetc/fstab
# Created by anaconda on Wed Nov  4 14:12:46 2020
#
# Accessible filesystems, by reference, are maintained under '/dev/disk/'.
# See man pages fstab(5), findfs(8), mount(8) and/or blkid(8) for more info.
#
```

```
# After editing this file, run 'systemctl daemon-reload' to update systemd
# units generated from this file.
#
/dev/mapper/cl_unknown080027d84f32-root /                            xfs
 defaults        0 0
UUID=935596d0-8156-4518-9f43-32afb6239947 /boot                      ext4
defaults        1 2
/dev/mapper/cl_unknown080027d84f32-swap swap                         swap
defaults        0 0
$
```

This /etc/fstab file references the devices by their udev UUID value, ensuring the correct drive partition is accessed no matter in what order it appears in the raw device table. The first partition is mounted at the root (/) of the virtual directory. The second partition is at the /boot mount point in the virtual directory, and the third partition is mounted as a swap area for virtual memory.

USING ENCRYPTED FILESYSTEMS

These days, environments that require additional security measures require the use of encrypted partitions. If you use the encryptfs filesystem type on any partitions, they will appear in the /etc/crypttab file, and they will be mounted automatically at boot time. While the system is running, you can also view all the currently mounted devices, whether they were mounted automatically by the system or manually by users, by viewing the /etc/mtab file.

You can manually add devices to the /etc/fstab file so that they are mounted automatically when the Linux system boots. However, if they don't exist at boot time, that will generate a boot error.

 ### Real World Scenario

MOUNTING A PARTITION

In the previous case study, you created a filesystem on a USB memory stick partition, but you can't access it until you mount it within the virtual directory on your Linux system. Follow these steps to do that:

1. If you're not already logged into your Linux system, log in now.

2. Insert the USB memory stick that you formatted in the "Formatting a New Storage Device" case study if it's not already loaded on your system. If you're using a virtual machine (VM) environment, you may need to configure the VM to recognize the new USB device. For VirtualBox, click the Devices menu bar item, and then select USB and the USB device name.

3. The Linux system may mount the device automatically. Type **dmesg | tail** to display the last few lines from the system console output. This should show the device name assigned to the USB device, such as /dev/sdb1, and if it was mounted.

4. Create a new mount point in your Home folder. Type `mkdir mediatest1`.

5. Mount the new filesystem to the mount point. Type `sudo mount -t ext4 /dev/` `xxx1 mediatest1`, where *xxx* is the device name. Type `ls mediatest1` to list any files currently in the filesystem.

6. Remove the USB stick by typing `sudo umount /dev/xxx1`, where *xxx* is the device name.

7. If you want to return the USB memory stick to a Windows format, you can change the filesystem type of the USB memory stick to VFAT, or you can reformat it using the Windows format tool in File Manager.

Managing Filesystems

Once you've created a filesystem and mounted it to the virtual directory, you may have to manage and maintain it to keep things running smoothly. This section walks through some of the Linux utilities available for managing the filesystems on your Linux system.

Retrieving Filesystem Stats

As you use your Linux system, there's no doubt that at some point you'll need to monitor disk performance and usage. There are a few different tools available to help you do that, as shown in Table 11.4.

TABLE 11.4:   Linux Filesystem Stats Commands

COMMAND	DESCRIPTION
df	Displays disk usage by partition
du	Displays disk usage by directory; good for finding users or applications that are taking up the most disk space
iostat	Displays a real-time chart of disk statistics by partition
lsblk	Displays current partition sizes and mount points

In addition to these tools, the `/proc` and `/sys` folders are special filesystems that the kernel uses for recording system statistics. Two directories that can be useful when working with filesystems are the `/proc/partitions` and `/proc/mounts` folders, which provide information on system partitions and mount points, respectively. Additionally, the `/sys/block` folder contains separate folders for each mounted drive, showing partitions and kernel-level stats.

DISK SPACE VS. INODES

Some filesystems, such as `ext3` and `ext4`, allocate a specific number of *inodes* when created. An inode is an entry in the index table that tracks files stored on the filesystem. If the filesystem runs out of inode entries in the table, you can't create any more files, even if there's available space on the drive. Using the `-i` option with the `df` command will show you the percentage of inodes used on a filesystem and can be a lifesaver.

Filesystem Tools

Linux uses the e2fsprogs package of tools to provide utilities for working with ext filesystems (such as ext3 and ext4). Table 11.5 shows the most popular tools in the e2fsprogs package.

TABLE 11.5:   Popular e2fsprogs Programs

PROGRAM	DESCRIPTION
blkid	Displays information about block devices, such as storage drives
chattr	Changes file attributes on the filesystem
debugfs	Manually views and modifies the filesystem structure, such as undeleting a file or extracting a corrupt file
dumpe2fs	Displays block and superblock group information
e2label	Changes the label on the filesystem
resize2fs	Expands or shrinks a filesystem
tune2fs	Modifies filesystem parameters

These tools help you fine-tune parameters on an ext filesystem, but if corruption occurs on the filesystem, you'll need the fsck program.

The XFS filesystem also has a set of tools available for tuning the filesystem. The two that you'll most likely run across are the following:

xfs_admin: Display or change filesystem parameters such as the label or UUID assigned

xfs_info: Display information about a mounted filesystem, including the block sizes and sector sizes, as well as label and UUID information.

While these ext and XFS tools are useful, they can't help fix things if the filesystem itself has errors. For that, the fsck program is the tool to use.

```
$ sudo fsck -f /dev/sdb1
fsck from util-linux 2.31.1
e2fsck 1.44.1 (24-Mar-2018)
Pass 1: Checking inodes, blocks, and sizes
Pass 2: Checking directory structure
Pass 3: Checking directory connectivity
Pass 4: Checking reference counts
Pass 5: Checking group summary information
/dev/sdb1: 11/655360 files (0.0% non-contiguous), 66753/2621440 blocks
$
```

The fsck program is a front end to several different programs that check the various filesystems to match the index against the actual files stored in the filesystem. If any discrepancies occur, run the fsck program in repair mode, and it will attempt to reconcile the discrepancies and fix the filesystem.

Storage Alternatives

Standard partition layouts on storage devices do have their limitations. Once you create and format a partition, it's not easy to make it larger or smaller. Individual partitions are also susceptible to disk failures, in which case all of the data stored in the partition will be lost.

To accommodate more dynamic storage options, as well as fault-tolerance features, Linux has incorporated a few advanced storage management techniques. This section covers three of the more popular techniques you'll run into.

Multipath

The Linux kernel now supports Device Mapper Multipathing (DM-multipathing), which allows you to configure multiple paths between the Linux system and network storage devices. Multipathing aggregates the paths providing for increased throughout while all of the paths are active, or fault tolerance if one of the paths becomes inactive.

The Linux DM-multipathing tools include the following:

`dm-multipath`: The kernel module that provides multipath support

`multipath`: A command-line command for viewing multipath devices

`multipathd`: A background process for monitoring paths and activating/deactivating paths

`kpartx`: A command-line tool for creating device entries for multipath storage devices

The `dm-multipath` feature uses the dynamic `/dev/mapper` device file folder in Linux. Linux creates a `/dev/mapper` device file named `mpathN` for each new multipath storage device you add to the system, where *N* is the number of the multipath drive. That file acts as a normal device file in the Linux system, allowing you to create partitions and filesystems on the multipath device just as you would a normal drive partition.

Logical Volume Manager

The Linux *Logical Volume Manager* (LVM) also utilizes the `/dev/mapper` dynamic device folder to allow you to create virtual drive devices. You can aggregate multiple physical drive partitions into virtual volumes, which you then treat as a single partition on your system.

The benefit of LVM is that you can add and remove physical partitions as needed to a logical volume, expanding and shrinking the logical volume as needed.

Using LVM is somewhat complicated. Figure 11.1 demonstrates the layout for an LVM environment.

FIGURE 11.1
The Linux LVM layout

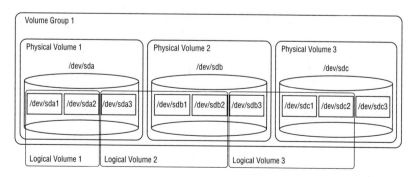

In the example shown in Figure 11.1, three physical drives each contain three partitions. The first logical volume consists of the first two partitions of the first drive. The second logical volume spans drives, combining the third partition of the first drive, with the first and second partitions of the second drive to create one volume. The third logical volume consists of the third partition of the second drive and the first two partitions of the third drive. The third partition of the third drive is left unassigned and can be added later to any of the logical volumes when needed.

For each physical partition, you must mark the partition type as the Linux LVM filesystem type in fdisk or gdisk. Then, you must use several LVM tools to create and manage the logical volumes.

pvcreate: Creates a physical volume

vgcreate: Groups physical volumes into a volume group

lvcreate: Creates a logical volume from partitions in each physical volume

The logical volumes create entries in the /dev/mapper folder, which represent the LVM device you can format with a filesystem and use like a normal partition. Listing 11.2 shows the steps you'd take to create a new LVM logical volume and mount it to your virtual directory.

LISTING 11.2:   Creating, Formatting, and Mounting a Logical Volume

```
$ sudo gdisk /dev/sdb

Command (? for help): n
Partition number (1-128, default 1): 1
First sector (34-10485726, default = 2048) or {+-}size{KMGTP}:
Last sector (2048-10485726, default = 10485726) or {+-}size{KMGTP}:
Current type is 'Linux filesystem'
Hex code or GUID (L to show codes, Enter = 8300): 8e00
Changed type of partition to 'Linux LVM'

Command (? for help): w

Final checks complete. About to write GPT data.
THIS WILL OVERWRITE EXISTING PARTITIONS!!

Do you want to proceed? (Y/N): Y
OK; writing new GUID partition table (GPT) to /dev/sdb.
The operation has completed successfully.

$ sudo pvcreate /dev/sdb1
  Physical volume "/dev/sdb1" successfully created.

$ sudo vgcreate newvol /dev/sdb1
```

```
    Volume group "newvol" successfully created

$ sudo lvcreate -l 100%FREE -n lvdisk newvol
  Logical volume "lvdisk" created.

$ sudo mkfs -t ext4 /dev/mapper/newvol-lvdisk
mke2fs 1.44.1 (24-Mar-2018)
Creating filesystem with 1309696 4k blocks and 327680 inodes
Filesystem UUID: 06c871bc-2eb6-4696-896f-240313e5d4fe
Superblock backups stored on blocks:
        32768, 98304, 163840, 229376, 294912, 819200, 884736

Allocating group tables: done
Writing inode tables: done
Creating journal (16384 blocks): done
Writing superblocks and filesystem accounting information: done

$ sudo mkdir /media/newdisk
$ sudo mount /dev/mapper/newvol-lvdisk /media/newdisk
$ cd /media/newdisk
$ ls -al
total 24
drwxr-xr-x 3 root root  4096 Jan 10 10:17 .
drwxr-xr-x 4 root root  4096 Jan 10 10:18 ..
drwx------ 2 root root 16384 Jan 10 10:17 lost+found
$
```

While the initial setup of a LVM is complicated, it does provide great benefits. If you run out of space in a logical volume, just add a new disk partition to the volume.

Using RAID Technology

Redundant Array of Inexpensive Disks (RAID) technology has changed the data storage environment for most data centers. RAID technology allows you to improve data access performance and reliability, as well as implement data redundancy for fault tolerance by combining multiple drives into one virtual drive. There are several versions of RAID commonly used.

RAID 0: Disk striping; spreads data across multiple disks for faster access.

RAID 1: Disk mirroring; duplicates data across two drives.

RAID 10: Disk mirroring and striping; provides striping for performance, and mirroring for fault-tolerance.

RAID 4: Disk striping with parity; adds a parity bit stored on a separate disk so that data on a failed data disk can be recovered.

RAID 5: Disk striping with distributed parity; adds a parity bit to the data stripe so that it appears on all of the disks so that any failed disk can be recovered.

RAID 6: Disk striping with double parity stripes both the data and the parity bit so two failed drives can be recovered.

The downside is that hardware RAID storage devices can be somewhat expensive (despite what the *I* stands for) and are often impractical for most home uses. Because of that, Linux has implemented a software RAID system that can implement RAID features on any disk system.

The mdadm utility allows you to specify multiple partitions to be used in any type of RAID environment. The RAID device appears as a single device in the /dev/mapper folder, which you can then partition and format to a specific filesystem.

The Bottom Line

Create Linux partitions on storage devices. Once you connect a drive to the Linux system, you'll need to create partitions on the drive. For MBR disks, you can use the fdisk or parted command-line tool. For GPT disks, you can use the gdisk tool. When you partition a drive, you must assign it a size and a filesystem type.

> **Master It** Your company has just purchased a new external USB 5TB drive that you need to connect to your Linux server to store customer data. How would you create a partition on the drive to be used in the Linux system?

Format partitions with a Linux filesystem and mount them in the virtual directory. After you partition the storage device, you must format it using a filesystem that Linux recognizes. The mkfs program is a front-end utility that can format drives using most of the filesystems that Linux supports. The ext4 filesystem is currently the most popular Linux filesystem. It supports journaling and provides good performance. Linux also supports more advanced filesystems, such as btrfs, xfs, zfs, and, of course, the Windows vfat and ntfs filesystems. After creating a filesystem on the partition, you'll need to mount the filesystem into the Linux virtual directory using a mount point and the mount command. The data contained in the partition's filesystem appears under the mount point folder within the virtual directory. To automatically mount partitions at boot time, make an entry for each partition in the /etc/fstab file.

> **Master It** Format the new external USB storage device you just partitioned so that it can be used by your Linux server, and then mount the new partition in the /data directory on your server.

Examine storage devices using Linux tools. There are a host of tools available to help you manage and maintain filesystems. The df and du command-line commands are useful for checking disk space for partitions and the virtual directory, respectively. The fsck utility is a vital tool for repairing corrupt partitions, and it's run automatically at boot time against all partitions automatically mounted in the virtual directory.

> **Master It** In your daily system administration checks, you determined that the partition that contains the /home directory has become full. How can you tell which storage device the /home directory is located on and what user account is using up the most space?

Chapter 12

Configuring Network Settings

For servers, it's a necessity to have your Linux system connected to some type of network. Whether it's the need to share files and printers on a local network or serve web pages on the Internet, your Linux server will most likely require some type of network connection.

IN THIS CHAPTER, YOU WILL LEARN TO

◆ Find and examine the network configuration files for your server

◆ View and change network configuration settings using command-line tools

◆ Troubleshoot common network problems

Network Settings

When you first installed your Linux server software (see Chapter 2, "Installing an Ubuntu Server," or Chapter 4, "Installing a Red Hat Server"), you were required to specify the network settings for your server to operate in your network environment. Most Linux workstation setups can use the Dynamic Host Configuration Protocol (DHCP), which allows the workstation to request network information from a DHCP server on the network automatically—you don't have to configure anything. Unfortunately, Linux servers are a bit different.

Since clients must know exactly where to find the server on the network, Linux servers should have a static IP address assigned. While that's possible to do via DHCP, depending on your network it's also possible that you'll need to set the static IP address manually in the server configuration. That makes the job of configurating a Linux server for the network a little bit harder.

There are five main pieces of information you need to configure for your Linux system to interact on a network:

◆ The host address

◆ The network subnet address

◆ The default router (sometimes called the *gateway*)

◆ The system hostname

◆ A DNS server address for resolving hostnames

Unfortunately, different Linux distributions use different methods for storing the network information required for the system. The following sections walk through the standard network configurations for both Ubuntu and Red Hat servers.

Ubuntu Servers

If you choose to manually configure the network settings during the Ubuntu server installation, a form appears for you to select which network interface to configure, as shown in Figure 12.1.

FIGURE 12.1
Selecting the network interface during an Ubuntu server installation

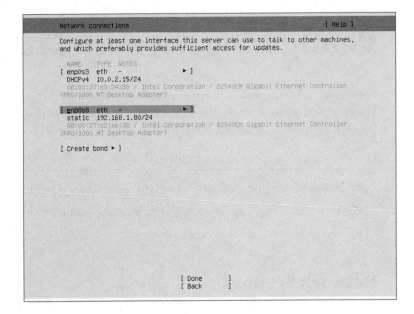

When you select a specific interface and set it to use Manual settings, a new form appears for you to fill out, as shown in Figure 12.2.

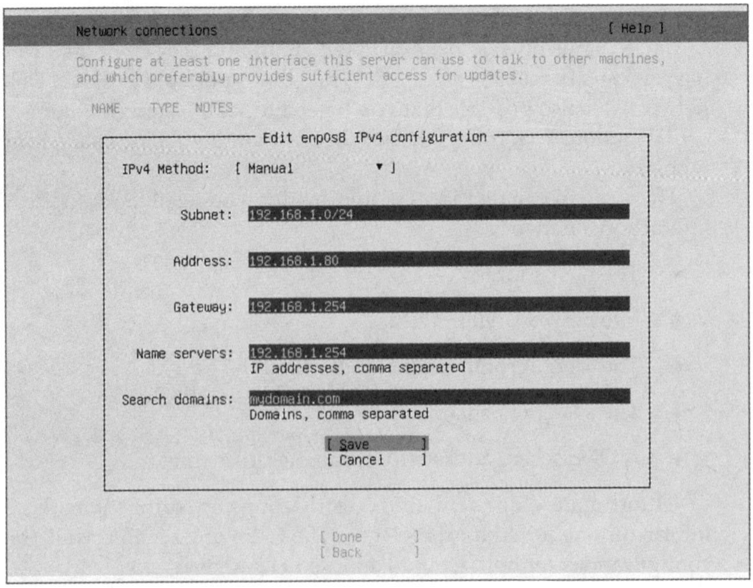

FIGURE 12.2
Setting network information during an Ubuntu server installation

In this form, you'll need to specify the values for each of the network settings. The installation service then automatically sets these values in the appropriate network configuration files for you. However, if you ever need to change the network settings, it helps to know where to find that information.

Since version 17.04, Ubuntu servers utilize the *Netplan* tool to manage network settings for the server. The Netplan tool doesn't actually handle the network traffic itself—that job is left to the `systemd-networkd` application. Instead, Netplan just makes the job of configurating network settings easier and then passes that information on to the `systemd-networkd` application.

Netplan uses a simple series of text-based configuration files located in the `/etc/netplan` directory to define all of the required network settings. These files use the YAML Ain't Markup Language (YAML) text format to define the network settings.

There can be multiple files in the `/etc/netplan` directory, and each file definition builds off prior files in the directory (in lexicographical order). This allows you to split multiple network settings into multiple files, making it easier to define settings for multiple network interfaces if necessary. Listing 12.1 shows a sample Netplan configuration file for an Ubuntu server.

LISTING 12.1:   Sample Ubuntu Server Network Configuration

```
# This is the network config written by 'subiquity'
network:
  ethernets:
    enp0s3:
      dhcp4: true
    enp0s8:
      addresses:
      - 192.168.1.80/24
      gateway4: 192.168.1.254
      nameservers:
        addresses:
        - 192.168.1.254
        search:
        - mydomain.com
  version: 2
```

In the example shown in Listing 12.1, the Ubuntu server has two network interface cards.

◆ The enp0s3 interface uses DHCP to obtain a dynamic IP address from a DHCP server on the network.

◆ The enp0s8 interface uses a static IP address of 192.168.1.80 on the network. The /24 at the end of the address indicates the subnet mask is 255.255.255.0. The file also specifies the default gateway (router) and the nameserver (DNS server) address.

If you make any changes to the YAML files, you'll need to either reboot the server for the changes to take effect or use the `netplan` command-line tool to have Netplan forward the changes to the `systemd-networkd` application by using the `apply` option.

```
netplan apply
```

The Netplan tool automatically informs the sytemd-networkd application that settings have been changed so it can update the information.

Red Hat Servers

When you select to configure network settings in the Red Hat installation process, a dialog box appears, showing you the available network interfaces, as shown in Figure 12.3.

FIGURE 12.3

The CentOS Network & Host Name dialog box

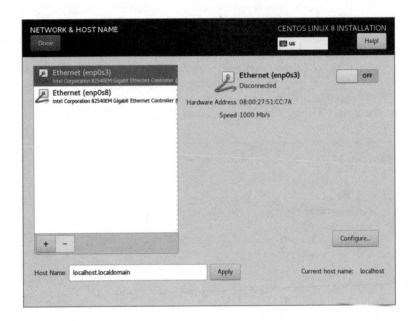

After you select an interface and click the Configure button, a form appears, allowing you to set the network configuration for that interface, as shown in Figure 12.4.

Select the IPv4 Settings tab at the top to set the necessary network information for the interface. The installation program saves the configuration settings you enter to one or more files in the /etc/sysconfig/network-scripts directory. Each network interface has its own file. Listing 12.2 shows an example from a CentOS Linux system.

LISTING 12.2: Sample CentOS Network Interface Configuration Settings

```
TYPE=Ethernet
PROXY_METHOD=none
BROWSER_ONLY=no
BOOTPROTO=none
DEFROUTE=yes
IPV4_FAILURE_FATAL=no
IPV6INIT=yes
IPV6_AUTOCONF=yes
```

```
IPV6_DEFROUTE=yes
IPV6_FAILURE_FATAL=no
IPV6_ADDR_GEN_MODE=stable-privacy
NAME=enp0s8
UUID=22982d8b-7a20-4c82-a9c3-7b0589037a24
DEVICE=enp0s8
ONBOOT=no
IPADDR=192.168.1.81
PREFIX=24
GATEWAY=192.168.1.254
DNS1=192.168.1.254
DOMAIN=mydomain.com
IPV6_PRIVACY=no
```

FIGURE 12.4

The CentOS network settings dialog box

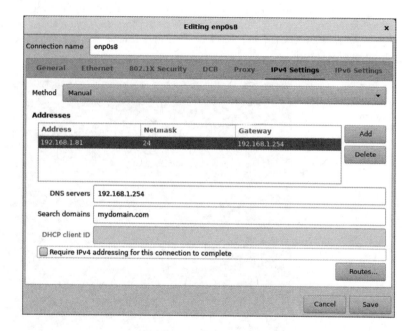

Red Hat servers use the *NetworkManager* tool to manage the network configurations and interfaces. If you make any changes to these files, you'll need to either reboot the server or restart the NetworkManager service using the following command:

```
systemctl restart NetworkManager
```

This forces the NetworkManager program to read the network configuration files and start the appropriate interfaces you have defined.

Using Network Command-Line Tools

Since most Linux server environments don't use a graphical desktop, you'll need to become familiar with the Linux command-line tools to change any of the network configuration settings after installation. There are quite a few different command-line tools that you have at your disposal. This section covers the ones you're most likely to run into.

NetworkManager Tools

While the NetworkManager tool is most often used in graphical workstation environments, Red Hat servers utilize the command-line tools that it provides:

nmtui—provides a simple text-based menu tool

nmcli—provides a text-only command-line tool

Both of these tools help guide you through the process of setting the required network information for your Linux system. The nmtui tool displays a stripped-down version of the graphical tool where you can select a network interface and assign network properties to it, as shown in Figure 12.5.

FIGURE 12.5
The Network Manager nmtui command-line tool

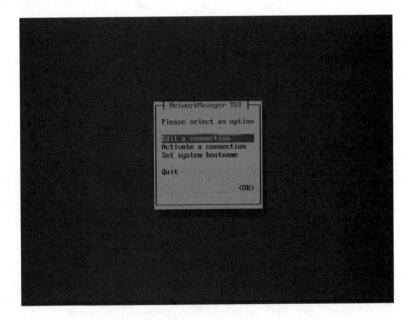

The nmcli tool doesn't attempt to use any type of graphics capabilities; it just provides a command-line interface where you can view and change the network settings. By default, the command displays the current network devices and their settings, as shown in Listing 12.3.

LISTING 12.3: The Default Output of the nmcli Command

```
$ nmcli
enp0s3: connected to enp0s3
        "Intel 82540EM"
        ethernet (e1000), 08:00:27:51:CC:7A, hw, mtu 1500
        ip4 default
        inet4 10.0.2.15/24
        route4 0.0.0.0/0
        route4 10.0.2.0/24
        inet6 fe80::990b:7cfd:20a9:cde8/64
        route6 fe80::/64
        route6 ff00::/8

enp0s8: connected to enp0s8
        "Intel 82540EM"
        ethernet (e1000), 08:00:27:2E:24:25, hw, mtu 1500
        ip6 default
        inet4 192.168.1.81/24
        route4 192.168.1.0/24
        route4 0.0.0.0/0
        inet6 2600:1702:1ce0:eeb0:ef6b:c9a9:33f6:28f/64
        inet6 2600:1702:1ce0:eeb0::5d0/128
        inet6 fe80::3458:6e68:8083:3ac4/64
        route6 2600:1702:1ce0:eeb0::/60
        route6 2600:1702:1ce0:eeb0::/64
        route6 ::/0
        route6 ff00::/8
        route6 fe80::/64
        route6 2600:1702:1ce0:eeb0::5d0/128

lo: unmanaged
        "lo"
        loopback (unknown), 00:00:00:00:00:00, sw, mtu 65536

DNS configuration:
        servers: 192.168.1.254
        domains: attlocal.net
        interface: enp0s3

        servers: 2600:1702:1ce0:eeb0::1
        interface: enp0s8

        servers: 192.168.1.254
        domains: mydomain.com
        interface: enp0s8

$
```

The `nmcli` command uses command-line options to allow you to set the network settings.

```
# nmcli con add type ethernet con-name eth1 ifname enp0s3 ip4
10.0.2.10/24 gw4 192.168.1.254
```

This is a quick way to change network settings directly from the command line.

Other Tools

If your Linux distribution doesn't support one of the NetworkManager tools (such as Ubuntu servers), there are a few legacy command-line tools that you can use.

`ethtool`—displays Ethernet settings for a network interface

`ifconfig`—displays or sets the IP address and netmask values for a network interface

`ip`—displays or sets the IP address, netmask, and router values for a network interface

`iwconfig`—sets the SSID and encryption key for a wireless interface

`route`—sets the default router address

`bond`—binds two or more network cards together

The following sections take a closer look at each of these tools.

THE *ETHTOOL* COMMAND

The `ethtool` command allows you to peek inside the network interface card Ethernet settings and change any properties that you may need to communicate with a network device, such as a switch.

By default, the `ethtool` command displays the current configuration settings for the network interface, as shown in Listing 12.4.

LISTING 12.4:   Output from the `ethtool` Command

```
$ ethtool enp0s8
Settings for enp0s8:
        Supported ports: [ TP ]
        Supported link modes:    10baseT/Half 10baseT/Full
                                 100baseT/Half 100baseT/Full
                                 1000baseT/Full
        Supported pause frame use: No
        Supports auto-negotiation: Yes
        Supported FEC modes: Not reported
        Advertised link modes:   10baseT/Half 10baseT/Full
                                 100baseT/Half 100baseT/Full
                                 1000baseT/Full
        Advertised pause frame use: No
        Advertised auto-negotiation: Yes
        Advertised FEC modes: Not reported
```

```
        Speed: 1000Mb/s
        Duplex: Full
        Port: Twisted Pair
        PHYAD: 0
        Transceiver: internal
        Auto-negotiation: on
        MDI-X: off (auto)
Cannot get wake-on-lan settings: Operation not permitted
        Current message level: 0x00000007 (7)
                               drv probe link
        Link detected: yes
$
```

You can change feature settings on the Ethernet card such as speed, duplex, and whether the network interface attempts to autonegotiate features with the switch.

THE *IFCONFIG* COMMAND

In the early days of Linux, the ifconfig command was the only tool available for working with network settings. It allows you to easily set the network address and subnet mask for a network interface.

```
$ sudo ifconfig enp0s3 down 10.0.2.10 netmask 255.255.255.0
```

While still available, with the advent of fancier tools it's not as common anymore and often is not installed by default in Linux systems. It helps to know that it exists in case you run into an older Linux server that has only ifconfig, but for modern servers, you'll want to use the ip command.

THE *IP* COMMAND

The ip command is more robust in what it can do and has become the more popular method to use for defining network settings from the command line. The ip utility uses several command options to display the current network settings or define new network settings. Table 12.1 shows these commands.

TABLE 12.1:   The ip Utility Command Options

PARAMETER	DESCRIPTION
address	Display or set the IPv4 or IPv6 address on the device.
addrlabel	Define configuration labels.
l2tp	Tunnel Ethernet over IP.
link	Define a network device.

TABLE 12.1:   The `ip` Utility Command Options   *(CONTINUED)*

PARAMETER	DESCRIPTION
`maddress`	Define a multicast address for the system to listen to.
`monitor`	Watch for netlink messages.
`mroute`	Define an entry in the multicast routing cache.
`mrule`	Define a rule in the multicast routing policy database.
`neighbor`	Manage ARP or NDISC cache entries.
`netns`	Manage network namespaces.
`ntable`	Manage the neighbor cache operation.
`route`	Manage the routing table.
`rule`	Manage entries in the routing policy database.
`tcpmetrics`	Manage TCP metrics on the interface.
`token`	Manage tokenized interface identifiers.
`tunnel`	Tunnel over IP.
`tuntap`	Manage TUN/TAP devices.
`xfrm`	Manage IPSec policies for secure connections.

Each command option utilizes parameters to define what to do, such as display network settings or modify existing network settings. Listing 12.5 demonstrates how to display the current network settings using the show parameter.

LISTING 12.5:   The `ip address` Command Output

```
$ ip address show
1: lo: <LOOPBACK,UP,LOWER_UP> mtu 65536 qdisc noqueue state UNKNOWN group
default qlen 1000
    link/loopback 00:00:00:00:00:00 brd 00:00:00:00:00:00
    inet 127.0.0.1/8 scope host lo
       valid_lft forever preferred_lft forever
    inet6 ::1/128 scope host
       valid_lft forever preferred_lft forever
2: enp0s3: <BROADCAST,MULTICAST,UP,LOWER_UP> mtu 1500 qdisc fq_codel state
UP group default qlen 1000
```

```
        link/ether 08:00:27:e0:34:86 brd ff:ff:ff:ff:ff:ff
        inet 10.0.2.15/24 brd 10.0.2.255 scope global dynamic enp0s3
           valid_lft 86012sec preferred_lft 86012sec
        inet6 fe80::a00:27ff:fee0:3486/64 scope link
           valid_lft forever preferred_lft forever
    3: enp0s8: <BROADCAST,MULTICAST,UP,LOWER_UP> mtu 1500 qdisc fq_codel state
    UP group default qlen 1000
        link/ether 08:00:27:c2:a6:38 brd ff:ff:ff:ff:ff:ff
        inet 192.168.1.80/24 brd 192.168.1.255 scope global enp0s8
           valid_lft forever preferred_lft forever
        inet6 2600:1702:1ce0:eeb0::4ce/128 scope global dynamic noprefixroute
           valid_lft 2591617sec preferred_lft 604417sec
        inet6 2600:1702:1ce0:eeb0:a00:27ff:fec2:a638/64 scope global dynamic
    mngtmpaddr noprefixroute
           valid_lft 3434sec preferred_lft 3434sec
        inet6 fe80::a00:27ff:fec2:a638/64 scope link
           valid_lft forever preferred_lft forever
     $
```

This example shows three network interfaces on the Linux system:

lo—the local loopback interface

enp0s3—a wired network interface

enp0s8—a second wired network interface

The *local loopback interface* is a special virtual network interface. Any local program can use it to communicate with other programs just as if they were across a network. That can simplify transferring data between programs.

The enp0s3 and enp0s8 network interfaces are the wired network connection for the Linux system. The ip command shows the IP address assigned to each interface (there's both an IP and an IPv6 link local address assigned), the netmask value, and some basic statistics about the packets on the interface.

If the output doesn't show a network address assigned to an interface, you can use the ip command to specify the host address and netmask values for the interface.

```
# ip address add 10.0.2.15/24 dev enp0s3
```

Then use the ip command to set the default router for the network interface.

```
# ip route add default via 192.168.1.254 dev enp0s3
```

Finally, make the network interface active by using the link option.

```
# ip link set enp0s3 up
```

The ip command has become the Swiss Army knife for command-line network configuration and is typically installed in most Linux server distributions.

THE *IWCONFIG* COMMAND

While generally not recommended for servers, some Linux systems do use wireless network cards to connect to the network. Before you can use the ip command to assign an address to a wireless interface, you must assign the wireless SSID and encryption key values using the iwconfig command.

```
# iwconfig wlan0 essid "MyNetwork" key s:mypassword
```

The essid parameter specifies the access point SSID name, and the key parameter specifies the encryption key required to connect to it. Notice that the encryption key is preceded by an s:. That allows you to specify the encryption key in ASCII text characters; otherwise, you'll need to specify the key using hexadecimal values.

If you don't know the name of a local wireless connection, you can use the iwlist command to display all of the wireless signals your wireless card detects. Just specify the name of the wireless device and use the scan option.

```
$ iwlist wlan0 scan
```

THE *ROUTE* COMMAND

While the ip command is a one-stop method for changing network settings, an alternative way to specify network routing settings for your network is the route command.

```
# route add default gw 192.168.1.254
```

You can also use the route command by itself to view the current default router configured for the system.

```
$ route
Kernel IP routing table
Destination     Gateway         Genmask         Flags Metric Ref Use Iface
default         192.168.1.254   0.0.0.0         UG    0      0   0   enp0s3
192.168.1.0     *               255.255.255.0   U     1      0   0   enp0s3
$
```

The default router defined for the Linux system is 192.168.1.254 and is available from the enp0s3 network interface. The output also shows that to get to the 192.168.1.0 network, you don't need a gateway, as that's the local network the Linux system is connected to.

If your network is connected to multiple networks via multiple routers, you can manually create the routing table in the system by using the add or del command-line options for the route command. The format for that is as follows:

```
route [add] [del] target gw gateway
```

where *target* is the target host or network, and *gateway* is the router address.

THE *BOND* COMMAND

One final network configuration setting you may run into in Linux distributions has to do with network interface *bonding*. Bonding allows you to aggregate multiple interfaces into one virtual network device.

You can then tell the Linux system how to treat the virtual network device using three different basic types.

Load balancing—Network traffic is shared between two or more network interfaces.

Aggregation—Two or more network interfaces are combined to create one larger network pipe.

Active/passive—One network interface is live while the other is used as a backup for fault tolerance.

There are seven different bonding modes you can choose from, as described in Table 12.2.

TABLE 12.2:   Network Interface Bonding Modes

MODE	NAME	DESCRIPTION
0	balance-rr	Provides load balancing and fault tolerance using interfaces in a round-robin approach
1	active-backup	Provides fault tolerance using one interface as the primary and the other as a backup
2	balance-xor	Provides load balancing and fault tolerance by transmitting on one interface and receiving on the second
3	broadcast	Transmits all packets on both interfaces
4	802.3ad	Aggregates the interfaces to create one connection combining the interface bandwidths
5	balance-tlb	Provides load balancing and fault tolerance based on the current transmit load on each interface
6	balance-alb	Provides load balancing and fault tolerance based on the current receive load on each interface

To initialize network interface bonding, you must first load the bonding module in the Linux kernel.

```
$ sudo modprobe bonding
```

This creates a bond0 network interface, which you can then define using the ip utility.

```
$ sudo ip link add bond0 type bond mode 4
```

Once you've defined the bond type, you can add the appropriate network interfaces to the bond using the ip utility.

```
$ sudo ip link set eth0 master bond0
$ sudo ip link set eth1 master bond0
```

The Linux system will then treat the bond0 device as a single network interface utilizing the load balancing or aggregation method you defined.

NETWORK BRIDGING

If you have multiple network interface cards on your Linux system and choose to connect them to separate networks, you can configure your Linux system to act as a bridge between the two networks. The brctl command allows you to control how the bridging behaves. To do this though, you must set the ip_forward kernel parameter in the /etc/sysctl.conf file to 1 to enable bridging.

USING DHCP TOOLS

If your network uses DHCP servers to assign static IP addresses to application servers, you'll need to ensure that a proper DHCP client program is running on your Linux server. The DHCP client program communicates with the network DHCP server in the background and assigns the necessary IP address settings as directed by the DHCP server. There are three common DHCP programs available for Linux systems:

◆ dhcpcd

◆ dhclient

◆ pump

The dhcpcd program is becoming the most popular of the three, but you'll still see the other two used in some Linux distributions.

When you use your Linux system's software package manager utility to install the DHCP client program, it sets the program to automatically launch at boot time and handle the IP address configuration needed to interact on the network.

RUNNING YOUR OWN DHCP SERVER

If you're working with a Linux server that acts as a DHCP server, the /etc/dhcpd.conf file contains the IP address settings that the server offers to DHCP clients. The file contains a section for each subnet the DHCP server services.

```
subnet 10.0.2.0 netmask 255.255.255.0 {
        option routers                  192.168.1.254;
        option subnet-mask              255.255.255.0;

        option domain-name              "mynetwork.com";
        option domain-name-servers       192.168.1.254;

        option time-offset              -18000;     # Eastern Standard Time

      range 10.0.2.1 10.0.2.100;
  }
```

It's good to get some practice using these network command-line tools before something goes wrong with your Linux server. Here's a case study to help guide you through how to document your existing network configuration.

 Real World Scenario

DETERMINING THE NETWORK ENVIRONMENT

This exercise will demonstrate how to quickly assess the network configuration and programs for your Linux system without having to dig through lots of configuration files. To document your system network information, follow these steps:

1. Log into your Linux server using the user account you created in Chapter 2 or Chapter 4, and acquire root privileges by using su or by using sudo with each of the following commands.

2. First, determine the network interfaces installed on the server. Type **ip address show** to display the current network interfaces. You will most likely see a loopback interface (named l0) and one or more network interfaces. Write down the IP address (called *inet*) and IPv6 address (called *inet6*) assigned to each network interface, along with the hardware address and the network mask address.

3. Use the ethtool command to determine the connection speed of the network interfaces. Type **ethtool *int***, where *int* is the name of each interface displayed in step 2. Note the speed and duplex settings for each interface.

4. Disable one of the network interfaces on your Linux server. Type **ip link set *int* down**, where *int* is the interface name displayed in step 2.

5. Type **ip address show** to display the network interfaces. Note the status displayed for the interface you disabled. It should show DOWN for the status.

6. Enable the interface by typing **ip link set *int* up**, where *int* is the interface you disabled in step 6. Type **ip address show** and note the status of the interface.

Basic Network Troubleshooting

After you've installed and configured the network interface in your Linux server, there are a few things you can do to check to make sure things are operating properly. This section walks through the commands you should know to monitor the network activity, including watching what processes are listening on the network and what connections are active from your system.

Sending Test Packets

One way to test network connectivity is to send test packets to known hosts. Linux provides the ping and ping6 commands to do that. The ping and ping6 commands send Internet Control Message Protocol (ICMP) packets to remote hosts using either the IPv4 (ping) or IPv6 (ping6) protocol. ICMP packets work behind the scenes to track connectivity and provide control messages between systems. If the remote host supports ICMP, it will send a reply packet when it receives a ping packet.

The basic format for the `ping` command is to just specify the IP address of the remote host.

```
$ ping 10.0.2.2
PING 10.0.2.2 (10.0.2.2) 56(84) bytes of data.
64 bytes from 10.0.2.2: icmp_seq=1 ttl=63 time=14.6 ms
64 bytes from 10.0.2.2: icmp_seq=2 ttl=63 time=3.82 ms
64 bytes from 10.0.2.2: icmp_seq=3 ttl=63 time=2.05 ms
64 bytes from 10.0.2.2: icmp_seq=4 ttl=63 time=0.088 ms
64 bytes from 10.0.2.2: icmp_seq=5 ttl=63 time=3.54 ms
64 bytes from 10.0.2.2: icmp_seq=6 ttl=63 time=3.97 ms
64 bytes from 10.0.2.2: icmp_seq=7 ttl=63 time=0.040 ms
^C
--- 10.0.2.2 ping statistics ---
7 packets transmitted, 7 received, 0% packet loss, time 6020ms
rtt min/avg/max/mdev = 0.040/4.030/14.696/4.620 ms
$
```

The `ping` command continues sending packets until you press Ctrl+C. You can also use the `-c` command-line option to specify a set number of packets to send, then stop.

For the `ping6` command, things get a little more complicated. If you're using an IPv6 link local address, you also need to tell the command which interface to send the packets out on.

```
$ ping6 -c 4 fe80::c418:2ed0:aead:cbce%enp0s3
PING fe80::c418:2ed0:aead:cbce%enp0s3(fe80::c418:2ed0:aead:cbce) 56 data
bytes
64 bytes from fe80::c418:2ed0:aead:cbce: icmp_seq=1 ttl=128 time=1.47 ms
64 bytes from fe80::c418:2ed0:aead:cbce: icmp_seq=2 ttl=128 time=0.478 ms
64 bytes from fe80::c418:2ed0:aead:cbce: icmp_seq=3 ttl=128 time=0.777 ms
64 bytes from fe80::c418:2ed0:aead:cbce: icmp_seq=4 ttl=128 time=0.659 ms

--- fe80::c418:2ed0:aead:cbce%enp0s3 ping statistics ---
4 packets transmitted, 4 received, 0% packet loss, time 3003ms
rtt min/avg/max/mdev = 0.478/0.847/1.475/0.378 ms
$
```

The `%enp0s3` part tells the system to send the ping packets out on the network using the enp0s3 network interface for the link local address.

USING PING TO TROUBLESHOOT WITH REMOTE HOSTS

Unfortunately, these days many network routers and firewalls block ICMP packets because they can be used to create a denial-of-service (DOS) attack against the host. Don't be surprised if you try to ping a remote host and don't get any responses.

Finding Host Information

Sometimes the problem isn't with network connectivity, but with the DNS hostname system. You can test a hostname using the host command.

```
$ host www.linux.org
www.linux.org is an alias for linux.org.
linux.org has address 107.170.40.56
linux.org mail is handled by 20 mx.iqemail.net.
$
```

The host command queries the DNS server to determine the IP addresses assigned to the specified hostname. By default, it returns all IP addresses associated with the hostname. Some hosts are supported by multiple servers in a load balancing configuration. The host command will show all of the IP addresses associated with those servers.

```
$ host www.google.com
www.google.com has address 74.125.138.104
www.google.com has address 74.125.138.105
www.google.com has address 74.125.138.147
www.google.com has address 74.125.138.99
www.google.com has address 74.125.138.103
www.google.com has address 74.125.138.106
www.google.com has IPv6 address 2607:f8b0:4002:c0c::67
$
```

You can also specify an IP address for the host command, and it will attempt to find the hostname associated with it.

```
$ host 107.170.40.56
56.40.170.107.in-addr.arpa domain name pointer iqdig11.iqnection.com.
$
```

However, an IP address will often resolve to a generic server hostname that hosts the website and not the website alias, as is the case with the www.linux.org IP address in the preceding code snippet.

Another great tool to use is the dig command. The dig command displays all the DNS data records associated with a specific host or network. For example, you can look up the information for a specific hostname.

```
$ dig www.linux.org

; <<>> DiG 9.9.4-RedHat-9.9.4-18.el7_1.5 <<>> www.linux.org
;; global options: +cmd
;; Got answer:
;; ->>HEADER<<- opcode: QUERY, status: NOERROR, id: 45314
```

```
;; flags: qr rd ra; QUERY: 1, ANSWER: 2, AUTHORITY: 0, ADDITIONAL: 1

;; OPT PSEUDOSECTION:
; EDNS: version: 0, flags:; udp: 4096
;; QUESTION SECTION:
;www.linux.org.              IN    A

;; ANSWER SECTION:
www.linux.org.        3600  IN    A     104.21.80.209
www.linux.org.        3600  IN    A     172.67.153.210


;; Query time: 75 msec
;; SERVER: 192.168.1.254#53(192.168.1.254)
;; WHEN: Sat Jan 30 17:44:29 EST 2021
;; MSG SIZE  rcvd: 72
$
```

Or you can look up DNS data records associated with a specific network service, such as a mail server.

```
$ dig linux.org MX

; <<>> DiG 9.9.5-3ubuntu0.5-Ubuntu <<>> linux.org MX
;; global options: +cmd
;; Got answer:
;; ->>HEADER<<- opcode: QUERY, status: NOERROR, id: 16202
;; flags: qr rd ra; QUERY: 1, ANSWER: 1, AUTHORITY: 0, ADDITIONAL: 1

;; OPT PSEUDOSECTION:
; EDNS: version: 0, flags:; udp: 4096
;; QUESTION SECTION:
;linux.org.               IN    MX

;; ANSWER SECTION:
linux.org.    3600     IN    MX    20    mx.iqemail.net.

;; Query time: 75 msec
;; SERVER: 127.0.1.1#53(127.0.1.1)
;; WHEN: Sat Jan 30 17:47:43 EST 2021
;; MSG SIZE  rcvd: 68

$
```

If you need to look up DNS information for multiple servers or domains, the nslookup command provides an interactive interface where you can enter commands.

```
$ nslookup
> www.google.com
Server:      192.168.1.254
```

```
Address:     192.168.1.254#53

Non-authoritative answer:
Name:    www.google.com
Address:     172.217.2.228
> www.wikipedia.org
Server:      192.168.1.254
Address:     192.168.1.254#53

Non-authoritative answer:
Name:    www.wikipedia.org
Address: 208.80.153.224
> exit

$
```

You can also dynamically specify the address of another DNS server to use for the name lookups, which is a handy way to determine if your default DNS server is at fault if a name resolution fails.

Advanced Network Troubleshooting

Besides the simple network tests shown in the previous section, Linux has some additional programs that can provide more information about the network environment. Sometimes it helps to be able to see just what network connections are active on a Linux system. There are two ways to troubleshoot that issue: the netstat command and the ss command.

The *netstat* Command

The netstat command can provide a wealth of network information for you. While often not installed by default, you can find it in the net-tools package in most Linux distributions. By default, it lists all the open network connections on the system.

```
$ netstat
Active Internet connections (w/o servers)
Proto Recv-Q Send-Q Local Address           Foreign Address         State
tcp        0      0 ubuntu-server:ssh        192.168.1.71:64733 ESTABLISHED
udp        0      0 ubuntu-server:58059      homeportal:domain   ESTABLISHED
udp6       0      0 ubuntu-server:47458      homeportal:domain   ESTABLISHED
Active UNIX domain sockets (w/o servers)
Proto RefCnt Flags       Type   State    I-Node   Path
unix  2      [ ]         DGRAM           24495    /run/user/1000/systemd/notify
unix  3      [ ]         DGRAM           15598    /run/systemd/notify
unix  2      [ ]         DGRAM           15615    /run/systemd/journal/syslog
unix  8      [ ]         DGRAM           15623    /run/systemd/journal/dev-log
unix  9      [ ]         DGRAM           15627    /run/systemd/journal/socket

...
```

The netstat command produces lots of output, as there are normally lots of programs that use network services on Linux systems. The output shows both network connections and internal *socket connections*. A socket connection is a file that allows one program running on the server to pass data to another program by reading from the file and writing to the file using standard network protocols.

You can limit the output to just TCP or UDP connections by using the –t command-line option for TCP connections, or –u for UDP connections.

```
$ netstat -t
Active Internet connections (w/o servers)
Proto Recv-Q Send-Q Local Address       Foreign Address        State
tcp        0      0 ubuntu-server2:ssh  192.168.1.71:64733     ESTABLISHED
$
```

You can also get a list of what applications are listening on which network ports by using the –l option.

```
$ netstat -l
Active Internet connections (only servers)
Proto Recv-Q Send-Q Local Address        Foreign Address      State
tcp        0      0 localhost:domain     0.0.0.0:*            LISTEN
tcp        0      0 0.0.0.0:ssh          0.0.0.0:*            LISTEN
tcp6       0      0 [::]:ssh             [::]:*              LISTEN
udp        0      0 localhost:domain     0.0.0.0:*
udp        0      0 ubuntu-server2:bootpc 0.0.0.0:*
udp6       0      0 ubuntu-se:dhcpv6-client [::]:*
raw6       0      0 [::]:ipv6-icmp       [::]:*              7
raw6       0      0 [::]:ipv6-icmp       [::]:*              7
Active UNIX domain sockets (only servers)
Proto RefCnt Flags  Type       State      I-Node  Path
unix  2      [ ACC ] SEQPACKET LISTENING  15630 /run/udev/control
unix  2      [ ACC ] STREAM    LISTENING  24498 /run/user/1000/systemd/private
unix  2      [ ACC ] STREAM    LISTENING  24507 /run/user/1000/bus
...
```

As you can see, just a standard Linux workstation still has lots of things happening in the background, waiting for connections.

Yet another great feature of the netstat command is that the –s option displays statistics for the different types of packets the system has used on the network.

```
$ netstat -s
Ip:
    Forwarding: 2
    58301 total packets received
    2 with invalid addresses
    0 forwarded
    0 incoming packets discarded
    58299 incoming packets delivered
    31415 requests sent out
    20 outgoing packets dropped
```

```
Icmp:
    44 ICMP messages received
    0 input ICMP message failed
    ICMP input histogram:
        destination unreachable: 44
    121 ICMP messages sent
    0 ICMP messages failed
    ICMP output histogram:
        destination unreachable: 121
IcmpMsg:
        InType3: 44
        OutType3: 121
Tcp:
    12 active connection openings
    2 passive connection openings
    0 failed connection attempts
    0 connection resets received
    1 connections established
    57794 segments received
    31023 segments sent out
    3 segments retransmitted
    0 bad segments received
    6 resets sent
Udp:
    195 packets received
    123 packets to unknown port received
    0 packet receive errors
    277 packets sent
    0 receive buffer errors
    0 send buffer errors
    IgnoredMulti: 115
UdpLite:
TcpExt:
    2 TCP sockets finished time wait in fast timer
    6 delayed acks sent
    Quick ack mode was activated 6 times
    16945 packet headers predicted
    216 acknowledgments not containing data payload received
    199 predicted acknowledgments
    TCPLossProbes: 3
    TCPLossProbeRecovery: 1
    TCPBacklogCoalesce: 1
    TCPDSACKOldSent: 7
    3 connections reset due to unexpected data
    TCPRcvCoalesce: 43797
    TCPOFOQueue: 34968
    TCPAutoCorking: 93
    TCPOrigDataSent: 597
```

```
        TCPDelivered: 594
        TCPAckCompressed: 23859
IpExt:
        InMcastPkts: 25
        InBcastPkts: 115
        InOctets: 110055874
        OutOctets: 2357683
        InMcastOctets: 900
        InBcastOctets: 24533
        InNoECTPkts: 75126
$
```

The netstat statistics output can give you a rough idea of how busy your Linux system is on the network or if there's a specific issue with one of the protocols installed.

Examining Sockets

The netstat tool provides a wealth of network information, but it can often be hard to determine just which program is listening on which open port. The ss command can come to your rescue for that.

A program connection to a port is called a *socket*. The ss command can link which system processes are using which network sockets that are active.

```
$ ss -anpt
State Recv-Q Send-Q Local Address:Port Peer Address:Port Process
LISTEN 0   4096   127.0.0.53%lo:53 0.0.0.0:*          users:(("systemd-
resolve",pid=582,fd=13))
LISTEN 0   128    0.0.0.0:22        0.0.0.0:* users:(("sshd",pid=630,fd=3))
ESTAB  0    64    192.168.1.80:22  192.168.1.71:64934 users:(("sshd",
pid=2556,fd=4),("sshd",pid=2474,fd=4))
LISTEN 0   128    [::]:22           [::]:*     users:(("sshd",pid=630,fd=4))
$
```

The -anpt option displays both listening and established TCP connections, as well as the process (if any) they're associated with. This output shows that the SSH port (port 22) has an established connection with a remote client and is using the sshd process.

Here's another case study to get some practice troubleshooting network issues on your Linux server.

 Real World Scenario

WATCHING FOR NETWORK CONNECTIONS

In this case study, you'll use the netstat and ss commands to monitor the network connections on your Linux server. Just follow these steps:

1. Log into your Linux server using the user account you created in Chapter 2 or Chapter 4, and acquire root privileges by using su or by using sudo with each of the following commands.

2. Type **netstat -l** to display the programs listening for incoming network connections. The entries marked as unix are using the loopback address to communicate with other programs internally on your system.

> **3.** Type **ss -anpt** to display the processes that have active network ports open on your system.
>
> It's a good idea to document the programs that are listening on your servers, as well as any that are actively communicating with external hosts. By being vigilant in watching network connections, you can often determine if something is going wrong with your system, or even if an attacker is trying to connect into your system.

The Bottom Line

Find and examine the network configuration files for your server.   Linux stores network connection information in configuration files. The installer program that runs when you install the Linux software typically asks you for the network configuration information and creates these files automatically. However, it's a good idea to find where these files are located on your Linux system in case anything goes wrong or you need to change anything. Ubuntu servers store the configuration files in the /etc/netplan directory. Red Hat servers store the configuration files in the /etc/sysconfig/network-scripts directory. Files in those directories define the network settings for each interface.

> **Master It**   You've been asked to help a colleague solve a network problem on an Ubuntu Linux server. What file would you look at to determine the current network configuration settings?

View and change network configuration settings using command-line tools.   If you must configure your network settings from the command line, there are a few different tools you'll need to use. For both wireless and wired connections, you need to use the ifconfig or ip command to set the IP address and netmask values for the interface. You may also need to use the route command to define the default router for the local network. For wireless connections, you'll need to use the iwconfig command to set the wireless access point and SSID key.

> **Master It**   Customers can't connect to your Red Hat Linux server, but the server is running, and the network cable is plugged in. What commands should you run to view the status of the network interface and make it active if it's down?

Troubleshoot common network problems.   Once your network configuration is complete, you may have to do some additional troubleshooting for network problems. The ping and ping6 commands allow you to send ICMP packets to remote hosts to test basic connectivity. If you suspect issues with hostnames, you can use the host and dig commands to query the DNS server for hostnames.

For more advanced network troubleshooting, you can use the netstat and ss commands to display what applications are using which network ports on the system.

> **Master It**   The web administrator for your company called you to say none of the customers can connect to the company's website running on an Ubuntu server. What commands should you use to see first if the Ubuntu server can communicate with remote hosts and then that the web server software is listening for HTTPS connections?

Chapter 13

Managing Users and Groups

At the core of Linux security is the user account. Each individual who accesses a Linux system should have a unique account assigned to them. Adding, modifying, and deleting user account authorizations are some of the most basic, but important, tasks you do to protect your system. Access granted to user accounts are more easily managed by putting the various accounts into groups. Managing these groups of users and defining what they are allowed to access also provides base-level protection.

In addition to these user accounts and groups, it is important to understand basic Linux file and directory permissions, including how to view them and interpret their meanings. The codes used to set and modify permissions can be a little cryptic, and without full understanding, you risk leaving files or directories opened to unauthorized access.

Our goal in this chapter is to provide a basic understanding of managing user accounts and groups as well as file and directory permissions. We'll provide guidance that will help you avoid basic security problems, while increasing your system's usability for authorized users.

IN THIS CHAPTER, YOU WILL LEARN TO

- ◆ Change a file's owner

- ◆ Create user accounts

- ◆ Modify a user's password

- ◆ Find an environment file

- ◆ Delete a user group

Understanding Linux Permissions

The core security feature of Linux is file and directory permissions. Linux accomplishes this by assigning each file and directory an owner and allowing that owner to set the basic security settings to control access to the file or directory. This section walks through how Linux handles ownership of files and directories, as well as the basic permissions settings that you can assign to any file or directory on your Linux system.

You can view permission settings for a specified file by adding the -l option to the ls command. To see these settings on a directory, add the -d option to the -l option.

```
$ history > keepHistory.txt
$ ls -l keepHistory.txt
-rw-rw-r-- 1 sysadmin sysadmin 12933 Jan 19 19:14 keepHistory.txt
$
$ ls -ld /etc/
drwxr-xr-x 94 root root 4096 Dec 12 15:50 /etc/
$
```

Figure 13.1 shows a chart that provides names for all of the various information displayed using the ls -l command. You'll want to refer to this graphic as you progress through this chapter section.

FIGURE 13.1

File information chart

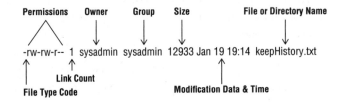

Understanding Ownership

The owner and group information of a file (or directory) is important, because Linux uses this information in a three-tiered approach for protecting files and directories.

Owner—Within the Linux system, each file and directory is assigned to a single user account. Permissions set in this tier apply only to the file's owner. Because the owner is a user account name, this tier is also called the *user* category.

Group—The Linux system also assigns each file and directory to a single group of users. The administrator can then assign that group specific privileges to the file or directory that differ from the owner privileges.

World—This permission category is assigned to any user account that is not the owner nor in the assigned group. Permissions set in this level are often sparse due to the wide range of accounts to which they apply. This tier is also called *others*, because it applies to those who are neither the file's owner or in its group.

Many Linux distributions (such as Ubuntu and Red Hat) assign each user account to a separate group with the same name as the user account. This helps prevent accidental sharing of files. However, this can also make things a little confusing when you're working with owner and group permissions and you see the same name appear in both areas. Here is an example where the owner and group names differ—the owner is root, and the group is shadow:

```
$ ls -l /etc/shadow
-rw-r----- 1 root shadow 1027 Dec  4 20:13 /etc/shadow
$
```

When a user creates a file or directory, by default the Linux system automatically assigns that user as the owner and uses the primary group (discussed later in this chapter) the user belongs to as the group for the file or directory. You can change the default owner and group assigned to files and directories using Linux commands. The following sections show how to do that.

CHANGING FILE OR DIRECTORY OWNERSHIP

The root user or an account with super user privileges can change the owner assigned to a file or directory by using the chown command. This command's format looks like this:

```
chown [OPTIONS] NEWOWNER FILENAMES
```

The *NEWOWNER* parameter is the username of the new owner to assign to the file or directory, and *FILENAMES* is the name of the file or directory to change.

```
$ ls -l keepHistory.txt
-rw-rw-r-- 1 sysadmin sysadmin 12933 Jan 19 19:14 keepHistory.txt
$
$ sudo chown root keepHistory.txt
[sudo] password for sysadmin:
$
$ ls -l keepHistory.txt
-rw-rw-r-- 1 root sysadmin 12933 Jan 19 19:14 keepHistory.txt
$
```

If needed, you can specify more than one file or directory by placing a space between each file or directory name. There are a few command-line options available for the chown command, but many are not used much. One that may be helpful for you is the -R option, which recursively changes the owner of all files under the specified directory.

CHANGING THE FILE OR DIRECTORY GROUP

The file or directory owner, or an account with super user privileges, can change the group assigned to the file or directory by using the chgrp command. This command's syntax format is as follows:

```
chgrp [OPTIONS] NEWOWNER FILENAMES
```

The *NEWGROUP* parameter is the name of the new user group assigned to the file or directory, and the *FILENAMES* parameter is the name of the file or directory to change. If you're the owner of the file, you can only change the group to one that you belong to. The root user, or an account with super user privileges, can change the group to any group on the system.

```
$ whoami
sysadmin
$ ls -l keepHistory.txt
-rw-rw-r-- 1 root sysadmin 12933 Jan 19 19:14 keepHistory.txt
$
$ sudo chgrp users keepHistory.txt
[sudo] password for sysadmin:
$
```

```
$ ls -l keepHistory.txt
-rw-rw-r-- 1 root users 12933 Jan 19 19:14 keepHistory.txt
$
```

The chgrp command also uses the -R option to recursively change the group assigned to all files and directories under the specified directory.

Besides changing a file's group with chgrp, you can also change it with the chown command. Just put a colon (:) in the front of the new group name.

```
$ ls -l keepHistory.txt
-rw-rw-r-- 1 root users 12933 Jan 19 19:14 keepHistory.txt
$
$ sudo chown :games keepHistory.txt
$
$ ls -l keepHistory.txt
-rw-rw-r-- 1 root games 12933 Jan 19 19:14 keepHistory.txt
```

Even more convenient is the ability to change the file's owner and group at the same time with the chown command. Put the new owner first, followed by a colon, and end with the new group.

```
$ ls -l keepHistory.txt
-rw-rw-r-- 1 root games 12933 Jan 19 19:14 keepHistory.txt
$
$ sudo chown root:sysadmin keepHistory.txt
$
$ ls -l keepHistory.txt
-rw-rw-r-- 1 root sysadmin 12933 Jan 19 19:14 keepHistory.txt
$
```

Keep in mind that you still have to use the root account or an account with super user privileges to perform these chown command changes to files.

Controlling Access Permissions

Once you've established the file or directory owner and group, you can assign specific permissions to each. Linux uses three types of permission controls on files and directories.

Read—The ability to access the data stored within the file or display a directory's contents

Write—The ability to modify the data stored within the file or create, rename, modify attributes of, and delete files within a directory

Execute—The ability to run the file on the system, or the ability for a user to change their working directory to this directory (if also set on all parent directories)

You can assign each tier of protection (owner, group, and world) different read, write, and execute permissions. This creates a set of nine different permissions that are assigned to each file and directory on the Linux system. These permissions appear in the ls output after the file type code when you use the -l option (shown previously in Figure 13.1). The r stands for read, w for write, and x for execute.

Figure 13.2 shows an example of file and directory permission data with the owner, group, and world tiers identified.

FIGURE 13.2
Permissions with tier identification

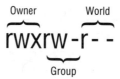

The order of the permissions within each tier is important. It is always in rwx order, and if a dash (-) is shown in one of the permission's place, that means that particular permission is not granted.

The root user account, an account with super user privileges, or the owner of the file or directory can change the assigned permissions. The command to change permissions is chmod. The chmod command can use two different modes for denoting the permission settings: symbolic mode and octal mode.

In *symbolic mode*, you denote permissions by using a letter code for the tier: user (u), group (g), others (o), or all (a). Notice that this mode refers to the owner tier as "user" and the world tier as "others," so you have to pay attention when using this command!

With this mode, the permissions syntax code is fairly easy: read (r), write (w), or execute (x). The tier and permission codes are separated with a plus sign (+) if you want to add the permission, a minus sign (-) to remove the permission, or an equal sign (=) to set the permission as the only permission. Here is an example of using symbolic mode with the chmod command:

```
$ history > newHistory.txt
$ ls -l newHistory.txt
-rw-rw-r-- 1 sysadmin sysadmin 14296 Jan 21 16:06 newHistory.txt
$
$ chmod g-w newHistory.txt
$
$ ls -l newHistory.txt
-rw-r--r-- 1 sysadmin sysadmin 14296 Jan 21 16:06 newHistory.txt
$
```

In this example, the g-w code in the chmod command indicates to remove the write permission for the group tier from the newHistory.txt file.

Using symbolic mode, you can combine the letter codes for the various tiers and permissions both to make multiple changes in a single chmod command, as shown here:

```
$ chmod ug=rwx newHistory.txt
$ ls -l newHistory.txt
-rwxrwxr-- 1 sysadmin sysadmin 14296 Jan 21 16:06 newHistory.txt
$
```

The ug code assigns the change to both the owner and the group levels, while the rwx code assigns the read, write, and execute permissions. The equal sign indicates to set those permissions.

The second mode available in chmod is called *octal mode*. With octal mode, the nine permission bits are represented as three octal numbers, one each for the owner, group, and world permission tiers. Table 13.1 shows how the octal number matches the three symbolic mode permissions.

TABLE 13.1: Octal Mode Permissions

OCTAL VALUE	PERMISSION	MEANING
0	---	No permissions
1	--x	Execute only
2	-w-	Write only
3	-wx	Write and execute
4	r--	Read only
5	r-x	Read and execute
6	rw-	Read and write
7	rwx	Read, write, and execute

In octal mode syntax, there is a single digit placed in the location to represent the permissions for that tier: *OwnerGroupWorld*. So, the octal mode number 640 would set read and write (6) permissions in the owner tier, it would set only read (4) in the group level, and no permissions (0) would be granted in the world tier. Here is an example of using chmod with octal mode syntax:

```
$ ls -l newHistory.txt
-rwxrwxr-- 1 sysadmin sysadmin 14296 Jan 21 16:06 newHistory.txt
$
$ chmod 651 newHistory.txt
$
$ ls -l newHistory.txt
-rw-r-x--x 1 sysadmin sysadmin 14296 Jan 21 16:06 newHistory.txt
$
```

The 651 octal mode set the owner-level permissions to read and write (6), the group permissions to read and execute (5), and the world level permission to execute only (1). This is a handy way to set all of the permissions for a file or directory in a single command.

Exploring Special Permissions

There are three special permission bits that Linux uses for controlling the advanced behavior of files and directories.

The *Set User ID (SUID)* bit is used with executable files. It tells the Linux kernel to run the program with the permissions of the file owner and not the user account actually running the file. This feature is most commonly used in server applications that must run as the root user account to have access to all files on the system, even if the user launching the process is a standard user.

The SUID bit is indicated by an s in place of the execute permission letter for the file owner: rwsr-xr-x. The execute permission is assumed for the system to run the file. If the SUID bit is set on a file that doesn't have execute permission for the owner, it's indicated by a capital S.

To set the SUID bit for a file, in symbolic mode add s to the owner permissions, or in octal mode include a 4 at the start of the octal mode setting.

```
# chmod u+s myapp
# chmod 4750 myapp
```

The *Set Group ID (GUID)* bit works differently in files and directories. For files, it tells Linux to run the program file with the file's group permissions. It's indicated by an s in the group execute position: rwxrwsr--. Like SUID, the execute permission is assumed for the system to run the file, and if the SGID bit is set on a file without group tier execute permission, it's indicated by a capital S.

For directories, the GUID bit helps us create an environment where multiple users can share files. When a directory has the GUID bit set, any files that users create in the directory are assigned the group of the directory and not that of the user. That way, all users in that group can have the same permissions to all of the files in the shared directory.

To set the GUID bit, in symbolic mode add s to the group permissions, or in octal mode include a 2 at the start of the octal mode setting.

```
# chmod g+s /sales
# chmod 2660 /sales
```

Finally, the *sticky bit* is used to protect a file from being deleted by those who don't own the file, even if they belong to the group that has write permissions to the file. The sticky bit is denoted by a t in the execute bit position for others: rwxrw-r-t.

The sticky bit is often used on directories shared by groups. The group members have read and write access to the data files contained in the directory, but only the file owners can remove files from the shared directory.

To set the sticky bit, in symbolic mode add t to the world tier permissions, or in octal mode include a 1 at the start of the octal mode setting:

```
# chmod o+t /sales
# chmod 1777 /sales
```

Managing Default Permissions

When a user creates a new file or directory, the Linux system assigns it a default owner, group, and permissions. The default owner, as expected, is the user who created the file. The default group is the owner's primary group.

The *user mask* feature defines the default permissions that Linux assigns to the file or directory. The user mask is an octal value that represents the bits to be removed from the octal mode 666 permissions for files, or the octal mode 777 permissions for directories.

The user mask value is set with the umask command. You can view your current umask setting by simply entering the command by itself on the command line.

```
$ umask
0022
$
```

The output of the umask command shows four octal values. The first octal value represents the mask for the SUID (4), GUID (2), and sticky (1) bits assigned to files and directories you create. The next three octal values mask the owner, group, and world level permission settings.

The mask is a bitwise mask applied to the permission bits on the file or directory. Any bit that's set in the mask is removed from the permissions for the file or directory. If a bit isn't set, the mask doesn't change the setting. Table 13.2 demonstrates how the umask values work in practice when creating files and directories on your Linux system.

TABLE 13.2: Results from Common umask Values for Files and Directories

UMASK	CREATED FILES	CREATED DIRECTORIES
000	666 (rw-rw-rw-)	777 (rwxrwxrwx)
002	664 (rw-rw-r--)	775 (rwxrwxr-x)
022	644 (rw-r--r--)	755 (rwxr-xr-x)
027	640 (rw-r-----)	750 (rwxr-x---)
077	600 (rw-------)	700 (rwx------)
277	400 (r--------)	500 (r-x------)

You can test this by creating a new file and directory on your Linux system:

```
$ umask
0002
$
$ mkdir test1
$ ls -ld test1
drwxrwxr-x 2 sysadmin sysadmin 4096 Jan 21 16:35 test1
$
$ touch test2
$ ls -l test2
-rw-rw-r-- 1 sysadmin sysadmin 0 Jan 21 16:35 test2
$
```

The umask value of 0002 created the default file permissions of rw-rw-r-- , or octal 664, on the test2 file, and rwxrwxr-x , or octal 775, on the test1 directory, as expected.

You can change the default umask setting for your user account by using the umask command from the command line.

```
$ umask 027
$ touch test3
$ ls -l test3
-rw-r----- 1 sysadmin sysadmin 0 Jan 21 16:40 test3
$
```

The default permissions for the new file have changed to match the umask setting. Note that you can use a three-digit number for indicating a new user mask setting, if you do not want to subtract any of the special permissions.

 Real World Scenario

EXPLORING THE EFFECT OF THE USER MASK ON PERMISSIONS

The user mask subtracts permissions from the default permission settings on files and directories. Different users can have different masks set. Understanding the effect of these various mask settings is important in achieving desired results for your own files.

The following steps will take you through exploring the user mask and the effects on file and directory permissions when it is modified:

1. Log into a Linux system using the `sysadmin` account and the password you created for it.

2. View your account's current user mask by typing **umask** and pressing Enter. Record the displayed number.

3. Determine the default permissions for a file on Linux. You can find this information near the beginning of the "Managing Default Permissions" section of this chapter. Record the octal code of default file permissions.

4. From the information you recorded in the previous two steps, calculate the permission settings for a newly created file on your system and record your answer.

5. Create a blank empty file. Type **touch umaskFile.txt** and press Enter.

6. View the file's current permission settings by typing **ls -l umaskFile.txt** and pressing Enter. Record the owner, group, and world level permissions.

7. Compare the information you recorded in step 6 to your calculation in step 4. If the data does not match, determine where you made a mistake in your calculations.

8. Determine the default permissions for a directory on Linux. You can find this information near the beginning of the "Managing Default Permissions" section of this chapter. Record the octal code of default directory permissions.

9. From the information you recorded in step 2 and step 8, calculate the permission settings for a newly created directory on your system and record your answer.

10. Create a new directory. Type **mkdir umaskDir** and press Enter.

11. View the directory's current permission settings by typing **ls -ld umaskDir** and pressing Enter. Record the owner, group, and world tier permissions.

12. Compare the information you recorded in step 11 to your calculation in step 9. If the data does not match, determine where you made a mistake in your calculations.

13. Modify your user mask by typing **umask 077** and pressing Enter.

14. Check that the user mask was set correctly by typing **umask** and pressing Enter. The number displayed should be 0077. If not, go back and redo step 13.

15. With this new user mask setting, determine the permission settings for a newly created directory on your system and record your answer.

16. Create another new directory by typing `mkdir umaskDir2` and pressing the Enter key.

17. View the newly created directory's current permission settings by typing `ls -ld umaskDir2` and pressing Enter. Record the owner, group, and world tier permissions.

18. Compare the information you recorded in step 17 to your calculation in step 15. If the data does not match, determine where you made a mistake in your calculations.

The umask value is normally set in a script that the Linux system runs at login time, such as in the /etc/profile file. If you override the setting at the command line, that will apply only for the duration of your session. You can override the system default umask setting by adding it to an environment file in your home directory. Environment files are covered later in this chapter.

Using Access Control Lists

The basic Linux method of permissions has one drawback in that it's somewhat limited. You can only assign permissions for a file or directory to a single group and a user account. In a complex business environment with different groups of people needing different permissions to files and directories, that doesn't work.

Linux developers have devised a more advanced method of file and directory security called an *access control list (ACL)*. The ACL allows you to specify a list of multiple users or groups and the permissions that are assigned to them. Like the basic security method, ACL permissions use the same read, write, and execute permission bits, but now can be assigned to multiple users and groups.

To employ the ACL feature in Linux, you use the setfacl and getfacl commands. With getfacl, you can view the ACLs assigned to a file or directory. If you've only assigned basic security permissions to the file, those still appear in the getfacl output.

```
$ touch testFile.txt
$ ls -l testFile.txt
-rw-rw-r--. 1 sysadmin sysadmin 0 Jan 21 13:11 testFile.txt
$
$ getfacl testFile.txt
# file: testFile.txt
# owner: sysadmin
# group: sysadmin
user::rw-
group::rw-
other::r--

$
```

To assign permissions for additional users or groups, you use the setfacl command.

```
setfacl [OPTIONS] RULE FILENAMES
```

The setfacl command allows you to modify the permissions assigned to a file or directory using the -m option or to remove specific permissions using the -x option. You define the *RULE* with three formats.

```
u[ser]:uid:perms
g[roup]:gid:perms
o[ther]::perms
```

To assign permissions for additional owner (user) accounts, use the user format; for additional groups, use the group format; and for world (other), use the other format. For the uid or gid values, either you can use the numerical user ID or group ID or you can use the names. The setfacl command in this example adds read and write permissions for the games group to the testFile.txt file.

```
$ setfacl -m g:games:rw testFile.txt
$ ls -l testFile.txt
-rw-rw-r--+ 1 sysadmin sysadmin 0 Jan 21 13:11 testFile.txt
$
```

Notice that there's no output from the setfacl command. When you list the file, only the standard owner, group, and world permissions are shown, but notice that there's a plus sign (+) added to the permissions list. This indicates that the file has additional ACLs applied to it. To view the additional ACLs, use the getfacl command.

```
$ getfacl testFile.txt
# file: testFile.txt
# owner: sysadmin
# group: sysadmin
user::rw-
group::rw-
group:games:rw-
mask::rw-
other::r--

$
```

The getfacl output now shows that there are permissions assigned to two groups. The default file group is assigned read and write permissions, and also the games group has read and write permissions to the file.

To remove the permissions, use the -x option along with the setfacl command.

```
$ setfacl -x g:games testFile.txt
$ getfacl testFile.txt
# file: testFile.txt
```

```
# owner: sysadmin
# group: sysadmin
user::rw-
group::rw-
mask::rw-
other::r--

$
```

Linux also allows you to set a default ACL on a directory that is automatically incorporated into any file created in the directory. This feature is called *inheritance*. To create a default ACL on a directory, you'll need to have super user privileges and start the rule with a d: followed by the normal rule definition. That looks like this:

```
$ sudo setfacl -m d:g:games:rw /games
```

This example assigns the read and write permissions to the games group for the /games directory. Now all files created in that directory will automatically be assigned read and write permissions for the games group.

File and directory permissions are only one layer of security in a Linux system. Another layer that is rather important involves user accounts. We'll look at that topic next.

Managing User Accounts

Adding, modifying, and deleting user account credentials—which includes usernames, account information, and passwords—is an important (but tedious) part of system administration. Managing user accounts and looking at the underlying configuration is covered in the following sections.

Adding Accounts

To add a new user account on the system, the useradd utility is typically used. On some distributions, such as Ubuntu, a script called adduser is used when adding users to the system, but it invokes the useradd program to handle the actual task.

The adding accounts process actually involves several players besides the core useradd program. Figure 13.3 depicts the process.

FIGURE 13.3
Adding a user account

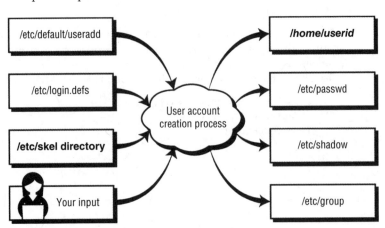

You can see in Figure 13.3 that there are several team players involved in the account creation process. Notice that the /etc/skel directory is bolded. This is because, depending upon the other configuration files, it may not be used in the process. The same goes for the /home/*userid* directory. It may not be created or it may have an alternative name, depending upon the system's account creation configuration. You'll learn more about these directories shortly.

Before we jump into the useradd utility details, let's look at the two files and the directory involved in the creation side of the process.

THE /ETC/LOGIN.DEFS FILE

This configuration file is typically installed by default on most Linux distributions. It contains directives for use in various shadow password suite commands. *Shadow password suite* is an umbrella term for commands dealing with account credentials, such as the useradd, userdel, and passwd commands.

The directives in this configuration file control password length, how long until the user is required to change the account's password, whether a home directory is created by default, and so on. The file is typically filled with comments and commented-out directives (which make the directives inactive). The following snipped output shows some of the active directives within a /etc/login.defs file:

```
$ cat /etc/login.defs
[...]
MAIL_DIR         /var/spool/mail
[...]
PASS_MAX_DAYS    99999
PASS_MIN_DAYS    0
PASS_MIN_LEN     5
PASS_WARN_AGE    7
[...]
UID_MIN                   1000
UID_MAX                  60000
[...]
SYS_UID_MIN                201
SYS_UID_MAX                999
[...]
GID_MIN                   1000
GID_MAX                  60000
[...]
SYS_GID_MIN                201
SYS_GID_MAX                999
[...]
CREATE_HOME      yes
[...]
$
```

Notice the UID_MIN directive within the preceding example. A *user identification number (UID)* is the number used by Linux to identify user accounts. A *user account*, sometimes called a *normal* or *standard account*, is any account an authorized person has been given to access the system, with the appropriate credentials, and perform daily tasks. While humans use account names,

Linux uses UIDs. The UID_MIN indicates the lowest UID allowed for user accounts. On the system, UID_MIN is set to 1000. This is typical, though some systems set it at 500.

System accounts are accounts that provide services (daemons) or perform special tasks. According to the settings in the previous example file, a system account's minimum UID is set by the SYS_UID_MIN, and its maximum is set by the SYS_UID_MAX directive.

Table 13.3 covers some additional /etc/login.def settings that are critical to common user account creation.

TABLE 13.3:   A Few Vital /etc/login.defs Directives

NAME	DESCRIPTION
PASS_MAX_DAYS	Number of days until a password change is required. This is the password's expiration date.
PASS_MIN_DAYS	Number of days after a password is changed until the password may be changed again
PASS_MIN_LENGTH	Minimum number of characters required in a password
PASS_WARN_AGE	Number of days a warning is issued to the user prior to a password's expiration
CREATE_HOME	Default is no. If set to yes, a user account home directory is created.
ENCRYPT_METHOD	The method used to hash account passwords

THE /ETC/DEFAULT/USERADD FILE

The /etc/default/useradd file is another configuration file that directs the process of creating accounts. It typically is a much shorter file than the /etc/login.defs file.

```
$ cat /etc/default/useradd
# useradd defaults file
GROUP=100
HOME=/home
INACTIVE=-1
EXPIRE=
SHELL=/bin/bash
SKEL=/etc/skel
CREATE_MAIL_SPOOL=yes
$
$ useradd -D
GROUP=100
HOME=/home
INACTIVE=-1
EXPIRE=
SHELL=/bin/bash
SKEL=/etc/skel
CREATE_MAIL_SPOOL=yes
$
```

Notice that there are two different ways to display the active directives in this file. You can use the cat command or invoke the useradd -D command. Both are equally simple to use. One cool fact about the useradd -D command is that you can use it to modify the directives within the /etc/default/useradd file.

Also in the preceding example, notice the HOME directive. It is currently set to /home, which means that any newly created user accounts will have their account directories located within the /home directory. Keep in mind that if CREATE_HOME is not set or set to no within the /etc/login.defs file, a home directory is *not* created by default.

Some additional directives are critical to common user account creation. These are covered briefly in Table 13.4.

TABLE 13.4: A Few Vital /etc/default/useradd Directives

NAME	DESCRIPTION
HOME	Base directory for user account directories
INACTIVE	Number of days after a password has expired and has not been changed until the account will be deactivated. See PASS_MAX_DAYS in Table 13.3.
SKEL	The skeleton directory
SHELL	User account default shell program

The SHELL directive needs a little more explanation. Typically it is set to /bin/bash, which means when you access the command line, your user process is running the /bin/bash shell program. This program provides you with the prompt at the command line and handles any commands you enter there.

THE /ETC/SKEL/ DIRECTORY

The /etc/skel directory, or the *skeleton directory* (see Figure 13.3) as it is commonly called, holds files. If a home directory is created for a user, these files are to be copied to the user account's home directory when the account is created. The following shows the files within the /etc/skel directory:

```
$ ls -a /etc/skel
.  ..  .bash_logout  .bash_profile  .bashrc
$
```

The ls command output shows three files. These particular files are environment files. We'll cover environment files later in this chapter. In the /etc/skel directory, you can modify any of these files or add new files and directories to meet your particular system's needs.

Now that we've covered the files in the creation side of the user account creation process, let's look at the files and directories that are built or modified when an account is created.

THE /ETC/PASSWD FILE

Account information is stored in the /etc/passwd file. Each account's data occupies a single line in the file. When an account is created, a new record for that account is added to the /etc/ passwd file.

```
$ cat /etc/passwd
root:x:0:0:root:/root:/bin/bash
bin:x:1:1:bin:/bin:/sbin/nologin
daemon:x:2:2:daemon:/sbin:/sbin/nologin
[...]
sysadmin:x:1000:1000:Christine Bresnahan:/home/sysadmin:/bin/bash
$
```

The /etc/passwd records contain several fields. Each field in a record is delimited by a colon (:). Table 13.5 describes the seven fields in a /etc/passwd record.

TABLE 13.5: The /etc/passwd File's Record Fields

FIELD NO.	DESCRIPTION
1	User account's username
2	Password field. Typically this file is no longer used to store passwords. An x in this field indicates passwords are stored in the /etc/shadow file.
3	User account's user identification number (UID)
4	User account's group identification number (GID)
5	Comment field. This field is optional. Usually, it contains the user's full name.
6	User account's home directory
7	User account's default shell. If set to /sbin/nologin or /bin/false, then the user cannot interactively log into the system.

You would think that the password file would hold passwords, but because of its file permissions, the password file can be compromised. Therefore, passwords are stored in the more permission-restricted /etc/shadow file.

THE /ETC/SHADOW FILE

Another file that is updated when an account is created is the /etc/shadow file. It contains information regarding the account's password, even if you have not yet provided a password for the account. Like the /etc/passwd file, each account's data occupies a single file line. Because the file is more protected than the password file, you'll need to either use the root account or use the super user privileges to view it.

```
# cat /etc/shadow
root:[...]::0:99999:7:::
```

```
bin:*:18358:0:99999:7:::
daemon:*:18358:0:99999:7:::
[...]
tcpdump:!!:18565::::::
sysadmin:[...]::0:99999:7:::$
```

The /etc/shadow records contain several fields. Each field in a record is delimited by a colon (:). There are nine fields in total, described in Table 13.6.

TABLE 13.6:   The /etc/shadow File's Record Fields

FIELD NO.	DESCRIPTION
1	User account's username
2	Password field. The password is a salted and hashed password. A ! ! or ! indicates a password has not been set for the account. A ! or * indicates the account cannot use a password to log in. A ! in front of a password indicates the account has been locked.
3	Date of last password change in Unix epoch time (days) format
4	Number of days after a password is changed until the password may be changed again
5	Number of days until a password change is required. This is the password's expiration date
6	Number of days a warning is issued to the user prior to a password's expiration (See field 5.)
7	Number of days after a password has expired (see field 5) and has not been changed until the account will be deactivated
8	Date of account's expiration in Unix epoch time (days) format
9	Called the special flag. It is a field for a special future use, is currently not used, and is blank.

Notice that field 1 is the account's username. This is the only field shared with the /etc/passwd file.

It's vital to understand the different possible expirations. When password expiration has occurred, there is a grace period. The user will have a certain number of days (designated in field 7) to log into the account using the old password but must change the password immediately. However, if password expiration has occurred and the user does *not* log in to the system in time, the user is effectively locked out of the system.

With account expiration, there is no grace period. After the account expires, the user cannot log into the account with its password.

You may have noticed that we have not yet covered the /etc/group file. It does get modified as part of the account creation process. However, that discussion is saved for the section "Managing Groups" later in this chapter.

CREATING AN ACCOUNT

The useradd command is the primary tool for creating user accounts on most distributions. This utility has many useful options for various needs, and Table 13.7 lists the most typical ones.

TABLE 13.7:   The useradd Command's Commonly Used Options

SHORT	LONG	DESCRIPTION
-c	--comment	Comment field contents. Traditionally, it contains the user's full name. Optional.
-d	--home or --home-dir	User's home directory specification. The default action is set by the HOME and CREATE_HOME directives.
-D	--defaults	Display /etc/default/useradd directives.
-e	--expiredate	Date of account's expiration in *YYYY-MM-DD* format. The default action is set by the EXPIRE directive.
-f	--inactive	Number of days after a password has expired and has not been changed until the account will be deactivated. A -1 indicates the account will never be deactivated. The default action is set by the INACTIVE directive.
-g	--gid	Account's group membership, which is active when the user logs into the system (default group)
-G	--groups	Account's additional group memberships
-m	--create-home	If it does not exist, create the user account's home directory. The default action is set by the CREATE_HOME directive.
-M	N/A or --no-create-home	Do *not* create the user account's home directory. Default action is set by the CREATE_HOME directive.
-s	--shell	Account's shell. Default action is set by the SHELL directive.
-u	--uid	Account's user identification (UID) number
-r	--system	Create a system account instead of a user account.

Distributions tend to vary greatly in their configuration when it comes to user accounts. Therefore, before you launch into creating accounts with the useradd utility, it's wise to review some directives within each distro's user account configuration files (see Table 13.3 and Table 13.4). That way, you'll know what useradd options you'll need to include when creating accounts.

Here, before creating an account, the CREATE_HOME and SHELL directives are checked on a Red Hat-based distribution.

```
$ grep CREATE_HOME /etc/login.defs
CREATE_HOME     yes
$
```

```
$ useradd -D | grep SHELL
SHELL=/bin/bash
$
```

You can see on this distribution that the home directory will be created by default, because CREATE_HOME is set to yes. The SHELL directive is pointing to the Bash shell, /bin/bash, which is the typical shell for most interactive user accounts.

An example of creating an account on this Red Hat–based distribution with the useradd utility is shown here using the root user account:

```
# whoami
root
#
# useradd -c "Takoda A. Puddle" tpuddle
#
```

Because the Red Hat–based distribution we are using has the CREATE_HOME directive set to yes and SHELL set to /bin/bash, there is no need to include any useradd command options. However, we did use the -c option to include the user's full name in the account's /etc/passwd record. The argument following the useradd command, tpuddle, is the actual username of the account.

Once you've created an account, it's a good idea to make sure that records now exist for the new user account in both the /etc/passwd and /etc/shadow files. The getent command is helpful here. You'll need to log into the root user account or use super user privileges to see the shadow files.

```
# getent passwd tpuddle
tpuddle:x:1001:1001:Takoda A. Puddle:/home/tpuddle:/bin/bash
#
# getent shadow tpuddle
tpuddle:!!:18652:0:99999:7:::
#
```

A password hasn't been added to the tpuddle account yet. That is why its record in the /etc/shadow file shows !! in the file's second field (the password field). Refer to Table 13.6 for all the fields in the shadow file.

Let's take a look at creating an account on a different Linux distribution. The Ubuntu server distro does things a little differently. You can see that CREATE_HOME is *not* set, so it will default to no, and that the SHELL directive is set to /bin/sh instead of the Bash shell.

```
$ grep CREATE_HOME /etc/login.defs
$
$ useradd -D | grep SHELL
SHELL=/bin/sh
$
```

Because of these settings, when creating a user account on this Ubuntu distribution, if you want the account to have a home directory and use the Bash shell, you will need to employ additional useradd command options listed in Table 13.7. Here is an example:

```
$ sudo useradd -c "London K. Radford" -md /home/lradford \
> -s /bin/bash lradford
[sudo] password for sysadmin:
$
```

Notice in the example that four options are used along with the useradd command. Because this system does not have the CREATE_HOME directive set, the -m option is needed to force useradd to make a home directory for the account. The -d switch designates that the directory name should be /home/lradford. Because the SHELL directive is set to /bin/sh on this system, the -s option is needed to set the account's default shell to /bin/bash. And the -c option was used to add a full name in the account's /etc/passwd record contents.

Now that this account is created, let's check to ensure the useradd options worked correctly.

```
$ getent passwd lradford
lradford:x:1001:1001:London K. Radford:/home/lradford:/bin/bash
$
$ sudo getent shadow lradford
lradford:!:18653:0:99999:7:::
$
$ ls -a /home/lradford
.  ..  .bash_logout  .bashrc  .profile
$
$ ls -a /etc/skel
.  ..  .bash_logout  .bashrc  .profile
$
```

Notice that records now exist for the new user account in the passwd and shadow files. Also, a new directory was created, /home/lradford, which contains files from this distro's /etc/skel/ directory. Keep in mind at this point that no password has been added to the lradford account yet, and thus its record in the shadow file shows ! in the password field.

Maintaining Accounts

Throughout an account's lifetime, you'll need to make modifications to it. A user can join new workgroups, change their name, and/or have their home directory moved to a new location, which all require changes to their account.

MANAGING PASSWORDS

When you first create an interactive account, you should immediately afterward create a password for that account using the passwd utility. You can create or update an account's password by passing the username as an argument to the command. Here a password is created for the new lradford account on an Ubuntu distribution:

```
$ sudo passwd lradford
[sudo] password for sysadmin:
New password:
Retype new password:
passwd: password updated successfully
$
```

If you need to update your own account's password, just enter **passwd** with no additional command arguments. With the passwd utility, you can lock or unlock accounts, set an account's password to expired, delete an account's password, and so on. Table 13.8 shows the more commonly used passwd switches; all of these options require super user privileges.

TABLE 13.8: The passwd Command's Commonly Used Options

SHORT	LONG	DESCRIPTION
-d	--delete	Removes the account's password
-e	--expire	Sets an account's password as expired. The user is required to change the account password at next login.
-i	--inactive	Sets the number of days after a password has expired and has not been changed until the account will be deactivated
-l	--lock	Places an exclamation point (!) in front of the account's password within the /etc/shadow file, effectively preventing the user from logging into the system via using the account's password
-n	--minimum	Sets the number of days after a password is changed until the password may be changed again
-S	--status	Displays the account's password status
-u	--unlock	Removes a placed exclamation point (!) from the account's password within the /etc/shadow file
-w	--warning or --warndays	Sets the number of days a warning is issued to the user prior to a password's expiration
-x	--maximum or --maxdays	Sets the number of days until a password change is required. This is the password's expiration date.

The chage utility displays password information, but in a more human-readable format than viewing the records in the /etc/shadow file or using the getent shadow command. It does require super user privileges to operate.

```
$ sudo chage -l lradford
Last password change                               : Jan 26, 2021
Password expires                                   : never
Password inactive                                  : never
Account expires                                    : never
Minimum number of days between password change     : 0
Maximum number of days between password change     : 99999
Number of days of warning before password expires  : 7
$
```

Notice that the password for this account never expires. Be sure to review your company's policies for password management to ensure that the accounts on your system are following them.

MODIFYING ACCOUNTS

Besides adding and managing passwords, the accounts on your systems may have additional changes needed. The utility employed to modify accounts is the usermod program. The type of user account modification(s) is determined by which options are used with the usermod utility. Table 13.9 shows the commonly used options.

TABLE 13.9:   The usermod Command's Commonly Used Options

SHORT	LONG	DESCRIPTION
-c	--comment	Modify the comment field contents.
-d	--home	Set a new user home directory specification. Use with the -m option to move the current directory's files to the new location.
-e	--expiredate	Modify the account's expiration date. Use YYYY-MM-DD format.
-f	--inactive	Modify the number of days after a password has expired and has not been changed that the account will be deactivated. A -1 indicates the account will never be deactivated.
-g	--gid	Change the account's default group membership.
-G	--groups	Update the account's additional group memberships. If only specifying new group membership, use the -a option to avoid removing the other group memberships.
-l	--login	Modify the account's username to the specified one. Does not modify the home directory
-L	--lock	Lock the account by placing an exclamation point in front of the password within the account's /etc/shadow file record.
-s	--shell	Change the account's shell.
-u	--uid	Modify the account's user identification (UID) number.
-U	--unlock	Unlock the account by removing the exclamation point from the front of the password within the account's /etc/shadow file record.

Notice that you can change an account's default group and provide memberships to additional groups. Accounts' groups are covered in detail later in this chapter.

Where usermod comes in really handy is in a situation where you've created an account but forgot to check the distribution's account creation configuration settings, such as on an Ubuntu distribution.

```
$ sudo useradd -md /home/tpuddle tpuddle
$
$ sudo getent passwd tpuddle
tpuddle:x:1002:1002::/home/tpuddle:/bin/sh
$
$ sudo usermod -s /bin/bash tpuddle
$
$ sudo getent passwd tpuddle
tpuddle:x:1002:1002::/home/tpuddle:/bin/bash
$
```

In the example, when the user account tpuddle is created and the account record is checked using the getent utility, it shows that the /bin/sh shell is being used instead of the Bash shell. To fix this problem, the usermod command is employed with the -s option, and the account's shell is modified to the /bin/bash shell instead.

Removing Accounts

Deleting an account on Linux is fairly simple. The userdel utility is the key tool in this task. The most common option to use is the -r switch. This option will delete the account's home directory tree and any files within it.

```
$ sudo ls -d /home/tpuddle
/home/tpuddle
$ sudo getent passwd tpuddle
tpuddle:x:1002:1002::/home/tpuddle:/bin/bash
$
$ sudo userdel -r tpuddle
userdel: tpuddle mail spool (/var/mail/tpuddle) not found
$
$ sudo ls -d /home/tpuddle
ls: cannot access '/home/tpuddle': No such file or directory
$ sudo getent passwd tpuddle
$
```

The first two commands in the example show that the /home/tpuddle directory exists and that the account does have a record within the /etc/passwd file. The third command includes the userdel -r command to delete the account as well as the home directory. Notice that an error message is generated stating that the /var/mail/tpuddle file could not be found. This is not a problem. It just means that this file was not created when the account was created. Finally, the last two commands show that both the /home/tpuddle directory was removed and that the /etc/passwd file no longer contains a record for the tpuddle account.

Adding, modifying, and deleting accounts are common system admin activities. So is managing a user's environment. We'll cover that topic next.

Maintaining the Environment

After a user authenticates with the Linux system and prior to reaching the Bash shell's command-line prompt, the user environment is configured. This environment consists of environment variables, command aliases, and various other settings.

The user environment configuration is accomplished via environment files. These files contain Bash shell commands to perform the necessary operations and are covered in the following sections along with a few environment variable highlights.

Setting Environment Variables

The Bash shell uses a feature called *environment variables* to store information about the shell session and the working environment, which were covered in Chapter 6, "Working with the Shell." While you can modify these variables on the fly as shown in Chapter 6, the focus here is on how these parameters are persistently set or modified for user login processes.

When you start a Bash shell by logging in to the Linux system, by default Bash checks several files for the configuration. These files are called *environment files*, which are sometimes called *startup files*. The environment files that Bash processes depend on the method you use to start the Bash shell. You can start a Bash shell in three ways.

- As a default login shell, such as when logging into the system at a tty terminal

- As an interactive shell that is started by spawning a subshell, such as when opening a terminal emulator in a Linux GUI

- As a noninteractive shell (also called *nonlogin shell*) that is started, such as when running a shell script

The environment files are actually shell scripts. Shell scripting is covered more thoroughly in Chapter 19, "Writing Scripts." The following sections take you through the various available environment files.

Exploring User Entries

There are four potential files found in the user's home directory, $HOME, that are environmental files. For a default login or interactive shell, the first file found in the following order is run, and the rest are ignored:

- .bash_profile

- .bash_login

- .profile

Typically, the fourth file, .bashrc, is run from the file found in the preceding list. However, anytime a noninteractive shell is started, the .bashrc file is run.

In the following example, a user's directory is checked for all four environment files. Notice that two of them are not found. Therefore, only the .bash_profile and .bashrc files are employed on this system.

```
$ pwd
/home/sysadmin
$
```

```
$ ls .bash_profile .bash_login .profile .bashrc
ls: cannot access '.bash_login': No such file or directory
ls: cannot access '.profile': No such file or directory
.bash_profile  .bashrc
$
```

If you want to modify your shell's primary prompt (PS1) persistently, you can do so via adding the modification to one of your local environment configuration files. Here a user has persistently modified their prompt by setting the PS1 environment variable within their .bash_profile file:

```
Bash Prompt: grep PS1 .bash_profile
PS1="Bash Prompt: "
Bash Prompt:
```

These individual user environment files are typically populated from the /etc/skel/ directory, depending on your account creation configuration settings. For future accounts, you can make changes to the skeleton environment files. Just keep in mind that any individual user who can access the command line has the ability to modify their own files. Thus, for environment configurations that need to apply to all users, it is better to make a global entry in one of the global environment files, which are covered next.

Exploring Global Entries

Global configuration files modify the working environment and shell sessions for all users starting a Bash shell. As mentioned earlier, the global entries in these files can be modified by the account user via adding user entries into their $HOME environment files.

The global environment files consist of the following:

♦   The /etc/profile file

♦   Files within the /etc/profile.d/ directory

♦   The /etc/bashrc or the /etc/bash.bashrc file

Whether your Linux system has the /etc/bashrc or the /etc/bash.bashrc file depends on which distribution you are running. Either file is typically called from the user's $HOME/ .bashrc file.

It is recommended that instead of changing the /etc/profile or other files for global environment needs, you create a custom environment file, give it a .sh file extension, and place it in the /etc/profile.d/ directory. All the .sh files within the /etc/profile.d/ directory are run via the /etc/profile environment file for logins to the Bash shell.

 Real World Scenario

DETERMINING THE EXISTENCE OF SYSTEM ENVIRONMENT FILES

Because different Linux distributions use different environment files to set things such as environment variables, it is critical to know which files are on your systems. A quick audit will provide you with the necessary information to make informed decisions when adding user environment files to /etc/skel and/or making modifications to global environment files.

The following steps will take you through exploring the user-level and global environment files on your system:

1. Log into a Linux system using the sysadmin account and the password you created for it.

2. View your system's skeleton directory by typing **ls -a /etc/skel** and pressing Enter. Record the names of the files found there.

3. From the reading, determine which of the files you found in the previous step are user environment files. Record the names of those files here.

4. View the files in your home directory by typing **ls -a** and pressing Enter. Determine if you have the same user environment files you recorded in step 3.

5. See if the global environment file, /etc/profile, exists on your system. Type **ls /etc/profile** and press Enter.

6. Determine if there are already any files in the /etc/profile.d/ directory where you can create customized environment scripts. Type **ls /etc/profile.d/** and press Enter. You should find some files in this directory.

7. See which global environment file your system has on it, /etc/bashrc or /etc/bash.bashrc. Type **ls /etc/*bashrc** and press Enter. Record your findings.

Besides managing a user's environment, you also need to manage their groups. We'll explore that subject next.

Managing Groups

Groups are an organizational structure that is a part of Linux's *discretionary access control (DAC)*. DAC is the traditional Linux security control, where access to a file, or any object, is based upon the user's identity and current group membership. When a user account is created, it is given membership to a particular group, called the account's *default group*. Though a user account can have lots of group memberships, its process can have only one designated current group at a time. The default group is an account's current group, when the user first logs into the system.

Groups are identified by their name as well as their *group identification number (GID)*. This is similar to how users are identified by UIDs in that the GID is used by Linux to identify a particular group, while humans use group names.

If a default group is not designated when a user account is created, then a new group is created. This new group has the same name as the user account's name, and it is assigned a new GID. To see an account's default group, use the getent command to view the /etc/passwd record for that account. The fourth field in the record is the GID for the account's default group.

```
$ getent passwd lradford
lradford:x:1001:1001:London K. Radford:/home/lradford:/bin/bash
$
$ sudo groups lradford
[sudo] password for sysadmin:
lradford : lradford
$
```

```
$ getent group lradford
lradford:x:1001:
$
$ grep 1001 /etc/group
lradford:x:1001:
$
```

The first command shows that the `lradford` account's default group has a GID of 1001, but it does not provide a group name. The groups command does show the group name, which is the same as the user account name, `lradford`. This is typical when no default group was designated at account creation time. The third command, another `getent` command, shows that the group `lradford` does indeed map to the 1001 GID. The fourth command confirms this information.

Adding Groups

To add a user to a new group or change the account's default group, the group must preexist. This task is accomplished via the groupadd utility and super user privileges.

```
$ sudo groupadd training
$
$ getent group training
training:x:1002:
$
```

The `getent` utility shows the new group record in the group file. The fields in the `/etc/group` file are delimited by a colon (:) and are as follows:

- Group name

- Group password (An x indicates that, if a group password exists, it is stored in the `/etc/gshadow` file.)

- GID

- Group members (user accounts that belong to the group, separated by a comma)

Once a new group is created, you can add individual members to the group with the usermod command.

```
$ sudo groups lradford
lradford : lradford
$
$ sudo usermod -aG training lradford
$
$ sudo groups lradford
lradford : lradford training
$
$ getent group training
training:x:1002:lradford
$
```

Notice that the usermod command uses two options, -aG. The -G adds the lradford account as a member of the training group, but the -a switch is important because it preserves any previous lradford account group memberships. After the lradford account is added as a training group member, you can see in the last two command results that the /etc/group file record for training was updated.

For a user to access a group that they are a member of when it is not their default or current group, they need to use a special command, newgrp. View your current group via the id -gn command; then switch your current group with the newgrp command.

```
$ whoami
lradford
$
$ id -gn
lradford
$
$ newgrp training
$
$ id -gn
training
$
$ groups
training lradford
$
```

Notice that after the newgrp command was used, the id -gn command shows that training is the current group for the lradford account. You can also see all your group memberships along with the current group through the groups command. Your current group is the first one in the displayed list.

For an account user to change back to their default group, they can use newgrp again followed by the group's name. Alternatively, the exit command will also switch a user back to the default group, because newgrp creates a new user process when it is used.

Removing Groups

To remove a group, use the groupdel utility.

```
$ sudo groupdel training
$
$ getent group training
$
$ sudo groups lradford
lradford : lradford
$
```

Notice that after the training group is deleted, the getent command shows that the training group record has been removed from the /etc/group file. What is really nice is that any member of that deleted group has also had their group information updated as shown in the third command.

Now that you can add and managing user accounts and their environments, you can start to increase the number of users on your Linux systems. You also can set up more groups to refine access to various files and directories within the virtual directory structure.

The Bottom Line

Change a file's owner.   A file or directory owner setting allows certain control over that file or directory. Some control is dictated by the permissions set at the owner level, but also only certain commands can be used on a file or directory by its owner. For example, you cannot change the group on a file if you do not own it (or don't have super user privileges).

> **Master It**   Imagine you are either logged into the root account or have access to super user privileges, and you have a copied a file projectData.txt to the lradford home directory. This user will need access to the file, which includes being able to change its group. What command syntax should you employ to accomplish this task?

Create user accounts.   The useradd command is a command at the basic system level that allows you to create new accounts on the system. The needed various options are often determined by settings in the /etc/login.defs and the /etc/default/useradd files.

> **Master It**   You need to create a new account for a newly hired project manager, Takoda Puddle, who needs access to the Bash shell on your server. In your system's /etc/login .defs, you find that CREATE_HOME is defined as no, and UID_MIN is set to 1000. Within the /etc/default/useradd file, SHELL is defined as /bin/bash, and SKEL is set to the /etc/ skel directory. The user's home directory should end up being /home/tpuddle. Assuming you are either logged into the root account or have access to super user privileges, what is the command syntax to create an account for the new project manager?

Modify a user's password.   The passwd command along with the correct privileges allows you to create an account's password. However, besides just creating a password, you can change an account's password, delete its password, force a user to change their password at the next login, and so on. In addition, without any extra privileges, you can modify your own account's password through the passwd command.

> **Master It**   You are the system administration for several Linux servers at your company. An HR representative and your boss have come to your office to let you know that a fellow employee, Jay Snow, is being fired from the company. They have asked you to lock the jsnow account while they wait. What command do you enter to lock this account?

Find an environment file.   Environment files on your system consist of both global files and local user files. Which environment files reside on a system depends on the Linux distribution being used. Global files reside in the /etc/ directory, and local user files reside in each user's home directory after being copied from the /etc/skel/ directory, if your system is configured to do so.

> **Master It**   You are the system admin for a development system. A programmer recently asked how a particular environment variable can be redefined, not only when they log into the system, but also when they run various Bash shell scripts on the system. What should you do or suggest?

Delete a user group. Managing groups of users on a Linux system is an important task. Several groups are permanent once created, but other groups, such as those related to special work projects, may come and go. You need to know how to create, modify, and even remove a user group.

> **Master It** A small development project, abc123, on the system you administer has come to an end. The project files are no longer needed by the former team, and you've been asked to change the group on these project files to the manager group. Once you've completed that task, you'll need to remove the old abc123 project group. What is the command to accomplish this removal task?

Chapter 14

Working with Processes and Jobs

Linux servers have to keep track of lots of different applications running on the system. Your goal as the Linux administrator is to make sure everything runs smoothly and at the correct time! This chapter shows just how Linux keeps track of all the active programs and how you can manage that information.

IN THIS CHAPTER, YOU WILL LEARN TO

- ◆ Monitor programs running on the server

- ◆ Manage programs running on the server

- ◆ Schedule programs to run in the future

Looking at Processes

At any given time, there are lots of active programs running on the Linux system. Linux calls each running program a *process*. A process can run in the foreground, displaying output on a console display or graphical desktop window, or it can run in the background, working on data behind the scenes. The Linux system assigns each process a *process ID* (or PID) and manages how the process uses memory and CPU time based on that PID.

When a Linux system first boots, it starts a special process called the *init process*. The init process is the core of the Linux system; it runs scripts that start all of the other processes running on the system, including the processes that start any text consoles or graphical windows you use to log in.

You can watch just which processes are currently running on your Linux system by using the ps command. The default output of the ps command looks like this:

```
$ ps
PID    TTY      TIME      CMD
 2797 pts/0   00:00:00 bash
 2884 pts/0   00:00:00 ps
$
```

By default, the ps command only shows the processes that are running in the current user shell. In this example, we only had the command prompt shell running (bash) and, of course, the ps command itself.

The basic output of the ps command shows the PID assigned to each process, the terminal (TTY) that they were started from, and the CPU time that the process has used.

The tricky feature of the ps command (and the reason that makes it so complicated) is that at one time there were two versions of it in Linux. Each version had its own set of command-line parameters controlling the information it displayed. That made switching between systems somewhat complicated.

The GNU developers decided to merge the two versions into a single ps program and, of course, added some additional parameters of their own. The current ps program used in Linux supports these three styles of command-line parameters:

◆ Unix-style parameters, which are preceded by a dash

◆ BSD-style parameters, which are not preceded by a dash

◆ GNU long parameters, which are preceded by a double dash

This makes for lots of possible parameters and options to use with the ps command. You can consult the ps manual page to see all of the possible parameters that are available. Most Linux administrators have their own set of commonly used parameters that they remember for extracting pertinent information. For example, if you need to see every process running on the system, use the Unix-style -ef parameter combination, like this:

```
$ ps -ef
UID        PID    PPID  C  STIME TTY  TIME      CMD
root         1       0  1  18:25 ?    00:00:03 /sbin/init maybe-ubiquity
root         2       0  0  18:25 ?    00:00:00 [kthreadd]
root         3       2  0  18:25 ?    00:00:00 [rcu_gp]
root         4       2  0  18:25 ?    00:00:00 [rcu_par_gp]
root         5       2  0  18:25 ?    00:00:00 [kworker/0:0-cgroup_destroy]
root         6       2  0  18:25 ?    00:00:00 [kworker/0:0H-kblockd]
root         7       2  0  18:25 ?    00:00:00 [kworker/0:1-events]
root         8       2  0  18:25 ?    00:00:00 [kworker/u2:0-events_unbound]
root         9       2  0  18:25 ?    00:00:00 [mm_percpu_wq]
root        10       2  0  18:25 ?    00:00:00 [ksoftirqd/0]
root        11       2  0  18:25 ?    00:00:00 [rcu_sched]
...
$
```

This format provides some useful information about the processes running:

UID: The user responsible for running the process

PID: The process ID of the process

PPID: The process ID of the parent process (if the process was started by another process)

C: The processor utilization over the lifetime of the process

STIME: The system time when the process was started

TTY: The terminal device from which the process was started

TIME: The cumulative CPU time required to run the process

CMD: The name of the program that was started in the process

Also notice in the -ef output that some process command names are shown in brackets. That indicates processes where ps could not determine the command arguments, which normally occurs with system processes and kernel threads. Often, the Linux kernel places a process into sleep mode while the process is waiting for an event. This is called a *sleeping process*. When the event triggers, the kernel sends the process a signal. If the process is in *interruptible sleep* mode, it will receive the signal immediately and wake up. If the process is in *uninterruptible sleep* mode, it only wakes up based on an external event, such as hardware becoming available. It will accumulate any other signals sent while it was sleeping and act on them once it wakes up.

ATTACK OF THE ZOMBIES

If a process has ended, but its parent process hasn't acknowledged the termination signal because it's sleeping, the process is considered a *zombie*. It's stuck in a limbo state between running and terminating until the parent process acknowledges the termination signal.

Monitoring Processes in Real Time

The ps command is a great way to get a snapshot of the processes running on the system, but sometimes you need to see more information to get an idea of just what's going on in your Linux system. If you're trying to find trends about processes that are frequently swapped in and out of memory, it's hard to do that with the ps command.

Instead, the top command can solve this problem. The top command displays process information similar to the ps command, but it does it in real-time mode. Figure 14.1 shows a snapshot of the top command in action.

FIGURE 14.1 The output of the top command

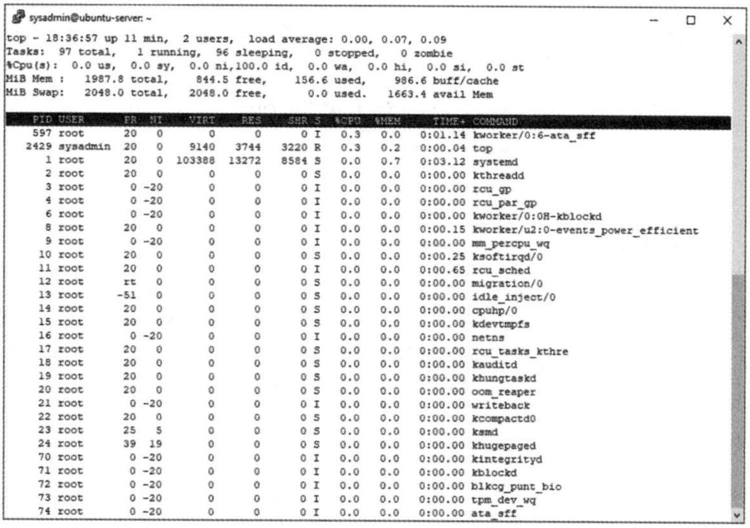
```
sysadmin@ubuntu-server: ~
top - 18:36:57 up 11 min,  2 users,  load average: 0.00, 0.07, 0.09
Tasks:  97 total,   1 running,  96 sleeping,   0 stopped,   0 zombie
%Cpu(s):  0.0 us,  0.0 sy,  0.0 ni,100.0 id,  0.0 wa,  0.0 hi,  0.0 si,  0.0 st
MiB Mem :   1987.8 total,    844.5 free,    156.6 used,    986.6 buff/cache
MiB Swap:   2048.0 total,   2048.0 free,      0.0 used.   1663.4 avail Mem

    PID USER      PR  NI    VIRT    RES    SHR S  %CPU  %MEM     TIME+ COMMAND
    597 root      20   0       0      0      0 I   0.3   0.0   0:01.14 kworker/0:6-ata_sff
   2429 sysadmin  20   0    9140   3744   3220 R   0.3   0.2   0:00.04 top
      1 root      20   0  103388  13272   8584 S   0.0   0.7   0:03.12 systemd
      2 root      20   0       0      0      0 S   0.0   0.0   0:00.00 kthreadd
      3 root       0 -20       0      0      0 I   0.0   0.0   0:00.00 rcu_gp
      4 root       0 -20       0      0      0 I   0.0   0.0   0:00.00 rcu_par_gp
      6 root       0 -20       0      0      0 I   0.0   0.0   0:00.00 kworker/0:0H-kblockd
      8 root      20   0       0      0      0 I   0.0   0.0   0:00.15 kworker/u2:0-events_power_efficient
      9 root       0 -20       0      0      0 I   0.0   0.0   0:00.00 mm_percpu_wq
     10 root      20   0       0      0      0 S   0.0   0.0   0:00.25 ksoftirqd/0
     11 root      20   0       0      0      0 I   0.0   0.0   0:00.65 rcu_sched
     12 root      rt   0       0      0      0 S   0.0   0.0   0:00.00 migration/0
     13 root     -51   0       0      0      0 S   0.0   0.0   0:00.00 idle_inject/0
     14 root      20   0       0      0      0 S   0.0   0.0   0:00.00 cpuhp/0
     15 root      20   0       0      0      0 S   0.0   0.0   0:00.00 kdevtmpfs
     16 root       0 -20       0      0      0 I   0.0   0.0   0:00.00 netns
     17 root      20   0       0      0      0 S   0.0   0.0   0:00.00 rcu_tasks_kthre
     18 root      20   0       0      0      0 S   0.0   0.0   0:00.00 kauditd
     19 root      20   0       0      0      0 S   0.0   0.0   0:00.00 khungtaskd
     20 root      20   0       0      0      0 S   0.0   0.0   0:00.00 oom_reaper
     21 root       0 -20       0      0      0 I   0.0   0.0   0:00.00 writeback
     22 root      20   0       0      0      0 S   0.0   0.0   0:00.00 kcompactd0
     23 root      25   5       0      0      0 S   0.0   0.0   0:00.00 ksmd
     24 root      39  19       0      0      0 S   0.0   0.0   0:00.00 khugepaged
     70 root       0 -20       0      0      0 I   0.0   0.0   0:00.00 kintegrityd
     71 root       0 -20       0      0      0 I   0.0   0.0   0:00.00 kblockd
     72 root       0 -20       0      0      0 I   0.0   0.0   0:00.00 blkcg_punt_bio
     73 root       0 -20       0      0      0 I   0.0   0.0   0:00.00 tpm_dev_wq
     74 root       0 -20       0      0      0 I   0.0   0.0   0:00.00 ata_sff
```

The first section of the top output shows general system information. The first line shows the current time, how long the system has been up, the number of users logged in, and the load average on the system.

The load average appears as three numbers: the 1-minute, 5-minute, and 15-minute load averages. The higher the values, the more load the system is experiencing. It's not uncommon for the 1-minute load value to be high for short bursts of activity. If the 15-minute load value is high, your system may be in trouble.

The second line shows general process information (called tasks in top): how many processes are running, sleeping, stopped, or in a zombie state.

The next line shows general CPU information. The top display breaks down the CPU utilization into several categories depending on the owner of the process (user versus system processes) and the state of the processes (running, idle, or waiting).

Following that, there are two lines that detail the status of the system memory. The first line shows the status of the physical memory in the system, how much total memory there is, how much is currently being used, and how much is free. The second memory line shows the status of the swap memory area in the system (if any is installed), with the same information.

Finally, the next section shows a detailed list of the currently running processes, with some information columns that should look familiar from the ps command output:

PID: The process ID of the process

USER: The username of the owner of the process

PR: The priority of the process

NI: The nice value of the process

VIRT: The total amount of virtual memory used by the process

RES: The amount of physical memory the process is using

SHR: The amount of memory the process is sharing with other processes

S: The process status (D = interruptible sleep, R = running, S = sleeping, T = traced or stopped, or Z = zombie)

%CPU: The share of CPU time that the process is using

%MEM: The share of available physical memory the process is using

TIME+: The total CPU time the process has used since starting

COMMAND: The command-line name of the process (program started)

By default, when you start top, it sorts the processes based on the %CPU value. You can change the sort order by using one of several interactive commands while top is running. Each interactive command is a single character you can press while top is running and changes the behavior of the program. Table 14.1 describes these commands.

TABLE 14.1: The top Interactive Commands

COMMAND	DESCRIPTION
1	Toggle the single CPU and Symmetric Multiprocessor (SMP) state.
b	Toggle the bolding of important numbers in the tables.
I	Toggle Irix/Solaris mode.
z	Configure color for the table.
l	Toggle the displaying of the load average information line.
t	Toggle the displaying of the CPU information line.
m	Toggle the displaying of the MEM and SWAP information lines.
f	Add or remove different information columns.
o	Change the display order of information columns.
F or O	Select a field on which to sort the processes (%CPU by default).
< or >	Move the sort field one column left (<) or right (>).
r	Toggle the normal or reverse sort order.
h	Toggle the showing of threads.
c	Toggle the showing of the command name or the full command line (including parameters) of the processes.
i	Toggle the showing of idle processes.
S	Toggle the showing of the cumulative CPU time or relative CPU time.
x	Toggle highlighting of the sort field.
y	Toggle highlighting of running tasks.
z	Toggle color and mono mode.
u	Show processes for a specific user.
n or #	Set the number of processes to display.
k	Kill a specific process (only if the process owner or if a root user).

TABLE 14.1:   The top Interactive Commands   *(CONTINUED)*

COMMAND	DESCRIPTION
r	Change the priority (renice) of a specific process (only if the process owner or if a root user).
d or s	Change the update interval (default is three seconds).
W	Write current settings to a configuration file.
q	Exit the top command.

You have lots of control over the output of the top command. Use the F or 0 command to toggle which field the sort order is based on. You can also use the r interactive command to reverse the current sorting. Using this tool, you can often find offending processes that have taken over your system.

Managing Processes

One of the jobs of a Linux system administrator is to be on the watch for runaway processes that can take down the Linux system. You've already seen how to use the ps and top commands (or the System Monitor graphical tool) to monitor how processes are doing on the system. The next step is to see how to stop a runaway process.

Setting Priorities

By default, all processes running on the Linux system are created equal; that is, they all have the same priority to obtain CPU time and memory resources. However, you may run some applications that either don't need to have the same level of priority, or that may need a higher level of priority.

The nice and renice commands allow you to set and change the priority level assigned to an application process. The nice command allows you to start an application with a nondefault priority setting. The format looks like this:

```
nice -n value command
```

The *value* parameter is a numeric value from -20 to 19. The lower the number, the higher priority the process receives. The default priority is 0. The *command* parameter specifies the program to start at the specified priority.

To change the priority of a process that's already running, use the renice command.

```
renice priority [-p pids] [-u users] [-g groups]
```

The renice command allows you to change the priority of multiple processes based on a list of PID values, all of the processes started by one or more users, or all of the processes started by one or more groups. Only the root user account can set a priority value less than 0 or decrease the priority value (increase the priority) of a running process.

Stopping Processes

Sometimes a process gets hung up and just needs a gentle nudge to either get going again or stop. Other times, a process runs away with the CPU and refuses to give it up. In both cases, you need a command that will allow you to control a process. To do that, Linux follows the Unix method of interprocess communication.

In Linux, processes communicate with each other using process signals. A process signal is a predefined message that processes recognize and may choose to ignore or act on. The developers program how a process handles signals. Most well-written applications have the ability to receive and act on the standard Unix process signals. Table 14.2 shows these signals.

TABLE 14.2:   Linux Process Signals

NUMBER	NAME	DESCRIPTION
1	HUP	Hang up.
2	INT	Interrupt.
3	QUIT	Stop running.
9	KILL	Unconditionally terminate.
11	SEGV	Segment violation.
15	TERM	Terminate if possible.
17	STOP	Stop unconditionally, but don't terminate.
18	TSTP	Stop or pause, but continue to run in the background.
19	CONT	Resume execution after STOP or TSTP.

As shown in Table 14.2, Linux handles signals as numbers, but also assigns names to each signal. In commands that use signals you can refer to a signal by either its name or number. While a process can send a signal to another process, there are two commands available in Linux that allow you to send process signals to running processes.

THE *KILL* COMMAND

The kill command allows you to send signals to processes based on their process ID (PID). By default, the kill command sends a TERM signal to all the PIDs listed on the command line. Unfortunately, you can only use the process PID instead of its command name, making the kill command difficult to use sometimes.

To send a process signal, you must either be the owner of the process or be logged in as the root user.

```
$ kill 3940
 -bash: kill: (3940) - Operation not permitted
 $
```

The TERM signal only asks the process to kindly stop running. Unfortunately, if you have a runaway process, most likely it will ignore the request. When you need to get forceful, the -s parameter allows you to specify other signals (either using their name or signal number).

The generally accepted procedure is to first try the TERM signal. If the process ignores that, try the INT or HUP signal. If the program recognizes these signals, it will try to gracefully stop doing what it was doing before shutting down. The most forceful signal is the KILL signal. When a process receives this signal, it immediately stops running. Use this as a last resort, as it can lead to corrupt files.

One of the scary things about the kill command is that there's no output from it.

```
$ sudo kill -s HUP 3940
$
```

Alternatively, you can just specify the signal name or number and the kill command will assume the -s option.

```
$ sudo kill -HUP 2940
$
```

To see if the command was effective, you'll have to perform another ps or top command to see if the offending process stopped.

WATCH OUT FOR OPEN FILES

Be careful of killing processes that may have open files. Files can be damaged and unrepairable if the process is abruptly stopped. It's usually a good idea to run the lsof command first to see a list of the open files and their processes before issuing a KILL signal to a process.

THE *PKILL* COMMAND

The pkill command is a powerful way to stop processes by using their names rather than the PID numbers. The pkill command allows you to use wildcard characters as well, making it a useful tool when you've got a system that's gone awry.

```
$ sudo pkill http*
$
```

This example will kill all of the processes that start with http, such as the httpd services for the Apache web server. Be careful with the search capability of the pkill command. It's usually a good idea to check the search term against the currently running processes to make sure you don't accidentally kill any other processes that match the search. The pgrep command allows you to display all processes that match the search term.

The following exercise walks through how to monitor the processes and manage them using the pgrep and kill commands.

Real World Scenario

MANAGING A RUNNING PROCESS

This exercise demonstrates how to monitor the running processes on your Linux system and how to remove a process you no longer want running.

1. Log into your Linux system and open two new command prompt windows. If you're using virtual terminals, open two separate virtual terminal sessions.

2. In the first command prompt, enter a command to run the sleep program for 1,000 seconds by typing **sleep 1000**.

3. In the second command prompt window or virtual terminal session, look for the PID of the sleep program by typing **pgrep sleep**.

4. Once you know the PID, use the kill command to stop it prematurely by typing **sudo kill -HUP** *pid*, where *pid* is the PID of the sleep program you found in step 3.

5. Observe the command prompt in the first window. It should return, indicating that the sleep program is no longer running.

6. Check the running processes to ensure the command is no longer running by typing **pgrep sleep**.

Running Programs in Background Mode

There are times when running a program directly from the command-line interface is inconvenient. Some programs can take a long time to process, and you may not want to tie up the command-line interface waiting. While the program is running, you can't do anything else in your terminal session. Fortunately, there's a simple solution to that problem.

When you use the ps command, you see a whole bunch of different processes running on the Linux system. Obviously, all of these processes are not running on your terminal monitor. This is called running processes in the *background*. In background mode, a process runs without being associated with a terminal session.

You can exploit this feature with your programs as well, allowing them to run behind the scenes and not lock up your terminal session. The following sections describe how to run programs in background mode on your Linux system.

Running in the Background

Running a program or script in background mode is a fairly easy thing to do. To run something in background mode from the command-line interface, just place an ampersand symbol after the command.

```
$ ./test1.sh &
[1] 1976
```

```
$ This is Test Program 1
Loop #1
Loop #2
ls
test1.sh test2.sh test3.sh test4.sh
$ Loop #3
Loop #4
...
[1]+  Done                  ./test1.sh
$
```

When you place the ampersand symbol after a command, it separates the command from the Bash shell and runs it as a separate background process on the system. The first thing that displays is the following line:

```
[1] 1976
```

The number in the square brackets is the job number assigned to the background process by the shell. The next number is the PID assigned to the process.

As soon as the system displays these items, a new command-line interface prompt appears. You are returned to the shell, and the command you executed runs safely in background mode.

At this point, you can enter new commands at the prompt (as shown in the example). However, while the background process is still running, it still uses your terminal monitor for messages. You'll notice from the example that the output from the test1.sh script appears in the output intermixed with any other commands that are run from the shell.

When the background process finishes, it displays a message on the terminal.

```
[1]+  Done                  ./test1.sh
```

This shows the job number and the status of the job (Done), along with the command used to start the job.

Running Multiple Background Jobs

You can start any number of background jobs at the same time from the command-line prompt.

```
$ ./test1.sh &
[3] 2174
$ This is Test Program 1

$ ./test2.sh &
[4] 2176
$ I am Test Program 2

$ ./test3.sh &
[5] 2178
$ Well this is Test Program 3

$ ./test4.sh &
[6] 2180
```

```
$ This is Test Program 4

$
```

Each time you start a new job, the Linux system assigns it a new job number and PID. You can see that all of the scripts are running using the ps command.

```
$ ps au
USER         PID %CPU %MEM   VSZ   RSS TTY     STAT START TIME COMMAND
...
user        1826  0.0  0.3  6704  3408 pts/0   Ss   14:07 0:00 bash
user        2174  0.0  0.1  4860  1076 pts/0   S    15:23 0:00 /bin/bash ./test1.sh
user        2175  0.0  0.0  3884   504 pts/0   S    15:23 0:00 sleep 300
user        2176  0.0  0.1  4860  1068 pts/    S    15:23 0:00 /bin/bash ./test2.sh
user        2177  0.0  0.0  3884   508 pts/0   S    15:23 0:00 sleep 300
user        2178  0.0  0.1  4860  1068 pts/0   S    15:23 0:00 /bin/bash ./test3.sh
user        2179  0.0  0.0  3884   504 pts/0   S    15:23 0:00 sleep 300
user        2180  0.0  0.1  4860  1068 pts/0   S    15:23 0:00 /bin/bash ./test4.sh
user        2181  0.0  0.0  3884   504 pts/0   S    15:23 0:00 sleep 300
user        2182  0.0  0.1  4592  1100 pts/0   R+   15:24 0:00 ps au
$
```

Each of the background processes you start appears in the ps command output listing of running processes. If all of the processes display output in your terminal session, things can get pretty messy pretty quickly. The next section walks through a solution.

Running Programs Without a Console

There will be times when you want to start a shell script from a terminal session and then let the script run in background mode until it finishes, even if you exit the terminal session. You can do this by using the nohup command.

The nohup command runs another command blocking any SIGHUP signals that are sent to the process. This prevents the process from exiting when you exit your terminal session.

The format used for the nohup command is as follows:

```
$ nohup ./test1.sh &
[1] 19831
$ nohup: ignoring input and appending output to  'nohup.out'
$
```

As with a normal background process, the shell assigns the command a job number, and the Linux system assigns a PID number. The difference is that when you use the nohup command, the script ignores any SIGHUP signals sent by the terminal session if you close the session.

Because the nohup command disassociates the process from the terminal, the process loses the output links to the terminal. To accommodate any output generated by the command, the nohup command automatically redirects any output messages to a file, called nohup.out.

The nohup.out file contains all of the output that would normally be sent to the terminal monitor. After the process finishes running, you can view the nohup.out file for the output results.

```
$ cat nohup.out
This is Test Program 1
Loop #1
Loop #2
Loop #3
Loop #4
Loop #5
Loop #6
Loop #7
Loop #8
Loop #9
Loop #10
This is the end of the test program
$
```

The output appears in the nohup.out file just as if the process ran on the command line! Be careful, though; if you run multiple programs using nohup, they all send their output to the same nohup.out file.

Job Control

The function of starting, stopping, killing, and resuming jobs is called *job control*. With job control, you have full control over how processes run in your shell environment. This section describes the commands to use to view and control jobs running in your shell.

Viewing Jobs

The key command for job control is the jobs command. The jobs command allows you to view the current jobs being handled by the shell.

```
$ cat test5.sh
#!/bin/bash
# testing job control

echo "This is a test program running on PID $$"
count=1
while [ $count -le 10 ]
do
    echo "Loop #$count"
    sleep 10
    count=$[ $count + 1 ]
done
echo "This is the end of the test program"
$
$ ./test5.sh
This is a test program running on PID 29011
Loop #1
^Z
```

```
[1]+  Stopped                    ./test5.sh
$
$ ./test5.sh > test5out &
[2] 28861
$
$ jobs
[1]+  Stopped                    ./test5.sh
[2]-  Running                    ./test5.sh >test5out &
$
```

The script uses the $$ variable to display the PID that the Linux system assigns to the script; then it goes into a loop, sleeping for 10 seconds at a time for each iteration. In the example, the first script is started from the command-line interface and then stopped using the Ctrl+Z key combination. Next, another job is started as a background process, using the ampersand symbol. To make life a little easier, the output of that script is redirected to a file so that it doesn't appear on the screen.

After the two jobs were started, we used the jobs command to view the jobs assigned to the shell. The jobs command shows both the stopped and the running jobs, along with their job numbers and the commands used in the jobs.

The jobs command uses a few different command-line parameters, as shown in Table 14.3.

TABLE 14.3:   The jobs Command Parameters

PARAMETER	DESCRIPTION
-l	List the PID of the process along with the job number.
-n	List only jobs that have changed their status since the last notification from the shell.
-p	List only the PIDs of the jobs.
-r	List only the running jobs.
-s	List only stopped jobs.

You probably noticed the plus and minus signs in the jobs command output. The job with the plus sign is considered the default job. It would be the job referenced by any job control commands if a job number isn't specified in the command line. The job with the minus sign is the job that would become the default job when the current default job finishes processing. There will only be one job with the plus sign and one job with the minus sign at any time, no matter how many jobs are running in the shell.

The following is an example showing how the next job in line takes over the default status, when the default job is removed:

```
$ ./test5.sh
This is a test program running on PID 29075
Loop #1
^Z
```

```
[1]+  Stopped                      ./test5.sh
$
$ ./test5.sh
This is a test program running on PID 29090
Loop #1
^Z
[2]+  Stopped                      ./test5.sh
$
$ ./test5.sh
This is a test program runnin on PID 29105
Loop #1
^Z
[3]+  Stopped                      ./test5.sh
$
$ jobs -l
[1]   29075 Stopped                  ./test5.sh
[2]- 29090 Stopped                   ./test5.sh
[3]+ 29105 Stopped                   ./test5.sh
$
$ kill -9 29105
$
$ jobs -l
[1]- 29075 Stopped                   ./test5.sh
[2]+ 29090 Stopped                   ./test5.sh
$
```

In this example, three separate scripts were started and then stopped. The jobs command listing shows the three processes and their status. Note that the default process (the one listed with the plus sign) is the last process started.

Then the kill command was issued to send a SIGHUP signal to the default process. In the next jobs listing, the job that previously had the minus sign is now the default job.

Restarting Stopped Jobs

You can restart any stopped job as either a background process or a foreground process. A foreground process takes over control of the terminal you're working on, so be careful about using that feature.

To restart a job in background mode, use the bg command, along with the job number.

```
$ bg 2
[2]+ ./test5.sh &
Loop #2
$ Loop #3
```

```
    Loop #4

$ jobs
[1]+  Stopped                 ./test5.sh
[2]-  Running                 ./test5.sh &
$ Loop #6
Loop #7
Loop #8
Loop #9
Loop #10
This is the end of the test program
[2]-  Done                    ./test5.sh
$
```

Because the job was restarted in background mode, the command-line interface prompt appears, allowing other commands to be entered. The output from the jobs command now shows that the job is indeed running (as you can tell from the output now appearing on the monitor).

To restart a job in foreground mode, use the fg command, along with the job number.

```
$ jobs
[1]+  Stopped                 ./test5.sh
$ fg 1
./test5.sh
Loop #2
Loop #3
```

Since the job is running in foreground mode, the command-line interface prompt does not appear until the job finishes.

Scheduling Jobs

As a system administrator, there will be situations in which you will want to run a program or script at a preset time, usually at a time when you're not there. The Linux system provides a couple of ways to run a script at a preselected time: the at command and the cron table. Each method uses a different technique for scheduling when and how often to run scripts. The following sections describe each of these methods.

Scheduling a Job Using the *at* Command

The at command allows you to specify a time when the Linux system will run a script. The at command submits a job to a queue with directions on when the shell should run the job. The at daemon, atd, runs in the background and checks the job queue for jobs to run. Most Linux distributions start this daemon automatically at boot time.

The atd daemon checks a special directory on the system (usually /var/spool/at) for jobs submitted using the at command. By default, the atd daemon checks this directory every 60 seconds. When a job is present, the atd daemon checks the time the job is set to be run. If the time matches the current time, the atd daemon runs the job.

The following sections describe how to use the at command to submit jobs to run and how to manage jobs.

THE *AT* COMMAND FORMAT

The basic at command format is pretty simple.

```
at [-f filename] time
```

By default, the at command submits input from the terminal to the queue. You can specify a filename used to read commands from using the -f parameter.

The *time* parameter specifies when you want the Linux system to run the job. You can get pretty creative with how you specify the time. The at command recognizes lots of different time formats.

◆ A standard hour and minute, such as 10:15

◆ An AM/PM indicator, such as 10:15 PM

◆ A specific named time, such as now, noon, midnight, or teatime (4 PM)

If you specify a time that has already past, the at command runs the job at that time on the next day.

In addition to specifying the time to run the job, you can also include a specific date, using a few different date formats, shown here:

◆ A standard date format, such as MMDDYY, MM/DD/YY, or DD.MM.YY.

◆ A text date, such as Jul 4 or Dec 25, with or without the year.

◆ You can also specify a time increment.

    ◆ Now + 25 minutes

    ◆ 10:15~PM tomorrow

    ◆ 10:15 + 7 days

When you use the at command, the job is submitted into a *job queue*. The job queue holds the jobs submitted by the at command for processing. There are 26 different job queues available for different priority levels. Job queues are referenced using lowercase letters, *a* through *z*.

The higher alphabetically the job queue, the lower the priority (higher nice value) the job will run under. By default, at jobs are submitted to the at job queue. If you want to run a job at a higher priority, you can specify a different queue letter using the -q parameter.

RETRIEVING JOB OUTPUT

When the job runs on the Linux system, there's no monitor associated with the job. Instead, the Linux system uses the email address of the user who submitted the job for any output messages. Any output destined to the terminal is mailed to the user via the mail system.

Here's a simple example of using the at command to schedule a job to run:

```
$
$ cat test6.sh
#!/bin/bash
#
# testing the at command
```

```
#
echo This script ran at `date`
echo This is the end of the script >&2
$
$ date
Sat Feb 13 14:38:17 EDT 2021
$
$ at -f test6.sh 14:39
warning: commands will be executed using /bin/sh
job 57 at Sat Feb 13 14:39:00 2021
$
$ mail
"/var/mail/user": 1 message 1 new
>N   1 user              Sat Feb 13 14:39  15/538   Output from your job
& 1
Date: Sat, 13 Feb 2021 14:39:00 -0400
Subject: Output from your job       57
To: sysadmin@ubuntu-server
From: sysadmin <sysadmin@ubuntu-server>

This script ran at Sat Feb 13 14:39:00 EDT 2021
This is the end of the script

& exit
$
```

The at command produces a warning message, indicating what shell the system uses to run the script, /bin/sh, along with the job number assigned to the job and the time the job is scheduled to run.

When the job completes, nothing appears on the monitor, but the system generates an email message. The email message shows the output generated by the script. If the script doesn't produce any output, it won't generate an email message, by default. You can change that by using the -m option in the at command. This generates an email message, indicating the job completed, even if the script doesn't generate any output.

LISTING PENDING JOBS

The atq command allows you to view what jobs are pending on the system.

```
$
$ at -f test6.sh 15:05
warning: commands will be executed using /bin/sh
job 58 at Sat Feb 13 15:05:00 2021
$
$ at -f test6.sh 15:10
warning: commands will be executed using /bin/sh
job 59 at Sat Febt 13 15:10:00 2021
$
```

```
$ at -f test6.sh 15:15
warning: commands will be executed using /bin/sh
job 60 at Sat Feb 13 15:15:00 2021
$
$ at -f test6.sh 15:20
warning: commands will be executed using /bin/sh
job 61 at Sat Feb 13 15:20:00 2021
$$ atq
61      Sat Feb 13 15:20:00 2021 a user
58      Sat Feb 13 15:05:00 2021 a user
59      Sat Feb 13 15:10:00 2021 a user
60      Sat Feb 13 15:15:00 2021 a user
$
```

The job listing shows the job number, the date and time the system will run the job, and the job queue the job is stored in.

REMOVING JOBS

Once you know the information about what jobs are pending in the job queues, you can use the atrm command to remove a pending job.

```
$
$ atq
59      Sat Feb 13 15:10:00 2021 a user
60      Sat Feb 13 15:15:00 2021 a user
$
$ atrm 59
$
$ atq
60      Sat Feb 13 15:15:00 2021 a user
$
```

Just specify the job number you want to remove. You can only remove jobs that you submit for execution. You can't remove jobs submitted by others; only the root user can do that.

Scheduling Recurring Programs

Using the at command to schedule a program or script to run at a preset time is great, but what if you need it to run at the same time every day, or once a week, or once a month? Instead of having to continually submit at jobs, you can use another feature of the Linux system.

The Linux system uses the cron program to allow you to schedule jobs that need to run on a regular basis. The cron program runs in the background and checks special tables, called cron *tables*, for jobs that are scheduled to run.

THE CRON TABLE

The cron table uses a special format for allowing you to specify when a job should be run. The format for the cron table is as follows:

```
min hour dayofmonth month dayofweek command
```

The cron table allows you to specify entries as specific values, ranges of values (such as 1–5), or as a wildcard character (the asterisk). For example, if you want to run a command at 10:15 on every day, you would use the following cron table entry:

```
15 10 * * * command
```

The wildcard character used in the *dayofmonth, month,* and *dayofweek* fields indicates that cron will execute the command every day of every month at 10:15 a.m. To specify a command to run at 4:15 p.m. every Monday, you would use the following:

```
15 16 * * 1 command
```

You can specify the *dayofweek* entry as either a three-character text value (mon, tue, wed, thu, fri, sat, or sun) or as a numeric value, with 0 being Sunday and 6 being Saturday.

Here's another example: to execute a command at 12 noon on the first day of every month, you would use the following format:

```
00 12 1 * * command
```

The *dayofmonth* entry specifies a date value (1–31) for the month.

The command list must specify the full pathname of the command to run. You can add any command-line parameters or redirection symbols you like, as a regular command line.

```
15 10 * * * /home/sysadmin/test4.sh > test4out
```

The cron program runs the script using the user account that submitted the job. Thus, you must have the proper permissions to access the command and output files specified in the command listing.

BUILDING THE *CRON* TABLE

Each system user can have their own cron table (including the root user) for running scheduled jobs. Linux provides the crontab command for handling the cron table. To list an existing cron table, use the -l parameter.

```
$ crontab -l
no crontab for sysadmin
$
```

By default, each user's cron table file doesn't exist. To add entries to your cron table, use the -e parameter. When you do that, the crontab command starts a text editor with the existing cron table (or an empty file if it doesn't yet exist).

CRON DIRECTORIES

When you create a script that has less precise execution time needs, it is easier to use one of the preconfigured cron script directories. There are four basic directories: hourly, daily, monthly, and weekly.

```
$ ls /etc/cron.*ly
/etc/cron.daily:
apport       bsdmainutils  logrotate  mlocate         update-notifier-common
```

```
apt-compat  dpkg           man-db      popularity-contest

/etc/cron.hourly:

/etc/cron.monthly:

/etc/cron.weekly:
man-db  update-notifier-common
$
```

Thus, if you have a script that needs to be run one time per day, just copy the script to the daily directory, and `cron` executes it each day.

The Bottom Line

Monitor programs running on the server.   You can view the running applications and the resources they consume by using the `ps` command. There are many different ways to view process information using the `ps` command, allowing you to customize the display exactly how you like. For real-time monitoring of applications, use the `top` command. With the `top` command, you can view a real-time display of applications, their system state, and the resources they consume; plus it allows you to sort the display based on many different features.

> **Master It**   Your server users are complaining that the server seems slow today. How can you tell what programs are using the most resources on the server?

Manage programs running on the server.   The `nice` command allows you to start an application at a different priority level than the applications that are already running. This allows users to run applications in the background at a lower priority or allows the system administrator to start applications with a higher priority. With the `renice` command, you can change the priority of an application that's already running. If an application causes problems and needs to be stopped, you can use the `kill` command, but you need to know the PID assigned to the application by the system. The `pkill` command is customized for stopping applications by their name instead of the PID.

> **Master It**   A software developer has contacted you to tell you that she made a coding error in her program named `inventory`, and now it's stuck running in an endless loop on the system. What command(s) should you run to find and safely stop the runaway program?

Schedule programs to run in the future.   Linux provides a couple of different ways for you to schedule programs to start at a future time or even a different date. The `at` command lets you schedule in individual program to run at a specific time/date. If you need to schedule a program to start on a regular schedule, use the `crontab` command to add the program to the system cron table. You must specify the schedule format to tell Linux when to start the program.

> **Master It**   The software developer has worked out all of the bugs in her `inventory` program and would like for it to run automatically every month on the first of the month at 1 AM. The program is stored in the `/applications` directory. What command should she use to make that happen?

Chapter 15

Managing Log Files

Lots of things happen on a Linux system while it's running. Part of your job as a Linux administrator is watching over all that is happening and watching for when things go wrong. The primary tools for accomplishing that task are the logging and journaling services.

All Linux distributions implement some method of *logging*. Logging or journaling directs short messages that indicate what events happen, and when they happen, to users, files, or even remote hosts for storage. If something goes wrong, the Linux administrator can review the entries in the log or journal to help determine the cause of the problem. Most logging methods allow manually entered messages, so local script utilities can create their own log and journal entries.

Managing the logging and journaling services is critical, and you need to understand the important aspects of maintaining the log and journal files, and their configurations. Configuring a system's method of logging is more than setting what is recorded. You'll also have to determine how large you'll allow log and journal files to get, when to remove journal files from the system, and whether to compress them beforehand. Administrators also need to protect their system's log and journal files, know where they are located in the virtual directory structure, and know how to sync them, when needed.

IN THIS CHAPTER, YOU WILL LEARN TO

- ◆ View journal entries
- ◆ Maintain the journal file's size
- ◆ Make a journal file continuous
- ◆ Modify a logging level

The systemd Journaling System

The systemd system services package includes the `systemd-journald` journal utility for logging. Notice that we called it a journal utility instead of a logging utility. The `systemd-journald` program uses its own method of storing event messages completely different from the older Linux logging protocol specifications.

This section discusses how to use the `systemd-journald` program to track event messages on your Linux system.

Configuring *systemd-journald*

The systemd-journald service reads its configuration from the /etc/systemd/journald.conf configuration file. When you examine this file, you'll notice settings that control how the application works and controls items, such as the journal file's size. Table 15.1 describes commonly modified directives.

TABLE 15.1: The journald.conf File Commonly Modified Directives

DIRECTIVE	DESCRIPTION
Storage	Set to auto, persistent, volatile, or none. Determines how systemd-journald stores event messages. (Default is auto.)
Compress	Set to yes or no. If yes, journal files are compressed. (Default is yes.)
ForwardToSyslog	Set to yes or no. If yes, any received messages are forwarded to a separate syslog program, such as rsyslogd, running on the system. (Default is yes.)
ForwardToWall	Set to yes or no. If yes, any received messages are forwarded as wall messages to all users currently logged into the system. (Default is yes.)
MaxFileSec	Set to a number followed by a time unit (such as month, week, or day) that sets the amount of time before a journal file is rotated (archived). Typically, this is not needed if a size limitation is employed. To turn this feature off, set the number to 0 with no time unit. (Default is 1month.)
RuntimeKeepFree	Set to a number followed by a unit (such as K, M, or G) that sets the amount of disk space systemd-journald must keep free for other disk usages when employing volatile storage. (Default is 15% of current space.)
RuntimeMaxFileSize	Set to a number followed by a unit (such as K, M, or G) that sets the amount of disk space systemd-journald journal files can consume if it is volatile.
RuntimeMaxUse	Set to a number followed by a unit (such as K, M, or G) that sets the amount of disk space systemd-journald can consume when employing volatile storage. (Default is 10% of current space.)
SystemKeepFree	Set to a number followed by a unit (such as K, M, or G) that sets the amount of disk space systemd-journald must keep free for other disk usages when employing persistent storage. (Default is 15% of current space.)
SystemMaxFileSize	Set to a number followed by a unit (such as K, M, or G) that sets the amount of disk space systemd-journald journal files can consume if it is persistent.
SystemMaxUse	Set to a number followed by a unit (such as K, M, or G) that sets the amount of disk space systemd-journald can consume when employing persistent storage. (Default is 10% of current space.)

Changing a journal file from being volatile to persistent is covered later in this chapter. Thus, the Storage directive settings in Table 15.1 need a little more explanation, because they are involved in this activity:

- **auto**: Causes systemd-journald to look for the /var/log/journal directory and store event messages there. If that directory doesn't exist, it stores the event messages in the temporary /run/log/journal directory, which is deleted when the system shuts down.

- **persistent**: Causes systemd-journald to automatically create the/var/log/journal directory if it doesn't currently exist, and store event messages there.

- **volatile**: Forces systemd-journald to store only event messages in the temporary /run/log/journal directory.

- **none**: Event messages are discarded.

There are quite a few settings that allow you to customize exactly how systemd-journald works in your system. If you'd like to explore a full list and explanation of all the settings, type **man journald.conf** at the command-line prompt.

Looking at Journal Files

You may have one or more active journal files on your system, depending on how systemd-journald is configured. For example, if you have Storage set to persistent, you can employ the SplitMode directive to divide up the journal file into multiple active files—one per user as well as a system journal file.

The file(s) directory location is contingent on whether the journal is persistent. In either case, the system's active journal file is named system.journal, with user active journal files (if used) named user-*UID*.journal.

These journal files are rotated automatically when a certain size or time is reached, depending on the directives set in the journal.conf file. After the files are rotated, they are renamed and considered archived. The archived journal filenames start with either system or user-*UID*, contain an @ followed by several letters and numbers, and end in a .journal file extension.

Here is a snipped example of both active and archived journal files on an Ubuntu distribution:

```
$ ls /var/log/journal/97be830906c6403080531940216d9d58/
system.journal
system@0005b1a4fa2a3f11-ccebd7a67a3fac0e.journal~
system@0005b1ba77b40dbf-746bd77e61dfd702.journal~
system@0005b85104386367-0f9a91515ce90123.journal~
system@2f6af80fdbf44d0d946eeed38d4d[...].journal
system@2f6af80fdbf44d0d946eeed38d4d[...].journal
user-1000.journal
user-1000@3367a2ef66d648b498adedab8[...].journal
user-1000@ce192e7a8484423d8ad44e590[...].journal
user-1001.journal
$
```

Notice that this system uses both system and user journal files and that several of the files have been archived. The systemd-journald configuration dictates when the archived journal files are removed from the system based on size directives, such as SystemMaxFileSize, or time directives, such as MaxFileSec.

On some systems that have persistent files, you can manually rotate (archive) active journals. If this feature is available on your system, you do this with the journalctl --rotate command.

Making the Journal Persistent

On some distributions, the journal entries are stored in the /run/log/journal directory, which is *volatile*, meaning the directory is removed and the journal entries are lost whenever the system is shut down.

Here is an example of a journal file on a Red Hat–based distribution, where the journal is configured as volatile:

```
# ls /run/log/journal/0c00adfd05364b9d921be2a22c59e3ed/
system.journal
#
```

If desired, system admins can change a journal file from volatile to persistent. To accomplish this, set the Storage directive within the journald.conf file, changing it to persistent.

When this configuration is loaded (via a systemctl restart, which was covered earlier), systemd-journald automatically creates the /var/log/journal directory, moves the journal file to its new location, and starts storing journal entries in it. Also, since this file is *persistent*, the file survives system shutdowns and reboots, and its entries are not removed.

While you can set the Storage directory to auto and create the /var/log/journal directory yourself, it's a little tricky getting the directory permissions set correctly. Thus, it's best to let systemd-journald do the work for you.

Viewing Journal Entries

The systemd-journald program doesn't store journal entries in text files. Instead, it uses its own binary file format that works similar to a database. Although this makes it a little harder to view journal entries, it does provide for quick searching for specific event entries.

The journalctl program is our interface to the journal files. The basic format for the journalctl command is as follows:

```
journalctl [OPTIONS...] [MATCHES...]
```

The OPTIONS control how data returned by the MATCHES is displayed and/or additionally filtered. Table 15.2 lists commonly used switches.

TABLE 15.2:   The journalctl Utility's Commonly Used Options

SHORT OPTION	LONG OPTION	DESCRIPTION
-a	--all	Display all data fields, including unprintable characters.
-e	--pager-end	Jump to the end of the journal and display the entries.

SHORT OPTION	LONG OPTION	DESCRIPTION
-g *pattern*	--grep *pattern*	Display only entries that match *pattern*.
-k	--dmesg	Display only kernel entries.
-n *number*	--lines=*number*	Show the most recent *number* of journal entries.
-r	--reverse	Reverse the order of the journal entries in the output.
-S *date*	--since=*date*	Show journal entries starting at *date*, where date is formatted as YYYY-MM-DD:HH:MM:SS. If a time specification is left off of date, then 00:00:00 is assumed. Keywords such as yesterday, today, tomorrow, and now can all replace date.
-U *date*	--until=*date*	Show journal entries until *date* is reached in the entries. *date* formatting is the same as it is for the -S option.
-u *unit* or *pattern*	--unit=*unit* or *pattern*	Show only journal entries for the systemd *unit* or systemd units that match *pattern*.

By default, the journalctl utility employs the less pager to display its entries. To turn off this feature, use the --no-pager option. Here is a simple snipped example of using journalctl without *MATCHES* and showing the last 20 messages without using the less pager on an Ubuntu system:

```
$ sudo journalctl -n 20 --no-pager
-- Logs begin [...] end at Wed 2021-02-03 19:44:38
Feb 03 19:08:32 [...]sysadmin from [...] port 63155 ssh2
Feb 03 19:08:32 [...]pam_unix(sshd:[...]user sysadmin by (uid=0)
Feb 03 19:08:32 ubuntu-server [...] of user sysadmin.
Feb 03 19:08:32 ubuntu-server [...] of user sysadmin.
Feb 03 19:17:01 ubuntu-server [...]root by (uid=0)
Feb 03 19:17:01 [...]CMD (   cd / && run-parts --report [...]
Feb 03 19:17:01 [...]:session): session closed for user root
Feb 03 19:21:52 [...]Cleanup of Temporary Directories...
Feb 03 19:21:53 [...]clean.service: Succeeded.
Feb 03 19:21:53 [...]Cleanup of Temporary Directories.
Feb 03 19:31:34 [...]Starting Message of the Day...
Feb 03 19:31:35 [...]Using degraded feature set[...]
Feb 03 19:31:35 [...]Using degraded feature set[...]
Feb 03 19:31:43 ubuntu-server 50-motd-news[...]
Feb 03 19:31:43 ubuntu-server 50-motd-news[...]
Feb 03 19:31:43 ubuntu-server 50-motd-news[...]
Feb 03 19:31:43 ubuntu-server systemd[1]: [...].
Feb 03 19:31:43 ubuntu-server systemd[1]: [...]
Feb 03 19:44:30 ubuntu-server sudo[1228]: [...]
Feb 03 19:44:32 ubuntu-server sudo[1228]: [...]
$
```

Real World Scenario

EXPLORING THE USE OF THE JOURNALCTL UTILITY

The journalctl program allows you to view various journal entries in the journal file. There are many options that allow you to format the display to assist in information search efforts.

The following steps will take you through exploring the journal file entries using the journalctl program:

1. If you are on an Ubuntu distribution, log into your Linux system using the sysadmin account and the password you created for it. If you are on a Red Hat–based distro, such as CentOS, log into your Linux system using the root account and the password you created for it.

2. View the oldest entries in the journal file by typing **journalctl** and pressing Enter. This will display the journal file entries using the less pager.

3. Press the spacebar to go to the next page in the journal file display. Notice the date and time stamps to the far left of the display.

4. Note the system hostname in the display, which should be one column to the right of the date and time stamps. Record the hostname.

5. Press Q to quit out of the less pager.

6. View your system's hostname, by typing **echo $HOSTNAME** and pressing Enter. Record the hostname.

7. Determine if the hostnames you recorded in steps 4 and 6 match. They should.

8. View the newest entries in the journal file by typing **journalctl -e** and pressing Enter. Take a look at the latest events on your system that have entries in the journal.

9. Press Q to quit out of the less pager.

10. Now, search for particular information in the journal, by typing **journalctl -g sysadmin** and pressing Enter. Look at the various items recorded concerning your sysadmin account. (If there is more than one page of information, press the spacebar to view a few pages.)

11. Press Q to quit the less pager.

The *MATCHES* for the journalctl utility filter what type of journal entries to display. Table 15.3 lists the various commonly used filters that are available.

TABLE 15.3: The Common journalctl *MATCHES* Parameters Used for Filtering

MATCH	DESCRIPTION
field	Match the specific *field* in the journal. You can enter multiple occurrences of *field* on the same line, but they must be separated with a space. You can separate multiple *field* specifications with a plus sign (+) to use a *logical OR* between them.

Match	Description
OBJECT_PID=*pid*	Match only entries made by the specified application *pid*.
PRIORITY=*value*	Match only entries with the specified priority *value*. The value can be set to one of the following numbers or keywords: emerg (0), alert (1), crit (2), err (3), warning (4), notice (5), info (6), or debug (7).
_HOSTNAME=*host*	Match only entries from the specified *host*.
_SYSTEMD_UNIT=*unit.type*	Match only entries made by the specified systemd *unit.type*.
_TRANSPORT=*transport*	Match only entries received by the specified *transport* method.
_UDEV_SYSNAME=*dev*	Match only entries received from the specified device.
_UID=*userid*	Match only entries made by the specified user ID.

To use journalctl to view all the various journal entries, you'll need to be logged in as the root user, use super user privileges, or typically belong to the systemd-journal group. Recognize that your distribution may use a different group for this task.

When you are looking for specific event entries in the journal, use the desired filters and options to target specific items. In the following example, only today's entries for the ssh .service systemd service unit are displayed:

```
$ sudo journalctl --no-pager --since=today _SYSTEMD_UNIT=ssh.service
-- Logs begin at Wed 2020-10-14 17:34:10 UTC, end at Wed 2021-02-03 19:56[...]
Feb 03 18:54:29 ubuntu-server sshd[696]: Server listening on 0.0.0.0 port 22.
Feb 03 18:54:29 ubuntu-server sshd[696]: Server listening on :: port 22.
Feb 03 19:05:58 ubuntu-server sshd[696]: Received signal 15; terminating.
[...]
Feb 03 19:06:54 ubuntu-server sshd[684]: Server listening on 0.0.0.0 port 22.
Feb 03 19:06:54 ubuntu-server sshd[684]: Server listening on :: port 22.
Feb 03 19:08:32 ubuntu-server sshd[1024]: Accepted password for sysadmin[...]
Feb 03 19:08:32 ubuntu-server sshd[1024]: pam_unix(sshd:session): sessio[...]
$
```

Employing various journalctl filters makes digging through journal files much easier.

The journalctl utility has a nice feature that allows you to watch the journal as entries are being added. Just employ the journalctl -f or --follow switch, and you will see the last few entries and additional entries as they are added to the journal. When you are done watching, press the Ctrl+C key combination to quit.

Maintaining the Journal

Besides configuring a persistent journal and keeping the journal disk usage in check, you have a few manual management activities you can employ for maintaining your journal file(s).

You can check the current disk usage of the persistent journal file(s) by employing the journalctl --disk-usage command:

```
$ journalctl --disk-usage
Archived and active journals take up 104.0M in the file system.
$
```

While systemd-journald can automatically clean up disk space via settings in the journald .conf file, you can do so manually as well. In this case, you employ a vacuum . . . well, actually its vacuum options available on the journalctl command:

```
--vacuum-size
--vacuum-time
```

As you would expect, --vacuum-size removes journal files until the disk space consumed by journal files reaches the designated size. You follow the option with a number and tack on a unit (K, M, G, or T) to set the size. Be aware that this removes only *archived* journal files and has no effect on any active journal files.

For the --vacuum-time option, you designate the oldest journal entries allowed, and the rest are deleted. The time is denoted with a number as well as a time unit (s, min, h, days, months, weeks, or years), such as 10months. Like the size option, the time option affects only archived journal files. The active files are left untouched.

While you can combine the two different switches if needed, this snipped example uses only the size option to pare down on disk usage:

```
$ journalctl --disk-usage
Archived and active journals take up 104.0M in the file system.
$
$ sudo journalctl --vacuum-size=10M
[...]
Deleted archived journal /var/log/journal/97be[...](8.0M).
Deleted archived journal /var/log/journal/97be[...] (8.0M).
Deleted archived journal /var/log/journal/97be[...] (8.0M).
Deleted archived journal /var/log/journal/97be[...] (8.0M).
Deleted archived journal /var/log/journal/97be[...] (16.0M).
Deleted archived journal /var/log/journal/97be[...](8.0M).
Deleted archived journal /var/log/journal/97be[...] (16.0M).
Vacuuming done, freed 72.0M of archived journa[...]
$
$ journalctl --disk-usage
Archived and active journals take up 32.0M in the file system.
$
```

Notice that after the vacuuming was completed, another journalctl --disk-usage command was issued, but it shows 32.0M instead of the 10M size set on the vacuum option. This is because though the disk-usage switch shows both active and archived journal files, the vacuum options work *only* on archived journal files.

Viewing Different Journal Files

If you need to retrieve a journal file from a rescued system but view it first or look at the entries in an archived or copied journal file, a few `journalctl` switches are available that can help.

Because `journalctl` looks for the active journal files in either the `/run/log/journal` or `/var/log/journal` directory, you can point it to a different directory location where a copied or another system's journal file is located by using the `-D directory-name` or `--directory= directory-name` option.

If the file you are trying to view has a different name than `system.journal` or `user-UID .journal`, use the `--file=pattern` option on the `journalctl` command. Set the `pattern` to be the exact name of the file you want to view. However, if there are several files, you can employ filename pattern-matching within the `pattern` to match several files.

If you have recently rescued your system and now have two or more journal files with entries to view, you can merge them. To do this, use the `-m` or `--merge` switches on the `journalctl` utility. Keep in mind that this does not *physically* merge the journal files but instead merges their entries in the output for your perusal.

Protecting Journal Files

If you'd like to back up your active journal file(s), you can simply copy them. However, right before you make a copy, run the `journalctl --sync` command to ensure all the entries are moved from their queue into the file.

The `systemd-journald` journal utility allows you to send your system's journals to a centralized journal host system via `systemd-journal-remote`. To view all the various journal files' entries on the central host, you'll need to employ the `-m` or `--merge` option when using the `journalctl` command.

Making Journal Entries

If needed, you can add journal entries from the command line or scripts using the `systemd-cat` tool. To do so, you must pipe your command's STDOUT into the utility:

```
COMMAND | systemd-cat
```

A quick test of employing the `systemd-cat` command is easily checked using the `--grep` option on the `journalctl` command:

```
# echo "Hello World Test" | systemd-cat
#
# journalctl --no-pager --grep "Hello World Test"
[...]
Feb 03 15:25:53 localhost.localdomain cat[1762]: Hello World Test
#
```

This feature of adding your own journal entries is handy for adding additional tracking information, such as when installing new apps on a server or modifying configurations. It leaves a nice "trail of breadcrumbs" should you encounter problems due to these changes later.

Real World Scenario

ADDING ENTRIES TO THE JOURNAL

You can manually add entries to the journal file. This feature is nice for troubleshooting. Understanding how this feature works will allow you to create journal entries from scripts, which assist in tracking when a script ran or isolating problems that occurred in the script.

The following steps will take you through trying out adding your own journal file entries using the systemd-cat program:

1. If you are on an Ubuntu distribution, log into your Linux system using the sysadmin account and the password you created for it. If you are on a Red Hat–based distro, such as CentOS, log into your Linux system using the root account and the password you created for it.

2. If you are on an Ubuntu system, create a journal entry by typing **sudo echo "Journal Entry Test" | systemd-cat** and pressing Enter. If you are on a Red Hat–based system, such as CentOS, create a journal entry by typing **echo "Journal Entry Test" | systemd-cat** and pressing Enter.

3. Locate your entry in the journal by typing **journalctl --no-pager -e -g "Journal Entry Test"** and pressing Enter. Do you see your journal entry? You should. If not, go back and reattempt step 2.

4. Try adding additional journal entries and then finding them using the appropriate **journalctl** command.

The rsyslog Legacy System

In the early days of Unix, there were many different logging methods used to track system and application events. Applications used different logging methods, making it difficult for system administrators to troubleshoot issues.

With the development of an important core logging protocol, and many open source logging tools that rapidly evolved into utilities with familiar configuration-file settings and interfaces, logging systems were now providing admins more useful troubleshooting information. The utilities and remnants of these advances still exist on many Linux distributions to this day.

The syslog Protocol

In the mid-1980s, Eric Allman defined a protocol for logging events from his Sendmail mail application, called *syslog*. The syslog protocol quickly became a standard for logging both system and application events in Unix and made its way to the Linux world.

What made the syslog protocol so popular is that it defines a standard message format that specifies the time stamp, type, severity, and details of an event. That standard can be used by the operating system, applications, and even devices that generate errors.

The type of event is defined as a *facility* value. The facility defines what is generating the event message, such as a system resource or an application. Table 15.4 lists the facility values defined in the syslog protocol.

TABLE 15.4:   The syslog Protocol Facility Values

CODE	KEYWORD	DESCRIPTION
0	kern	Messages generated by the system kernel
1	user	Messages generated by user events
2	mail	Messages from a mail application
3	daemon	Messages from system applications running in the background
4	auth	Security or authentication messages
5	syslog	Messages generated by the logging application itself
6	lpr	Printer messages
7	news	Messages from the news application
8	uucp	Messages from the Unix-to-Unix copy program
9	cron	Messages generated from the cron job scheduler
10	authpriv	Security or authentication messages
11	ftp	File Transfer Protocol application messages
12	ntp	Network Time Protocol application messages
13	security	Log audit messages
14	console	Log alert messages
15	solaris-cron	Another scheduling daemon message type
16–23	local0–local7	Locally defined messages

As you can tell from Table 15.4, the syslog protocol covers many different types of events that can appear on a Linux system.

Each event is also marked with a *severity*. The severity value defines how important the message is to the health of the system. Table 15.5 shows the severity values as defined in the syslog protocol.

TABLE 15.5:   The syslog Protocol Severity Values

CODE	KEYWORD	DESCRIPTION
0	emerg	An event causes the system to be unusable.
1	alert	An event that requires immediate attention.

TABLE 15.5: The syslog Protocol Severity Values *(CONTINUED)*

CODE	KEYWORD	DESCRIPTION
2	crit	An event that is critical, but doesn't require immediate attention.
3	err	An error condition that allows the system or application to continue.
4	warning	A non-normal warning condition in the system or application.
5	notice	A normal but significant condition message.
6	info	An informational message from the system.
7	debug	Debugging messages for developers.

Combining the facility and severity codes with a short informational message provides enough logging information to troubleshoot almost any problem in Linux.

Basic Logging Using *rsyslogd*

Over the years, there have been many open source logging projects for Linux systems. One that uses the syslog protocol is the rsyslog project, whose developers' claim that the *r* stands for "rocket fast." Speed is the focus of the rsyslog project, and the rsyslog application quickly became a standard logging package for many Linux distributions.

The rsyslog application uses the `rsyslogd` program to monitor events and log them as directed, using the `/etc/rsyslogd.conf` configuration file to define what events to listen for, and how to handle them. Many Linux distributions also use a `/etc/rsyslog.d/` directory to store individual configuration files that are included as part of the `rsyslog.conf` configuration. This allows applications to define their own log settings.

The configuration file contains rules that define how the program handles syslog events received from the system, kernel, or applications. The format of an `rsyslogd` rule is as follows:

```
facility.priority action
```

The `facility` entry uses one of the standard syslog protocol facility keywords. The `priority` entry uses the severity keyword as defined in the syslog protocol, but with a twist. When you define a severity, `rsyslogd` will log all events with that severity or higher. Thus, the following entry logs all kernel event messages with a severity of critical, alert, or emergency:

```
kern.crit
```

To log only messages with a specific severity, use an equal sign before the priority keyword:

```
kern.=crit
```

You can also use wildcard characters for either the facility or priority. The entry logs all events with an emergency severity level:

```
*.emerg
```

The `action` entry defines what `rsyslogd` should do with the received syslog protocol message. There are six action options you have available:

- ◆ Forward to a regular file.

- ◆ Pipe the message to an application.

- ◆ Display the message on a terminal or the system console.

- ◆ Send the message to a remote host.

- ◆ Send the message to a list of users.

- ◆ Send the message to all logged-in users.

Some of the entries for directing log messages in the /etc/rsyslogd.conf file on a CentOS system are shown here:

```
$ cat /etc/rsyslog.conf
# rsyslog configuration file
[...]
# Include all config files in /etc/rsyslog.d/
include(file="/etc/rsyslog.d/*.conf" mode="optional")


#### RULES ####


# Log all kernel messages to the console.
# Logging much else clutters up the screen.
#kern.*                          /dev/console

[...]
# The authpriv file has restricted access.
authpriv.*                      /var/log/secure

# Log all the mail messages in one place.
mail.*                          -/var/log/maillog


# Log cron stuff
cron.*                          /var/log/cron

# Everybody gets emergency messages
*.emerg                         :omusrmsg:*

# Save news errors of level crit and higher in a special file.
uucp,news.crit                  /var/log/spooler

# Save boot messages also to boot.log
local7.*                        /var/log/boot.log

[...]
$
```

Notice the dash in front of the /var/log/maillog filename. This lets rsyslogd know that there is no need to update the log file (sync) after every single mail event. Typically, this configuration speeds logging up a little, but on certain filesystems, it runs the risk of losing some events.

Layering Your Logging

If desired (or required), you can have both systemd-journald and a syslog protocol application, such as rsyslog, running and working together. There are two primary ways to accomplish this:

Journal Client Method This method allows a syslog protocol program to act as a *journal client*, reading entries stored in the journal file(s). It is typically the preferred way, because it avoids losing any important messages that may occur during the system boot, before the syslog service starts. Also for rsyslog, this is commonly already configured, which is handy.

For rsyslog, if this method is not already configured or you'd like to check your system, look in the /etc/rsyslog.conf file. It needs to have the imuxsock and/or imjournal module being loaded via module without a preceding pound sign (#), as shown snipped here:

```
$ cat /etc/rsyslog.conf
module(load="imuxsock"  #[...] local system logging[...]
module(load="imjournal" #[...] access to the systemd journal
$
```

Forward to Syslog Method This method employs the file /run/systemd/journal/syslog. Messages are forwarded to the file (called a *socket*) where a syslog protocol program can read them.

To use this method, you need to modify the journal configuration file, /etc/systemd/journald.conf, and set the ForwardToSyslog directive to yes. Keep in mind that you'll need to load the modified journald.conf file into systemd-journald for it to take effect. Unfortunately, you cannot employ the systemctl reload option to load the new configuration for systemd-journald. Instead, using super user privileges, you must restart the service using the systemctl restart systemd-journald command.

 Real World Scenario

LOOKING AT THE RSYSLOG CONFIGURATION FILES

The legacy rsyslog logging application is still often employed on modern distributions. If it is used on a system you administer, it's wise to understand its configuration, such as looking to see if it works with systemd-journald.

The following steps will take you through auditing your system to see if rsyslog may be used and viewing its configuration file:

1. Log into your Linux system using the sysadmin account and the password you created for it.

2. Determine if the rsyslog configuration is on your system, by typing **ls /etc/rsyslog.conf** and pressing Enter. If the configuration file is on your system, continue with these steps. If it is not, then there is no need to continue, because your system does not have rsyslog.

3. Determine if there are any configurations files in the /etc/rsyslog.d/ directory by typing **ls /etc/rsyslog.d/** and pressing Enter. Do you see files? If so, record their names.

4. Take a look at the rsyslog configuration file's contents by typing **less /etc/rsyslog.conf** and pressing Enter. Stay in the less pager for the next several steps.

5. From the journal client method information covered in the preceding "Layering Your Logging" section, as well as the modules loaded through your system's /etc/rsyslog.conf file, determine whether your rsyslog application is acting as a journal client.

6. From the information covered in "The syslog Protocol" and "Basic Logging Using *rsyslogd*" sections in this chapter, locate the syslog protocol severity value of emerg in the /etc/rsyslog.conf file. If you find it here, record what happens when this type of event occurs on the system.

7. Press q to quit the less pager.

8. If in step 6, you did not locate the emerg severity value in the /etc/rsyslog.conf file, and you have files in the /etc/rsyslog.d/ directory, look through those files for what happens when this type of event occurs on the system, and record your findings.

Making Log Entries

If you create and run scripts on your Linux system (Bash shell scripts are covered in Chapter 19, "Writing Scripts"), you may want to log your own application events using rsyslog. You can do that with the logger command-line tool:

```
logger [-isd] [-f file] [-p priority] [-t tag] [-u socket] [message]
```

The -i option specifies the process ID (PID) of the program that created the log entry as part of the event message. The -p option allows you to specify the event priority. The -t option allows you to specify a tag to add to the event message to help make finding the message in the log file easier. Either you can specify the message as text in the command line or you can specify it as a file using the -f option. The -d and -u options are advanced options for sending the event message to the network. The -s option sends the event message to the standard error output.

An example of using logger looks like this:

```
$ logger This is a test message from script123.sh
$
```

On an Ubuntu system, you can look at the end of the /var/log/syslog file to see the manually created log entry:

```
$ tail -n 2 /var/log/syslog
Feb 10 18:07:32 ubuntu-server systemd[1]:
Started Session 3 of user sysadmin.
Feb 10 18:08:09 ubuntu-server sysadmin:
This is a test message from script123.sh
$
```

Notice that rsyslogd added the time stamp, hostname, and user account for the message. This provides a lot of information for use in troubleshooting!

Finding Event Messages

Generally, most Linux distributions create log files in the /var/log directory. Depending on the security of the Linux system, many log files are readable by everyone, but some may not be.

Most Linux distributions create separate log files for different event message types. However, they don't always agree on the log filenames.

It's also common for individual applications to have a separate directory under the /var/log directory for their own application event messages, such as /var/log/apache2 for the Apache web server.

The easiest way to find the rsyslog log files for your system is to examine the /etc/ rsyslogd.conf configuration file. Just remember to also look at the files stored in the /etc/ rsyslog.d directory.

As you can guess, for busy Linux systems, it doesn't take long to generate large log files. To help combat that, many Linux distributions install the logrotate utility. It automatically splits rsyslogd log files into archive files based on a time or the size of the file. You can usually identify archived log files by the numerical extension added to the log filename, so if the event information you are searching for is older, you may need to go perusing through those log files.

Since rsyslogd log files are text files, you can use any of the standard text tools available in Linux, such as cat, head, tail, and less, to view them. One common trick for administrators is to use the -f option with the tail command. That displays the last few lines in the log file, but then monitors the file for any new entries and displays those too.

The Bottom Line

View journal entries. The journalctl program is needed to view journal file entries, because unlike some logging utilities, systemd-journald doesn't store events in text files. Instead, it uses its own binary file format that works similar to a database. Thus, you cannot use the typical programs used to view text files, such as cat, head, or tail, to view journal file entries.

Master It You're an administrator on a rather under-resourced server with problems concerning two different apps that run on it. The problems are sporadic, but seem to start occurring during the app's peak use time. You decide to keep an eye on the error messages being logged to the journal during that time. What's the most efficient journalctl command(s) to use in this scenario?

Maintain the journal file's size. The systemd-journald journal file(s) can get rather large. Because the various services on the system are sending messages to this file, if multiple events are occurring on a regular basis, disk space can quickly become consumed. It's important to make some decisions on journal file size limits prior to lack of disk space becoming a critical emergency issue.

Master It Imagine you are administering a new server and are currently accessing the persistent systemd-journald journal files. After running the journalctl --disk-usage program, you've made some decisions on journal file size limits and determine a rotation schedule, which includes an archival process for the old files. Which directives should you consider modifying in the /etc/systemd/journald.conf file to match your decisions concerning this and prevent a critical emergency issue with disk space due to journal files?

Make a journal file continuous. On some distributions, the journal file entries are stored in the /run/log/journal directory. The /run/ directory and its contents are deleted when a system is shut down, so any journal entries are lost at that time. It is typical to change this behavior by modifying a directive in the /etc/systemd/journald.conf file to force systemd-journald to keep entries in a journal that is not removed when the system is shut down or reboots. The /var/log/journal directory is used in these cases to store the journal file(s).

> **Master It** Currently, the servers you administer have temporary journal files, which are lost when these systems are shut down or reboot. You'd like to make these journal files continuous and manage their size through rotation and archival settings in the systemd-journald configuration file. What directive should you change in the configuration files on these servers, and what should you set it to?

Modify a logging level. The legacy rsyslog application uses the syslog protocol. It uses either a single configuration file, /etc/rsyslogd.conf, or a combination of that configuration file and additional configuration files within the /etc/rsyslog.d/ directory. Modifying the rsyslog application's configuration is fairly straightforward with the *facility .priority action* syntax in its configuration rules.

> **Master It** You are the system admin for a server that uses the legacy rsyslog application for its event logging. You'd like to direct the rsyslogd program to send the following severity level of events for all systems to everyone: crit, alert, and emerg. What do you need to do?

Chapter 16

Managing Printers

Printing in a Linux environment can be somewhat complex. With a myriad of different types of printers available, trying to manually install the correct printer drivers as well as using the correct printer protocol to communicate with the printer can be a nightmare. Fortunately, there's a simpler solution available that you can easily install and configure on your Linux server to handle all of your printing issues.

IN THIS CHAPTER, YOU WILL LEARN TO

- ◆ Install and configure the CUPS software

- ◆ Create printers on your Linux server

- ◆ Manage print jobs submitted by clients on your local network

The Common Unix Printing System

The *Common Unix Printing System* (CUPS) is an open source software package developed at Apple to make printing in a Unix environment simple. Fortunately for us, a group of developers has ported the CUPS software to the Linux world, making it easier for Linux system administrators to manage printing on their systems and networks.

The CUPS software isn't a single program, but rather a package of different server and client programs, as well as printer drivers and tools. This section describes the different features of the CUPS software.

Printer Drivers

In the past, one of the hurdles of printing in Linux was finding printer drivers for any given printer. Often, manufacturers wouldn't bother releasing Linux drivers for their printers because different Linux distributions would handle printing differently, making it difficult if not impossible for Linux administrators to get printers working. One of the amazing features of CUPS is that it defines a standard printer driver format for printers. With CUPS, printer manufacturers just need to create one set of files that work in all Unix-based environments.

The CUPS software uses the Ghostscript program to convert standard PostScript documents into a format understood by the different printers. The Ghostscript program still requires drivers for the different printer types to know how to convert the document to make it printable on that type of printer, but at least it's a unified standard. CUPS installs many different drivers for common printers on the market and automatically sets the configuration requirements to use them.

Web Interface

CUPS provides a web interface for both admin and normal user printer functions. You don't need to have a web server installed on your Linux server; the CUPS software has it built-in. Figure 16.1 shows the basic CUPS web interface when you first open the web page.

FIGURE 16.1

The main CUPS web interface page

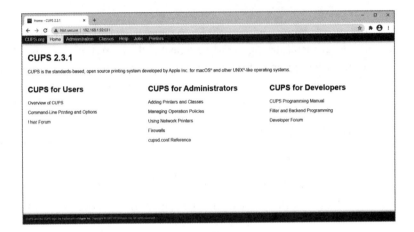

The web interface provides access to both user and admin features in CUPS. As a normal user, you can use the web interface to do the following:

◆ Submit print jobs to printers or printer classes.

◆ Monitor and control your own print jobs.

In the administration section of the web interface, you can do the following:

◆ Create/modify/delete printers.

◆ Group printers into a pool.

◆ Enable features on printers.

◆ Share printers on the network.

Besides these features, the CUPS web interface also provides links to CUPS documentation and simple tutorials, making it a useful resource to have.

Command-Line Commands

Aside from the CUPS web interface, there are a few command-line tools you can use for interacting with the printers and print queues:

cancel: Cancels a print request

cupsaccept: Enables queuing of print requests

cupsdisable: Disables the specified printer

cupsenable: Enables the specified printer

cupsreject: Rejects queuing of print requests

Besides the standard CUPS command-line commands, CUPS also accepts commands from the legacy BSD command-line printing utility:

lpc: Starts, stops, or pauses the print queue

lpq: Displays the print queue status, along with any print jobs waiting in the queue

lpr: Submits a new print job to a print queue

lprm: Removes a specific print job from the print queue

If you're working from the command line, you can check the status of any print queue, as well as submit print jobs, as shown in Listing 16.1.

LISTING 16.1:   Printing from the Command Line in Linux

```
$ lpq -P EPSON_ET_3750_Series
EPSON_ET_3750_Series is ready
no entries
$ lpr -P EPSON_ET_3750_Series test.txt
$ lpq -P EPSON_ET_3750_Series
EPSON_ET_3750_Series is ready and printing
Rank    Owner   Job     File(s)                 Total Size
active  rich    1       test.txt                1024 bytes
$
```

The first line in Listing 16.1 uses the lpq command to check the status of the print queue, which shows the printer is ready to accept new jobs, and doesn't currently have any jobs in the print queue. The lpr command submits a new print job to print a file. After submitting the new print job, the lpq command shows the printer is currently printing and shows the print job that's being printed.

Printer Sharing

With the printer sharing feature, client workstations on your local network can see any CUPS printer that you configure to share. Clients using the Microsoft Windows or Apple macOS operating systems can connect to the shared printers directly using their desktop graphical tools, usually without much work required on their part.

CUPS uses the standard Internet Printing Protocol (IPP) to advertise and share printers on the local network. With IPP, the server and client exchange printer information, such as the printer manufacturer and model and the features the printer supports, making it easy for workstations to detect the printer and install the correct drivers automatically. CUPS also supports other common network sharing protocols, such as these:

◆ Server Message Block (SMB), a Microsoft protocol for sharing files and printers on a network

◆ AirPrint, an Apple protocol for connecting iPad, iPhone, and macOS clients to printers using WiFi networks

Printer Classes

Printer classes in CUPS provides some versatility in your printer sharing. There are two basic features provided by printer classes:

Customized Printer Queues With printer classes, you can create multiple classes pointing to the same printer, with each class configured for a different printer feature. For example, you can create separate printer classes to use a particular paper tray for printers that support multiple paper sizes in multiple trays. For a print job to use the appropriate paper size, you just send it to the appropriate printer class instead of directly to the printer.

Printer Pools With printer classes, you can create a single printer class that points to multiple printers. The CUPS server will send new print jobs to the next available printer in the pool, without you having to worry about finding an available printer. This also accounts for printers that may be down due to hardware issues, or printers that are tied up printing large print jobs.

SHARING NETWORKED PRINTERS

You may be wondering why all the fuss about creating a shared printer in CUPS when nowadays most printers are already network-ready. The answer is versatility. Network-connected printers are somewhat simple—they just receive print jobs from network clients and process them. There's typically no way to manage print jobs that are sent directly to network printers, especially when multiple clients are sending print jobs to the same printer. By having everyone on the network send print jobs to a CUPS server as a step before the network printer, you gain a common way to manage the print jobs. Any client can use the CUPS web interface to check the status of a print job, as well as pause or cancel their own submitted print job (a printer admin can pause or cancel other people's print jobs). With the printer class feature in CUPS, you can see how CUPS can add versatility to any network printer environment.

Installing and Configuring CUPS

Unfortunately, neither the Ubuntu nor Red Hat server distribution installs the CUPS software by default. However, both include the CUPS software in their software repositories, so installing CUPS is easy. This section walks through the process of installing and configuring CUPS for both Ubuntu and Red Hat servers.

Installing CUPS

Since the CUPS software is already in the standard software repositories for both Ubuntu and Red Hat servers, installing the software is easy, using the standard package management tools for each server. For Ubuntu, you just need to use the apt tool:

```
$ sudo apt install cups
```

In a Red Hat server environment, use the dnf tool:

```
$ sudo dnf install cups
```

In both server environments, the CUPS software package installs quite a few things. Listing 16.2 shows the output from installing on a CentOS server.

LISTING 16.2:   Installing CUPS on a CentOS Server

```
# dnf install cups
Dependencies resolved.
========================================================================
 Package                          Arch    Version          Repo      Size
========================================================================
Installing:
 cups                             x86_64  1:2.2.6-38.el8   appstream 1.4 M
Installing dependencies:
 adobe-mappings-cmap              noarch  20171205-3.el8   appstream 2.1 M
 adobe-mappings-cmap-deprecated   noarch  20171205-3.el8   appstream 119 k
 adobe-mappings-pdf               noarch  20180407-1.el8   appstream 707 k
 cups-client                      x86_64  1:2.2.6-38.el8   appstream 169 k
 cups-filesystem                  noarch  1:2.2.6-38.el8   appstream 109 k
 cups-filters                     x86_64  1.20.0-20.el8    appstream 779 k
 cups-filters-libs                x86_64  1.20.0-20.el8    appstream 134 k
 ghostscript                      x86_64  9.25-7.el8       appstream  82 k
 google-droid-sans-fonts          noarch  20120715-13.el8  appstream 2.5 M
 jbig2dec-libs                    x86_64  0.14-4.el8_2     appstream  67 k
 jbigkit-libs                     x86_64  2.1-14.el8       appstream  55 k
 lcms2                            x86_64  2.9-2.el8        appstream 165 k
 libICE                           x86_64  1.0.9-15.el8     appstream  74 k
 libSM                            x86_64  1.2.3-1.el8      appstream  48 k
 libXcursor                       x86_64  1.1.15-3.el8     appstream  36 k
 libXfixes                        x86_64  5.0.3-7.el8      appstream  25 k
 libXi                            x86_64  1.7.10-1.el8     appstream  49 k
 libXinerama                      x86_64  1.1.4-1.el8      appstream  16 k
 libXmu                           x86_64  1.1.3-1.el8      appstream  75 k
 libXrandr                        x86_64  1.5.2-1.el8      appstream  34 k
 libXt                            x86_64  1.1.5-12.el8     appstream 186 k
 libXxf86misc                     x86_64  1.0.4-1.el8      appstream  23 k
 libXxf86vm                       x86_64  1.1.4-9.el8      appstream  19 k
 liberation-fonts-common          noarch  1:2.00.3-7.el8   baseos     25 k
```

```
liberation-mono-fonts           noarch 1:2.00.3-7.el8    baseos    505 k
libfontenc                      x86_64 1.1.3-8.el8       appstream  37 k
libgs                           x86_64 9.25-7.el8        appstream 3.1 M
libidn                          x86_64 1.34-5.el8        appstream 239 k
libijs                          x86_64 0.35-5.el8        appstream  30 k
libjpeg-turbo                   x86_64 1.5.3-10.el8      appstream 156 k
libmcpp                         x86_64 2.7.2-20.el8      appstream  81 k
libpaper                        x86_64 1.1.24-22.el8     appstream  45 k
libtiff                         x86_64 4.0.9-18.el8      appstream 188 k
mcpp                            x86_64 2.7.2-20.el8      appstream  31 k
openjpeg2                       x86_64 2.3.1-6.el8       appstream 154 k
poppler                         x86_64 0.66.0-27.el8     appstream 929 k
poppler-data                    noarch 0.4.9-1.el8       appstream 2.1 M
poppler-utils                   x86_64 0.66.0-27.el8     appstream 225 k
qpdf-libs                       x86_64 7.1.1-10.el8      appstream 338 k
urw-base35-bookman-fonts        noarch 20170801-10.el8   appstream 857 k
urw-base35-c059-fonts           noarch 20170801-10.el8   appstream 884 k
urw-base35-d050000l-fonts       noarch 20170801-10.el8   appstream  79 k
urw-base35-fonts                noarch 20170801-10.el8   appstream  12 k
urw-base35-fonts-common         noarch 20170801-10.el8   appstream  23 k
urw-base35-gothic-fonts         noarch 20170801-10.el8   appstream 654 k
urw-base35-nimbus-mono-ps-fonts noarch 20170801-10.el8   appstream 801 k
urw-base35-nimbus-roman-fonts   noarch 20170801-10.el8   appstream 865 k
urw-base35-nimbus-sans-fonts    noarch 20170801-10.el8   appstream 1.3 M
urw-base35-p052-fonts           noarch 20170801-10.el8   appstream 982 k
urw-base35-z003-fonts           noarch 20170801-10.el8   appstream 279 k
xorg-x11-font-utils             x86_64 1:7.5-40.el8      appstream 103 k
xorg-x11-server-utils           x86_64 7.7-27.el8        appstream 198 k
Installing weak dependencies:
avahi                           x86_64 0.7-19.el8        baseos    282 k
cups-ipptool                    x86_64 1:2.2.6-38.el8    appstream 5.8 M

Transaction Summary
================================================================================
Install  56 Packages

Total download size: 30 M
Installed size: 92 M
Is this ok [y/N]:
```

Notice in Listing 16.2 all of the different font packages that are installed as part of CUPS. This is another indication of the versatility CUPS provides.

For the Ubuntu server, after the package management script installs the software the CUPS server, it automatically starts the CUPS service. You can verify that by using the systemctl command.

```
sysadmin@ubuntu-server:~$ sudo systemctl status cups
[sudo] password for sysadmin:
```

```
  cups.service - CUPS Scheduler
     Loaded: loaded (/lib/systemd/system/cups.service; enabled; vendor preset: >
     Active: active (running) since Sat 2021-02-27 14:26:19 UTC; 49s ago
TriggeredBy:  cups.path
              cups.socket
       Docs:  man:cupsd(8)
   Main PID:  654 (cupsd)
      Tasks:  1 (limit: 2282)
     Memory:  5.0M
     CGroup:  /system.slice/cups.service
              └─654 /usr/sbin/cupsd -l

Feb 27 14:26:19 ubuntu-server systemd[1]: Started CUPS Scheduler.
sysadmin@ubuntu-server:~$
```

For the Red Hat server environment, the package management script doesn't automatically start the CUPS service:

```
[root@unknown080027D84F32 ~]# systemctl status cups
  cups.service - CUPS Scheduler
    Loaded: loaded (/usr/lib/systemd/system/cups.service; enabled; vendor preset>
    Active: inactive (dead)
      Docs: man:cupsd(8)
[root@unknown080027D84F32 ~]#
```

So you'll need to start it yourself, as well as tell the system to automatically start it at boot time, again with the systemctl command:

```
[root@centos-server ~]# systemctl start cups
[root@centos-server ~]# systemctl enable cups
```

You won't see any output from either command. You can then use the systemctl command to check to ensure CUPS is running:

```
[root@centos-server ~]# systemctl status cups
  cups.service - CUPS Scheduler
    Loaded: loaded (/usr/lib/systemd/system/cups.service; enabled; vendor preset>
    Active: active (running) since Sat 2021-02-27 09:31:49 EST; 55s ago
      Docs: man:cupsd(8)
 Main PID: 6555 (cupsd)
    Status: "Scheduler is running..."
     Tasks: 1 (limit: 11412)
    Memory: 2.6M
    CGroup: /system.slice/cups.service
            └─6555 /usr/sbin/cupsd -l

Feb 27 09:31:49 unknown080027D84F32 systemd[1]: Starting CUPS Scheduler...
Feb 27 09:31:49 unknown080027D84F32 systemd[1]: Started CUPS Scheduler.
[root@centos-server ~]#
```

The CUPS software also has the ability to detect printers on your local network using the separate cups-browsed service. This service is started by default in Ubuntu servers, but is not in

Red Hat server environments. You can start it, as well as ensure that it starts automatically at system startup by using the start and enable systemctl commands:

```
systemctl start cups-browsed
systemctl enable cups-browsed
```

In either environment, you can stop or restart the CUPS service at any time, again using the systemctl command:

```
systemctl stop cups
systemctl restart cups
```

Once you get CUPS installed and running, you'll need to make a few configuration changes from the default setup to get things to work. We cover that in the next section.

Preparing the Server to Use CUPS

By default, the CUPS software only allows connection to the web interface from the localhost. While that works fine for workstations, in a server environment that doesn't have a graphical desktop, it's somewhat impractical. To fix that situation, you'll need to make a few changes in the CUPS configuration file.

CONFIGURATION FILE CHANGES

The CUPS configuration file is located in the /etc/cups/cupsd.conf file. You can edit it with any text editor that you're familiar with. There are three places you'll need to make the changes.

First, you'll need to allow CUPS to listen for incoming network connections on all network cards on the system. Look for the following line:

```
Listen localhost:631
```

and change it to this:

```
Listen *:631
```

Second, you'll need to enable the browsing feature in CUPS so that network clients can see any printers that you share from CUPS. Look for the following line:

```
Browsing Off
```

and change it to this:

```
Browsing On
```

Next up, you'll need to configure CUPS to allow connections to both the user and admin interfaces from devices on your local network. This is done using the Allow directive. You can specify a single IP address, an IP address range, or the special @LOCAL keyword to allow any client on the local network to connect.

That's done in two sections. First, look for this section in the configuration file:

```
# Restrict access to the server...
<Location/>
  Order allow,deny
</Location>
```

and add an `Allow` line so that it looks like this:

```
# Restrict access to the server...
<Location/>
  Order allow,deny
  Allow @LOCAL
</Location>
```

You'll need to do the same thing to the /admin location definition:

```
# Restrict access to the admin pages...
<Location /admin>
  Order allow,deny
  Allow @LOCAL
</Location>
```

After you make these changes, save the updated `cupsd.conf` configuration file, and restart the CUPS service.

USER ACCOUNT CHANGES

To perform any printer administration functions using the web interface, you'll need to add your Linux user account to a group that has administrator privileges to the CUPS server. Unfortunately, not all Linux distributions use the same group to control this feature. You can find which group your distribution uses by looking in the /etc/cups/cups-files.conf file for the `SystemGroup` setting. For Ubuntu servers the line is as follows:

```
SystemGroup lpadmin
```

So, you'll need to add your user account to the `lpadmin` group using the `usermod` command. For Red Hat servers the line is as follows:

```
SystemGroup sys root wheel
```

So, you can add your user account to the `wheel` group:

For Ubuntu: `usermod sysadmin -G lpadmin`

For Red Hat: `usermod sysadmin -G wheel`

Once your user account is added to the appropriate user group, you'll be able to use the printer administration features in the CUPS web interface.

FIREWALL CHANGES

If your Linux server has a firewall activated to block network traffic, you'll need to allow the connections to the CUPS web interface through the firewall. Instead of the default HTTP port, the CUPS web interface uses TCP port 631. Assuming your network is 192.168.0.0, the command for the Ubuntu firewall is as follows:

```
sudo ufw allow in from 192.168.0.0/24 to any port 631
```

and the command for the Red Hat firewall is as follows:

```
sudo firewall-cmd --permanent --add-port=631/tcp
sudo systemctl reload firewalld
```

After you've completed all of these changes, you're ready to start your printer administration duties. The next section walks through that part.

Using CUPS

Now that you have the CUPS software installed and everything properly configured, you can define and configure printers. This section walks through how to do both using the web interface.

As shown in Figure 16.1, the CUPS web interface has several tabs:

◆ **Home**—the main page that contains links to tutorials and documentation

◆ **Administration**—allows the printer administrator to create and manage printers and printer classes, as well as manage print jobs submitted to the printers

◆ **Classes**—provides an interface to manage existing printer classes

◆ **Help**—provides access to the CUPS online documentation, including a search feature

◆ **Jobs**—allows you to manage your own print jobs, or allows administrators to manage all print jobs

◆ **Printers**—shows the status of printers, and print jobs currently pending

Each tab provides quick access to different features and functions of the CUPS print server. The following sections walk through how to manage printers and print jobs using the CUPS web interface.

Administration Functions

Clicking the Administration tab at the top of the main CUPS page opens the Administration web page, shown in Figure 16.2.

The following sections walk through the different administration functions you can perform from the CUPS web interface.

SERVER SETTINGS

The right side of the Administration page contains a button that allows you to manually edit the `cupsd.conf` configuration file, easily making changes to the overall configuration of the server. Once you make any changes, click the Save Changes button for them to take effect. There's also a button that allows you to revert to the default configuration if necessary. If you're accessing the CUPS web interface from a remote workstation, be careful, as the default configuration disables remote connections.

FIGURE 16.2
The CUPS
Administration web page

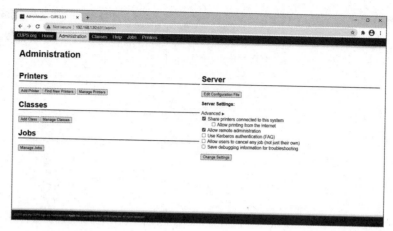

Beneath the configuration button is a series of check boxes that allow you to quickly enable or disable common server settings, such as the following:

♦ Sharing printers on the server

♦ Allowing remote administration

♦ Using Kerberos authentication

♦ Allowing users to cancel any print job (not just their own)

♦ Save debugging information

After making a selection from the feature menu, you'll need to click the Change Settings button to make them take effect.

PRINTER SETTINGS

As shown in Figure 16.2, on the left side of the Administration page are controls for managing printers, printer classes, and jobs. The Printer section contains three buttons:

♦ Add Printer

♦ Find New Printers

♦ Manage Printers

Clicking the Add Printer button produces the Add Printer web page (after you authenticate your user account), as shown in Figure 16.3.

FIGURE 16.3

The Add Printer web page in CUPS

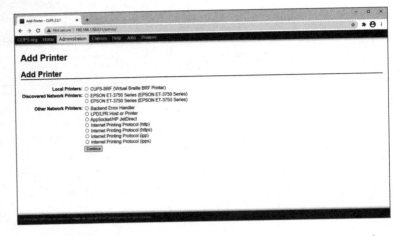

At the top of the page is a list of printers the CUPS service has detected on the server. If the cups-browsed service is running on the server, CUPS will also display a list of any detected network printers. You can also manually define a new printer using one of several common network protocols:

◆ LPD/LPR

◆ AppSocket

◆ IPP

◆ IPPS (secure IPP)

◆ IPP using HTTP

◆ IPP using HTTPS

Selecting any of the detected or manual options walks you through a wizard that helps configure the printer with the correct settings and driver.

While working through the wizard, the CUPS web interface will prompt you for the printer driver to use (it will attempt to automatically detect the printer type and provide the appropriate options). After setting up the printer driver, it will take you to the Set Printer Options page, shown in Figure 16.4.

From this page, you can set some common options that are available for the printer from four classes of options:

◆ **General**—set the paper size, tab stops, and margins.

◆ **Options Installed**—select which specialty options are available for the printer, such as the character encoding, what characters to set to indicate a line feed, and the page size.

◆ **Banners**— set if you want opening and/or closing banners set for each print job.

◆ **Policies**—set what CUPS should do if it encounters a printer error, such as retry the print job or pause it, as well as set if the printer requires authentication to print.

FIGURE 16.4

The Set Printer Options page in CUPS

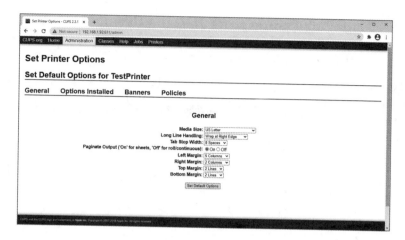

Once you've completed the Add Printer wizard process, the printer will appear in the list of available printers and is ready to accept print jobs.

 Real World Scenario

CREATING A TEST PRINTER

Even if you don't have a printer available, you can still define a test printer in CUPS; it just won't print to anything. Follow these steps to create a test printer so you can experiment with the other features in CUPS:

1. Connect to the CUPS web interface for your server. Open a browser on a workstation and enter the URL **http://server address:631**, where *server address* is the IP address of your Linux server.

2. Click the Administration tab at the top of the page.

3. Click the Add Printer button and then enter your user ID and password for authentication.

4. On the Add Printer page, select the Internet Printing Protocol (ipp) radio button, and then click the Continue button.

5. For the Connection text box, type **ipp://localhost:631**, and then click the Continue button.

6. In the Name text box, type **TestPrinter**. In the Description text box, type **A fictitious printer used for testing**. Click the Continue button.

7. In the Make selection box, choose Generic, and then click the Continue button.

8. In the Model selection box, choose Generic Text-Only Printer, and then click the Add Printer button.

9. Click the Printers tab at the top of the page to view the list of printers. You should see the TestPrinter printer appear in the list.

Managing Printers and Jobs in CUPS

Once you've installed a printer in CUPS, you can manage the printer operation from the web interface by clicking the Printers tab at the top of the page, as shown in Figure 16.5.

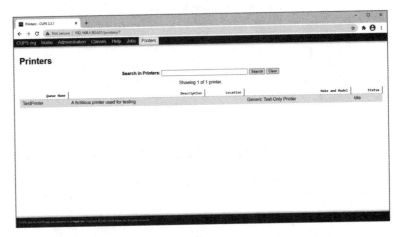

FIGURE 16.5
The Printers
page in CUPS

The main Printers page shows a list of all the printers configured in CUPS, along with their status, providing a quick dashboard to detecting any problems with printers.

When you click the name of an individual printer, the printer and jobs management web interface appears, as shown in Figure 16.6.

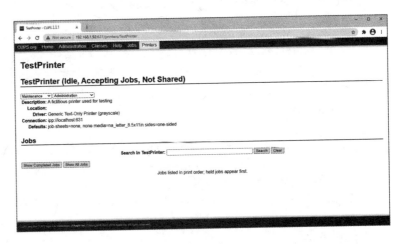

FIGURE 16.6
The printer management
page in CUPS

As shown in Figure 16.6, the printer management page shows a more detailed description of the printer status, along with the list of any print jobs currently assigned to the printer. There are two drop-down boxes available: Maintenance and Administration.

From the Maintenance drop-down box, you can select one of the following actions:

♦ Print a test page.

♦ Pause the printer.

♦ Reject print jobs.

♦ Move all print jobs to another printer.

♦ Cancel all print jobs.

From the Administration drop-down box, you can select one of the following actions:

♦ Modify the printer settings.

♦ Delete the printer.

♦ Set the default printer options.

♦ Set the printer as the server default.

♦ Set a list of allowed users for the printer.

Below that is the Jobs section. This lists all the pending print jobs assigned to the printer and their status. As the printer administrator, you can cancel an individual print job or move it to another printer if necessary.

As you can see, CUPS provides a full set of features for controlling all aspects of printer management for Linux servers and is a useful tool to install and have available in a network environment.

The Bottom Line

Install and configure the CUPS software. Most Linux distributions provide the Common Unix Printing System (CUPS) to make it easy to connect, use, and even share printers with your Linux system. Both Ubuntu and CentOS provide the CUPS software in their default software repositories, so you can install CUPS using apt in Ubuntu, or dnf in CentOS. Once you install the software, you'll need to make a few configuration changes to allow remote clients to use CUPS, especially if your server doesn't provide a graphical desktop. You'll also need to ensure your administrator user account has access to the CUPS administrator features by adding it to the appropriate user group.

Master It Your boss wants to allow all of the clients on your local network to be able to use the CUPS web interface to manage their own print jobs, but wants to restrict access to the CUPS administrator privileges to just your workstation, which has the static IP address of 192.168.1.100. What do you need to change in the cupsd.conf configuration file to accommodate that configuration?

Create printers on your Linux server. The CUPS web interface provides an administration section that allows you to create new printers for the Linux server. Clicking the Add Printer button starts a wizard that walks through the process of defining and creating the printer.

CUPS has the ability to automatically detect both local and network printers and can aid you in setting them up on the system.

Master It   The network team has installed a new printer on the network, but customers are complaining that their print output keeps getting mixed up with others. How can you assist in separating each print job sent to the printer using CUPS?

Manage printers and print jobs submitted by clients on your local network.   The CUPS web interface allows you to manage both printer settings as well as print jobs submitted to the printer. Click the Printer tab from the main CUPS web page, and then select the printer you want to manage. On the Printer page, you can select from several different printer administration functions, such as modify the printer settings, delete the printer, pause print jobs, and cancel print jobs. Under the printer settings is also a list of jobs currently assigned to the printer. From here, you can select a job to either cancel it or move it to another printer.

Master It   Customers are complaining that someone sent a large print job to the printer yesterday that's not printing, and blocking any other print job from processing. What process do you need to perform to solve the problem?

Part 3

Advanced Admin Functions

Chapter 17

Exploring Ubuntu Security

Securing an Ubuntu system includes setting up user accounts with passwords and setting permissions on files and directories, which are part of *discretionary access controls* (DAC). However, these methods are no longer considered enough to properly secure a server. You also need to implement *mandatory access controls* (MAC), which allow or block user and application access to data. Software that implements MAC on a system typically uses what is called *least privilege*. This means applications and users are provided access to only the data needed to accomplish their defined tasks.

The least privilege principal actually goes a bit deeper by giving users and applications only the privileges they need to complete their work and no more. This is one of the concepts behind privilege escalation. While you need only a basic set of privileges to look at file listings or edit a simple text file, there are times you, as a system administrator, need greater privileges to accomplish tasks, such as installing software and managing user accounts. Ubuntu provides a secure method for escalating your system admin account's privileges when needed.

Finally, to protect against individuals who have malicious intents, called *bad actors*, from snooping on your communications, you need a form of encryption to protect your network connections to remote servers. We cover these topics and more in this chapter as we look at the various components that make up a layered approach to security, which is called *defense in depth*.

IN THIS CHAPTER, YOU WILL LEARN TO

- ◆ Safely escalate privileges to accomplish tasks

- ◆ Use OpenSSH to connect to remote systems

- ◆ Manage Ubuntu MAC protection software

- ◆ Configure the Ubuntu firewall

Locking Down Root

Ubuntu security is a little different when it comes to the root user account. It defaults to a least privilege approach at installation. This may cause you some confusion if you are accustomed to how other Linux distributions handle root. In this section, we'll cover the different types of accounts you'll find, how root is treated by default, and how to securely obtain super user privileges when needed.

Looking at Linux Account Types

While in Linux, all user accounts are typically created the same way using the `useradd` utility (see Chapter 13, "Managing Users and Groups"), not all user accounts behave the same way. There are three basic types of user accounts in Linux:

Root: The `root` user account is historically the main administrator user account on the system. It is identified by being assigned the special user ID value of 0. The `root` user account has permissions to access all files and directories on the system, regardless of any permission settings assigned.

Standard: Standard Linux user accounts are used to log into the system and perform standard tasks, such as run desktop applications or shell commands. Standard Linux users normally are assigned a `$HOME` directory, with permissions to store files and create subdirectories. Standard Linux users cannot access files outside of their `$HOME` directory unless they're given permission by the file or directory owner. Most Linux distributions assign standard user accounts user IDs over 1000.

Service: Service Linux accounts are used for applications that start in the background, such as network services like the Apache web server or MySQL database server. Though these accounts are required, they are also restricted so that they cannot log into the system by setting the password value in the shadow file to an asterisk. Also, the login shell defined in `/etc/passwd` is set to the `/sbin/nologin` value to prevent access to a command shell. Service accounts normally have a user ID less than 1000.

The `root` account does exist on the Ubuntu distribution, as shown here with the `getent` command:

```
$ getent passwd root
root:x:0:0:root:/root:/bin/bash
$
```

However, by default on Ubuntu, `root` is blocked from logging into the system, because its account password is set to an asterisk:

```
$ sudo getent shadow root
[sudo] password for sysadmin:
root:*:18474:0:99999:7:::
$
```

Blocking the `root` account from logging into the system is considered a good security practice. The account originates from a time when each server had a single administrator. As systems evolved, administration grew from one person to a team of administrators.

If a team is sharing one account, logging individual actions is not possible, and an administrator who is acting unlawfully can deny that they were the one responsible for logging into `root` and causing problems. This is called a *repudiation environment*.

Next, we'll show you how to implement a *nonrepudiation environment*, where each user has their own account and their actions are properly logged.

Gaining Super User Privileges

To safely gain super user privileges and provide a nonrepudiation environment, Ubuntu uses *privilege escalation*. This method allows administrators to use their standard Linux user account to run programs with preconfigured root administrator privileges.

The sudo command is short for "substitute user do," though many still refer to its older name, "super user do," because of its ability to provide super user privilege access. It lets a standard user account run any pre-authorized command as another pre-authorized user account, including the root user account. The use of the sudo command provides the following benefits and features:

♦ When used, sudo prompts the user for their own password to validate who they are.

♦ An account once validated to use sudo does not have to re-enter their password until after a time period of not using the sudo command.

♦ Actions taken with the sudo command are logged.

♦ Groups of users can be configured to use sudo, instead of granting individual account authorized access.

♦ Properly configured, sudo provides a least privilege and nonrepudiation environment contributing to a system's security.

The /etc/sudoers configuration file defines what users are allowed to run the sudo command along with what they have access to do. The sudoers file may contain a list of user accounts, aliases, and/or groups whose users are allowed to escalate privileges.

```
$ sudo cat /etc/sudoers
[sudo] password for sysadmin:
#
# This file MUST be edited with the 'visudo' command as root.
#
# Please consider adding local content in /etc/sudoers.d/[...]
# directly modifying this file.
#
# See the man page for details on how to write a sudoers file.
#
Defaults        env_reset
Defaults        mail_badpass
Defaults        secure_path="/usr/local/sbin:/usr/local/bin:
/usr/sbin:/usr/bin:/sbin:/bin:/snap/bin"

# Host alias specification

# User alias specification

# Cmnd alias specification

# User privilege specification
```

```
root     ALL=(ALL:ALL) ALL

# Members of the admin group may gain root privileges
%admin ALL=(ALL) ALL

# Allow members of group sudo to execute any command
%sudo    ALL=(ALL:ALL) ALL

# See sudoers(5) for more information on "#include" directives:

#includedir /etc/sudoers.d
$
```

Ubuntu uses the group sudo to designate those who can access full super user privileges. Often the initial account created at installation time is assigned to this group. You can determine if your account is a member of the sudo group through the groups command:

```
$ groups
sysadmin adm cdrom sudo dip plugdev lxd
$
```

If you'd like to modify the sudo configuration, you'll need to use the visudo command. It's a special text editor that prevents multiple system administrators from making changes at the same time, causing file corruption, and using incorrect syntax.

However, instead of directly adding your configuration in the /etc/sudoers file, it's a good idea to create your sudo command configuration file(s) in the /etc/sudoers.d/ directory. If you do this, be sure to uncomment the includedir line located at the bottom of the sudoers file to load your configuration.

LOOKING AT THE su COMMAND

On systems that allow administrators to log into the root account, you'll find that the su command (short for "substitute user") is used to escalate privileges. It allows a standard user account to run commands as another user account, including the root user account.

However, to run the su command, the standard user must provide the password for the substitute user account password, because they are temporarily logging into that account. While this solves the problem of knowing who is performing an administrator task, it doesn't solve the problem of multiple people knowing the other account's password.

If you stick with the default Ubuntu configuration that blocks logging into the root account, using the su command to escalate privileges isn't even an option. This is the best practice for a secure system.

There is another nice command that provides privilege escalation. The sudoedit command allows a standard user to open a file in a text editor with privileges of another pre-authorized user account, including the root user account. Similar to the sudo command, sudoedit also prompts the user for their own password to validate who they are.

Real World Scenario

DETERMINING YOUR PRIVILEGE ELEVATION STATUS

On Ubuntu, the common method for escalating privileges is to use the sudo command. However, you must either belong to a group listed for accessing higher privileges in the /etc/sudoers file or have a record authorizing the privileges within the file.

The following steps will take you through determining your privilege elevation status:

1. Using your Ubuntu Linux distribution, log into the sysadmin account and enter the password you created for it.

2. Look at your account name by typing **whoami** and pressing Enter. The account name should be sysadmin.

3. Determine the groups to which this account belongs by typing **groups** and pressing Enter. Record the group names.

4. Typically, Ubuntu Linux allows those users who belong to the group sudo to access full super user privileges. From the names you recorded in the previous step, determine if you belong to that group. Record your finding.

5. Try to display the /etc/sudoers file without using escalated privileges by typing **cat /etc/ sudoers** and pressing Enter. You should receive a "permission denied" error message and not be able to view the file.

6. Now attempt to display the file by using escalated privileges by typing **sudo cat /etc/ sudoers** and pressing Enter. If asked, enter your account's password. Record whether you were able to display the file.

   If you were able to display the file, then you do have access to escalated privileges.

7. Assuming you do have access to escalated privileges, use the group names you recorded in step 3 to search for a record in the /etc/sudoers file that shows what escalated privileges you are allowed to use, by typing **grep *group-name* /etc/sudoers** and pressing Enter. Continue to enter this command until grep finds a record for one of your groups, if any. (If you cannot find a group record, try substituting your username, sysadmin, for the *group-name* in the command.) Record your findings.

Using OpenSSH on Ubuntu

When you connect over a network to a remote server, if it is not via an encrypted method, bad actors using network sniffers can view the data being sent and received. Secure Shell (SSH) has resolved this problem by providing an encrypted means for communication. It is the de facto standard software used by those wanting to send data securely to/from remote systems.

Exploring Basic SSH Concepts

Linux uses OpenSSH for providing Secure Shell functionality, and it is typically installed by default on Ubuntu. However, if for some reason you are unable to use basic SSH services, you may want to check the needed OpenSSH packages' status (installing software was covered in Chapter 3, "Installing and Maintaining Software in Ubuntu"). Ubuntu uses the openssh-server and openssh-client packages:

```
$ sudo apt list openssh-server
[sudo] password for sysadmin:
openssh-server[...][installed]
[...]
$
$ sudo apt list openssh-client
Listing... Done
openssh-client[...][installed,automatic]
[...]
$
```

To create a secure OpenSSH connection between two systems, use the ssh command. The basic syntax is as follows:

```
ssh [options] username@hostname
```

For a successful encrypted connection, both systems (client and remote) must have the OpenSSH software installed and the sshd daemon running. Here is an example of connecting from an Ubuntu system to a CentOS server:

```
$ echo $HOSTNAME
ubuntu-server
$
$ lsb_release --id
Distributor ID: Ubuntu
$
$ ssh sysadmin@192.168.0.102
The authenticity of host '192.168.0.102 (192.168.0.102)'
can't be established.
ECDSA key fingerprint is SHA256:4K3wFeVOFMUXgmeAGWWkUogxe6
gP+QpQ+ROCuZr7aW0.
Are you sure you want to continue connecting
(yes/no/[fingerprint])? yes
Warning: Permanently added '192.168.0.102' (ECDSA) to the
list of known hosts.
sysadmin@192.168.0.102's password:
Activate the web console with: systemctl enable
```

```
--now cockpit.socket

Last login: Mon Feb 22 14:54:28 2021
$
$ echo $HOSTNAME
localhost.localdomain
$
$ cat /etc/centos-release
CentOS Linux release 8.2.2004 (Core)
$
$ exit
logout
Connection to 192.168.0.102 closed.
$
$ lsb_release --id
Distributor ID: Ubuntu
$
```

In the example, the ssh command uses no options, includes the remote system account
username, and uses the remote system's IPv4 address instead of its hostname. Note that you do
not have to use the remote system account username if the local account name is identical.
However, in this case, you do have to enter the remote account's password to gain access to the
remote system.

Within the user's home directory, the OpenSSH application keeps track of any previously
connected hosts in a hidden directory file, .ssh/known_hosts. This data contains remote servers'
public keys used for encrypting traffic.

If you have not used ssh to log in to a particular remote host in the past, you'll get a
scary-looking message like the one shown in the previous example. The message just lets you
know that this particular remote host is not in the known_hosts file. When you type **yes** at the
message's prompt, it is added to the collective.

INTERPRETING OpenSSH MESSAGES

If you attempt to use the ssh command and get a no route to host message, first check if the
sshd daemon is running. On a systemd system, the command to use is **systemctl status sshd**.
If the daemon is running, check your firewall settings, which are covered later in this chapter.

If you have previously connected to the remote server and you get a warning message that says
WARNING: REMOTE HOST IDENTIFICATION HAS CHANGED, pay attention. It's possible that the
remote server's public key has changed. However, it may also indicate that the remote system is
being spoofed or has been compromised by a bad actor. So pay attention to this message.

You can also use the ssh command to send commands to a remote system. Just add the
command, between quotation marks, to the ssh command's end:

```
$ ssh sysadmin@192.168.0.102 "ls -ld /var/log/"
sysadmin@192.168.0.102's password:
drwxr-xr-x. 10 root root 4096 Feb 22 15:17 /var/log/
$
```

Real World Scenario

USING OpenSSH TO LOG INTO A SYSTEM

Often, servers you manage are headless, which means they do not have a terminal or keyboard attached to them. In these cases, defense-in-depth security requires an encrypted means of communicating with your computers in a server room. OpenSSH is the standard for completing this task.

The following steps will take you through using OpenSSH for logging into a system:

1. Using your Ubuntu Linux distribution, log into the sysadmin account and the password you created for it.

2. Determine your system's hostname by typing **echo $HOSTNAME** and pressing Enter. Record your system's hostname.

3. You will be logging into the current system by going out onto the network and back into the system via OpenSSH. Do this by typing **ssh sysadmin@*hostname***, where *hostname* is the system's hostname you recorded in the previous step, and pressing Enter.

    Note that if you have problems in this step, you may need to enter the system's IP address instead of its hostname. If after using the IP address you continue to have problems, there may be a firewall setting blocking your access. (Firewalls are covered later in this chapter.)

4. If you receive a message stating something similar to "The authenticity of host [...] cannot be established [...]," type **yes** at the question prompt and press Enter.

5. At the password prompt, enter the password for the sysadmin account.

    If you receive a prompt, you have successfully used OpenSSH to log into a system. Congratulations.

6. At the command prompt, type **who** to see all the accounts that are currently logged into the system and from what IP address they have accessed the system, if any. More than likely, you will see that you accessed this system from 127.0.0.1 (IPv4) or ::1 (IPv6).

7. Type **exit** and press Enter to log out of the connection.

Configuring SSH

It's a good idea to review the various OpenSSH configuration files and their directives. Ensuring that your encrypted connection is properly configured is critical for securing remote system communications. Table 17.1 lists the primary OpenSSH configuration files.

If you need to make SSH configuration changes, it is essential to know which configuration file(s) to modify. The following guidelines can help:

◆ For an individual user's connections to a remote system, create and/or modify the client side's ~/.ssh/config file.

◆ For every user's connection to a remote system, create and modify the client side's /etc/ssh/ssh_config file.

◆ For incoming SSH connection requests, modify the /etc/ssh/sshd_config file on the server side.

TABLE 17.1   Primary OpenSSH Configuration Files

CONFIGURATION FILE	DESCRIPTION
~/.ssh/config	Contains OpenSSH client configurations. May be overridden by ssh command options.
/etc/ssh/ssh_config	Contains OpenSSH client configurations. May be overridden by ssh command options or settings in the ~/.ssh/config file.
/etc/ssh/sshd_config	Contains the OpenSSH daemon (sshd) configurations.

Keep in mind that for an SSH client connection to be successful, besides proper authentication, the client and remote server's SSH configuration must be compatible.

There are several OpenSSH configuration directives. You can peruse them all via the man pages for the ssh_config and sshd_config files. However, there are two vital directives related to security for the sshd_config file:

◆ PermitRootLogin: Permits the root user to log in through an SSH connection. (The default is prohibit-password.) Typically, this should be set to no.

◆ Port: Sets the port number on which the OpenSSH daemon (sshd) listens for incoming connection requests. (The default is 22.)

System admins will wisely change the OpenSSH default port from port 22 to another port. On public-facing servers, this port is often targeted by malicious attackers.

An example of why you might change the client's ssh_config or ~/.ssh/config file is when the remote system's SSH port is modified in the sshd_config file. In this case, if the client-side configuration files were not changed to match this new port, the remote user would have to modify their ssh command's options and include -p with the correct SSH port.

Generating SSH Keys

OpenSSH uses what is called *public/private key pairs* to encrypt and decrypt the communication transmissions between two systems. When a connection is attempted, typically OpenSSH will search for its system's public/private key pairs. If they are not found, OpenSSH automatically generates them. These key pairs, also called *host keys*, are stored in the /etc/ssh/ directory within files. The following example shows key files in a single column via the ls -1 command on an Ubuntu distribution:

```
$ ls -1 /etc/ssh/*key*
/etc/ssh/ssh_host_dsa_key
/etc/ssh/ssh_host_dsa_key.pub
/etc/ssh/ssh_host_ecdsa_key
/etc/ssh/ssh_host_ecdsa_key.pub
/etc/ssh/ssh_host_ed25519_key
/etc/ssh/ssh_host_ed25519_key.pub
/etc/ssh/ssh_host_rsa_key
/etc/ssh/ssh_host_rsa_key.pub
$
```

Public key files end in the .pub filename extension, while the private keys have no filename extension. The filenames follow this standard:

```
ssh_host_KeyType_key
```

The key filename's *KeyType* corresponds to the digital signature algorithm used in the key's creation. The different types you may see on your system are as follows:

◆ dsa

◆ rsa

◆ ecdsa

◆ ed25519

There may be times you need to manually generate these keys or create new ones. To do so, the ssh-keygen utility is used as shown snipped here:

```
$ ls /etc/ssh/ssh_host_rsa_key*
ls: cannot access '/etc/ssh/ssh_host_rsa_key*':
No such file or directory
$
$ sudo ssh-keygen -t rsa -f /etc/ssh/ssh_host_rsa_key
Generating public/private rsa key pair.
Enter passphrase (empty for no passphrase):
Your identification has been saved in /etc/ssh/ssh_host_rsa_key
Your public key has been saved in /etc/ssh/ssh_host_rsa_key.pub
The key fingerprint is:
[...]
$ ls /etc/ssh/ssh_host_rsa_key*
/etc/ssh/ssh_host_rsa_key  /etc/ssh/ssh_host_rsa_key.pub
$
```

While the ssh-keygen command has several options, in the preceding example only two are used. The -t option sets the *KeyType*, which is rsa in the example. The -f switch designates the private key file to store the key. The public key is stored in a file with the same name, but the .pub file extension is added. Notice that this command asks for a passphrase, which is associated with the private key, but you can just press Enter to bypass adding it.

Authenticating with SSH Keys

Entering the password for every command employing SSH can be tiresome. However, you can use keys instead of a password to authenticate. Typically, sites where you deploy remote virtual Linux systems, such as Amazon Web Services (AWS), use this method to allow you to securely connect to your virtual systems that they manage.

To manually set up this authentication method for your own systems, the following steps are needed:

1. Log into the SSH client system.

2. Generate an SSH ID key pair.

3. Securely transfer the public SSH ID key to the SSH server computer.

4. Log into the SSH server system.

5. Add the public SSH ID key to the `~/.ssh/authorized_keys` file on the server system.

Let's look at these steps in a little more detail. First, you should log into the client system via the account you will be using as the SSH client. On that system, generate the SSH ID key pair via the `ssh-keygen` utility. You must designate the correct key pair filename, which is `id_TYPE`, where *TYPE* is dsa, rsa, or ecdsa. An example of creating an SSH ID key pair on a client system is shown snipped here:

```
$ ssh sysadmin@192.168.0.102
sysadmin@192.168.0.102's password:
[...]
$
$ ssh-keygen -t ecdsa -f ~/.ssh/id_ecdsa
Generating public/private ecdsa key pair.
Created directory '/home/sysadmin/.ssh'.
Enter passphrase (empty for no passphrase):
Enter same passphrase again:
Your identification has been saved in /home/sysadmin/.ssh/id_ecdsa.
Your public key has been saved in /home/sysadmin/.ssh/id_ecdsa.pub.
The key fingerprint is:
[...]
$
```

Notice in the example the key file's name. The `ssh-keygen` command in this case generates a private key, stored in the `~/.ssh/id_ecdsa` file, and a public key, stored in the `~/.ssh/id_ecdsa.pub` file. You may enter a passphrase if desired.

Once these keys are generated on the client system, the public key must be copied to the server system. The `ssh-copy-id` utility allows you to do this using a secure method. Not only does it copy over your public key, it also stores it in the server system's `~/.ssh/authorized_keys` file for you. In essence, it completes steps 3 through 5 in a single command, as shown here:

```
$ ssh-copy-id sysadmin@192.168.0.100
/usr/bin/ssh-copy-id: INFO: Source of key(s) to be installed:
"/home/sysadmin/.ssh/id_ecdsa.pub"
/usr/bin/ssh-copy-id: INFO: attempting to log in with the new key(s), to filter out
any that are already installed
/usr/bin/ssh-copy-id: INFO: 1 key(s) remain to be installed -- if you are prompted now
it is to install the new keys
sysadmin@192.168.0.100's password:

Number of key(s) added: 1

Now try logging into the machine, with:   "ssh 'sysadmin@192.168.0.100'"
and check to make sure that only the key(s) you wanted were added.

$
```

If you'd like, you can do a "dry run" first, which means you can see what keys would be copied and installed on the remote system, but not allow the command to perform the task. To perform a dry run, just add the -n option on your ssh-copy-id command.

Now that the public ID key has been copied over to the SSH server system, the ssh command can be used to connect from the client system to the server system with no need to enter a password:

```
$ ssh sysadmin@192.168.0.100
Welcome to Ubuntu 20.04.1 LTS (GNU/Linux 5.4.0-53-generic x86_64)

[...]
Last login: Mon Feb 22 21:08:07 2021 from 192.168.0.102
sysadmin@ubuntu-server:~$ PS1="$ "
$
$ lsb_release --id
Distributor ID: Ubuntu
$
$ exit
logout
Connection to 192.168.0.100 closed.
$ $
```

If your Linux distribution does not have the ssh-copy-id command, you can employ the scp command to copy over the public ID key. In this case, you would have to manually add the key to the bottom of the ~/.ssh/authorized_keys file. To do this, you can use the cat command and the >> symbols to redirect and append the public ID key's standard output to the authorized keys file.

Encrypting your network communications is another important layer in a defense-in-depth security strategy. Another layer includes using MAC software to implement least privilege access. We cover that topic next.

The AppArmor System

Ubuntu use the AppArmor MAC system, which controls the files and network ports each application can access through an *allowed list*. An allowed list is a catalog of what a particular entity, in this case an application, can access. The opposite of an allowed list, a *block list*, is a menu of what an entity *cannot* access. At the heart of AppArmor is the principle of least privilege.

AppArmor calls its allowed lists *profiles*. Profiles are text-based and defined for each application in the /etc/apparmor.d directory structure. Normally, each application package installs its own profiles.

As of Ubuntu 18.04LTS, AppArmor is installed by default, but the utilities and profile packages aren't. To get the needed software, use apt to install both the apparmor-utils and apparmor-profiles packages shown snipped here:

```
$ sudo apt install apparmor-utils apparmor-profiles
Reading package lists... Done
Building dependency tree
Reading state information... Done
The following additional packages will be installed:
```

```
   python3-apparmor python3-libapparmor
Suggested packages:
  vim-addon-manager
The following NEW packages will be installed:
  apparmor-profiles apparmor-utils python3-apparmor
  python3-libapparmor
0 upgraded, 4 newly installed, 0 to remove and 61 not [...]
Need to get 189 kB of archives.
After this operation, 1324 kB of additional disk space[...]
Do you want to continue? [Y/n] Y
[...]
Setting up apparmor-profiles (2.13.3-7ubuntu5.1) ...
Setting up python3-apparmor (2.13.3-7ubuntu5.1) ...
Setting up apparmor-utils (2.13.3-7ubuntu5.1) ...
Processing triggers for man-db (2.9.1-1) ...
$
```

Each profile is a text file that defines the files and network ports the application is allowed to communicate with, and the access permissions allowed for each. The name of the profile usually references the path to the application executable file, replacing the slashes with periods. For example, the profile name for the rsyslogd application program is called usr.sbin.rsyslogd as shown in the following code snippet, which displays both the files and the directories (indicated by the trailing /) in the /etc/apparmor.d/ directory:

```
$ ls -Fw 60 /etc/apparmor.d/
abstractions/                  usr.bin.man
apache2.d/                     usr.lib.snapd.snap-confine.real
bin.ping                       usr.sbin.avahi-daemon
disable/                       usr.sbin.dnsmasq
force-complain/                usr.sbin.identd
local/                         usr.sbin.mdnsd
lsb_release                    usr.sbin.nmbd
nvidia_modprobe                usr.sbin.nscd
sbin.dhclient                  usr.sbin.rsyslogd
sbin.klogd                     usr.sbin.smbd
sbin.syslog-ng                 usr.sbin.smbldap-useradd
sbin.syslogd                   usr.sbin.tcpdump
tunables/                      usr.sbin.traceroute
usr.bin.chromium-browser
$
```

AppArmor profiles can use variables, called *tunables*, within the profile definition. The variables are then defined in files contained in the /etc/apparmor.d/tunables directory. This allows you to easily make changes to the variables to alter the behavior of a profile without having to modify the profile itself. Here is a listing of the files and directories contained within AppArmor's tunables directory:

```
$ ls -Fw 60 /etc/apparmor.d/tunables
alias       home        multiarch.d/   sys
```

```
apparmorfs   home.d/      proc         xdg-user-dirs
dovecot      kernelvars   securityfs   xdg-user-dirs.d/
global       multiarch    share
$
```

To determine the status of AppArmor on your Linux system, use the `aa-status` command with super user privileges shown snipped here:

```
$ sudo aa-status
[sudo] password for sysadmin:
apparmor module is loaded.
50 profiles are loaded.
31 profiles are in enforce mode.
[...]
   /usr/bin/man
   /usr/lib/NetworkManager/nm-dhcp-client.action
   /usr/lib/NetworkManager/nm-dhcp-helper
   /usr/lib/connman/scripts/dhclient-script
[...]
   /usr/sbin/tcpdump
   /{,usr/}sbin/dhclient
   chromium_browser//browser_java
   chromium_browser//browser_openjdk
   chromium_browser//sanitized_helper
   lsb_release
   man_filter
   man_groff
[...]
19 profiles are in complain mode.
   /usr/sbin/dnsmasq
   /usr/sbin/dnsmasq//libvirt_leaseshelper
   avahi-daemon
   chromium_browser
   chromium_browser//chromium_browser_sandbox
   chromium_browser//lsb_release
   chromium_browser//xdgsettings
   identd
   klogd
   mdnsd
   nmbd
   nscd
   ping
   smbd
   smbldap-useradd
   smbldap-useradd///etc/init.d/nscd
   syslog-ng
   syslogd
   traceroute
```

```
1 processes have profiles defined.
1 processes are in enforce mode.
   /usr/sbin/dhclient (1016) /{,usr/}sbin/dhclient
0 processes are in complain mode.
0 processes are unconfined but have a profile defined.
$
```

The output from the aa-status command shows all of the profiles in enforce, complain, or disabled status:

- enforce mode: This is the default mode, and profile violations are logged and blocked.

- complain mode: Any violations of the profile are logged, but not blocked, except in the case when deny rules exist in the profile.

- disable mode: Violations are ignored because the profile is unloaded and will not be loaded for any reason, until the mode is changed.

To turn off a specific profile, use the aa-complain command, which places the profile in complain mode:

```
$ sudo aa-complain /usr/bin/ping
Setting /usr/bin/ping to complain mode.
[...]
$
```

If you want to completely disable an individual profile, use the aa-disable command:

```
$ sudo aa-disable /usr/bin/ping
Disabling /usr/bin/ping.
$
```

To turn a profile back on, use the aa-enforce command:

```
$ sudo aa-enforce /usr/bin/ping
Setting /usr/bin/ping to enforce mode.
Warning: profile ping represents multiple programs
$
```

You can see that AppArmor does not always follow its rule of one profile per application. In the case of /usr/bin/ping, it represents multiple programs.

You can view a listing of active network ports on your system that don't have a profile defined by using the aa-unconfined command with super user privileges:

```
$ sudo aa-unconfined
615 /usr/lib/systemd/systemd-networkd
(/lib/systemd/systemd-networkd) not confined
685 /usr/sbin/sshd (sshd: /usr/sbin/sshd -D
[listener] 0 of 10-100 startups) not confined
1016 /usr/sbin/dhclient confined by '/{,usr/}
sbin/dhclient (enforce)'
1061 /usr/lib/systemd/systemd-resolved
(/lib/systemd/systemd-resolved) not confined
$
```

Be aware that AppArmor will not break any pre-established DAC rules (file and directory permission settings) on a system. For instance, if a text file does not allow read access to the world tier and the application is not the owner of the text file nor belongs to its group, no matter what is in the profile, the app is out of luck—it has no read access to the file.

Using MAC software to implement least privilege access to processes on your system is another important layer in a defense-in-depth security strategy. But how do you implement least privilege for programs and users who are coming into and out of the system via the network? We'll tell you how to implement that security layer next.

Network Security Using Firewalls

A firewall in a building is a fireproof wall that helps to prevent fire from spreading throughout the structure. In computer security, firewalls prevent the spread of unwanted, unauthorized, or malicious network traffic.

Firewalls are implemented in different forms. You can provide layered security by using multiple firewall structures. A firewall is either a hardware device or a software application, network-based or host-based, and a network-layer or application-layer filter.

Firewalls provide access control to your system or network. An access control list (ACL) implemented within a firewall identifies which network packets are allowed in or out. This is often referred to as *packet filtering*. In this section, we'll take a look at Ubuntu's software application firewall that is host-based and operates at the OSI's Network layer.

Understanding UFW

Embedded in the Linux kernel is *netfilter*. This software provides code hooks into the kernel, which allow other packages to implement firewall technologies. From a functionality standpoint, think of netfilter as a network sniffer that is planted in the Linux kernel and that offers up packet filtering services.

The Uncomplicated Firewall (UFW) is the default firewall service on Ubuntu distributions that uses netfilter's services. It is configured with the ufw command-line utility.

By default, the UFW service is disabled. You start the service and set it to start at boot time by using the sudo ufw enable command, but do not use a system initialization tool, such as systemctl. This is because the firewall services covered here are not systemd services, but instead are interface services for the netfilter firewall.

There are several UFW commands that control the firewall's state as well as view its status. Table 17.2 describes these commands. Each one requires super user privileges.

TABLE 17.2   The ufw Commands to Control State and View Status

COMMAND	DESCRIPTION
ufw enable	Starts the UFW firewall and enables it to start at system boot
ufw disable	Stops the UFW firewall and disables it from starting at system boot
ufw reset	Disables the UFW firewall and resets it to installation defaults
ufw reload	Reloads the UFW firewall
ufw status	Displays the UFW firewall's current state

To view the current state of the UFW service, use the `sudo ufw status verbose` command, if you need more information than just `status` provides. Enabling the UFW firewall service and viewing its current state is shown here:

```
$ sudo ufw enable
[...]
Firewall is active and enabled on system startup
$
$ sudo ufw status verbose
Status: active
Logging: on (low)
Default: deny (incoming), allow (outgoing), disabled (routed)
New profiles: skip
$
```

Viewing the verbose status of the UFW firewall provides information that helps to explain its configuration:

◆ Status: UFW service is running and will start on system boot (`active`), or the services stopped and a system boot does not change this (`disabled`).

◆ Logging: The service's logging feature can be set to `off`; log all blocked packets (`low`), which is the default; log all blocked, invalid, no-policy-match, and new connection packets (`medium`) with rate limiting; log medium-log-level packets and all other packets (`high`) with rate limiting; and log everything with no rate limits (`full`).

◆ Default: Shows the default policy for `incoming`, `outgoing`, and `routed` packets, which can be set to `allow` the packet, drop (`deny`) the packet, or `reject` the packet and send a rejection message back.

◆ New profiles: Shows the default policy for automatically loading new profiles into the firewall, which can be set to `ACCEPT`, `DROP`, `REJECT`, or `SKIP`, where `ACCEPT` is considered a security risk.

Configuring UFW

The various default UFW policies are stored in the `/etc/default/ufw` configuration file. When first installed, these settings allow all outgoing connections and block all incoming connections. You can make modifications to the firewall as needed using the `ufw` command and its various arguments. Table 17.3 describes a few of the more common arguments.

When creating new UFW rules, you can use either simple or full syntax. Simple syntax involves designating the rule using only the port number or its service name. You can also add the protocol to the port number:

```
$ sudo ufw allow 22/tcp
Rule added
Rule added (v6)
$
```

```
$ sudo ufw status
Status: active

To                        Action      From
--                        ------      ----
22/tcp                    ALLOW       Anywhere
22/tcp (v6)               ALLOW       Anywhere (v6)


$
```

TABLE 17.3   The ufw Command's Commonly Used Arguments

ARGUMENT	DESCRIPTION
allow *Identifiers*	Sets the rule identified by *Identifiers* to allow packets
deny *Identifiers*	Sets the rule identified by *Identifiers* to deny (drop) packets
reject *Identifiers*	Sets the rule identified by *Identifiers* to reject packets
delete *RULE* | *NUM*	Deletes the rule identified by *RULE* or *NUM*
insert *NUM RULE*	Inserts the *RULE* at index *NUM*
default *POLICY DIRECTION*	Modifies the default *DIRECTION* policy, where *POLICY* is allow, deny, or reject, and *direction* is incoming, outgoing, or routed
logging *LEVEL*	Sets the logging level, where *LEVEL* is on, off, low (default), medium, high, or full

Notice that when the rule is added, two rules were applied—one for IPv4 and one for IPv6 packets. With full syntax, there are many options. For example, you can employ settings such as those listed in Table 17.4.

One of the nice features of UFW is that you do not need to issue the ufw reload command after you add, delete, or modify a rule. The change automatically takes effect.

You can specify a rule via a service name (e.g., telnet) with the ufw command. When doing this, ufw checks the /etc/services file to determine the appropriate port and protocol information for that service.

Here is an example of using the UFW full syntax:

```
$ sudo ufw deny from 192.168.0.0/24 to any port 80
Rule added
$
$ sudo ufw show added
Added user rules (see 'ufw status' for running firewall):
ufw allow 22/tcp
ufw deny from 192.168.0.0/24 to any port 80
$
```

TABLE 17.4   The ufw Command's Full Syntax Common Settings

SETTING	DESCRIPTION
comment "*string*"	Displays this comment for rejected traffic
in	Applies rule only to incoming traffic
out	Applies rule only to outgoing traffic
proto *protocol*	Applies rule to this *protocol*
port *port#*	Applies rule to this *port#*
from *source*	Applies rule to traffic from this *source*, which may be a single IP address, subnet, or any traffic
on *interface*	Applies rule to traffic on this network *interface*
to *destination*	Applies rule to traffic going to this *destination*, which may be a single IP address, subnet, or any traffic

In this case, network packets coming from any systems in the 192.168.0.0 class C subnet will be denied access to port 80 on this system. Once a rule is added, you can view all the user-added rules using the ufw show added command.

The UFW rules are stored in the /etc/ufw/ directory, and user-added rules are placed into the user.rules file within that directory:

```
$ ls /etc/ufw/
after.init     applications.d   before6.rules   user.rules
after.rules    before.init      sysctl.conf     user6.rules
after6.rules   before.rules     ufw.conf
$
```

If you need to delete a rule, it's easiest to do it by the rule number. First view the rules via their numbers, and then employ the ufw delete command:

```
$ sudo ufw status numbered
Status: active

     To                    Action      From
     --                    ------      ----
[ 1] 22/tcp               ALLOW IN    Anywhere
[ 2] 80                   DENY IN     192.168.0.0/24
[ 3] 22/tcp (v6)          ALLOW IN    Anywhere (v6)

$
```

```
$ sudo ufw delete 2
Deleting:
 deny from 192.168.0.0/24 to any port 80
Proceed with operation (y|n)? y
Rule deleted
$
```

 Real World Scenario

VIEWING AND CONFIGURING UFW

A firewall is another layer of security in a defense-in-depth strategy for a system. This particular item is rather popular in its use throughout the systems and network components inside and outside a server room. Therefore, it's important to have experience in using the applications that control firewalls.

The following steps assume you have access to escalated privileges and will take you through trying out the UFW application for managing firewalls on Ubuntu Linux:

1. Using your Ubuntu Linux distribution, log into the sysadmin account and enter the password you created for it.

2. Determine if your system's UFW firewall application is enabled by typing

   sudo ufw status verbose and pressing Enter. If your password is asked for, enter the account's password. Record the status.

3. If the status you determined in the previous step is inactive, type **sudo ufw enable** and press Enter. If your password is asked for, enter the account's password.

4. View any added rules (there may be none) in UFW by typing **sudo ufw show added** and pressing Enter. Record what you find.

5. Determine what service may use port 23 by typing **grep "23/tcp" /etc/services** and pressing Enter. Record the service name.

6. Block the service using port 23 you discovered in the previous step from any incoming network traffic via UFW by typing **sudo ufw deny from any port 23** and pressing Enter.

7. See if the rule was added to UFW by typing **sudo ufw show added** and pressing Enter.

8. Now determine your new rule's number by typing **sudo ufw status numbered** and pressing Enter. The rule number will appear in the first column within brackets. You may see two different rules—one for IPv4 and one for IPv6. Record its number(s).

9. Remove the new rule by typing **sudo ufw delete** *rule#* and pressing Enter, where *rule#* is the first number you recorded in the previous step. When you receive the message Proceed with operation (y|n)?, type **y** and press Enter.

10. If you recorded two rules in step 8, be aware that the rule number will change after a rule deletion. To delete the second rule, if you have one:

    a. Type **sudo ufw status numbered** and press Enter. The rule number will appear in the first column within brackets. Record its number.

> **b.** Remove the second rule by typing **sudo ufw delete** *rule#* and pressing Enter, where *rule#* is the number you recorded in the previous step. When you receive the message `Proceed with operation (y|n)?`, type **y** and press Enter.
>
> **11.** Ensure the new rule(s) was deleted by typing **sudo ufw show added** and pressing Enter.
>
> **12.** Compare the output of the previous step's command with what you recorded for step 4. You should find that they are now identical.
>
> **13.** If you determined that your UFW firewall was `inactive` in step 2, disable it again by typing **sudo ufw disable** and pressing Enter.

UFW uses profiles for common applications and daemons. These profiles are stored in the /etc/ufw/applications.d/ directory. Use the ufw app list command to see the currently available UFW application profiles:

```
$ sudo ufw app list
Available applications:
  OpenSSH
$
$ sudo ufw app info OpenSSH
Profile: OpenSSH
Title: Secure shell server, an rshd replacement
Description: OpenSSH is a free implementation of
the Secure Shell protocol.

Port:
  22/tcp
$
```

You can also view detailed information on these profiles as shown in the previous example. The profiles not only provide application documentation, they allow you to modify the ports and protocols used by the applications as well as create nontypical application profiles for your system's needs.

Be aware that you should not modify the profile files in the /etc/ufw/applications.d/ directory. Instead, create a subdirectory there and name it **custom.d**. This will prevent your custom profiles from being overwritten during UFW software package updates. See the ufw man pages for more details on profile specifications.

Once you have created a new profile or updated an old one, use the ufw app update all command to update UFW on the profile changes. Also, when using a profile to specify a rule's ports and protocols, you must employ app instead of port within your syntax for creating new rules.

The Bottom Line

Safely escalate privileges to accomplish tasks.   Ubuntu implements privilege escalation through the sudo command. This method allows administrators to log into their standard Linux user account and run programs with higher-level administrator privileges, as needed.

Master It   You're an administrator on an Ubuntu Linux system. There is a new member on your team who will be performing the same administrator duties that you do. This team member will need to use sudo to safely escalate privileges when needed. The record in the /etc/sudoers configuration file that provides your account with privilege escalation is the following: %sudo ALL=(ALL:ALL) ALL. What do you need to do to set up this new team member to use the sudo command?

Use OpenSSH to connect to remote systems.   OpenSSH provides an encrypted means for communication when you connect over a network to a remote server. Ubuntu Linux typically has OpenSSH installed by default, but you may need to perform additional configuration steps to customize it for your secure communication requirements.

Master It   Imagine you are administering an Ubuntu server that already uses OpenSSH. Connections are set to use key pairs instead of passwords for command-line access. While you currently have rsa keys, the decision was made to switch to ecdsa key pairs, which don't exist at this time on the system. What steps do you need to take in order to implement this functionality for your accounts on the systems?

Manage Ubuntu MAC protection software.   AppArmor is the MAC protection system used on Ubuntu. This software controls the files and network ports each application accesses through access lists, which are text-based files called profiles. These files reside in the /etc/apparmor.d/ directory and are typically installed for a particular application, when it is installed.

Master It   You're an administrator on an Ubuntu Linux system that uses AppArmor as its MAC system. All of the AppArmor utility and profile packages are installed. The primary application on this system is run only on Tuesday through Sunday of every week. The development team would like to test a large app modification on Monday. What should you do to the firewall to log potential firewall violation issues with the modification, but not stop the application from accomplishing its test tasks?

Configure the Ubuntu firewall.   Ubuntu's software application firewall is host-based and works at the Network layer. It uses an ACL to identify which network packets are allowed in or out of the system. Ubuntu's UFW uses netfilter's services and is configured with the ufw command-line utility.

Master It   You are the system admin for several Ubuntu servers that reside in server rooms spread across the world. To access these servers remotely and securely, you use OpenSSH. However, you've decided not to use the default port 22 for this service. Instead, you are going to use a different and available port number. What do you need to do to the firewall on all the Ubuntu servers to make this work?

Chapter 18

Exploring Red Hat Security

These days, security is a hot topic, especially for servers. The Red Hat server distribution provides many security features by default to help keep your server safe, but depending on your environment, you may need to still do some tweaking. This chapter explores three areas where you should consider making changes to the security of your server.

IN THIS CHAPTER, YOU WILL LEARN TO

- ◆ Control access from the root user account
- ◆ Manage the SELinux environment
- ◆ Control network access using `firewalld`

Working with Root Access

As discussed in Chapter 17, "Exploring Ubuntu Security," Linux systems utilize three types of user accounts:

Root: The administrator account with full privileges to all files, directories, and services

Standard: Normal user accounts

Service: Application accounts

Because of its power, the root user account can be somewhat dangerous to have active on your Linux server. As discussed in Chapter 17, the Ubuntu server distribution blocks the ability to log in or change to the root user account to help manage the security environment. However, that's not the case in the Red Hat server distribution.

If you check in a Red Hat environment, the root user account exists:

```
$ getent passwd root
root:x:0:0:root:/root:/bin/bash
$
```

This account should have been assigned a password at the time of installation:

```
$ sudo getent shadow root
[sudo] password for sysadmin:
root:$6$P92P.wjWGerpM8Zz4PqYcSfIn6UqS1hLY.K7aNEdpEssjK8ES6C1::0:99999:7:::
$
```

Because the `root` user account is active in the Red Hat server, there are a few things that you should be careful about when using a Red Hat server. This section walks through a few security practices related to the `root` user account you should consider when working on a Red Hat server.

Keeping Track of Root Logins

If the `root` user account is active on your Linux server, it's always a good idea to monitor the times it's used on your server. You can do that using the `aulast` command. The `aulast` command displays a list of users who have logged into the system as found in the system audit logs. Listing 18.1 shows a sample output.

LISTING 18.1 The `aulast` Command Output

```
$ sudo aulast | grep root
root     tty1        unknown080027D84 Fri Feb 26 19:04 - 09:12  (00:07)
root     pts/0       192.168.1.71     Fri Feb 26 19:13 - 11:20  (02:06)
root     tty1        unknown080027D84 Fri Feb 26 19:12 - 11:30  (02:17)
root     tty1        DESKTOP-1NP6J2S  Fri Feb 26 21:04 - 16:04  (00:00)
root     pts/0       192.168.1.71     Sat Mar  6 15:46 - 15:49  (00:03)
root     pts/0       192.168.1.71     Sat Mar  6 15:49 - 15:49  (00:00)
root     tty1        unknown080027D84 Sat Mar  6 15:31 - 16:06  (00:34)
root     pts/0       192.168.1.71     Sat Mar 13 08:52 - 08:52  (00:00)
root     tty1        unknown080027D84 Sat Mar 13 08:51    still logged in
$
```

The second column in the `aulast` output shows the terminal the root user account logged in from. If the terminal was a remote terminal (such as an SSH connection), the third column shows the IP address of the remote device. It's a good idea to monitor this on a regular basis to watch for unknown login activity.

Disabling Root Access from SSH

The OpenSSH software package includes an SSH server that allows connections from remote clients using the secure SSH protocol. The `/etc/ssh/sshd_config` file controls the behavior of the SSH server. By default, the configuration used in Red Hat servers allows the `root` user account to log in from a remote device. To prevent the `root` user account from logging in from a remote device using the SSH protocol, you'll need to modify the configuration file.

The line in the configuration file that allows this feature is as follows:

```
PermitRootLogin yes
```

To block access for the `root` user account, edit the line to the following:

```
PermitRootLogin no
```

Then restart the OpenSSH service for the change to take effect:

```
$ sudo systemctl restart sshd
```

After restarting OpenSSH, you should now be denied access as the `root` user account in a remote SSH connection:

```
login as: root
root@192.168.1.81's password:
Access denied
root@192.168.1.81's password:
```

Now the `root` user account can log in only from a console device on the server.

Enabling Automatic Logout

If you allow administrators on the Linux server to log in using the `root` user account, it's a good idea to set a timeout for the Bash shell. An unattended Bash shell prompt with the `root` login is a huge security risk for your Linux server environment.

The timeout feature in the Bash shell is controlled by the TMOUT environment variable. To implement a shell timeout, you just need to set the TMOUT environment variable to the number of seconds you want an idle session to terminate.

For the setting to apply to all logins, you should enable it in the `/etc/profile` script, which the Bash shell runs at each login. However, to make adding login scripts easier, Red Hat systems also look for scripts in the `/etc/profile.d` directory. You can create a file in the `/etc/profile.d` directory that sets the TMOUT environment variable, and it will run each time a user account logs into the system and opens a Bash shell. It's also a good idea to make the TMOUT environment variable read-only so users can't override that feature. You do that with the `readonly` command.

So to implement this feature, all you need to do is create the file `/etc/profile.d/timeout.sh` and include these two lines:

```
TMOUT=300
readonly TMOUT
```

In this example, we set the timeout to 300 seconds (5 minutes). Now if any user account session on the server sits idle for 5 minutes (300 seconds), the server will terminate the session.

 Real World Scenario

TESTING THE TIMEOUT FEATURE

In this exercise, you will set the TMOUT environment variable for your Linux server, and test to see if it works. Follow these steps:

1. Log into your CentOS server either as the root user account or as a user account that has root privileges.

2. From the command prompt, type **echo "TMOUT=120"> /etc/profile.d/timeout.sh**.

3. Again from the command prompt, type **echo "readonly TMOUT" >> /etc/profile.d/timeout.sh**.

4. Log out from the terminal session, and then log back in.

(continued)

5. Let the session sit idle at the command prompt for more than 2 minutes. The system should log out your session.

6. If you want to remove the timeout feature, from the command prompt, type **rm   /etc/ profile.d/timeout.sh**.

Blocking Root Access

If you prefer for your Red Hat server to block all access to the root user account similar to what Ubuntu does, you can do that as well. There are a couple of ways to do that:

- Similar to the Ubuntu method, you can use an asterisk as the password value for the root user account.

- You can assign the root user account the special nologin shell.

While Ubuntu's method of using the asterisk as a password is perfectly valid, it's not typically the preferred way of blocking access from a user account. The /sbin/nologin file is a special program that displays a message to the user and then exits. To activate it, just set it as the default shell for the root user account in the /etc/passwd file:

```
root:x:0:0:root:/root:/sbin/nologin
```

Then when you try to log in using the root user account, you'll see the default warning message and be disconnected:

```
$ ssh root@localhost
root@localhost's password:

Last login: Sat Mar 13 10:34:55 2021 from ::1
This account is currently not available.
Connection to localhost closed.
$
```

You can customize the message that appears by creating the /etc/nologin.txt file and entering the following text message:

```
# echo "The root account not available. Please use sudo to gain root
Privileges." > /etc/nologin.txt
```

Now when you attempt to log in using the root user account, you'll see the custom message:

```
$ ssh root@localhost
root@localhost's password:

Last login: Sat Mar 13 10:36:21 2021 from ::1
The root account is not available. Please use sudo to gain root privileges.
Connection to localhost closed.
$
```

CHANGING ROOT FEATURES

Be extremely careful when restricting the root user account on your Linux server. It's best to make sure you have a standard user account that has access to the sudo command (it's a member of the sudo group) so that you can still gain administrator privileges if something goes wrong and completely locks out the root user account!

Using SELinux

In Chapter 13, "Managing Users and Groups," we introduced the concept of file and directory permissions. By default, Linux uses two layers of file and directory protection:

♦ Standard user, group, and everyone permissions

♦ Discretionary access controls (DAC) using access control lists (ACLs)

As discussed in Chapter 17, in Linux you can take file and directory security even further by implementing Mandatory Access Control (MAC) security. MAC security allows you to set policy rules for controlling access between various types of objects on the Linux system, including users, files, directories, memory, network ports, and processes. Each time a user or process attempts to access any object on the Linux system, the MAC security software intercepts the attempt and evaluates it against any defined policy rules.

The Red Hat Linux distribution uses the Security-Enhanced Linux (SELinux) application to provide MAC security. SELinux is a project of the United States National Security Agency (NSA) and has been integrated into the Linux kernel since version 2.6.x. It is now a standard part of Red Hat-based Linux distributions, including Fedora and CentOS, and an optional install for Debian-based distributions.

SELinux implements MAC security by allowing you to set policy rules for controlling access between various types of objects on the Linux system, including users, files, directories, memory, network ports, and processes. Each time a user or process attempts to access an object on the Linux system, SELinux intercepts the attempt and evaluates it against the defined policy rules.

Enabling SELinux

The /etc/selinux/config file controls the basic operation of SELinux. There are two primary settings that you need to set:

SELINUX: This setting determines the operation of SELinux. Set this to enforcing to enable the policy rules on the system and block any unauthorized access. By setting this to permissive, SELinux monitors policy rules and logs any policy violations, but doesn't enforce them. The disabled setting value completely disables SELinux from monitoring actions on the system.

SELINUXTYPE: This setting determines which policy rules are enforced. The targeted setting is the default and only enforces network daemon policy rules. The mls setting uses multilayer security, providing advanced policies following the Bell-LaPadula model of security control. The strict setting enforces policy rules for all daemons but is not recommended for use anymore.

To change the state of SELinux, you can also use the setenforce utility from the command line. However, you can only use the utility to change SELinux between enforcing and permissive modes. To disable SELinux, you must make the change in the SELinux configuration file manually. To see the current mode of SELinux, use the getenforce utility:

```
$ sudo getenforce
Enforcing
$
```

For a more detailed listing of the SELinux status, use the sestatus utility:

```
$ sudo sestatus
SELinux status:                 enabled
SELinuxfs mount:                /sys/fs/selinux
SELinux root directory:         /etc/selinux
Loaded policy name:             targeted
Current mode:                   enforcing
Mode from config file:          enforcing
Policy MLS status:              enabled
Policy deny_unknown status:     allowed
Memory protection checking:     actual (secure)
Max kernel policy version:      32
$
```

Once you've enabled SELinux, it starts enforcing access rules on the objects defined in a set of policies. The next sections explain how SELinux policies work.

Understanding Security Context

SELinux labels each object on the system with a *security context*. The security context defines what policies SELinux applies to the object. The security context format is as follows:

user:*role*:*type*:*level*

The *user* and *role* attributes are only used in the multilayer security mode and can get quite complex. Systems running in the default targeted security mode only use the *type* attribute to set the object security type, and control access based on that. The *level* attribute sets the security sensitivity level and clearance level. It is optional under the targeted security mode and is mostly used in high-secure environments.

To view the security context assigned to objects, add the -Z option to common Linux commands such as id, ls, ps, and netstat. For example, to view your user security context, use the following:

```
$ id -Z
unconfined_u:unconfined_r:unconfined_t:s0-s0:c0.c1023
$
```

The unconfined_u user security context means the user account is not assigned to a specific security policy. Likewise, the unconfined_r for the role and the unconfined_t for the type also mean no security policy is assigned. The level security context of `s0-s0:c0.c10123` means the security and clearance levels for the object are also not set.

To view the security context for a file, use the following:

```
$ ls -Z test1.txt
unconfined_u:object_r:user_home_t:s0 test1.txt
$
```

Again, the user and role attributes are unconfined, but now the type attribute is set to `user_home_t`. You can use this attribute in a security policy to set the access for files in each user account's $HOME directory.

To examine the security context assigned to a process, use this:

```
$ ps -axZ | grep firewalld
system_u:system_r:firewalld_t:s0     899 ?        Ssl    0:00
 /usr/libexec/platform-python -s /usr/sbin/firewalld --nofork --nopid
$
```

The process required for the `firewalld` firewall application is set to the `system_u` user security context and the `system_r` role security context. These indicate the process is system-related. Notice that the type security context contains the program name; each program has its own security context. This means you can control each program running on the system with separate policies. SELinux assigns policies to each object on the system when SELinux is first enabled, which can be a long process, so be prepared if you're first enabling SELinux on your system.

The `semanage` utility allows you to view and set the security context for user accounts on the system. For files and directories, the Linux system sets their security context when they are created, based on the security context of the parent directory. You can change the default security context assigned to a file by using the `chcon` or `restorecon` utilities.

The chcon format is as follows:

```
chcon -u newuser -r newrole -t newtype filename
```

The *newuser*, *newrole*, and *newtype* values define the new user, role, and type security contexts you want assigned to the specified file.

The `restorecon` utility restores the security context of a file or directory back to the default settings as defined in the policies. You can use the `-R` option to recursively restore the security context on all files under a specified directory.

The `runcon` utility allows you to start an application with a specified security context, but be careful. If an application starts without having access to any required configuration or logging files, strange things can, and usually will, happen.

Using Policies

SELinux controls access to system objects based on policies. In the targeted security mode, each policy defines what objects within a specific type security context can access objects within another type security context. This is called *type enforcement*.

For example, an application labeled with the type security context `firewalld_t` is only allowed to access files labeled with the type security context `firewalld_t`. This restricts access from the application to only certain files on the system.

SELinux maintains policies as text files within the /etc/selinux directory structure. For example, all policies for the targeted security mode are under the /etc/selinux/targeted directory.

Creating your own policies can be somewhat complicated. Fortunately, SELinux includes policy groups, called *modules*, that you can install as standard rpm packages. Use the semodule utility to list, install, and remove policy modules in your system.

To make things even easier for us, SELinux uses a method of enabling and disabling individual policies without having to modify a policy file. A *Boolean* is a switch that allows you to enable or disable a policy rule from the command line based on its policy name. To view the current setting of a policy, use the getsebool command:

```
$ getsebool antivirus_can_scan_system
antivirus_can_scan_system --> off
$
```

To view all of the policies for the system, include the -a option, as shown in Listing 18.2.

LISTING 18.2   Using the -a Option with the getsebool Command

```
$ sudo getsebool -a
abrt_anon_write --> off
abrt_handle_event --> off
abrt_upload_watch_anon_write --> on
antivirus_can_scan_system --> off
antivirus_use_jit --> off
auditadm_exec_content --> on
authlogin_nsswitch_use_ldap --> off
authlogin_radius --> off
authlogin_yubikey --> off
awstats_purge_apache_log_files --> off
boinc_execmem --> on
cdrecord_read_content --> off
cluster_can_network_connect --> off
cluster_manage_all_files --> off
cluster_use_execmem --> off
cobbler_anon_write --> off
cobbler_can_network_connect --> off
cobbler_use_cifs --> off
cobbler_use_nfs --> off
collectd_tcp_network_connect --> off
colord_use_nfs --> off
condor_tcp_network_connect --> off
conman_can_network --> off
conman_use_nfs --> off
...
```

Listing 18.2 just shows a partial output from the getsebool command; there are lots of different policies installed by default in most Red Hat Linux environments.

To change the Boolean setting, use the setsebool command:

```
$ sudo setsebool antivirus_can_scan_system on
$ getsebool antivirus_can_scan_system
antivirus_can_scan_system --> on
$
```

This setting applies only to your current session. To make the change permanent, you must add the -P option to the command. This gives you full control over the policy settings defined for SELinux.

Network Security Using Firewalls

Firewall software helps protect your Linux server from unwanted network access. It uses ACLs to define what network connections can be allowed and which ones should be blocked.

The Red Hat Linux distribution uses the firewalld software package to provide firewall services. This section describes the firewalld program and shows how you can use it to help protect your Red Hat server on different types of networks.

Red Hat Firewall Concepts

The firewalld software uses the concept of *zones* to define protection for the network interfaces on your Red Hat server. A zone defines the type of network the interface is connected to and what type of network traffic should be allowed or blocked. Different types of network connections require different levels of protection. For example, consider the network shown in Figure 18.1.

FIGURE 18.1

A Linux server connected to two networks

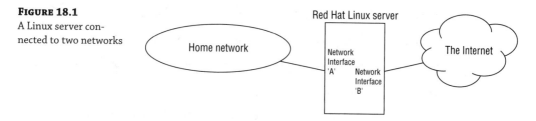

In Figure 18.1, the Linux server has two network interfaces. Network card A is connected to a home network, which includes other network devices that need to connect to the Linux server. Network card B in the server is connected to the Internet. You most likely will want to define different ACL rules for each network interface. Network card A should allow the local clients to connect to server resources, such as shared files, printers, and possibly even establish SSH connections to login.

However, network card B needs extra security protections so that unknown attackers lurking on the Internet can't gain access to your server. With a myriad of different network applications and protocols, you can see how it would quickly become difficult to keep things straight on the system.

The solution is to implement zone-based ACL rules. The `firewalld` program allows you to define multiple zones and assign each zone a different set of rules to control network access. Typically, each network interface on the server is assigned to a specific zone, based on the network requirements. The `firewalld` program applies the zone rules to the network interface.

By default, the Red Hat server defines 10 zones. You can list the currently defined zones using the `firewall-cmd` command:

```
$ firewall-cmd --get-zones
block dmz drop external home internal nm-shared public trusted work
$
```

Table 18.1 provides a basic description of what each of these default zones is used for.

TABLE 18.1   The Default `firewalld` Zones

ZONE	DESCRIPTION
block	Rejects all incoming network connections and sends an ICMP prohibited message. Only outgoing network connections are allowed.
dmz	Only selected incoming connections are accepted.
drop	Rejects all incoming network connections with no reply message. Only outgoing network connections are allowed.
external	Enables masquerading feature to hide the server's true IP address. Only specified incoming connections are accepted.
home	Allows only specified incoming connections, but all outgoing connections are allowed.
internal	Only specified incoming connections are accepted.
nm-shared	Special zone defined for sharing on the network.
public	For use on untrusted networks; only select incoming connections are accepted.
trusted	All network connections are accepted.
work	For use on mostly trusted networks; only select incoming connections are accepted.

Each zone has a different set of rules assigned to it, controlling what network traffic can come in or go out from network interfaces assigned to that zone. To manage the access on a network interface, you just assign it to a specific zone.

Besides zones, `firewalld` uses ACL rules. The ACL rules define what network connections should be allowed or blocked. With `firewalld`, you can define the rules using two different methods:

◆ Define the service name

◆ Define the protocol port

By using service names, you can allow or block connections by application, such as FTP, SSH, or HTTP. By using ports, you can allow or block connections based on TCP or UDP port numbers.

The following sections show you how to use `firewalld` in your Red Hat server environment.

Checking the Firewall Status

While the `firewalld` program uses standard text configuration files, you can use the `firewall-cmd` command-line command for most of the things you need to do. To check if `firewalld` is running, just use the following command:

```
$ sudo firewall-cmd --state
running
$
```

You can check what zone a specific interface is currently in by using the `--get-zone-of-interface` option:

```
$ sudo firewall-cmd --get-zone-of-interface=enp0s8
public
$
```

Or, if you have multiple network interface cards, you can use the `--get-active-zones` option to list all zones that are currently active on network interfaces:

```
$ sudo firewall-cmd --get-active-zones
public
   interfaces: enp0s3, enp0s8
$
```

You can see the current configuration for a zone by using the `--list-all` option and specifying the zone name using the `--zone` option:

```
$ sudo firewall-cmd --zone=public --list-all
public (active)
   target: default
   icmp-block-inversion: no
   interfaces: enp0s8
   sources:
   services: cockpit dhcpv6-client ssh
   ports: 631/tcp
   protocols:
   masquerade: no
   forward-ports:
   source-ports:
   icmp-blocks:
   rich rules:
$
```

The output shows the features and what items are allowed through the firewall for that zone. The `target` feature defines the action for the zone:

default: Rejects all packets not matching the zone rules, but sends an ICMP packet to the client indicating why.

ACCEPT: Accepts packets not matching the zone rules.

DROP: Drop packets not matching the zone rules.

%%REJECT%%: Rejects all packets not matching the zone rules.

The `sources`, `services`, `ports`, and `protocols` features define the rule items that are either allowed or blocked, based on the target setting. In this example, the Red Hat web cockpit service, the DHCPv6 client service, and the OpenSSH service are all allowed. Likewise, traffic on TCP port 631 (the CUPS application, described in Chapter 16, "Managing Printers") is allowed.

Working with Zones

Besides the default zones, you can create your own zones to help customize your server's network environment. The `--new-zone` option of the `firewall-cmd` command defines the zone name:

```
$ sudo firewall-cmd --permanent --new-zone=mytest
Success
$
```

The `--permanent` option is required to make the change permanent in the configuration files. Before you can use the zone, you must tell `firewalld` to reload the configuration file so it knows about the new zone:

```
$ sudo firewall-cmd --reload
Success
$
```

Then you can list the zones to see if the new zone exists:

```
$ sudo firewall-cmd --get-zones
block dmz drop external home internal mytest nm-shared public trusted work
$
```

Once you've created the zone, you can move a network interface to the zone using the `--add-interface` option:

```
$ sudo firewall-cmd -zone=mytest --add-interface=enp0s8
Success
$
```

Be careful, though, as the new zone doesn't have any ACL rules applied to it:

```
$ sudo firewall-cmd --zone=mytest --list-all
mytest
  target: default
  icmp-block-inversion: no
```

```
      interfaces:
      sources:
      services:
      ports:
      protocols:
      masquerade: no
      forward-ports:
      source-ports:
      icmp-blocks:
      rich rules:
  $
```

If you add the network interface that you're currently connected to the server, this will cause your connection to drop and possibly be a problem! The next section shows how you can add rules to the zones.

Working with Firewall Rules

ACL rules are the core of the firewall. They define what type of network traffic is allowed or blocked by the network interface. Mistakes when adding or removing rules can be costly, especially if you're remotely connected to the server!

The firewalld program is robust in how it allows you to define rules. You can define rules to allow or block access based on a well-known application service name by using the --add-service option:

```
$ sudo firewall-cmd --zone=mytest --add-service=https --permanent
success
$ sudo firewall-cmd --reload
success
$ sudo firewall-cmd --zone=mytest --list-all
mytest
   target: default
   icmp-block-inversion: no
   interfaces:
   sources:
   services: https
   ports:
   protocols:
   masquerade: no
   forward-ports:
   source-ports:
   icmp-blocks:
   rich rules:
  $
```

Notice again that you should add the --permanent option to ensure the new rule applies when the system reloads.

You can also specify rules as TCP or UDP port values:

```
$ sudo firewall-cmd --zone=mytest --add-port=631/tcp --permanent
success
$ sudo firewall-cmd --reload
success
$ sudo firewall-cmd --zone=mytest --list-all
mytest
  target: default
  icmp-block-inversion: no
  interfaces:
  sources:
  services: https
  ports: 631/tcp
  protocols:
  masquerade: no
  forward-ports:
  source-ports:
  icmp-blocks:
  rich rules:
$
```

The   program also uses what it calls *rich rules*, which allow you to customize a rule to specify a specific object, such as a single IP address and a port or service:

```
$ sudo firewall-cmd --zone=mytest --permanent --add-rich-rule='rule
family=ipv4 source address=192.168.1.70 port port=22 protocol=tcp reject'
success
$ sudo firewall-cmd --reload
success
$
```

This rich rule example rejects SSH packets (port 22) coming from a specific source address, 192.168.1.70. The command applies this rich rule to the mytest zone. You can then check if the rule was applied:

```
$ sudo firewall-cmd --zone=mytest --list-all
mytest
  target: default
  icmp-block-inversion: no
  interfaces:
  sources:
  services:
  ports: 631/tcp
  protocols:
  masquerade: no
  forward-ports:
  source-ports:
  icmp-blocks:
  rich rules:
```

```
        rule family="ipv4" source address="192.168.1.70" port port="22"
    protocol="tcp" reject
  $
```

With the firewalld program, you can lock down your Red Hat server as tight as you need, only opening it up to specific network clients.

The Bottom Line

Control access from the root user account.   The Red Hat server distribution enables the root user account by default, which could cause security issues if not managed correctly. You should always check for uses of the root user account by using the aulast command to view the logins on the server. Depending on your environment, you may also want to restrict the root user account from accessing the server from a remote device. You can do that using the /etc/ssh/sshd_config configuration file in OpenSSH. Finally, if you do allow root user access on your system, it's a good idea to restrict the idle time at the command prompt. You do that using the TMOUT environment variable.

> **Master It**   Your boss came into your office saying that someone deleted his user account on the server and wants to know how he can find out who did it. He thinks it happened yesterday afternoon. What command should you use to see who logged in with the root user account on the system during that time period?

Manage the SELinux environment.   While standard Linux file and directory permissions can help with locking down files and directories, they can't provide mandatory access controls required for some environments. The SELinux package allows you to write policy rules that control access to not only files and directories but also applications and network ports. This helps provide MAC-level of security on the Linux server.

> **Master It**   After you enabled SELinux on the Red Hat server, the web administrator notified you that his web application can't connect to the MySQL database anymore. What commands should you use to troubleshoot and fix the problem?

Control network access using firewalld.   In today's world, managing access to the Linux server is a must, especially if your Linux server has some type of connection to the Internet. Red Hat servers utilize the firewalld program to block unwanted network connections and allow approved connections on the network. The firewalld program defines connections as rules and applies those rules to specific zones. You can then assign network interfaces to the zone that supports the network connections needed.

> **Master It**   The database administrator contacted you to complain she just installed MySQL on the Red Hat server, but none of the remote clients can connect to it. She indicated that MySQL uses TCP port 3306 for communications by default and just assumed it would be open on the server. What commands should you use to troubleshoot and fix the problem?

Chapter 19

Writing Scripts

While you can enter individual shell commands at the command line, there are times when doing so is not efficient. For example, if you need to enter the same 15 commands to accomplish a certain task, a single shell script can handle the job faster than you can type in those commands. However, shell scripts go beyond just repeating commands. They allow you to modify their behavior through the use of variables and change the course of their actions based on results of conducted tests.

In addition, you can configure shell scripts to run at night unattended, while you're asleep. Even better is that you can write a single set of shell scripts and then deploy them to all the various servers you administer. If written well, these scripts will need little to no modifications for the different systems on which they reside. Due to their effectiveness, flexibility, and efficiency, creating well-written shell scripts is a core function of properly administering a system.

IN THIS CHAPTER, YOU WILL LEARN TO

- ◆ Create basic scripts to automatically run commands
- ◆ Use variables in shell scripts
- ◆ Provide compound conditions to guide scripts
- ◆ Determine the best loops to use in a script, when needed
- ◆ Create and use functions in shell scripts

Beginning a Shell Script

When you are first learning, writing shell scripts is often an intimidating task. It's helpful to try some basic scripts in order to get comfortable with the process, before you launch into more complicated and intricate script writing. The basic scripts and methods in this section will help you build a solid base for creating shell scripts.

Creating a Script File

To place shell commands in a text file, first you'll need to use a text editor (covered in Chapter 8, "Working with Text Files") to create a file. It is considered good form to use the .sh file extension in your script file's name. While it's not required, it is helpful to be able to quickly glance at a directory and see which files are scripts by their filename extension.

When creating a shell script file, you should specify the shell you are using in the first line of the file. The format (also called *syntax*) for this is as follows:

```
#!/bin/bash
```

This first line of a shell script file, which is a pound sign (#) followed by the exclamation point (!) and an absolute directory reference to a shell (/bin/bash), tells the current shell which shell to use for running the script.

USING OTHER SHELLS

You are not limited to only the Bash shell (/bin/bash) in your script's first line. You can use any shell that you desire, such as zsh, tcsh, and dash.

However, if you use a different shell than Bash, be aware that some of the structures and commands in this chapter will not work. For example, tcsh uses elements from the C programming language. We focus on the Bash shell in this chapter, because it's the most commonly used shell.

Also, you may see #!/bin/sh used as the first line in the shell script. The /bin/sh file is typically a pointer to another file, usually the Bash shell, but not always! On Ubuntu systems, the /bin/sh file points to the Dash shell, so it's a good idea not to use #!/bin/sh as the first line in your shell scripts.

After indicating the shell, commands are entered onto each line of the file. The shell will process commands in the order in which they appear in the file. An example shell script file looks like this:

```
$ cat sampleScript1.sh
#!/bin/bash
# This sample script dislays the date/time
# and who is logged onto the system
#
date
who
$
```

Notice that three additional lines were included that start with the pound symbol and add a description of the script. Lines that start with the pound symbol (other than the first #! line) aren't interpreted by the shell. This is a great way to leave comments for yourself about what the script does and what's happening in the script, so when you come back to it two years later, you can easily remember what you did.

There are several different methods for running a shell script. We'll just cover three basic ones here.

Precede the script name with the bash command. This method is the easiest and is often used by those who are just learning how to write and run shell scripts. Your current working directory needs to be the same directory where the script is located. You type in **bash** and follow with the script's name:

```
$ bash sampleScript1.sh
```

Precede the script name with ./. This method requires a little more work. Before attempting to run the script for the first time, you must ensure that the script file has the execution privilege bit set prior to running it. Here is an example of this:

```
$ chmod u+x sampleScript1.sh
$ ./sampleScript1.sh
```

The example assumes you are the owner of the file, and thus the chmod u+x was used. Keep in mind that you only need to set the execution privilege one time. Once set, you can just enter ./ and follow it with your script's name, but your current working directory needs to be the same directory where the script is located.

Precede the script name with nothing. This method requires that the script is located in a directory within the PATH environment variable (covered in Chapter 6, "Working with the Shell"), or you have modified the variable to include the script's directory. The convenience of this method is that you can be located anywhere on the Linux system to run the script, and nothing other than the script name will launch it:

```
$ sampleScript1.sh
```

The downside of this method is that your script must reside in a PATH directory. Also, you'll need to give the script a unique name so that its name isn't the same as another script on the system or shell command.

When you run a script, you'll see output from the script's commands. Here's an example of using bash to run a sample script:

```
$ pwd
/home/sysadmin/Scripts
$
$ ls sampleScript1.sh
sampleScript1.sh
$
$ bash sampleScript1.sh
Fri Mar  5 19:19:11 UTC 2021
sysadmin tty1        2021-03-05 18:45
sysadmin pts/0       2021-03-05 18:48 (192.168.0.103)
$
```

Success! Now all of the pieces are in the right places to execute the new shell script file.

Displaying Messages

Most shell commands produce their own output, which is displayed on the terminal where the script is running. Many times, however, you will want to add your own text messages to help the script user know what is happening within the script. You can do this with the echo command. The echo command can display a simple text string if you add the string following the command:

```
$ echo This is a test
This is a test
$
```

Notice that, by default, you don't need to use quotes to delineate the string you're displaying. However, sometimes this can get tricky if you are using quotes within your string:

```
$ echo Let's see if this'll work
Lets see if thisll work
$
```

The echo command uses either double or single quotes to delineate text strings. If you use them within your string, you need to use one type of quote within the text and the other type to delineate the string:

```
$ echo "This is a test to see if you're paying attention"
This is a test to see if you're paying attention
$
$ echo 'Rich says "scripting is easy".'
Rich says "scripting is easy".
$
```

Now all of the needed quotation marks appear properly in the output.

You can add echo statements anywhere in your shell scripts where you need to display additional information:

```
$ cat sampleScript2.sh
#!/bin/bash
# This sample script dislays the date/time
# and who is logged onto the system
#
echo "The date and time are: "
date
echo "The following users are logged on: "
who
$
```

When you run this script, it produces the following output:

```
$ chmod u+x sampleScript2.sh
$ ./sampleScript2.sh
The date and time are:
Fri Mar  5 19:41:16 UTC 2021
The following users are logged on:
sysadmin tty1         2021-03-05 18:45
sysadmin pts/0        2021-03-05 18:48 (192.168.0.103)
$
```

That's nice, but what if you want to echo a text string on the same line as a command output? You can use the −n parameter for the echo statement to do that. Just change the first echo statement line to this:

```
echo -n "The time and date are: "
```

You'll need to use quotes around the string to ensure that there's a space at the end of the echoed string. The command output begins exactly where the string output stops. The output will now look like this:

```
$ ./sampleScript2.sh
The date and time are: Fri Mar  5 19:42:50 UTC 2021
The following users are logged on:
sysadmin tty1         2021-03-05 18:45
sysadmin pts/0        2021-03-05 18:48 (192.168.0.103)
$
```

Perfect! The echo command is a crucial piece of shell scripts that interact with users. You'll find yourself using it in many situations, especially when you want to display the values of script variables. Let's look at that next.

Using Variables

Just running individual commands from the shell script is useful, but this has its limitations. Often you'll want to incorporate other data in your shell commands to process information. You can do this by using variables. Variables allow you to temporarily store information within the shell script for use with other commands in the script. This section shows how to use variables in your shell scripts.

Environment Variables

You've already seen one type of Linux variable in action. (Chapter 6 described the environment variables available in the Linux system.) You can access these values from your shell scripts as well.

The shell maintains environment variables that track specific system information, such as the name of the system, the name of the user logged in to the system, the user's system ID (called UID), the default home directory of the user, and the search path used by the shell to find programs.

You can tap into these environment variables from within your scripts by using the environment variable's name preceded by a dollar sign. This is demonstrated in the following script:

```
$ cat sampleScript3.sh
#!/bin/bash
# Display a user's information
#
echo "User info for userid: $USER"
echo UID: $UID
echo HOME: $HOME
$
```

The *$USER, $UID,* and *$HOME* environment variables are used to display the pertinent information about the logged-in user. The output should look something like this:

```
$ chmod u+x sampleScript3.sh
$ ./sampleScript3.sh
User info for userid: sysadmin
```

```
UID: 1000
HOME: /home/sysadmin
$
```

Notice that the environment variables in the echo commands are replaced by their current values when the script is run. Also notice that we were able to place the *$USER* system variable within the double quotation marks in the first string, and the shell script was still able to figure out what we meant.

User Variables

In addition to the environment variables, a shell script allows you to set and use your own variables within the script. Setting variables allows you to temporarily store data and use it throughout the script.

User variables can be any text string of up to 20 letters, digits, or an underscore character. User variables are case sensitive, so the variable *Var1* is different from the variable *var1*. This little rule often gets novice script writers in trouble.

Values are assigned to user variables using an equal sign. No spaces can appear between the variable, the equal sign, and the value (another trouble spot for novices). Here are a few examples of assigning values to user variables:

```
var1=10
var2=-57
var3=testing
var4="still more testing"
```

The shell script stores all variable values as text strings, so it's up to the individual commands in the shell to properly handle the data type used for the variable's value.

Just like system variables, user variables are referenced using the dollar sign:

```
$ cat sampleScript4.sh
#!/bin/bash
# Trying out user variables
#
days=10
guest="London Radford"
echo "$guest checked in $days days ago."
#
days=5
guest="Takoda Puddle"
echo "$guest checked in $days days ago."
$
```

Running the script produces the following output:

```
$ chmod u+x sampleScript4.sh
$ ./sampleScript4.sh
London Radford checked in 10 days ago.
Takoda Puddle checked in 5 days ago.
$
```

Each time the variable is referenced, it produces the value currently assigned to it. Variables defined within the shell script maintain their values throughout the life of the shell script but are deleted when the shell script completes.

Command Substitution

One of the most useful features of shell scripts is the ability to extract information from the output of a command and assign it to a variable. Once you assign the output to a variable, you can use that value anywhere in your script. This comes in handy when processing data in your scripts.

There are two ways to assign the output of a command to a variable:

◆ The backtick character

◆ The $() format

Be careful with the backtick character, which is not the normal single quotation mark character you are used to using for strings. Because it is not used often outside of shell scripts, you may not even know where to find it on your keyboard. On a U.S. keyboard, it is usually on the same key as the tilde symbol (~).

Command substitution allows you to assign the output of a shell command to a variable. While this doesn't seem like much, it is a major building block in script programming.

You must surround the entire command-line command with either the backtick characters:

```
testDate=`date`
```

or using the $() format:

```
testDate="$(date)"
```

The shell runs the command within the command substitution characters and assigns the output to the variable testDate. Notice that there aren't any spaces between the assignment equal sign and the command substitution character. Also notice that we enclosed the $(date) command in quotation marks. This helps to avoid unusual problems that can occur with a command's output and is considered good form.

Here's an example of creating a variable using the output from a normal shell command:

```
$ cat sampleScript5.sh
#!/bin/bash
# Trying out command subsitution variables
#
testDate="$(date)"
echo "The date and time are: $testDate"
$
```

The variable testDate receives the output from the date command, and it is used in the echo statement to display it. Notice that this user variable name, testDate, starts with a lowercase letter and has an uppercase letter in its middle. This naming convention is called *camel case* and allows easier reading of variable names created out of multiple words by shell script writers. It's often used when naming shell scripts too.

Running the shell script produces the following output:

```
$ chmod u+x sampleScript5.sh
$ ./sampleScript5.sh
The date and time are: Fri Mar  5 20:23:02 UTC 2021
$
```

That's not all that exciting in this example (you could just as easily put the command in the echo statement), but once you capture the command output in a variable, you can do anything with it.

Exiting the Script with Status

When a shell script ends, it returns an *exit status* back to the parent shell that launched it. The exit status tells us if the shell script completed successfully.

Linux provides us with the special $? variable, which holds the exit status value from the last command that executed. To check the exit status of a command, you must view the $? variable immediately after the command ends. It changes values according to the exit status of the last command executed by the shell:

```
$ ls *.sh
sampleScript1.sh   sampleScript3.sh   sampleScript5.sh
sampleScript2.sh   sampleScript4.sh
$ echo $?
0
$
$ ls *.txt
ls: cannot access '*.txt': No such file or directory
$ echo $?
2
$
```

By convention, the exit status of a command that successfully completes is 0. If a command completes with an error, a positive integer value appears as the exit status.

You can change the exit status of your shell scripts by using the exit command and using a number as an argument. While you don't have to include an exit status with your script's exit command, it is helpful in certain situations, such as debugging a script problem. To use an exit status, just specify the status value you want in the exit command:

```
$ cat sampleScript6.sh
#!/bin/bash
# Trying out an exit status
#
testDate="$(date)"
echo "The date and time are: $testDate"
exit 42
$
$ chmod u+x sampleScript6.sh
$ ./sampleScript6.sh
The date and time are: Mon Mar  8 15:45:17 UTC 2021
```

```
$ echo $?
42
$
```

In this example script, an `exit` command was used to exit the script using an exit status code of 42. After the script was run, we displayed the $? variable value to see if it matched what we had set in the `exit` command, which it did.

As you write more complicated scripts, you can indicate errors by changing the exit status value. That way, by checking the exit status, you can easily debug your shell scripts. If you don't want to include an exit status in your script, it is still considered good form to use the `exit` command—just don't add an exit status to it.

Passing Parameters

The most basic method of passing data to your shell script is to use *command-line parameters*. These parameters allow you to add data values to the command line when you execute the script:

```
$ ./sampleScript7.sh 3 7
[...]
$
```

This example passes two command-line parameters (3 and 7) to the script `sampleScript7.sh`. The script handles the command-line parameters using special variables. This section describes how to use command-line parameters in your Bash shell scripts.

The Bash shell assigns special variables, called *positional parameters*, to all of the command-line parameters entered. This includes the name of the script the shell is executing. The positional parameter variables are standard numbers, with $0 being the script's name, $1 being the first parameter, $2 being the second parameter, and so on, up to $9 for the ninth parameter.

Here's a simple example of using two command-line parameters in a shell script:

```
$ cat sampleScript7.sh
#!/bin/bash
# Trying out using command-line parameters
#
total=$[ $1 + $2 ]
echo "When you add $1 to $2,"
echo "the result is: $total"
exit
$
$ chmod u+x sampleScript7.sh
$ ./sampleScript7.sh 3 7
When you add 3 to 7,
the result is: 10
$
```

You can use the $1 and $2 variables just like any other variables in the shell script. The shell script automatically assigns the value from the command-line parameter to the variable, so you don't need to do anything special.

In the preceding example, the command-line parameters used were both numerical values. You can also use text strings as parameters:

```
$ cat sampleScript8.sh
#!/bin/bash
# Trying out using a string parameter
#
echo Hello $1, glad to meet you.
exit
$
$ chmod u+x sampleScript8.sh
$ ./sampleScript8.sh Kathi
Hello Kathi, glad to meet you.
$
```

The shell passes the string value entered into the command line to the script. However, you'll have a problem if you try to do this with a text string that contains spaces:

```
$ ./sampleScript8.sh Kathi Duggan
Hello Kathi, glad to meet you.
$
```

Remember that each of the parameters is separated by a space, so the shell interpreted the space as just separating the two values. To include a space as a parameter value, you must use quotation marks (either single or double quotation marks), which are not included as part of the data, but just delineate the beginning and the end of the data:

```
$ ./sampleScript8.sh 'Kathi Duggan'
Hello Kathi Duggan, glad to meet you.
$
$ ./sampleScript8.sh "Kathi Duggan"
Hello Kathi Duggan, glad to meet you.
$
```

If your script needs more than nine command-line parameters, you can continue, but the variable names change slightly. After the ninth variable, you must use braces around the variable number, such as ${10}. Here's an example of doing that:

```
$ cat sampleScript9.sh
#!/bin/bash
# Trying out using 12 parameters
#
totalA=$[ $1 + $2 + $3 + $4 ]
totalB=$[ $5 + $6 + $7 + $8 +$9 ]
totalC=$[ ${10} + ${11} + ${12} ]
#
total=$[ $totalA + $totalB + $totalC ]
#
echo
echo "When you add all these numbers together,"
echo "the result is: $total"
```

```
echo
echo "When you add ${10}, ${11} and ${12} together,"
echo "the result is: $totalC"
#
exit
$
$ chmod u+x sampleScript9.sh
$ ./sampleScript9.sh 1 2 3 4 5 6 7 8 9 10 11 12

When you add all these numbers together,
the result is: 78

When you add 10, 11 and 12 together,
the result is: 33
$
```

This technique allows you to add as many command-line parameters to your scripts as you could possibly need.

 Real World Scenario

WRITING A SIMPLE SHELL SCRIPT WITH VARIABLES

When writing Bash shell scripts, you need to include a few basic items, such as the shell you want to use in the first line of the file and the various shell commands you need to run. It's also considered good form to place an `exit` command at the script's end. To incorporate other data in your shell commands to process information, you can use variables in your scripts too.

The following steps will take you through writing a simple Bash shell script that uses variables:

1. Log into your Linux system, using the `sysadmin` account and the password you created for it.

2. Start creating a shell script by typing **nano myScript.sh** and pressing Enter. This will create the file `myScript.sh` and put you into the `nano` text editor to start editing it.

3. On the file's first line, type **#!/bin/bash** and press Enter. This will select the Bash shell to run the script when it is executed.

4. On the file's second line, type **# A simple script that uses variables** and press Enter. This is a comment line. You can add your name to the end of the comment line if you want.

5. On the third line of the file, type **echo "I am logged into the $USER account."** and press Enter. This will display the text along with the username of the current account you are using.

6. On the file's last line, type **exit**.

7. Save the entered text to the script file by pressing Ctrl+O and pressing Enter when the file's name displays on the text editor's status line.

8. Exit the `nano` text editor by pressing Ctrl+X.

9. Try running the script by typing **bash myScript.sh** and pressing Enter.

10. If the script did not run successfully, go back and edit the file, making any needed corrections.

11. Once you have the script running correctly, try adding a new echo command that uses the $0 parameter value, which is the script's filename.

12. After you get the script modification working with the $0 parameter value, add another echo command that uses a parameter you pass to the script ($1).

Adding Conditional Expressions

So far, all the shell scripts presented process commands in a linear fashion—one command after another. However, not all programming is linear. There are times when you'd like your program to test for certain conditions, such as if a file exists or if a mathematical expression is 0, and perform different commands based on the results of the test. For that, the Bash shell provides *logic statements*.

Logic statements allow us to test for a specific condition or conditions and then branch to different sections of code based on whether the condition evaluates to a zero (true) or nonzero (false) exit value. There are a couple of different ways to implement logic statements in Bash scripts.

Working with the *if-then* Statement

The most basic logic statement is the *if-then condition statement*. The format for the if-then condition statement is as follows:

```
if [ condition ]
then
    commands
fi
```

If the *condition* you specify evaluates to a zero exit value (true), the shell runs the commands in the then section of code. If the *condition* evaluates to a nonzero exit value (false), the shell script skips the commands in the then section of code.

The if-then condition syntax is typically tricky for those who are new to shell script writing. It is critical to ensure a space is included after the first bracket and before the condition, as well as after the condition and before the last bracket: [condition].

The condition expression has quite a few different formats in the Bash shell programming. There are built-in tests for numerical values, string values, and even files and directories. Table 19.1 lists the different built-in tests that are available.

TABLE 19.1   Condition Tests

TEST	TYPE	DESCRIPTION
n1 -eq *n2*	Numeric	Checks if *n1* is equal to *n2*
n1 -ge *n2*	Numeric	Checks if *n1* is greater than or equal to *n2*
n1 -gt *n2*	Numeric	Checks if *n1* is greater than *n2*
n1 -le *n2*	Numeric	Checks if *n1* is less than or equal to *n2*
n1 -lt *n2*	Numeric	Checks if *n1* is less than *n2*
n1 -ne *n2*	Numeric	Checks if *n1* is not equal to *n2*
str1 = *str2*	String	Checks if *str1* is the same as *str2*
str1 != *str2*	String	Checks if *str1* is not the same as *str2*
str1 < *str2*	String	Checks if *str1* is less than *str2*
str1 > *str2*	String	Checks if *str1* is greater than *str2*
-n *str1*	String	Checks if *str1* has a length greater than zero
-z *str1*	String	Checks if *str1* has a length of zero
-d *file*	File	Checks if *file* exists and is a directory
-e *file*	File	Checks if *file* exists
-f *file*	File	Checks if *file* exists and is a file
-r *file*	File	Checks if *file* exists and is readable
-s *file*	File	Checks if *file* exists and is not empty
-w *file*	File	Checks if *file* exists and is writable
-x *file*	File	Checks if *file* exists and is executable
-O *file*	File	Checks if *file* exists and is owned by the current user
-G *file*	File	Checks if *file* exists and the default group is the same as the current user
file1 -nt *file2*	File	Checks if *file1* is newer than *file2*
file1 -ot *file2*	File	Checks if *file1* is older than *file2*

Here is an example of using several if-then condition statements in a shell script:

```
$ cat sampleScript10.sh
#!/bin/bash
```

```
# Trying out if-then conditions
#
if [ -z $1 ]
then
    echo "You did not provide any parameters"
    exit
fi
#
if [ -z $2 ]
then
    echo "You did not provide a second parameter"
    exit
fi
#
if [ $1 -eq $2 ]
then
    echo "Both values are equal"
    exit
fi
#
if [ $1 -gt $2 ]
then
    echo "$1 is greater than $2"
    exit
fi
#
if [ $1 -lt $2 ]
then
    echo "$1 is less than $2"
fi
#
exit
$
```

We'll try not providing enough parameters first and see how the if-then statement tests string length using the -z condition test. This is an excellent condition test to include, if command-line parameters are used in a shell script.

```
$ chmod u+x sampleScript10.sh
$ ./sampleScript10.sh
You did not provide any parameters
$
$ ./sampleScript10.sh 73
You did not provide a second parameter
$
```

Now we can try providing enough parameters and have the script determine information concerning them:

```
$ ./sampleScript10.sh 73 42
73 is greater than 42
$
```

```
$ ./sampleScript10.sh 42 73
42 is less than 73
$
$ ./sampleScript10.sh 42 42
Both values are equal
$
```

Whenever the command from an if-then statement in the script evaluated to a zero exit value, the statements between then and fi were processed by the shell script.

Using Compound Tests

You can reduce the number of if-then statements through the use of Boolean logic to combine tests. These operators are available:

◆ [*conditionA*] && [*conditionB*]

◆ [*conditionA*] || [*conditionB*]

The first operator is an "and" test, where both conditions must return a zero exit status (true). The second operator performs an "or" test. In this case, only one condition must return a zero exit status.

Modifying our if-then sample script in this manner allows us to consolidate the first two tests, as shown snipped here:

```
$ cat sampleScript11.sh
#!/bin/bash
# Trying out if-then conditions
# and compound tests
#
if [ -z $1 ] || [ -z $2 ]
then
    echo "You didn't provide the correct number of parameters."
    exit
fi
#
if [ $1 -eq $2 ]
[...]
exit
$
```

The script still works as needed, but with a less code:

```
$ chmod u+x sampleScript11.sh
$
$ ./sampleScript11.sh
You didn't provide the correct number of parameters.
$
$ ./sampleScript11.sh 42
You didn't provide the correct number of parameters.
$
$ ./sampleScript11.sh 42 73
42 is less than 73
$
```

Working with the *if-then-else* Statement

In the if-then statement, you have only one option for whether a command is successful. If the command returns a nonzero exit value (false), the Bash shell just moves on to the next command in the script. In this situation, it would be nice to be able to execute an alternate set of commands. That's exactly what the if-then-else statement is for.

The if-then-else statement provides another group of commands in the statement:

```
if [ condition ]
then
    commands
else
    commands
fi
```

When the command in the if statement line returns with a zero exit value, the commands listed in the then section are executed, just as in a normal if-then statement. When the command in the if statement line returns a nonzero exit value, the Bash shell executes the commands in the else section.

Modifying our if-then sample script to include an if-then-else statement allows us to provide more information concerning the parameters, as shown snipped here:

```
$ cat sampleScript12.sh
#!/bin/bash
# Trying out if-then-else statments
[...]
#
if [ $1 -eq $2 ]
then
    echo "Both values are equal"
    exit
else
    echo "The values are not equal"
fi
#
if [ $1 -gt $2 ]
then
    echo "$1 is greater than $2"
    exit
fi
#
if [ $1 -lt $2 ]
then
    echo "$1 is less than $2"
fi
#
exit
$
$ chmod u+x sampleScript12.sh
$
```

```
$ ./sampleScript12.sh 42 42
Both values are equal
$
$ ./sampleScript12.sh 42 73
The values are not equal
42 is less than 73
$
```

The script still works as needed but allows additional information to be provided through the else section of the if-then-else statement. However, there are additional methods to provide more information and consolidate code. We'll explore one technique next.

Trying the *case* Statement

Often, you'll find yourself trying to evaluate the value of a variable, looking for a specific value within a set of possible values, similar to what we demonstrated in earlier scripts. Instead of having to write multiple if-then statements testing for all of the possible conditions, you can use a case statement.

The case statement allows you to check multiple values of a single variable in a list-oriented format:

```
case variable in
pattern1) commands1;;
pattern2 | pattern3) commands2;;
*) default commands;;
esac
```

The case statement compares the variable specified against the different patterns. If the variable matches the pattern, the shell executes the command(s) specified for the pattern. You can list more than one pattern on a line, using the bar operator to separate each pattern as an "or" operator. The asterisk (*) symbol is the catchall for values that don't match any of the listed patterns.

Here is an example of using the case statement within a script:

```
$ cat sampleScript13.sh
#!/bin/bash
# Trying out case statements
#
case $PWD in
/home/sysadmin)
     echo "You are in your home directory"
;;
/home/sysadmin/Scripts)
     echo "You are in your Scripts directory"
;;
*)
     echo "You are not in your home directory, and"
     echo "you are not in your Scripts directory"
;;
esac
```

```
#
exit
$
```

In this script, the variable being matched against the patterns is an environment variable ($PWD) that contains the user's current working directory. Notice that you do not have to put the ;; syntax on the same line as your last command within a selected pattern. This flexibility of the case statement allows you to create easy-to-read shell code.

Here's this script in action:

```
$ echo $PWD
/home/sysadmin/Scripts
$
$ chmod u+x sampleScript13.sh
$
$ ./sampleScript13.sh
You are in your Scripts directory
$
$ cd
$ echo $PWD
/home/sysadmin
$
$ ./Scripts/sampleScript13.sh
You are in your home directory
$
```

The case statement provides a much cleaner way of specifying the various options for each possible variable value.

Using Loops

Iterating through a series of commands is a common programming practice. Often, you need to repeat a set of commands until a specific condition has been met, such as processing all the files in a directory, all the users on a system, or all the lines in a text file.

The Bash shell provides three structures for controlling loops: for, while, and until. They each have value for iterating through commands, and we cover them next.

Looking at the *for* Command

The Bash shell provides the for command to allow you to create a loop that iterates through a series of values. Each iteration performs a predefined set of commands using one of the values in the series. Here's the basic format of the Bash shell for command:

```
for var in list
do
     commands
done
```

You supply the series of values used in the iterations in the *list* parameter. The values can be specified in several ways.

In each iteration, the variable *var* contains the current value in the list. The first iteration uses the first item in the list, the second iteration uses the second item, and so on, until all the items in the list have been used.

The *commands* entered between the do and done statements can be one or more standard Bash shell commands. Within the commands, the *$var* variable contains the current list item value for the iteration.

The most basic use of the for command is to iterate through a list of values defined within the for command itself:

```
$ cat sampleScript14.sh
#!/bin/bash
# Trying out the for command
#
for wordVar in Alpha Bravo Charlie Delta
do
    echo The current word is $wordVar
done
#
exit
$
$ chmod u+x sampleScript14.sh
$
$ ./sampleScript14.sh
The current word is Alpha
The current word is Bravo
The current word is Charlie
The current word is Delta
$
```

Each time the for command iterates through the list of values provided, it assigns the $wordVar variable the next value in the list. The $wordVar variable can be used just like any other script variable within the for command statements. After the last iteration, $wordVar remains valid throughout the remainder of the shell script. It retains the last iteration value (unless you change its value).

For large series of numbers in your for loops, it's convenient to use the seq command, instead of typing in all the numbers. You just enter seq followed by the starting number and then the last number in the series, but you'll need to employ command substitution to make it work correctly:

```
$ cat sampleScript15.sh
#!/bin/bash
# Trying out the for with seq
#
for numVar in $(seq 1 10)
do
    echo The current number is $numVar
done
#
exit
$
```

```
$ chmod u+x sampleScript15.sh
$
$ ./sampleScript15.sh
The current number is 1
The current number is 2
The current number is 3
The current number is 4
The current number is 5
The current number is 6
The current number is 7
The current number is 8
The current number is 9
The current number is 10
$
```

Using the $(seq 1 10) syntax within the for commands list allows the Bash shell to handle generating all the numbers in the list automatically. Notice that in this case of command substitution, we did not enclose the $(seq 1 10) command in quotation marks. This is because the list would be treated as a single item, which is not what we want.

Command substitution in the *list* lets you get rather fancy with your for loops:

```
$ cat sampleScript16.sh
#!/bin/bash
# Getting fancy with the for loop
#
for fileVar in $(ls *.sh)
do
      echo The current file is $fileVar
done
#
exit
$
$ chmod u+x sampleScript16.sh
$
$ ./sampleScript16.sh
The current file is sampleScript1.sh
The current file is sampleScript10.sh
The current file is sampleScript11.sh
The current file is sampleScript12.sh
The current file is sampleScript13.sh
The current file is sampleScript14.sh
The current file is sampleScript15.sh
The current file is sampleScript16.sh
The current file is sampleScript2.sh
The current file is sampleScript3.sh
The current file is sampleScript4.sh
The current file is sampleScript5.sh
The current file is sampleScript6.sh
```

```
The current file is sampleScript7.sh
The current file is sampleScript8.sh
The current file is sampleScript9.sh
$
```

In this example, all the script files in the current directory are listed using the $(ls *.sh) command. This list of files is then processed through the command that's between do and done. You can use multiple commands here too, if needed.

Working with the *while* Format

The while command is somewhat of a cross between the if-then statement and the for loop. The while command allows you to define a command to test and then loop through a set of commands for as long as the defined *test command* returns a zero exit value (true). It tests the *test command* at the start of each iteration. When the *test command* returns a zero exit value, the while command stops executing the set of commands.

Here's the format of the while command:

```
while test command
do
  other commands
done
```

The *test command* defined in the while command is the same format as in if-then statements. As in the if-then statement, you can use any normal Bash shell command, or you can use the *test command* to test for conditions, such as variable values.

The key to the while command is that the exit status of the *test command* specified must change, based on the commands run during the loop. If the exit status never changes, the while loop will get stuck in an infinite loop.

The most common use of the *test command* is to use brackets to check a value of a shell variable that's used in the loop commands:

```
$ cat sampleScript17.sh
#!/bin/bash
# Trying out the while loop
#
numVar=10
#
while [ $numVar -gt 0 ]
do
    echo The current number is $numVar
    numVar=$[ $numVar - 1 ]
done
#
exit
$
$ chmod u+x sampleScript17.sh
$
$ ./sampleScript17.sh
```

```
The current number is 10
The current number is 9
The current number is 8
The current number is 7
The current number is 6
The current number is 5
The current number is 4
The current number is 3
The current number is 2
The current number is 1
$
```

The `while` command defines the test condition to check for each iteration:

```
while [ $numVar -gt 0 ]
```

As long as the test condition is true, the `while` command continues to loop through the commands defined. Within the commands, the variable used in the test condition must be modified, or you'll have an infinite loop. In this example, we use shell arithmetic to decrease the variable value by one:

```
numVar=$[ $numVar - 1 ]
```

The `while` loop stops when the test condition is no longer true.

Using the *until* Command

The `until` command works in exactly the opposite way from the `while` command. The `until` command requires that you specify a `test command` that normally produces a nonzero exit value (false). As long as the exit status of the `test command` is a nonzero exit value, the Bash shell executes the commands listed in the loop. When the `test command` returns a zero exit value (true), the loop stops.

As you would expect, the format of the `until` command is as follows:

```
until test command
do
    other commands
done
```

Only the exit status of the last command determines if the Bash shell executes the *other commands* defined. The following is an example of using the `until` command:

```
$ cat sampleScript18.sh
#!/bin/bash
# Trying out the until loop
#
numVar=10
#
until [ $numVar -eq 0 ]
do
    echo The current number is $numVar
    numVar=$[ $numVar - 1 ]
```

```
done
#
exit
$
$ chmod u+x sampleScript18.sh
$
$ ./sampleScript18.sh
The current number is 10
The current number is 9
The current number is 8
The current number is 7
The current number is 6
The current number is 5
The current number is 4
The current number is 3
The current number is 2
The current number is 1
$
```

This example tests the numVar variable to determine when the until loop should stop. As soon as the value of the variable is equal to zero, the until command stops the loop.

 Real World Scenario

ADDING CONDITIONAL EXPRESSIONS AND LOOPS TO A SHELL SCRIPT

In Bash shell scripts, often you need to repeat certain commands for a series of data. Using a loop structure helps in these situations. Also, the script's flexibility and usability typically increase when you include tests and conditional expressions that direct the script to proceed in one direction or another, depending on the outcome of the tests.

The following steps will take you through writing a Bash shell script that uses a conditional expression and a loop:

1. Log into your Linux system, using the sysadmin account and the password you created for it.

2. Start creating a shell script by typing **nano myScript2.sh** and pressing Enter. This creates the file myScript2.sh, and puts you into the nano text editor to start editing it.

3. On the file's first line, type **#!/bin/bash** and press Enter to select the Bash shell to run the script when it is executed.

4. On the file's second line, type
 # A script that uses conditional expressions and loops and press Enter. You can add your name to the end of the comment line, if you want to.

5. On the third line of the file, create a variable and give it a value by typing **count=10** and pressing Enter.

6. On the next file line, begin a while loop by typing **while [$count -gt 0]** and pressing Enter.

7. On the file's next line, type **do** and press Enter.

8. Now add a command to the loop by pressing Tab, typing **echo The loop count is $count**, and pressing Enter.

9. Add a second command to the loop by pressing Tab, typing **count=[$count - 1]**, and pressing Enter.

10. End the loop by typing **done** and pressing Enter.

11. Add a blank comment line by typing **#** and pressing Enter. This will help the readability of the script.

12. On the file's next line, start adding a conditional expression by typing **if [$count -eq 0]** and pressing Enter.

13. Type **then** and press Enter.

14. Add a command to execute, if the test returns a zero exit status (true), by pressing Tab, typing **echo "Count is set to zero: $count"**, and pressing Enter.

15. Type **else** and press Enter.

16. Add a command to execute if the test returns a nonzero exit status (false), by pressing Tab, typing **echo "Count is not set to zero: $count"**, and pressing Enter.

17. On the file's last line, type **exit**.

18. Before saving your shell script file, review the following code and make sure your code is the same (though your comment lines do not have to match). Make any needed changes.

```
#!/bin/bash
# A script that uses conditional expressions and loops
count=10
while [ $count -gt 0 ]
do
        echo The loop count is $count
        count=[ $count - 1 ]
done
#
if [ $count -eq 0 ]
then
        echo "Count is set to zero: $count"
else
        echo "Count is not set to zero: $count"
fi
exit
```

19. Save the entered text to the script file by pressing Ctrl+O and pressing Enter when the file's name displays on the text editor's status line.

20. Exit the nano text editor by pressing Ctrl+X.

21. Try running the script by typing **bash myScript2.sh** and pressing Enter.

22. If the script did not run successfully, go back and edit the file, making any needed corrections.

23. Once you have the script running correctly, try turning your `while` loop into an `until` loop, making changes to the `count` variable's original definition and math expression as needed.

Using Functions

Often while writing shell scripts, you'll find yourself using the same code in multiple locations. If it's just a small code snippet, it's usually not that big of a deal. However, rewriting large chunks of code multiple times in your shell script can get tiring and is not good form.

The Bash shell provides a way to help you out by supporting user-defined functions. *Functions* are blocks of script code that you assign a name to and reuse anywhere in your code. Anytime you need to use that block of code in your script, you simply use the function name you assigned it (referred to as *calling* the function).

Creating Functions

There are two formats you can use to create functions in Bash shell scripts. The first format uses the keyword `function`, along with the function name you assign to the block of code:

```
function name {
    commands
}
```

The *name* attribute defines a unique name assigned to the function. Each function you define in your script must be assigned a unique name.

The *commands* are one or more Bash shell commands that make up your function. When you call the function, the Bash shell executes each of the commands in the order they appear in the function, just as in a normal script.

The second format for defining a function in a Bash shell script more closely follows how functions are defined in other programming languages:

```
name() {
commands
}
```

The empty parentheses after the function name indicate that you're defining a function. The same naming rules apply in this format as in the original shell script function format.

Calling Functions

To use a function in your script, specify the function name on a line, just as you would any other shell command:

```
$ cat sampleScript19.sh
#!/bin/bash
# Trying out functions
#
```

```
function func1 {
    echo "This is a function example"
}
numVar=5
#
until [ $numVar -eq 0 ]
do
    func1
    echo The current number is $numVar
    numVar=$[ $numVar - 1 ]
done
#
exit
$
$ chmod u+x  sampleScript19.sh
$
$ ./sampleScript19.sh
This is a function example
The current number is 5
This is a function example
The current number is 4
This is a function example
The current number is 3
This is a function example
The current number is 2
This is a function example
The current number is 1
$
```

Each time you reference the func1 function name, the Bash shell returns to the function func1 definition and executes any commands you defined there.

The function definition doesn't have to be the first thing in your shell script, but be careful. If you attempt to use a function before it's defined, you'll get an error message:

```
$ cat sampleScript20.sh
#!/bin/bash
# Trying out two functions
#
echo "This line is before func1 is defined"
function func1 {
    echo "This is a function example"
}
numVar=5
#
until [ $numVar -eq 0 ]
do
    func1
    echo The current number is $numVar
    numVar=$[ $numVar - 1 ]
done
```

```
        echo "The loop is done"
        func2
        #
        echo "This line is before func2 is defined"
        #
        function func2 {
            echo "This is the second function"
        }
        #
        exit
$
$ chmod u+x sampleScript20.sh
$
$ ./sampleScript20.sh
This line is before func1 is defined
This is a function example
The current number is 5
This is a function example
The current number is 4
This is a function example
The current number is 3
This is a function example
The current number is 2
This is a function example
The current number is 1
The loop is done
./sampleScript20.sh: line 17: func2: command not found
This line is before func2 is defined
$
```

The first function, func1, was defined after the first statement in the script, which is perfectly fine. When the func1 function was used in the script, the shell knew where to find it.

However, the script attempted to use the func2 function before it was defined. Because the func2 function wasn't defined, when the script reached the place where we used it, it produced an error message.

You also need to be careful about your function names. Remember, each function name must be unique, or you'll have a problem. If you redefine a function, the new definition overrides the original function definition, without producing any error messages:

```
$ cat sampleScript21.sh
#!/bin/bash
# Trying out redefining a function
#
function myFunc1 {
    echo "This is the first function definition"
}
myFunc1
#
```

```
function myFunc1 {
    echo "This overrides the first function definition"
}
#
numVar=3
#
until [ $numVar -eq 0 ]
do
    myFunc1
    echo The current number is $numVar
    numVar=$[ $numVar - 1 ]
done
#
exit
$
$ chmod u+x sampleScript21.sh
$
$ ./sampleScript21.sh
This is the first function definition
This overrides the first function definition
The current number is 3
This overrides the first function definition
The current number is 2
This overrides the first function definition
The current number is 1
$
```

The original definition of the myFunc1 function works fine, but after the second definition of the myFunc1 function, any subsequent uses of the function use the second definition.

Ideally you are now inspired to pursue more shell script writing to make your system admin work a little easier. If you'd like to learn more, one of our favorite resources is the *Linux Command Line and Shell Scripting Bible* by Richard Blum and Christine Bresnahan (Wiley, 2021).

The Bottom Line

Create basic scripts to automatically run commands. Basic Bash shell scripts require a few, but important, items. For example, on the first line of a shell script file, you use special syntax that indicates to the current shell which shell to use for running the script. You also need to include the commands you want to run within the script. In addition, it's helpful for the script users, even if it is only you, to have the script produce messages so that the script user knows what is happening within the script.

Master It You have written a basic Bash shell script that assists in viewing who is logged onto the system currently as well as looking at log files that indicate who logged in previously to the system. For some reason, the script is not functioning properly. You are getting error messages as if the Dash shell is running the script, but you want the Bash shell to run the script and are even using the bash command to run it. What is most likely the problem?

Use variables in shell scripts. You can integrate data into your shell script commands to process information using variables. Variables allow you to temporarily store information within the shell script for use with other commands in the script. Variables can be environment variables, user-defined variables, or even data passed to the script through the use of parameters.

Master It Imagine you are writing a shell script to assist in the deletion of individual user accounts. This script will be used by an admin intern from the local college, so it needs to include the username of the account to delete in a variable. How will you accomplish this?

Provide compound conditions to guide scripts. Compound conditions are ones in which two or more conditions need checking so that the script can decide which commands to execute or the course of action to take. You can handle compound conditions through multiple `if-then` statements or, if there are only two conditions to check, through the use of Boolean logic to combine the tests.

Master It You are writing a script that needs to check a compound condition. In this case, the `machine0087.log` file's existence needs to be checked. In addition, a counter variable, `logCount`, must be examined as well. If the file exists and the counter has reached `100`, the script should exit. What `if-then` statement(s) should you write to make this test as consolidated as possible?

Determine the best loops to use in a script, when needed. There are times in a shell script that you need to repeat a set of commands until a specific condition has been met. This need occurs when processing all the files in a directory, all the users on a system, or all the lines in a text file. The loop types available for Bash shell scripts include `for`, `while`, and `until`.

Master It You are writing a shell script that needs to process lines in a text file. One particular line toward the bottom of the file contains only the text `stop here`. You are reading in the text file lines one at a time, keeping only the line's text, and putting it into the variable `fileLine`. What type of loop should you use in your script, and what is the syntax of that loop's first line?

Create and use functions in shell scripts. User-defined functions are blocks of script code that you assign a name to and reuse anywhere in your shell script. When you need your script to execute that block of code, you call the function using the name you assigned to it. This provides scripts with the ability to keep blocks of code within a single location, so any changes that the code needs are done in only one place in the script.

Master It As you are creating a shell script, you recognize that you are writing these four lines of code over and over again:

```
echo "Error in processing file, $1."
echo "Check that the $1 file exists and contains data."
echo "This script will now exit..."
exit
```

Properly write a function named `errorMessage` that will allow you to turn these four lines of code into a single line (except for the function declaration) throughout the script.

Chapter 20

Managing Web Servers

The most popular use of Linux in the server environment is as a web server. Linux web servers dominate the Internet and are also popular for hosting internal corporate intranet applications. Everything from serving static web pages to hosting dynamic web applications often runs faster and more efficiently on a Linux server platform.

IN THIS CHAPTER, YOU'LL LEARN HOW TO

- Determine the right web server for your environment
- Install and configure the Apache web server
- Install and configure the nginx web server

Linux Web Servers

There are lots of different types of web server software packages available for the Linux platform. However, two have risen to the top and are most commonly used in the Linux environment:

- Apache
- nginx

This section describes some background on each server and how to use them in your network environment.

Apache

By far the most used web server on the Internet is the Apache web server application. It is an open source project maintained by the Apache Software Foundation. Since it's open source, it is available free of charge for any purpose, both commercial and private, and now is commonly included in most Linux distribution repositories, making it easy to install.

Over the years, the Apache web server project has pioneered many new features that define just what web servers should support:

Loadable dynamic modules—The ability to activate and deactivate features on the fly as the web server is running.

Scalable multi-session support—The ability to easily handle multiple client requests at the same time is crucial for modern web servers.

Limiting concurrent connections—While multiuser support is crucial, so is the ability to limit the number of clients that can connect at the same time to help prevent system overload.

Bandwidth throttling—The ability to regulate the output from the web server to prevent overloading the network, even if the system can handle more connections.

Web caching (also called web proxy)—The ability to store web pages requested by multiple clients and reading additional requests from the cache rather than from the original data source.

Load balancing (also called reverse proxy)—The ability to act as a single point of connection for clients and then redirect requests to multiple back-end servers for processing.

Common Gateway Interface (CGI)—The ability to forward web page content to internal server programs, commonly used for processing embedded scripting code.

Virtual hosting—The ability to host multiple domains on a single web server.

User-based web page hosting—The ability to allow individual users on the system to host their own web pages.

With Apache, all of these features, plus a lot more, are easily enabled or disabled using simple text-based configuration files.

APACHE SERVER VERSIONS

One confusing issue with the Apache web server is that there are currently two separate versions supported. The 1.3.x version thread supports older installations of the Apache web server. It's mostly maintained to support bug fixes and security patches for legacy systems. New Apache web server installations should use the 2.x version thread. Most Linux distributions differentiate the two versions by calling the 2.x version by the name Apache2.

---

nginx

While it too can operate as a standard web server, the nginx (pronounced "engine-X") web server is better known as a *reverse proxy* server. As you can probably guess, a reverse proxy server does the opposite of what a web proxy server does. Instead of processing requests from multiple clients to a single web server, a reverse proxy server processes requests from a single client to multiple web servers. This technique is also known as *load balancing*.

A load balancing server receives HTTP requests from clients and sends them to a specific server in a pool of common web servers for processing. Each web server in the pool contains the same data and can process the same HTTP requests. The load balancing process helps distribute the client load on multiple web servers in a high-traffic environment, helping prevent overloading and slow performance.

The remainder of this chapter walks through how to install and set up each of these web servers in your Linux environment.

The Apache Web Server

With the overall popularity of the Apache web server, most Linux distributions have installation packages that make setting up a basic Apache web server easy. The difficult part comes if you need to customize special features. This section walks through both the installation of a basic Apache web server setup and how to dig into the Apache configuration files to help customize your web environment.

Installing an Apache Server

As mentioned, most Linux server distributions include the Apache web server software as easy-to-install software packages. For example, in the Ubuntu Linux server distribution, the Apache web server package is called apache2. You install the basic Apache server using a single package:

```
$ sudo apt-get install apache2
```

This installs the latest version of the Apache 2.x web server supported by the Ubuntu server version. Once you install the Apache server, the installation package automatically configures the server to start at boot time and serve data files from the /var/www/html directory on the server.

After the Apache server is running, you can open a browser and connect to your Linux server. Figure 20.1 shows the default index.html file that is created for Ubuntu servers.

FIGURE 20.1
The default Apache web page for Ubuntu

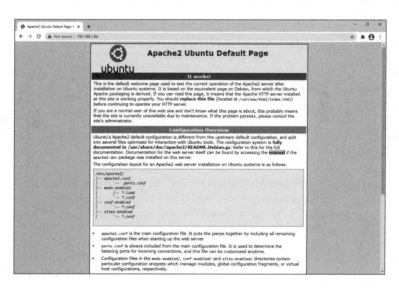

For Red Hat–based Linux servers, the Apache package is called httpd (this is because the name of the Apache server program is httpd). You can use the standard dnf package installer to install it:

```
# dnf install httpd
```

While not specified in the filename, this is the Apache 2.x version of the server. Unlike the Ubuntu Linux distribution, the Red Hat package doesn't automatically start the Apache web server, nor does it start it at boot time. To do that, you'll need to use the systemctl command:

```
# systemctl start httpd
# systemctl enable httpd
```

Since Red Hat servers have firewall protection enabled by default, you'll also need to allow HTTP connections through the firewall:

```
# firewall-cmd --zone=public --add-service=http --permanent
```

The Red Hat–based distributions also serve data files from the /var/www/html directory by default. Figure 20.2 shows the default index.html file that is created for CentOS.

FIGURE 20.2
The default Apache web page for CentOS

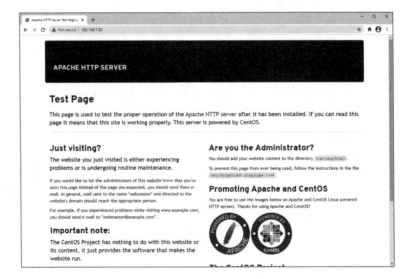

You can start, stop, restart, and check the status of the Apache program using the apache2ctl utility. (Some Red Hat–based distributions such as CentOS use apachectl even for the 2.x versions.) Table 20.1 shows the commands you can use with apache2ctl.

The status and fullstatus commands are a handy way to check on the Apache web server. However, they display the Apache status as a web page, which requires a text-based command-line browser. Most Linux distributions don't install a command-line browser by default. The Lynx command-line browser is the most popular, and it's available in most Linux distribution repositories.

TABLE 20.1: The apache2ctl Utility Commands

COMMAND	DESCRIPTION
start	Starts the Apache server
stop	Stops the Apache server, terminating any active connections
restart	Sends a SIGHUP signal to the Apache server to restart it, closing any existing connections
fullstatus	Displays a full status report from the Apache server
status	Displays a short status report from the Apache server
graceful	Restarts the Apache server, but existing connections are not terminated
graceful-stop	Stops the Apache server, but existing connections are not terminated
configtest	Parses the configuration files and reports any syntax errors
help	Displays the list of commands.

ADVANCED FEATURES

The core Apache software package for both Ubuntu and Red Hat installs a basic web server without many additional features. To customize the web server to support advanced features such as server-side programming, you'll have to install additional software packages. Unfortunately, different Linux distributions bundle different Apache features into different software packages. Consult your specific Linux distribution documentation to determine which packages you need to install to support the Apache features you want to use.

Configuring the Apache Server

A great feature of the Apache web server is that it uses simple text-based configuration files to manage the behavior of the server. The configuration file controls every feature of the server, giving you complete control over just how the Apache web server operates.

Unfortunately, there isn't a standard location or filename for the Apache configuration file. The main locations and files that you'll need to remember are as follows:

/etc/apache/apache.conf—Apache 1.3.x installation for Ubuntu servers

/etc/apache2/apache2.conf—Apache2 installation for Ubuntu servers

/etc/httpd/conf/httpd.conf—Apache 1.3.x and 2.x installation for Red Hat servers

---

MULTIPLE CONFIGURATION FILES

Another confusing issue that you'll most likely run into is that not all of the Apache configuration settings are necessarily stored in one configuration file. Often, Linux distributions move configuration settings for separate features into their own configuration files, and they use the INCLUDE directive in the main configuration file to include them in the configuration. You will need to consult the documentation for your specific Linux distribution to find out how the Apache configuration files are arranged.

The following sections walk through some of the different configuration settings that you'll run into in standard Apache configurations.

BASIC SETUP

When you look inside an Apache configuration file, the first thing you'll see are lots of lines that start with a pound sign (#). The pound sign denotes a comment line, allowing you to embed comments within the configuration file.

You define actual configuration settings using a directive keyword and then, optionally, a value for the setting, such as the following:

```
DocumentRoot "/var/www/html"
```

This directive sets the default directory for the Apache server to the /var/www/html directory on the Linux server. As you peruse through the configuration file, you'll see lots of directives setting basic features for the server. Table 20.2 shows the main settings that you'll be interested in.

By default, settings that you define in the main configuration area are called *global settings*. They apply to the main Apache web server when it starts.

You can also define *conditional settings* that apply only when specific conditions are met, such as if an environment variable is defined.

You define conditional settings as a block of directives. The block uses the following format:

```
<IfDefine variable>
    Directive
</IfDefine>
```

The <IfDefine> marker defines the start of the block, and the </IfDefine> marker defines the end of the block. The Apache server only processes the directives listed in the block if the variable is set.

Likewise, you can use *module settings* that apply only when specific modules are loaded. The <IfModule> condition specifies directives that are processed only when a specified module is loaded using the LoadModule directive.

Finally, you can use *directory settings* that apply only to specific directories on the server. The <Directory> condition specifies the directives that apply only to the directory path specified in the setting:

TABLE 20.2:   Common Apache Configuration Directives

DIRECTIVE	DESCRIPTION
Listen	The TCP port (and optional IP address) to listen for client requests
User	The user account used to start the Apache server daemon
Group	The group account used to start the Apache server daemon
ServerAdmin	The email address of the server administrator
ServerName	The domain name of the server
ServerRoot	The location of the base configuration files
DocumentRoot	The location of the default data directory
DirectoryIndex	The default file served when a client requests an index of a directory
ErrorDocument	The file to serve when a specific error type occurs
ErrorLog	The log file location to use for logging error messages
LogFormat	The format of each log file entry
AccessFileName	The file that lists restrictions on web page files in a directory
Include	Includes configuration settings defined in an external file
StartServers	The number of servers to start to handle concurrent requests
MaxClients	The maximum number of servers to handle concurrent requests
MinSpareServers	The minimum number of extra servers to have running
MaxSpareServers	The maximum number of extra servers to have running
LoadModule	Load and enable the specified feature module into the server

```
<Directory /var/www/html/mydata>
    Directive
</Directory>
```

The directives specified in this block apply only when clients attempt to access files stored in that directory.

APACHE LOGS

The Apache web server creates two types of log files by default:

◆   Error logs

◆   Access logs

As you can probably guess, the error log keeps track of any errors that occur while the Apache web server is running. The location of the error log is defined using the ErrorDocument directive in the configuration file. Usually, the error log is located in the /var/log/apache2/error.log file in Ubuntu servers, and in the /var/log/httpd/error_log file in Red Hat servers (note the underscore instead of the period in the filename).

You can customize the format for entries in the error log using the LogFormat directive in the configuration file. By default, error log entries look like this:

```
# cat error_log
[Sat Mar 27 09:55:58.296217 2021] [core:notice] [pid 6142:tid
 140605549128000] SELinux policy enabled; httpd running as context
system_u:system_r:httpd_t:s0
[Sat Mar 27 09:55:58.298306 2021] [suexec:notice] [pid 6142:tid
140605549128000] AH01232: suEXEC mechanism enabled (wrapper:
/usr/sbin/suexec)
AH00558: httpd: Could not reliably determine the server's fully qualified
domain name, using 192.168.1.92. Set the 'ServerName' directive globally to
suppress this message
[Sat Mar 27 09:55:58.336220 2021] [lbmethod_heartbeat:notice] [pid 6142:tid
140605549128000] AH02282: No slotmem from mod_heartmonitor
[Sat Mar 27 09:55:58.336554 2021] [http2:warn] [pid 6142:tid
140605549128000] AH02951: mod_ssl does not seem to be enabled
[Sat Mar 27 09:55:58.337692 2021] [mpm_event:notice] [pid 6142:tid
140605549128000] AH00489: Apache/2.4.37 (centos) configured -- resuming
normal operations
[Sat Mar 27 09:55:58.337702 2021] [core:notice] [pid 6142:tid
140605549128000] AH00094: Command line: '/usr/sbin/httpd -D FOREGROUND'
[Sat Mar 27 09:58:37.678050 2021] [autoindex:error] [pid 6146:tid
140604646274816] [client 192.168.1.71:60218] AH01276: Cannot serve
directory /var/www/html/: No matching DirectoryIndex (index.html) found,
and server-generated directory index forbidden by Options directive
```

Notice that the entries in the error log aren't necessarily all errors. In this example, the Apache web server is documenting notices that appear when it starts up.

The *access log* is normally located in the same directory as the error log and is called either access.log (for Ubuntu servers) or access_log (for Red Hat servers). It documents all requests made by clients. By default, the access log entries look like this:

```
192.168.1.71 - - [27/Mar/2021:09:58:37 -0400] "GET / HTTP/1.1" 403 4288 "-"
"Mozilla/5.0 (Windows NT 10.0; Win64; x64) AppleWebKit/537.36 (KHTML, like
Gecko) Chrome/89.0.4389.90 Safari/537.36"
192.168.1.71 - - [27/Mar/2021:09:58:37 -0400] "GET
/noindex/common/css/styles.css HTTP/1.1" 200 71634 "http://192.168.1.92/"
"Mozilla/5.0 (Windows NT 10.0; Win64; x64) AppleWebKit/537.36 (KHTML, like
Gecko) Chrome/89.0.4389.90 Safari/537.36"
192.168.1.71 - - [27/Mar/2021:09:58:37 -0400] "GET
/noindex/common/css/bootstrap.min.css HTTP/1.1" 200 99548
"http://192.168.1.92/" "Mozilla/5.0 (Windows NT 10.0; Win64; x64)
AppleWebKit/537.36 (KHTML, like Gecko) Chrome/89.0.4389.90 Safari/537.36"
```

```
192.168.1.71 - - [27/Mar/2021:09:58:37 -0400] "GET
/noindex/common/images/pb-apache.png HTTP/1.1" 200 103267
"http://192.168.1.92/" "Mozilla/5.0 (Windows NT 10.0; Win64; x64)
AppleWebKit/537.36 (KHTML, like Gecko) Chrome/89.0.4389.90 Safari/537.36"
192.168.1.71 - - [27/Mar/2021:09:58:37 -0400] "GET
/noindex/common/images/pb-centos.png HTTP/1.1" 200 13122
"http://192.168.1.92/" "Mozilla/5.0 (Windows NT 10.0; Win64; x64)
AppleWebKit/537.36 (KHTML, like Gecko) Chrome/89.0.4389.90 Safari/537.36"
192.168.1.71 - - [27/Mar/2021:09:58:37 -0400] "GET
/noindex/common/images/centos-header.png HTTP/1.1" 200 28888
"http://192.168.1.92/noindex/common/css/styles.css" "Mozilla/5.0 (Windows
NT 10.0; Win64; x64) AppleWebKit/537.36 (KHTML, like Gecko)
Chrome/89.0.4389.90 Safari/537.36"
192.168.1.71 - - [27/Mar/2021:09:59:29 -0400] "-" 408 - "-" "-"
192.168.1.71 - - [27/Mar/2021:10:06:53 -0400] "GET /badpage.html HTTP/1.1"
404 196 "-" "Mozilla/5.0 (Windows NT 10.0; Win64; x64) AppleWebKit/537.36
(KHTML, like Gecko) Chrome/89.0.4389.90 Safari/537.36"
192.168.1.71 - - [27/Mar/2021:10:06:53 -0400] "GET /favicon.ico HTTP/1.1"
404 196 "http://192.168.1.92/badpage.html" "Mozilla/5.0 (Windows NT 10.0;
Win64; x64) AppleWebKit/537.36 (KHTML, like Gecko) Chrome/89.0.4389.90
Safari/537.36"
192.168.1.71 - - [27/Mar/2021:10:07:45 -0400] "-" 408 - "-" "-"
```

The access log not only documents the file request, but can also document the browser type of the client, the OS of the client, and the IP address. You can customize the output using the LogFormat directive as well.

USER WEB HOSTING

The default configuration for most Linux distribution Apache servers is to provide one location for hosting files, called the *document root*. The DocumentRoot directive defines this location, and for both Ubuntu and Red Hat servers, it is set to the /var/www/html directory by default. Any files or directories that you want to make available to web clients are normally placed under that directory structure.

The Apache web server also provides a feature that allows each individual user on the Linux system to host their own files. To enable this feature, add the UserDir directive to the global configuration settings. The UserDir directive specifies the name of the directory in each user's HOME directory where they can host files. The most common setting is as follows:

```
UserDir public_html
```

To access files in the user's public_html directory, you must specify the username in the URL. For example, to access the file /home/rich/public_html/test.html, you'd use the URL http://localhost/~rich/test.html.

> ### WEB DIRECTORY PERMISSIONS
>
> To allow access to files in your `public_html` directory, you must grant read and execute privileges to the user or group account that runs the Apache web server. Not only will that user or group need read and execute privileges to the `public_html` directory, but also to the user's HOME directory. This can make things somewhat complicated for protecting other files in the user's HOME directory.

VIRTUAL WEB HOSTING

The basic configuration for an Apache web server assumes the host is serving files for a single server, namely, the server name or IP address that the Apache software is running on. However, Apache also allows you to host web pages for multiple domain names or IP addresses on a single physical server. This is ideal for businesses that support multiple customers, such as Internet service providers (ISPs).

The ability to host multiple web environments on a single physical server is called *virtual web hosting*. There are two ways to implement virtual web hosting in Apache:

◆ Name-based virtual hosting

◆ IP-based virtual hosting

With *name-based virtual hosting*, the physical server has multiple hostnames that point to its IP address in the DNS system. You then must configure the Apache web server to use separate directories based on the hostname the client uses in the URL request to connect. You do that using the `NameVirtualHost` directive and separate `<VirtualHost>` blocks, one for each virtual host:

```
NameVirtualHost 192.168.1.77

<VirtualHost 192.168.1.77>
    ServerName www.myhost1.com
    DocumentRoot /var/www/html/host1
</VirtualHost>

<VirtualHost 192.168.1.77>
    ServerName www,myhost2.com
    DocumentRoot /var/www/html/host2
</VirtualHost>
```

The `NameVirtualHost` directive defines the IP address that the server listens on. Then, you must create a separate `<VirtualHost>` block to define the IP address and use the `ServerName` directive to define the hostname that the client uses in the request. Each separate hostname points to a different `DocumentRoot` area by specifying separate `DocumentRoot` directives.

With *IP-based virtual hosting*, the server must listen for incoming requests on multiple IP addresses. Each IP address is assigned a different hostname in the DNS system.

With IP-based virtual hosting, you must define multiple IP addresses on the server either by having separate physical network cards in the server or by defining multiple IP addresses for the same network interface using the ifconfig network command.

After you configure your Linux server to support multiple IP addresses, you must configure the Apache web server to listen to each IP address using multiple Listen directives. After that, just define separate <VirtualHost> blocks to define the hostname and DocumentRoot area for each IP address:

```
Listen 192.168.1.77:80
Listen 192.168.1.78:80
<VirtualHost 192.168.1.77>
    Servername www.myhost1.com
    DocumentRoot /var/www/html/myhost1
</VirtualHost>
<VirtualHost 192.168.1.78>
    Servername www.myhost2.com
    DocumentRoot /var/www/html/myhost2
</VirtualHost>
```

One advantage to IP-based virtual hosting is that you can have two separate Apache programs running at the same time, each one listening on a different IP address. Each Apache program can have a separate configuration, making it easier to separate out settings for each server.

ACCESS RESTRICTION

While the original intention of web servers was to provide easy access to public data, there are times when it would be handy to provide restricted access to data, such as an internal corporate intranet application. The Apache web server provides a few different methods for implementing authentication, forcing clients to log in before granting access to documents based on the provided authentication.

Apache provides authentication features using separate loadable modules. Originally, the Apache web server accomplished that with the mod_auth module, which provided authentication using a text-based file that lists user accounts and encrypted passwords. However, that module has been replaced as of Apache 2.1 with other more advanced modules. The more common authentication modules in newer versions of Apache are the following:

mod_authn_file—Uses a text-based file to list user accounts and encrypted passwords for access (the direct replacement for mod_auth)

mod_authn_anon—Uses a list of usernames but no passwords to restrict access

mod_authn_db—Uses a Berkeley database format file to list user accounts and passwords to restrict access

mod_authn_dbm—Uses a Unix dbm–formatted database file to list user accounts and passwords to restrict access

mod_authnz_ldap—Uses an LDAP network database for user authentication mod_authnz_mysql—Uses a MySQL database for user authentication

mod_access—Uses a list of IP address, hostnames, or domains to restrict access

The mod_auth method (now called mod_authn_file) uses a text-based user file that's created using the htpasswd utility in Apache. To add a new user account to the authentication user file, specify the file using the -c option and then specify the user account to add, like this:

```
# htpasswd -c /var/www/html/passwords rich
New password:
Re-type new password:
Adding password for user rich
#
```

Once you create the user file, you must reference it in the Apache configuration file to use for authentication. There are two approaches to doing that.

One method is to add the authentication configuration settings in the <Directory> section for the block you need to protect in the main Apache configuration file:

```
<Directory /var/www/html>
    AuthName "Restricted Area"
    AuthType Basic
    AuthUserFile /var/www/html/passwords
    Require valid-user
</Directory>
```

There are a few different directives needed to tell Apache about the authentication protection. The AuthName directive provides the title of the login dialog box that appears when it asks for the user ID and password. The AuthUserFile directive points to the password file created using the htpasswd utility. When a user attempts to access a file in that directory, the browser will produce a login dialog box, as shown in Figure 20.3.

FIGURE 20.3

Basic web page authentication

The other method to provide basic authentication is to use a special filename called `.htaccess` in the directory that you need to protect. The `.htaccess` file contains the same authentication directives that we used in the main configuration file. To tell Apache to use the `.htaccess` file, the `<Directory>` block must contain the `AllowOverride` directive. Using the `.htaccess` file decentralizes the authentication configurations instead of placing them all in the main configuration file.

There's also an `AuthGroupFile` directive that allows you to bundle user accounts into groups. You can then grant the entire group access to specific areas on the web server.

The `mod_access` authentication method is another popular way to restrict access to web pages. Instead of using a user ID/password challenge, it allows you to restrict pages based on the IP address of the clients. It uses simple `Deny` and `Allow` directives to list individual IP addresses or network addresses to deny or allow access. Here's an example of using that method:

```
<Directory /var/www/html>
    Order Deny,Allow
    Deny from All
    Allow from 192.168.1.0/255.255.255.0
</Directory>
```

The `Order` directive determines which rule set is checked first. In this example, we set it to deny (block) all clients, but only allow clients that are on the 192.168.1.0 subnet.

Hosting Dynamic Web Applications

In the old days, all content provided in web pages was static. To update the information on your website, you had to manually open the appropriate HTML file, enter the changes to the content, and then save the new version. In this day of constantly changing content, that just doesn't work. It would be impossible for a large online store to have programmers making manual changes to web pages for each new product that came in.

Instead, modern websites use *dynamic web programming*. Dynamic web programming uses embedded program code inside an HTML file to dynamically generate content. Often, the content is based on external data, such as items stored in a database. With dynamic web programming, you just need to write the web application once and then modify the data stored in the database as needed to update the web page content.

Apache supports dynamic web pages by supporting a host of different programming languages. There are, however, two different ways that Apache uses to do that. The following sections describe each of these methods and how to implement them in your Apache web server.

THE COMMON GATEWAY INTERFACE

The simple way for the Apache web server to process program code is to pass it off to another program to process. The Apache server acts as a gateway to the main program interpreter. This feature in Apache is thus called the *Common Gateway Interface* (CGI).

The CGI feature uses the filename extension to detect when a web page file has embedded code and then passes the file off to an external program language interpreter based on the filename extension. The interpreter then processes the code and passes any output from the interpreter back to the Apache web server to send to the client as content. The output must be standard HTML code for the client to process it as a web page.

The programming languages that you can use with CGI are limited only by the languages that are installed on your Linux system. Because of the text nature of HTML pages, CGI applications commonly use scripting languages, such as Perl, Python, and Bash shell scripts. However, there are CGI interfaces for more advanced languages such as C and C++.

To configure Apache to pass code to an external interpreter, you must first have the CGI feature installed in your Apache setup. For Ubuntu servers running Perl scripts, this means installing the `libapache2-mod-perl2` module. For Red Hat servers, it's the `perl-CGI` module.

After you install the appropriate module, you must make some changes to the Apache configuration file. You'll need to add the `ScriptAlias` directive to point to the directory that can contain scripts, and the `AddHandler` directive to tell Apache which filenames to process with CGI:

```
ScriptAlias /cgi-bin/ /var/www/cgi-bin
AddHandler cgi-script .cgi .pl
```

These lines allow you to place Perl scripts in the /var/www/cgi-bin directory. The scripts must end with the .pl file extension for the Apache server to process them properly. Also, the scripts must start with a line that invokes the required language interpreter:

```
#!/usr/bin/perl
```

This tells the Bash shell to invoke the Perl interpreter to process the script.

PROGRAMMING MODULES

A faster way of handling embedded program scripts in web pages is to use installable modules. Apache includes modules for most popular web programming languages, such as the following:

- `mod_perl`
- `mod_php`
- `mod_python`
- `mod_ruby`

The tricky part of using Apache programming modules is finding them in the Linux distribution. In Red Hat servers, the PHP module package is just called php, while the Perl module package is called mod_perl. For Ubuntu, you'll need the php5 and libapache2-mod-php5 packages for PHP, and the libapache2-mod-perl2 package for Perl.

The nice thing about using the module packages is that they usually do all of the configuration work for you. For example, after installing the PHP module, you should see some new lines in your Apache configuration file:

```
LoadModule php5_module modules.libphp5.so
AddHandler php5-script .php
AddType application/x-httpd-php .php
DirectoryIndex index.html index.php
```

The `AddHandler` directive tells the Apache server that the PHP module should redirect files ending with the .php file extension to the PHP server process.

PROGRAMMING SUPPORT WARNINGS

Adding program processing to the Apache web server does open your server to additional attack entry points. Be careful when adding these features. For CGI, make sure you restrict scripts to a specific directory and that you monitor the scripts placed in that directory for unauthorized activity. For program modules such as PHP and Perl, you have to be more careful, as any document served on the server can contain embedded program code.

Creating a Secure Web Server

Protecting data transmitted across the Internet has become a high priority for most corporations. These days, it's recommended to use the secure version of HTTP—HTTPS—for all web transactions.

The Apache web server supports HTTPS sessions, but it requires quite a bit of work. You must have a private/public key pair to use for the encryption, plus have a signed certificate to validate your public key to clients. Creating an HTTPS server with Apache involves six steps:

1. Install the Apache SSL module.

2. Create a public/private key pair.

3. Create a certificate signing request (CSR).

4. Have the CSR signed by a trusted certificate authority (CA) to create a certificate.

5. Install the certificate and key files in your Apache setup.

6. Configure Apache to use the certificate.

To use encryption on your Linux system, you'll need to ensure that the mod_ssl Apache module is installed. You'll also need the OpenSSL software package installed so your server can handle certificates.

There are a few additional configuration items you'll need to add or change to support HTTPS connections. For the Listen directive, ensure that you have a separate line to listen on TCP port 443, the default port for HTTPS:

```
Listen 443
```

Also, look for the <VirtualHost> directive that defines the area that you want to protect with encrypted communication. In that configuration block, add these new directives:

```
SSLEngine On
SSLCertificateFile    /etc/apache2/certs/mycert.pem
SSLCertificateKeyFile    /etc/apache2/certs/myserver.key
```

These lines enable encryption on the Apache server and add the certificate and private key needed for HTTPS. Now your network clients should be able to connect to your Apache web server using the HTTPS protocol.

The nginx Server

While the Apache web server is by far the most popular web server running on the Internet, it's starting to get some competition from a new player. The nginx web server has made some great strides in popularity, as it's used for some high-profile commercial websites.

One of the benefits of nginx is that it doesn't use separate program threads to handle each client like Apache does. Instead, it uses an asynchronous architecture that allows it to spawn client threads within the main program as needed. This helps reduce the memory footprint required for each client that connects to the web server, and thus the same server can handle more clients.

Another benefit of nginx is its ability to work as a reverse proxy server. This allows you to place a main nginx server at the front end of your network and place your application servers behind a firewall, protected from the Internet. Your website visitors connect to the nginx server on the front, and it forwards the requests to the back-end servers.

This section walks through the basics of setting up an nginx server and how to use it as a basic reverse proxy server.

Installing nginx

Because it's relatively new, many Linux distributions don't include the nginx software in their main software repositories. Fortunately, the Ubuntu and Red Hat Linux server distributions do, so installing it is easy. For an Ubuntu server, use the following:

```
$ sudo apt-get install nginx
```

And for a Red Hat server, use this:

```
$ sudo dnf install nginx
```

These commands install the nginx server program and configuration files. For Ubuntu servers, the nginx server starts automatically, but for Red Hat servers, you'll need to manually start it and set it to start at boot time:

```
$ sudo systemctl start nginx
$ sudo systemctl enable nginx
```

Unlike Apache, the nginx software doesn't have a command-line application to control the server, so in both Ubuntu and Red Hat environments, you have to use the standard `systemctl` command to determine the status of the server or to start or stop the server.

Also, remember that if you haven't already done so, you'll need to open the HTTP service on the firewall for Red Hat servers.

RUNNING MULTIPLE WEB SERVERS

Because nginx works as a normal web server, it will start on TCP port 80, the default HTTP network port. If you already have the Apache web server installed on your system, you'll need to stop it while testing nginx and then stop nginx if you want to restart the Apache web server. Alternatively, you can configure them to listen on different TCP ports so they can both run at the same time.

When you've successfully installed nginx, you can test the default web settings by opening your browser and going to the server address, as shown in Figure 20.4.

FIGURE 20.4

The nginx default web page in CentOS

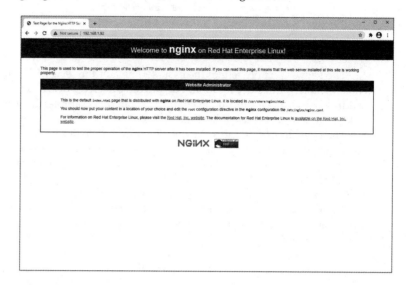

Configuring nginx

As you would expect, the configuration files for nginx are stored in the /etc/nginx directory. The nginx.conf file is the main configuration file, but as with the Apache web server, nginx uses the include directive to allow configuration settings to be defined in external files. For Ubuntu servers, the main website directives are defined in the /etc/nginx/sites-enabled/default file.

The nginx configuration has many of the same features as the Apache web server, so looking at the basic configuration, you'll probably be able to pick out most of the settings:

```
server {
        listen          80 default_server;
        listen          [::]:80 default_server;
        server_name     _;
        root            /usr/share/nginx/html;

        # Load configuration files for the default server block.
        include /etc/nginx/default.d/*.conf;

        location / {
        }

        error_page 404 /404.html;
            location = /40x.html {
```

```
        }

        error_page 500 502 503 504 /50x.html;
            location = /50x.html {
        }
    }
```

The server section defines the basic settings for the server. The root directive defines the document root directory location. The listen directives define the TCP ports and network addresses to listen for incoming connections. In this example, the server is listening on both the IPv4 and IPv6 addresses of the Linux server.

The root directive defines the document root directory for the server. The location directive defines settings unique for specific locations on the server. The entry shown in this example defines the error messages that should be returned when a file is not found in the root directory or is temporarily unavailable.

The beauty of nginx is in the location section. In here, you can define proxy addresses for multiple back-end web servers to implement the reverse proxy feature. Thanks to this feature, the nginx web server is gaining in popularity and may soon become the de facto web server in Linux.

 Real World Scenario

TESTING YOUR WEB SERVER FROM THE COMMAND LINE

This exercise demonstrates how to test a web server using the Telnet command-line command. This allows you to submit HTTP requests to the server and see the HTTP response codes that it returns. To do that, follow these steps:

1. Log in as root or acquire root privileges by using su or sudo with each of the following commands.

2. Ensure that you have the Apache web server installed. Open a command prompt and then type **sudo apt-get install apache2** to install the Apache web server package on your Ubuntu server, or **sudo dnf install httpd** to install Apache on your Red Hat server.

3. For Red Hat servers, start the Apache web server by typing **sudo systemctl start httpd**.

4. Test the Apache web server by typing **telnet localhost 80** at a command line (you may have to also install the Telnet package on your system). If your system has the Apache web server running, you should be greeted by the Telnet banner, but nothing from the Apache web server as it's waiting for your request.

5. Request the default web page from the server by typing **GET /**, and then hit the Enter key to submit the request.

6. The Apache web server should return the HTML code contained in the index.html file from the /var/www/html directory.

7. Now test attempting to retrieve an invalid web page. Connect to the Apache web server by typing **telnet localhost 80** at a command line. At the prompt, type **GET /badfile.html** and then hit the Enter key. You should see some HTML code for a generic error message web page that the browser would display to inform you that it could not find the file on the system.

8. Remove the Telnet package from your server, as it can be a security risk if left enabled.

The Bottom Line

Determine the right web server for your environment. Web servers are the heart of the Internet, and Linux is the main server platform used for supporting them. There are many different web server software packages available for Linux, but the two most popular are Apache and nginx. The Apache web server is the oldest and most popular web server package. It is highly customizable and has defined many of the features expected from web servers. The nginx web server is relatively new to the web server game but is a powerful player. It can support larger client bases on the same physical hardware than Apache, making it ideal for high-traffic environments. It also has made a name for itself in the reverse web proxy world. A reverse web proxy sits in front of multiple back-end application servers and provides load balancing for clients.

> **Master It** Your company wants to implement load balancing using several web servers to host your corporate website. The website uses PHP to retrieve data stored in a database to produce the website content. Describe a good web server solution to meet these requirements.

Install and configure the Apache web server. The Apache web server is available for installation from the standard Ubuntu and Red Hat repositories. Adding features to the Apache web server often requires installing additional packages. Customizing the Apache web server is as easy as changing configuration settings. You use the UserDir directive to allow users to create their own websites on the server, separate from each other. You use the VirtualHost directives to host web pages for multiple domains on the same physical server. You can also implement client authentication on your website, requiring clients to log in to access content. The Apache server also provides for secure transactions by using HTTPS and encrypting network traffic between the client and the server.

> **Master It** You've received a frantic phone call from the company web administrator informing you that after changing the configuration file she can't start the Apache web server, it keeps failing. What command should you use to see why the Apache server won't start?

Install and configure the nginx web server. With the growing popularity of the nginx web server, both the Ubuntu and Red Hat server repositories include it. After installing nginx, you can customize it by changing the nginx.conf configuration file. Many of the configuration directives for nginx are similar to the Apache, so migrating from one to the other is a fairly simple process.

> **Master It** Customers are complaining that they can't connect to your corporate website running on the nginx web server. What commands can you use to check the status of the server and restart it if necessary?

Chapter 21

Managing Database Servers

Data is as important as talent, strategy, and sales, and is often central to a business's success. In fact, data is typically considered a company's most important asset. We are now in a data-driven society, and the sheer volume of useful data is growing astronomically. Protecting and managing this data provides your organization with a base for data analysis that can lead to a competitive advantage . . . or just plain survival.

While you may not be involved in the data analytics side of your company, as a system administrator, you are on the data management side. Whatever data your establishment decides to keep and scrutinize, it is up to you to make sure your fellow employees have fast and appropriate access to it through your administration of the database servers.

IN THIS CHAPTER, YOU WILL LEARN TO

- ◆ Understand basic DBMS components
- ◆ Create user accounts within MariaDB
- ◆ Use SQL to query a MariaDB database
- ◆ Install PostgreSQL on Linux
- ◆ Set up roles within PostgreSQL

Linux Database Servers

We've looked at a lot of text files so far in this book, and they are useful for many different purposes such as storing configuration information, boot messages, Bash scripts, and so on. However, when you have complex data that needs to be stored, processed, and analyzed, simple text files don't work well. Text files are often referred to as *flat files*, because only basic relationships can exist between the data they contain.

Databases were created to fill the need for complex connections between individual data items. While data is the focus, there are other pieces that make up a *database management system* (DBMS). A DBMS typically consists of the following parts:

- ◆ Database data file(s)
- ◆ Query-language interface
- ◆ Database engine

Organizing the Data

Back in the 1970s, a database management system architecture, called a *relational DBMS* (RDBMS), was first conceived. This still-popular model organizes data into three levels:

Database A database is the largest of the three levels, and it is used to group together related data. While you can have a large single database on a system, it's typical to create a database for every application on a server that needs one. Each database is required to have its own unique name, so it's wise to name the database in a way that relates to the application.

Table There are typically multiple tables per database. This mid-level organization further refines the data's groupings. For example, if the database contains tree information for a site that sells live fruit trees through a website, one table in the database might be specifically for apple trees, another table for cherry trees, another table for pear trees, and a fourth table for orange trees. Grouping data in a database into tables is called *data normalization*.

Field The finest level of detail for data in a database is the *field*. Using the apple tree table in our tree database as an example, the fields for a single apple tree may be item number, apple tree type, description, tree size, apple color, blooming period, pollinator group, harvest period, and growth zones.

In the apple tree table, each apple tree sold by the company would have its own *record*. A table record is a collection of fields about the same item. So, in our apple tree table, each type of apple tree sold would have its own record, identified by the item number. This item number is a *primary key*. Primary keys are used to uniquely identify each record within a table.

It's helpful to see a pictorial view of a database table. Sticking with our fruit-trees-for-sale application, a representation of the database's apple tree table is shown snipped in Figure 21.1.

FIGURE 21.1

Apple tree table representation

Apple Tree Table

Item #	Tree Type	Description	Tree Size	Apple Color	Blooming Period	Pollinator Group	Harvest Period	Grow Zones
[...]								
3247	Baldwin	Impressive American variety...	Std	Red and Green	Mid-Late Spring	4	October	5-8
3248	Baldwin	Impressive American variety...	Dwarf	Red and Green	Mid-Late Spring	4	October	5-8
3249	Sundance	Favorite dessert apple...	Std	Yellow and Red	Mid-Late Spring	4	Mid to Late October	5-8
3250	Sundance	Favorite dessert apple...	Dwarf	Yellow and Red	Mid-Late Spring	4	Mid to Late October	5-8
3251	Redfree	Sweet and a little acidic...	Std	Red and Green	Early-Mid Spring	3	August	4-8
[...]								

In the representation, each row is a record in the table, which is why sometimes database table records are called *rows*. Each column within the apple tree table is a field, which are why fields are sometimes called *columns*. Notice that some fields for the records contain the same data, while others do not. For example, item numbers 3247 and 3248 share all the same data in their record fields, except for their primary key (Item #) and TreeSize—one record has standard (Std) in that field, and one contains Dwarf. A record in a table is a single occurrence of *all* the values in the record's data fields.

Fields can be different types of data. Table 21.1 shows these standard database data types for an RDBMS.

TABLE 21.1: RDBMS Data Types

DATA TYPE	DESCRIPTION
bool	Boolean value representing either true or false
char(*n*)	Character string of a fixed *n* characters in length
date	Date expressed in *YYYY–MM–DD* format
datetime	Date and time expressed in *YYYY–MM–DD HH:MM:SS* format
float	Floating-point number
int	Integer number
text	Character string of a variable length
varchar(*n*)	Character string of a variable *n* or fewer characters in length

These data types are slightly different depending on which RDMBS you use. Also, they may add a few additional types of data.

Querying the Data

Created in the 1970s, Structured Query Language (SQL) was declared a standard by the American National Standards Institute (ANSI) in the mid-1980s. Pronounced *sequel*, this language is still used to communicate with databases using an RDBMS, and the standard has continued to evolve, making it stronger and more flexible.

What's exciting about SQL is that when you learn the language's syntax, you can use it on nearly all relational databases with few modifications. So, when you have a Linux RDBMS installed on your system, you'll have a place to learn and practice using SQL.

SQL consists of specific instruction commands that are crafted into statements to interface with the database. SQL commands are typically grouped into four different categories (though some special SQL commands fall outside of these categorizations):

◆   Data definition language (DDL)

◆   Data manipulation language (DML)

- ◆ Transaction control language (TCL)

- ◆ Data control language (DCL)

We'll only be using a few basic commands in this chapter that fall into the DDL and DML categories as well as a few that don't fall into any of these groupings. Table 21.2 describes the commands.

TABLE 21.2:   A Few Basic SQL Commands

COMMAND	CATEGORY	DESCRIPTION
CREATE	DDL	Creates a table, database, or user account
DESCRIBE	n/a	Lists a table's field definitions
DROP	DDL	Deletes a table, a database, or a user account
GRANT	DDL	Grants access to the selected item for the designated user account
INSERT	DML	Adds new data records to a table
SELECT	DML	Queries data in a table
SHOW	n/a	Displays the selected item
UPDATE	DML	Modifies current data records in a table
USE	n/a	Selects a database to use

Notice that the commands are in uppercase. This is typical of most SQL commands. Be aware that with some RDBMSs, you can use either lowercase or uppercase, but good form dictates using only uppercase for SQL commands.

Controlling the Data

Access to the data that resides in the database is managed by the database engine. When an application wants to view or modify data, it has to go through the database engine to do so, as portrayed in Figure 21.2.

The database engine in some DBMSs continues to run in the background as a daemon on Linux. Daemons, covered in Chapter 10, "Booting Linux," are programs that continue to run in the background, offering a specific service. In the case of a DBMS, that service is access to data managed by the database engine.

One nice aspect about this structure is that the application doesn't have to reside on the same computer system as the database engine. Various instances of the app could run on different systems, sending requests to the database engine on the primary database server similar to what is shown in Figure 21.3.

FIGURE 21.2
App using a database
engine to access data
stored in a database

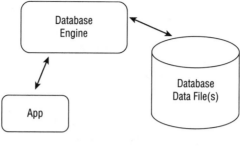

FIGURE 21.3
Apps using a database
engine to access data
stored in a database
across a network

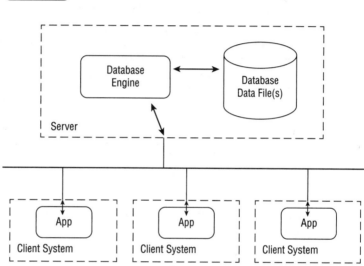

The Linux RDBMSs we're going to focus on in this chapter include MySQL, MariaDB, and PostgreSQL. They each are relational and use a SQL interface.

Installing and Using MySQL/MariaDB

Released in 1996, MySQL is one of the more popular RDBMSs used for web servers on Linux. The LAMP (Linux system, Apache web server, MySQL database server, and PHP programming language) platform can be found in Linux servers around the world still today.

MySQL was revolutionary at the time of its release, because it used indexing data to speed up data queries. The MySQL developers didn't start out trying to compete with commercial databases. Instead, they just wanted to create a simple but fast database system. So, the fancy RDBMS features were left out, and speed was the focus. Because of this development emphasis, MySQL quickly became the standard RDBMS used in many high-profile Internet web applications.

Over time, while continuing to maintain the emphasis on speedy data queries, additional RDBMS features were added, which strengthened MySQL's popularity. MySQL can run on many different platforms besides Linux, can scale its processing into multiple CPUs, provides security at the user and host levels, supports many different human languages, and so on.

UNDERSTANDING THE DIFFERENCE BETWEEN MYSQL AND MARIADB

You can think of MariaDB and MySQL as identical twins, but their developers may disagree with that statement. A more accurate claim concerning these two database systems is that MariaDB maintains nearly 100 percent compatibility with MySQL. So, the code that you wrote for a MySQL database system should work perfectly to interact with a MariaDB server.

In 2010, Oracle purchased Sun Microsystems, which had purchased MySQL AB (the original developers of MySQL) in 2008. When Oracle took over the development of MySQL, the original developer and some of the team left the project to start their own open source RDBMS project, MariaDB. This is perfectly legal with open source licensing.

Over the last several years, the MariaDB project has gained respect. Due to this and its MySQL compatibility, many Linux distributions have moved to MariaDB as a MySQL replacement package in their repositories. These distributions include Red Hat Linux and Ubuntu.

Conducting a MariaDB Installation

Installing MariaDB is fairly simple. You need super user privileges, of course, and the correct package name: `mariadb-server`. (Installing packages was covered in Chapter 3 "Installing and Maintaining Software in Ubuntu," and Chapter 5, "Installing and Maintaining Software in Red Hat.")

Here is a snipped example of installing MariaDB on Ubuntu, after updating the system's package information:

```
$ sudo apt update
[sudo] password for sysadmin:
[...]
Fetched 4124 kB in 22s (187 kB/s)
Reading package lists... Done
Building dependency tree
Reading state information... Done
[...]
$
$ sudo apt install mariadb-server
Reading package lists... Done
Building dependency tree
Reading state information... Done
[...]
The following NEW packages will be installed:
[...]
  mariadb-common mariadb-server mariadb-server-10.3 mar[...]
  mysql-common socat
[...]
Need to get 21.1 MB of archives.
After this operation, 173 MB of additional disk space will
be used.
```

```
Do you want to continue? [Y/n] Y
[...]
Fetched 21.1 MB in 39s (536 kB/s)
Preconfiguring packages ...
Selecting previously unselected package mysql-common.
[...]
Unpacking mariadb-server-10.3 (1:10.3.25-0ubuntu0.20.04.1)
[...]
Setting up mariadb-server-10.3 (1:10.3.25-0ubuntu0.20.04.1)
[...]
$ dpkg -s mariadb-server | grep Status
Status: install ok installed
```

Installing MariaDB on a Red Hat–based distribution is also fairly straightforward. Here is a snipped example of an installation on CentOS using the root account:

```
# dnf install mariadb-server
[...]
Last metadata expiration check: [...].
Dependencies resolved.
[...]
Installing:
 mariadb-server      [...]
 mariadb             [...]
 mariadb-common      [...]
[...]
Installing weak dependencies:
 mariadb-backup      [...]
[...]
Install  54 Packages

Total download size: 43 M
Installed size: 191 M
Is this ok [y/N]: y
Downloading Packages:
(1/54): mariadb-common-[...]
[...]
(7/54): mariadb-server-utils[...]
[...]
Total       1.6 MB/s |  43 MB      00:27
Running transaction check
Transaction check succeeded.
Running transaction test
Transaction test succeeded.
Running transaction
[...]
Installed products updated.
Installed:
```

```
 mariadb-[...]
 mariadb-backup[...]
 mariadb-common[...]
[...]
Complete!
#
# dnf list installed mariadb-server
Installed Packages
mariadb-server.x86_64 [...]
#
```

Even though some distribution's installation process sets the MariaDB service to start when the system boots, it's a good idea to go ahead and enable it yourself. Also start the service as shown in this snipped example on CentOS using the root account:

```
# systemctl status mariadb
• mariadb.service - MariaDB 10.3 database server
  Loaded: loaded [...] disabled; vendor pr>
  Active: inactive (dead)
    Docs: man:mysqld(8)
          https://mariadb.com/kb/en/library/systemd/
#
# systemctl enable mariadb
Created symlink /etc/systemd/system/mysql.service
/usr/lib/systemd/system/mariadb.service.
Created symlink /etc/systemd/system/mysqld.service →
/usr/lib/systemd/system/mariadb.service.
Created symlink /etc/systemd/system/
multi-user.target.wants/mariadb.service →
/usr/lib/systemd/system/mariadb.service.
#
# systemctl start mariadb
#
# systemctl status mariadb
• mariadb.service - MariaDB 10.3 database server
  Loaded: loaded [...] enabled; vendor pre>
  Active: active (running) since [...] 42s ago
    Docs: man:mysqld(8)
          https://mariadb.com/kb/en/library/systemd/
[...]
 Main PID: 27112 (mysqld)
   Status: "Taking your SQL requests now..."
    Tasks: 30 (limit: 11479)
   Memory: 84.7M
   CGroup: /system.slice/mariadb.service
```

```
       └27112 /usr/libexec/mysqld --basedir=/usr

[...]
lines 1-23)
#
```

The MariaDB server is now enabled to start when the system boots. Also, it is currently active. After you've accomplished installing the server and enabling it, MariaDB is ready to start managing your data.

 Real World Scenario

INSTALLING THE MARIADB SERVER ON YOUR UBUNTU SYSTEM

SQL code you write for MariaDB will also work for a MySQL server. Since many modern Linux distributions now support MariaDB as a replacement package for MySQL, it makes sense to install and focus on the MariaDB server. When you have the RDBMS installed, you can work on creating SQL statements to interact with it.

The following steps will take you through installing the MariaDB server RDBMS software on an Ubuntu distribution:

1. Log into your Ubuntu Linux system, using the sysadmin account and the password you created for it.

2. Update the package information on your Ubuntu system by typing **sudo apt update** and pressing Enter. Enter your account's password, if the system asks for one.

3. After you receive the command-line prompt back, install the MariaDB package by typing **sudo apt install mariadb-server** and pressing Enter. Enter your account's password, if the system asks for one.

4. During the installation process, when you receive the Do you want to continue? [Y/n] prompt, type **Y** and press Enter.

5. When you receive the command-line prompt back, check to see if the installation was successful by typing **dpkg -s mariadb-server | grep Status** and pressing Enter. If you receive a message similar to Status: install ok installed, continue on to the next step. If you do not receive this message, troubleshoot the installation. You can get additional help from Chapter 3.

6. Set the MariaDB server to start when the system is booted, by typing **sudo systemctl enable mariadb** and pressing Enter. Enter your account's password, if the system asks for one.

7. Start the MariaDB server by typing **sudo systemctl start mariadb** and pressing Enter. Enter your account's password, if the system asks for one.

8. Check to ensure that the MariaDB service is enabled (will start at boot) and active (is currently running), by typing **systemctl status mariadb** and pressing Enter. Look through the command's output for the words enabled and active. If you do not see these words, go back to step 6 and reissue the commands in steps 6 and 7, noting any error messages. If you do see these words, congratulations! Your installation of MariaDB on Ubuntu was successful, and the RDBMS is ready to manage your data.

If you are running a Red Hat–based Linux system, the process for installation is different enough from Ubuntu that it is worth your time to try it for yourself.

Real World Scenario

INSTALLING THE MARIADB SERVER ON YOUR RED HAT–BASED SYSTEM

SQL code you write for MariaDB will also work for a MySQL server. Since many modern Linux distributions now support MariaDB as a replacement package for MySQL, it makes sense to install and focus on the MariaDB server. When you have the RDBMS installed, you can work on creating SQL statements to interact with it.

The following steps will take you through installing the MariaDB server RDBMS software on a CentOS distribution:

1. Log into your CentOS system, using the `sysadmin` account and the password you created for it.

2. Jump into the `root` account by typing `su -` (don't miss that dash!) and pressing Enter. Enter the `root` account's password, when the system asks for it.

3. Update the system's package information and install the MariaDB package by typing **`dnf install mariadb-server`** and pressing Enter. Enter your account's password, if the system asks for one.

4. During the installation process, when you receive the `Is this ok [y/N]:` prompt, type **y** and press Enter.

5. When you receive the command-line prompt back, check to see if the installation was successful by typing **`dnf list installed mariadb-server`** and pressing Enter. If you receive the MariaDB package name under the heading `Installed Packages`, the installation was successful. If you do not receive this information, troubleshoot the installation. You can get additional help from Chapter 5.

6. Set the MariaDB server to start when the system is booted by typing **`systemctl enable mariadb`** and pressing Enter.

7. Start the MariaDB server by typing **`systemctl start mariadb`** and pressing Enter.

8. Check to ensure that the MariaDB service is enabled (will start at boot) and active (is currently running) by typing **`systemctl status mariadb`** and pressing Enter. Look through the command's output for the words `enabled` and `active`. If you do not see these words, go back to step 6 and reissue the commands in steps 6 and 7, noting any error messages. If you do see these words, congratulations! Your installation of MariaDB on CentOS was successful, and the RDBMS is ready to manage your data.

Accessing a MariaDB Database

You access and manage data within the MariaDB server through database user accounts. By default, a special all-powerful account called `root` (sound familiar?) is installed as an account in the RDBMS. However, since this account has full access to everything in MariaDB, it is considered a poor security practice to use it for user-level access and management of data.

It's best to create a single database account for every user account that needs access. This good security practice allows you to limit a user's access to a particular application's database and protect other managed MariaDB databases from accidental or intentional disturbance.

When you've newly installed a MariaDB server, you will need to either log into the root system account or use sudo to gain super user privileges to interface with MariaDB and create the first user account. The command to access the SQL interface to MariaDB is mysql. When you are in the interface, your prompt will look like this: MariaDB [(none)]>. This is one difference between MySQL and MariaDB. For MySQL, the prompt looks like this: MySQL [(none)]>.

To create your first user account, you may want the system's hostname, which can be obtained a variety of ways, including through the hostname command. The hostname can be used within the database account username.

It's a good practice to use the same username for the database account as the Linux system account's username. The SQL interface syntax to create a database user account is as follows:

```
CREATE USER username@hostname IDENTIFIED BY 'password';
```

Notice that at the end of the SQL syntax line, there is a semicolon (;). This lets the SQL interface know that you have completed entering the syntax for this statement. That small, but important, piece of SQL syntax is easy for those who are new to SQL to miss!

An example of creating a first MariaDB database user account on an Ubuntu system using sudo to gain super user privileges is shown here:

```
$ hostname
ubuntu-server
$
$ sudo mysql
[sudo] password for sysadmin:
Welcome to the MariaDB monitor.  Commands end with ; or \g.
Your MariaDB connection id is 42
Server version: 10.3.25-MariaDB-0ubuntu0.20.04.1 Ubuntu 20.04

Copyright (c) 2000, 2018, Oracle, MariaDB Corporation Ab
and others.

Type 'help;' or '\h' for help. Type '\c' to clear the current
input statement.

MariaDB [(none)]> CREATE USER 'sysadmin@ubuntu-server'
    -> IDENTIFIED BY 'Project42Password';
Query OK, 0 rows affected (0.037 sec)
MariaDB [(none)]>
```

You don't have to put the user account name and hostname in single quotation marks, but it's needed in this case because of the dash (-) in the hostname. Notice that you can put the SQL statement on two lines. That's because the interface doesn't care about line returns produced by the Enter key like the Bash shell does. Instead, the SQL interface is watching for a semicolon to end the statement.

After you've created a user account, you can view it as shown here:

```
MariaDB [(none)]> SELECT user FROM mysql.user;
+------------------------+
| user                   |
+------------------------+
| sysadmin@ubuntu-server |
| root                   |
+------------------------+
2 rows in set (0.000 sec)

MariaDB [(none)]> exit
Bye
$
```

Notice that the exit command (no semicolon needed) allows you to leave the SQL interface and return to the command line.

Now that you've created a MariaDB user account for yourself, use it to log into the SQL interface. An example of doing this is shown here:

```
$ mysql --user 'sysadmin@ubuntu-server' --password
Enter password:
Welcome to the MariaDB monitor.  Commands end with ; or \g.
Your MariaDB connection id is 47
Server version: 10.3.25-MariaDB-0ubuntu0.20.04.1 Ubuntu 20.04

Copyright (c) 2000, 2018, Oracle, MariaDB Corporation Ab
 and others.

Type 'help;' or '\h' for help. Type '\c' to clear the current
input statement.

MariaDB [(none)]>
```

For your MariaDB account's password, instead of entering it on the same line as the mysql command, you just use the --password option with no argument. When you do this, the SQL interface will prompt you for the password, and your password is not displayed as you type it.

Besides creating an account to access the MariaDB database server, you'll need to grant permissions to access tasks and items within MariaDB for the account. If this is not done, when the user account tries to perform a task, such as creating a database, access will be denied as shown here:

```
$ mysql --user 'sysadmin@ubuntu-server' --password
Enter password:
Welcome to the MariaDB monitor.  Commands end with ; or \g.
[...]
MariaDB [(none)]> CREATE DATABASE FruitTrees;
ERROR 1044 (42000): Access denied for user
'sysadmin@ubuntu-server'@'%' to database 'FruitTrees'
```

```
MariaDB [(none)]> exit
Bye
$
```

To grant access for the first account, you'll again need to use super user privileges. The basic syntax for doing this is as follows:

```
GRANT access ON objects TO user;
```

The *access* is essentially commands that the *user* can use when dealing with the listed *objects*. Wildcards are allowed when specifying *objects*. For example, to allow a user to issue the SQL SELECT command on any database in the system, you'd use the GRANT SELECT ON *.* TO *user*; SQL statement syntax.

In the case of granting access for the first account, assuming it is an administrative account, it's best to provide full-blown access by using ALL as the *access* granted, as shown snipped here:

```
$ sudo mysql
[sudo] password for sysadmin:
Welcome to the MariaDB monitor.  Commands end with ; or \g.
[...]
MariaDB [(none)]> SHOW GRANTS FOR 'sysadmin@ubuntu-server';
+------------------------------------[...]+
| Grants for sysadmin@ubuntu-server@%  [...]|
+------------------------------------[...]
| GRANT USAGE ON *.* TO `sysadmin@ubuntu-server`@`%`
IDENTIFIED BY PASSWORD '*3429168B1E2FE4[...]|
+------------------------------------[...]+
1 row in set (0.000 sec)

MariaDB [(none)]> GRANT ALL ON *.* TO 'sysadmin@ubuntu-server';
Query OK, 0 rows affected (0.001 sec)

MariaDB [(none)]> SHOW GRANTS FOR 'sysadmin@ubuntu-server';
+------------------------------------[...]+
| Grants for sysadmin@ubuntu-server@%  [...]|
+------------------------------------[...]+
| GRANT ALL PRIVILEGES ON *.* TO `sysadmin@ubuntu-server`@`%`
IDENTIFIED BY PASSWORD '*3429168B1E2FE4[...]|
+------------------------------------[...]+|
1 row in set (0.000 sec)

MariaDB [(none)]> exit
Bye
$
```

The SHOW GRANTS FOR *user*; SQL statement shows the current access granted to that user. When the access was modified by the GRANT command, the user now has ALL PRIVILEGES granted.

Populating and Using MariaDB Database

After you have the database server installed and appropriate access granted, you can begin creating databases and their tables and populating them with data.

The SQL command to create a database is logically CREATE DATABASE. Using the fruit tree example from previously, an appropriately named database is created in MariaDB through the SQL interface as shown snipped here:

```
$ mysql --user 'sysadmin@ubuntu-server' --password
Enter password:
Welcome to the MariaDB monitor.  Commands end with ; or \g.
[...]
MariaDB [(none)]> CREATE DATABASE FruitTrees;
Query OK, 1 row affected (0.001 sec)

MariaDB [(none)]> SHOW DATABASES;
+--------------------+
| Database           |
+--------------------+
| FruitTrees         |
| information_schema |
| mysql              |
| performance_schema |
+--------------------+
4 rows in set (0.036 sec)

MariaDB [(none)]>
```

Notice you can see all the databases within MariaDB using the SHOW DATABASES; command, including the newly created FruitTrees database.

After a database is created, assuming you have normalized your data, you are ready to begin creating tables. The USE *database*; command is needed to select the database to create a table in, as shown here:

```
MariaDB [(none)]> USE FruitTrees;
Database changed
MariaDB [FruitTrees]> CREATE TABLE AppleTrees (
    -> item_number int not null,
    -> tree_type text,
    -> description text,
    -> tree_size text,
    -> apple_color text,
    -> blooming_period text,
    -> pollinator_group int,
    -> harvest_period text,
    -> grow_zones text,
    -> primary key (item_number));
Query OK, 0 rows affected (0.755 sec)

MariaDB [FruitTrees]>
```

The CREATE TABLE command starts the process of creating a designated table (AppleTrees in the example). While you could type the field information for the table all on the same line, it's easier to see what you are doing by putting a single field designation on each line. Each field designation has a name and a data type (see Table 21.1), as well as any options. Also, you have to designate a primary key, and you need to prevent that particular field from being set to blank or null. In the example, the item_number is the primary key, and it is blocked from being empty through the not null option in its field designation.

To view any tables, use the SHOW TABLES syntax as shown in the example here:

```
MariaDB [FruitTrees]> SHOW TABLES IN FruitTrees;
+---------------------+
| Tables_in_FruitTrees |
+---------------------+
| AppleTrees          |
+---------------------+
1 row in set (0.000 sec)

MariaDB [FruitTrees]>
```

To view field description details within a particular table of a selected database, you can use the DESCRIBE command, as shown here:

```
MariaDB [FruitTrees]> DESCRIBE AppleTrees;
+------------------+---------+------+-----+---------+-------+
| Field            | Type    | Null | Key | Default | Extra |
+------------------+---------+------+-----+---------+-------+
| item_number      | int(11) | NO   | PRI | NULL    |       |
| tree_type        | text    | YES  |     | NULL    |       |
| description      | text    | YES  |     | NULL    |       |
| tree_size        | text    | YES  |     | NULL    |       |
| apple_color      | text    | YES  |     | NULL    |       |
| blooming_period  | text    | YES  |     | NULL    |       |
| pollinator_group | int(11) | YES  |     | NULL    |       |
| harvest_period   | text    | YES  |     | NULL    |       |
| grow_zones       | text    | YES  |     | NULL    |       |
+------------------+---------+------+-----+---------+-------+
9 rows in set (0.046 sec)

MariaDB [FruitTrees]>
```

Now that you have a table created, you can start populating it with data. Sticking with our AppleTrees table scenario, we added three data records to it in this example:

```
MariaDB [FruitTrees]> INSERT INTO AppleTrees VALUES (3247,
    -> 'Baldwin', 'Impressive American variety…',
    -> 'Std', 'Red and Green',
    ->  'Mid-Late Spring', 4, 'October', '5-8');
```

```
Query OK, 1 row affected (0.067 sec)

MariaDB [FruitTrees]> INSERT INTO AppleTrees VALUES (3248,
    -> 'Baldwin', 'Impressive American variety…',
    -> 'Dwarf', 'Red and Green',
    -> 'Mid-Late Spring', 4, 'October', '5-8');
Query OK, 1 row affected (0.074 sec)

MariaDB [FruitTrees]> INSERT INTO AppleTrees VALUES (3251,
    -> 'Redfree', 'Sweet and a little acidic…',
    -> 'Std', 'Red and Green',
    -> 'Early-Mid Spring', 4, 'August', '4-8');
Query OK, 1 row affected (0.075 sec)
```

It's a good idea to check the data you've entered into your database tables to ensure all is well. Using the SELECT * FROM *tablename*; SQL statement will allow you to view all the current data in *tablename,* as shown snipped here:

```
MariaDB [FruitTrees]> SELECT * FROM AppleTrees;
[...]
| item_number | tree_type | description
| tree_size | apple_color  | blooming_period  | pollinator_group
| harvest_period | grow_zones |
[...]
|        3247 | Baldwin   | Impressive American variety...
| Std       | Red and Green | Mid-Late Spring  |               4
| October        | 5-8      |
|        3248 | Baldwin   | Impressive American variety...
| Dwarf     | Red and Green | Mid-Late Spring  |               4
| October        | 5-8      |
|        3251 | Redfree   | Sweet and a little acidic...
| Std       | Red and Green | Early-Mid Spring |               4
| August         | 4-8      |
[...]
3 rows in set (0.001 sec)

MariaDB [FruitTrees]>
```

If you find mistakes in your data or just need to update information, you can do that rather easily. Just use the UPDATE command along with the data field you'd like to change and a WHERE statement to select the record identified by its primary key (item_number in this case):

```
MariaDB [FruitTrees]> UPDATE AppleTrees SET
    -> pollinator_group=3 WHERE item_number=3248;
Query OK, 1 row affected (0.120 sec)
Rows matched: 1  Changed: 1  Warnings: 0

MariaDB [FruitTrees]> SELECT * FROM AppleTrees;
[...]
| item_number | tree_type | description
| tree_size | apple_color  | blooming_period  | pollinator_group
```

```
| harvest_period | grow_zones |
[...]
|        3247 | Baldwin   | Impressive American variety...
| Std       | Red and Green | Mid-Late Spring  |              4
| October      | 5-8       |
|        3248 | Baldwin   | Impressive American variety...
| Dwarf      | Red and Green | Mid-Late Spring  |              4
| October      | 5-8       |
|        3251 | Redfree   | Sweet and a little acidic...
| Std       | Red and Green | Early-Mid Spring |              3
| August      | 4-8       |
[...]
3 rows in set (0.001 sec)

MariaDB [FruitTrees]> exit
Bye
$
```

After your database and its tables are created and you have populated the tables and checked their data, you are ready to let your database applications roll.

 Real World Scenario

CREATING A DATABASE WITH MARIADB

One of the best ways to get started with understanding how to manage a MariaDB server is to use one as a storehouse for data that is important to you. Setting up access to this database, determining the appropriate structure for your data, and then populating the database will give you some practical experience that is invaluable later.

The following steps assume you have installed the MariaDB RDBMS on your system and will take you through setting up access to it and filling a database with data:

1. Log into your Linux system using the sysadmin account and the password you created for it.

2. Using the appropriate privilege escalation method for your Linux distribution, use super user privileges (such as entering **sudo** or logging into the root account), type **mysql**, and press Enter.

3. At the MariaDB SQL interface prompt, type **CREATE USER sysadmin IDENTIFIED BY 'password';**, replacing *password* with the password of your choice, and press Enter.

4. Leave the SQL interface by typing **exit** at the prompt and pressing Enter.

5. Pick one of your favorite hobbies to create a database for. Using word processing software or even just a few pieces of paper, list all the data concerning this hobby that you want to track.

6. Normalize your hobby data by determining the different categories the data should go into.

7. For your categorized data, determine what tables should be created, what they should be named, and what data fields they will contain. Record this information in your document.

(continued)

8. Determine what data field will be the primary key or create one, such as an identification number. This field will exist in every table. Record this information in your document.

9. Decide the data type for every data field, and record this in your document.

10. Choose a name for your hobby database.

11. Access the MariaDB server's SQL interface by typing `mysql --user sysadmin --password`, and press Enter. When asked for a password, enter the one you created in step 3 for this interface.

12. Create your hobby database by typing **CREATE DATABASE** *database-name;*, replacing *database-name* with the name of your hobby database, and press Enter.

13. Select your hobby database by typing **USE** *database-name;*, replacing *database-name* with the name of your hobby database, and press Enter.

14. Create your first table in your database. Gather your table's field information from your document, and begin the process by typing **CREATE TABLE** *table-name* (, replacing *table-name* with the name of your first table, and press Enter.

15. Using your documented table field information and guidance from this section, continue to create the table by putting in each table field and its data type. Don't forget to include the primary key information.

16. After you have completed creating your first table, review its structure by typing **DESCRIBE** *table-name;*, replacing *table-name* with the name of your first table, and press Enter. If you find any problems, you can use the **DROP** command to delete the table and re-create it properly.

17. When you are satisfied with your first table's structure, begin populating the table with your hobby data using the appropriate INSERT INTO commands along with guidance from this section.

18. After you have completed your data entry into your first table, review the data by typing **SELECT * FROM** *table-name;*, replacing *table-name* with the name of your first table, and press Enter. If you find any incorrect data, modify it using the **UPDATE** command along with guidance from this section.

19. When your first table is completed to your satisfaction, continue creating and populating the tables needed for your hobby database.

20. When you are done, type **exit** and press Enter to leave the SQL interface for MariaDB. Congratulations! We hope your hobby database will assist in your enjoyment of your favorite hobby.

Knowing how to install and use the MySQL and MariaDB databases will provide you with invaluable skills in your system administration career. However, it's always a good idea to expand your database knowledge so that your experience has some variety to it. We'll explore another RDBMS next.

Installing and Using PostgreSQL

PostgreSQL has a history that goes all the way back to the 1980s, though its current name wasn't designated until 1995. In fact, many administrators still refer to it by a variant of its previous name, Postgres.

PostgreSQL's evolutionary life has brought about some popular features. It supports standard SQL, with a few exceptions, and has data integrity structures, such as multiversion concurrency control (MVCC), which allows each database transaction to have a copy of the data. This way, creating or modifying data does not prevent any data queries and vice versa. MVCC not only provides higher levels of data integrity, but it speeds things up.

Security-wise, PostgreSQL has the ability to provide mandatory access control (MAC) security levels similar to that of SELinux (see Chapter 18, "Exploring Red Hat Security"). In addition, it can work with several different authentication systems, such as Kerberos, Lightweight Directory Access Protocol (LDAP), pluggable authentication modules (PAM), and so on.

Conducting a PostgreSQL Installation

Installing PostgreSQL is a little different depending on the Linux distribution you are using. You need super user privileges and the correct package name, which is `postgresql` for Ubuntu and `postgresql-server` for Red Hat–based distributions.

Here is a snipped example of installing PostgreSQL on Ubuntu, after updating the system's package information:

```
$ sudo apt update
[sudo] password for sysadmin:
[...]
Fetched 4124 kB in 22s (187 kB/s)
Reading package lists... Done
Building dependency tree
Reading state information... Done
[...]
$
$ sudo apt install postgresql
[sudo] password for sysadmin:
Reading package lists... Done
Building dependency tree
Reading state information... Done
The following additional packages will be installed:
  libllvm10 libpq5 libsensors-config libsensors5
  postgresql-12 postgresql-client-12
  postgresql-client-common postgresql-common
  ssl-cert sysstat
[...]
0 upgraded, 11 newly installed, 0 to remove [...]
Need to get 30.6 MB of archives.
After this operation, 122 MB of additional [...]
Do you want to continue? [Y/n] Y
Get:1 http://us.archive.ubuntu.com/ubuntu focal/main
```

```
amd64 libllvm10 amd64 1:10.0.0-4ubuntu1 [15.3 MB]
[...]
Fetched 30.6 MB in 46s (659 kB/s)
Preconfiguring packages ...
[...]
Unpacking sysstat (12.2.0-2) ...
Setting up postgresql-client-common (214ubuntu0.1) ...
[...]
Setting up postgresql-common (214ubuntu0.1) ...
Adding user postgres to group ssl-cert
[...]
The files belonging to this database system will be owned
by user "postgres".
This user must also own the server process.
[...]
syncing data to disk ...
[...]
[...]
Processing triggers for libc-bin [...]
$
$ systemctl status postgresql
•   postgresql.service - PostgreSQL RDBMS
       Loaded: loaded [...] enabled; vendor pr>
       Active: active (exited) since [...]
    Main PID: 2690 (code=exited, status=0/SUCCESS)
        Tasks: 0 (limit: 2282)
       Memory: 0B
       CGroup: /system.slice/postgresql.service

[...]ubuntu-server systemd[1]: Starting PostgreSQL RDBMS...
[...]ubuntu-server systemd[1]: Finished PostgreSQL RDBMS.
lines 1-10/10 (END)
$
$ which createdb
/usr/bin/createdb
$
```

When you install PostgreSQL on Ubuntu, it is automatically enabled to start when the system boots. Also, the service is started for you. One simple check you can perform to see if PostgreSQL is installed on a system outside of package management is through the which createdb command. If you see a file when this command is issued, PostgreSQL is installed on your system, as was done in the preceding installation example.

Installing PostgreSQL on a Red Hat–based distribution is a little different. In the following snipped example, we used the su -c 'command' syntax to issue single commands as the root user to escalate to super user privileges, when needed:

```
$ su -c 'dnf install postgresql-server'
Password:
```

```
Last metadata expiration check: [...]
Dependencies resolved.
[...]
Installing:
 postgresql-server [...]
Installing dependencies:
 libpq             [...]
 postgresql        [...]
Enabling module streams:
 postgresql        [...]

Transaction Summary
[...]
Install  3 Packages

Total download size: 6.7 M
Installed size: 26 M
Is this ok [y/N]:y
Downloading Packages:
[...]
Running transaction check
Transaction check succeeded.
Running transaction test
Transaction test succeeded.
Running transaction
[...]
Installed products updated.

Installed:
  libpq[...]
  postgresql[...]
  postgresql-server[...]

Complete!
$
```

When you install PostgreSQL on CentOS, it is not automatically enabled or started, so you'll have to issue those systemctl commands manually. But before you do that, you have to run a PostgreSQL database initialization with super user privileges, as shown here:

```
$ su -c '/usr/bin/postgresql-setup --initdb'
Password:
 * Initializing database in '/var/lib/pgsql/data'
 * Initialized, logs are in /var/lib/pgsql/initdb_postgresql.log
$
```

After the database is initialized, you can enable the PostgreSQL to start during the system's boot and get the service running. The process is shown snipped in this example:

```
$ systemctl status postgresql
•   postgresql.service - PostgreSQL database server
    Loaded: loaded ([...]disabled; vendor>
    Active: inactive (dead)
$
$ su -c 'systemctl enable postgresql'
Password:
Created symlink
[...]
$
$ su -c 'systemctl start postgresql'
Password:
$
$ systemctl status postgresql
•   postgresql.service - PostgreSQL database server
    Loaded: loaded [...]enabled; vendor >
    Active: active (running) since [...]
[...]
$
```

When you have your PostgreSQL RDBMS software installed and properly initialized, you can move forward on setting up proper access to it and then loading data into the database.

Accessing a PostgreSQL Database

You access and manage data within the PostgreSQL server through database user accounts, which are called *roles*. Instead of using the root account, a special all-powerful account called postgres is a role created in this RDBMS. The postgres role has full access to everything in PostgreSQL, so it is a good security practice to create a single database role for every user account that needs access to it.

A quick check lets you determine whether your current user account has a role set up for it within a PostgreSQL server. Attempt to create a database with the createdb command. If you get a role "*username*" does not exist message when issuing the command, a role for you is not yet created:

```
$ createdb AppleTrees
createdb: error: could not connect to database template1:
FATAL:  role "sysadmin" does not exist
$
```

To create your role, you first have to log into the *postgres* account. To do this, you need super user privileges as shown here:

```
$ sudo --login -u postgres
postgres@ubuntu-server:~$ whoami
postgres
postgres@ubuntu-server:~$
```

```
postgres@ubuntu-server:~$ psql
psql (12.6 (Ubuntu 12.6-0ubuntu0.20.04.1))
Type "help" for help.

postgres=#
```

The command to access the SQL interface to PostgreSQL is psql. When you are in the interface, your prompt will look like this: postgres=#. The name (postgres) lets you know the current role you are using in the RDBMS. The pound sign (#) indicates that this role has super user privileges within the database. A greater-than sign (>) in place of the pound sign indicates that the super user privileges are not granted for a role.

It's a good practice to use the same role name for the database account as the Linux system account's username. The SQL interface syntax to create a database user account is as follows:

```
CREATE ROLE role-name access;
```

When you create a role in PostgreSQL, you grant the allowed access for that role at the same time. The access portion of the CREATE command is what grants access, and it can be set to one or more of the items listed in Table 21.3.

TABLE 21.3:   A Few PostgreSQL Role Access Settings

ACCESS NAME	DESCRIPTION
CREATEDB	Creation of databases is permitted.
CREATEROLE	Creation of database roles is permitted. This is a potential security risk, because the role can create other roles with SUPERUSER access.
LOGIN	Sets the role as a database user. Passwords for database authentication are set with PASSWORD 'password'.
SUPERUSER	Grants full access to all database objects. This is a dangerous access level and should be used with caution.

The access list in Table 21.3 is not complete, but it will get you started on your journey of exploring PostgreSQL. If you make a mistake or need to grant more privileges later, you can use the ALTER ROLE command. Use DROP ROLE if you need to remove a role from the database.

An example of creating a role for the user sysadmin in the psql SQL interface with the postgres role is shown snipped here:

```
$ sudo --login -u postgres
postgres@ubuntu-server:~$ psql
psql (12.6 (Ubuntu 12.6-0ubuntu0.20.04.1))
Type "help" for help.

postgres=# CREATE ROLE sysadmin
postgres-# CREATEDB LOGIN PASSWORD 'Project42Password';
CREATE ROLE
postgres=#
```

To see all the roles you've created and the ones that came with the default installation, use the special psql command of \du. This command will show the role information using a pager, so you'll need to press the Q key to exit out of the display when you are done viewing the role information. A snipped example of this using this command is shown here:

```
postgres=# \du

                            List of roles
  Role name |                         Attributes [...]
-----------+-----------------------------------[...]
  postgres  | Superuser, Create role, Create DB, [...]
  sysadmin  | Create DB                          [...]

(END)
postgres=#
```

After you're done creating the initial role, it's a good idea to exit from the psql interface and log out of the postgres account. You can use the exit command to do both actions:

```
postgres=# exit
postgres@ubuntu-server:~$
postgres@ubuntu-server:~$ exit
logout
$ whoami
sysadmin
$
```

After a role has been created for a user and prior to them entering into the psql SQL interface for the first time, they will need to perform an initialization by issuing the createdb command with no database name listed after it. An example of this is shown here:

```
$ whoami
sysadmin
$
$ createdb
$
$ psql
psql (12.6 (Ubuntu 12.6-0ubuntu0.20.04.1))
Type "help" for help.

sysadmin=>
```

Notice that the SQL interface prompt in psql has changed. It now shows the role name of the user who is accessing the interface. When the RDBMS has been installed and an initial role is created, you're ready to start creating and using a PostgreSQL database.

Populating and Using a PostgreSQL Database

PostgreSQL generally follows standardized SQL. For example, creating a database looks the same as it did when using MariaDB:

```
sysadmin=> CREATE DATABASE FruitTrees;
CREATE DATABASE
sysadmin=>
```

However, you'll find that within the psql SQL interface, some SQL statements do not work, such as the SHOW DATABASES command. Instead, you need to use \l (a lowercase *L*) to see all the databases, as shown snipped here:

```
sysadmin-> \l
                             List of databases
     Name    |   Owner   | Encoding | Collate  |[...]
------------+----------+----------+---------+[...]
 fruittrees | sysadmin | UTF8     | C.UTF-8  |[...]
 postgres   | postgres | UTF8     | C.UTF-8  |[...]
 sysadmin   | sysadmin | UTF8     | C.UTF-8  |[...]
 template0  | postgres | UTF8     | C.UTF-8  |[...]
 template1  | postgres | UTF8     | C.UTF-8  |[...]
 (5 rows)

sysadmin->
```

Notice in the preceding example that even though we named our database FruitTrees when we created it, PostgreSQL changed the name to fruittrees. If you want an object name to be a different case than lowercase, you'll have to enclose it in quotation marks. This is important to note, because you have to have the right case when you use an object, such as a database name, in your SQL command syntax.

Before creating tables in your newly created database, you need to connect to it. Use the \c command to accomplish this as shown here:

```
sysadmin-> \c fruittrees;
You are now connected to database "fruittrees" as user "sysadmin".
fruittrees->
```

When you connect to a database, the psql prompt will change and replace your role name with the current database. Creating a table follows standard SQL syntax, as shown in this test example:

```
fruittrees=> CREATE TABLE test (
fruittrees(> id_number int not null,
fruittrees(> type text,
fruittrees(> brand text,
fruittrees(> primary key (id_number));
CREATE TABLE
```

However, displaying a table is a little different. Instead of using the SHOW TABLES SQL command, you need to use the \dt command, which stands for *display table*:

```
fruittrees=> \dt
        List of relations
 Schema | Name | Type  |  Owner
--------+------+-------+----------
 public | test | table | sysadmin
(1 row)


fruittrees=>
```

After a table is created and defined, you can start populating it with data. An example of doing this is shown here:

```
fruittrees=> INSERT INTO test VALUES (1,'first test','data1');
INSERT 0 1
fruittrees=> INSERT INTO test VALUES (2,'2nd test','data2');
INSERT 0 1
fruittrees=>
```

Viewing data in a table follows standard SQL syntax, which is nice:

```
fruittrees=> SELECT * FROM test;
 id_number |    type    | brand
-----------+------------+-------
         1 | first test | data1
         2 | 2nd test   | data2
(2 rows)


fruittrees=> exit
$
```

When you have completed your work within the psql SQL interface, be sure to use the exit command to leave. If you need to access this database or its table again through this interface, you'll need to reconnect to the database using the \c command.

Database administration is a rather deep topic, and we've just scratched the surface. However, you've got a little experience now that will assist you as you continue your database server management journey.

The Bottom Line

Understand basic DBMS components. A database management system typically consists of a database engine, the data files for the database, and a query-language interface, which typically uses standard SQL or something relatively compliant with standard SQL. These components assist in fulfilling the need to manage complex connections between individual data items.

Master It You have installed an RDBMS on your Linux system. The various applications that access this database reside on different servers across your local network. However, these servers are in different buildings on your company's campus. Recently, the power was cut to the campus due to a mistake by the power utility supply company. You did not have any backup power systems in place, and all your servers went down. Now that the power has been restored and your systems are back up and running again, none of the applications can access the database. The system on which your RDBMS resides is running (the primary database server), and there are no network firewall problems. What should you investigate next to resolve this issue?

Create user accounts within MariaDB. Managing and querying data within a MariaDB server is accomplished through database user accounts. Typically, an account is created for every user account on the Linux system that needs to manage and/or query data in the database. It is also considered a good practice to limit user access to only those databases associated with applications the user can access.

Master It Imagine you are the system administrator on a new Linux server. You have completed the installation of MariaDB and need to create a database for the application that will be using MariaDB as its RDMS. What are the next few steps to take, after starting the MariaDB service and enabling it to start at system boot?

Use SQL to query a MariaDB database. MariaDB uses several standard SQL commands, plus a few more, to manage databases, create tables, populate them with data, and query that data. The times that may cause you a little heartburn are when you need to use SQL commands that fall outside of the standards. However, that is fairly rare when interacting with the MariaDB SQL interface.

Master It You have recently created a table named `ArtificialFlowers` within the `Florist` database. The artificial flower records listed in this table have only a few fields: `ProductID` (which is the primary key), `FlowerName`, `FlowerColor`, and `StemColor`. The store manager of the florist shop wants to check the data you've entered into this table. What steps should you take after you have logged into the MariaDB server's command line where this data exists?

Install PostgreSQL on Linux. The PostgreSQL (also called Postgres) RDBMS has some features that make it popular in segments of the Linux community. For instance, it has data reliability structures and generally supports standard SQL, with a few exceptions. Installing PostgreSQL can be a little tricky, as its installation process is slightly different depending on the Linux distribution you are using.

Master It You are a system administrator for a Linux system whose customers want to use the PostgreSQL RDBMS on the system. This particular system is a Red Hat Linux distribution. What steps do you need to take to accomplish this task?

Set up roles within PostgreSQL. Roles are used to access and manage data within a PostgreSQL server. It is considered a good practice to determine what privileges a user needs for using a PostgreSQL database and then create a role with the appropriate privileges. This structure provides protection for the data and appropriate security tracking of database users.

Master It You are the database administrator of the PostgreSQL database on your Linux system. Your database user role is named `admin`. This role has super user privileges in the database as well as the ability to create roles and databases. What, if any, changes should be made to your account to improve the security levels of administering this database?

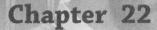

Chapter 22

Exploring the Virtualization Environment

When something is virtualized, it no longer physically exists, but instead is simulated. In the information technology world, this simulation can apply to computer systems, which is accomplished through special software. Within the last few decades, virtualization has revolutionized the server room. By moving many systems or portions of systems to a virtualized environment, the amount of physical hardware housed in server rooms has been reduced, lowering the overall footprint required. In addition, these reductions have lowered the total amount of electricity needed by these rooms, which is not only better for the environment, but costs less. Server virtualization is a win-win on many levels.

Virtualization can now also be applied directly to software applications. Using special package management systems, apps are sandboxed along with all their needed dependencies. This allows an additional layer of security running on either a physical system or a virtualized one.

IN THIS CHAPTER, YOU WILL LEARN TO

- ◆ Understand basic hypervisor components
- ◆ Generate a container with a Bash shell
- ◆ Manage the Snap universal package system
- ◆ Install the Flatpak framework

Hypervisors

Virtual machines (VMs) are simulated computer systems that appear and act as physical machines to their users. The process of creating these virtual machines is called *virtualization*.

Managing VMs

The primary software tool used to create and manage VMs is a *hypervisor*, which has been historically called either a *virtual machine monitor* or a *virtual machine manager* (VMM). Hypervisors come in two basic flavors: Type 1 and Type 2. However, you'll find that some hypervisor software doesn't neatly fit into either category.

The easier to understand is the Type 2 hypervisor, so we'll start there. A Type 2 hypervisor is a software application that operates between its created virtual machine (*guest*) and the physical system (*host*) on which the hypervisor is running. Figure 22.1 shows a diagrammed example of a Type 2 hypervisor.

FIGURE 22.1
Example of a Type 2
hypervisor

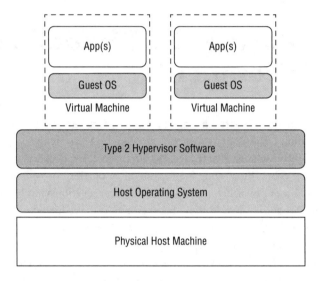

A Type 2 hypervisor acts as a typical software application in that it interacts with the host's operating system. However, its distinction lies in the fact that it provides one or more virtualized environments or virtual machines. These VMs each have their own operating system (guest OS) and can have various applications running on them. The host OS on the physical system is often completely different than the VM's guest OS.

There are several Type 2 hypervisors from which to choose. A few options that run on Linux include Oracle VirtualBox and VMware Workstation Player. Figure 22.2 shows Oracle VirtualBox with two Linux server systems installed.

FIGURE 22.2
Oracle VirtualBox Type
2 hypervisor

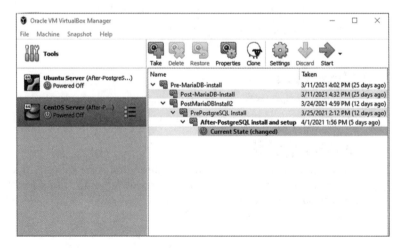

There are many considerations when setting up a virtualized environment. Some Type 2 hypervisors, such as Oracle VirtualBox, need a graphical user interface (GUI) on which to operate. Therefore, if you are managing a Linux system running a server distro that has no desktop capabilities, VirtualBox is not a good choice for your situation.

Also, when creating VMs with a Type 2 hypervisor, it is important to determine if you have enough resources, such as RAM, on your physical host machine. Keep in mind that you will need to accommodate the host OS and Type 2 hypervisor software, as well as the guest OS and applications on each VM.

A Type 1 hypervisor eliminates the need for the physical host's OS. This software runs directly on the physical system and therefore is sometimes called a *bare-metal* hypervisor. Figure 22.3 shows a diagrammed example of a Type 1 hypervisor.

FIGURE 22.3
Example of a Type 1 hypervisor

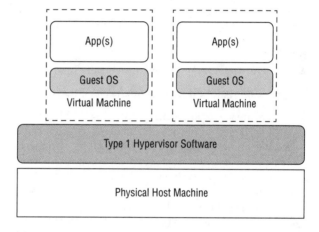

There are also several Type 1 hypervisors from which to choose. A few options include KVM, Xen, and Hyper-V. For Linux, KVM is built-in. KVM's kernel component has been included in the Linux kernel since v2.6.20.

An interesting feature with KVM and Hyper-V is that they can both be started while the host OS is running. These hypervisors then take over for the host OS and run as a Type 1 hypervisor. This is a case where the hypervisors don't neatly fit into the Type 1 category.

Creating a Virtual Machine

A virtual machine is made up of either one file or a series of files that resides on the host machine. Whether it is a single file or multiple files depends on the hypervisor used. The file (or files) contains configuration information, such as how much RAM is needed, as well as the VM's data, such as the guest OS and any installed application binaries.

There are many ways to create a virtual machine. When first starting out, most people will create a Linux virtual machine from the ground up; they set up the VM specifications within the hypervisor software of their choice and use an ISO file (live or otherwise) to install the guest operating system.

Lots of choices exist for creating VMs. Which methods you use depend on your organization's needs as well as the number of VMs you must deploy. Here are brief descriptions of some common options:

Clone   A *clone* is essentially a copy of another guest VM. Just like in science fiction, a VM clone is identical to its original. The files that make up the original VM are copied to a new filesystem location, and the VM is given a new name.

Hypervisors typically have easy methods for creating clones. However, before you start up a cloned VM, it is important to check the VM's settings. For example, some hypervisors do not issue a new network interface card (NIC) media access control (MAC) address when creating a VM clone. This could cause network issues should you have two running VMs that have identical NIC MAC addresses. The following is a brief list of items that may need to be modified for a Linux clone:

◆   Host name

◆   NIC MAC address

◆   NIC internet protocol (IP) address, if using a static IP

◆   Machine ID

◆   Any items employing a universally unique identifier (UUID)

◆   Configuration settings on the clone that employ any item in this list

There are some potentially interesting problems with cloning. For example, your system's machine ID is a unique hexadecimal 32-character identifier. The ID is stored in the /etc/ machine-id file. D-Bus will use this ID if its own machine ID file, /var/lib/dbus/ machine-id, does not exist. Typically on modern distributions, the D-Bus machine ID file will not exist or will be symbolically linked to the /etc/machine-id file. Problems can ensue if you clone a machine and boot it so that the two machines share the same ID. These problems may include not being able to get an IP address if your network manager is configured to use the machine's ID instead of a NIC's MAC address for dynamic host control protocol (DHCP) services. To prevent this problem, after you clone a VM, you'll need to address the duplicate machine ID. Typically, you can do this on the clone by performing the following steps:

1. Delete the machine ID file: rm /etc/machine-id.

2. Delete the D-Bus ID file: rm /var/lib/dbus/machine-id.

3. Regenerate the ID: dbus-uuidgen --ensure.

Keep in mind that a distribution may require additional steps, such as linking the /var/ lib/dbus/machine-id file to /etc/machine-id. Be sure to look at your distro's documentation prior to changing a machine's identity.

Open Virtualization Format   Another method employs the Open Virtualization Format (OVF). The OVF is a standard administered by the Distributed Management Task Force (DMTF) organization. This standard allows the hypervisor to export a VM's files into the OVF for use in other hypervisors. After you export the files, you can import them into any other hypervisor that honors the standard. It's like cloning a machine between two different hypervisor software applications. You'll need to change the appropriate settings on the new VMs, such as the hostname, if the VMs will be running on the same local network.

While the OVF file standard creates multiple files, some hypervisors recognize a single compressed archive file of OVF files, called an Open Virtualization Archive (OVA). This is useful if you need to transfer a VM's files across a network to a different host system.

Template Outside of computing, a template is a pattern or mold that is used to guide the process of creating an item. In word processing, a template is often employed to provide formatting models, such as when creating a business letter.

In virtualization, a VM *template* is a master copy. It is similar to a VM clone, except you cannot boot it. Virtual machines are created using these templates as their base.

To create a template, you need a *system image* (sometimes called a *VM image*). This image contains the guest OS and any installed applications, as well as configuration and data files. The system image is created from a VM you have configured as your base system. You direct the hypervisor software to generate a template, which is often a file or set of files. Now, you can employ this system image to create several virtual machines based on that template.

Keep in mind that for a template-created VM, you may need to modify items prior to booting it. The same list covered in the previous "Clone" description applies here.

There are additional choices for creating virtual machines besides the ones listed here. For example, some companies offer software that will scan your current system and create a VM of it. The term used for these software offerings is *physical-to-virtual* (P2V).

Integrating via Linux Extensions

Before you jump into creating virtual machines, it's important to check that your Linux host system will support virtualization and the hypervisor product you have chosen. This support is accomplished via various extensions and modules.

A hardware extension is based within the system's CPU. It grants the hypervisor the ability to access the CPU directly, instead of going through the host OS, which improves performance.

First, you should determine whether your system's CPU has these hardware extensions available. You can research this via the /proc/cpuinfo file's flag information. Type in **grep ^flags /proc/cpuinfo** at the command line to view the various enabled features of your server's CPU. If enabled, you should see one of the following:

- **For Intel CPUs:** vmx

- **For AMD CPUs:** svm

If you see the hypervisor flag (instead of vmx or svm), this means your Linux OS is not running on a physical machine, but a virtual one. You can check to see which hypervisor is being employed via the virt-what utility, which may or may not be installed on your Linux distro by default.

To use one of the required CPU extensions and support the chosen hypervisor software, the appropriate Linux modules must be loaded. You'll need to review your hypervisor's documentation to determine what modules are needed.

To check if a needed module is already loaded, use the lsmod command. An example is shown here, checking for support of the KVM hypervisor:

```
lsmod | grep -i kvm
```

If you find that the needed hypervisor modules are not loaded, employ the `modprobe` command to insert them. An example of loading up a needed KVM hypervisor module is shown here:

```
sudo modprobe kvm-amd
```

While your server may have everything it needs to run VMs, including the Linux extensions, if the virtualization is disabled in the startup firmware, it won't work. Check your system's firmware documentation and ensure that virtualization is enabled.

Containers

Containers are virtual entities, but they are different from virtual machines and serve distinct purposes. Whereas a VM provides an entire guest operating system, a container's focus is typically on a single app, application stack, or environment. A container gathers all the files necessary to run an application—the runtime files, library files, database files, and any operating system–specific files. The container becomes self-sufficient for the application to run, and everything the application needs is stored within the container.

Instead of a hypervisor, a container is managed by a container engine. Figure 22.4 shows a diagrammed example of a container.

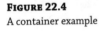

FIGURE 22.4
A container example

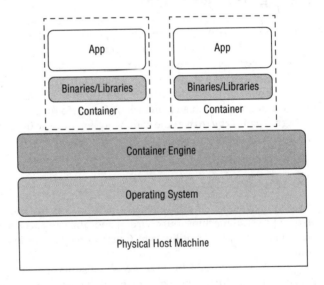

Notice in the figure that the physical machine's operating system is shared among the containers. However, each container has its own set of binaries and needed libraries to support its app, application stack, or environment.

Exploring Container Types

A container's focus depends on its purpose in life. Two container focal points are described here:

Application Containers   These containers focus on a single application, or an application stack, such as a web server. Application containers are heavily used in development and operations (DevOps). Software developers can modify their company's app in a newly created container. This same container, with the modified app, is then tested and eventually moved into production on the host machine. The old production container is destroyed. Using containers in this way eliminates production and development environment differences and provides little to no downtime for app users. Thus, containers are popular in continuous software deployment environments. The example in Figure 22.4 showed two application containers.

Operating System Containers   While containers are useful for developers, system admins can love them too. You can use a container that provides a fully functioning Linux OS space and is isolated from your host machine. Some in systems administration use containers to test their applications and needed libraries on various Linux distributions. Other system admins, prior to upgrading their host system distro, try out their environment on an upgraded Linux distribution. You can also employ VMs for these different evaluations, but containers provide a faster-to-deploy and more lightweight test area.

Keep in mind that virtualizing an application typically does not make it perform faster and should not be the primary motivation for moving it to a virtualized environment. Although containers allow you to quickly deploy applications, they will not cause an app to run more swiftly. Some hypervisors are termed *efficient hypervisors,* but that is only when there is a small performance difference between the physical environment and its virtualized self.

Looking at Container Software

Linux has been in the forefront of container development, making it a popular choice for developers. Two main container packages are commonly used in Linux, as described here:

LXC   The LXC package was developed as an open source standard for creating containers. Each container in LXC is a little more involved than just a standard lightweight application container, but not quite as heavy as a full virtual machine, placing it somewhere in the middle. LXC containers include their own bare-bones operating system that interfaces with the host system hardware directly, without requiring a host operating system. Because LXC containers include their own mini operating system, they are sometimes referred to as virtual machines although that term isn't quite correct as LXC containers still require a host operating system to operate.

Docker   The Docker package was developed by Docker Incorporated and released as an open source project. Docker is extremely lightweight, allowing several containers to run on the same host Linux system. Docker uses a separate daemon that runs on the host Linux system that manages the installed Docker images. The daemon listens for requests from the individual containers as well as from a Docker command-line interface that allows you to control the container environment.

Real World Scenario

TRYING OUT DOCKER ON YOUR LINUX SYSTEM

Docker is actually built on top of LXC and is a popular container engine that has been widely accepted throughout the industry. In addition, early adoption and strong partnerships not only helped this leadership, but brought about many container standards now in existence.

The following steps will take you through installing the Docker engine on a CentOS distribution and trying basic commands with it to manage a container environment:

1. Log into your CentOS Linux system using the sysadmin account and the password you created for it.

2. Install the docker package:

   a. If your sysadmin account is not configured to use sudo, log into the root account using the su - command and the root password, type **dnf install docker**, and press Enter.

      If your sysadmin account is configured to use sudo, then type **sudo dnf install docker** and press Enter.

   b. Type **y** to answer any questions, and press Enter after doing so.

   c. If you used the root account for privilege escalation, type **exit** and press Enter to leave the account.

3. Once the installation is complete, test Docker by typing **docker run hello-world** and pressing Enter. You may see some error messages, and that's OK. You know the installation was successful when you receive a message similar to the following along with additional information:

   ```
   Hello from Docker!
   This message shows that your installation appears to be working correctly.
   ```

4. When you issued the previous command (docker run hello-world), you actually created a container called Hello-World. View this container's information by typing **docker ps -a** and pressing Enter.

5. Find the Container ID number from the previous step's command output and record it. (Hint: The Container ID number will contain both letters and numbers and will be listed under the Container ID column.)

6. Delete the Hello-World container by typing **docker rm *Container-ID*** and pressing Enter, where ***Container-ID*** is the number you recorded in the previous step.

7. Start up an Ubuntu container on your CentOS system by typing **docker run -it ubuntu bash** and pressing Enter. Besides starting the container, this command will put you into the container. The -it options on the run command allow you to enter into interactive mode (i) and use a pseudo-terminal (t). Once you are in the container, your prompt will look similar to the following:

   ```
   root@8a7a39343829:/#
   ```

8. At the container prompt, type **whoami** and press Enter. Surprise! You're logged in as the root user, and that's OK, because you are contained.

9. See where you are in the container's virtual directory system by typing **pwd** and pressing Enter. You should see that you are at the root (/) of the directory structure.

10. View the version of Ubuntu you are running in this container by typing **cat /etc/debian_version** and pressing Enter. Record your findings.

11. Leave the Ubuntu container by typing **exit** and pressing Enter. You should see your prompt change.

12. Double-check that you are out of the container by typing **whoami** and pressing Enter. You should now be logged into the sysadmin account, instead of the root account.

13. View the available containers by typing **docker ps -a** and pressing Enter. You should see only one container. Record its Container ID.

14. Start the container you viewed in the previous step by typing **docker start** *Container-ID* and pressing Enter, where *Container-ID* is the number you recorded in the previous step.

15. Jump back into the Ubuntu container by typing **docker attach** *Container-ID* and pressing Enter, where *Container-ID* is the number you recorded in step 13. You should see that your prompt has changed.

16. At the container prompt, type **whoami** and press Enter. You should see that you are logged in as the root user.

17. View the version of Ubuntu you are running in this container by typing **cat /etc/debian_version** and pressing Enter. Check that the version information matches what you recorded in step 10. It should.

18. If you want, do a little exploring in the container. Try different commands you have learned in this book, and look through the Linux virtual directory structure.

19. Leave the Ubuntu container by typing **exit** and pressing Enter. You should see your prompt change.

20. Delete the Ubuntu container by typing **docker rm** *Container-ID* and pressing Enter, where *Container-ID* is the number you recorded in step 13.

Because containers are still relatively new in the computing world, container packages are often confused with Linux orchestration packages. We cover the orchestration topic next.

Organizing Containers

Orchestration refers to the organization of a process that is balanced, coordinated, and achieves consistency in the results. Orchestration of containers requires various orchestration engines (also called *orchestration systems*). These orchestration packages help you to manage the numerous containers you typically end up managing on your Linux systems.

No one orchestration system can do it all. The best combination is a set of general and specialized orchestration tools. We cover just a few here.

EMBRACING KUBERNETES

Originally designed and used by Google, Kubernetes is an open source orchestration system that is considered by many to be the de facto standard. Not only is Kubernetes popular and free, it also is highly scalable, fault tolerant, and easy to learn.

In some documentation, you will see the word *k8s* in reference to Kubernetes. The 8 replaces the "ubernete" portion of the Kubernetes name.

This system contains years of Google's orchestration experience, and because it is open source, additional community-desired features have been added. This is one reason so many companies have adopted its use for container orchestration.

Each Kubernetes managed service or application has the following primary components:

Cluster service: Uses a markup language file to deploy and manage app pods

Pod: Contains one or more running app containers

Worker: Pod host system that uses a kubelet (agent) to communicate with cluster services

YAML file: Contains a particular app container's automated configuration management and desired state settings

This distributed component configuration allows high scalability and great flexibility. It also works well for continuous software delivery desired by companies employing those development models.

INSPECTING DOCKER SWARM

Docker, the popular app container management utility, created its own orchestration system, called Docker Swarm (also called *Swarm*). A group of Docker containers is referred to as a *cluster*, which appears to a user as a single container. To orchestrate a Docker cluster, you can employ Swarm.

With the Swarm system, you can monitor the cluster's health and return the cluster to the desired state should a container within the cluster fail. You can also deploy additional Docker containers if the desired app performance is not currently being met. Swarm is typically faster than Kubernetes when it comes to deploying additional containers.

While not as popular as the Kubernetes orchestration system, Docker Swarm has its place. It is often used by those who are new to orchestration and already familiar with Docker tools.

SURVEYING MESOS

Mesos (also called *Apache Mesos*) is not a container orchestration system. Instead, Apache Mesos, created at the University of California, Berkeley, is a distributed systems kernel. It is similar to the Linux kernel, except it operates at a higher construct level. One of its features is the ability to create containers. The bottom line is that Apache Mesos combined with another product, Marathon, does provide a type of container orchestration system framework. You could loosely compare Mesos with Marathon to Docker with Swarm.

Mesos with Marathon provides high availability and health monitoring integration and can support both Mesos and Docker containers. This orchestration framework has a solid history for large container deployment environments.

If you desire to find out more about Mesos with Marathon, don't use search engine terms like *Mesos orchestration*. Instead, go straight to the source at `https://mesosphere.github.io/marathon/`.

A whole or partial Linux server is not the only thing you can virtualize nowadays. Software packaging is also getting in on this movement. We cover that topic next.

Software Packaging

Software packaging has some troublesome issues. As an example, there are several packages and libraries needed (called *dependencies*) to make PostgreSQL (covered in Chapter 21, "Managing Database Servers") fully functional. So when you install the postgresql using apt or the postgresql-server package using dnf, the needed dependencies are installed too. If a dependency is not available or the wrong version of it is installed, your database may not function correctly or securely. In addition, when the database server is set up and run, it is not fully isolated from the other software and services on the system.

At some point in time, software package developers (sometimes called *publishers*) realized that system administrators and app developers were having all the fun with containers. It became apparent that software could be delivered and implemented on Linux systems in their own container-like environment. As a result, package developers began exploring this brave new world of software distribution.

Using a container-like package system resolves many of the problems in our PostgreSQL example. A compressed software package holds all the needed dependencies, and each is the correct version. These packages are installed and run in a protected sandbox, making them unable to adversely affect other software and services on the system. This includes newer versions of the software package itself, so you could run two versions of PostgreSQL on the same system!

In this section, we take a look at two container-like package formats, more appropriately called *universal package systems*. One is Snap, and the other is Flatpak.

Looking at Ubuntu Snap

Canonical (keepers of the Ubuntu distribution) introduced a new package system around 2015. However, it was released to the world in a limited form—focused on only cloud-based applications and available only on the Ubuntu distribution.

Over time, this package format, called Snap, became so popular that it was made available to other major Linux distributions, including Red Hat. Snap is now used not only for cloud-based applications, but also for desktop, server, and Internet of Things (IoT) apps.

EXPLORING THE SNAP PACKAGE SYSTEM

The Snap package system consists of many different components in its framework. The following parts are important for system administrators:

Snap Packages   Software packages in the Snap format are called *snaps* and focus on a single software application. For example, you could install the Multipass orchestration snap on your system. The snaps download as a single self-contained compressed package file that holds all the binaries and dependencies needed for the app to work.

Snaps are distribution independent. In other words, they don't require any modification for their apps to run on a different Linux distribution than the one for which they were originally packaged. This simplifies application version testing for the system administrator and package building for the package managers. However, keep in mind not *all* Linux distributions support Snap.

A popular aspect of snaps concerns heightened security. When you run an app installed from a snap package, it operates in a sandbox. This way, it is isolated from other data and applications on a Linux system, including other running snaps.

Snap Channels   A common problem with managing system applications is maintaining an older version of the app. There could be additional products or hardware that need to be upgraded prior to the installation of the latest and greatest software version. Sometimes your customers may refuse to sanction an application upgrade. Whatever the reason, a snap channel can help.

Snap channels are snap delivery pathways. Your snap package is updated using a set channel, though you can switch channels if desired. What's even nicer is that you can have two different snaps, each updating from a separate channel. This is a wonderful feature for testing the latest and greatest app modifications.

The channels are named to indicate items such as app stability, using the following format:

track/*risk*/*branch*

A *track* is typically set to latest for normal production updates, or insider for app developers, with latest being the default. A *risk* is stable, candidate, beta, or edge, with stable being the least risky all the way to edge being the most daring for those who like to use software on the bleeding edge. Be aware that some snaps use alpha in place of edge for the risk level. A branch is a temporary channel naming for quick fixes and is generally closed after 30 days of no updates.

The snaps on your system are updated continuously. You can pause the updates, but only for a certain period of time, such as a few days. Also, a snap channel may close if the publisher no longer believes the channel fits the snap package.

The Snap Daemon   One of the primary duties of the snap daemon, snapd, is checking the snaps' channels for app updates. This is typically done multiple times per day.

Potentially confusing is that snapd is also the package name for the Snap package management framework.

The snap **Command**   The gateway to managing snaps is the snap command. Using this command-line interface, you can install and remove snaps. You can also view snaps that are available to install and get detailed information concerning them, such as their current snap channels and publishers. The snap command even allows you to manage the entire Snap framework after it is installed, which is handy.

BUILDING SNAPS

The art of creating snaps is called Snap Craft. Well, that's not true, but it would be a great name for it! Actually, snapcraft is a tool and framework you used to create snaps. So, if you are not only a system administrator, but also a software publisher, you'll want to check out this utility. You can find out more at snapcraft.io/docs/snapcraft-overview and get started building snaps and loading them into the snap store.

The Snap Store You can think of the snap store as a type of package repository. What's a little different about it is that it's a central location where publishers can share their snaps, and system administrators can view what's available.

The snap store is a GUI-based app. So if you want to view what's available using this method, you'll need to install it on your Linux desktop and not any GUI-less servers. However, you don't have to use the snap store to see all the available snaps. The snap command also allows you to list information concerning snaps available for installation, so you're covered on those servers without a GUI.

Be aware that there is a web-based store with an identical name. However, it is for the Snapchat messaging app, and not snap packages.

While snaps sound wonderful, there are a few potential disadvantages to consider. For one, you cannot stop a snap update on a channel. You can only delay it. When your snap is updated, you receive more than just a few changes to the software. Instead, you'll receive an entirely new snap package, some of which are rather large.

Finally, while a publisher may be an entire team of people, typically it's just one individual. Often with a software package maintained by a distribution, many eyes have viewed the code for flaws before it hits the repository. However, there have been cases where even a team of people have missed large security holes in an application's code. You need to be aware of these problems, in case any of them cause snaps to not fit well into your organization's requirements.

INSTALLING THE SNAP FRAMEWORK

On modern Ubuntu distributions, the Snap package management framework comes pre-installed. The package name for Snap is snapd, which is a little confusing, since it's the same name as the Snap daemon. Here's a snipped example of checking the package's status on Ubuntu, using the dpkg -s command:

```
$ dpkg -s snapd
Package: snapd
Status: install ok installed
[...]
```

On other distributions, you'll have to install the Snap framework. On CentOS, you'll also need to install the epel repository, as snapd isn't available in the standard repos. This is shown snipped using the root account here:

```
# dnf install epel-release
[...]
Is this ok [y/N]: y
Downloading Packages:
[...]
Installed:
  epel-release-8-8.el8.noarch

Complete!
#
# dnf install snapd
[...]
```

```
Install  3 Packages
Upgrade  2 Packages

Total download size: 39 M
Is this ok [y/N]: y
[...]
Importing GPG key [...]:
 Userid     : "Fedora EPEL [...]"
 Fingerprint: [...]
 From       : [...]
Is this ok [y/N]: y
Key imported successfully
Running transaction check
Transaction check succeeded.
Running transaction test
[...]
Installed:
  snap-confine-2.49-2.el8.x86_64
  snapd-2.49-2.el8.x86_64
  snapd-selinux-2.49-2.el8.noarch

Complete!
#
```

Once you've installed snapd on your system, be sure to enable it at system boot and start it, using super user privileges and the systemctl command as follows:

```
# systemctl enable snapd
# systemctl start snapd
```

USING BASIC COMMANDS

The snap command has many subcommands. You can see all of them by typing in **snap --help** at the command line, but Table 22.1 describes the basic ones you'll use when getting started with snaps.

TABLE 22.1:   Basic snap Subcommands

SUBCOMMAND	DESCRIPTION
find *query*	Searches the snap store for snaps containing *query* in their description
info *snaps-name*	Displays detailed information concerning the *snaps-name* snap package
install *snaps-name*	Installs the *snaps-name* snap package, if you use super user privileges when issuing a command
list	Displays a list of installed snaps along with their version and revision number, channel, publisher, and any notes
remove *snaps-name*	Uninstalls the *snaps-name* snap package, if you use super user privileges when issuing a command

On Ubuntu, you'll have a few pre-installed snaps that you can view using the snap list command, as shown here:

```
$ snap list
Name     Version    Rev    Tracking        Publisher   Notes
core18   20210309   1997   latest/stable   canonical✓  base
lxd      4.0.5      19647  4.0/stable/...  canonical✓  -
snapd    2.49.2     11588  latest/stable   canonical✓  snapd
$
```

If your distribution doesn't have any pre-installed snaps, you'll receive the following message when you attempt the list subcommand:

```
$ snap list
No snaps are installed yet. Try 'snap install hello-world'.
$
```

One nice feature about using the snap find command to search through the snap store for snaps is that the query you use can be the snap package's name, the publisher's name, or some subset of information in the description. In Figure 22.5, we issued the command **snap find canonical | less** to take our time in viewing all the snaps available from the canonical publisher in the less pager.

FIGURE 22.5

Using the snap find command

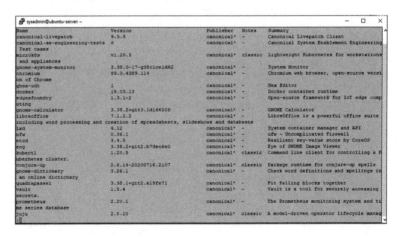

To get more detailed information on a particular snap package than the find subcommand provides, use snap info as shown here:

```
$ snap info cvescan
name:      cvescan
summary:   Security/CVE vulnerability monitoring for Ubuntu
publisher: Canonical✓
store-url: https://snapcraft.io/cvescan
[...]
channels:
```

```
latest/stable:     2.5.0 2020-09-01 (281) 43MB -
latest/candidate: ↑
latest/beta:       ↑
latest/edge:       ↑
$
```

Though many of the snap basic commands work without any special privileges, you will need super user privileges to install and remove snaps. We decided to install the cvescan snap on Ubuntu as shown snipped here:

```
$ sudo snap install cvescan
[sudo] password for sysadmin:
Download snap "cvescan" (281) from channel "stable"   [...]
[...]
Setup snap "cvescan" (281) security profiles
cvescan 2.5.0 from Canonical✓ installed
$
$ which cvescan
/snap/bin/cvescan
$
```

Once you have a snap package installed, you run the app just as you would normally, as shown here for the cvescan software:

```
$ cvescan -p critical
✓ Ubuntu vulnerability datbase successfully downloaded!
✓ Scan complete!

Summary
----------------------------------    ------------------
Ubuntu Release                        focal
Installed Packages                    620
CVE Priority                          critical or higher
Unique Packages Fixable by Patching   0
Unique CVEs Fixable by Patching       0
Vulnerabilities Fixable by Patching   0
Fixes Available by `apt-get upgrade`  0
----------------------------------    ------------------
$
```

Removing snaps is just as easy as installing them. Just use the required super user privileges and the snap remove *snap-name* command. We don't want to remove our cvescan snap package just yet because there is further exploration we'd like to do with it.

VIEWING THE *SNAP* DIRECTORIES

An interesting activity to do once you've installed a snap package and tried it out is to view where its files are located, as we've done here using the find command:

```
$ sudo find / -name cvescan
/snap/bin/cvescan
/snap/cvescan
```

```
/snap/cvescan/281/bin/cvescan
/snap/cvescan/281/lib/python3.6/site-packages/cvescan
/home/sysadmin/snap/cvescan
/var/snap/cvescan
$
```

When installing snaps, you'll find that their file locations are slightly different than traditional packages:

◆ Binaries are stored in the /snap/bin/ directory.

◆ Any needed libraries and configuration files are located within the /snap/*snap-name*/ directory tree.

◆ User data associated with the snap application is a snap subdirectory of the user's $HOME directory.

◆ Variable data typically stored in the /var/ directory for nonsnap apps is stored in the /var/snap/*snap-name*/ directory for snaps.

Recall that for each app, snaps are a single self-contained compressed package file that holds all the binaries and dependencies needed for the application to work. One difference between snaps and other package files is that snaps are never unpacked. They also stay in a compressed format, living in the /var/lib/snapd/ directory, as shown here:

```
$ ls -Fw 50 /var/lib/snapd/snaps/
core18_1988.snap  lxd_19647.snap
core18_1997.snap  partial/
cvescan_281.snap  snapd_11402.snap
lxd_19188.snap    snapd_11588.snap
$
```

The snap package files have a .snap file extension. Notice that the cvescan snap package name has a number in it. This is the revision number, which we can see using the snap list command:

```
$ snap list cvescan
Name     Version  Rev  Tracking       Publisher   Notes
cvescan  2.5.0    281  latest/stable  canonical√  -
```

Using the snap list command, you can also see what channel the cvescan app is set to update. In this case, it's using the latest/stable snap channel.

 Real World Scenario

USING SNAP ON YOUR LINUX SYSTEM

The Snap universal package format makes installing and using software applications rather easy. Earlier in this chapter, we covered Docker. Installing Docker on Ubuntu using apt is rather tedious, but installing it as a snap package on Ubuntu is simple!

The following steps will take you through installing a Docker snap on an Ubuntu distribution and trying basic commands with it to manage a container environment:

1. Log into your Ubuntu Linux system using the sysadmin account and the password you created for it.

2. Install the docker snap package by typing **sudo snap install docker** and pressing Enter. If you're asked for a password, type in the sysadmin account's password. If asked, type **y** to answer any questions, and press Enter after doing so.

3. Once the installation is complete, test Docker by typing **sudo docker run hello-world** and pressing Enter. If asked for a password, type in the sysadmin account's password. You may see some error messages, and that is OK. You know the installation was successful when you receive a message similar to the following along with additional information:

   ```
   Hello from Docker!
   This message shows that your installation appears to be working correctly.
   ```

4. When you issued the previous command (sudo docker run hello-world), you actually created a container called Hello-World. View this container's information by typing **sudo docker ps -a** and pressing Enter. If you're asked for a password, type in the sysadmin account's password.

5. Find the Container ID number from the previous step's command output and record it. (Hint: The Container ID number will contain both letters and numbers and will be listed under the Container ID column.)

6. Delete the Hello-World container by typing **sudo docker rm *Container-ID*** and pressing Enter, where ***Container-ID*** is the number you recorded in the previous step. If you're asked for a password, type in the sysadmin account's password.

7. Start up a CentOS container using Docker running in a snap sandbox on your Ubuntu system by typing **sudo docker run -it centos bash** and pressing Enter. Besides starting the container, this command will put you into the container. The -it options on the run command allow you to enter into interactive mode (i) and use a pseudo-terminal (t). If you're asked for a password, type in the sysadmin account's password. After you are in the container, your prompt will look similar to the following:

   ```
   [root@8a7a39343829 /]#
   ```

8. At the container prompt, type **whoami** and press Enter. Surprise! You're logged in as the root user, and that's OK, because you are contained.

9. See where you are at in the container's virtual directory system by typing **pwd** and pressing Enter. You should see that you are at the root (/) of the directory structure.

10. View the version of CentOS you are running in this container by typing **cat /etc /redhat-release** and pressing Enter. Record your findings.

11. Leave the CentOS container by typing **exit** and pressing Enter. You should see your prompt change.

12. Double-check that you are out of the container by typing **whoami** and pressing Enter. You should now be logged into the sysadmin account, instead of the root account.

13. View the available containers by typing **sudo docker ps -a** and pressing Enter. If you're asked for a password, type in the sysadmin account's password. You should see only one container. Record its Container ID.

14. Start the container you viewed in the previous step by typing
dsudo docker start *Container-ID* and pressing Enter, where ***Container-ID*** is the number you recorded in the previous step. If you're asked for a password, type in the sysadmin account's password.

15. Jump back into the Ubuntu container by typing **sudo docker attach *Container-ID*** and pressing Enter, where ***Container-ID*** is the number you recorded in step 13. If you're asked for a password, type in the sysadmin account's password. You should see that your prompt has changed.

16. At the container prompt, type **whoami** and press Enter. You should see that you are logged in as the root user.

17. View the version of CentOS you are running in this container by typing **cat /etc /redhat-release** and pressing Enter. Check that the version information matches what you recorded in step 10. It should.

18. If you want, do a little exploring in the container that was started from the Docker snap. Try different commands you have learned in this book, and look through the Linux virtual directory structure.

19. Leave the CentOS container by typing **exit** and pressing Enter. You should see your prompt change.

20. Delete the CentOS container by typing **sudo docker rm *Container-ID*** and pressing Enter, where ***Container-ID*** is the number you recorded in step 13. If you're asked for a password, type in the sysadmin account's password.

Snap is still relatively new to the package management world. Now that you have some basic concepts, you can start exploring more with snaps.

Looking at Flatpak

Flatpak is a package format similar to Snap. Software packages are called *flatpaks*, focused on a single software application, and are a single self-contained compressed package file that holds all the binaries and dependencies needed for the app to work. Flatpak packages are distribution independent, earning Flatpak the same designation as Snap, a universal package system.

When you run an app installed from a flatpak package, it operates in a sandbox. Thus, it is isolated from other data and applications on a Linux system, including other running flatpaks. This provides increased security of the apps and the host system.

Though the concept of Flatpak has been around longer than Snap, this universal package system is only now starting to gain ground. Currently, flatpaks are available only for desktop applications on Linux, not server applications. However, it's still important for you to know the general concepts around Flatpak, since all things tend to evolve to greater heights in Linux.

EXPLORING THE FLATPAK PACKAGE SYSTEM

Flatpak has some terms and structures that are unique to it. The following are some of those items you should know:

Application Sandboxes Each app installed from a flatpak runs in a sandboxed environment. Within that environment are all the application's binaries, and some or all of the needed libraries. The application can access only items in the sandbox or items through portals to which clear access has been given. However, the apps cannot directly access other running programs. Application sandboxes also include a runtime.

Runtimes Think of these structures as container engines that run on a host's operating system. Each flatpak app sandbox operates with a runtime environment. These environments include all the needed libraries that are not bundled into the app itself.

Portals Flatpak apps running in a sandbox can access items outside the sandbox, such as files. This is done through portals. Only those items to which clear access has been given through sandbox permissions are accessible.

An interesting feature of Flatpak is the ability to install flatpaks without using elevated privileges. In other words, your users can install their own flatpaks and runtimes without involving you and your ability to use super user privileges in the process. That can be a benefit to some Linux environments, while a security nightmare for those organizations that need to restrict apps installed and used on their systems.

INSTALLING THE FLATPAK FRAMEWORK

On modern Red Hat–based server distributions, the Flatpak package management framework does not necessarily come pre-installed. You can quickly check to see if your system has the Flatpak universal package system by looking for the flatpak command with which, as shown here on a CentOS server distribution:

```
$ which flatpak
/usr/bin/which: no flatpak in (/home/sysadmin/.local/bin:
/home/sysadmin/bin:/usr/local/bin:/usr/bin:/usr/local/sbin:
/usr/sbin:/var/lib/snapd/snap/bin)
$
```

The package name for Flatpak is flatpak, which keeps things simple. Here's a snipped example of installing the Flatpak package framework on a CentOS server distro using the root account:

```
$ su -
Password:
[root@localhost ~]# dnf install flatpak
Last metadata expiration check:[...].
Dependencies resolved.
[...]
```

```
Install  29 Packages

Total download size: 6.7 M
Installed size: 25 M
Is this ok [y/N]: y
Downloading Packages:
[...]
Running transaction check
Transaction check succeeded.
Running transaction test
Transaction test succeeded.
Running transaction
[...]
Complete!
[root@localhost ~]# which flatpak
/usr/bin/flatpak
[root@localhost ~]#
```

If you'd like to install the Flatpak framework on Ubuntu, you'll need to use super user privileges, update the apt repository information, and install the flatpak package with these commands:

```
$ sudo apt update
$ sudo apt install flatpak
```

There is no service to enable or start. So you're ready to start using Flatpak once the package installation is completed.

USING BASIC COMMANDS

Once installed, the flatpak command is available, and the next step is to add a Flatpak remote repository. A repository is a location on the Internet that contains various flatpak packages to choose from. There are several repositories, but the most popular one is flathub. Adding this particular repository is shown here:

```
[root@localhost ~]# flatpak remote-add flathub \
> https://flathub.org/repo/flathub.flatpakrepo
[root@localhost ~]#
[root@localhost ~]# flatpak remotes
Name    Options
flathub system
[root@localhost ~]#
```

Now that there is a Flatpak remote repository, you can start installing flatpak apps. Table 22.2 shows a few basic subcommands you can use with flatpak to install and manage your flatpaks.

TABLE 22.2:   Basic flatpak Subcommands

SUBCOMMAND	DESCRIPTION
info *name*	Displays detailed information concerning the *name* flatpak package or runtime
install *name*	Installs the *name* flatpak package or runtime
list	Displays a list of installed flatpaks and/or runtimes
uninstall *name*	Removes the *name* flatpak package or runtime
update *name*	Updates the installed *name* flatpak package
search *query*	Searches the added flatpak repository(ies) for flatpaks containing *query* in their description

Once you have a flatpak name that you'd like to install, just use super user privileges, if desired, and use flatpak install *flatpak-name* to complete the task. An example of installing the gedit flatpak on CentOS using the root account is shown snipped here:

```
[root@localhost ~]# flatpak install gedit
Looking for matches...
Found similar ref(s) for 'gedit' in remote 'flathub'[...]
Use this remote? [Y/n]: Y
Found ref 'app/org.gnome.gedit/[...]in remote 'flathub'[...]
Use this ref? [Y/n]: Y
Required runtime for org.gnome.gedit/x86_64/stable
(runtime/org.gnome.Platform/x86_64/40) found in remote flathub
Do you want to install it? [Y/n]: n
error: The application org.gnome.gedit/x86_64/stable requires the runtime
org.gnome.Platform/x86_64/40 which is not installed
[root@localhost ~]#
```

Notice that this installation was not successful. Because we answered n to installing the gnome runtime, the gedit flatpak would not install. For a flatpak installation to complete successfully, you'll have to install any required runtimes.

Because these universal package systems are fairly new to the Linux environment, it is wise to determine exactly what your company needs in package management. Then, before installing either the Snap or Flatpak software framework on your system, do some research and determine if the current state of these software systems meets your particular organization's app management and security needs.

The Bottom Line

Understand basic hypervisor components.   Hypervisors are used to create and manage VMs and are generally categorized as Type 1, Type 2, or hybrid. There are pros and cons associated with each category. For example, when creating a VM using a Type 2 hypervisor, host machine resources need auditing to determine if the VM's requirements can be met. While a Type 1 hypervisor eliminates the need for the physical host's OS, it still can consume significant resources to run VMs. Creating a VM using hypervisor software is done using many different methods, such as P2V, cloning, using templates, or employing OVF files.

> **Master It**   You need to create and deploy several VMs that contain the same brand new application and need the same environment. After reviewing the various options, which method would you choose to create these VMs and why?

Generate a container with a Bash shell.   Containers each have their own set of binaries and needed libraries to support their app, application stack, or environment, but they share the physical host's operating system. Starting and stopping containers, instead of performing software upgrades within them, is one reason why they are so popular for development and operations (DevOps). Docker is one such container engine that is extremely popular. It uses a daemon on the Linux system to listen for requests from the individual containers as well as from a Docker command-line interface that allows you to control the container environment.

> **Master It**   Imagine you are a system administrator for an Ubuntu Linux system, and the development team is considering Docker containers to use in their production of applications. To let them try this environment, you need to install Docker to create and manage containers. Your Ubuntu system is specifically a server distro, so you want to manage the containers from the command line. What steps can you take to quickly install the Docker engine and generate a test CentOS container with access to the Bash shell for the software developers to try?

Manage the Snap universal package system.   The Snap universal package system employs the snap command to install and manage snap packages. The snapd daemon updates these packages on a regular basis through the appropriate Snap channel. When run, snaps operate in an isolated sandbox, protecting other data and applications on a Linux system, including other running snaps.

> **Master It**   You have recently visited the snap store and found a wonderful snap application that will assist in your orchestration management of containers, Multipass. After installing it and running it through several tests, you decide to use it in your production environment. However, you'd like to also keep up-to-date with the new developments in this special snap package. Besides reading about up-and-coming Multipass features, how can you stay informed using a snap package?

Install the Flatpak framework.   Software packages, flatpaks, in the Flatpak universal package system focus on a single software application and are a single self-contained compressed package file that holds all the binaries and dependencies needed for the app to work. Though Flatpak is similar to Snap, flatpaks are currently available only for Desktop applications on Linux systems.

> **Master It**   You are a system administrator for a CentOS Desktop Linux system used by developers for creating the company's main software product. The developers are

interested in a different text editor that will allow them to efficiently operate as they update the company's software app. Because there is a consideration to move development from the current Linux distro to another one that also uses Flatpak, you decide to install this text editor's flatpak package that is available in `flathub`. What steps should you take to get this framework and text editor installed for the developers on this current system?

Appendix

The Bottom Line

Each of The Bottom Line sections in the chapters suggest exercises to deepen skills and understanding. Sometimes there is only one possible solution, but often you are encouraged to use your skills and creativity to create something that builds on what you know and lets you explore one of many possible solutions.

Chapter 1: Understanding the Basics

List the components of a standard Linux system.   The main components of a Linux system include the Linux kernel, the GNU utilities, a user interface, and application programs. The kernel controls how memory, programs, and hardware all interact with one another. The GNU utilities provide useful functions such as text and file manipulation. The Linux user interfaces range from fancy graphical desktops, such as GNOME or KDE Plasma, to simple command-line interfaces, such as the Bash Shell.

Master It   The Linux kernel is constantly updated and managed by a group of developers. They publish their work at the kernel.org website. Go to that website and determine the version number of the latest stable release. What version is currently under development?

Solution   At the time of this writing, the current stable version of the Linux kernel is version 5.9.6 and is available for download. The current development release is 5.10.

Explain how GNU utilities are used within Linux.   The GNU utilities provide command-line functions for creating, modifying, moving, and deleting files, as well as working with data inside text files. The main GNU utilities are in the coreutils package.

Master It   The GNU community is constantly making improvements to the core GNU utilities used in Linux. You can find the latest released utilities at www.gnu.org/software/coreutils/. Go to that website and determine the current version of the GNU coreutils package.

Solution   At the time of this writing, the GNU coreutils website has version coreutils-8.32 available for download.

Describe the various Linux user interface environments.   There are many graphical desktop environments available in Linux. The two most popular ones are GNOME and KDE Plasma. Both provide common desktop features most desktop users are comfortable with. However, for server environments, it's most common to use a command-line interface (CLI) provided by a Linux shell program. The most common Linux shell is bash.

Master It The GNU Bash Shell is continually being updated, with updates available at www.gnu.org/software/bash/. According to that website, what is the most recent version of bash available for download?

Solution At the time of this writing, the latest production release for GNU bash is 5.0. The 5.1 version is available for beta testing, so it may be available for production systems by the time you read this!

Explain why there are different Linux distributions. A Linux distribution bundles the various parts of a Linux system into a simple package that you can easily install on your PC. The Ltinux distribution world consists of full-blown Linux distributions that include just about every application imaginable, as well as specialized Linux distributions that only include applications focused on a special function.

Master It There are many websites that track Linux distributions. The www .distrowatch.com website is a popular place to get information on new releases for lots of different distributions. Go to that site and list the current top five Linux distribution downloads.

Solution At the time of this writing, the top five desktop Linux systems are MX Linux, Manjaro, Mint, Pop!_OS, and Ubuntu.

Chapter 2: Installing an Ubuntu Server

Review needed Ubuntu server hardware resources. Determining the hardware resources required for an Ubuntu installation on a physical or virtualized server helps to ensure a successful completion of the install. It also avoids wasting time.

Master It Imagine that you need to install the Ubuntu Server on a physical server that has a dual-core 1 GHz CPU, a 200 GB hard drive, and 10 GB of RAM. Are the server's resources sufficient? Why or why not?

Solution The server's resources of a dual-core 1 GHz CPU, a 200 GB hard drive, and 10 GB of RAM are sufficient to install the Ubuntu Server distribution. The minimum needed is a 1 GHz CPU, 2.5 GB of disk space, and 1 GB of memory. Thus, this physical server can properly handle the load of the Ubuntu Server distro.

Determine the requirements for a virtual Ubuntu system. Installing the Ubuntu Server distribution on as a VM on a host system has different requirements than a direct installation on a physical server. It is critical to evaluate the host system so that the installation is successful.

Master It Your project team is planning on installing two Ubuntu Server VMs on a host system that has a dual-core 1 GHz CPU, a 200 GB hard drive, and 10 GB of RAM. Are the host system's resources sufficient? Why or why not?

Solution The host system does not meet the minimum CPU requirements for a single Ubuntu Server VM, which is a 2 GHz dual core processor. While there is sufficient disk space for two VMs, the RAM is potentially a little low, since 16 GB is recommended (but not required) for a single Ubuntu Server VM.

Obtain Ubuntu Server software.   To install the Ubuntu Server Linux distribution, you must have the proper ISO image file. This is true whether you are installing it directly on hardware or as a VM. Besides getting the ISO file, you need to ensure that it is not corrupted so that the installation proceeds well.

Master It   You've downloaded the Ubuntu Server ISO image file but are concerned that during the download process, file corruption occurred. What should you do to see whether the ISO image file is corrupt?

Solution   Get a hash value by using a hashing algorithm program that uses the SHA256 algorithm on the downloaded Ubuntu Server ISO image file. After you get the hash value, compare it to the hash value listed on the Ubuntu Server website. If they match, your ISO image file is not corrupted. If they don't match, you'll need to download it again.

Conduct an installation of an Ubuntu Server.   There are several steps to successfully install an Ubuntu Server, and it is critical that you complete all of them. Skipping a step can cause problems immediately, and problems later, if you can even get the system to boot.

Master It   Your sysadmin team has correctly installed the Ubuntu Server software from the ISO image file and the system booted without any problems. What's the next step?

Solution   After your sysadmin team has correctly installed the Ubuntu Server software from the ISO image file and the system booted without any problems, the team needs to update the software information via the `sudo apt update` command. After that is completed, they will need to update the software through the `sudo apt dist-upgrade` command.

Audit the Ubuntu Server's installation.   If you had some problems while booting the system, there are a few commands you can use to look at helpful boot messages. But even a successful installation still requires a few additional checks.

Master It   At your company, you have completed the entire Ubuntu Server installation process on a new system without any problems for the development team. The team wants to know what version of the Linux kernel is used on this new system. How do you get that information?

Solution   There are two ways to get the Linux kernel version information on the new system for the development team. You can log into the system and issue either the `uname -r` or the `cat /proc/version` command.

Chapter 3: Installing and Maintaining Software in Ubuntu

Explore different Linux software package management systems.   Developers bundle the files required for an application into a package to make it easier to install. A package management system allows you to easily track, install, and remove application packages on your Linux system. There are two popular Linux package management systems: dpkg for Debian-based systems, and `rpm` for Red Hat–based systems.

Master It The Debian Linux distribution maintains an official website that tracks all software packages as they're developed for the Debian environment. Go to the packages .debian.org website and determine what version of the systat application is available as a stable Debian package.

Solution After you go to the packages.debian.org website, enter **sysstat** in the search text box to search for that package name. In the Exact Hits section, notice that there are different versions of sysstat available in the different Debian distribution versions. At the time of this writing, the current stable version (called *buster*) only supports sysstat version 12.0.3-2. However, the testing version (called *bullseye*) supports version 12.4.0-1.

Use Debian software packages to install software. The Debian-based Linux distributions use the dpkg utility to interface with the package management system from the command line, and they use the apt-cache and apt-get utilities to interface with a common repository to easily download and install new software. A front end to these utilities is apt. It provides simple command-line options for working with software packages in the dpkg format.

Master It The C shell provides an alternative to the Bash Shell, handy for writing advanced shell scripts. For Ubuntu, the C shell is bundled as part of the csh package. What commands should you use to install the csh package from the standard Ubuntu software repository?

Solution To install the csh package, you would use the apt utility. Just enter the command **sudo apt install csh** at the command prompt. To test the new shell, enter the command **csh** at the command prompt. This opens an instance of the C shell, which uses the percent symbol (%) as the shell prompt. To return to your Bash Shell, type **exit**.

Install applications using Debian snap containers. Application containers are a relatively new player in software package management. An application container bundles all the files necessary for an application to run in one installable package. This means the application doesn't rely on any external dependencies such as library files, and the container bundle can be installed in any Linux distribution and run. Currently, the two most popular container packages are snap, common in the Ubuntu Linux distribution, and flatpak, used in Red Hat Linux environments.

Master It The PowerShell package provides a powerful scripting language similar to that found on Microsoft Windows servers. Ubuntu distributes the PowerShell package as a snap container. What command should you use to install PowerShell on your Ubuntu server?

Solution Since the PowerShell application uses an old container format, if you try to install it using the standard snap install powershell, you'll receive an error message warning you that it uses the old format and telling you to use the --classic option. So, to install the PowerShell snap package, you must enter the command **sudo snap --classic install powershell**.

Install software from source code. The chapter closed with a discussion on how to install software packages that are only distributed in source code tarballs. The tar command allows you to unpack the source code files from the tarball, and then the configure and make commands allow you to build the final executable program from the source code.

Master It   There are lots of handy utilities created and shared by Linux developers. One such utility is the sysstat tool. The sysstat tool provides statistics for various features of your Linux system. You can find the sysstat tool on the developer's website, sebastien .godard.pagesperso-orange.fr. After downloading the package tarball, what commands would you need to use to compile the software and install it on your Linux server?

Solution   The sysstat source code is provided using several different package types. The one that creates the smallest package size is the .xz version. At the time of this writing you should download the sysstat-12.5.1.tar.xz package. Once you have that package downloaded, extract it using the command tar -Jxvf sysstat-12.5.1.tar .xz. This creates the sysstat-12.5.1 directory. Change to that directory using the command cd sysstat-12.5.1. The next step is to run the configuration script using the command ./configure. This generates the Makefile file. The next step is to run the make command. After the software compiles, you can install it on your system using the command sudo make install.

Chapter 4: Installing a Red Hat Server

Review needed CentOS hardware resources.   Determining the hardware resources required for a CentOS installation on a physical or virtualized server helps to ensure a successful completion of the install. It also avoids important project delays due to under-resourced systems.

Master It   Imagine that you need to install the CentOS distribution on a physical server that has a dual-core 2 GHz CPU, 200 GB hard drive, and 2 GB of RAM. Are the server's resources at the recommended level? Why or why not?

Solution   The server's resources of a dual-core 2 GHz CPU, 200 GB hard drive, and 2 GB of RAM are sufficient to install the CentOS distribution. The minimum needed is a 1.8 GHz CPU, 10 GB of disk space, and 2 GB of memory. However, they do not meet the recommended level. Because the recommendation requires 2 GB of RAM per logical CPU and this system has a dual-core CPU, 4 GB RAM is recommended. Thus, this physical server needs more RAM to meet the recommended resource levels.

Determine the requirements for a virtual CentOS system.   Installing the CentOS distribution as a VM on a host system has different requirements than a direct installation on a physical server. It is critical to evaluate the host system so that the installation is successful.

Master It   Your project team is planning on installing two CentOS VMs on a host system that has a quad-core 2.8 GHz CPU, 200 GB of free disk space, and 32 GB of RAM. Are the host system resources sufficient? Why or why not?

Solution   The host system does have enough resources for two CentOS VMs. The recommendations for a single CentOS VM are a 2 or more GHz dual-core processor, 16 or more GB of memory, and 30 or more GB of free disk space. However, the host system's OS needs should also be considered before declaring the resources sufficient.

Obtain CentOS software.   To install the CentOS Linux distribution, you must have the proper ISO image file. This is true whether you are installing it directly on hardware or as a VM. Besides getting the ISO file, you need to ensure that it is not corrupted so that the installation proceeds well.

Master It   You've downloaded the CentOS ISO image file, but you are concerned that during the download process, file corruption occurred. What should you do to see whether the ISO image file is corrupt?

Solution   Get a hash value by using a hashing algorithm program that uses the SHA256 algorithm on the downloaded CentOS ISO image file. After you get the hash value, compare it to the hash value listed on the website from which you downloaded the ISO image file. If they match, your ISO image file is not corrupted. If they don't match, you'll need to download the ISO image file again.

Conduct an installation of a CentOS distribution.   There are several steps to successfully install a CentOS distribution, and it is critical to make sure you complete all of them. Skipping a step can cause problems immediately as well as problems later, if you can even get the system to boot.

Master It   Your sysadmin team has correctly installed the CentOS software from the ISO image file, and the system booted without any problems. What's the next step?

Solution   After your sysadmin team has correctly installed the CentOS software from the ISO image file and the system booted without any problems, the team needs to install the update stream via the `dnf install -y centos-release-stream` command, using super user privileges. After that is completed, they will need to update the software using super user privileges through the `dnf update` command.

Audit the CentOS distribution's installation.   If you had some problems while booting the system, there are a few commands you can use to look at helpful boot messages. But even a successful installation still requires a few additional checks.

Master It   At your company, you have completed the entire CentOS distro installation process on a new system without any problems, but you then ran into issues the last time the server was rebooted. You need to review the boot messages to track down the problem(s). What log file can you use to view these messages?

Solution   There are three ways on a CentOS system to look at boot messages. If the system was recently booted, you can use the `dmesg` command. The `journalctl` command will also contain boot messages. However, the log file that contains boot messages on a CentOS system is `/var/log/boot.log`, and it is best to use the `less` command to view it for finding boot problems.

Chapter 5: Installing and Maintaining Software in Red Hat

Recognize Red Hat packages.   Developers bundle the files required for an application into a package to make it easier to install. A package management system allows you to easily track what software packages are installed on your Linux system, as well as install, update, and remove them. Red Hat–based Linux distributions use the Red Hat Package Management (RPM) system for managing application software. The `rpm` command-line tool provides access to the package management database, allowing you to quickly determine the status of installed packages.

Master It The curl software package allows you to easily transfer data using a multitude of protocols (such as FTP, HTTP, and SCP) from the command line. What command would you use to determine whether curl is installed on your Linux system? If the package is installed, what command would you use to view the version and a description of the package?

Solution To query the package management database, use the rpm -q command. At the command prompt, type **rpm -q curl**. If the package is installed, you will see it listed in the output. To obtain additional information on the installed package, type the command **rpm -qi curl**.

Use automated Red Hat package managers. Most Red Hat–based Linux distributions are based on the rpm utility but use different front-end tools at the command line. Red Hat, CentOS, and Fedora use dnf for installing and managing software packages. The dnf tool automatically installs any software packages required by the package you install.

Master It The perf utility allows you to monitor the performance of a Linux system. What command would you use to check whether the perf software is available as an rpm package for your Linux system, and what command would you use to install it? What command would you use to remove it?

Solution You would use the dnf command to check whether the perf software package is available, install it, and remove it when necessary. Enter the command **dnf list perf** to see if the package is available for installation. Then, to install the package, type the command **dnf install perf.** After you've installed the perf package, remove it using the command **dnf remove perf**. Remember, you will need to have root privileges to install the package.

Manually install Red Hat packages. Not all Linux systems are connected to the Internet, allowing the automated package management tools to connect to a repository. In those situations, you'll need to manually find and download RPM software packages and then use the rpm command to manually install the package. The most common options used to install software are the -Uvh options, which will update the package if it's already installed and provide verbose information on the installation progress.

Master It What steps would you need to take to install the perf utility if your Linux system is not connected to the Internet?

Solution First you would need to download the perf rpm package file. You can do this from another Linux system connected to the Internet by typing the command **yumdownloader perf** (you don't need root privileges to do this). At the time of this writing, the download file is perf-4.18.0-240.1.1.el8_3.x86_64.rpm. Once you have the RPM file transferred to your Linux system, you can manually install it by typing the command **rpm -Uvh perf-4.18.0-240.1.1.el8_3.x86_64.rpm**. You will need root privileges to install the software.

Install flatpak application containers. Application containers are relatively new in software package management. Containers bundle all of the software required for an application to run, including all files the application is dependent on. This makes containers portable and easily moved between systems. Red Hat Linux–based distributions use the flatpak container format.

Master It Cointop is a terminal-based application for tracking cryptocurrencies. What command would you use to check if there's a flatpak container for it, and what command would you use to install it?

Solution To check whether the cointop application container exists in the current repository, enter the command **flatpak search cointop**. The output indicates that the package exists and displays the software version. To install the container, enter the command **flatpak install cointop**. Remember that you must have root privileges to install the software.

Chapter 6: Working with the Shell

Decode the shell prompt and the manual pages. The prompt is where you enter shell commands. It provides access to the utilities needed to manage a system. In addition, the shell prompt often gives additional information that can help you at the CLI.

Master It Imagine that you recently successfully logged in to a Linux system. This particular system uses the CentOS Linux distribution. What sort of items might you see in the shell prompt?

Solution Typically, you'll see the dollar sign ($) character in your prompt, as long as you have not logged into the root account. In addition, your username and the system's host name are often also displayed in the prompt within a set of brackets for a CentOS distro. (You may also see a ~, which is a special character that represents your home directory.)

Decode the shell prompt and the manual pages. The man pages are an online manual that provide information on various shell utilities, special files, system administrator commands, and so on. They are a source of quick help and can be searched to determine the information you need.

Master It You are attempting to become proficient at using the man pages. However, the pager utility it employs is causing you some frustration, so you attempt to learn more about it without leaving the CLI. How can you accomplish learning more about the pager utility used for the man pages?

Solution The less utility is the pager used for the man pages. Type **man less** and press Enter at the shell prompt to view the information on this command from the online manual.

Enter, recall, and redirect shell commands. To function efficiently and effectively at the CLI, recalling shell commands is a critical task. A system admin must be proficient at quickly retrieving, potentially modifying, and using previously issued commands.

Master It Your main production app on the server is experiencing some performance problems, and you are working as fast as possible to determine and correct the issue(s). You need to recall and reenact a command you used previously. You can see from this history list that it is command 42. What's the fastest way to recall and reuse this command?

Solution The fastest way to recall and reuse the command that is numbered 42 in the history list is to type **!42** and press the Enter key. These four simple keystrokes will display the command and then reenact it at the CLI.

Enter, recall, and redirect shell commands. Being efficient and effective at the command line is more than just being fast. It also requires smart habits. One of these is using command redirection to manage STDIN, STDOUT, and STDERR.

Master It You created a nice pipeline of commands to filter and format some needed text file information. You want to view the information but keep a copy of it at the same time. How can you accomplish this?

Solution To view produced information as well as keep a copy of it, you'll need to use the tee command within your pipeline. The tee command will allow you to save the information to a designated file, but in addition, it sends the data to STDOUT for viewing (or further processing).

Set and use environment variables. Variables help to define your CLI environment. In addition, they allow you to store data in memory that can be easily accessed by any program. Defining a variable, removing a definition, and globalizing a variable are all important management activities.

Master It You are creating a user-defined environment variable for an application. Because of the nature of the application, this variable must be available in subshells. What needs to be done to ensure this happens?

Solution When, or immediately after, you define the environment variable, use the export command on the variable. By using export, the variable definition is available to the current parent shell as well as any subshells.

Chapter 7: Exploring Linux File Management

Describe how Linux handles files and directories. File management is an important part of the Linux system, and it helps to know the basics of how to manage files from the CLI. This chapter first showed you how to use both absolute and relative filepaths in commands to reference files and directories. Next, it showed the standard Linux file naming conventions used by Linux distributions, along with how Linux uses inodes to handle files.

Master It Your boss has given you a list of files he saw being used on the server and wants you to find out what type of files they are. The files are as follows:

/usr/bin/grep

/usr/bin/zcat

/etc/hosts

~/.bashrc

What command should you use to determine those file types?

Solution To determine the file type of a Linux file, you use the file command. From the command prompt, enter these commands:

file /usr/bin/grep

file /usr/bin/zcat

file /etc/hosts

file ~/.bashrc

Explain the different options available to list files and directories. The ls command is how to list the contents of directories from the command prompt. While there are lots of parameters associated with the ls command, you'll soon find yourself using just a handful of them to view the information that you need.

Master It A user on your Linux server has an important project and needs access to the file /share/HR/employees.txt. However, the user doesn't know who owns the file to ask for permission to access the file. What command and parameters should you use to determine the owner of the file?

Solution The -l parameter of the ls command produces a long-format listing of the files in a directory. Part of that output shows the owner of the files. Use the command **ls -l /share** to view the file properties and determine the file owner.

Submit commands to manage files and directories. The chapter showed you how to use the Linux CLI to create, move, and remove both directories and files. The chapter also went through how to use globbing to specify file and directory ranges instead of single files in the commands, as well as how to use quoting to work with file and directory names that incorporate spaces.

Master It You have been assigned the task of creating a new directory for the Engineering team on the Linux server. Under that directory they'd also like to have separate directories for the automotive project group and the truck project group. What commands should you enter to create these directories?

Solution To create new directories, you'll use the mkdir command. From the CLI prompt, enter the command **mkdir /Engineering** (you must have root permissions to create a directory under the root directory). Then to create the project directories, first enter the command **mkdir /Engineering/automotive** and then the command **mkdir /Engineering/truck**.

Use Linux commands to find files and directories. There are a few common Linux commands used to help find files on the Linux system. The which, locate, and whereis commands can be useful for general searches, but the find command allows you to customize your search by specifying specific file or directory properties to look for.

Master It You have been tasked to find all files on your filesystem that are larger than 10 MB in size. What command would you use to easily find those files?

Solution The find command allows you to search for files based on file size by using the -size parameter. To explore all directories on the server, you'll need to run the command with root privileges: **find / -size +10MG -print**.

Use Linux commands to compress and archive files and directories. There are many different utilities available for compressing and archiving files in Linux. For archiving files, the gzip family of commands is a popular option. For archiving multiple files into a single file, the tar command is common. You can also compress a tar archive file to facilitate moving it to off-site storage.

Master It What commands should you use to create a backup archive file of the new /Engineering directory and compress it?

Solution To archive all the files and subdirectories in the /Engineering directory, enter the command **tar -cvf engineering.tar /Engineering**. Since this directory is at the root level, you'll need to have root permissions to do this. Then to compress the file using the gzip utility, enter the command **gzip engineering.tar**.

Chapter 8: Working with Text Files

Use the vim editor's basic features.   The vim editor is one of the most popular text editors in use. Though it can be tricky to use, modifying text files using vim is worth the time to learn. Grasping the basics of the vim editor is all that is needed for a system admin.

> **Master It**   Imagine that you just opened up a configuration file in the vim editor. You only want to quickly add a paragraph of comments to the top of the file. What editor commands can you employ to accomplish this task quickly?

> **Solution**   The fastest way to accomplish this task, from what you have learned in this chapter, is to enter into Insert mode by pressing the I key. Once you are in Insert mode, type in the needed paragraph of comments. After the comments are properly entered, leave Insert mode by pressing the Esc key. Now you have three choices to save the needed text modifications and leave the editor: type **ZZ**, **:x**, or **:wq**.

Employ the nano editor for everyday text file editing.   The nano text editor is a simple and quick editor to use in your daily work. You can quickly get into a file, make any needed modifications, save your work, and go on with other tasks. It's a favorite editor of system administrators because of its simplicity.

> **Master It**   You need to quickly edit a text file by copying two lines of text from the top of the file to the bottom of the text file. Assuming you are already in the nano editor with this file in the buffer, what editor commands covered in this chapter can you use to accomplish this task quickly?

> **Solution**   The fastest way to accomplish this task, from what you have learned in this chapter, is to use the Ctrl+K key combination two times to cut the first two lines of the text file. Use the Ctrl+U key combination one time to paste those two lines back into place. To quickly reach the file's bottom, use the Ctrl+V key combination to move one page down, until you reach the bottom. Now press Ctrl+U again to paste the two lines from the editing buffer to current lines. To save your modifications and leave the nano editor, press Ctrl+O one time, and then press Enter to select the filename displayed. Press Ctrl+X to leave the nano text editor and return to a shell prompt.

Find data in a text file, and reduce its size.   To quickly find files that contain certain data, the grep command is a utility to learn. With its ability to conduct simple or complex searches, locating the information or the files you need is a snap.

> **Master It**   You need to find all the files in the /etc directory (but not its subdirectories) that contain the word host. The search must be case-insensitive, and you don't want to see any error messages concerning directory files. Assuming you need to use the sudo command along with your grep command, what will your command look like to conduct this search?

> **Solution**   Assuming you need to use the sudo command along with your grep command to conduct a case-insensitive search through all the files in the /etc directory, find the

ones that contain the word host, and not display any error messages concerning directory files, the command is as follows: sudo grep -d skip -i host /etc/*.

Back up and organize text file data. The tar utility has been around for a long time. It provides useful options to create archive files. While tar has the ability to compress files on the fly, you can also use the gzip, bzip2, and xz compression utilities to compress tar archive files as well as other files.

Master It You created a tar archive file, myArchive.tar, but did not compress it with a tar option, because you needed to verify each file as it was processed with the -W option. Now that the archive file was successfully created and verified, what command will you use to compress it to the highest level, and what will the resulting file's name be?

Solution The command to compress the tar archive file, myArchive.tar, to the highest level will use the xz compression utility. The command is xz myArchive.tar, and the resulting file's name will be myArchive.tar.xz.

Chapter 9: Managing Hardware

Use Linux device driver modules. Similar to other operating systems, Linux uses device drivers to communicate with hardware devices connected to the system. The Linux kernel supports device modules, which allow you to dynamically insert or remove device driver software in the kernel as needed.

Master It What command should you use to determine what hardware modules are currently installed on your Linux server?

Solution From the command prompt, type **lsmod** to list all the device driver modules currently installed on the Linux server.

Find device information for the system. Besides the physical interfaces, Linux also uses files to communicate with devices. When you connect a device to the system, Linux automatically creates a file in the /dev directory that's used for applications to send data to and receive data from the devices. The kernel uses the /proc directory to create virtual files that contain information about the devices and system status. The /sys directory is also used by the kernel to create files useful for troubleshooting device issues.

Master It Your boss just sent you an email asking what CPU and memory are installed in the Linux server. You know that you can find the information in the /proc/cpuinfo and /proc/meminfo files, but what command(s) should you use to obtain that information?

Solution The /proc directory files are text-based, so you can use any text editor to view them, or use the cat command to display the contents on the monitor. Use the command **cat /proc/cpuinfo** to see information about the CPU, and the command **cat /proc/meminfo** to see information about the system memory.

Work with PCI and USB devices. Linux provides a handful of command-line tools that are useful when you're trying to troubleshoot device problems. The lsdev command allows you to view the status and settings for all devices on the system. The lsblk command provides information about block devices, such as hard drives and network cards, that are connected. The dmesg command lets you peek at the kernel ring buffer to view kernel event messages as it detects and works with devices. The lspci and lsusb commands allow you to view the PCI and USB devices that are connected to the Linux system.

Master It You've just plugged in a USB storage device, but the server doesn't recognize it. What command should you use to determine if the correct device module loaded or if there's some other problem?

Solution From the command prompt, type the command **dmesg**. Look toward the bottom of the output to view the most recent kernel event messages. You should see messages related to the USB device, and what (if any) kernel modules the Linux system tried to load.

Chapter 10: Booting Linux

Diagnose the Linux boot process. The process of booting a Linux server is typically free of problems. The firmware performs a POST, the bootloader finds and loads the Linux kernel, and systemd starts the desired services. Each part is critical in getting a system ready to offer services.

Master It Imagine that you booted your Linux system, and as you were watching the boot messages, it seemed that several error messages were generated. However, the messages went by so fast, you did not have time to analyze them. The system is now up and running, but you'd like to review those messages to see if they were indeed errors. How can you do that?

Solution Though some systems keep boot log files that you can view, since the system just booted, you can use the dmesg utility. This utility displays the kernel ring buffer, which holds kernel messages, and most Linux distributions copy the boot kernel messages into it. If, for some reason, you cannot locate the messages within the kernel ring buffer with dmesg, look to see if your distro keeps boot log files in the /var/log directory, such as boot, bootstrap.log, or boot.log.

Configure a bootloader. The GRUB2 bootloader is the most typical and popular bootloader on Linux systems. It provides flexibility and supports advanced features. Often there is little need to make changes to its configuration.

Master It After installing Linux on your new server, you notice that the GRUB2 bootloader menu does not display when the system boots. You'd like to modify this behavior. What setting(s) should you look to potentially change and in what configuration file?

Solution The settings, called keys, you should look to potentially change are in the /etc/default/grub file. You can directly edit this file with super user privileges. Look for the GRUB_TIMEOUT key and make sure it is not set to 0. If it is, the boot menu will not display, and you'll need to set it to the number of seconds you want the menu to show at boot time. The other key to look at is the GRUB_TIMEOUT_STYLE. If it is set to hidden, the boot menu will not display; you'll need to either comment it out with a hash mark (#) or set it to menu. When you make a change in this GRUB2 configuration file, you'll need to rebuild the grub.cfg file using the appropriate privileges and utility.

Interact with a bootloader. At boot time, if configured to do so, the GRUB2 boot menu will display. This allows you to pick different Linux kernels to boot as well as modify parameters set in the menu entries, which is often helpful when troubleshooting problems that adversely affect the system's boot.

Master It Your Linux system is currently not booted, and due to some trouble shooting, you need to select the `multi-user.target` for the next boot. How can you accomplish this?

Solution Assuming the GRUB2 menu is configured to display or is accessible at boot time, you can edit the boot menu choice that typically boots your system. When you see the boot menu, move your cursor to the menu option and press the E key to edit it. Using your arrow keys, scroll down and find the line that starts with the `linux16` or `linux` command. Press the End key or use the arrow key to reach that line's end. Once your cursor is there, press the spacebar and type **systemd.unit=multi-user.target**. Then press the B key to boot the system using the new service target.

Stop and start services after boot. The systemd daemon and its `systemctl` utility help in managing system services. They allow you to control what services are started at boot time, start and stop services, and analyze service issues and troubleshoot problems.

Master It By accident, the `ntpd` service was not enabled to start at boot time, and you need to immediately get this service up and running. Assuming you have super user privileges, how can you use systemd to start the service and check that it is indeed started?

Solution To start the service, you'll need to use the `systemctl` command and access super user privileges through either using the `sudo` command or logging into the root account, depending on your Linux distribution's configuration. The full command to enter at the command line (without the potentially needed `sudo`) is `systemctl start ntpd`. Once you have issued that command, you can check on the service's status by typing **systemctl status ntpd** at the command line and pressing Enter. Look for `Active: active (running)` in the command's output.

Analyze service startup times. The systemd daemon has some special utilities that can assist in tracking down the sources of various problems. One of those utilities is `systemd-analyze`, which has several commands you can use in troubleshooting situations.

Master It Imagine that you've installed several new services on your Linux server, but they are not starting at boot time. The services are enabled, but something seems to be going wrong with their unit file configurations. What can you do to quickly narrow down the problem?

Solution Use the `systemd-analyze verify` command on the newly installed service unit files to scan the files and locate any errors. This will assist in quickly determining the problem(s).

Chapter 11: Working with Storage Devices

Create Linux partitions on storage devices.   Once you connect a drive to the Linux system, you'll need to create partitions on the drive. For MBR disks, you can use the `fdisk` or `parted` command-line tool. For GPT disks, you can use the `gdisk` tool. When you partition a drive, you must assign it a size and a filesystem type.

> **Master It**   Your company has just purchased a new external USB 5TB drive that you need to connect to your Linux server to store customer data. How would you create a partition on the drive to be used in the Linux system?

> **Solution**   After connecting the external drive, determine the device name by using the command **dmesg | tail**. Next, use either the `fdisk` or `gdisk` tool, depending on your server's firmware. For systems using the BIOS firmware, type **sudo fdisk /dev/*xxx***, where *xxx* is the device name. Type **d** at the first prompt to delete the existing partition, and then type **n** to create a new partition. Press Enter to select the default starting and ending blocks. Type **w** to save the new partition and exit the `fdisk` utility.

Format partitions with a Linux filesystem and mount them in the virtual directory.   After you partition the storage device, you must format it using a filesystem that Linux recognizes. The `mkfs` program is a front-end utility that can format drives using most of the filesystems that Linux supports. The ext4 filesystem is currently the most popular Linux filesystem. It supports journaling and provides good performance. Linux also supports more advanced filesystems, such as btrfs, xfs, zfs, and, of course, the Windows vfat and ntfs filesystems. After creating a filesystem on the partition, you'll need to mount the filesystem into the Linux virtual directory using a mount point and the `mount` command. The data contained in the partition's filesystem appears under the mount point folder within the virtual directory. To automatically mount partitions at boot time, make an entry for each partition in the /etc/fstab file.

> **Master It**   Format the new external USB storage device you just partitioned so that it can be used by your Linux server, and then mount the new partition in the /data directory on your server.

> **Solution**   To format the new partition, type the command **sudo mkfs -t ext4 /dev/*xxx*1**, where *xxx* is the device name you used to create the new partition. After Linux completes the partition formatting, you can manually mount the partition to test it. First, create a mount point by typing the command **sudo mkdir /data**. Then, you can mount the new partition by typing the command **sudo mount /dev/*xxx*1 /data**, where *xxx* is the device name of the partition. After copying and deleting a few test files in the new partition, modify the /etc/fstab text file to automatically mount the new partition by opening it in an editor and adding the following line:

> **/dev/*xxx*1 /data ext4 defaults 1 2**

> where *xxx* is the device name of the storage device.

Examine storage devices using Linux tools.   There are a host of tools available to help you manage and maintain filesystems. The `df` and `du` command-line commands are useful for checking disk space for partitions and the virtual directory, respectively. The `fsck` utility is a vital tool for repairing corrupt partitions, and it's run automatically at boot time against all partitions automatically mounted in the virtual directory.

Master It In your daily system administration checks, you determined that the partition that contains the /home directory has become full. How can you tell which storage device the /home directory is located on and what user account is using up the most space?

Solution To determine the partition that contains the /home directory, type the command **df -h**. This displays the currently mounted storage devices, along with their capacities and how much space is currently being used. This allows you to determine if the /home directory is on its own partition or under the root (/) partition. To determine what user account has the most data stored, type the command **du /home**. This displays the disk space used by each user's Home directory.

Chapter 12: Configuring Network Settings

Find and examine the network configuration files for your server. Linux stores network connection information in configuration files. The installer program that runs when you install the Linux software typically asks you for the network configuration information and creates these files automatically. However, it's a good idea to find where these files are located on your Linux system in case anything goes wrong or you need to change anything. Ubuntu servers store the configuration files in the /etc/netplan directory. Red Hat servers store the configuration files in the /etc/sysconfig/network-scripts directory. Files in those directories define the network settings for each interface.

Master It You've been asked to help a colleague solve a network problem on an Ubuntu Linux server. What file would you look at to determine the current network configuration settings?

Solution From the command line, change to the netplan directory by typing the command **cd /etc/netplan**. List the files in that directory by typing the command **ls -l**. View the current network configuration by using the cat command on each of the configuration files in that directory. For example, you can view the configuration defined in the 00-installer-comnfig.yaml file by typing the command **cat 00-installer-config .yaml**. Note the interfaces listed, along with the IP addresses assigned.

View and change network configuration settings using command-line tools. If you must configure your network settings from the command line, there are a few different tools you'll need to use. For both wireless and wired connections, you need to use the ifconfig or ip command to set the IP address and netmask values for the interface. You may also need to use the route command to define the default router for the local network. For wireless connections, you'll need to use the iwconfig command to set the wireless access point and SSID key.

Master It Customers can't connect to your Red Hat Linux server, but the server is running, and the network cable is plugged in. What commands should you run to view the status of the network interface and make it active if it's down?

Solution To view the current status of a network interface, type the command **ip address show**. If the status of the interface enp0s3 shows DOWN, you can make it active also using the ip command. Type **ip link set enp0s3 up** at the command prompt to make the interface active. Then type **ip address show** at the command prompt and note the status of the network interface to ensure it's active.

Troubleshoot common network problems.   Once your network configuration is complete, you may have to do some additional troubleshooting for network problems. The ping and ping6 commands allow you to send ICMP packets to remote hosts to test basic connectivity. If you suspect issues with hostnames, you can use the host and dig commands to query the DNS server for hostnames.

For more advanced network troubleshooting, you can use the netstat and ss commands to display what applications are using which network ports on the system.

Master It   The web administrator for your company called you to say none of the customers can connect to the company's website running on an Ubuntu server. What commands should you use to see first if the Ubuntu server can communicate with remote hosts and then that the web server software is listening for HTTPS connections?

Solution   To first check for network connectivity from the Ubuntu server, type the command **ping www.linux.org**. You should get a response from the remote server, indicating that your server is communicating. Next, to check for the web server, type **ss -anpt** from the command line to view all open TCP sockets on the server. You should see a line with the local address/port of 0.0.0.0:443, indicating that a web server is listening on TCP port 443 for HTTPS connections. If not, it may be time for the web administrator to restart the web server software!

Chapter 13: Managing Users and Groups

Change a file's owner.   A file or directory owner setting allows certain control over that file or directory. Some control is dictated by the permissions set at the owner level, but also only certain commands can be used on a file or directory by its owner. For example, you cannot change the group on a file if you do not own it (or don't have super user privileges).

Master It   Imagine you are either logged into the root account or have access to super user privileges, and you have a copied a file projectData.txt to the lradford home directory. This user will need access to the file, which includes being able to change its group. What command syntax should you employ to accomplish this task?

Solution   To change the owner of the projectData.txt file to the lradford user, you'll need to use the chown command. The exact syntax to accomplish the task, if you are logged into the root account, is chown lradford projectData.txt. If you are using super user privileges to accomplish this task, the syntax is sudo chown lradford projectData.txt. It's a good idea to double-check that the change of ownership was successful by issuing the command **ls -l projectData.txt** when you are done with the chown command.

Create user accounts.   The useradd command is a command at the basic system level that allows you to create new accounts on the system. The needed various options are often determined by settings in the /etc/login.defs and the /etc/default/useradd files.

Master It   You need to create a new account for a newly hired project manager, Takoda Puddle, who needs access to the Bash shell on your server. In your system's /etc/login.defs, you find that CREATE_HOME is defined as no, and UID_MIN is set to 1000. Within the /etc/default/useradd file, SHELL is defined as /bin/bash, and SKEL is set to the /etc/skel directory. The user's home directory should end up being /home/tpuddle.

Assuming you are either logged into the root account or have access to super user privileges, what is the command syntax to create an account for the new project manager?

Solution To create an account, you'll need to use the useradd command. With the current system configuration settings, and if you are logged into the root account, the command is useradd -md /home/tpuddle tpuddle. If you are using super user privileges to accomplish this task, the syntax is sudo useradd -md /home/tpuddle tpuddle. You don't necessarily have to add a comment field through the use of the -c option. It is wise to double-check that the account addition was successful by issuing the command **getent passwd tpuddle** when you are done with the useradd command. However, don't forget that you also need to create a password for this new account using the command passwd tpuddle or sudo passwd tpuddle!

Modify a user's password. The passwd command along with the correct privileges allows you to create an account's password. However, besides just creating a password, you can change an account's password, delete its password, force a user to change their password at the next login, and so on. In addition, without any extra privileges, you can modify your own account's password through the passwd command.

Master It You are the system administration for several Linux servers at your company. An HR representative and your boss have come to your office to let you know that a fellow employee, Jay Snow, is being fired from the company. They have asked you to lock the jsnow account while they wait. What command do you enter to lock this account?

Solution The passwd command will allow you to lock accounts if you are logged into the root account or have super user privileges. The syntax needed if you are logged into the root account is either passwd -l jsnow or passwd --lock jsnow. If you are using super user privileges, use the same syntax but with sudo before the rest of the command. Keep in mind that if the user jsnow is already logged into the system, this command will not remove the user jsnow. It only prevents the user from logging in again to the system after logging out.

Find an environment file. Environment files on your system consist of both global files and local user files. Which environment files reside on a system depends on the Linux distribution being used. Global files reside in the /etc/ directory, and local user files reside in each user's home directory after being copied from the /etc/skel/ directory, if your system is configured to do so.

Master It You are the system admin for a development system. A programmer recently asked how a particular environment variable can be redefined, not only when they log into the system, but also when they run various Bash shell scripts on the system. What should you do or suggest?

Solution Because a noninteractive shell (also called a non-login shell) is started when a user runs a Bash script, the best place to redefine this particular environment variable is in the user's .bashrc file. However, you should determine if other developers on the system need the same thing, and if they do, put the variable in a global environment file instead.

Delete a user group. Managing groups of users on a Linux system is an important task. Several groups are permanent once created, but other groups, such as those related to special work projects, may come and go. You need to know how to create, modify, and even remove a user group.

Master It A small development project, abc123, on the system you administer has come to an end. The project files are no longer needed by the former team, and you've been asked to change the group on these project files to the manager group. Once you've completed that task, you'll need to remove the old abc123 project group. What is the command to accomplish this removal task?

Solution   Use the groupdel abc123 command on the system to remove the abc123 user group. You'll need to be logged into the root account or have access to super user privileges to successfully complete this task.

Chapter 14: Working with Processes and Jobs

Monitor programs running on the server.   You can view the running applications and the resources they consume by using the ps command. There are many different ways to view process information using the ps command, allowing you to customize the display exactly how you like. For real-time monitoring of applications, use the top command. With the top command, you can view a real-time display of applications, their system state, and the resources they consume; plus it allows you to sort the display based on many different features.

Master It   Your server users are complaining that the server seems slow today. How can you tell what programs are using the most resources on the server?

Solution   From the command line, type **top** to start the interactive display of processes. By default, top sorts the display based on CPU usage. Note the two or three processes using the most CPU resources.

Manage programs running on the server.   The nice command allows you to start an application at a different priority level than the applications that are already running. This allows users to run applications in the background at a lower priority or allows the system administrator to start applications with a higher priority. With the renice command, you can change the priority of an application that's already running. If an application causes problems and needs to be stopped, you can use the kill command, but you need to know the PID assigned to the application by the system. The pkill command is customized for stopping applications by their name instead of the PID.

Master It   A software developer has contacted you to tell you that she made a coding error in her program named inventory, and now it's stuck running in an endless loop on the system. What command(s) should you run to find and safely stop the runaway program?

Solution   First try to send a HUP signal to the runaway program so it can gently stop by typing the command **sudo pkill --signal HUP inventory**. Check if the program has stopped by typing the command **ps -ef** and looking for the program. If the program continues to run, you must send a KILL signal to stop it. Type the command
sudo pkill --signal KILL inventory.

Schedule programs to run in the future.   Linux provides a couple of different ways for you to schedule programs to start at a future time or even a different date. The at command lets you schedule in individual program to run at a specific time/date. If you need to schedule a program to start on a regular schedule, use the crontab command to add the program to the system cron table. You must specify the schedule format to tell Linux when to start the program.

Master It   The software developer has worked out all of the bugs in her `inventory` program and would like for it to run automatically every month on the first of the month at 1 AM. The program is stored in the `/applications` directory. What command should she use to make that happen?

Solution   To schedule a recurring program, add it to your user `cron` table using the `crontab` command. To edit your user `cron` table, type **crontab -e**. In the editor, go to input mode by typing **i** and then enter the schedule and command to run. To run the inventory program at 1 a.m. on the first of every month, type the following:

```
00 1 1 * * /applications/inventory
```

Save the entry by typing **:qw!**.

Chapter 15: Managing Log Files

View journal entries.   The `journalctl` program is needed to view journal file entries, because unlike some logging utilities, `systemd-journald` doesn't store events in text files. Instead, it uses its own binary file format that works similar to a database. Thus, you cannot use the typical programs used to view text files, such as `cat`, `head`, or `tail`, to view journal file entries.

Master It   You're an administrator on a rather under-resourced server with problems concerning two different apps that run on it. The problems are sporadic, but seem to start occurring during the app's peak use time. You decide to keep an eye on the error messages being logged to the journal during that time. What's the most efficient `journalctl` command(s) to use in this scenario?

Solution   To keep an eye on the error messages being logged to the journal during the problematic apps' peak usage time, it is the most efficient to set a watch on the journal file. The `journalctl` command that allows you to see the entries as they are being logged to the journal is `journalctl -f` or `journalctl --follow`. This is similar to using the `tail -f` command on a text-based log file to watch as messages are added to it.

Maintain the journal file's size.   The `systemd-journald` journal file(s) can get rather large. Because the various services on the system are sending messages to this file, if multiple events are occurring on a regular basis, disk space can quickly become consumed. It's important to make some decisions on journal file size limits prior to lack of disk space becoming a critical emergency issue.

Master It   Imagine you are administering a new server and are currently accessing the persistent `systemd-journald` journal files. After running the `journalctl --disk-usage` program, you've made some decisions on journal file size limits and determine a rotation schedule, which includes an archival process for the old files. Which directives should you consider modifying in the `/etc/systemd/journald.conf` file to match your decisions concerning this and prevent a critical emergency issue with disk space due to journal files?

Solution   Within the `/etc/systemd/journald.conf` file, the three directives related to persistent journal file size are `SystemKeepFree`, `SystemMaxFileSize`, and `SystemMaxUse`. Reviewing these particular directives and modifying them to meet your decisions will work. The other directives related to journal file size are for volatile journal files and do not apply in this case. You also will want to turn off the `MaxFileSec` directive by setting it to 0, because this setting is not needed when size limitations are in place.

Make a journal file continuous. On some distributions, the journal file entries are stored in the `/run/log/journal` directory. The `/run/` directory and its contents are deleted when a system is shut down, so any journal entries are lost at that time. It is typical to change this behavior by modifying a directive in the `/etc/systemd/journald.conf` file to force `systemd-journald` to keep entries in a journal that is not removed when the system is shut down or reboots. The `/var/log/journal` directory is used in these cases to store the journal file(s).

> **Master It** Currently, the servers you administer have temporary journal files, which are lost when these systems are shut down or reboot. You'd like to make these journal files continuous and manage their size through rotation and archival settings in the `systemd-journald` configuration file. What directive should you change in the configuration files on these servers, and what should you set it to?
>
> **Solution** To force `systemd-journald` to keep entries in a journal that is not removed when the system is shut down or reboots, you'll need to modify the `Storage` directive in these servers' `journald.conf` file in their `/etc/systemd/` directory. If the `/var/log/journal` directory already exists (or you plan on creating it), you can set the `Storage` directive to `auto`. Otherwise, you'll want to set it to `persistent` to create the `/var/log/journal` directory, if it is not there already.

Modify a logging level. The legacy rsyslog application uses the syslog protocol. It uses either a single configuration file, `/etc/rsyslogd.conf`, or a combination of that configuration file and additional configuration files within the `/etc/rsyslog.d/` directory. Modifying the rsyslog application's configuration is fairly straightforward with the *facility* *.priority action* syntax in its configuration rules.

> **Master It** You are the system admin for a server that uses the legacy rsyslog application for its event logging. You'd like to direct the `rsyslogd` program to send the following severity level of events for all systems to everyone: `crit`, `alert`, and `emerg`. What do you need to do?
>
> **Solution** First, you'll need to find the proper configuration file in which to set the configuration for that rule. Check to see if the rules that define how the program handles syslog events received from the system, kernel, or applications are set in the `/etc/rsyslogd.conf` file. If not, check for them in the files within the `/etc/rsyslog.d/` directory. Once you find the correct configuration file, look for a rule similar to the following:

```
# Everybody gets emergency messages
*.emerg                     :omusrmsg:*
```

> If you find this rule, you'll only need to change `emerg` to `crit`, because `rsyslogd` will log all events with the `crit` severity or higher (`alert` and `emerg`). If you don't find this rule, add a similar line, changing `emerg` to `crit`.

Chapter 16: Managing Printers

Install and configure the CUPS software. Most Linux distributions provide the Common Unix Printing System (CUPS) to make it easy to connect, use, and even share printers with your Linux system. Both Ubuntu and CentOS provide the CUPS software in their default software repositories, so you can install CUPS using apt in Ubuntu, or dnf in CentOS. Once you install the software, you'll need to make a few configuration changes to allow remote clients to use CUPS, especially if your server doesn't provide a graphical desktop. You'll also need to ensure your administrator user account has access to the CUPS administrator features by adding it to the appropriate user group.

Master It Your boss wants to allow all of the clients on your local network to be able to use the CUPS web interface to manage their own print jobs, but wants to restrict access to the CUPS administrator privileges to just your workstation, which has the static IP address of 192.168.1.100. What do you need to change in the cupsd.conf configuration file to accommodate that configuration?

Solution In the cupsd.conf configuration file, you'll first need to set the root location to allow connection from any client on the local network by adding the line **ALLOW @LOCAL** to the <Location /> block. However, in the <Location /admin> block, add the line **ALLOW from 192.168.1.100** to only allow your workstation to connect to the administrative features in CUPS.

Create printers on your Linux server. The CUPS web interface provides an administration section that allows you to create new printers for the Linux server. Clicking the Add Printer button starts a wizard that walks through the process of defining and creating the printer. CUPS has the ability to automatically detect both local and network printers and can aid you in setting them up on the system.

Master It The network team has installed a new printer on the network, but customers are complaining that their print output keeps getting mixed up with others. How can you assist in separating each print job sent to the printer using CUPS?

Solution From the CUPS web interface, select the Administration tab, and then click the Add Printer button to define a new printer. Select the network printer, and then select the appropriate drivers. On the Default Options page, click the Banners tab, and select the option to print a banner at the start of each print job.

Manage printers and print jobs submitted by clients on your local network. The CUPS web interface allows you to manage both printer settings as well as print jobs submitted to the printer. Click the Printer tab from the main CUPS web page, and then select the printer you want to manage. On the Printer page, you can select from several different printer administration functions, such as modify the printer settings, delete the printer, pause print jobs, and cancel print jobs. Under the printer settings is also a list of jobs currently assigned to the printer. From here, you can select a job to either cancel it or move it to another printer.

Master It Customers are complaining that someone sent a large print job to the printer yesterday that's not printing, and blocking any other print job from processing. What process do you need to perform to solve the problem?

Solution From the CUPS web interface, select the Printers tab, and then click the name of the printer the job was sent to. On the Printer page, you will see a list of the jobs currently assigned to the printer for processing. The offending print job will be listed first and possibly show the error that's causing the issue. Click the Cancel job button to remove the job from the printer queue so other jobs can process.

Chapter 17: Exploring Ubuntu Security

Safely escalate privileges to accomplish tasks. Ubuntu implements privilege escalation through the sudo command. This method allows administrators to log into their standard Linux user account and run programs with higher-level administrator privileges, as needed.

Master It You're an administrator on an Ubuntu Linux system. There is a new member on your team who will be performing the same administrator duties that you do. This team member will need to use sudo to safely escalate privileges when needed. The record in the /etc/sudoers configuration file that provides your account with privilege escalation is the following: %sudo ALL=(ALL:ALL) ALL. What do you need to do to set up this new team member to use the sudo command?

Solution To set up this new team member to use the sudo command and have the ability to perform the same administrator duties that you do, you'll need to add the team member's account to the sudo group. To do this, you'll need to use the usermod -aG command covered in Chapter 13, "Managing Users and Groups."

Use OpenSSH to connect to remote systems. OpenSSH provides an encrypted means for communication when you connect over a network to a remote server. Ubuntu Linux typically has OpenSSH installed by default, but you may need to perform additional configuration steps to customize it for your secure communication requirements.

Master It Imagine you are administering an Ubuntu server that already uses OpenSSH. Connections are set to use key pairs instead of passwords for command-line access. While you currently have rsa keys, the decision was made to switch to ecdsa key pairs, which don't exist at this time on the system. What steps do you need to take in order to implement this functionality for your accounts on the systems?

Solution To implement OpenSSH connections to use ecdsa key pairs, the first step is to log into a client system and generate ecdsa keys via the ssh-keygen -t ecdsa -f ~/.ssh/id_ecdsa command. After that, copy the new public key to the server system's ~/.ssh/authorized_keys filesystem using the ssh-copy-id utility. Be aware you will need to do these steps for each client system.

Manage Ubuntu MAC protection software. AppArmor is the MAC protection system used on Ubuntu. This software controls the files and network ports each application accesses through access lists, which are text-based files called profiles. These files reside in the /etc/apparmor.d/ directory and are typically installed for a particular application, when it is installed.

Master It You're an administrator on an Ubuntu Linux system that uses AppArmor as its MAC system. All of the AppArmor utility and profile packages are installed.

The primary application on this system is run only on Tuesday through Sunday of every week. The development team would like to test a large app modification on Monday. What should you do to the firewall to log potential firewall violation issues with the modification, but not stop the application from accomplishing its test tasks?

Solution To log potential MAC violation issues with the modification, but not stop the application from accomplishing its test tasks, use the `aa-complain` command on the application's profile. You will also need to do this on any applications' profiles that this modified application uses on the system. By putting the various profiles into complain mode, any violations of the profile are logged, but not blocked. In addition, check all the profiles for deny rules, which will block violations whether or not the profile is in complain mode.

Configure the Ubuntu firewall. Ubuntu's software application firewall is host-based and works at the Network layer. It uses an ACL to identify which network packets are allowed in or out of the system. Ubuntu's UFW uses netfilter's services and is configured with the `ufw` command-line utility.

Master It You are the system admin for several Ubuntu servers that reside in server rooms spread across the world. To access these servers remotely and securely, you use OpenSSH. However, you've decided not to use the default port 22 for this service. Instead, you are going to use a different and available port number. What do you need to do to the firewall on all the Ubuntu servers to make this work?

Solution You'll need to open traffic in the firewall for the chosen OpenSSH port. Just as an example, say you'll use port 1138, instead of 22, for OpenSSH services. To open the port, type in **sudo ufw allow 1138/tcp** at the servers' command line. It is wise to only allow traffic to this port from any of the client systems, so also consider adding the `from source`, where `source` is either a set of IP addresses or subnets of the client systems from where you are logging in. If UFW firewalls are implemented on the client systems, you'll need to perform similar commands on them.

Chapter 18: Exploring Red Hat Security

Control access from the root user account. The Red Hat server distribution enables the `root` user account by default, which could cause security issues if not managed correctly. You should always check for uses of the `root` user account by using the `aulast` command to view the logins on the server. Depending on your environment, you may also want to restrict the `root` user account from accessing the server from a remote device. You can do that using the `/etc/ssh/sshd_config` configuration file in OpenSSH. Finally, if you do allow `root` user access on your system, it's a good idea to restrict the idle time at the command prompt. You do that using the `TMOUT` environment variable.

Master It Your boss came into your office saying that someone deleted his user account on the server and wants to know how he can find out who did it. He thinks it happened yesterday afternoon. What command should you use to see who logged in with the root user account on the system during that time period?

Solution   From the command prompt as root, type **sudo aulast | grep root**. This displays the times the root user account logged into the system and, if from a remote device, the IP address of the device.

Manage the SELinux environment.   While standard Linux file and directory permissions can help with locking down files and directories, they can't provide mandatory access controls required for some environments. The SELinux package allows you to write policy rules that control access to not only files and directories but also applications and network ports. This helps provide MAC-level of security on the Linux server.

Master It   After you enabled SELinux on the Red Hat server, the web administrator notified you that his web application can't connect to the MySQL database anymore. What commands should you use to troubleshoot and fix the problem?

Solution   First, you'll need to find out if there's a security policy that manages the database connection from the web server. From the command prompt, type **sudo getsebool | grep httpd**. From this list, you see the policy httpd_can_network_connect_db is turned off. To enable it, from the command prompt, type **sudo setsebool -P httpd_can_network_connect_db 1**.

Control network access using `firewalld`.   In today's world, managing access to the Linux server is a must, especially if your Linux server has some type of connection to the Internet. Red Hat servers utilize the `firewalld` program to block unwanted network connections and allow approved connections on the network. The `firewalld` program defines connections as rules and applies those rules to specific zones. You can then assign network interfaces to the zone that supports the network connections needed.

Master It   The database administrator contacted you to complain she just installed MySQL on the Red Hat server, but none of the remote clients can connect to it. She indicated that MySQL uses TCP port 3306 for communications by default and just assumed it would be open on the server. What commands should you use to troubleshoot and fix the problem?

Solution   First, determine the zone the network interface card is assigned to. Open the command prompt and type **sudo firewall-cmd --list-all**. This displays the active zones on the server and what network interface is in each one. Look for the zone the active network interface is assigned to, and enable TCP port 3306 for it by typing **sudo firewall-cmd --zone=public --permanent --add-port=3306/tcp**. Then reload the configuration by typing **sudo firewall-cmd --reload**.

Chapter 19: Writing Scripts

Create basic scripts to automatically run commands.   Basic Bash shell scripts require a few, but important, items. For example, on the first line of a shell script file, you use special syntax that indicates to the current shell which shell to use for running the script. You also need to include the commands you want to run within the script. In addition, it's helpful for the script users, even if it is only you, to have the script produce messages so that the script user knows what is happening within the script.

Master It You have written a basic Bash shell script that assists in viewing who is logged onto the system currently as well as looking at log files that indicate who logged in previously to the system. For some reason, the script is not functioning properly. You are getting error messages as if the Dash shell is running the script, but you want the Bash shell to run the script and are even using the bash command to run it. What is most likely the problem?

Solution If you are getting error messages as if the Dash shell is running the script, the most likely cause is incorrect code on the first line of your shell script. If the first line uses #!/bin/sh, your script will be run by whatever shell the /bin/sh file points to. On some systems, this file points to the Dash shell. Modify the script to use #!/bin/bash in its first line.

Use variables in shell scripts. You can integrate data into your shell script commands to process information using variables. Variables allow you to temporarily store information within the shell script for use with other commands in the script. Variables can be environment variables, user-defined variables, or even data passed to the script through the use of parameters.

Master It Imagine you are writing a shell script to assist in the deletion of individual user accounts. This script will be used by an admin intern from the local college, so it needs to include the username of the account to delete in a variable. How will you accomplish this?

Solution To create a shell script to assist in the deletion of individual user accounts, which requires the username of the account to delete it, you can use the $1 variable in the script. This will allow the intern who is running the program to run the script and include the username as a parameter to the shell script. However, you may want to include some additional safeguards in your script to avoid typographical errors on the username and prevent the intern from entering valid but incorrect usernames into the script.

Provide compound conditions to guide scripts. Compound conditions are ones in which two or more conditions need checking so that the script can decide which commands to execute or the course of action to take. You can handle compound conditions through multiple if-then statements or, if there are only two conditions to check, through the use of Boolean logic to combine the tests.

Master It You are writing a script that needs to check a compound condition. In this case, the machine0087.log file's existence needs to be checked. In addition, a counter variable, logCount, must be examined as well. If the file exists and the counter has reached 100, the script should exit. What if-then statement(s) should you write to make this test as consolidated as possible?

Solution To exit the script if the machine0087.log file exists and the logCount counter has reached 100, you'll need to use Boolean logic in your if-then test statement as follows:

```
if [ -f machine0087.log ] && [ $logCount -eq 100 ]
then
    exit
fi
```

You could also use the -e test on the machine0087.log file, and it would be best to use the file's absolute directory reference, instead of a relative one.

Determine the best loops to use in a script, when needed. There are times in a shell script that you need to repeat a set of commands until a specific condition has been met. This need occurs when processing all the files in a directory, all the users on a system, or all the lines in a text file. The loop types available for Bash shell scripts include for, while, and until.

Master It You are writing a shell script that needs to process lines in a text file. One particular line toward the bottom of the file contains only the text stop here. You are reading in the text file lines one at a time, keeping only the line's text, and putting it into the variable fileLine. What type of loop should you use in your script, and what is the syntax of that loop's first line?

Solution While you could use any type of loop in your script, most likely the easiest one to write for this particular set of conditions is an until loop. The format of the loop's first line would look like this:

```
until [ $fileLine = "stop here" ].
```

Create and use functions in shell scripts. User-defined functions are blocks of script code that you assign a name to and reuse anywhere in your shell script. When you need your script to execute that block of code, you call the function using the name you assigned to it. This provides scripts with the ability to keep blocks of code within a single location, so any changes that the code needs are done in only one place in the script.

Master It As you are creating a shell script, you recognize that you are writing these four lines of code over and over again:

```
echo "Error in processing file, $1."
echo "Check that the $1 file exists and contains +data."
echo "This script will now exit..."
exit
```

Properly write a function named errorMessage that will allow you to turn these four lines of code into a single line (except for the function declaration) throughout the script.

Solution A function named errorMessage that will allow you to turn the four lines of code into a single line (except for the function declaration) throughout the script would look like this:

```
function errorMessage {
echo "Error in processing file, $1."
echo "Check that the $1 file exists and contains data."
echo "This script will now exit..."
exit
}
```

or this:

```
errorMessage () {
echo "Error in processing file, $1."
echo "Check that the $1 file exists and contains data."
echo "This script will now exit..."
exit
}
```

and then would be called by simply using errorMessage in place of those four lines of code throughout the script.

Chapter 20: Managing Web Servers

Determine the right web server for your environment. Web servers are the heart of the Internet, and Linux is the main server platform used for supporting them. There are many different web server software packages available for Linux, but the two most popular are Apache and nginx. The Apache web server is the oldest and most popular web server package. It is highly customizable and has defined many of the features expected from web servers. The nginx web server is relatively new to the web server game but is a powerful player. It can support larger client bases on the same physical hardware than Apache, making it ideal for high-traffic environments. It also has made a name for itself in the reverse web proxy world. A reverse web proxy sits in front of multiple back-end application servers and provides load balancing for clients.

Master It Your company wants to implement load balancing using several web servers to host your corporate website. The website uses PHP to retrieve data stored in a database to produce the website content. Describe a good web server solution to meet these requirements.

Solution The nginx web server is good at providing reverse proxy services and handling multiple clients, while the Apache web server is good at processing PHP code and communicating with a database. A good solution would be to use an nginx web server as the main server and to use several Apache web servers in a load balancing configuration behind the nginx web server.

Install and configure the Apache web server. The Apache web server is available for installation from the standard Ubuntu and Red Hat repositories. Adding features to the Apache web server often requires installing additional packages. Customizing the Apache web server is as easy as changing configuration settings. You use the UserDir directive to allow users to create their own websites on the server, separate from each other. You use the VirtualHost directives to host web pages for multiple domains on the same physical server. You can also implement client authentication on your website, requiring clients to log in to access content. The Apache server also provides for secure transactions by using HTTPS and encrypting network traffic between the client and the server.

Master It You've received a frantic phone call from the company web administrator informing you that after changing the configuration file she can't start the Apache web server, it keeps failing. What command should you use to see why the Apache server won't start?

Solution From an Ubuntu server command line, type **sudo apache2ctl configtest**, or from a Red Hat server command line, type **sudo apachectl configtest**. The configtest option parses the Apache configuration file and displays any errors that would prevent the Apache web server from starting.

Install and configure the nginx web server. With the growing popularity of the nginx web server, both the Ubuntu and Red Hat server repositories include it. After installing nginx, you can customize it by changing the nginx.conf configuration file. Many of the configuration directives for nginx are similar to the Apache, so migrating from one to the other is a fairly simple process.

Master It   Customers are complaining that they can't connect to your corporate website running on the nginx web server. What commands can you use to check the status of the server and restart it if necessary?

Solution   To check the status of the nginx web server, you'll need to use the `systemctl` command. From a command-line prompt, type **sudo `systemctl` `status` `nginx`**. If the status shows that the server is stopped, start it by typing the command **sudo `systemctl` `start` `nginx`**.

Chapter 21: Managing Database Servers

Understand basic DBMS components.   A database management system typically consists of a database engine, the data files for the database, and a query-language interface, which typically uses standard SQL or something relatively compliant with standard SQL. These components assist in fulfilling the need to manage complex connections between individual data items.

Master It   You have installed an RDBMS on your Linux system. The various applications that access this database reside on different servers across your local network. However, these servers are in different buildings on your company's campus. Recently, the power was cut to the campus due to a mistake by the power utility supply company. You did not have any backup power systems in place, and all your servers went down. Now that the power has been restored and your systems are back up and running again, none of the applications can access the database. The system on which your RDBMS resides is running (the primary database server), and there are no network firewall problems. What should you investigate next to resolve this issue?

Solution   The database engine typically runs in the background as a daemon on Linux and provides access to the database data to local and, if configured, remote applications. The next item to investigate is whether the RDBMS daemon is currently running. If it is not, use super user privileges and the `systemctl` command to start the service; then enable the service so that the next time the database server reboots, the RDBMS daemon is started automatically.

Create user accounts within MariaDB.   Managing and querying data within a MariaDB server is accomplished through database user accounts. Typically, an account is created for every user account on the Linux system that needs to manage and/or query data in the database. It is also considered a good practice to limit user access to only those databases associated with applications the user can access.

Master It   Imagine you are the system administrator on a new Linux server. You have completed the installation of MariaDB and need to create a database for the application that will be using MariaDB as its RDMS. What are the next few steps to take, after starting the MariaDB service and enabling it to start at system boot?

Solution   Your next major step is to create a database administrator account for yourself so that you do not have to use super user privileges or the `root` account to create the database. To do this, you will need to escalate your privileges to super user and issue the `mysql` command to enter into the SQL interface. After that, your next step is to issue the appropriate CREATE USER command along with the username of the account, the hostname of the system (optional), and a password to access the SQL interface of MariaDB. After you have completed creating this account, you should log out of the mysql interface and log back in using the new credentials. Now that this is accomplished, you can move forward with creating the database.

Use SQL to query a MariaDB database. MariaDB uses several standard SQL commands, plus a few more, to manage databases, create tables, populate them with data, and query that data. The times that may cause you a little heartburn are when you need to use SQL commands that fall outside of the standards. However, that is fairly rare when interacting with the MariaDB SQL interface.

Master It You have recently created a table named ArtificialFlowers within the Florist database. The artificial flower records listed in this table have only a few fields: ProductID (which is the primary key), FlowerName, FlowerColor, and StemColor. The store manager of the florist shop wants to check the data you've entered into this table. What steps should you take after you have logged into the MariaDB server's command line where this data exists?

Solution The first step is to log into the MariaDB's SQL interface, using your database server username and password. Next, in the SQL interface, connect to the database using the USE Florist; command. After that, you can display the data to the screen, using the SQL command SELECT * FROM ArtificialFlowers;. Keep in mind that if there is a lot of data in this table, it will scroll off the screen. The store manager may prefer a report from which they can view the data as opposed to looking at it on your computer screen.

Install PostgreSQL on Linux. The PostgreSQL (also called Postgres) RDBMS has some features that make it popular in segments of the Linux community. For instance, it has data reliability structures and generally supports standard SQL, with a few exceptions. Installing PostgreSQL can be a little tricky, as its installation process is slightly different depending on the Linux distribution you are using.

Master It You are a system administrator for a Linux system whose customers want to use the PostgreSQL RDBMS on the system. This particular system is a Red Hat Linux distribution. What steps do you need to take to accomplish this task?

Solution The package name for PostgreSQL on a Red Hat or Red Hat–based system is postgresql-server. So, to install it, you'll need to escalate your privileges to super user status and issue a command similar to dnf install postgresql-server. After the installation, to finish this task, you will need to again escalate your account's privileges and run a PostgreSQL database initialization by issuing the following command with super user privileges: /usr/bin/postgresql-setup --initdb. When this is completed, be sure to enable PostgreSQL to start at boot, and start the daemon.

Set up roles within PostgreSQL. Roles are used to access and manage data within a PostgreSQL server. It is considered a good practice to determine what privileges a user needs for using a PostgreSQL database and then create a role with the appropriate privileges. This structure provides protection for the data and appropriate security tracking of database users.

Master It You are the database administrator of the PostgreSQL database on your Linux system. Your database user role is named admin. This role has super user privileges in the database as well as the ability to create roles and databases. What, if any, changes should be made to your account to improve the security levels of administering this database?

Solution   Providing permissions of CREATEROLE and SUPER USER to other database roles besides postgres is considered risky. It would be best to remove the CREATEROLE and SUPER USER from the admin role, and only use the postgres account for those functions. While it is troublesome to have to log in to the postgres account to add roles to the database, it does provide an extra layer of security around the data.

Chapter 22: Exploring the Virtualization Environment

Understand basic hypervisor components.   Hypervisors are used to create and manage VMs and are generally categorized as Type 1, Type 2, or hybrid. There are pros and cons associated with each category. For example, when creating a VM using a Type 2 hypervisor, host machine resources need auditing to determine if the VM's requirements can be met. While a Type 1 hypervisor eliminates the need for the physical host's OS, it still can consume significant resources to run VMs. Creating a VM using hypervisor software is done using many different methods, such as P2V, cloning, using templates, or employing OVF files.

Master It   You need to create and deploy several VMs that contain the same brand new application and need the same environment. After reviewing the various options, which method would you choose to create these VMs and why?

Solution   Almost any method will work to create multiple VMs that contain the same application and need the same environment. However, using a P2V method is not possible, since the application is new and not already deployed on a system. Cloning is most likely the most time-saving method, as long as you properly handle issues, such as the NIC MAC address and machine IDs. A template is also a logical choice that will allow you to quickly create the needed VMs. Creating OVF files (or compressing them into a single OVA file, if needed) is also a reasonable option for this type of need. Since the same environment is needed for this single brand new app, you may want to consider exploring using containers, instead of VMs managed by a hypervisor.

Generate a container with a Bash shell.   Containers each have their own set of binaries and needed libraries to support their app, application stack, or environment, but they share the physical host's operating system. Starting and stopping containers, instead of performing software upgrades within them, is one reason why they are so popular for development and operations (DevOps). Docker is one such container engine that is extremely popular. It uses a daemon on the Linux system to listen for requests from the individual containers as well as from a Docker command-line interface that allows you to control the container environment.

Master It   Imagine you are a system administrator for an Ubuntu Linux system, and the development team is considering Docker containers to use in their production of applications. To let them try this environment, you need to install Docker to create and manage containers. Your Ubuntu system is specifically a server distro, so you want to manage the containers from the command line. What steps can you take to quickly install the Docker engine and generate a test CentOS container with access to the Bash shell for the software developers to try?

Solution   To quickly get Docker on an Ubuntu server distribution, you should install the docker snap package using the command sudo snap install docker. The Snap framework comes pre-installed on Ubuntu, so there is no need to install it. Once you have the docker snap package successfully installed, you can start a Docker CentOS container with access to the Bash shell for the software developers to test using the command `sudo docker run -it centos bash`.

Manage the Snap universal package system.   The Snap universal package system employs the snap command to install and manage snap packages. The snapd daemon updates these packages on a regular basis through the appropriate Snap channel. When run, snaps operate in an isolated sandbox, protecting other data and applications on a Linux system, including other running snaps.

Master It   You have recently visited the snap store and found a wonderful snap application that will assist in your orchestration management of containers, Multipass. After installing it and running it through several tests, you decide to use it in your production environment. However, you'd like to also keep up-to-date with the new developments in this special snap package. Besides reading about up-and-coming Multipass features, how can you stay informed using a snap package?

Solution   You can try new features before they've reached production quality by installing the Multipass snap package from the `latest/edge` channel. You can run this snap package alongside your production Multipass snap (which you should have installed from the `latest/stable` channel). This way, you'll gain hands-on access and can try newfangled features before they hit the `latest/stable` channel and your production Multipass snap.

Install the Flatpak framework.   Software packages, flatpaks, in the Flatpak universal package system focus on a single software application and are a single self-contained compressed package file that holds all the binaries and dependencies needed for the app to work. Though Flatpak is similar to Snap, flatpaks are currently available only for Desktop applications on Linux systems.

Master It   You are a system administrator for a CentOS Desktop Linux system used by developers for creating the company's main software product. The developers are interested in a different text editor that will allow them to efficiently operate as they update the company's software app. Because there is a consideration to move development from the current Linux distro to another one that also uses Flatpak, you decide to install this text editor's flatpak package that is available in `flathub`. What steps should you take to get this framework and text editor installed for the developers on this current system?

Solution   First you need to install the Flatpak framework. Using super user privileges, install it by issuing the `dnf install flatpak` command. After that step is successfully completed, connect to the `flathub` repository by using super user privileges and typing in **`flatpak remote-add flathub https://flathub.org/repo/flathub.flatpakrepo`** at the command line. Once the Flatpak framework is installed and your system is connected to the repository, install the desired text editor flatpak by using super user privileges and entering the command **`flatpak install package`**, where **`package`** is the name of the flatpak package.

Index